SHURLEY ENGLISH

English Made Easy

Student Textbook Level **6**

06-07
ISBN 978-1-58561-102-7 (Level 6 Student Textbook)

For additional information or to place an order, write to: Shurley Instructional Materials, Inc.
366 SIM Drive
Cabot, AR 72023

Table of Contents

SHURLEY ENGLISH

CHAPTER 1

CHAPTER 2

Table of Contents

CHAPTER 4

CHAPTER 5

CHAPTER 6

Table of Contents

CHAPTER 8

CHAPTER 9

CHAPTER 10

CHAPTER 11

CHAPTER 12

CHAPTER 13

CHAPTER 14

CHAPTER 15

CHAPTER 16

CHAPTER 17

CHAPTER 18

CHAPTER 19

CHAPTER 20

English Made Easy

PRETEST TIME

As you begin a new year, it is important for you to evaluate what you know about grammar, mechanics, usage, editing, and writing by taking a pretest. Later in the school year, you will take a posttest. Then, you will be able to compare the pretest and posttest to tell how much you have learned in English

GOALS

Learn It: SETTING GOALS

In order to make the most of your time, setting goals is important. Goals will keep you pointed in the direction you want to go, will focus your efforts, and will keep you on track. With a list of goals, you can check your progress. Long-term goals are what you want to accomplish in life, usually focused on your education and your career. Short-term goals will help you plan for a week or a month at a time. Getting organized and setting aside study time are always important short-term goals because they help you achieve your long-term goals.

Examples of Goals for a Sixth-Grade Student

Long-Term Goals:

1. Make good grades in sixth grade.
2. Graduate from high school.
3. Go to college or to a technical school.
4. Get a good job.

Short-Term Goals:

1. Make a daily schedule to plan my time.
2. Keep my schoolwork and supplies organized.
3. Make good grades each day.
4. Schedule study time each night.

Apply It: SETTING GOALS

Make a Goal Booklet of your long-term and short-term goals. The information in Reference 1 will guide you.

 Reference 1 **Activity for Goal Booklets**

Directions for your Goal Booklet:

1. Write the title **Long-Term Goals** on a sheet of white paper.
2. Write your long-term goals on another sheet of white paper.
3. Write the title **Short-Term Goals** on a sheet of white paper.
4. Write your short-term goals on another sheet of white paper.
5. Make goal-evaluation pages that will be used throughout the year.
   Write **Evaluation 1**, **Evaluation 2**, **Evaluation 3**, **Evaluation 4** on four separate sheets.
   Put them at the back of the booklet.
6. Use a folder or two sheets of construction paper as the cover of your booklet.
   Write the title **My Goal Booklet** and your name on the front cover.
7. Put the pages in order. Staple them on the left side or use a folder with brads.
8. Illustrate the cover page. (*Suggestions: clock, books, pencils, diploma, school building, etc.*)

Lesson 1

You will
- take pretest.
- write goals.
- do a Goal Book activity.

START LESSON 2

Lesson 2

You will

- recite new jingle (Study Skills).
- listen and respond to the Quigley stories.
- assess study skills.

LISTENING AND SPEAKING:

Recite the new jingle.

♪ Jingle 1	The Study Skills Jingle

Un-Quigley, Un-Quigley,
What are you going to do?
You've got a frown on your face,
And you're singing the blues!
You're not organized, Quigley;
You are not prepared.
You're not listening,
And your mind's not there.
You don't have plans, and you don't have goals.
Your homework's unfinished,
And you've been told.
You need to get your act together
'Cause you don't have a clue.
You've got the Study Skills Blues!

O-Quigley, O-Quigley,
Now, you see what to do.
You've got a smile on your face,
And you're lookin' cool!
You're so organized, Quigley;
You are so prepared.
You're listening carefully,
And your mind is there.
You've got plans, and you've got goals.
Your homework is finished;
You don't have to be told.
You've got your act together, Quigley,
'Cause you followed the clues.
And you're not singing the Study Skills Blues!

QUIGLEY AND STUDY SKILLS

Read It: QUIGLEY AND STUDY SKILLS

All through school, Quigley had a big problem with organization. He had no organizational plan at all, and it affected everything he did. He was a bright student, but he had not been able to keep up with his work at home or school. He would get sidetracked easily, and he would forget books and assignments and other responsibilities.

When Quigley was unorganized and unprepared, he was stressed and felt terrible. This resulted in Quigley having **Un-Quigley** days because he was "**Un**-organized." But when Quigley was organized and prepared, he felt in control and had confidence in himself. This resulted in Quigley having **O-Quigley** days because he was "**So**-organized." The type of day Quigley had affected how he felt about school. In the past, Quigley's mom and all his teachers had tried to help him get organized, but somehow it never clicked—until this summer.

Every summer since second grade, Quigley's mother had tried to teach him good organizational habits. She had tried different things, but nothing worked. However, this summer was different because Quigley was different. He worked hard at listening to what his mother said and tried to do everything she told him to do. As usual, he made a daily schedule to plan his time. At first, Quigley had to account for every minute, and his mother inspected everything he did. It was hard, but, suddenly, planning made sense, and he was able to do things that he only dreamed about before. Eventually, he found that he did not need such a detailed schedule. He learned how to write his schedule for the week, adding or changing things as needed. Quigley couldn't believe how much a written schedule helped him. When he began consulting his schedule regularly, he was amazed at the results. After he completed ALL his assigned work and his chores, he still had plenty of free time! Since he also made an effort to respond immediately to requests made of him, he no longer felt stressed and in trouble all the time.

This year, for the first time, Quigley did not dread school. He had surprised even himself over the summer. He guessed it was what his mom called "growing up." All the good study habits that his parents and his teachers had tried to teach him were beginning to soak in. Quigley had finally realized that good study habits and good work habits were the keys to making his life easier and happier. All his work and self-discipline were finally paying off. He was actually excited about a new school year without his old habits.

Read the Quigley stories to find out what happens to Quigley in the sixth grade.

The O-Quigley Story:
When Quigley Was Organized

Quigley walked into his classroom brimming with confidence. He looked around and wondered if anyone else could see the big change in him. Then, Mrs. Harper, his new teacher, walked into the room. Quigley was a little nervous, but he paid close attention to everything she said. He was determined that this school year was going to be different. He was going to be a good student, and he was going to like school

The first thing Quigley did this year was organize his desk. No more messy desk for him! He was a new man, and he was going to have a new look–the organized look. Quigley was surprised that it did not take very long to get his desk organized. He decided to take a few minutes every day to keep it that way. Now, he looked around with a satisfied smile. He felt so good. Then, he noticed that Tommy, the new boy on his left, was trying to find his pencil and paper in a very messy desk. Quigley just shook his head in sympathy as he began his work. Mrs. Harper was frowning at the new boy, but she was smiling at him!

Discuss It:

1. What had Quigley decided to do this year that was different than last year?
2. What problems was Tommy having?
3. Why do you think Quigley felt sympathy for Tommy?
4. Why did Quigley feel good?

Learn It: GETTING ORGANIZED

 Reference 2 | **Study Skills for Getting Organized**

GET ORGANIZED...

1. **Be prepared!** Have pencils sharpened and supplies handy before you begin the day. Keep an assignment notebook to record assignments, page numbers, and due dates.
2. **Organize your desk!** Each time you put something in it, know exactly where it goes. Avoid "stuffing." Start today by having a complete clean-out and fix-up. Put all folders and notebooks on one side of your desk, and put all textbooks on the other side. Small items should be kept in the front in a zippered bag.
3. **Everything has a place!** Keep each subject in a separate folder so that you can find papers easily.
4. **Directions are important!** Take time to read carefully and understand each direction even if you know what to do. Look at your teacher and concentrate on what your teacher is saying.
5. **Proofread your work!** Check it over. Read everything you have written. Do your answers make sense? Have you skipped any items?

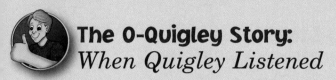

The O-Quigley Story:
When Quigley Listened

Quigley was having a great year so far! Mrs. Harper was a really good teacher even though she worked her students hard. Quigley enjoyed learning all the new things that he never had time to learn before because he was always behind and in trouble. Now, he listened to every lesson with interest. He really got involved in the discussions, and he learned to listen to others and to ask questions.

The new boy was still having problems. Quigley could see that Tommy couldn't follow even simple directions. He was always behind or couldn't find his work. "That boy needs to develop better study habits," Quigley thought to himself as Mrs. Harper made her way back to Tommy's desk. Quigley sighed with relief. Mrs. Harper had not scolded him one time so far. Quigley sure did like school this year.

Discuss It:

1. How did Quigley feel about school this year?

2. How did Quigley feel about his teacher, Mrs. Harper?

3. What did Quigley do in this story that helped him do better in school?

4. How could you tell that Tommy was having trouble listening?

5. What did Quigley think Tommy should do?

Learn It: LISTENING

 Reference 3 | **Study Skills for Listening**

LISTEN...

1. **Listen with your whole body!** Turn your body toward the speaker and look directly at him. Keep your legs and hands still. Try to be interested in what the speaker is saying. You will learn more, and you will show him that he is important.

2. **Ask questions!** Try to understand what the speaker is saying. When the speaker says something you don't understand, raise your hand and wait to be acknowledged. Remember to ask your question before the speaker moves on to something else.

3. **Write it down!** Write down anything that you think you might forget.

4. **Concentrate!** Think about what the speaker is saying. Listen with your brain as well as your ears.

5. **Listen to directions!** Listen to understand each step. Ask questions if you do not understand the directions.

>>>>>>>>> **Student Tip...**

For additional information and activities on following directions, refer to the Resource Tools Section on pages 522–523.

The 0-Quigley Story:
When Quigley Planned His Time

As soon as Mrs. Harper gave the class a study period, Quigley made a list of the most important things to do first. He wanted to make the most of this study period because he wouldn't have much time over the weekend to study. Quigley and his family were going on a canoe trip, and he was so excited. But that meant that he had to use his time wisely in order to get everything done so that he could enjoy his trip and not have to worry about unfinished homework.

He checked his supplies and started the first job on his list. He worked hard the whole time without looking up. By the time his study period was over, Quigley had gotten almost all of his homework completed. He carefully put his finished papers in the proper folders where he could easily find them on Monday. Then, he started getting ready to go home for his big weekend.

As he prepared to go home, Quigley noticed that Tommy was still trying to keep his supplies from tumbling out of his desk. Tommy hadn't finished one assignment. "Well, it looks like Tommy needs a friend to give him some advice," Quigley thought to himself as Mrs. Harper walked impatiently to Tommy's desk again.

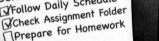

SCHOOL:
☑ Follow Daily Schedule
☑ Check Assignment Folder
☐ Prepare for Homework

HOME:
☐ Eat Snack
☐ Do Chores
☐ Do Homework
☐ Free time
☐ Eat Dinner

Discuss It:

1. What did Quigley do first to help him get his work done during study period?

2. What else did Quigley do before he began working?

3. Why did Quigley work so hard during study period?

4. What did Quigley do with his finished papers?

5. What did Quigley notice about Tommy?

6. What do you think Quigley has decided to do about Tommy?

Learn It: PLANNING YOUR TIME

Reference 4   Study Skills for Planning Your Time

PLAN YOUR TIME...

1. **Set goals for yourself!** Choose one study skill at a time that you need to improve. Think of reasons why you need help in this area. Make a list of the things you can do to improve. Then, stick to it.

2. **Plan your day!** Make an assignment folder and check it every day. Know what you need to do and plan time to work on it. Check off completed assignments.

3. **Do what is important first!** Assignments that are due first should be completed first.

4. **Make each minute count!** Concentrate on the job at hand. If you don't waste time, you will have more time to do the things you like to do. Keep your eyes on your work and keep your pencil moving. Don't give yourself a chance to stop working by breaking your concentration.

5. **Reward yourself!** When you complete a goal, allow yourself to feel proud for a job well done.

The O-Quigley Story:
When Quigley Did His Homework

Quigley was getting ready to go home. He made sure he had his assignments written down, and he checked to make sure he had the books and supplies that he would need. He carefully put everything into his book bag.

Then, he glanced at Tommy. Last week, he had talked to Tommy and offered to help him. Now, Tommy was doing everything that Quigley did. "That talk really helped Tommy," Quigley thought to himself as he grinned at Tommy. Tommy smiled back and gave him the OK sign. Lately, Mrs. Harper was smiling at Quigley and at Tommy. Tommy was really trying hard, and it was paying off. His desk looked just like Quigley's, and he worked hard, just like Quigley. He listened to Mrs. Harper and asked only necessary questions, just like Quigley. And, Tommy said he even liked school—just like Quigley!

"And I bet he gets his homework done again tonight, just like me!" Quigley laughed to himself as he walked happily out the door with Tommy.

Discuss It:

1. How did Quigley prepare for his homework before he left school?
2. How did Tommy prepare for his homework before he left school?
3. How did Quigley help Tommy?
4. How was Tommy different after their talk?
5. How did Mrs. Harper's attitude change in the story?
6. How do you think Quigley felt as he watched Tommy improve?

Learn It: DOING HOMEWORK

Reference 5	Study Skills for Doing Homework

DO YOUR HOMEWORK...

1. **Think before you leave school!** Check your assignment folder and decide what you need to take home. Put books and folders you will need in your book bag.
2. **Schedule a time to study!** Think about your family's routine and decide on a good study time. Stick to your schedule.
3. **Study where you can concentrate!** You can get homework done in a very short time if you do it away from TV, conversations, or other distractions. Have all the supplies you will need at your study area.
4. **Set a time limit to study!** See how long you can concentrate. You might use a timer to set a time for a focused study period and then give yourself a break or a reward at the end of that time.
5. **Have a special place to keep homework!** When your homework is finished, put it in your book bag, and you will always have it ready to take to school.

Discuss It: A REVIEW

1. What do you think about the new Quigley?
2. How does the organized Quigley differ from the unorganized Quigley?
3. Do you think good study skills helped Quigley and Tommy become better students?
4. Do you think good study skills could help you become a better student?
5. What study habits would you like to improve?

Apply It: EVALUATING INDIVIDUAL STUDY HABITS

Do you enjoy learning new things at school? Do you work hard to improve your study skills? Do you use good study habits? Most of you know the answers to these questions by the time you are in sixth grade.

Being a good student involves more than how fast you learn. Most students who do well in school know how to get organized, how to listen, how to plan their time, and how to get their homework finished.

Use the Study Skills Assessment on the next page to help you evaluate your personal study habits. This assessment is designed to help you make improvements.

>>>>>>>>>>>> Student Tip...

Ask your parents to help you practice these study skills until they become good habits. Make posters of the study skills for your room to remind you what to do.

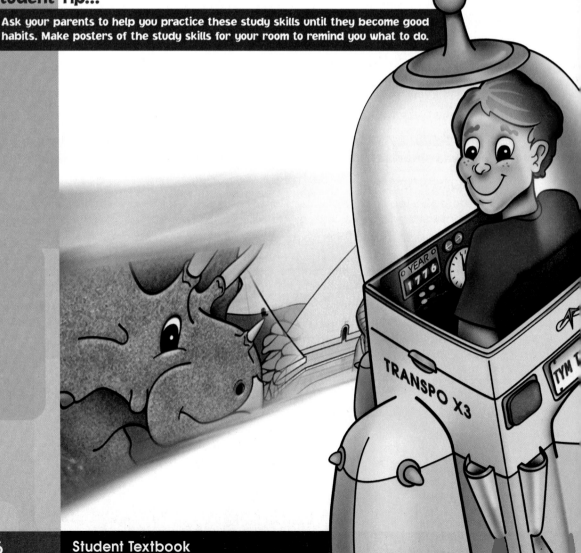

Study Skills Assessment

Name:_____ Date:_____

Directions: Rate your skills in each category by marking the appropriate column with an **X**.

GET ORGANIZED: Reference 2

	Excellent	Average	Needs Improvement
1. Being prepared	☐	☐	☐
2. Organizing your desk	☐	☐	☐
3. Putting everything in its place	☐	☐	☐
4. Realizing the importance of directions	☐	☐	☐
5. Proofreading your work	☐	☐	☐

LISTEN: Reference 3

	Excellent	Average	Needs Improvement
1. Listening with your whole body	☐	☐	☐
2. Asking questions	☐	☐	☐
3. Taking notes	☐	☐	☐
4. Concentrating	☐	☐	☐
5. Listening to directions	☐	☐	☐

PLAN YOUR TIME: Reference 4

	Excellent	Average	Needs Improvement
1. Setting goals for yourself	☐	☐	☐
2. Planning your day	☐	☐	☐
3. Doing what is important first	☐	☐	☐
4. Making each minute count	☐	☐	☐
5. Rewarding yourself	☐	☐	☐

DO YOUR HOMEWORK: Reference 5

	Excellent	Average	Needs Improvement
1. Collecting assignments before you leave school	☐	☐	☐
2. Scheduling a time to study	☐	☐	☐
3. Studying where you can concentrate	☐	☐	☐
4. Setting a time limit to study	☐	☐	☐
5. Having a special place to keep homework	☐	☐	☐

If you marked any areas as "Average" or "Needs Improvement," look back at the references in those areas to help you find ways to improve. Find a study-skills partner to check your progress, to encourage you, and to give you advice and help.

START LESSON 3

Lesson 3

You will

- practice Jingle 1.
- implement study plans for school and home.
- read, listen, and implement journal writing.
- write in your journal.

LISTENING AND SPEAKING:

 Jingle Time

Recite It: Practice Jingle 1 in the Jingle Section on page 506.

STUDY PLANS

Learn It: A STUDY PLAN TO ORGANIZE SCHOOLWORK

You have learned that goals are important because they are a constant reminder of what you want to happen in your future. Remember that goals are your destination. A schedule is your road map. You may take a few detours, but you still know the general direction in which you are headed and how to get there.

The first step in good organization is to make and follow a plan of action.

 Reference 6 **Study Plan to Organize Schoolwork**

You should use this plan to keep things in order!

1. Keep all necessary school supplies in a handy, heavy-duty plastic bag or a pencil bag that zips shut.

2. Make a folder labeled **Unfinished Work**. Put all unfinished work for every subject in this folder so that any unfinished work is easy to find. *(Keep this folder on the top left side of your desk so that it is available to you and the teacher at all times.)*

3. Make a folder labeled **Finished Work** for each school subject. (Finished Work for Math, Finished Work for English, etc.) Place only the finished papers for a subject in the left pocket of the appropriate folder immediately after finishing the work. Put notes to study, graded tests, and study guides in the brads so that you will have them to study for scheduled tests. *(Choose a different-colored folder for each subject to make it easier to find a specific subject.)*

4. Make a folder labeled **Progress** for all graded work that will be sent home for parents to view.

5. Make a folder labeled **Paper** to store two kinds of paper: unused paper and papers to throw away. Place clean sheets of unused paper in the right pocket and keep it full at all times. In the left pocket, place papers that need to be thrown away. Check this pocket and empty it at the end of every day. Make sure you do not stuff trash papers in your subject folders or your desk!

6. Make a folder labeled **Assignments** and review it every day. Ideas for your Assignments folder are listed below.

   A. Keep a monthly calendar of assignments, test dates, report-due dates, project-due dates, extra activities, important dates and times, review dates, etc.

   B. Keep a grade sheet to record the grades received in each subject. *(You might also consider keeping your grades on the inside cover of each subject folder. However you keep track of your grades, just remember to record them accurately. Your grades are your business, so keep up with them! Grades help you know which subject areas need attention.)*

   C. Make a list every day of the things you want to do. Mark off tasks as you complete them and move the unfinished items to a new list the next day. *(Making this list takes time, but it's your road map to success. You will always know at a glance what you set out to accomplish and what still needs to be done.)*

Learn It: A STUDY PLAN FOR SCHOOL

A study plan for school gives you a daily routine to follow.

 Reference 7   Study Plan for School

You should check this plan every day!

1. Eat a nutritious breakfast to start your day.

2. Attend class regularly.

3. Develop the "I'm-willing-to-do-what-it-takes-to-get-the-job-done-right" attitude. Schoolwork is your job; so, make it an important part of your daily life.

4. Work with your teachers and parents to correct any attitudes or habits that keep you from learning.

5. Make the effort to listen. Ask questions if you don't understand and answer questions if you are asked.

6. Write it down! Write it down! Write it down! Make a habit of taking notes in class. Put the notes in the correct subject folder.

7. Write down your assignments. Then, check your assignment folder every day. Know what is on your calendar. Remember to record everything on your calendar so you won't forget things.

8. Do what is important first! Assignments that are due first should be completed first. Turn your daily assignments in on time. If you are absent, ask about make-up work and turn it in on time.

9. Concentrate on the job at hand. If you don't waste time, you will get more work finished. Keep your eyes on your work and keep your pencil moving. Don't break your concentration; just keep working. Every time your eyes leave your paper to look around, you lose working time!

10. Think before you leave school! Check your assignment folder and decide what you need to take home. Put the books and folders you will need in a book bag so you won't forget them.

Learn It: A STUDY PLAN FOR HOME

A study plan for home gives you a checklist of important things to consider when studying at home.

 Reference 8   Study Plan for Home

Stick to this plan every evening!

1. Schedule a time to study. Think about your family's routine and decide on a good study time. Stick to your schedule.

2. Study where you can concentrate. Complete your homework and studying before watching TV, playing computer games, or talking on the telephone.

3. Make a personal decision to concentrate 100 percent on completing your homework assignments. By doing this, you can accomplish more in less time.

4. Check your assignment folder every day. This puts you in charge!

5. Have a special place to keep homework. When your homework is finished, put it in your book bag or another designated place immediately. You will always have it ready to take to school, no matter how rushed you are the next morning.

6. Use your home study time to complete your assignments and/or to review for a test. Don't wait until the last minute to study for a test. Study a little every night so that you won't overload the night before the test. (You might have something unexpected come up the night before the big test!)

7. If possible, set a weekly meeting time to discuss your progress and problems with your parents. If this is not possible, evaluate your own progress. You need to decide which study skills you did not follow. Figure out how to "fix" the problem and try again! You will get better with practice.

Write It: JOURNAL WRITING

Reference 9 — Journal Writing

What is journal writing? **Journal Writing** is a written record of your personal thoughts and feelings about people, things, or events that are important to you. Recording your thoughts in a journal is a good way to remember how you felt about what was happening in your life at a particular time. You can record your dreams, memories, feelings, and experiences. You can ask questions. You can answer questions. A journal can also be a place to look for future writing topics, creative stories, poems, etc. Keeping a journal should develop into a lifelong habit. Later, you will enjoy looking back at what you have written because it shows how you have matured and the changes that have taken place in your life.

WHAT DO I WRITE ABOUT?

Journals are personal, but sometimes it helps to have ideas to get you started. Remember, in a journal, you do not have to stick to one topic. Write about someone or something you like. Write about what you did last weekend or on vacation. Write about what you hope to do this week or on your next vacation. Write about home, school, friends, hobbies, special talents (yours or someone else's), or the hopes and fears you have about things now and in the future. Looking at what's wrong with your world, what would you do to "fix" it? Write about the good things in your world and how you feel about them.

A journal can also be an excellent record of events. You can record details about past or present events. You could write opinions of past, present, or future events that have changed or could change the way you think about things. If something bothers you, record it in your journal. If something interests you, write about it in your journal. If you just want to write about something that does not seem important at all, record it in your journal. After all, it is *your* journal!

HOW DO I GET STARTED?

Use a spiral notebook or folder for your journal writing. Write the title, **My Personal Journal for the Year 20——**, on the front cover of your notebook or folder. Ask your teacher if you should write with a pen or pencil in your journal. On the first line of the journal entry, put the journal entry number and the date. Example: **Journal Entry 1 for September ____, 20——**. Skip the next line and begin your entry. You might write one or two sentences, a paragraph, a whole page, or several pages. If you have several entries on one page, skip three lines between each entry.

Except for the journal entry number and date, no particular organizational style is required for journal writing unless you are given instructions for a special assignment. You decide how best to organize and express your thoughts. Feel free to include sketches, diagrams, lists, etc., if these will help you remember your thoughts about a topic or an event. You will need a quiet place and at least 5-10 minutes of uninterrupted writing time. If you do not finish your journal entry during the assigned time, finish it during a study period. If you need to review what to do during Journal Writing, refer to this page.

Possible Topics:

| My best friend | I am thankful for... | This is the way I feel about... | My vacation |
| Three wishes | Favorite subjects | Things I would like to learn | I am good at... |

JOURNAL WRITING — 1

Write an entry in your journal.
Use Reference 9 above.

English Made Easy

LISTENING AND SPEAKING:

Recite It: Practice Jingle 1 in the Jingle Section on page 506.

Learn It: THE IMPORTANCE OF CAPITALIZATION AND PUNCTUATION

It is important for you to know how to capitalize and punctuate any type of writing correctly.

Lesson 4

You will

- practice Jingle 1.
- read and discuss capitalization and punctuation rules.
- read and discuss editing guide.
- do Classroom Practice 1.
- write in your journal.

Reference 10	The Importance of Capitalization and Punctuation

Can you imagine trying to read something with no capitalization or punctuation? How would you know when a writer's thought was complete? How would you know when to pause and when to take a breath? Read this short paragraph aloud and see if it makes sense to you. Read it with no pauses and without expression because there are no punctuation marks to tell you what to do.

our family has a yearly reunion every may aunts uncles and cousins gather at our favorite lake for camping fishing and eating good food is a specialty of the women in our family during the get-together everyone sings songs and tells stories around the campfire while the children laugh and play games at midnight the family gong sounds for everyone to go to bed

---

Learn It: CAPITALIZATION RULES

The capitalization rules are organized into sections of similar rules.
Read the titles of each section.

Reference 11	Capitalization Rules

SECTION 1: CAPITALIZE THE FIRST WORD

1. The first word of a sentence. *(He likes to take a nap.)*
2. The first word in the greeting and closing of letters. *(Dear, Yours truly, Sincerely, etc.)*
3. The first, last, and important words in titles of literary works.
   (books, songs, short stories, poems, articles, movie titles, magazines, newspapers, etc.) (Note: Conjunctions, articles, and prepositions with fewer than five letters are not capitalized unless they are the first or last words.)
4. The first word of a direct quotation. *(Dad said, "We are going home.")*
5. The first word in the topics, subtopics, and details of an outline.

SECTION 2: CAPITALIZE NAMES, INITIALS, AND TITLES OF PEOPLE

6. The pronoun I. *(May I go with you?)*
7. The names and nicknames of people. *(Sam, Joe, Jones, Slim, Junior, etc.)*
8. Family names when used in place of or with a person's name.
   (Grandmother, Auntie, Uncle Joe, etc.) (Note: Do not capitalize family names when a possessive noun or pronoun is used with it: My mom, Her father, His aunt, etc.)
9. Titles used with, or in place of, people's names. *(Mr., Ms., Prime Minister, Dr. Lin, Captain, President, Sir, etc.)*
10. People's initials. *(J. D., C. Smith, K. C. Jones, etc.)*

Continued on next page. >>>

Reference 11 continued from previous page.

SECTION 3: CAPITALIZE DESIGNATIONS OF TIME

11. The days of the week and months of the year. *(Monday, Wednesday, July, February, etc.)*
12. The names of holidays. *(Christmas, Thanksgiving, New Year's Day, etc.)*
13. The names of historical events, periods, laws, documents, conflicts, and distinguished awards.
    (Civil War, Middle Ages, Bill of Rights, Medal of Honor, etc.)

SECTION 4: CAPITALIZE NAMES OF PLACES

14. The names and abbreviations of cities, towns, counties, states, countries, nations, and continents.
    (Dallas, Texas, Fulton County, Africa, America, USA, CA, TX, etc.)
15. The names of avenues, streets, roads, highways, routes, and post office boxes.
    (Main Street, Jones Road, Highway 89, Rt. 1, Box 2, P.O. Box 45, etc.)
16. The names of lakes, rivers, oceans, other bodies of water, mountain ranges, deserts, parks, stars, planets, and constellations. *(Beaver Lake, New York Harbor, Rocky Mountains, Glacier National Park, Sahara Desert, etc.)*
17. The names of schools and specific school courses that are either numbered or name a language.
    (Walker Elementary School, Mathematics II, French, English, etc.)
18. North, South, East, and West when they refer to geographical regions of the country.
    (up North, lives in the East, traveled out West, Southern gentleman, etc.)
    (Note: Do not capitalize directional words: Go south two miles.)

SECTION 5: CAPITALIZE NAMES OF OTHER NOUNS AND PROPER ADJECTIVES

19. The names of pets. *(Spot, Tweety Bird, Muffin, etc.)*
20. The names of products. *(Dixie cups, Dove soap, Ford automobiles, etc.)*
21. The names, abbreviations, or acronyms of companies, buildings, stores, monuments, ships, airplanes, spaceships. *(Empire State Building, Titanic, IBM, The Big Tire Co., Statue of Liberty, Challenger, etc.)*
22. Proper adjectives. *(the English language, Italian restaurant, French test, etc.)*
23. The names of clubs, organizations, groups, or teams. *(Lion's Club, Jaycees, Beatles, Dallas Cowboys, etc.)*
24. The names of political parties, religious preferences, nationalities, and races.
    (Democratic party, Republican, Jewish synagogue, American flag, etc.)

Learn It: PUNCTUATION RULES

The punctuation rules are also organized into sections of similar rules.
Read the titles of each section.

Reference 12 Punctuation Rules

SECTION 1: END-MARK PUNCTUATION

1. Use a period (.) for the end punctuation of a sentence that makes a statement. *(Mom baked us a cake.)*
2. Use a question mark (?) for the end punctuation of a sentence that asks a question.
   (Are you going to town?)
3. Use an exclamation point (!) for the end punctuation of a sentence that expresses strong feeling.
   (That bee stung me!)
4. Use a period (.) for the end punctuation of a sentence that gives a command or makes a request.
   (Close the door.)

Continued on next page. >>>

Reference 12 continued from previous page.

SECTION 2:   **COMMAS TO SEPARATE TIME WORDS**

5. Use a comma between the day of the week and the month and day. *(Friday, July 23)*
Use a comma between the day and year. *(July 23, 2009)*
6. Use a comma after the year when the complete date is used in the middle of the sentence.
(We spent July 23, 2004, with Grandmother.)
Note: When just the month and the year appear in a sentence, no comma is required.
(We leave in May 2006 for our first vacation.)

SECTION 3:   **COMMAS TO SEPARATE LOCATION WORDS**

7. Use a comma to separate the city from the state (or country) or route numbers from the street address
(or box number). *(I will go to Dallas, Texas.   He is from Paris, France.   Rt. 2, Box 55   Rt. 4, Smokey Lane)*
8. Use a comma to separate the state or country from the rest of the sentence when the name of the state
or country follows the name of a city. *(We flew to Dallas, Texas, in June.   We flew to Paris, France, in July.)*

SECTION 4:   **COMMAS TO MAKE MEANINGS CLEAR**

9. Use a comma to separate words or phrases in a series. *(We had soup, crackers, and milk.)*
10. Use a comma **after** an introductory word, an introductory prepositional phrase, or an introductory clause.
(Oh, I see.   In the morning, the ship will dock.   If you go, I will go.)
(Other introductory words: well, today, now, yes, no, so)
Use a comma **before** the conjunction in a compound sentence and before *too* when it means "also."
(Jim mowed the yard, and Larry raked the leaves.   I want a brownie, too.)
11. Use commas to set off most appositives. An appositive is a word, phrase, title, or degree used directly
after another word to explain or rename it. *(Sue, my friend, likes to draw.   My brother, Tim, is working today.)*
12. Use commas to separate a noun of direct address (the name of a person directly spoken to)
from the rest of the sentence. *(Mom, do you want some tea?)*

SECTION 5:   **PUNCTUATION IN GREETINGS AND CLOSINGS OF LETTERS**

13. Use a comma (**,**) after the salutation (greeting) of a friendly letter. *(Dear Sam,)*
14. Use a comma (**,**) after the closing of any letter. *(Yours truly,)*
15. Use a colon (**:**) after the salutation (greeting) of a business letter. *(Dear Madam:)*

📖 **Reference 13** | **Punctuation Rules**

SECTION 6: PERIODS

16. Use a period after most abbreviations or titles that are accepted in formal writing.
   (Mr., Ms., Dr., Capt., St., Ave., St. Louis, etc.)
   (Note: These abbreviations should not be used alone. They should be used with a proper noun.)
   In the abbreviations or acronyms of many well-known organizations or words, periods are not required.
   (USA, GM, TWA, GTE, AT&T, TV, AM, FM, GI, etc.)
   Use only one period after an abbreviation at the end of a statement. Do not put an extra period for the end-mark punctuation.

17. Use a period after initials. *(C. Smith, D. J. Brewton, Thomas A. Jones, etc.)*

18. Place a period after Roman numerals, Arabic numbers, and letters of the alphabet in an outline.
   (II., IV., 5., 25., A., B., etc.)

SECTION 7: APOSTROPHES

19. Form a contraction by using an apostrophe in place of a letter or letters that have been left out.
   (I'll, he's, isn't, wasn't, can't, etc.)

20. Form the possessive of singular and plural nouns by using an apostrophe.
   (boy's football, boys' football, child's football, children's football, James's football, Jameses' football, etc.)

21. Form the plurals of letters, symbols, numbers, and signs with an apostrophe and *s* ('s).
   (9's, B's, b's, etc.)

SECTION 8: UNDERLINING

22. Use underlining for writing the titles of ships, books, magazines, newspapers, motion pictures, full-length plays, works of art, and long musical compositions. (Our newspaper is the <u>Gazette</u>.)
   (<u>Titanic</u>, <u>Charlotte's Web</u>, <u>Reader's Digest</u>, <u>Macbeth</u>, etc.) These titles may also be italicized instead of underlined. (Our newspaper is the *Gazette*.) (*Titanic, Charlotte's Web, Reader's Digest, Macbeth*, etc.)

SECTION 9: QUOTATIONS

23. Use quotation marks around titles of book chapters, magazine articles, short stories and plays, essays, single poems, television and radio programs, songs, and short pieces of music.
   (Do you like to sing the song "America" in music class?)

24. Use quotation marks at the beginning and end of the speaker's words to separate what the speaker said from the rest of the sentence. Since the quotation tells what is being said, it should always have quotation marks around it.

25. Do not use quotation marks to set off explanatory words, the words that tell who is speaking.
   (Fred said, "I'm here.") (**Fred said** *is explanatory and should not be set off with quotation marks.)*

26. Use a new paragraph to indicate a change of speaker.

27. When a speaker's speech is longer than one paragraph, use quotation marks at the beginning of each paragraph and at the end of the last paragraph of that speaker's speech.

28. Use single quotation marks to enclose a quotation within a quotation.
   ("My bear says 'I love you' four different ways," said little Amy.)

29. Use a period at the end of explanatory words that come at the end of a sentence.

30. Use a comma to separate a direct quotation from the explanatory words.

Learn It: **CAPITALIZATION AND PUNCTUATION RULES AND CORRECTIONS**

Look at Sentence 1 in Reference 14. The capitalization rule numbers have been written above the corrections to verify the reasons for the corrections. The punctuation rule numbers have been written below the corrections to verify the reasons for the corrections. When you are required to write rule numbers, it is helpful to work with capitalization rules first and then to work with punctuation rules.

Reference 14 | **Capitalization & Punctuation Rules and the Editing Guide**

For the first sentence, write the capitalization and punctuation rule numbers for each correction in **blue** print to verify the reason for the correction. Use References 11–13 to look up the capitalization and punctuation rule numbers.

```
   1  6      14      14        11
1. Yes, I'll go to Lincoln, Nebraska, in July for our family reunion.
   10 19              7        8                                    1
```

Checking a sentence or a paragraph for mistakes is called **proofreading**. Correcting these mistakes is called **editing**. You will have an **Editing Guide** that will tell you how many mistakes of each kind you will find in the sentence or paragraph to be edited.

For the second sentence, put punctuation corrections within the sentence. Write all other corrections above the sentence.

Editing Guide: Capitals: 8   Periods: 1   Commas: 3   Misspelled Words: 1   End Marks: 1

```
   m L        S             C    I              S   N   Mountains
2. mr. lee, did the swedish tourists leave chicago, illinois, on their way to the sierra nevada mountins?
```

Learn It: THE EDITING GUIDE

Look at Sentence 2. An **Editing Guide** shows how many mistakes of each kind you will correct in an editing sentence or paragraph. As a capitalization mistake or misspelled word is found, the correction is written above it. As a punctuation mistake is found, the correction is written within the sentence.

The second sentence has an Editing Guide that tells how many capitalization, punctuation, and spelling mistakes are in the sentence. The number 8 after the word **Capitals** means that there are eight capitalization mistakes to correct. A number after the word **Periods** refers to periods used after abbreviations and initials within the sentence. A number after The number 3 written after the word **Commas** means that there are three comma mistakes. The number 1 after **Misspelled Words** means that there is one spelling mistake to correct. **End Marks** refers to any period, question mark, or exclamation point at the end of a sentence.

After you have made the corrections listed in the Editing Guide, you must always double-check your work by counting each type of correction you made to make sure the total matches the Editing Guide.

 Classroom Practice 1

It is time to practice the skills you are learning. You will use the classroom practice on the next page to apply these skills.

Student Tip...

If you need a more in-depth study of how to use the dictionary, refer to the Resource Tools Section on pages 531-532.

JOURNAL WRITING 2

Write an entry in your journal. Use Reference 9 on page 12 for ideas.

Classroom Practice 1

Name:_____ Date:_____

SKILLS

▶ **Exercise 1:** Using Reference 11 on page 13, write the capitalization rule number in column A and the letter that best illustrates each rule in column B.

A	B		
		1. Capitalize the names of products.	A. Tuesday, June, August
		2. Capitalize the names of holidays.	B. English test, French fries
		3. Capitalize proper adjectives.	C. Mike, Meg, Junior
		4. Capitalize the names of pets.	D. Dear,
		5. Capitalize the names and nicknames of people.	E. Whiskers, Spot, Fido
		6. Capitalize people's initials.	F. Mr., Mrs., Dr., Sir
		7. Capitalize the first word in the greeting of letters.	G. Chicago, Illinois
		8. Capitalize the names of cities, towns, and states.	H. Ford, Kleenex
		9. Capitalize titles used with, or in place of, people's names.	I. T. J., P. Allen
		10. Capitalize the days of the week and months of the year.	J. Christmas, Labor Day

▶ **Exercise 2:** Using References 12–13 on pages 14, 16, write the punctuation rule number in column A and the letter that best illustrates each rule in column B.

A	B		
		1. Use an apostrophe to form a contraction.	A. T. S. Eliot
		2. Use a period after initials.	B. Dear Sir:
		3. Use a colon after the salutation of a business letter.	C. you'll, she's, won't
		4. Use a comma between the day and the year.	D. girl's dress
		5. Use a comma to separate words or phrases in a series.	E. Miami, Florida
		6. Use a comma after the salutation of a friendly letter.	F. January 1, 2010
		7. Use an apostrophe to make a noun possessive.	G. A's, a's
		8. Use an apostrophe to form the plural of letters.	H. TIME, Old Yeller
		9. Use underlining for titles of books and magazines.	I. juice, tea, and milk
		10. Use a comma to separate the city from the state.	J. Dear Kate,

EDITING

▶ **Exercise 3:** Write the capitalization and punctuation rule numbers for each correction in **bold type.**
Use References 11–13 on pages 13–16 to look up the capitalization and punctuation rule numbers.

Our guide, **Mr. H. G. M**artinez, took us camping on Table Rock Lake near Branson, Missouri.

▶ **Exercise 4:** Put punctuation corrections within the sentence. Write all other corrections above the sentence.
Editing Guide: Capitals: 6   Commas: 4   Misspelled Words: 1   End Marks: 1

we exspect my sister maria to arrive in dallas texas on the fourth of july

English Made Easy

LISTENING AND SPEAKING:

Jingle Time

Recite It: 1. Practice Jingle 1 in the Jingle Section on page 506.
2. Recite the new jingle.

♪	Jingle 2	**The Sentence Jingle**

A sentence, sentence, sentence
Is complete, complete, complete
When five simple rules
It meets, meets, meets.

It has a subject, subject, subject
And a verb, verb, verb.
And it makes sense, sense, sense
With every word, word, word.

Add a capital letter
And a punctuation mark.
And now our sentence has all its parts!

But REMEMBER—
Subject and **verb** and **complete sense**,
With a **capital letter** and an **end mark**, too.
Our sentence is complete,
And now we're through!

Skill Time

Learn It: SYNONYMS AND ANTONYMS

You are able to communicate more effectively when you do not use the same words over and over again. That is why it is necessary to add a wide variety of synonyms and antonyms to your vocabulary.

📖	Reference 15	**Synonyms and Antonyms**

Synonyms are words that have similar, or almost the same, meanings.
Antonyms are words that have opposite meanings.

1. guess, surmise
<u>Synonyms</u> or Antonyms

2. fatigue, exhaustion
<u>Synonyms</u> or Antonyms

3. fragile, strong
Synonyms or <u>Antonyms</u>

>>>>>>>>>> **Student Tip...**

You will learn new synonyms and antonyms during Vocabulary and Analogy Time. Use the dictionary for a more in-depth study of any synonym or antonym presented. Refer to the Resource Tools Section on pages 531-532 for more information on using the dictionary.

You will
- practice Jingle 1; recite new jingle (Sentence).
- analyze synonyms/ antonyms.
- learn new vocabulary word.
- learn new analogy.
- respond to oral analogy exercise.
- study new vocabulary; make card 1; write own sentence using the vocabulary word.
- analyze new analogy; make card 1; write own analogy.
- do Classroom Practice 2.

Vocabulary & Analogy Time

Learn It: VOCABULARY WORDS

Notice how the vocabulary section is arranged. For each vocabulary word, there is a definition of the word, a synonym and antonym for the word, and a sentence that helps you understand the word and remember how it is used.

Reference 16	Vocabulary & Analogy Words

Word: sarcasm (sär'kăz'əm)
    Definition: words designed to hurt
    Synonym: ridicule   **Antonym:** encouragement
    Sentence: The **sarcasm** in Pam's response hurt Brittany's feelings.

Analogy: open : close :: run : walk
    Antonym relationship: Just as **open** is the opposite of **close**,
    run is the opposite of **walk**.

Vocabulary Card 1: Record the vocabulary information above and write your own sentence, using the new word.

Analogy Card 1: Record the analogy information and write your own analogy, using the same relationship as the analogy above.

Learn It: WORD ANALOGIES

Reference 17	Word Analogies

An **analogy** is a way of looking at pairs of words to find out what they have in common or how they are related. An analogy usually has one word missing. An analogy has symbols that must be read a certain way. Notice how the colons are placed in the analogy below.

This is an analogy statement: **puppy : dog :: kitten : _cat_ .**

This is the proper reading of the analogy: puppy is to dog as kitten is to <u>cat</u>.

To solve an analogy, you must divide it into two parts. In one part, you are given two words. You must decide how these two words relate to each other. Some ways that words can be related are listed below.

Common Relationships	Analogy	How the Words Are Related
1. Synonym	daybreak : dawn	**Daybreak** means nearly the same as **dawn**.
2. Antonym	fear : confidence	**Fear** is the opposite of **confidence**.
3. Part-to-whole	leaf : tree	A **leaf** is part of a **tree**.
4. Purpose or use	glove : hand	A **glove** goes on a **hand**.
5. Progression or sequence	puppy : dog	A **puppy** grows into a **dog**.
6. Type or kind	rose : flower	A **rose** is a kind of **flower**.
7. Descriptive or characteristic	green : grass	**Green** describes **grass**.
8. Rhyming	peace : lease	**Peace** rhymes with **lease**.
9. Grammatical	break : broke	**Break** is the present tense of **broke**.
10. Homonym	hare : hair	**Hare** and **hair** sound alike but have different meanings and spellings.

In the other part of the analogy, you are given only one of the two words. Since you must supply the missing word, you must think about how the first pair of words is related. Then, choose the word that makes the second pair relate in the same way.

Continued on next page. >>>

Reference 17 continued from previous page.

1. **daybreak : dawn :: vacant : _____.**
(Read as: Daybreak is to dawn as vacant is to _____.)
Thinking process: **Synonym** - Just as daybreak means nearly the same as dawn, vacant means nearly the same as <u>empty</u>.

2. **fear : confidence :: hate : _____.**
(Read as: Fear is to confidence as hate is to _____.)
Thinking process: **Antonym** - Just as fear is the opposite of confidence, hate is the opposite of <u>love</u>.

3. **leaf : tree :: finger : _____.**
(Read as: Leaf is to tree as finger is to _____.)
Thinking process: **Part-to-whole** - Just as a leaf is a part of a tree, a finger is a part of a <u>hand</u>.

4. **glove : hand :: _____ : foot**
(Read as: Glove is to hand as _____ is to foot.)
Thinking process: **Purpose or use** - Just as a glove goes on a hand, a <u>sock</u> goes on a foot.

5. **puppy : dog :: kitten : _____.**
(Read as: Puppy is to dog as kitten is to _____.)
Thinking process: **Progression or sequence** - Just as a puppy grows into a dog, a kitten grows into a <u>cat</u>.

6. **rose : flower :: _____ : insect**
(Read as: Rose is to flower as _____ is to insect.)
Thinking process: **Type or kind** - Just as a rose is a kind of flower, a <u>grasshopper</u> is a kind of insect.

7. **green : grass :: _____ : water**
(Read as: Green is to grass as _____ is to water.)
Thinking process: **Descriptive or characteristic** - Just as green describes grass, <u>wet</u> describes water.

8. **peace : lease :: _____ : rain**
(Read as: Peace is to lease as _____ is to rain.)
Thinking process: **Rhyming** - Just as peace rhymes with lease, <u>pain</u> rhymes with rain.

9. **break : broke :: _____ : swam**
(Read as: Break is to broke as _____ is to swam.)
Thinking process: **Grammatical** - Just as break is the present tense of broke, <u>swim</u> is the present tense of swam.

10. **hare : hair :: _____ : blew**
(Read as: Hare is to hair as _____ is to blew.)
Thinking process: **Homonym** - Just as hare is a homonym of hair, <u>blue</u> is a homonym of blew.

Review: Step 1: Decide how the completed pair of words is related.
 Step 2: Think how the incomplete pair of words show the same kind of relationship.
 Step 3: Choose a word for the incomplete pair that makes both pairs relate in the same way.

Word Analogy Exercise: Choose the correct missing word and put the letter in the blank.

1. lazy : energetic :: introduction : <u>b</u>   a. preface   b. conclusion   c. epilogue   d. critique

2. finger : touch :: <u>c</u> : taste   a. sweet   b. saliva   c. tongue   d. lip

3. verse : <u>d</u> :: chapter : novel   a. painting   b. book   c. biography   d. poem

4. cub : bear :: <u>c</u>   a. colt : saddle   b. colt : hoof   c. colt : horse   d. colt : animal

Apply It: MAKING CARDS FOR VOCABULARY AND ANALOGY WORDS

Making cards for vocabulary and analogies will help you remember them.

Reference 18   **Making Cards for Vocabulary & Analogy Words**

TO MAKE A VOCABULARY CARD

Use a 4x6 index card with lines to record vocabulary information. Write the vocabulary word on the blank side of the card, and write the other information about the vocabulary word on the side with lines. At the bottom of the card, write your own sentence, using the new vocabulary word. Use the index cards as flash cards to study vocabulary words with a study partner at home or at school. Keep the vocabulary cards in plastic zip bags or recipe boxes.

TO MAKE AN ANALOGY CARD:

Use a 4x6 or a 3x5 index card with lines. Write all the analogy information on the side with lines. At the bottom of the card, write your own analogy, using the same relationship as the analogy in the reference. Use the index cards to study analogies with a study partner at home or at school. Keep the analogy cards in plastic zip bags or recipe boxes.

Classroom Practice 2

It is time to practice the skills you are learning. You will use the classroom practice on the next page to apply these skills.

Classroom Practice 2

Name:_____ Date:_____

SKILLS

▶ **Exercise 1:** Match the definitions by writing the correct letter beside each number.

_____ 1. periods, commas, apostrophes, end marks

_____ 2. words with similar meanings

_____ 3. words with opposite meanings

_____ 4. comparisons of words with similar relationships

A. synonyms

B. antonyms

C. analogies

D. punctuation

▶ **Exercise 2:** Identify each pair of words as synonyms or antonyms by underlining the correct answer.

1. brief, short

Synonyms or Antonyms

2. verify, confirm

Synonyms or Antonyms

3. entire, partial

Synonyms or Antonyms

▶ **Exercise 3:** Choose the correct missing word and put the letter in the blank.

1. button : shirt :: buckle : ____   a. brace   b. belt   c. ornament   d. bend

2. rake : leaves :: ____ : dirt   a. mud   b. shirt   c. dirty   d. shovel

3. pool : ____ :: pillow : willow   a. stool   b. water   c. splash   d. wood

4. foot : head :: ____   a. oak : tree   b. snout : tail   c. move : go   d. water : fish

EDITING

▶ **Exercise 4:** Write the capitalization and punctuation rule numbers for each correction in **bold type**. Use References 11–13 on pages 13–16 to look up the capitalization and punctuation rule numbers.

Henri Dunant, founder of the Red Cross, accepted the Nobel Peace Prize in Oslo, Norway, in

December 1901.

▶ **Exercise 5:** Put punctuation corrections within the sentence. Write all other corrections above the sentence.

Editing Guide: Capitals: 9   Commas: 5   Apostrophes: 1   Misspelled Words: 1   End Marks: 1

are mom dad and ashley going to uncle dans brithday party in tampa florida on may 2 2009

LISTENING AND SPEAKING:
Oral Review Questions

Lesson 6

You will
- respond to oral review questions.
- take Chapter 1 Test.

Discuss It:

1. What are words with opposite meanings?

2. What are words with similar meanings?

3. What is the relationship between the words *spell* and *bell*?

4. What is the relationship between the words *yellow* and *lemon*?

5. What is the relationship between the words *thermometer* and *temperature*?

6. What is proofreading?

7. When you correct mistakes in a sentence or paragraph, what are you doing?

8. What does an editing guide tell you?

9. True or False. Except for the journal entry number and date, no particular organizational style is required for journal writing.

10. True or False. As a student in the sixth grade, short-term goals should include your plans for college and career.

11. What punctuation would you use to separate words in a series?

CHAPTER TEST

It is time to evaluate your knowledge of the skills you have learned in this chapter. Your teacher will give you the Chapter 1 Test to help you assess your progress.

>>>>>>>>>>>>>>>> **Student Tip...**

For information about test-taking strategies, refer to the Resource Tools Section on page 528.

Lesson 1

You will

- study new vocabulary; make card 2; write own sentence using the vocabulary word.
- analyze new analogy; make card 2; write own analogy.
- practice Jingles 1-2; recite new jingles (Noun and Verb).
- identify nouns, subject nouns, and verbs.
- learn how to classify sentences.
- classify Introductory Sentences.
- identify a Pattern 1 sentence.
- identify the five parts of a sentence.
- use **SN V** to write a Practice Sentence.
- do Classroom Practice 3.

LISTENING AND SPEAKING:
Vocabulary & Analogy Time

Learn It: Recite the new vocabulary and analogy words.

 Reference 19	Vocabulary & Analogy Words

Word: audacity (ô dăs'ĭtē)
    Definition: bold disregard of others
    Synonym: nerve   **Antonym:** discretion
    Sentence: She had the **audacity** to ask me to do her homework.

Analogy: leg : table :: key : piano
    Part-to-whole relationship: Just as a **leg** is part of a **table**, a **key** is part of a **piano**.

Vocabulary Card 2: Record the vocabulary information above and write your own sentence, using the new word.
Analogy Card 2: Record the analogy information and write your own analogy, using the same relationship as the analogy above.

Jingle Time

Recite It: 1. Practice Jingles 1–2 in the Jingle Section on page 506.
          2. Recite the new jingles.

♪ Jingle 3	The Noun Jingle

This is a noun jingle, my friend,
A noun jingle, my friend.
You can shake it to the left
And shake it to the right.
Find yourself a noun,
And then recite:

A noun names a person.
A noun names a thing.
A noun names a person,
Place, or thing,
And sometimes an idea.

Person, place, thing, idea!
Person, place, thing, idea!

So, shake it to the left,
And shake it to the right.
Find yourself a noun,
And feel just right!

♪ Jingle 4	The Verb Jingle

A verb, a verb.
What is a verb?
Haven't you heard?
There are two kinds of verbs:
The **action verb**
And the **linking verb**.

The action verb
Shows a state of action,
Like **stand** and **sit** and **smile**.
The action verb is always in motion
Because it tells what the subject does.
*We **stand**! We **sit**! We **smile**!*

The linking verb shows a state of being,
Like *am, is, are, was,* and *were,*
Looks, becomes, grows, and *feels.*
The linking verb shows no action
Because it tells what the subject is.
*He **is** a clown. He **looks** funny.*

Grammar Time

Learn It: NOUN, SUBJECT NOUN, AND VERB

Reference 20   **Noun, Subject Noun, and Verb**

NOUN AND SUBJECT NOUN

1. A **noun** names a person, place, thing, or idea. A noun is a naming word. Words like *nurse* and *Jonathan* name people. Words like *airport* and *ocean* name places. Words like *dog* and *train* name things. Animals are grouped in the category of *things*. Words like *freedom* and *beauty* name ideas.

2. The **subject** of a sentence tells who or what a sentence is about. Every sentence has a subject. Since a noun names a person, place, thing, or idea, a *subject noun* tells who or what a sentence is about.

3. A **subject noun** is labeled with the abbreviation **SN**.

VERB

4. A **verb** tells what the subject does or what the subject is. Every sentence has a verb. **Verbs** that tell what people or things do are called **action verbs**. Children *walk*. Children *play*. Kittens *walk*. Kittens *play*.

5. A **verb** is labeled with the abbreviation **V**.

Learn It: THE QUESTION AND ANSWER FLOW

Reference 21   **The Question & Answer Flow**

1. The **Question and Answer Flow** is a series of questions and answers used to identify the parts of a sentence.

2. **Classifying** is naming or identifying each word in a sentence by using the Question and Answer Flow. As you classify the words of a sentence, you will label each word with an abbreviation to identify its function.

3. To classify a subject noun in the Question and Answer Flow, ask a subject question to find the noun that serves as the subject of the sentence. The subject questions are **who** or **what**. Ask *who* if the sentence is *about people*. Ask *what* if the sentence is **not about people**, but about places, things, or ideas. Then, label the subject noun with the abbreviation **SN**.

4. To classify a verb in the Question and Answer Flow, ask the verb question *what is being said about* _____ *(the subject)* since the verb tells what the subject does. Then, label the verb with the abbreviation **V**.

The Question and Answer Flow for the Subject Noun and Verb

Practice Sentence: Detectives looked.

1. Who looked? **detectives – subject noun (SN)**
2. What is being said about detectives? **detectives looked – verb (V)**

     SN   V
Detectives looked.

Learn It: PATTERN 1

📖 **Reference 22** | **Pattern 1**

1. The **pattern**, or core, of a sentence identifies the **order of its main parts**.
2. A **Pattern 1** has only two main parts as its core: a subject noun (**SN**) and a verb (**V**).
3. A Pattern 1 sentence is identified with the abbreviations of its main parts and pattern number: **SN V P1**. It is also known as a noun-verb (**N V**) core.
4. In the Question and Answer Flow, the pattern of a sentence is identified after all the words in a sentence have been classified.
5. To identify a Pattern 1 sentence, say "Subject Noun, Verb, Pattern 1" and write **SN V P1** on the line in front of a Pattern 1 sentence.

Adding Pattern 1 to the Question and Answer Flow

Practice Sentence: Detectives looked.

1. Who looked? **detectives – subject noun (SN)**
2. What is being said about detectives? **detectives looked – verb (V)**
3. **Subject Noun, Verb, Pattern 1 (SN V P1)**

```
            SN        V
 SN  V      Detectives looked.
 P1
```

LISTENING AND SPEAKING:

Grammar Time

Apply It: These Introductory Sentences are used to apply the new grammar concepts taught. Classify these sentences orally with your teacher. You will say the **questions** and **answers** with your teacher. The Question and Answer Flow should have a lively rhythm and should be recited in unison.

Introductory Sentences | **Chapter 2: Lesson 1**

1. _____ Clowns raced.

2. _____ Swans flew.

3. _____ Squirrels climbed.

Skill Time

Learn It: THE FIVE PARTS OF A COMPLETE SENTENCE

A **complete sentence** is a group of words that has a subject and a verb and states a complete idea. A complete sentence should also begin with a capital letter and end with a punctuation mark. The five parts of a sentence are identified in the Sentence Jingle.

English Made Easy

GRAMMAR & WRITING CONNECTION:
Practice Sentence

Learn It: THE PRACTICE SENTENCE FOR *SN V*

A **Practice Sentence** is a sentence you write from the grammar labels that you are learning, like **SN** and **V**. To write a Practice Sentence, you must follow the labels and think of words that fit the labels and that make sense.

Reference 23	Practice Sentence for SN V
Labels: SN V	
Practice: Bumblebees buzzed.	

Look at the labels **SN** and **V** in Reference 23. First, think of a noun that you want to use as the subject noun. The example uses the word *bumblebees* as the subject noun. Notice that the word *bumblebees* is written *under* the label **SN** to identify it as the subject noun.

Next, think of a verb that tells what the subject does. You must make sure that the verb makes sense with the subject noun. The example uses the word *buzzed* as the verb. The word *buzzed* is written *under* the label **V** to identify it as the verb.

Apply It: WRITE A PRACTICE SENTENCE, USING THE LABELS *SN V*

Write a Practice Sentence, using a subject noun and a verb. On the top line of a sheet of notebook paper, write the title *Practice Sentence*. After you write your title, skip down two lines. On the third line, write the sentence labels **SN V**. Be sure to leave plenty of writing space between each label.

1. Go to the **SN** label for the subject noun. Think of a noun that tells who or what you want to use as the subject of your sentence *(person, place, thing, or idea)*. Write the noun you have chosen on the line *under* the **SN** label.

2. Go to the **V** label for the verb. Ask the verb question, "*what is being said about _____ (the subject)?*" to help you think of a verb that tells what your subject does. Make sure that your verb makes sense with the subject noun. Write the verb you have chosen on the line *under* the **V** label.

Practice It:

Write four more sentences, using the same steps that you used to write the first Practice Sentence. Remember to check each Practice Sentence for the five parts of a correct sentence. Each sentence must have a subject and a verb, it must make sense, it must start with a capital letter, and it must end with an end mark.

Classroom Practice 3

It is time to practice the skills you are learning. You will use the classroom practice on the next page to apply these skills.

Classroom Practice 3

Name:_____ Date:_____

GRAMMAR

▶ **Exercise 1:** Fill in the blanks below for this sentence: **Flags flew.**

1. What flew?..................................... _____ Subject Noun _____

2. What is being said about flags? .... _____ _____ Verb _____

3. Subject Noun, Verb, Pattern 1................... _____

Classify this sentence: _____ Flags flew.

▶ **Exercise 2:** Match the definitions by writing the correct letter beside each number.

_____ 1. verb question   A. what

_____ 2. subject-noun question (thing)   B. a capital letter

_____ 3. parts of a complete sentence   C. action verb

_____ 4. subject-noun question (person)   D. noun

_____ 5. sentences should begin with   E. subject, verb, complete sense

_____ 6. tells what the subject does   F. who

_____ 7. person, place, thing, idea   G. what is being said about

SKILLS

▶ **Exercise 3:** Identify each pair of words as synonyms or antonyms by underlining the correct answer.

1. occasionally, frequently   2. colossal, huge   3. ridicule, praise
   Synonyms or Antonyms   Synonyms or Antonyms   Synonyms or Antonyms

▶ **Exercise 4:** Choose the correct missing word and put the letter in the blank.

1. pepper : spice :: carrot : ____   a. orange   b. rabbit   c. vegetable   d. karat

2. calf : cow :: ____ : deer   a. fawn   b. leer   c. buck   d. hoof

3. rainbow : ____ :: wave : ocean   a. sun   b. sky   c. indigo   d. storm

4. jockey : horse :: ____   a. trunk : tree   b. stop : go   c. passenger : bus   d. softball : game

EDITING

▶ **Exercise 5:** Write the capitalization and punctuation rule numbers for each correction in **bold type.**
Use References 11–13 on pages 13–16 to look up the capitalization and punctuation rule numbers.

Do **K**elly and **I** have a direct flight from **H**ouston**,** **T**exas**,** to **A**tlanta**,** **G**eorgia**?**

▶ **Exercise 6:** Put punctuation corrections within the sentence. Write all other corrections above the sentence.
Editing Guide: Capitals: 4   Commas: 1   Apostrophes: 1   Misspelled Words: 2   End Marks: 1

sam we will go to papas pizza palace tonite to celabrate your new job

English Made Easy

LISTENING AND SPEAKING:
Vocabulary & Analogy Time

Learn It: Recite the new vocabulary and analogy words.

📖 Reference 24	Vocabulary & Analogy Words

Word: reiterate (rēĭt'ərāt')
  Definition: to say something over again
  Synonym: repeat   **Antonym:** refrain
  Sentence: The speaker **reiterated** the main points in his talk.

Analogy: pen : write :: scissors : cut
  Purpose or use relationship: Just as a **pen** is used to **write**,
        scissors are used to **cut**.

Vocabulary Card 3: Record the vocabulary information above and write your own
        sentence, using the new word.
Analogy Card 3: Record the analogy information and write your own analogy,
        using the same relationship as the analogy above.

Lesson 2

You will

- study new vocabulary; make card 3; write own sentence using the vocabulary word.
- analyze new analogy; make card 3; write own analogy.
- practice Jingles 3-4; recite new jingles (Adverb and Adjective).
- identify adverbs and adjectives.
- classify Introductory Sentences.
- use **Adj SN V Adv** to write a Practice Sentence.
- do Classroom Practice 4.

Jingle Time

Recite It: 1. Practice Jingles 3–4 in the Jingle Section on page 507.
        2. Recite the new jingles.

♪ Jingle 5	**The Adverb Jingle**

An adverb modifies a verb, adjective, or another adverb.
An adverb asks, "HOW? WHEN? WHERE?"
To find an adverb: **Go,** *(snap)* **Ask,** *(snap)* **Get.** *(snap)*
But where do I **go**? *To a verb, adjective, or another adverb.*
What do I **ask**? *HOW? WHEN? WHERE?*
What do I **get**? *An adverb, man. Cool!*

♪ Jingle 6	**The Adjective Jingle**

An adjective modifies a noun or a pronoun.
An adjective asks, "WHAT KIND?"
An adjective asks, "WHICH ONE?"
An adjective asks, "HOW MANY?"
To identify an adjective: **Go!** *(stomp, stomp)* **Ask!** *(clap, clap)* **Get!** *(snap)*
Where do I **go**? *(stomp, stomp)* To a noun or a pronoun.
What do I **ask**? *(clap, clap)* WHAT KIND? WHICH ONE? or HOW MANY?
What do I **get**? *(snap, snap)* An Adjective!

Grammar Time

Apply It: These Introductory Sentences are used to apply the new grammar concepts taught. Classify these sentences orally with your teacher.

Introductory Sentences	Chapter 2: Lesson 2

1. _____ Clowns raced wildly around yesterday.

2. _____ Swans flew very gracefully away.

3. _____ Five funny clowns raced madly around today.

Learn It: ADVERBS

Reference 25	Adverbs

There are several things you should know about adverbs.

1. The Adverb Jingle gives a lot of information about an adverb quickly and easily.

2. The adverb definition says that an adverb modifies a verb, an adjective, or another adverb.

3. The adverb questions are *How? When? Where?*

4. The adverb definition uses the word *modifies.* The word **modify** means to describe. When the adverb definition says that an adverb modifies a verb, an adjective, or another adverb, it means that an adverb **describes** a verb, an adjective, or another adverb.

5. An *adverb* is labeled with the abbreviation **Adv.**

6. An adverb is not part of a sentence pattern because it is not considered a core part. Always identify the core parts of a sentence, the subject noun and verb, before identifying other parts of the sentence.

Adding Adverbs to the Question and Answer Flow

Practice Sentence: Detectives looked around thoroughly today.

1. Who looked around thoroughly today? **detectives – subject noun (SN)**
2. What is being said about detectives? **detectives looked – verb (V)**
3. Looked where? **around – adverb (Adv)**
4. Looked how? **thoroughly – adverb (Adv)**
5. Looked when? **today – adverb (Adv)**
6. **Subject Noun, Verb, Pattern 1 (SN V P1)**

	SN	V	Adv	Adv	Adv
SN V / P1	Detectives	looked	around	thoroughly	today.

Discuss It:

1. Where do you go to find an adverb?

2. Where do you go **first** to find an adverb?

3. What is the verb in the practice sentence?

Continued on next page. >>>

4. What do you ask after you go to the verb looked?

5. How do you know which adverb question to ask?

6. Which adverb question would you use to find the first adverb in this sentence?

7. Which adverb question would you use to find the second adverb in this sentence?

8. Which adverb question would you use to find the third adverb in this sentence?

Learn It: ADJECTIVES

 Reference 26 | **Adjectives**

There are several things you should know about adjectives.

1. The Adjective Jingle gives a lot of information about an adjective quickly and easily.

2. The adjective definition says that an adjective modifies a noun or pronoun.

3. The adjective questions are *What kind? Which one? How many?*

4. The adjective definition uses the word *modifies*. The word **modify** means to describe. When the adjective definition says that an adjective modifies a noun or pronoun, it means that an adjective **describes** a noun or pronoun.

5. An *adjective* is labeled with the abbreviation **Adj**.

6. An adjective is not part of a sentence pattern because it is not considered a core part. Always identify the core parts of a sentence, the subject noun and verb, before identifying other parts of the sentence.

Adding Adjectives to the Question and Answer Flow

Practice Sentence: Three special detectives looked around thoroughly today.

1. Who looked around thoroughly today? **detectives – subject noun (SN)**

2. What is being said about detectives? **detectives looked – verb (V)**

3. Looked where? **around – adverb (Adv)**

4. Looked how? **thoroughly – adverb (Adv)**

5. Looked when? **today – adverb (Adv)**

6. What kind of detectives? **special – adjective (Adj)**

7. How many detectives? **three – adjective (Adj)**

8. **Subject Noun, Verb, Pattern 1 (SN V P1)**

		Adj	Adj	SN	V	Adv	Adv	Adv
SN V		Three	special	detectives	looked	around	thoroughly	today.
P1								

Discuss It:

1. Where do you go to find an adjective?

2. Where do you go **first** to find an adjective?

3. What is the subject noun in the practice sentence?

4. What do you ask after you go to the subject noun *detectives*?

5. How do you know which adjective question to ask?

6. Which adjective questions would you use to find the adjectives in this sentence?

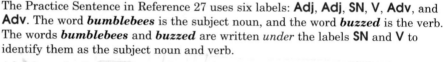

SHURLEY ENGLISH

GRAMMAR & WRITING CONNECTION:
Practice Sentence

Learn It: **THE PRACTICE SENTENCE FOR *ADJ, SN, V, ADV***

Add adjectives and adverbs to the **Practice Sentence**.

	Reference 27	**Practice Sentence for Adj Adj Sn V Adv Adv**
Labels:	*Adj Adj SN V Adv Adv*	
Practice:	Twelve yellow bumblebees buzzed calmly nearby.	

The Practice Sentence in Reference 27 uses six labels: **Adj, Adj, SN, V, Adv,** and **Adv**. The word ***bumblebees*** is the subject noun, and the word ***buzzed*** is the verb. The words ***bumblebees*** and ***buzzed*** are written *under* the labels **SN** and **V** to identify them as the subject noun and verb.

Adverbs and adjectives are used to expand the sentence. The words ***calmly*** and ***nearby*** are written *under* the labels **Adv** to identify them as the two adverbs in the sentence. The adverb ***calmly*** tells *how* the bumblebees buzzed, and the adverb ***nearby*** tells *where* the bumblebees buzzed. You may add more adverbs to a Practice Sentence, but the adverbs must make sense.

The words ***twelve*** and ***yellow*** are written *under* the labels **Adj** to identify them as the two adjectives in the sentence. The adjective ***yellow*** tells *what kind* of bumblebees, and the adjective ***twelve*** tells *how many* bumblebees. You may add more adjectives to a Practice Sentence, but the adjectives must make sense.

Apply It: **WRITE A PRACTICE SENTENCE,**
USING THE LABELS *ADJ, ADJ, SN, V, ADV, ADV*

Write a Practice Sentence, adding adjectives and adverbs. On the top line of a sheet of notebook paper, write the title **Practice Sentence**. After you write your title, skip down two lines. On the third line, write the sentence labels **Adj Adj SN V Adv Adv**. Be sure to leave plenty of writing space between each label.

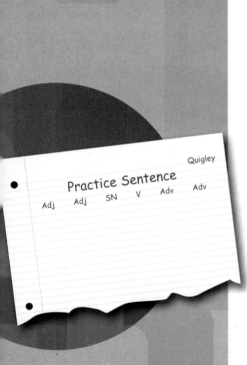

1. Go to the **SN** label for the subject noun. Think of a noun that tells who or what you want to use as the subject of your sentence *(person, place, thing, or idea)*. Write the noun you have chosen on the line *under* the **SN** label.

2. Go to the **V** label for the verb. Ask the verb question, *"What is being said about _____ (the subject)?"* to help you think of a verb that tells what your subject does. Make sure that your verb makes sense with the subject noun. Write the verb you have chosen on the line *under* the **V** label.

3. Go to the first **Adv** label for the first adverb. Go to the verb in your sentence and ask an adverb question. What are the adverb questions? *(How? When? Where?)* Choose one adverb question to ask and write your adverb answer *under* the first **Adv** label.

4. Go to the second **Adv** label for another adverb. Go to the verb again and ask another adverb question. You can ask the same question or a different question. *(How? When? Where?)* After choosing an adverb question, write your adverb answer *under* the second **Adv** label.

5. Go to the second **Adj** label for the adjective that is closest to the subject noun. Go to the subject noun of your sentence and ask an adjective question. What are the adjective questions? *(What kind? Which one? How many?)* Choose one adjective question to ask and write your adjective answer *under* the **Adj** label next to the subject noun.

Continued on next page. >>>

6. Go to the subject noun of your sentence again and ask another adjective question for the first **Adj** label. You can ask the same question or a different question. *(What kind? Which one? How many?)* After choosing an adjective question to ask, write your adjective answer *under* the first **Adj** label.

7. Always check to make sure your word choices make sense in the sentence.

Practice It:

Write one more sentence, using the same steps that you used to write the first Practice Sentence. Remember to check your Practice Sentence for the five parts of a complete sentence. Your sentence must have a subject and a verb, it must make sense, it must start with a capital letter, and it must end with an end mark.

Classroom Practice 4

It is time to practice the skills you are learning. You will use the classroom practice on the next page to apply these skills.

SHURLEY ENGLISH

Classroom Practice 4

Name:_____ Date:_____

GRAMMAR

▶ **Exercise 1:** Fill in the blanks below for this sentence: **Three frightened frogs jumped away hastily.**

1. What jumped away hastily? .... _____ Subject Noun _____

2. What is being said about frogs? .... _____ _____ Verb _____

3. Jumped where? .... _____ Adverb _____

4. Jumped how? .... _____ Adverb _____

5. What kind of frogs? .... _____ Adjective _____

6. How many frogs? .... _____ Adjective _____

7. Subject Noun, Verb, Pattern 1 .... _____

Classify this sentence: _____ Three frightened frogs jumped away hastily.

▶ **Exercise 2:** Write a Practice Sentence, using the following labels. **Adj Adj SN V Adv Adv**

_____

▶ **Exercise 3:** Write the correct answer.

1. What does an adverb modify? .... _____

2. What does an adjective modify? .... _____

3. What does a noun name? .... _____

4. What are the adverb questions? .... _____

5. What are the adjective questions? .... _____

EDITING

▶ **Exercise 4:** Write the capitalization and punctuation rule numbers for each correction in **bold type**.
Use References 11–13 on pages 13–16 to look up the capitalization and punctuation rule numbers.

Arizona**,** **N**ew **M**exico**,** and **O**klahoma are home to several tribes of **A**merican **I**ndians**.**

▶ **Exercise 5:** Put punctuation corrections within the sentence. Write all other corrections above the sentence.
Editing Guide: Capitals: 5   Commas: 2   Apostrophes: 1   Periods: 1   Misspelled Words: 2   End Marks: 1

we had sanwichs chips and soda at ms greens house on friday and saterday

English Made Easy

LISTENING AND SPEAKING:
Vocabulary & Analogy Time

Learn It: Recite the new vocabulary and analogy words.

Reference 28	Vocabulary & Analogy Words

Word: ambiguous (ăm bĭg'yo͞oəs)
   Definition: not clearly seen or understood
   Synonym: unclear   **Antonym:** unmistakable
   Sentence: Sam wrote **ambiguous** sentences in his essay.

Analogy: eagle : bird :: poodle : dog
   Type or kind relationship: Just as an **eagle** is a kind of **bird**,
                                    a **poodle** is a kind of **dog**.

Vocabulary Card 4: Record the vocabulary information above and write your own
                   sentence, using the new word.
Analogy Card 4: Record the analogy information and write your own analogy,
                  using the same relationship as the analogy above.

Jingle Time

Recite It: 1. Practice Jingles 3–6 in the Jingle Section on page 507.
             2. Recite the new jingle.

♪ Jingle 7	The Article Adjective Jingle

We are the article adjectives,
Teeny, tiny adjectives.
A, AN, THE — A, AN, THE

We are called article adjectives and noun markers.
We are memorized and used every day.
So, if you spot us, you can mark us
With a capital A.

We are the article adjectives,
Teeny, tiny adjectives.
A, AN, THE — A, AN, THE

Lesson 3
You will
- study new vocabulary; make card 4; write own sentence using the vocabulary word.
- analyze new analogy; make card 4; write own analogy.
- practice Jingles 3–6; recite new jingle (Article Adjective).
- identify article adjectives.
- classify Introductory Sentences.
- use **A Adj SN V Adv** to write a Practice Sentence.
- do Classroom Practice 5.

Apply It: These Introductory Sentences are used to apply the new grammar concepts taught. Classify these sentences orally with your teacher.

Introductory Sentences	**Chapter 2: Lesson 3**

1. _____ An inquisitive young child walked curiously around yesterday.

2. _____ The beautiful new planes flew extremely fast.

3. _____ A curious little kitten climbed everywhere today.

Learn It: ARTICLE ADJECTIVES

📖 **Reference 29**	**Article Adjectives**

There are several things you should know about article adjectives.

1. The Article Adjective Jingle gives a lot of information about an article adjective quickly and easily.
2. Only three adjectives are called articles. They are **a, an, the**. They are also known as noun markers.
3. Article adjectives must be memorized because you do not ask questions to find them.
4. Use the article **a** before singular words that begin with a consonant sound. Use the article **an** before singular words that begin with a vowel sound. The articles **a** and **an** are called *indefinite* articles, meaning *one* of several. (**a** book, meaning one of several books; **an** answer, meaning one of several answers)
5. Use the article **the** before words that begin with either a consonant or a vowel sound. Use the article **the** before either singular or plural words. The article **the** is called a *definite* article, meaning "a specific person, place, thing, or idea." (**the** book, meaning a specific book; **the** five books, meaning five specific books)
6. The article **the** has two pronunciations:
   a. A long **e** *(used when the article comes before a word that begins with a vowel sound: the egg, the igloo)*
   b. A short **u** *(used when the article comes before a word that begins with a consonant sound: the mop, the store)*
7. An *article adjective* is labeled with the abbreviation **A**.
8. An article adjective is not part of a sentence pattern because it is not part of the core. Always identify the core parts of a sentence, the subject noun and verb, before identifying other parts of the sentence.

Adding an Article Adjective to the Question and Answer Flow

Practice Sentence: The three excited children raced wildly around yesterday.

1. Who raced wildly around yesterday? **children - subject noun (SN)**
2. What is being said about children? **children raced - verb (V)**
3. Raced how? **wildly - adverb (Adv)**
4. Raced where? **around - adverb (Adv)**
5. Raced when? **yesterday - adverb (Adv)**
6. What kind of children? **excited - adjective (Adj)**
7. How many children? **three - adjective (Adj)**
8. **The - article adjective (A)**
9. **Subject Noun, Verb, Pattern 1 (SN V P1)**

```
     A  Adj  Adj   SN    V   Adv  Adv   Adv
 SN  V_____  The three excited children raced wildly around yesterday.
 P1
```

Discuss It:

1. What are the three article adjectives?
2. How do you find article adjectives?
3. What are article adjectives sometimes called?

GRAMMAR & WRITING CONNECTION:
Practice Sentence

Learn It: **A PRACTICE SENTENCE FOR *A, ADJ, ADJ, SN, V, ADV, ADV***

Add an article adjective to the **Practice Sentence**.

✎ **Reference 30**	**Practice Sentence for A Adj Adj Sn V Adv Adv**

Labels:	A	Adj	Adj		SN		V	Adv	Adv	
Practice:	The	twelve	yellow	bumblebees			buzzed	calmly	nearby.	

The Practice Sentence in Reference 30 uses seven labels: **A, Adj, Adj, SN, V, Adv,** and **Adv**. The words ***bumblebees*** and ***buzzed*** are written *under* the labels **SN** and **V** to identify them as the subject noun and verb. The words ***calmly*** and ***nearby*** are written *under* the **Adv** labels to identify them as the two adverbs in the sentence. The words ***twelve*** and ***yellow*** **Adj** are written *under* the labels to identify them as the two adjectives in the sentence.

The word ***the*** is written *under* the label **A** to identify it as an article adjective. Of the three articles, only the article adjective ***the*** can be used before the plural noun, ***bumblebees***.

Apply It: **WRITE A PRACTICE SENTENCE,**
USING THE LABELS *A, ADJ, ADJ, SN, V, ADV, ADV*

Write a Practice Sentence, adding an article adjective. On the top line of a sheet of notebook paper, write the title ***Practice Sentence***. After you write your title, skip down two lines. On the third line, write the sentence labels **A Adj Adj SN V Adv Adv**. Be sure to leave plenty of writing space between each label.

1. Go to the **SN** label for the subject noun. Think of a noun that tells who or what you want to use as the subject of your sentence (*person, place, thing, or idea*). Write the noun you have chosen on the line *under* the **SN** label.

2. Go to the **V** label for the verb. Ask the verb question, "*What is being said about _____ (the subject)?*" to help you think of a verb that tells what your subject does. Make sure that your verb makes sense with the subject noun. Write the verb you have chosen on the line *under* the **V** label.

3. Go to the first **Adv** label for the first adverb. Go to the verb in your sentence and ask an adverb question. What are the adverb questions? (*How? When? Where?*) Choose one adverb question to ask and write your adverb answer *under* the first **Adv** label.

4. Go to the second **Adv** label for another adverb. Go to the verb again and ask another adverb question. You can ask the same question or a different question. (*How? When? Where?*) After choosing an adverb question to ask, write your adverb answer *under* the second **Adv** label.

5. Go to the second **Adj** label for the adjective that is closest to the subject noun. Go to the subject noun of your sentence and ask an adjective question. What are the adjective questions? (*What kind? Which one? How many?*) Choose one adjective question to ask and write your adjective answer *under* the **Adj** label next to the subject noun.

6. Go to the subject noun of your sentence again and ask an adjective question for the first **Adj** label. You can ask the same question or a different question. (*What kind? Which one? How many?*) After choosing an adjective question to ask, write your adjective answer *under* the first **Adj** label.

Continued on next page. >>>

7. Go to the **A** label for the article adjective. What are the three article adjectives? *(a, an, and the)* You will choose the article adjective that makes the best sense in the sentence. After choosing the article adjective, write it *under* the **A** label.

8. Always check to make sure your word choices make sense in the sentence.

Practice It:

Write one more sentence, using the same steps that you used to write the first Practice Sentence. Remember to check your Practice Sentence for the five parts of a complete sentence. Your sentence must have a subject and a verb, it must make sense, it must start with a capital letter, and it must end with an end mark.

Classroom Practice 5

It is time to practice the skills you are learning. You will use the classroom practice on the next page to apply these skills.

Classroom Practice 5

Name:_____ Date:_____

GRAMMAR

▶ **Exercise 1:** Fill in the blanks below for this sentence: **The shy little girl spoke softly.**

1. Who spoke softly?................................... _____ Subject Noun _____
2. What is being said about girl? .... _____ _____ Verb _____
3. Spoke how?... _____ Adverb _____
4. What kind of girl?................................ _____ Adjective _____
5. What kind of girl?................................ _____ Adjective _____
6. _____ Article Adjective _____
7. Subject Noun, Verb, Pattern 1................... _____

Classify this sentence: _____ The shy little girl spoke softly.

▶ **Exercise 2:** Write a Practice Sentence, using the following labels. **A Adj Adj SN V Adv Adv**

_____

▶ **Exercise 3:** Write the correct answer in each blank.

1. What are the article adjectives? .... _____
2. What does an adverb modify?................. _____
3. What are the adverb questions?.............. _____
4. What does an adjective modify?.............. _____
5. What are the adjective questions?............ _____
6. What does a noun name?...................... _____

EDITING

▶ **Exercise 4:** Write the capitalization and punctuation rule numbers for each correction in **bold type**. Use References 11–13 on pages 13–16 to look up the capitalization and punctuation rule numbers.

The Tampa Bay Buccaneers, my favorite team, will play Seattle on Sunday.

▶ **Exercise 5:** Put punctuation corrections within the sentence. Write all other corrections above the sentence.
Editing Guide: Capitals: 7   Commas: 2   Periods: 1   Misspelled Words: 1   End Marks: 1

captain john m evans returned from spain on wendsday october 27 2004

START LESSON 4

Lesson 4

You will

- practice Jingles 2–7.
- identify four kinds of sentences and recite the End Mark Flow.
- classify Introductory Sentences.
- identify complete subject and complete predicate.
- recognize nouns, verbs, adjectives, and adverbs as parts of speech.
- do Classroom Practice 6.

LISTENING AND SPEAKING:

Jingle Time

Recite It: Practice Jingles 2–7 in the Jingle Section on pages 506–507.

Grammar Time

Apply It: These Introductory Sentences are used to apply the new grammar concepts. Classify these sentences orally with your teacher.

Introductory Sentences	Chapter 2: Lesson 4
1. _____ An impressive soccer team played extremely well yesterday.	
2. _____ The highly intelligent scientist works very intensely tonight.	
3. _____ The exceedingly meddlesome raccoon growled ominously!	

Learn It: **THE FOUR KINDS OF SENTENCES AND THE END MARK FLOW**

The top part of Reference 31 tells about the four kinds of sentences, and the bottom part tells about the End Mark Flow.

Reference 31 — The Four Kinds of Sentences and the End Mark Flow

1. A **declarative** sentence makes a statement. It is labeled with a **D**.
   Example: Cole played with his friends.
   (Period, statement, declarative sentence)

2. An **imperative** sentence gives a command. It is labeled with an **Imp**.
   Example: Stand in the line quietly.
   (Period, command, imperative sentence)

3. An **interrogative** sentence asks a question. It is labeled with an **Int**.
   Example: Did you hear about the new mall?
   (Question mark, question, interrogative sentence)

4. An **exclamatory** sentence expresses strong feeling. It is labeled with an **E**.
   Example: Our new house is on fire!
   (Exclamation point, strong feeling, exclamatory sentence)

END MARK FLOW

The **End Mark Flow** identifies the end mark, gives the definition, and names the kind of sentence.
(Example: period, statement, declarative sentence.)

Directions: Read each sentence, recite the End Mark Flow in parentheses, and put the end mark and the abbreviation for the kind of sentence in the blank at the end of each sentence.

1. Shane helped at the library **. D**
   (Period, statement, declarative sentence)

2. Listen to your teacher **. Imp**
   (Period, command, imperative sentence)

3. Are you going to the meeting **? Int**
   (Question mark, question, interrogative sentence)

4. The lion is coming toward me **! E**
   (Exclamation point, strong feeling, exclamatory sentence)

>>>>> **Student Tip...**

> Develop hand signals for the End Mark Flow. Suggestions: Make a fist in your palm as you say "period, statement, declarative sentence." Slap two fingers in your palm as you say "period, command, imperative sentence." Arch both arms high in the air with fingertips touching as you say "question mark, question, interrogative sentence." Make both hands into fists, bend your arms back to your chest, straighten your arms quickly, and point your index fingers as you say "exclamation point, strong feeling, exclamatory sentence."

Learn It: **SKILL CHECK, END MARK FLOW, COMPLETE SUBJECT, AND COMPLETE PREDICATE**

 Reference 32   **Skill Check, End Mark Flow, Complete Subject, & Complete Predicate**

After a sentence has been classified and the pattern identified, a **Skill Check** will be added to the Question and Answer Flow to identify specific skills. The Skill Check will identify the End Mark Flow, the complete subject, and the complete predicate. Other skills will be added to the Skill Check later.

A REVIEW OF THE END MARK FLOW FOR THE FOUR KINDS OF SENTENCES

When you say the End Mark Flow *(such as period, statement, declarative sentence)*, you are identifying the end mark, giving the definition, and naming the kind of sentence. As you write the abbreviation at the end of the sentence, you are verifying that you have gone through the End Mark Flow and have identified the kind of sentence.

1. Period, statement, declarative sentence (**D**)
2. Period, command, imperative sentence (**Imp**)
3. Question mark, question, interrogative sentence (**Int**)
4. Exclamation point, strong feeling, exclamatory sentence (**E**)

COMPLETE SUBJECT AND COMPLETE PREDICATE

The **complete subject** is the subject and all the words that modify it. The complete subject usually starts at the beginning of the sentence and includes every word up to the verb of the sentence. A vertical line in front of the verb shows where the subject parts end.

The **complete predicate** is the verb and all the words that modify it. The complete predicate usually starts with the verb and includes every word after the verb. A vertical line in front of the verb shows where the predicate parts begin.

To identify the complete subject and predicate in the Question and Answer Flow, say, "Go back to the verb. Divide the complete subject from the complete predicate." Draw a vertical line in front of the verb to divide the subject parts on the left from the predicate parts on the right.

Note: At this time, the Question and Answer Flow for the Practice Sentence below will use abbreviations to identify the sentence parts. You will continue saying the words for which the abbreviations stand.
(Example: For the abbreviation **SN**, you will continue to say the words *subject noun*.)

Adding a Skill Check to the Question and Answer Flow

Practice Sentence: The three special detectives looked around thoroughly today.

1. Who looked around thoroughly today?
   detectives - SN
2. What is being said about detectives?
   detectives looked - V
3. Looked where? **around - Adv**
4. Looked how? **thoroughly - Adv**
5. Looked when? **today - Adv**
6. What kind of detectives? **special - Adj**
7. How many detectives? **three - Adj**
8. **The - A**
9. **SN V P1**
10. Skill Check
11. **Period, statement, declarative sentence**
    *(Write **D** at the end of the sentence.)*
12. Go back to the verb. Divide the complete subject from the complete predicate.
    (As you say divide, draw a vertical line before the verb.)

```
              A    Adj   Adj    SN        V     Adv    Adv     Adv
 SN  V        The  three special detectives / looked around thoroughly today.  D
 P1
```

Learn It: PARTS OF SPEECH

Do you know that all words in the English language have been put into eight groups called the **Parts of Speech**? How a word is used in a sentence determines its part of speech. The sentences you have been classifying are made from four parts of speech. Do you know the names of these four parts of speech?

 Classroom Practice 6

It is time to practice the skills you are learning. You will use the classroom practice on the next page to apply these skills.

Classroom Practice 6

Name:_____ Date:_____

GRAMMAR

▶ **Exercise 1:** Fill in the blanks below for this sentence:
That frightened puppy whimpered miserably today.

1. What whimpered miserably today? .... _____ Subject Noun _____
2. What is being said about puppy?............. _____ _____ Verb _____
3. Whimpered how? .... _____ Adverb _____
4. Whimpered when?............................ _____ Adverb _____
5. What kind of puppy? .... _____ Adjective _____
6. Which puppy?............................... _____ Adjective _____
7. Subject Noun, Verb, Pattern 1................. _____
8. Skill Check
9. Period, statement, declarative sentence...... _____
10. Go back to the verb. Divide the complete subject from the complete predicate. _____

Classify this sentence: _____ That frightened puppy whimpered miserably today.

▶ **Exercise 2:** Name the four parts of speech that you have studied so far.

1._____   2._____   3._____   4._____

SKILLS

▶ **Exercise 3:** Put the end mark and the End Mark Flow for each kind of sentence in the blanks.
Use these words in your answers: *declarative, exclamatory, imperative, interrogative.*

1. Sit down for dinner___................. _____
2. Did you do well on your exam___...... _____
3. The fire is out of control___ .... _____
4. I'm leaving on my trip tomorrow___ ... _____

EDITING

▶ **Exercise 4:** Write the capitalization and punctuation rule numbers for each correction in **bold type**.
Use References 11–13 on pages 13–16 to look up the capitalization and punctuation rule numbers.

Will they ever sail the cruise liner, **Q**ueen **V**ictoria, to **A**ruba, **J**amaica, and the **B**ahamas**?**

▶ **Exercise 5:** Put punctuation corrections within the sentence. Write all other corrections above the sentence.
Editing Guide: Capitals: 5   Commas: 3   Misspelled Words: 1   End Marks: 1

dad spent the summer in boulder colorado with his brothers michael and kenneth

START LESSON 5

Lesson 5

You will
- practice Jingle 2.
- do Classroom Practice 7.
- create and label a sentence in a group activity.
- write in your journal.

LISTENING AND SPEAKING:

Jingle Time

Recite It: Practice Jingle 2 in the Jingle Section on page 506.

GRAMMAR & WRITING CONNECTION:
Practice and Revised Sentences

Learn It: **A REVISED SENTENCE**

You have been writing Practice Sentences, using all the parts of speech that you have studied. Now, you must learn how to improve your Practice Sentence by writing a Revised Sentence. A **Revised Sentence** is a sentence made from the Practice Sentence, which is changed and improved through the use of synonyms, antonyms, complete-word changes, and/or by adding or deleting words. Writing Revised Sentences helps you learn to make better word choices as you revise the content of your Practice Sentence.

| Reference 33 | Independent Practice and Revised Sentences |

1. Write a Practice Sentence according to the labels you choose. Use the **SN V** labels once. You may use the other labels in any order and as many times as you wish in order to make a Practice Sentence. Chapter 2 labels for a Practice Sentence: (**SN, V**, Adj, Adv, A)

2. Write a Revised Sentence. Use the following revision strategies: *synonym (**syn**), antonym (**ant**), word change (**wc**), added word (**add**), deleted word (**delete**),* or *no change (**nc**)*. Under each word, write the abbreviation of the revision strategy you use.

3. As you go through each word of your Practice Sentence, think about the changes and improvements you want to make. Think about what you really want to say. After a Practice Sentence is written, it is easier to look more critically at each word in the sentence to see if you can think of a better word to express your thought.

4. As you write a Revised Sentence, you may make several changes or only a few. Antonym changes and complete-word changes will alter the meaning and direction of your sentence. Knowing different ways to revise sentences gives you more flexibility as you work to improve your sentences.

5. When you have finished, your Practice and Revised Sentences should resemble the examples below.

Labels:	A	Adj	Adj	Adj	SN	V	Adv	Adv
Practice:	The	twelve		yellow	bumblebees	buzzed	calmly	nearby.
Revised:		Twelve	crazed	black	hornets	swarmed	furiously	nearby.
Strategies:	(delete)	(nc)	(add)	(wc)	(wc)	(syn)	(ant)	(nc)

Apply It:

You will write a Practice Sentence and a Revised Sentence for Classroom Practice 7. Since the directions for a Practice Sentence and a Revised Sentence are very important, they are listed and explained below.

1. Write a Practice Sentence according to the labels you choose. <u>Use the **SN V** labels once</u>. You may use the <u>other</u> labels in any order and as many times as you wish to make a Practice Sentence. Chapter 2 labels for Practice Sentence: **SN, V**, Adj, Adv, A

Continued on next page. >>>

2. Write a Revised Sentence. Use the following revision strategies: synonym (*syn*), antonym (*ant*), word change (*wc*), added word (*add*), deleted word (*delete*), or no change (*nc*). Under each word, write the abbreviation of the revision strategy you use.

In each chapter, new labels will be added. You must make your Practice Sentence only from the labels that are listed. The pattern labels, or core parts, are listed first in bold letters. The other labels are not pattern indicators, and they are not in bold type.

First, you will write the labels for your Practice Sentence. You will use your pattern label, **SN V**, only one time. You can use the other labels that are not in bold type (Adj, Adv, A) as many times as you want. For example, you can use the adjective label five times if you want your Practice Sentence to have five adjectives.

Next, you will write your Practice Sentence, following the label guides you have chosen. If you need to rearrange your labels, do it while you are writing the Practice Sentence. Then, you should look carefully at your Practice Sentence to find ways to improve and revise it. You will use the revision strategies listed on your page to help you write a Revised Sentence. Finally, you will write the abbreviation of the revision strategy you used under each word.

Use the information in Reference 34 to help you build and expand your Practice and Revised Sentences.

Reference 34	**A Guide for Using Nouns, Verbs, Adjectives, and Adverbs to Build and Expand Sentences**

1. **SN (subject noun)** Think of a noun that tells who or what *(person, place, thing, or idea)* will be the subject of your sentence. The subject is very important because it determines your choice of words for the rest of the sentence. Write the noun you have chosen for the subject of your sentence.

2. **V (verb)** Ask the verb question, "*What is being said about _____ (the subject)*?" to help you think of a verb that tells what your subject does. Make sure that the verb makes sense with the subject noun. Write the verb you have chosen for your sentence.

3. **Adv (adverb)** Go to the verb and ask an adverb question *(How? When? or Where?)* to help you think of an adverb. Write the adverb in your sentence. Repeat this step for each adverb you add to the sentence.

4. **Adj (adjective)** Go to a noun and ask an adjective question *(What kind? Which one? or How many?)* to help you think of an adjective. Write the adjective in your sentence. Repeat this step for each adjective you add to the sentence.

5. **A (article adjective)** Choose the article adjective *(a, an, or the)* that makes the best sense and write it in your sentence. Repeat this step for each article adjective you add to the sentence.

6. Always check to make sure all your word choices make sense in the sentence.

SHURLEY ENGLISH

Classroom Practice 7

It is time to practice the skills you are learning. You will use the classroom practice on the next page to apply these skills.

JOURNAL WRITING 3

Write an entry in your journal. Use Reference 9 on page 12 for ideas.

Student Activity

Create a sentence with other students. Divide into small groups. Each group will complete three jobs.

Job 1. Write each of these sentence labels on separate sheets of construction paper: **SN, V, A, Adj, Adj, Adj, Adv, Adv**

Job 2. Write a period (**.**) and an exclamation point (**!**) on separate sheets of construction paper. Write the words **capital letter** on another sheet of construction paper.

Job 3. Write 3 to 6 words on separate sheets of construction paper for each label below.

SN words: (3 to 6 nouns)   **Adj** words: (3 to 6 adjectives)

V words: (3 to 6 verbs)   **Adv** words: (3 to 6 adverbs)

A words: (3 article adjectives)

Now, each group exchanges its words with another group. Following the directions below, each group must create a sentence with the other group's words. The teacher will select enough class members to help each group construct its sentence.

1. **Group:** Decide the order of the sentence labels.
   Helpers: Hold up the labels in the selected sentence order.

2. **Group:** Select the words to fit each label.
   Helpers: Kneel in front of the appropriate labels, holding the selected words.

3. **Group:** Decide where the capital letter and the period or exclamation point should be placed.
   Helpers: Stand at the beginning and end of the sentence with the appropriate signs.

4. **Group:** Read the sentence aloud to the class.
   Class: Check to make sure the sentence has all its parts.
   (subject, verb, complete sense, capital letter, and end mark.)

The subject and verb are the main parts of a sentence. Notice that the subject and verb determine the choice of words for the rest of the sentence.

Classroom Practice 7

Name: _____ Date: _____

PRACTICE & REVISED SENTENCES

1. Write a Practice Sentence according to the labels you choose.
Use the **SN V** labels once. You may use the other labels in any order and as many times as you wish in order to make a Practice Sentence.
Chapter 2 labels for a Practice Sentence: **SN**, **V**, Adj, Adv, A

2. Write a Revised Sentence. Use the following revision strategies: *synonym (syn), antonym (ant), word change (wc), added word (add), deleted word (delete), or no change (nc)*. Under each word, write the abbreviation of the revision strategy you use.

Labels:

Practice:

Revised:

Strategies:

Labels:

Practice:

Revised:

Strategies:

Labels:

Practice:

Revised:

Strategies:

START LESSON 6

Lesson 6

You will
- identify topics.
- identify supporting/ nonsupporting ideas and sentences.
- do Classroom Practice 8.
- write a creative writing piece for WA 1.

 Skill Time

Learn It: TOPICS AND PARAGRAPHS

Reference 35 — Topics and Paragraphs

A **topic** can tell what a paragraph or what a group of words is about. A **paragraph** is a group of sentences that tells about one topic. The topic is also called the **subject** of a paragraph.

Directions for finding the topic: Write the name of the topic that best describes what each group of words is about.

Choose from these topics: Sports   Clothing   Animals   Colors

(1) Animals	(2) Clothing	(3) Sports
snail	vest	cycling
walrus	jacket	fencing
lynx	cap	rugby
hyena	smock	hockey

Learn It: SUPPORTING AND NONSUPPORTING IDEAS AND SENTENCES

When a topic has been selected, all sentences and ideas should tell about that topic. A sentence or idea that tells about the topic is called **supporting** and can be used to develop the topic. A sentence or idea that does not support the topic is called **nonsupporting** and should not be used.

Reference 36 — Supporting and NonSupporting Ideas and Sentences

In each column, cross out the one idea that does not support the underlined topic.

(1) Transportation	(2) Occupations	(3) Food
barge	beautician	pastry
submarine	librarian	~~hungry~~
blimp	~~aquatic~~	potato
helicopter	chef	radish
~~fish~~	lawyer	beef

Cross out the sentence below that does not support the topic.

Topic: Pilot Certification

In order to be a certified airplane pilot in the USA, you must receive a certificate from the Federal Aviation Administration. This certificate means that you have passed a physical exam and a written test for flying. ~~You must also take a written test to get a driver's license.~~ In addition, you must have flown under the supervision of a licensed instructor and have completed the required hours of flying solo in order to be certified.

Classroom Practice 8

It is time to practice the skills you are learning. You will use the classroom practice on the next page to apply these skills.

Writing Time

Write It: CREATIVE EXPRESSIONS

Your first writing assignment is creative writing. The top portion of Writing Assignment 1 gives you a list of writing topics. Choose one topic from this list. Before you begin any writing assignment, always check the special instructions at the bottom of the assignment box.

Writing Assignment 1

Choose one of the creative-writing topics below.

1. Describe your first day of school; then, tell how you feel about school today.

2. Tell about some of the rules you follow at home or at school; then, tell what you think it would be like if there were no rules.

3. Write a poem about the first day of school or about rules.

4. You may also choose your own topic.

Special Instructions: Do this creative-writing assignment in your journal.

Classroom Practice 8

Name:_____ Date:_____

GRAMMAR

▶ **Exercise 1:** Classify each sentence.

1. _____ That small speckled trout swam swiftly away yesterday.

2. _____ The new lawnmower worked extremely well.

3. _____ The extremely exasperated receptionist gazed wistfully outside today.

SKILLS

▶ **Exercise 2:** In each column, cross out the word that does not support the underlined topic at the top.

1. **Amphibians**	2. **Oceans**	3. **Planets**
frogs	Atlantic	Mars
jellyfish	Pacific	Earth
toads	Arctic	Peter
salamanders	Vermont	Venus
newts	Indian	Jupiter

▶ **Exercise 3:** Write the name of the topic that best describes what each column of words is about. Choose from these topics. **Weather   Cities   Electronics   Seasons   Gases   Holidays**

1._____	2._____	3._____
Independence Day	stereo	carbon monoxide
New Year's Day	computer	helium
Presidents Day	calculator	hydrogen
Armistice Day	television	oxygen

▶ **Exercise 4:** Cross out the sentence in each paragraph that does not support the topic.

Topic: A Hurricane

Store windows are boarded up before the mighty storm. Tall waves rush onto the coastline. Strong winds batter buildings. The ground shakes and splits. .

Topic: Underwater

Deep in the ocean, thousands of creatures move freely. Seals bask in the sun on the shore. Sea turtles glide between strands of algae. Starfish and sand dollars litter the ocean floor.

EDITING

▶ **Exercise 5:** Put punctuation corrections within the sentence. Write all other corrections above the sentence.
Editing Guide: Capitals: 8   Commas: 2   Quotations: 2   Periods: 3   Misspelled Words: 1   End Marks: 1

mr j c brewer sang the song america in the talent contest at webster elementery school

Writing Time

Plan It: WRITING FOLDERS

As you begin the writing process, you need four writing folders in which to organize your writing assignments.

START LESSON 7

Lesson 7

You will
- prepare writing folders.
- do Chapter Checkup 9.
- write in your journal.

📖	Reference 37	**Writing Folders**

You need four different-colored pocket folders for the writing process. (Check with your teacher for the color of each folder.)

1. Label the first folder **Rough Draft**. All rough drafts are held in this folder until they are revised, edited, and rewritten. After a rough draft has been rewritten, it will be moved to the Final Paper folder.

2. Label the second folder **Final Paper**. Final papers are held in this folder until they are graded. After a final paper has been graded, it will be moved to the Publishing folder.

3. Label the third folder **Publishing**. Graded papers are held in this folder until they are rewritten and published. After the graded paper has been rewritten and published, it will be moved to the Writing Portfolio.

4. Label the fourth folder **My Writing Portfolio**. Graded papers that have been rewritten and published are held in this folder until the end of the school year. Your teacher will keep this folder for you because the writing pieces in this folder may be used for parent conferences. At the end of the school year, your teacher will select several of your papers to keep as a record of your writing. The rest of the papers will be sent home.

JOURNAL WRITING [4]

Write an entry in your journal. Use Reference 9 on page 12 for ideas.

✏️ Chapter Checkup 9

It is time for a checkup of the skills you have learned in this chapter. You will use the chapter checkup on the next page to evaluate your progress.

Chapter 2 Checkup 9

Name:_____ Date:_____

GRAMMAR

▶ **Exercise 1:** Classify each sentence.

1. _____ The three incredibly tired little boys fell asleep instantly.

2. _____ An enraged black hornet buzzed very angrily nearby!

3. _____ Several large Canadian geese flew high overhead.

▶ **Exercise 2:** Name the four parts of speech that you have studied so far.

1._____   2._____   3._____   4._____

SKILLS

▶ **Exercise 3:** Read the topic and paragraph. Cross out the sentence that does not support the topic.

Topic: Saturn

   Saturn's pale butterscotch-colored surface and its huge halo of rings make it a planet of beauty. Its color is caused by ammonia gases, and its huge rings surround the planet. Saturn's rings are made of billions of chips of ice and dust that are the size of ice cubes. Uranus also has rings, but they are much smaller. Saturn has a very windy surface and more moons than any other planet.

▶ **Exercise 4:** Put the end mark and the End Mark Flow for each kind of sentence in the blanks. Use these words in your answers: *declarative, exclamatory, imperative, interrogative.*

1. Erase the chalkboard___ .... _____

2. Did you wash the car___ .... _____

3. A spider is in my soup___............. _____

4. I skated across the frozen pond___... _____

EDITING

▶ **Exercise 5:** Write the capitalization and punctuation rule numbers for each correction in **bold type**. Use References 11–13 on pages 13–16 to look up the capitalization and punctuation rule numbers.

Sandra, will you work in the nursery on **S**unday, **A**pril 18**?**

▶ **Exercise 6:** Put punctuation corrections within the sentence. Write all other corrections above the sentence.
   Editing Guide: Capitals: 3   Commas: 2   Misspelled Words: 2   End Marks: 1

my sister and i like to eat turkey sweet potatos and pumkin pie on thanksgiving

Discuss It:

1. What is a topic?
2. What is a paragraph?
3. What is another word for topic?
4. How is a subject like a topic?

Lesson 8

You will
- read and discuss a three-point expository paragraph.

Learn It: EXPOSITORY WRITING AND THE THREE-POINT FORMAT

Reference 38	Expository Writing and the Three-Point Format

Expository writing is the sharing of ideas. Its purpose is to inform, to give facts, to give directions, to explain, or to define something. Since expository writing is informational, it provides some type of information to the reader.

Since expository writing deals with information of some kind, it is very important to focus on making the meaning clear. The reader must be able to understand exactly what the writer means. So, first you will learn to organize your writing.

Expository writing may be organized in different ways. One of the most common ways to write an expository paragraph is by using a three-point format. A **three-point format** presents three points, or main ideas, and develops these main ideas with supporting sentences. The three-point format makes your writing understandable.

Before you begin writing a three-point paragraph, you must do two things. First, select a topic. Then, list the three main points about the topic that you will develop.

WRITING TOPIC: My Favorite Colors

LIST THE THREE POINTS ABOUT THE TOPIC

- Select three points to list about the topic. **1. orange 2. yellow 3. brown**

Learn It: WRITING THE INTRODUCTION
FOR A THREE-POINT EXPOSITORY PARAGRAPH

The sentences in a paragraph can be divided into three basic parts:
the **Introduction**, the **Body**, and the **Conclusion**.

Reference 39	Writing the Introduction for a Three-Point Expository Paragraph

THE INTRODUCTION

TOPIC AND NUMBER SENTENCE
The topic and number sentence will be the **first** sentence in the paragraph because it tells what the paragraph is about. A topic sentence is very important because it tells the main idea of the paragraph. Sometimes, the topic sentence is not the first sentence, but, for now, it is important to write it as the first sentence in a three-point paragraph.

Continued on next page. >>>

Reference 39 continued from previous page.

The topic sentence should not say, "I am going to tell you about my three favorite colors." You do not need to tell the reader you are going to tell him something; you simply do it. To say, "I am going to tell you about" is called *writing about your writing*. You should never begin a paragraph with "I am going to tell you about" because **good writers do not write about their writing**.

To write the Topic and Number Sentence, use some or all of the words in your topic and add a general or specific number word that tells the number of points that will be discussed.

General number words: *several, many, some, etc.*

Specific number words: *two, three, four, etc.*

In the sample sentence below, words from the topic (*favorite colors*) are used, and the specific number word (*three*) is used instead of a general number word.

Sentence 1 – **Topic and Number Sentence:**

Of all the colors I like, my three favorites are autumn colors.

THREE-POINT SENTENCE

Now that the topic sentence has been written, the next sentence will be the three-point sentence. The three-point sentence lists or names the three points to be discussed in the order that you will present them in the body of your paper.

To write the Three-Point Sentence, list the exact three points in the order you will develop them in the body of the paragraph. You should also repeat words from the topic that connect this sentence to the topic sentence.

In the sample sentence below, the specific points, *orange, yellow, and brown*, are named, and the topic word *colors* is repeated. Repetition is a good device for making your paragraph flow smoothly.

Sentence 2 – **Three-Point Sentence:**

Without a doubt, I would choose the colors orange, yellow, and brown.

Learn It: WRITING THE BODY
FOR A THREE-POINT EXPOSITORY PARAGRAPH

The body of a three-point paragraph contains six sentences. Notice that the body lists each of the three points, and each of the three main points has at least one supporting sentence.

Reference 40 | **Writing the Body for a Three-Point Expository Paragraph**

THE BODY

After the topic sentence and the three-point sentence have been written, you will present and support each point in the body. The three points will be developed, one at a time. Do not forget that the three points should be presented in the same order in which they were listed in the three-point sentence.

The third sentence states the first listed point. Next, a **supporting sentence** is written about the first point. The details in this sentence must **support** the first point. This is why it is called a **supporting sentence**. The supporting sentence can explain or describe, but it must be about the first point. Next, Sentence 5 is written to state the second point, and Sentence 6 supports it. Then, Sentence 7 is written to state the third point, and Sentence 8 supports it.

Sentence 3 – **First Point:** Write a sentence stating your first point.

Orange is the color I enjoy most of all the fall colors.

Sentence 4 – **Supporting Sentence:** Write a sentence that gives more information about the first point.

It is a color that reminds me of jack-o-lanterns, fields of ripe pumpkins, and sassafras leaves after a frost.

Continued on next page. >>>

Reference 40 continued from previous page.

Sentence 5 – Second Point: Write a sentence stating your second point.

Yellow, another autumn hue, is also a favorite color of mine.

Sentence 6 – Supporting Sentence: Write a sentence that gives more information about the second point.

It makes me think of flowering goldenrod along country roads and hickory leaves in my yard.

Sentence 7 – Third Point: Write a sentence stating your third point.

Brown is yet another favorite of mine.

Sentence 8 – Supporting Sentence: Write a sentence that gives more information about the third point.

Brown reminds me of hickory-nut shells and the crispness of autumn leaves rustling in the wind.

When you keep your writing focused on the topic, your paragraph will have what is called **unity**; it will be a **unified** paragraph. In a unified paragraph, all sentences work together to focus on one topic. Use only ideas that support your topic. Discard all nonsupporting ideas.

Learn It: WRITING THE CONCLUSION
FOR A THREE-POINT EXPOSITORY PARAGRAPH

The conclusion forms the last part of a three-point paragraph. It consists of only one sentence called the **concluding general sentence**.

Reference 41 | Writing the Conclusion for a Three-Point Expository Paragraph

THE CONCLUSION

CONCLUDING GENERAL SENTENCE

Now that the three points have been made and supported, you need to complete the paragraph, leaving the reader with the impression that he/she has read a finished product. In order to complete the paragraph, you need a conclusion, or final sentence. The concluding general sentence should tie all the important points together with a restatement of the main idea and your final comments on it.

To write the Concluding General Sentence, read the topic sentence again and then rewrite it, using some of the same words. The Concluding General Sentence is meant to be general in nature and restates the topic sentence. In the sample sentence, the general word, *colors*, is used instead of the particular points, *orange*, *yellow*, and *brown*.

Sentence 9 – Concluding General Sentence:

As long as I can see these colors in my mind, I can avoid the bleakness of winter.

Learn It: WRITING THE TITLE

The title forms the fourth part of a three-point paragraph.

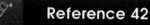

Reference 42	Writing the Title for a Three-Point Expository Paragraph

WRITING THE TITLE

Most paragraphs and longer pieces of writing have a title. A title will be the first item appearing at the top of a paragraph. The title not only tells what you are writing about, but it grabs the reader's attention. Since there are many possibilities for titles, the writer usually finds it easier to think of a title after the paragraph has been completed. In effect, the title will become the fourth and last part of a paragraph.

To write the title, look at the topic and the three points listed about the topic. You may use the topic as your title or choose another word or phrase that is interesting and that tells what your writing is about. Your title can be long or short. In your title, capitalize the first word, the last word, and all of the important words between them. Unless they are first or last words, prepositions, conjunctions, and articles are not normally capitalized.

In the sample title, the word *seasonal* has been added to the topic to express accurately what the paragraph is about.

Title: My Favorite Seasonal Colors

Sample Three-Point Paragraph

My Favorite Seasonal Colors

Of all the colors I like, my three favorites are autumn colors. Without a doubt, I would choose the colors orange, yellow, and brown. Orange is the color I enjoy most of all the fall colors. It is a color that reminds me of jack-o-lanterns, fields of ripe pumpkins, and sassafras leaves after a frost. Yellow, another autumn hue, is also a favorite color of mine. It makes me think of flowering goldenrod along country roads and hickory leaves in my yard. Brown is yet another favorite of mine. Brown reminds me of hickory-nut shells and the crispness of autumn leaves rustling in the wind. As long as I can see these colors in my mind, I can avoid the bleakness of winter.

Discuss It:

1. What does the **Introduction** contain?
2. What does the **Body** contain?
3. What does the **Conclusion** contain?

Reference 43	Main Parts of an Expository Paragraph

Topic:	My Favorite Colors
Three points about the topic:	Orange, yellow, brown
Introduction:	**Sentence 1:** Topic and number sentence
	Sentence 2: A three-point sentence
Body:	**Sentence 3:** A first-point sentence
	Sentence 4: A supporting sentence for the first point
	Sentence 5: A second-point sentence
	Sentence 6: A supporting sentence for the second point
	Sentence 7: A third-point sentence
	Sentence 8: A supporting sentence for the third point
Conclusion:	**Sentence 9:** A concluding general sentence
Title:	My Favorite Seasonal Colors

 Writing Time

Learn It: **PREWRITING, THE FIRST STEP IN THE WRITING PROCESS**

Lesson 9

You will
- read and discuss prewriting (Step 1 in the writing process).
- plan and write sentences on sentence outline form from prewriting map for WA 2, Part 1 (expository).

Reference 44	Prewriting Checklist for Step 1 in the Writing Process

The first step in the writing process is called prewriting. In the prewriting stage, you plan and organize your ideas and thoughts for writing. A graphic organizer, which is a visual aid, can help you organize your prewriting ideas. Lists, maps, outlines, and Venn diagrams are some of the graphic organizers you will use this year. Use the prewriting steps below as you begin the writing process.

1. **Know the purpose.** Before you begin writing, you should know the purpose of your writing. Knowing the purpose will help you focus on your topic. The purpose of your writing determines the type of writing you will do. The different types of writing and their purposes are listed below.

    Expository: to explain or inform

    Persuasive: to win over or convince

    Descriptive: to describe

    Narrative: to tell a story

    Creative: to entertain through different forms, or genres: stories, poems, plays, etc.

    Compare/Contrast: to tell how things are alike and/or how things are different

2. **Know the audience.** Who will read your writing? Is this writing intended for you, your classmates, friends, family, teacher, principal, or someone else?

3. **Choose a topic.** Sometimes your teacher will assign a topic. Other times, you will select your own topic. If you select your own topic, you should list several topic ideas from which to choose. You should consider all of your topic choices and then select the one that you can best develop with main points and details from your experience and/or knowledge.

4. **Narrow the topic.** If the topic is too broad for you to cover well, it must be narrowed. A narrowed topic makes it easier to develop the main points you want to make. Decide if you need to narrow the topic.

5. **Collect ideas and details.** Think about your topic. **Brainstorm** for ideas and details that can be used to develop the topic. This is the time you will broaden your original ideas and elaborate on existing ones. Use your experiences, books, or information from other people to collect ideas. Write these ideas on your prewriting map.

6. **Arrange ideas and details.** Make sure your ideas and details are grouped into some kind of visual order on a **graphic organizer**. A form for a prewriting map has been provided on page 59 as a sample graphic organizer. Your teacher will tell you when to use this form.

7. **Keep your prewriting map.** Use it to write your rough draft. Then, place it in your Rough Draft folder.

Learn It: THE PREWRITING MAP

The information in the Prewriting Checklist will help you complete a prewriting map. This map will give you a visual aid of how you will organize your ideas. The example below shows you how ideas are organized into a prewriting map.

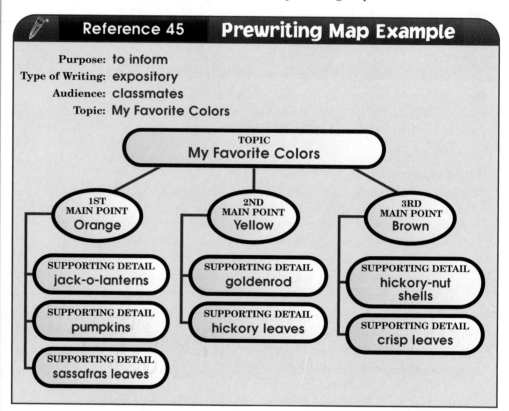

Reference 45 — **Prewriting Map Example**

Purpose: **to inform**
Type of Writing: **expository**
Audience: **classmates**
Topic: **My Favorite Colors**

TOPIC
My Favorite Colors

1ST MAIN POINT **Orange**

2ND MAIN POINT **Yellow**

3RD MAIN POINT **Brown**

SUPPORTING DETAIL **jack-o-lanterns**

SUPPORTING DETAIL **goldenrod**

SUPPORTING DETAIL **hickory-nut shells**

SUPPORTING DETAIL **pumpkins**

SUPPORTING DETAIL **hickory leaves**

SUPPORTING DETAIL **crisp leaves**

SUPPORTING DETAIL **sassafras leaves**

Discuss It: FEATURES OF THE PREWRITING MAP EXAMPLE

First, look at the list in the top left corner of the map.

1. What is the purpose for writing?

2. What is the type of writing?

3. Who is the intended audience?

4. What is the topic?

As you can see, the topic is listed again as it is placed in the topic oval.

Plan It: MAKING A PREWRITING MAP

Next, brainstorm for ideas about the topic. If you don't know very much about your topic, you will have to look in the library or on the Internet to find information. In the example, the writer listed his favorite colors as main points in the ovals directly under the topic. His favorite colors, **orange**, **yellow**, and **brown** will be used as the main points in his three-point expository paragraph.

After the main points were listed, the writer had to think of some interesting details to tell about each of his favorite colors. For the color **orange**, he listed the details *jack-o-lanterns, pumpkins,* and *sassafras leaves* on the prewriting map. For the color **yellow**, he wrote the details *goldenrod* and *hickory leaves*. For the color **brown**, the writer listed the details *hickory-nut shells* and *crisp leaves*. Then, he checked to make sure each detail on his map supported its main point.

In the example, all the ideas are organized into a simple map that shows the order in which the writer will write his three-point expository paragraph. Keep in mind, however, that this map is to help him get started. His ideas may change as he begins to write. He might add ideas to the map or even change them as he writes the actual paragraph.

Write It: WRITING ASSIGNMENT 2, PART 1

Look at Writing Assignment 2, Part 1. Follow the special instructions for this writing assignment. Use the prewriting map below and the sentence outline on the next page to help you.

Writing Assignment ②2 Part 1

Purpose: To inform

Type of Writing: Three-point expository paragraph

Audience: Classmates

Writing Topic: My Favorite Colors

Special Instructions:

1. Follow the Prewriting Checklist on page 57 and make a prewriting map, using your own brainstorming ideas. Write your ideas on a prewriting map.

2. Use your prewriting map as a guide and write the sentences for your expository paragraph on the form titled "Sentence Outline for an Expository Paragraph."

3. Use References 38–43 on pages 53–56 to help you write your paragraph.

4. Put your prewriting map and your sentence outline in your Rough Draft folder.

Prewriting Map

Name:_____ Date:_____

Purpose: _____

Type of Writing: _____

Audience: _____

Topic: _____

TOPIC

1ST MAIN POINT	2ND MAIN POINT	3RD MAIN POINT
SUPPORTING DETAIL	SUPPORTING DETAIL	SUPPORTING DETAIL
SUPPORTING DETAIL	SUPPORTING DETAIL	SUPPORTING DETAIL
SUPPORTING DETAIL	SUPPORTING DETAIL	SUPPORTING DETAIL

Sentence Outline for an Expository Paragraph

Name:_____ Date:_____

Purpose: _____

Type of Writing: _____

Audience: _____

Topic: _____

List 3 points about the topic:

1._____ 2._____ 3._____

Sentence 1 — Write a topic and number sentence.

_____

_____

Sentence 2 — Write a three-point sentence.

_____

_____

Sentence 3 — State your first point in a complete sentence.

_____

Sentence 4 — Write a supporting sentence for the first point.

_____

Sentence 5 — State your second point in a complete sentence.

_____

Sentence 6 — Write a supporting sentence for the second point.

_____

_____

Sentence 7 — State your third point in a complete sentence.

_____

Sentence 8 — Write a supporting sentence for the third point.

_____

_____

Sentence 9 — Write a concluding general sentence.

_____

_____

Writing Time

Lesson 10

You will
- read and discuss rough draft (Step 2 in the writing process).
- write an expository paragraph for WA 2, Part 2.

Learn It: WRITING A ROUGH DRAFT,
    THE SECOND STEP IN THE WRITING PROCESS

Reference 46	Rough Draft Checklist for Step 2 in the Writing Process

The second step in the writing process is writing the rough draft. Since you generally do not have a finished product the first time you write, your first writing attempt is called a **rough draft.** You do not have to worry about correcting mistakes as you write your rough draft because you will do that later. Use the rough draft guidelines below as you write a rough draft.

1. Your rough draft will be written in pencil on notebook paper.

2. On the left side of your paper, use the first seven lines to write the information below.

    Name:
    Date:
    WA: (Writing Assignment Number)
    Purpose: (to inform or explain, to persuade, to describe, or to entertain)
    Type of writing: (expository, persuasive, descriptive, narrative, creative, or comparison/contrast)
    Audience: (myself, classmates, friends, parents, relatives, teacher, principal, other)
    Topic: (name of assigned or chosen topic)

3. Skip the next line.

4. Begin writing your rough draft, using your prewriting map.

5. Use extra wide margins and skip every other line in your rough draft. This will give you room to revise and edit.

6. Skip two lines at the end of your rough draft and write the title on the left side of your paper.

    Title Information: You usually decide on a title after you write the rough draft. The title should not only tell what you are writing about but should also grab the reader's attention. You may use the topic as your title or choose another word or phrase that is interesting and that tells what your writing is about. Your title can be long or short. In your title, capitalize the first word, the last word, and all of the important words between them. Unless they are first or last words, prepositions, conjunctions, and articles are not normally capitalized.

7. Put the rough draft and prewriting map in your Rough Draft folder.

Discuss It: STEPS IN WRITING A ROUGH DRAFT

Look at the Rough Draft Example in Reference 47. This example demonstrates how to use the Rough Draft Checklist to write a rough draft.

Notice how the assignment information is placed on the left side of the paper on the first seven lines. Then, look at the extra wide margins that are used when writing a rough draft. Next, observe that every other line is skipped to give room for editing. Finally, a title is written at the end of the rough draft.

The mistakes in this rough draft have not been corrected. Learning how to correct a rough draft is presented in a later lesson.

Reference 47   Rough Draft Example

Name: John Doe
Date: September ___, 20—
WA 2
Purpose: to inform
Type of writing: expository
Audience: classmates
Topic: My Favorite Colors

Of all the colors there is, my three favorites is autumn colors. I would

choose the colors orange yellow and brown orange is is the color i enjoy

of all the fall colors. Orange is an color that reminds me of jack-o-lanterns

fields of pumpkens, and sassafras leafs after a frost. The jack-o-lanterns are

always interesting. Yellow, another autumn hue is another favorite color of mine.

It makes me think of flowering goldenrod along country roads and hickory leafs

in my yard brown is yet another color i like. Brown remind me of of hickory-nut

shells and the crispness of autumn leafs blowing in the wind as long as I

remember my favorite colors in my mind I can avoid the harsh winter.

Title: My Favorite Seasonal Colors

Write It: **WRITING ASSIGNMENT 2, PART 2**

Look at Writing Assignment 2, Part 2.
Follow the special instructions for this writing assignment.

Writing Assignment 2 Part 2

Purpose: To inform
Type of Writing: Three-point expository paragraph
Audience: Classmates
Writing Topic: My Favorite Colors

Special Instructions:

1. Copy your sentences from your sentence outline onto notebook paper, putting them in paragraph form.

2. Follow the Rough Draft Checklist in Reference 46 as you write your paragraph on paper.

3. Put your prewriting map and rough draft in your Rough Draft folder when you have finished.

START LESSON 11

Lesson 11

You will

- read and discuss revising and editing (Steps 3-4 in the writing process).

 Writing Time

Learn It: REVISING, THE THIRD STEP IN THE WRITING PROCESS

Reference 48	Revising Checklist for Step 3 in the Writing Process

The third step in the writing process is called revising. Revising is finding ways to improve the content and meaning of your writing. Since you are dealing with content, you must read your rough draft several times. First, read your rough draft silently, and, then, read it aloud to yourself. Next, read it to others. When your rough draft is read aloud, you usually hear mistakes that you would not discover otherwise.

To revise your rough draft, draw a line through the words or phrases you want to change or delete. Write the revisions above the words or phrases you want to change. If you want to insert words, phrases, or sentences, use the insert symbol (∧) and write the added part above it.

The **checkpoints** below will help you improve the content and meaning of your writing as you revise your rough draft.

1. Have you written according to the purpose, type of writing, and audience assigned?

2. Have you stayed on the topic assigned? Does each paragraph have a topic sentence? Does each sentence within a paragraph support the topic sentence?

3. Check each sentence. Are your sentences in the right order? Do you need to combine, rearrange, or delete any of the sentences? Are your sentences interesting and descriptive with appropriate examples? Have you used a variety of simple, compound, and complex sentences?

4. Check the words. Have any words been left out? Are any words repeated or unnecessary? Do you need to replace any word or phrase with a clearer or more expressive one? Did you elaborate by using examples and descriptive words to support your ideas? Do the words make sense and express the thoughts you want to share?

5. Check the content for interest and creativity.

6. Check the voice of the writing. Does your writing sound original and genuinely express your own personal viewpoint?

>>>>>>>>>>>> **Student Tip...**

In the Revising Example, a line is drawn through words to be deleted, and the revised text is written above it. An insert symbol (∧) is used to indicate where to insert new text.

Discuss It:

This revising example in Reference 49 demonstrates how to use the Revising Checklist to revise a rough draft. Compare the checkpoints in Reference 48 to the corrections made in the revising example.

Reference 49 Revising Example

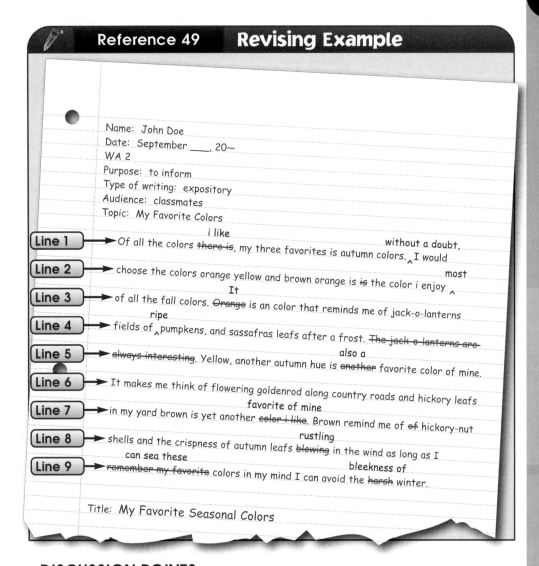

Name: John Doe
Date: September ___, 20—
WA 2
Purpose: to inform
Type of writing: expository
Audience: classmates
Topic: My Favorite Colors

Line 1 → Of all the colors ~~there is~~ , my three favorites *i like* is autumn colors. *without a doubt,* I would

Line 2 → choose the colors orange yellow and brown orange is ~~is~~ the color i enjoy *most*

Line 3 → of all the fall colors. *It* ~~Orange~~ is an color that reminds me of jack-o-lanterns

Line 4 → fields of *ripe* pumpkens, and sassafras leafs after a frost. ~~The jack-o-lanterns are~~

Line 5 → ~~always interesting~~. Yellow, another autumn hue is ~~another~~ *also a* favorite color of mine.

Line 6 → It makes me think of flowering goldenrod along country roads and hickory leafs

Line 7 → in my yard brown is yet another ~~color i like~~ *favorite of mine*. Brown remind me of ~~of~~ hickory-nut

Line 8 → shells and the crispness of autumn leafs ~~blowing~~ *rustling* in the wind as long as I

Line 9 → ~~remember my favorite~~ *can sea these* colors in my mind I can avoid the ~~harsh~~ *bleekness of* winter.

Title: My Favorite Seasonal Colors

DISCUSSION POINTS:

How did the writer use the Revising Checkpoints to revise his paragraph in Reference 49?

Checkpoint 1: Have you written according to the purpose, type of writing, and audience assigned?

Revising Example: The purpose, type of writing, and audience were identified because the writer used an expository paragraph to inform his classmates about his favorite colors.

Checkpoint 2: Have you stayed on the topic assigned? Does each paragraph have a topic sentence? Does each sentence within a paragraph support the topic sentence?

Revising Example: The writer checked over his sentences, looking for any sentence that did not support the topic. The sentence, ***The jack-o-lanterns are always interesting***, does not support the topic, *My Favorite Colors*. The writer drew a line through the sentence, ***The jack-o-lanterns are always interesting***, to indicate that it will be deleted when the final paper is written.

Checkpoint 3: Check each sentence. Are your sentences in the right order? Do you need to combine, rearrange, or delete any of the sentences? Are your sentences interesting and descriptive with appropriate examples? Have you used a variety of simple, compound, and complex sentences?

Continued on next page. >>>

Revising Example: As the writer checked each sentence, he was satisfied with the sentence order. The writer then checked and was sure his sentences were interesting and descriptive with appropriate examples. Finally, he checked and verified that he had used different types of sentences.

Checkpoint 4: Check the words. Have any words been left out? Are any words repeated or unnecessary? Do you need to change any word or phrase for a clearer or more expressive one? Did you elaborate by using examples and descriptive words to support your ideas? Do the words make sense and express the thoughts you want to share?

Revising Example: The writer checked the words within each sentence. He found several things he wanted to change. On the first line, he drew a line through the words *there is* and changed them to the words *i like*. He also decided to insert the words *without a doubt* at the beginning of the next sentence. Notice that he used the insert symbol ($_\wedge$) and wrote the words he wanted to insert above the symbol.

What are the other changes that the writer made as he continued using Checkpoint 4 to revise his paragraph?

Line 2: He marked through the repeated word *is* because he wanted to delete it; he inserted the word *most* after the word *enjoy*.

Line 3: He drew a line through the word *orange* and changed it to *it*.

Line 4: He inserted the word *ripe* in front of *pumpkens**. The sentence, ***The jack-o-lanterns are always interesting***, was already discussed in Checkpoint 2.

Line 5: He drew a line through *another* and changed it to *also a*.

Line 6: There are no revisions.

Line 7: He drew a line through *color I like* and changed it to *favorite of mine*; he marked through the repeated word *of* because he wanted to delete it.

Line 8: He drew a line through *blowing* and changed it to *rustling*.

Line 9: He drew a line through *remember my favorite* and changed it to *can sea* these*; he drew a line through *harsh* and changed it to *bleekness* of*. (*The misspelling of *pumpkins*, *bleakness* and *see* will be corrected during editing time.)

Checkpoint 5: Check the content for interest and creativity.

Revising Example: The writer read over his paragraph again and was satisfied that it was interesting and creative.

Checkpoint 6: Check the voice of the writing. Does the writing sound original and genuinely express your own personal viewpoint?

Revising Example: The writer was satisfied that his paragraph sounded original and expressed his personal viewpoint.

Learn It: **EDITING, THE FOURTH STEP IN THE WRITING PROCESS**

 Reference 50 — **Editing Checklist for Step 4 in the Writing Process**

The fourth step in the writing process is called editing. When you check a sentence or a paragraph for mistakes in spelling, grammar, usage, capitalization, and punctuation, it is called **proofreading**. When you correct these mistakes, it is called **editing**.

After you have completed your revisions, you will use the **checkpoints** below to edit your rough draft. As you find capitalization, spelling, and usage mistakes, write the corrections above them. As you find punctuation mistakes, write the punctuation corrections within the sentence.

Continued on next page. >>>

Reference 50 continued from previous page.

1. Did you indent each paragraph?
2. Did you capitalize the first word and put an end mark at the end of every sentence? Did you follow all other capitalization and punctuation rules?
3. Did you check for misspelled words, for incorrect spellings of plural and possessive forms, and for incorrect homonym choices?
4. Did you check for correct construction and correct punctuation of a simple sentence, a simple sentence with compound parts, a compound sentence, and/or a complex sentence?
5. Did you check for usage mistakes? This includes subject-verb agreement, a/an choices, contractions, pronoun-antecedent agreement, pronoun cases, degrees of adjectives, double negatives, verb tenses, and singular/plural word choices.
6. You are now ready to put the revised and edited paper back in the Rough Draft folder.

Discuss It:

This editing example demonstrates how to use the Editing Checklist to edit a rough draft. Compare the checkpoints in Reference 50 to the corrections made in the editing example below.

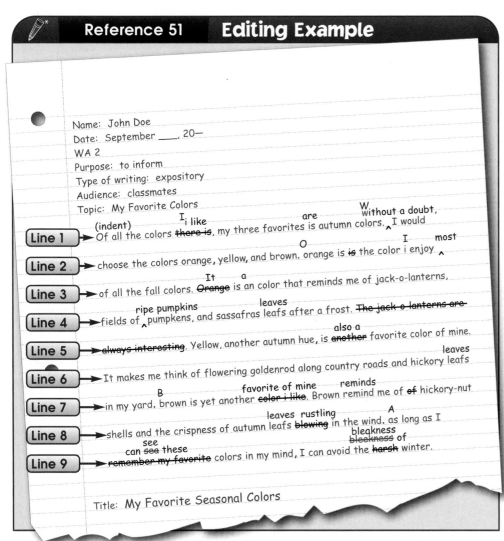

Reference 51   Editing Example

Name: John Doe
Date: September ___, 20—
WA 2
Purpose: to inform
Type of writing: expository
Audience: classmates
Topic: My Favorite Colors

Line 1 → (indent) Of all the colors there is, my three favorites is autumn colors. I would
Line 2 → choose the colors orange, yellow, and brown. orange is is the color i enjoy most
Line 3 → of all the fall colors. Orange is an color that reminds me of jack-o-lanterns,
Line 4 → fields of pumpkens, and sassafras leafs after a frost. The jack o lanterns are
Line 5 → always interesting. Yellow, another autumn hue, is another favorite color of mine.
Line 6 → It makes me think of flowering goldenrod along country roads and hickory leafs
Line 7 → in my yard. brown is yet another color i like. Brown remind me of of hickory-nut
Line 8 → shells and the crispness of autumn leafs blowing in the wind. as long as I
Line 9 → remember my favorite colors in my mind, I can avoid the harsh winter.

Title: My Favorite Seasonal Colors

DISCUSSION POINTS:

How did the writer use the Editing Checkpoints to edit his paragraph in Reference 51?

Checkpoint 1: Did you indent each paragraph?

Editing Example: The writer wrote the word *indent* at the beginning of the paragraph to remind him to correct this mistake on the final paper.

Checkpoint 2: Did you capitalize the first word and put an end mark at the end of every sentence? Did you follow all other capitalization and punctuation rules?

Editing Example: First, the writer checked each sentence for first-word capitalization and end-mark punctuation. How many first-word capitalization mistakes did he find? He found four mistakes: *without* in Line 1; *orange* in Line 2; *brown* in Line 7; and *as* in Line 8. How many end-mark punctuation mistakes did he find? He found three mistakes: *brown.* in Line 2; *yard.* in Line 7; and *wind.* in Line 8. He then checked the sentences for other capitalization and punctuation mistakes. He also corrected seven other capitalization and punctuation mistakes.

Checkpoint 3: Did you check for misspelled words, for incorrect spellings of plural and possessive forms, and for incorrect homonym choices?

Editing Example: The writer found and corrected five misspelled words. What are the misspelled words that were corrected? (Line 4: *pumpkens—pumpkins*, Line 4: *leafs—leaves*, Line 6: *leafs—leaves*, Line 8: *leafs—leaves*, Line 9: *bleekness—bleakness*) He also corrected one homonym spelling. Homonyms are words that sound alike but are spelled differently and have different meanings. What homonym mistake was found? (Line 9: *sea—see*)

Checkpoint 4: Did you check for correct construction and correct punctuation of a simple sentence, a simple sentence with compound parts, a compound sentence, or a complex sentence?

Editing Example: The writer checked his sentences and found that he had already corrected a complex sentence punctuation mistake by adding a comma during Checkpoint 2. (Lines 8–9: *As long as I can see these colors in my mind, I can avoid the bleakness of winter.*)

Checkpoint 5: Did you check for usage mistakes? This includes subject-verb agreement, a/an choices, contractions, pronoun-antecedent agreement, pronoun cases, degrees of adjectives, double negatives, verb tenses, and singular/plural word choices.

Editing Example: The writer corrected two subject-verb agreement mistakes and one a/an choice mistake. (Line 1: changed *favorites is* to *favorites are*, Line 7: changed *brown remind* to *brown reminds*, Line 3: changed *an color* to *a color*)

Checkpoint 6: You are now ready to put the revised and edited paper back in the Rough Draft folder.

You will use the Rough Draft Checklist, Revising Checklist, and the Editing Checklist in the next lesson as you write, revise, and edit your rough draft.

English Made Easy

 Writing Time

Learn It: THE REVISING AND EDITING SCHEDULE

The schedule in Reference 52 has special instructions for revising and editing in the top portion and for writing a final paper in the bottom portion. You will revise and edit your rough draft today, and you will write your final paper in the next lesson. Since the revising and editing steps are so important, your rough draft will go through several stages of revising and editing before you write a final paper. Do not get in a hurry when you revise and edit. It is a slow, precise job because you are checking many areas.

Lesson 12

You will
- read and discuss The Revising and Editing Schedule.
- revise and edit WA 2.

Reference 52	Revising & Editing Schedule and Writing a Final Paper

**SPECIAL INSTRUCTIONS FOR REVISING AND EDITING
(Steps 3-4 in the writing process):**

- Use the Revising and Editing Checklists in References 48 and 50 as you revise and edit your rough draft.

- Follow the revising and editing schedule below as directed by your teacher.

  1. **Individual.** First, read your rough draft to yourself. Use the Revising Checklist in Reference 48 on page 64. Go through your paper, checking each item on the list and making revisions to your rough draft. Then, use the Editing Checklist in Reference 50 on page 66. Go through your paper again, checking each item on the list and editing your rough draft.

  2. **Partner.** Next, get with your editing partner. Work together on each partner's rough draft, one paper at a time. Read each rough draft aloud and revise and edit it together, using the Revising and Editing Checklists. (The author of the paper should be the one to make the corrections on his own paper.)

  3. **Group.** Finally, read the rough draft to a revision group for feedback. Each student should read his paper while the others listen and offer possible revising and editing suggestions. (The author will determine whether to make corrections from the revision group's suggestions.)

**SPECIAL INSTRUCTIONS FOR FINAL PAPER
(Step 5 in the writing process):**

- Write your final paper, using the Final Paper Checklist in Reference 53 on page 70.

- Staple your writing papers in this order: the final paper on top, the rough draft in the middle, and the prewriting map on the bottom. Place the stapled papers in the Final Paper folder.

>>>>>>>>> Student Tip...

1. Be tactful and helpful in your comments during revising and editing time. The purpose of any suggestion should be to improve the writer's rough draft.

2. As you make your final corrections, you have the choice of accepting or rejecting any suggestions made by your partners or your revision group.

3. If you need to improve your handwriting, refer to the Resource Tools Section on pages 529–530 for information on writing legibly.

Chapter 2

START LESSON 13

Lesson 13

You will

- discuss final paper (Step 5 in the writing process).
- discuss the Writing Evaluation Guide.
- review The Steps in the Writing Process.
- write the final paper for WA 2.
- identify one part of speech.

Learn It: **FINAL PAPER, THE FIFTH STEP IN THE WRITING PROCESS**

Reference 53	Final Paper Checklist for Step 5 in the Writing Process

The fifth step in the writing process is writing the final paper. A final paper is a neat, corrected copy of your rough draft. You should follow these guidelines as you write your final paper.

1. Read through your rough draft one last time and make final corrections before beginning your final paper.
2. Write your final paper neatly in pencil.
3. Center the title on the top line.
4. Center your name under the title with the word **By** in front of your name.
5. Skip a line after your name before you begin your writing assignment.
6. Single-space your final paper.
7. Use wide margins for your final paper.
8. Use the Writing Evaluation Guide to check your final paper one last time.
9. Staple your writing papers in this order: the final paper on top, the rough draft in the middle, and the prewriting map on the bottom. Place the stapled papers and a copy of the Writing Evaluation Guide in the Final Paper folder.

Example of the Final Paper

My Favorite Seasonal Colors
By John Doe

Of all the colors I like, my three favorites are autumn colors. Without a doubt, I would choose the colors orange, yellow, and brown. Orange is the color I enjoy most of all the fall colors. It is a color that reminds me of jack-o-lanterns, fields of ripe pumpkins, and sassafras leaves after a frost. Yellow, another autumn hue, is also a favorite color of mine. It makes me think of flowering goldenrod along country roads and hickory leaves in my yard. Brown is yet another favorite of mine. Brown reminds me of hickory-nut shells and the crispness of autumn leaves rustling in the wind. As long as I can see these colors in my mind, I can avoid the bleakness of winter.

Learn It: WRITING EVALUATION GUIDE

You will have a Writing Evaluation Guide for each chapter. You will use it to check your final paper one last time. Your teacher will also use this guide to evaluate your writing and to discuss your final paper with you during writing conferences. Study the Writing Evaluation Guide on the next page.

Review It: STEPS IN THE WRITING PROCESS

Reference 54	**The Steps in the Writing Process**

The steps below will take you through the writing process and will give you the location of each checklist.

1. **Prewriting.** Use the Prewriting Checklist to plan and organize your writing. (Reference 44, page 57)
2. **Rough Draft.** Use the Rough Draft Checklist to set up and write the rough draft. (Reference 46, page 61)
3. **Revising.** Use the Revising Checklist to revise the content of your writing. (Reference 48, page 64)
4. **Editing.** Use the Editing Checklist to edit your writing for spelling, grammar, usage, capitalization, and punctuation mistakes. (Reference 50, page 66)
5. **Final Paper.** Use the Final Paper Checklist to set up and write the final paper. (Reference 53, page 70)
6. **Publishing.** Use the Publishing Checklist to choose a publishing form for sharing your writing with others. (Reference 66, page 98)

Write It: WRITING A FINAL PAPER
FOR WRITING ASSIGNMENT 2, PART 2

Get Writing Assignment 2, Part 2 from your Rough Draft folder, and write a final paper. Follow ALL the steps listed in the Final Paper Checklist. Make sure you use the Chapter 2 Writing Evaluation Guide on the next page to check your final paper one last time. After you have finished your paper, put it in your Final Paper folder.

Learn It: IDENTIFYING ONE PART OF SPEECH

You have been identifying the parts of a sentence by classifying every word. Now, you will use that knowledge to find only one part of speech on Part B of the Chapter Test. Use the steps below to learn the process for finding one part of speech.

1. Use the Question and Answer Flow to classify the sentence. Label each word mentally or with a pencil.
2. Start with the subject and verb. Continue classifying until you have classified the underlined word.
3. Look at the label of the underlined word.
4. Choose the answer that matches the classified word.

Example: Choose the part of speech for the underlined word.

Several specialty shops opened very <u>early</u> today.
ⓐ noun   ⓑ verb   ⓒ adjective   ⓓ adverb

SHURLEY ENGLISH

Chapter 2 Writing Evaluation Guide

Name:_____ Date:_____

ROUGH DRAFT CHECK

_____ 1. Did you write your rough draft in pencil?

_____ 2. Did you write the correct headings on the first seven lines of your paper?

_____ 3. Did you use extra wide margins and skip every other line?

_____ 4. Did you write a title at the end of your rough draft?

_____ 5. Did you place your edited rough draft in your Rough Draft folder?

REVISING CHECK

_____ 6. Did you identify the purpose, type of writing, and audience?

_____ 7. Did you check for a topic, topic sentence, and sentences supporting the topic?

_____ 8. Did you check sentences for the right order, and did you combine, rearrange, or delete sentences when necessary?

_____ 9. Did you check for a variety of simple, compound, and complex sentences?

_____ 10. Did you check for any left out, repeated, or unnecessary words?

_____ 11. Did you check for the best choice of words by replacing or deleting unclear words?

_____ 12. Did you check the content for interest and creativity?

_____ 13. Did you check the voice to make sure the writing says what you want it to say?

EDITING CHECK

_____ 14. Did you indent each paragraph?

_____ 15. Did you put an end mark at the end of every sentence?

_____ 16. Did you capitalize the first word of every sentence?

_____ 17. Did you check for all other capitalization mistakes?

_____ 18. Did you check for all punctuation mistakes?
(*commas, periods, apostrophes, quotation marks, underlining*)

_____ 19. Did you check for misspelled words and for incorrect homonym choices?

_____ 20. Did you check for incorrect spellings of plural and possessive forms?

_____ 21. Did you check for correct construction and punctuation of your sentences?

_____ 22. Did you check for usage mistakes? (*subject/verb agreement, a/an choices, contractions, verb tenses, pronoun/antecedent agreement, pronoun cases, degrees of adjectives, double negatives, etc.*)

_____ 23. Did you put your revised and edited paper in the Rough Draft folder?

FINAL PAPER CHECK

_____ 24. Did you write the final paper in pencil?

_____ 25. Did you center the title on the top line and center your name under the title?

_____ 26. Did you skip a line before starting the writing assignment?

_____ 27. Did you single-space, use wide margins, and write the final paper neatly?

_____ 28. Did you staple your papers in this order: final paper on top, rough draft in the middle, and prewriting map on the bottom? Did you put them in the Final Paper folder?

START LESSON 14

Lesson 14

You will
- hand in WA 2 for grading.
- respond to oral review questions.
- take Chapter 2 Test.

Hand It In: **WRITING ASSIGNMENT 2, PART 2**

Get your stapled sheets for Writing Assignment 2, Part 2 from your Final Paper folder, and give them to your teacher.

LISTENING AND SPEAKING:

Oral Review Questions

CHAPTER TEST

It is time to evaluate your knowledge of the skills you have learned in this chapter. Your teacher will give you the Chapter 2 Test to help you assess your progress.

Discuss It:

1. What are the three article adjectives?
2. What is the definition of a noun?
3. What is the definition of an adverb?
4. What is the definition of an adjective?
5. What are the three adverb questions?
6. What are the three adjective questions?
7. What are the four kinds of sentences?
8. What is the End Mark Flow for the declarative sentence?
9. What is the End Mark Flow for the imperative sentence?
10. What is the End Mark Flow for the exclamatory sentence?
11. What is the End Mark Flow for the interrogative sentence?
12. What are the five parts of a correct sentence?
13. What do you call a group of sentences that is written about one particular subject?
14. What do you call the sentence that tells what a paragraph is about?
15. What type of writing is used when your purpose is to inform, to give facts, to give directions, to explain, or to define something?

Learn It: **STANDARDIZED-TEST FORMAT**

There are two parts for the chapter test. The first part is called Chapter 2 Test, Part A. It looks like the Classroom Practices you have already been doing. The second part is called Chapter 2 Test, Part B. This part of the test is in a standardized-test format, so you will fill in the bubble beside the correct answer. Work each section of this page with your teacher to make sure you understand what to do.

>>>>>>>>>>>>>>>> **Student Tip...**

For information about test-taking strategies, refer to the Resource Tools Section on page 528.

Lesson 1

You will

- study new vocabulary; make card 5; write own sentence using the vocabulary word.
- analyze new analogy; make card 5; write own analogy.
- recite new jingles (Preposition, Object of the Preposition, Prepositional Phrase, Prepositional Flow).
- identify prepositions, objects of the prepositions, and prepositional phrases.
- identify/compare adverbs and prepositions.
- classify Introductory Sentences.
- do a Skill Builder to identify nouns.
- recognize prepositions as a part of speech.
- write in your journal.

LISTENING AND SPEAKING:
Vocabulary & Analogy Time

Learn It: Recite the new vocabulary and analogy words.

Reference 55	Vocabulary & Analogy Words

Word: fastidious (făst ĭd' ē əs)
  Definition: excessively attentive to detail
  Synonym: meticulous   **Antonym:** careless
  Sentence: My grandmother was a fastidious housekeeper.

Analogy: cold : frigid :: vigorous : strenuous
  Synonym relationship: Just as **cold** means nearly the same as **frigid**, **vigorous** means nearly the same as **strenuous**.

Vocabulary Card 5: Record the vocabulary information above and write your own sentence, using the new word.

Analogy Card 5: Record the analogy information and write your own analogy, using the same relationship as the analogy above.

Jingle Time

Recite It: Recite the new jingles.

♪ Jingle 8	The Preposition Jingle

A prep, prep, preposition
Is an extra-special word
That connects a
Noun, noun, noun
Or a pro, pro, pronoun
To the rest of the sentence.

♪ Jingle 9	The Object of the Preposition Jingle

An object of the preposition
Is a NOUN or PRONOUN.
An object of the preposition
Is a NOUN or PRONOUN

After the prep, prep, prep
After the prep, prep, prep
After the prep, prep, prep
That answers **WHAT** or **WHOM**.

♪ Jingle 10	The Prepositional Phrase Jingle

I've been working with prepositions
'Til I can work no more.
They're connecting their objects
To the rest of the sentence before.

When I put them all together,
The prep and its noun or pro,
I get a prepositional phrase
That could cause my mind to blow!

♪ Jingle 11	The Preposition Flow Jingle	
1. Preposition, Preposition, Starting with an **A**: **aboard, about, above,** **across, after, against,** **along, among, around, as, at!**	2. Preposition, Preposition, Starting with a **B**: **before, behind, below,** **beneath, beside, between,** **beyond, but,** and **by!**	3. Preposition, Preposition, Starting with a **D**: **despite, down, during** **despite, down, during!**
4. Oh, Preposition, Please, don't go away. Go to the middle of the alphabet, And see just what we say. **E** and **F** and **I** and **L** And **N** and **O** and **P**: **except, for, from,** **in, inside, into, like,** **near, of, off, on, out,** **outside, over, past!**	5. Preposition, Preposition, Almost through. Start with **S** and end with **W**: **since, through,** **throughout, to, toward,** **under, underneath,** **until, up, upon,** **with, within, without!**	6. Preposition, Preposition, Easy as can be. We just recited All **fifty-one** of these!

Grammar Time

Apply It: These Introductory Sentences are used to apply the new grammar concepts taught below. Classify these sentences orally with your teacher.

Introductory Sentences	Chapter 3: Lesson 1

1. _____ Chang Le looked curiously at the tall picture of the Southern gentleman on the wall in the hall.

2. _____ A tiny scorpion scurried quickly across the sand toward the big rock.

3. _____ The lion cubs at the back of the dark cave whimpered anxiously during the furious thunderstorm!

Learn It: PREPOSITION, OBJECTS OF THE PREPOSITIONS, AND PREPOSITIONAL PHRASES

 Reference 56 — **Prepositions, Objects of the Prepositions, and Prepositional Phrases**

Prepositions

Prepositions join other words in a special way. They show how words in a sentence are related. Read Example 1.

Example 1: The little boy walked *beside* his mother.

Which word tells you where the little boy is in relation to his mother? The word *beside* is placed before *mother* to show the relationship between *boy* and *mother*. The word *beside* is a preposition. If you use the preposition *near* or *behind*, this changes where the *boy* is in relation to his *mother*.

Example 2: The little boy walked **near** his mother.   **Example 3:** The little boy walked **behind** his mother.

The words *near* and *behind* give different ways of relating *boy* and *mother*. *Near* and *behind* are also prepositions. **A preposition relates the noun or pronoun that follows it to some other word in the sentence.** For example, the noun *mother* follows each of the prepositions. Therefore, each preposition relates *mother* to the word *boy* differently because they are different prepositions.

Continued on next page. >>>

Reference 56 continued from previous page.

To find a preposition, say the preposition word and ask *WHAT* or *WHOM*. If the answer is a noun or pronoun, then the word is a preposition. A preposition is labeled with the abbreviation **P**.

Objects of the Prepositions

In Example 1 above, the noun *mother* follows the preposition *beside*. **The noun or pronoun following a preposition is called the object of the preposition.** *Mother* is the object of the preposition *beside*. *Mother* is also the object of the prepositions *near* and *behind* in Examples 2 and 3.

To find an object of the preposition, say the preposition and ask *WHAT* or *WHOM*. If the answer is the noun or pronoun after the preposition, the word is an object of the preposition. An *object of the preposition* is labeled with the abbreviation **OP**.

Prepositional Phrases

A **prepositional phrase** starts with a preposition and ends with the object of the preposition. It also includes any words between the preposition and the object of the preposition. Prepositional phrases add meaning to sentences and can be located anywhere within a sentence.

Prepositional phrases are identified in the Question and Answer Flow after you say **Skill Check**. Mark prepositional phrases by putting parentheses around them. The examples below demonstrate how to identify prepositional phrases.

                   P   OP   P   OP   P   OP
The little boy walked (beside his mother). The plane flew (past my house). We laughed (at the funny clown).

| **Ask:** beside whom? **mother** | **Ask:** past what? **house** | **Ask:** at whom? **clown** |
| beside – P   mother – OP | past – P   house – OP | at – P   clown – OP |

Learn It: IDENTIFYING ADVERBS AND PREPOSITIONS

| **Reference 57** | **Identifying Adverbs and Prepositions** |

Some words can be used as both **adverbs** and as **prepositions**. To tell the difference, find out how the word is used in a particular sentence. For example, the word *down* can be an adverb or a preposition. How do you decide if the word *down* is an adverb or a preposition?

If *down* is used alone, it is probably an adverb. Prepositions are never used alone. They are used in phrases and always have objects. If *down* has a noun or pronoun after it that answers the question *what* or *whom*, then *down* is a preposition, and the noun or pronoun after *down* is an object of the preposition.

In the first sentence below, the word *down* is an adverb because it is used alone. In the second sentence, the word *down* is a preposition because it is used in a phrase and has an object, *stairs*.

              Adv   *P*   *noun* (OP)
1. Chuck fell **down**.   2. Chuck fell **down the stairs**.

How to classify adverbs and prepositions in the Question and Answer Flow	
Chuck fell down.	Chuck fell down the stairs.
Fell where? **down – Adv (down—adverb)**	**Down – P (down—preposition)**
	Down what? **stairs – OP (stairs—object of the preposition)**

>>>>>>>>> **Student Tip...**

For a comprehensive list of the most commonly used abbreviations in Shurley English, refer to the Resource Tools Section on page 520.

Learn It: A SKILL BUILDER FOR A NOUN CHECK

You will use the sentences you have just classified to do a Skill Builder. A **Skill Builder** is an oral review of certain skills. The first skill introduced in the Skill Builder is a **Noun Check**. A Noun Check is a check to find the nouns in a sentence.

A noun can do many jobs in a sentence. The first noun job is the subject noun, and it is marked **SN**. The second noun job is the object of a preposition, and it is marked **OP**.

To find nouns, you will go to these jobs. An example of a Skill Builder for a Noun Check is given below.

LISTENING AND SPEAKING:

FOR A NOUN CHECK

Circle the nouns in a Noun Check.

Sentence 1: Subject Noun Chang Le, *yes, it is a noun;*
Object of the Preposition picture, *yes, it is a noun;*
Object of the Preposition gentleman, *yes, it is a noun;*
Object of the Preposition wall, *yes, it is a noun;*
Object of the Preposition hall, *yes, it is a noun.*

Sentence 2: Subject Noun scorpion, *yes, it is a noun;*
Object of the Preposition sand, *yes, it is a noun;*
Object of the Preposition rock, *yes, it is a noun.*

Sentence 3: Subject Noun cubs, *yes, it is a noun;*
Object of the Preposition back, *yes, it is a noun;*
Object of the Preposition cave, *yes, it is a noun;*
Object of the Preposition thunderstorm, *yes, it is a noun.*

JOURNAL WRITING 5

Write an entry in your journal. Use Reference 9 on page 12 for ideas.

Learn It: ADDING THE PREPOSITION TO THE PARTS OF SPEECH

A preposition is a part of speech. You have learned five of the eight parts of speech. What are these five parts of speech?

START LESSON 2

Lesson 2

You will

- study new vocabulary; make card 6; write own sentence using the vocabulary word.
- analyze new analogy; make card 6; write own analogy.
- practice Jingles 8–11.
- classify Practice Sentences.
- do a Skill Builder to identify singular/plural nouns, common/proper nouns, and simple subject/simple predicate.
- do Classroom Practice 10.
- read and discuss Discovery Time.

LISTENING AND SPEAKING:

Vocabulary & Analogy Time

Learn It: Recite the new vocabulary and analogy words.

📖* Reference 58	Vocabulary & Analogy Words

Word: brevity (brĕv'ĭte)
   Definition: lasting a short time
   Synonym: briefness   **Antonym:** lengthiness
   Sentence: The brevity of her comments surprised everyone!

Analogy: thorns : rosebush :: quills : porcupine
   Part-to-whole relationship: Just as **thorns** are part of a **rosebush**,
               quills are part of a **porcupine**.

Vocabulary Card 6: Record the vocabulary information above and write your own sentence, using the new word.

Analogy Card 6: Record the analogy information and write your own analogy, using the same relationship as the analogy above.

Jingle Time

Recite It: Practice Jingles 8–11 in the Jingle Section on page 508.

Grammar Time

Apply It: Classify the Practice Sentences orally with your teacher.

Practice Sentences	Chapter 3: Lesson 2

1. _____ David arrived too late for the graduation party.
2. _____ The extremely hot fire burned amazingly fast through the dry forest during the night.
3. _____ The brave young canoeists fought frantically against the raging rapids of the river!

Skill Time

Review It: A SKILL BUILDER FOR A NOUN CHECK

FOR A noun CHECK

Circle the nouns in a Noun Check.

Sentence 1: Subject Noun (David) *yes, it is a noun;*
Object of the Preposition (party) *yes, it is a noun.*

Sentence 2: Subject Noun (fire) *yes, it is a noun;*
Object of the Preposition (forest) *yes, it is a noun;*
Object of the Preposition (night) *yes, it is a noun.*

Sentence 3: Subject Noun (canoeists) *yes, it is a noun;*
Object of the Preposition (rapids) *yes, it is a noun;*
Object of the Preposition (river) *yes, it is a noun.*

Learn It: SINGULAR AND PLURAL NOUNS

Study the definitions for singular and plural nouns in Reference 59.

 Reference 59 **Definitions of Words Used in a Skill Builder**

1. A **noun** names a person, place, thing, or idea.
2. A **singular noun** means only one. Most singular nouns do not end in -s or -es. (**Examples:** *cat, child*) Some singular nouns, however, end in -s. (**Examples:** *grass, glass, gas*)
3. A **plural noun** means more than one. Most plural nouns add -s or -es to form the plural. (**Examples:** *cats, glasses*) Some plural nouns, however, have different spellings for the plural. (**Examples:** *children, women*)

Read below and continue on next page. >>>

Apply It:

Add singular and plural nouns to the Skill Builder.

FOR A SINGULAR AND PLURAL CHECK

Mark the nouns with the letter **S** or **P**.

Sentence 1: (David) S – *singular (write S);*
(party) S – *singular (write S).*

Sentence 2: (fire) S – *singular (write S);*
(forest) S – *singular (write S);*
(night) S – *singular (write S).*

Sentence 3: (canoeists) P – *plural (write P);*
(rapids) P – *plural (write P);*
(river) S – *singular (write S).*

Learn It: COMMON AND PROPER NOUNS
Study the definitions for common and proper nouns in Reference 59.

Reference 59 continued from previous page.

4. A **common noun** names ANY person, place, or thing. A common noun is not capitalized because it does not name a specific person, place, or thing. (**Examples:** *girl, country*)

5. A **proper noun** is a noun that names a specific or particular person, place, or thing. Proper nouns are always capitalized no matter where they are located in the sentence. (**Examples:** *Carla, Peru*)

Continued below. >>>

Apply It:
Add common and proper nouns to the Skill Builder.

FOR A COMMON AND PROPER CHECK

Mark the nouns with the letter **C** or **P**.

Sentence 1: David - proper (write P);

party - common (write C).

Sentence 2: fire - common (write C);

forest - common (write C);

night - common (write C).

Sentence 3: canoeists - common (write C);

rapids - common (write C);

river - common (write C).

Learn It: COMPLETE SUBJECT AND COMPLETE PREDICATE
Study the definitions for complete subject and complete predicate in Reference 59.

Reference 59 continued from above.

6. The **complete subject** is the subject and all the words that modify it. The complete subject usually starts at the beginning of the sentence and includes every word up to the verb of the sentence.

7. The **complete predicate** is the verb and all the words that modify it. The complete predicate usually starts with the verb and includes every word after the verb.

Continued on next page. >>>

Apply It:
Add complete subject and complete predicate to the Skill Builder.

FOR A COMPLETE SUBJECT AND COMPLETE PREDICATE CHECK

Underline the complete subject once and the complete predicate twice.

Sentence 1: David <u>arrived too late for the graduation party</u>.

Sentence 2: The extremely hot fire <u>burned amazingly fast through the dry forest during the night</u>.

Sentence 3: The brave young canoeists <u>fought frantically against the raging rapids of the river</u>!

Learn It: SIMPLE SUBJECT AND SIMPLE PREDICATE

Study the definitions for simple subject and simple predicate in Reference 59.

> *Reference 59 continued from previous page.*

8. A **simple subject** is another name for the subject noun or subject pronoun in a sentence. The simple subject is just the subject, without the words that modify it.

9. A **simple predicate** is another name for the verb in a sentence. The simple predicate is just the verb without the words that modify it.

Apply It:

Add simple subject and simple predicate to the Skill Builder.

FOR A SIMPLE SUBJECT AND SIMPLE PREDICATE CHECK

Circle the simple subject and the simple predicate.

Sentence 1: (David) (arrived) too late for the graduation party.

Sentence 2: The extremely hot (fire) (burned) amazingly fast through the dry forest during the night.

Sentence 3: The brave young (canoeists) (fought) frantically against the raging rapids of the river!

Learn It: THE NOUN JOB CHART

| Reference 60 | Noun Job Chart |

Directions: Classify the sentence below. Underline the complete subject once and the complete predicate twice. Then, complete the table below.

SN V
Pl

A   Adj   SN   V   Adv   P A   OP
The exhausted athlete / walked slowly (off the field). D

List the Noun Used	List the Noun Job	Singular or Plural	Common or Proper	Simple Subject	Simple Predicate
athlete	SN	S	C	athlete	walked
field	OP	S	C		

Classroom Practice 10

It is time to practice the skills you are learning. You will use the classroom practice on the next page to apply these skills.

Enrichment: DISCOVERY TIME

Discovery Time is designed to broaden and enrich your knowledge of people in history. During this time, you will read interesting highlights about a notable person in history. These facts will follow the theme for Level 6, which is historical time travel. Each historical figure is also listed in the Resource Tools section on pages 519–520.

ENRICHMENT:

(French) 1412-1431— Saint Joan (Joan of Arc) was 17 years old when she successfully led French troops against a British attack on the French town of Orleans. She was captured and burned at the stake by the British in 1431 for heresy (going against the doctrine of the church) and for wearing men's clothing.

Discovery Questions:
• **What do you think it was like to grow up during Joan's time?**
• **Do you think Joan had a fair trial? Why or why not?**

Are you interested in learning more about Saint Joan?

1. You may explore this topic further by using the resources listed below.
   Computer resources: Internet, encyclopedia software
   Library resources: encyclopedias, books, magazines, newspapers
   Home/community resources: books, interviews, newspapers, magazines

2. A Discovery Share Time is provided in Lesson 7 of Chapter 4 if you wish to share your investigation results. You may share orally, or you may prepare a written report. You will put your written report in a class booklet titled "Notable People in History." This booklet will be placed in the class library for everyone to enjoy.

 **Student Tip...**

For an introduction to computer terminology and using the Internet, refer to the Resource Tools Section on pages 540–543.

Classroom Practice 10

Name:_____ Date:_____

GRAMMAR

▶ **Exercise 1:** Classify each sentence. Underline the complete subject once and the complete predicate twice.

1. _____ Several ripe red apples fell from the tree in the backyard.

2. _____ Ms. Johnson waited patiently in the long line of traffic on the highway.

▶ **Exercise 2:** Use sentence 2 above to complete the table below.

List the Noun Used	List the Noun Job	Singular or Plural	Common or Proper	Simple Subject	Simple Predicate

▶ **Exercise 3:** Name the five parts of speech that you have studied so far.
1. _____ 2. _____ 3. _____ 4. _____ 5. _____

▶ **Exercise 4:** Underline the complete subject once and the complete predicate twice.
1. The dangerous lion growled menacingly! 3. Several large Canadian geese honked loudly.
2. Ten black motorcycles raced away. 4. The political candidates argued heatedly.

▶ **Exercise 5:** Underline the simple subject once and the simple predicate twice.
1. A small mouse dashed across the room! 3. The nine orange balloons drifted across the sky.
2. A few rude students talked continuously. 4. The champion skater performed for the crowd.

SKILLS

▶ **Exercise 6:** Write **S** for singular or **P** for plural.

Noun	S or P
1. shepherd	_____
2. robots	_____
3. shoulder	_____
4. foreigners	_____

▶ **Exercise 7:** Write **C** for common or **P** for proper.

Noun	C or P
1. ostrich	_____
2. Smoky Mountains	_____
3. Albuquerque	_____
4. planetarium	_____

EDITING

▶ **Exercise 8:** Put punctuation corrections within the sentence. Write all other corrections above the sentence.
Editing Guide: Capitals: 7 Commas: 2 Periods: 1 End Marks: 1

james g jones the president of the valley rotary club gave dad an award for his excellent service

START LESSON 3

Lesson 3

You will

- study new vocabulary; make card 7; write own sentence using the vocabulary word.
- analyze new analogy; make card 7; write own analogy.
- practice Jingles 7-11.
- classify Practice Sentences.
- do a Skill Builder to build vocabulary.
- identify subject-verb agreement.
- do Classroom Practice 11.
- read and discuss Discovery Time.

LISTENING AND SPEAKING:
Vocabulary & Analogy Time

Learn It: Recite the new vocabulary and analogy words.

Reference 61	Vocabulary & Analogy Words

Word: adamant (ăd'ə mənt)
   Definition: refusing to change one's mind or position
   Synonym: unyielding   **Antonym:** compromising
   Sentence: He was adamant about not signing the document.

Analogy: farmer : tractor :: doctor : stethoscope
   Purpose or use relationship: Just as a **farmer** uses a **tractor**, a **doctor** uses a **stethoscope**.

Vocabulary Card 7: Record the vocabulary information above and write your own sentence, using the new word.

Analogy Card 7: Record the analogy information and write your own analogy, using the same relationship as the analogy above.

Jingle Time

Recite It: Practice Jingles 7–11 in the Jingle Section on pages 507–508.

Grammar Time

Apply It: Classify the Practice Sentences orally with your teacher.

Practice Sentences	Chapter 3: Lesson 3

1. _____ The small frugal woman shopped discerningly for food in the grocery store.
2. _____ Uncle Wade dressed warmly for the cold weather during the winter months.
3. _____ The opposing teams from local schools gathered for the final game of the season.

Learn It: **A SKILL BUILDER WITH A VOCABULARY CHECK**

A Vocabulary Check will be added to the Skill Builder. The purpose of this check is to improve your vocabulary. An example of a Skill Builder for a Vocabulary Check is given below.

FOR A VOCABULARY CHECK

For selected words, provide this information: a synonym, a new sentence, an antonym.

Sentence 1: The small frugal woman shopped discerningly for food in the grocery store.

Sentence 3: The opposing teams from local schools gathered for the final game of the season.

SENTENCE 1

1. **frugal: synonym:** thrifty, careful, saving
   new sentence: He was frugal with his money.
   antonym: wasteful

2. **discerningly: synonym:** wisely, sensibly, intelligently
   new sentence: He read the article discerningly.
   antonym: unwisely, irrationally, carelessly

3. A fun antonym sentence, using antonyms or word changes for the words **small, frugal, woman,** and **discerningly**: The **large wasteful man** shopped **unwisely** for food in the grocery store.

SENTENCE 3

1. **opposing: synonym:** competing, rivaling
   new sentence: The opposing candidates did not agree.
   antonym: supporting, helping

2. A fun antonym sentence, using antonyms or word changes for the words **opposing, teams, local,** and **final**: The **supporting fans** from **distant** schools gathered for the **first** game of the season.

Review It: **GUIDELINES FOR A VOCABULARY CHECK**

Guidelines for a Vocabulary Check

1. Look over the sentences just classified.
   Do a vocabulary check for any of the words your students may not know.

2. Name a synonym or give a definition for any word selected.

3. Use the vocabulary word correctly in a new sentence.

4. Name an antonym for the word, if possible.

5. For fun, make a new sentence, using antonyms for several words in the original sentence. *(For an example, see the previous Skill Builder that introduces the Vocabulary Check.)*

SHURLEY ENGLISH

Learn It: SUBJECT-VERB AGREEMENT

 | **Reference 62** | **Subject-Verb Agreement Rules**

The word **agreement** means *working together;* therefore, subject-verb agreement means the special way in which the subject and verb work together in a sentence. Whenever you work with subject-verb agreement, you must remember to look at only the subject and verb of a sentence.

RULE 1: A **singular** subject must use a singular verb that ends in **s** or **es**: *is, was, has, does, swims, pushes.*

In Rule 1, notice that all the singular verbs end in s or es. This should make them easier to identify as singular. If the subject is singular, use a singular verb that ends in s or es. Use Rule 1 to help you decide which verb to use with a singular subject.

Example 1. <u>otter</u> <u>swims</u> (swim**s**—singular form)

Look at Example 1 above. The subject *otter* is singular and needs a singular verb to be in agreement. According to Rule 1, adding an **s** to the verb *swim* makes it singular. The singular subject *otter* agrees with the singular verb *swims.* Since the subject and verb are both singular, there is subject-verb agreement.

The following examples show subject-verb agreement for singular forms: *snake crawls, duck quacks, kite flies, child laughs.* Each subject is singular; therefore, each verb must end in **s** or **es** for the singular form.

RULE 2: A **plural** subject, a compound subject, or the subject **YOU** must use a plural verb with **no s** or **es** ending: *are, were, have, do, swim, push.*

In Rule 2, notice that all plural verbs have a **plain form.** Plain form means that verbs do not end in s or es. This should make plural verbs easier to identify as plural. If the subject is plural, use a plural verb that does not end in **s** or **es**. Use Rule 2 to help you decide which verb to use with a plural subject.

Example 2. <u>otters</u> <u>swim</u> (swim—plural form)

Look at Example 2 above. The subject *otters* is plural and needs a plural verb to be in agreement. According to Rule 2, the plain form of the verb *swim* makes it plural. The plural subject *otters* agrees with the plural verb *swim.* Since the subject and verb are both plural, there is subject-verb agreement.

The following examples show subject-verb agreement for plural forms: *snakes crawl, ducks quack, kites fly, children laugh.* Each subject is plural; therefore, each verb must not end in **s** or **es** for the plural form.

Example 3. <u>Mom and Dad</u> <u>drive</u> (drive—plural form)

Look at the compound subject in Example 3 above. A compound subject occurs when there are two or more subjects in the sentence. According to Rule 2, the plain form of the verb *drive* makes it plural. The compound subject *Mom and Dad* agrees with the plural verb *drive.* Since the subject and verb are both plural, there is subject-verb agreement.

The following examples show subject-verb agreement for compound subjects and the plural verb forms: *shoes and socks are, aunt and uncle visit, Kim and Katy were.*

Example 4. <u>You</u> <u>drive</u> (drive—plural form)

Look at Example 4 above. The subject *you* always uses a plural verb to be in agreement. According to Rule 2, the plain form of the verb *drive* makes it plural. Since the subject *you* agrees with the plural verb *drive,* there is subject-verb agreement.

The following examples show subject-verb agreement for the subject *you* and the plural verb forms: *you walk, you run, you are, you were.*

Note: Subject-verb agreement is important only when verbs are in present tense. If a verb is past tense, it **does not** matter whether the subject is singular or plural because the verb remains in the same past-tense form. Even though the subject changes from singular to plural, the verb stays the same. (*dog barked; dogs barked; cat ran; cats ran*)

Continued on next page. >>>

Reference 62 continued from previous page.

RULE 1: A **singular** subject must use a singular verb that ends in **s** or **es**: *is, was, has, does, swims, pushes.*

RULE 2: A **plural** subject, a compound subject, or the subject **YOU** must use a plural verb with **no s** or **es** ending: *are, were, have, do, swim, push.*

Sample Exercise: For each sentence, do three things: (1) Write the subject. (2) Write **S** and **Rule 1** if the subject is singular, or write **P** and **Rule 2** if the subject is plural. (3) Underline the correct verb.

Subject	S or P	Rule #	
boy	S	1	1. The **boy** (jump, <u>jumps</u>) on his trampoline.
boys	P	2	2. The **boys** (<u>jump</u>, jumps) on their trampoline.
hat / coat	P	2	3. Your **hat** and **coat** (is, <u>are</u>) in the closet.
you	P	2	4. **You** (<u>help</u>, helps) with the chores today.

Student Note:

1. The subject *I* is an exception. It presents a special case of subject-verb agreement. These examples demonstrate plural verb forms used with the pronoun *I*: *I* want; *I* walk; *I* talk; etc.

2. The singular subject *I* and the verb be also present a special case of subject-verb agreement. These examples demonstrate other verb forms used with the pronoun *I*: *I* am; *I* was.

Classroom Practice 11

It is time to practice the skills you are learning. You will use the classroom practice on the next page to apply these skills.

ENRICHMENT:

(German) 1400(?)-1468— **Johannes Gutenberg** built the first printing press which used metal letters, called moveable type, to spell out words on a page. Gutenberg's press could print 300 pages a day, and he massed-produced the Bible for commoners.

Discovery Questions:
- **What do you think Gutenberg's printing press looked like?**
- **What was the impact of Gutenberg's invention on religion and education?**
- **What would Gutenberg think if he could see the printing presses of today?**

Are you interested in learning more about Johannes Gutenberg?

1. You may explore this topic further by using the resources listed below.
   Computer resources: Internet, encyclopedia software
   Library resources: encyclopedias, books, magazines, newspapers
   Home/community resources: books, interviews, newspapers, magazines

2. A Discovery Share Time is provided in Lesson 7 of Chapter 4 if you wish to share your investigation results. You may share orally, or you may prepare a written report. You will put your written report in a class booklet titled "Notable People in History." This booklet will be placed in the class library for everyone to enjoy.

Student Tip...

1. Recite the singular examples several times to hear the subject-verb agreement for singular forms: **snake crawls, duck quacks, kite flies, child laughs.**

2. Recite the plural examples several times to hear the subject-verb agreement for plurals forms: **snakes crawl, ducks quack, kites fly, children laugh.**

SHURLEY ENGLISH

Classroom Practice 11

Name:_____ Date:_____

GRAMMAR

▶ **Exercise 1:** Classify each sentence. Underline the complete subject once and the complete predicate twice.

1._____ The column of smoke rose high into the morning air.

2._____ Leah walked up the steep steps to a seat in the bleachers.

3._____ The cool water flowed openly from the mouth of the cave.

▶ **Exercise 2:** Use sentence 1 above to complete the table below.

List the Noun Used	List the Noun Job	Singular or Plural	Common or Proper	Simple Subject	Simple Predicate

SKILLS

▶ **Exercise 3:** For each sentence, do three things: (1) Write the subject. (2) Write **S** and **Rule 1** if the subject is singular, or write **P** and **Rule 2** if the subject is plural. (3) Underline the correct verb.

Rule 1: A singular subject must use a singular verb form that ends in **s** or **es**.

Rule 2: A plural subject, a compound subject, or the subject **YOU** must use a plural verb form that has **no s** or **es** endings. (A plural verb form is also called the *plain form*.)

Subject	S or P	Rule	
_____	_____	_____	1. The gopher (dig, digs) in the flowerbed.
_____	_____	_____	2. You (chew, chews) with your mouth closed.
_____	_____	_____	3. Lynn and Rose (was, were) studying diligently.
_____	_____	_____	4. The turkey (is, are) in the oven.
_____	_____	_____	5. Alex and Alicia (is, are) going to the game.
_____	_____	_____	6. The dog (need, needs) a bath before dark.
_____	_____	_____	7. The new lawnmower (do, does) a great job.
_____	_____	_____	8. The boys (wasn't, weren't) here today, Derrick.
_____	_____	_____	9. Your lotion (help, helps) my chapped hands.
_____	_____	_____	10. We (was, were) hunting yesterday.

EDITING

▶ **Exercise 4:** Put punctuation corrections within the sentence. Write all other corrections above the sentence.
Editing Guide: Capitals: 9   Commas: 4   Subject-Verb Agreement: 1   Misspelled words: 1   End Marks: 1

my three freinds nick trey and travis visits the statue of liberty on their tour of new york city today

English Made Easy

LISTENING AND SPEAKING:
Vocabulary & Analogy Time

Learn It: Recite the new vocabulary and analogy words.

Reference 63	Vocabulary & Analogy Words

Word: laudable (lô'də bəl)
  Definition: worthy of praise
  Synonym: commendable   **Antonym:** deplorable
  Sentence: Janet gave a laudable performance on her cello.

Analogy: goose : geese :: tooth : teeth
  Grammatical relationship: Just as **goose** is the singular form of **geese**, **tooth** is the singular form of **teeth**.

Vocabulary Card 8: Record the vocabulary information above and write your own sentence, using the new word.

Analogy Card 8: Record the analogy information and write your own analogy, using the same relationship as the analogy above.

Lesson 4

You will

- study new vocabulary; make card 8; write own sentence using the vocabulary word.
- analyze new analogy; make card 8; write own analogy.
- practice Jingles 1–6.
- classify Practice Sentences.
- do a Skill Builder.
- identify homonyms.
- edit a paragraph.
- do Classroom Practice 12.
- read and discuss Discovery Time.
- do a homework assignment.
- do a Home Connection activity.

Jingle Time

Recite It: Practice Jingles 1–6 in the Jingle Section on pages 506–507.

Grammar Time

Apply It: Classify the Practice Sentences orally with your teacher.

Practice Sentences	Chapter 3: Lesson 4

1. _____ The boisterous young crowd of fans yelled loudly for the victorious team.
2. _____ The elderly gentleman ran amazingly fast during the marathon race today.
3. _____ Hannah ran quickly to the corner store for a carton of milk before dinner.

SHURLEY ENGLISH

LISTENING AND SPEAKING:

Using the sentences just classified, do a Skill Builder orally with your teacher.

1. **Identify the nouns in a Noun Check.**
2. **Identify the nouns as singular or plural.**
3. **Identify the nouns as common or proper.**
4. **Identify the complete subject and the complete predicate.**
5. **Identify the simple subject and the simple predicate.**
6. **Do a Vocabulary Check.**

Learn It: HOMONYMS

The Homonym Chart contains a partial listing of the most common homonyms. Use a dictionary to look up other homonyms that you do not know.

📖	Reference 64	Homonym Chart

Homonyms are words which sound alike but have different meanings and different spellings.

1. **capital** - main; wealth 2. **capitol** - statehouse	11. **lead** - metal 12. **led** - guided; did lead	21. **their** - belonging to them 22. **there** - in that place 23. **they're** - contraction for they are
3. **coarse** - rough 4. **course** - route; subject	13. **no** - not so; negative 14. **know** - to understand	24. **threw** - did throw 25. **through** - from end to end
5. **council** - assembly 6. **counsel** - advice; to advise	15. **right** - correct; direction 16. **write** - to form letters	26. **to** - toward (a preposition) 27. **too** - denoting excess 28. **two** - the number 2; a couple
7. **forth** - forward 8. **fourth** - ordinal number	17. **principle** - a truth; rule; law 18. **principal** - primary; head person	29. **your** - owned by you (a pronoun) 30. **you're** - contraction for you are
9. **its** - ownership pronoun 10. **it's** - contraction for it is	19. **stationary** - motionless 20. **stationery** - letter-writing paper	

Exercise: Underline the correct homonym.

1. Mr. Bradley is a member of the state (<u>council</u>, counsel).

2. Mrs. Gordon (councils, <u>counsels</u>) students about opportunities in education beyond high school.

Learn It: EDITING PARAGRAPHS

When you correct mistakes in your writing, it is called editing. You have been editing sentences for capitalization, punctuation, and spelling mistakes. Now, you will edit a paragraph instead of a single sentence.

When you edit a paragraph, you will still have an Editing Guide to help you, but it will be arranged a little differently. In Reference 65, notice that the **End Marks** title has been moved to the front of the Editing Guide so you will know how many sentences are in the paragraph.

To edit a paragraph, find each sentence and write the end mark for each one before editing the rest of the paragraph. This allows you to identify the sentences before the paragraph gets crowded with other corrections. It also helps you find the first word of each sentence to check for capitalization. Notice that homonyms have also been added to the Editing Guide.

Reference 65   Editing a Paragraph

Correct each mistake. **Editing Guide: End Marks: 4   Capitals: 14   Commas: 8   Homonyms: 7   Apostrophes: 2 Subject-Verb Agreement: 1   Misspelled Words: 2**

O our   to S   S   C   A   C   I   some
on hour ski trip two steamboat springs, colorado, andrew, cassandra, and i learned sum interesting

         history I   C   H   N   immigrant
facts about the town's histrey. in 1912, carl howelson, a norwegian imigrant, introduced winter sports

to   H   H   one   him I like   new
too the area. howelson hill, won of the city's ski areas, was named after hem. i likes learning knew facts.

Classroom Practice 12

It is time to practice the skills you are learning. You will use the classroom practice on the next page to apply these skills.

ENRICHMENT:

Discovery Time

(Italian) 1452-1519— Leonardo da Vinci's most famous paintings are the *Last Supper* and the *Mona Lisa*. In 1962, the *Mona Lisa* was appraised for $100 million for insurance purposes. The *Mona Lisa* is now hanging in the Louvre Museum in Paris.

Discovery Questions:
- What did da Vinci do to improve his knowledge of physiology?
- What would you say to da Vinci if you could talk to him?
- What do you think da Vinci would say to you if he could see the modern world?

Are you interested in learning more about Leonardo da Vinci?

1. You may explore this topic further by using the resources listed below.
   Computer resources: Internet, encyclopedia software
   Library resources: encyclopedias, books, magazines, newspapers
   Home/community resources: books, interviews, newspapers, magazines

2. A Discovery Share Time is provided in Lesson 7 of Chapter 4 if you wish to share your investigation results. You may share orally, or you may prepare a written report. You will put your written report in a class booklet titled "Notable People in History." This booklet will be placed in the class library for everyone to enjoy.

Classroom Practice 12

Name:_____ Date:_____

GRAMMAR

▶ **Exercise 1:** Classify each sentence. Underline the complete subject once and the complete predicate twice.

1. _____ The small goldfish swam swiftly toward the large body of water.

2. _____ The motor of the large model airplane worked extremely well during the tryouts.

▶ **Exercise 2:** Use sentence 2 above to complete the table below.

List the Noun Used	List the Noun Job	Singular or Plural	Common or Proper	Simple Subject	Simple Predicate

SKILLS

▶ **Exercise 3:** Underline the correct homonym in each sentence.

1. The baby seal swam to (its, it's) mother.

2. I want cake for my last (coarse, course).

3. He (led, lead) his team to victory.

4. Chess is his (principal, principle) interest.

5. Our population is (stationery, stationary).

6. The tree put (forth, fourth) large green leaves.

7. (There, Their, They're) going to the office.

8. (Its, It's) a very hot day outside.

▶ **Exercise 4:** For each sentence, do three things: (1) Write the subject. (2) Write **S** and **Rule 1** if the subject is singular, or write **P** and **Rule 2** if the subject is plural. (3) Underline the correct verb.

Subject	S or P	Rule
_____	_____	_____
_____	_____	_____
_____	_____	_____
_____	_____	_____
_____	_____	_____
_____	_____	_____
_____	_____	_____
_____	_____	_____
_____	_____	_____

1. The mailman (deliver, delivers) the mail on time.
2. Cats and dogs (is, are) natural enemies.
3. You (drive, drives) to the game tonight.
4. Those two men (has, have) the same sunglasses.
5. The satellite slowly (circle, circles) the Earth.
6. You (turn, turns) your assignment in over there.
7. The woman in the store (give, gives) good directions.
8. Several boys (was, were) late for class.
9. An otter (play, plays) happily in the water.

EDITING

▶ **Exercise 5:** Correct each mistake. **Editing Guide: End Marks: 4   Capitals: 11   Commas: 3   Homonyms: 5   Subject-Verb Agreement: 2   Periods: 2   Misspelled Words: 3**

our neighbors mr and mrs bonelli has an italian resturant inn madison wisconsin

my hole family love too eat their we go every saterday knight it is delisious

Homework 1

Complete this homework assignment on notebook paper.

1. Number your paper 1–6.
   Write the correct homonym for each sentence. Write answers only.

   1. I would like a (peace, piece) of candy.
   2. Which (stationary, stationery) do you like?
   3. Let me know if (you're, your) allowed to go.

   4. We will go (to, two, too) town tomorrow.
   5. Do you like (there, their) new truck?
   6. I was (forth, fourth) in line for a drink of water.

2. Number your paper 1–7.
   For each sentence, do three things: (1) Write the subject. (2) Write **S** and **Rule 1** if the subject is singular, or write **P** and **Rule 2** if the subject is plural. (3) Write the correct verb.

   > **Rule 1:** A singular subject must use a singular verb form that ends in **s** or **es**: *is, was, has, does, swims, pushes.*
   >
   > **Rule 2:** A plural subject, a compound subject, or the subject **YOU** must use a plural verb form that has **no s** or **es** endings: *are, were, have, do, swim, push.*

	Subject	S or P	Rule	
1.	_____	_____	_____	The shrubs (grow, grows) quite well in a shaded area.
2.	_____	_____	_____	Susan and Jan (is, are) going to the state fair.
3.	_____	_____	_____	The boa constrictor (was, were) in its cage.
4.	_____	_____	_____	You (is, are) a hero in the eyes of our children.
5.	_____	_____	_____	(Doesn't, Don't) your sister drive an antique car?
6.	_____	_____	_____	(Do, Does) the band members receive free tickets to the show?
7.	_____	_____	_____	My permanent teeth (is, are) in good condition.

3. Rewrite the sentence below correctly. Use the editing guide to help you.
   Editing Guide: Capitals: 7   Commas: 3   Homonyms: 3   Misspelled Words: 1   End Marks: 1

   did the south american tourests visit phoenix arizona on there weigh too hollywood california

Home Connection

Family Activity for Subject-Verb Agreement

1. Gather 20 index cards. Write the words from the subject and verb columns below on separate cards. On the back of the index cards with singular subjects and verbs, write a number one. On the back of the index cards with plural subjects and verbs, write a number two. Place the cards face up with the words showing. Match the subject cards with any verb card that makes sense and agrees with the subject. After all matches have been made, flip the cards over. If the numbers on the back of each card pair match, the subject-verb agreement is correct. If the numbers do not match, a subject-verb agreement mistake has been made.

2. Have a timed contest between family members to see who can complete the most correct subject-verb agreement matches in the fastest time.

3. Make more subject and verb cards to play the game again.

(1) SINGULAR		(2) PLURAL	
Subjects	Verbs	Subjects	Verbs
mailman	flies	swans	crash
Judy	walks	children	race
pilot	laughs	cars	swim
tree	waves	Elizabeth and Cody	eat
dog	grows	cymbals	fly

START LESSON 5

Lesson 5

You will
- recite new jingle (Transition Words).
- classify Practice Sentences.
- do Chapter Checkup 13.
- write in your journal.
- read and discuss Discovery Time.

LISTENING AND SPEAKING:

Recite It: Recite the new jingle.

♪ Jingle 12	The Transition Words Jingle

Aw, listen, comrades, and you shall hear
About transition words
That make your writing smooth and clear.

Transition words are connecting words.
You add them to the beginning
Of sentences and paragraphs
To keep your ideas spinning and give your writing flow.

These words can clarify, summarize, or emphasize,
Compare or contrast, inform or show time.
Learn them now, and your writing will shine!

Transition, Transition,
For words that **SHOW TIME:**
first, second, third, before, during, after,
next, then, and *finally.*

Transition, Transition,
For words that **INFORM:**
for example, for instance, in addition, as well,
also, next, another, along with, and *besides.*

Transition, Transition,
For words that **CONTRAST:**
although, even though, but, yet, still,
otherwise, however, and *on the other hand.*

Transition, Transition,
For words that **COMPARE:**
as, also, like, and *likewise.*

Transition, Transition,
For words that **CLARIFY:**
for example, for instance, and *in other words.*

Transition, Transition,
For words that **EMPHASIZE:**
truly, again, for this reason, and *in fact.*

Transition, Transition,
For words that **SUMMARIZE:**
therefore, in conclusion, in summary, and *finally,*
to sum it up, all in all, as a result, and *last.*

TRANSITION WORD

Grammar Time

Apply It: Classify the Practice Sentences orally with your teacher.

Practice Sentences	Chapter 3: Lesson 5

1. _____ The people in the big auditorium applauded warmly for the guest speaker.

2. _____ The wild onions on the hill grew rapidly during the fall of the year.

3. _____ Roberta arrived too early for dinner at the new restaurant tonight.

Chapter Checkup 13

It is time for a checkup of the skills you have learned in this chapter. You will use the chapter checkup on the next page to evaluate your progress.

ENRICHMENT:

Discovery Time

(Italian) 1475-1564— Michelangelo Buonarroti's most memorable works include his painting of the Sistine Chapel (*The Last Judgment; The Creation of Adam*) and, *David* and *Pietà,* his sculptures. Michelangelo was very religious, and this was reflected in his art. Michelangelo favored marble carving and fresco painting because they required hard physical labor.

Discovery Questions:
- What gave Michelangelo his expert knowledge of human anatomy?
- What would you do if you had as much artistic talent as Michelangelo?
- What type of art would you like to create? Explain.

Are you interested in learning more about Michelangelo Buonarroti?

1. You may explore this topic further by using the resources listed below.
   Computer resources: Internet, encyclopedia software
   Library resources: encyclopedias, books, magazines, newspapers
   Home / community resources: books, interviews, newspapers, magazines

2. A Discovery Share Time is provided in Lesson 7 of Chapter 4 if you wish to share your investigation results. You may share orally, or you may prepare a written report. You will put your written report in a class booklet titled "Notable People in History." This booklet will be placed in the class library for everyone to enjoy.

Note: Reference 54 on page 71 gives the steps in the writing process and the location of all the writing checklists.

JOURNAL WRITING 6

Write an entry in your journal. Use Reference 9 on page 12 for ideas.

Chapter 3 Checkup 13

Name:_____ Date:_____

GRAMMAR

▶ **Exercise 1:** Classify each sentence. Underline the complete subject once and the complete predicate twice.

1. _____ Sarah drove too fast for safety on the icy roads during rush-hour traffic.

2. _____ A large, colorful peacock strutted confidently along the edge of the water.

3. _____ The extremely talented cast of actors performed especially well tonight.

▶ **Exercise 2:** Use sentence 1 above to complete the table below.

List the Noun Used	List the Noun Job	Singular or Plural	Common or Proper	Simple Subject	Simple Predicate

SKILLS

▶ **Exercise 3:** For each sentence, do three things: (1) Write the subject. (2) Write **S** and **Rule 1** if the subject is singular, or write **P** and **Rule 2** if the subject is plural. (3) Underline the correct verb.

Subject	S or P	Rule	
_____	_____	_____	1. You (pick, picks) your own topic for this assignment.
_____	_____	_____	2. The rooster (crows, crow) every morning.
_____	_____	_____	3. Glenn and Colleen (is, are) my new neighbors.
_____	_____	_____	4. Your articles (wasn't, weren't) in last week's paper.

EDITING

▶ **Exercise 4:** Correct each mistake. **Editing Guide: End Marks: 6   Capitals: 13   Commas: 3   Homonyms: 2   Subject-Verb Agreement: 2   Misspelled Words: 3**

lewis martinez my cousin pulled a muscle inn his write arm at the weight-lifting competiton

on thrsday in boise idaho he still placed second we was so proud of him mama even hugged

him papa and uncle ernest was taking rolls of film of lewis we had a fantasic time

English Made Easy

Writing Time

Write It: WRITING ASSIGNMENT 3

Lesson 6

You will
- conference with teacher about WA 2.
- write a creative writing piece for WA 3.

Writing Assignment ③: Creative Expressions

Purpose: To entertain

Type of Writing: Creative

Audience: Classmates, family, or friends

Choose one of the writing topics below:

1. If you could have been anyone in history, who would you have been and why? Would you have changed history? How would you have been different?

2. What are three traits an ideal friend would possess? Tell about someone you know with these qualities.

3. Write a poem about friends, an event in history, or a topic of your choice.

Special Instructions:

1. A prewriting map is not required for this creative-writing assignment.

2. Follow the Rough Draft Checklist in Reference 46 on page 61.

3. Put your creative-writing paper in your Rough Draft folder when you have finished.

Note: Reference 54 on page 71 gives the steps in the writing process and the location of all the writing checklists.

 **Student Tip...**

For more information about writing poetry, look at Chapter 18, pages 465–482.

Conference Time

Discuss It: TEACHER-STUDENT CONFERENCES
FOR WRITING ASSIGNMENT 6

Meet with your teacher to discuss Writing Assignment 2, Part 2.
After the conference, place this group of papers in your Publishing folder.

Lesson 7

You will

- read and discuss publishing (Step 6 in the writing process).
- publish WA 2.

Publishing Time

Learn It: PUBLISHING, THE SIXTH STEP IN THE WRITING PROCESS

Discuss the Publishing Checklist in Reference 66 with your teacher.
Then, choose a publishing form and publish Writing Assignment 2, Part 2.
After rewriting your paper for publication, give the stapled papers (evaluation guide, graded final paper, rough draft, and prewriting map) to your teacher to be placed in your Writing Portfolio.

Reference 66 | **Publishing Checklist for Step 6 in the Writing Process**

The sixth step in the writing process is called publishing. Publishing is sharing your writing with others. With so many forms of publishing available, finding a match for every project and personality is easy. At times, a written work is best read aloud. Other times, the biggest impact is made when a written work is read silently. You can also use media sources to enhance any publication.

SPECIAL INSTRUCTIONS FOR PUBLISHING:

- Rewrite the graded paper in ink or type it on a computer, correcting any marked errors.
  (Do not display or publish papers that have marked errors or grades on them.)
- Give your teacher the set of stapled papers to place in your Writing Portfolio.
  (Stapled papers: evaluation guide, graded final paper, rough draft, and prewriting map.)
- Select a publishing form from the list below and publish your rewritten paper.

  1. Have classmates, family members, neighbors, or others read your writing at school or home.
  2. Share your writing with others during a Share Time. *(Refer to Reference 67 for sharing guidelines.)*
  3. Display your writing on a bulletin board or wall.
  4. Put your writing in the classroom library or in the school library for checkout.
  5. Send your writing as a letter or an e-mail to a friend or relative.
  6. Frame your writing by gluing it on colored construction paper and decorating it.
  7. Make a book of your writing for your classroom, your family, or others.
  8. Illustrate your writing and give it to others to read.
  9. Dramatize your writing in the form of a play, puppet show, or radio broadcast.
  10. Send your writing to be placed in a waiting room (doctor, veterinarian, dentist, etc.), senior-citizen center, or a nursing home.
  11. Send your writing to a school newspaper, local newspaper, or a magazine for publication.
  12. Make a videotape, cassette tape, or slide presentation of your writing.
  13. Choose another publishing form that is not listed.

Learn It: SHARE TIME GUIDELINES

Sharing is one of the publishing forms listed in Reference 66. Study the Share Time Guidelines to help you know what to do as a speaker or as a member of the audience.

Reference 67 — Share Time Guidelines

Speaker Presentation

1. Have your paper ready to read when called upon.
2. Tell the title of your writing selection.
3. Tell the purpose and type of writing used.

PRESENTATION TIPS:

4. Stand with your feet flat on the floor and your shoulders straight. Do not shift your weight as you stand.
5. Hold your paper about chin high to help you project your voice to your audience.
6. Make sure you do not read too fast.
7. Read in a clear voice that can be heard so that your audience does not have to strain to hear you.
8. Change your voice tone for different characters or for different parts of the writing selection.

Audience Response

1. Look at the speaker.
2. Turn your body toward the speaker.
3. Listen attentively. Do not let your thoughts wander.
4. Do not make distracting noises as you listen.
5. Do not make distracting motions as you listen.
6. Show interest in what the speaker is saying.
7. Silently summarize what the speaker is saying. Take notes if necessary.
8. Ask questions about anything that is not clear.
9. Show appreciation by clapping after the speaker has finished.

Chapter 3

START LESSON 8

Lesson 8

You will

- practice Jingles 2 and 12.
- do Classroom Practice 14.
- write an independent expository paragraph (WA 4).

LISTENING AND SPEAKING:

Recite It: Practice Jingles 2 and 12 in the Jingle Section on pages 506, 509.

GRAMMAR & WRITING CONNECTION:
Practice and Revised Sentences

Apply It: BUILDING AND EXPANDING SENTENCES

 Reference 68 | **A Guide for Using Prepositions and Objects of the Prepositions to Build and Expand Sentences**

1. **P (preposition)** Use the Preposition Flow Jingle to help you think of a preposition for a prepositional phrase that describes and expands the subject and verb in your sentence. The preposition you choose must make sense with the noun you choose for the object of the preposition in your next step. Write the preposition you have chosen for your sentence. Repeat this step for each preposition you add to the sentence.

2. **OP (object of the preposition)** An object of the preposition is a noun or pronoun after a preposition. Think of an object of the preposition by asking **what** or **whom** after the preposition. The noun or pronoun you choose for an object of the preposition must make sense with the preposition and with the rest of the sentence. Write the word you have chosen for the object of the preposition in your sentence. Repeat this step for each object of the preposition you add to the sentence.

 Student Tip...

Use your vocabulary words in your Practice and Revised Sentences. Use a thesaurus, synonym-antonym book, or a dictionary to help you develop your writing vocabulary.

Classroom Practice 14

It is time to practice the skills you are learning. You will use the classroom practice on the next page to apply these skills.

Writing Time

Write It: WRITING ASSIGNMENT 4

As you write a rough draft for your independent writing assignment, you will do two of the six steps in the writing process: prewriting and rough draft.

Writing Assignment 4

Purpose: To inform

Type of Writing: Three-point expository paragraph

Audience: Classmates

Writing Topics: Favorite holiday
Favorite foods
Favorite season
(Brainstorm for other ideas, individually or in groups.)

Special Instructions:

1. Follow the Prewriting and Rough Draft Checklists in References 44 and 46 on pages 57, 61.

2. Use References 38–43 on pages 53–56 to help you write your expository paragraph.

3. Put your prewriting map and rough draft in your Rough Draft folder when you have finished.

Note: Reference 54 on page 71 gives the steps in the writing process and the location of all the writing checklists.

Student Note: **Some of your writing pieces will be selected for revision and editing later in the school year.**

Classroom Practice 14

Name: _____   Date: _____

INDEPENDENT PRACTICE & REVISED SENTENCES

1. Write a Practice Sentence according to the labels you choose.
Use the **SN V** labels once. You may use the other labels in any order and as many times as you wish in order to make a Practice Sentence.
Chapter 3 labels for a Practice Sentence: **SN, V,** Adj, Adv, A, P, OP

2. Write a Revised Sentence. Use the following revision strategies: *synonym (syn), antonym (ant), word change (wc), added word (add), deleted word (delete),* or *no change (nc).* Under each word, write the abbreviation of the revision strategy you use.

Labels:

Practice:

Revised:

Strategies:

Labels:

Practice:

Revised:

Strategies:

Labels:

Practice:

Revised:

Strategies:

LISTENING AND SPEAKING:

Jingle Time

Recite It: Practice Jingle 12 in the Jingle Section on page 509.

>>>>> **Student Tip...**

Reviewing the transition words will help you apply them in your writing.

Writing Time

Lesson 9

You will
- practice Jingle 12.
- read and discuss writing forms and point of view.
- plan and write rough drafts for expository paragraphs (WA 5 and 6).

Learn It: DIFFERENT WRITING FORMS

The information in Reference 69 will explain different ways to introduce the main points in a paragraph.

Reference 69 — Different Writing Forms

The way you introduce the points in your paragraph determines the form of the paragraph. Whichever form you choose must be used throughout the paragraph. You cannot mix forms within the same paragraph.

1. Standard Form – Uses possessive pronouns or article adjectives and *first, second, third.*

In the standard form, the main points begin with possessive pronouns or article adjectives followed by the time-order words, *first, second,* and *third.* The standard form is the easiest because it is the most consistent. For this reason, it is used often and is a good, reliable three-point writing form.

Standard words: My first, My second, My third. The first, The second, The third.

I have three favorite sports. These sports are football, ice skating, and diving. **My first** favorite sport is football. I like football because it has cheering fans, cheerleaders, and a team of fighting players who are trying to score. **My second** favorite sport is ice skating. I enjoy watching the exciting ice skaters do beautiful and even dangerous jumps that keep me on the edge of my seat. **My third** favorite sport is diving. I love watching divers leap from high diving boards or high cliffs. I could watch these three sports over and over because I love the excitement they produce.

2. Time-Order Form – Uses time-order words.

In the time-order form, the main points begin with transition words that suggest a definite time order, or number order, at the beginning of the sentence. Using time-order words is a superior way to accomplish sequence when it is important. The words, *first, second, third* or *first, next, last* or *finally,* are the most common time-order words. Whenever you use this form, you must put a comma after the time-order words at the beginning of the sentences because they are transitional words.

Time-order words: First, Second, Third. First, Next, Then, After that, Last, Lastly, Finally.

I have three favorite sports. These sports are football, ice skating, and diving. **First**, I am interested in football. I like football because it has cheering fans, cheerleaders, and a team of fighting players who are trying to score. **Next**, I like ice skating. I enjoy watching the exciting ice skaters do beautiful and even dangerous jumps that keep me on the edge of my seat. **Finally**, diving is on my list of favorites. I love watching divers leap from high diving boards or high cliffs. I could watch these three sports over and over because I love the excitement they produce.

Continued on next page. >>>

Reference 69 continued from previous page.

3. Transition Form – Uses different types of transition words.

In the transition form, the main points are stated by using transition words that denote addition instead of time-order. These transition words may be added to the beginning of the sentences or added within the sentences. The transition form provides a chance for variety because the main points are all presented with different transition words. This makes your writing unlike others and is highly favored if you choose not to use time-order words.

Transition words: one, also, other, another, besides, besides that, in addition to, furthermore, too.

    I have three favorite sports. These sports are football, ice skating, and diving. **Football is an exciting sport for me.** Football has cheering fans, cheerleaders, and a team of fighting players who are trying to score. Ice skating is **another** favorite sport of mine. I enjoy watching the exciting ice skaters do beautiful and even dangerous jumps that keep me on the edge of my seat. I **also** like diving. I love watching divers leap from high diving boards or high cliffs. I could watch these three sports over and over because I love the excitement they produce.

Learn It: POINT OF VIEW
                AND WRITING IN FIRST AND THIRD PERSON

Reference 70   Point of View

Point of view refers to the writer's use of personal pronouns to show who is telling a story. In order to use a point of view correctly, one must know the pronouns associated with the points of view listed below.

First-Person Point of View uses the first-person pronouns **I, me, my, mine, we, us, our,** and **ours** to name the speaker. If **any** of the first-person pronouns are used in a piece of writing, the writing is automatically considered a first-person writing, even though second- and third-person pronouns may also be used. **First person shows that you (the writer) are speaking, and that you (the writer) are personally involved in what is happening.**

(**Examples:** **I** am going sledding on **my** new sled. He likes **my** sled.)

Third-Person Point of View uses the third-person pronouns *he, his, him, she, her, hers, it, its, they, their, theirs,* and *them* to name the person or thing spoken about. You may **not** use the first-person pronouns *I, me, my, mine, we, us, our,* and *ours* because using any first-person pronouns automatically puts the writing in a first-person point of view. **Third person means that you (the writer) must write as if you are observing the events that take place.** Third person shows that you are writing about another person, thing, or event, and you are not involved.

(**Examples:** **He** is going sledding on **his** new sled. **She** likes **his** sled.)

Second-Person Point of View uses the second-person pronouns *you, your,* or *yours* to name the person or thing to whom you are speaking. Second-person point of view is not used very often in writing. Mostly, second-person point of view is used in giving directions, and it uses the pronoun **you** almost exclusively.

(**Examples:** (**You**) Make a ham sandwich for lunch. **You** may use wheat or white bread.)

Continued on next page. >>>

Review It:

The examples on the next page illustrate the different points of view.
All the pronouns are in blue type so you will notice the change in the point
of view of each paragraph.

Reference 70 continued from previous page.

First-Person Point of View

Yesterday, **my** friends and **I** went on a camping trip to Yosemite National Park. **We** packed sleeping bags, flashlights, food, and a tent into the car and drove to a quiet spot on the far side of the park. Scott put up the tent while Jim and **I** unpacked the food. Soon, **we** were feasting and enjoying the outdoors. A family of birds flew right up to the clearing near **us** and chirped for food. Before long, the birds were enjoying **our** feast, too!

Third-Person Point of View

Yesterday, Scott and **his** friends went on a camping trip to Yosemite National Park. **They** packed sleeping bags, flashlights, food, and a tent into the car and drove to a quiet spot on the far side of the park. Scott put up the tent while Jim and Casey unpacked the food. Soon, **they** were feasting and enjoying the outdoors. A family of birds flew right up to the clearing near **them** and chirped for food. Before long, the birds were enjoying **their** feast, too!

Second-Person Point of View

You should go on a camping trip to Yosemite National Park. **You** need to pack **your** sleeping bag, a flashlight, food, and a tent. **You** could drive to a quiet spot on the far side of the park. There, **you** should put up **your** tent, unpack the food, and enjoy the outdoors.

Look at the paragraph for third-person point of view again. Notice that all the first-person pronouns were changed to third-person pronouns or to a person's name. Remember that when you write in third person, you cannot use any of the first-person pronouns (*I, me, my, mine, we, us, our,* and *ours*) because this would automatically put your writing in a first-person point of view. As you look at the paragraph for second-person point of view, you can see why very few stories or paragraphs are written in second person.

Write It: WRITING ASSIGNMENTS 5 AND 6

As you write rough drafts for your two guided writing assignments, you will do two of the six steps in the writing process: prewriting and rough draft.

Writing Assignment 5 and 6

Purpose: To inform

Type of Writing: Three-point expository paragraphs

Audience: Classmates or family

Writing Topics: Favorite hobby/subject/towns
  (Brainstorm for other ideas, individually or in groups.)

Special Instructions:

1. Write rough draft 5 in third-person point of view. Use Reference 70 on page 104 and third-person pronouns: *he, his, him, she, her, hers, it, its, they, their, theirs,* and *them*.

2. Write rough draft 6 in first-person point of view. Use Reference 70 and first-person pronouns: *I, me, my, mine, we, us, our, and ours.*.

3. Follow the Prewriting and Rough Draft Checklists in References 44 and 46 on pages 57, 61.

4. Make only one prewriting map to use with both rough drafts.

5. Use References 38–43 on pages 53–56 to help you write your expository paragraphs.

6. Use standard, time-order, or transition writing form. See Reference 69 on page 103.

Note: Reference 54 on page 71 gives the steps in the writing process and the location of all the writing checklists.

START LESSON 10

Lesson 10

You will
- revise, edit, and write a final paper for WA 6.

Apply It: REVISE, EDIT, AND WRITE A FINAL PAPER

Following the schedule below, you will revise and edit Writing Assignment 6. Then, you will write a final paper. Use the Chapter 3 Writing Evaluation Guide on the next page to check your final paper one last time.

 Reference 52 | **Revising & Editing Schedule and Writing a Final Paper**

SPECIAL INSTRUCTIONS FOR REVISING AND EDITING (Steps 3-4 in the writing process):
- Use the Revising and Editing Checklists in References 48 and 50 as you revise and edit your rough draft.
- Follow the revising and editing schedule below as directed by your teacher.
  1. **Individual.** First, read your rough draft to yourself. Use the Revising Checklist in Reference 48 on page 64. Go through your paper, checking each item on the list and making revisions to your rough draft. Then, use the Editing Checklist in Reference 50 on page 66. Go through your paper again, checking each item on the list and editing your rough draft.
  2. **Partner.** Next, get with your editing partner. Work together on each partner's rough draft, one paper at a time. Read each rough draft aloud and revise and edit it together, using the Revising and Editing Checklists. (The author of the paper should be the one to make the corrections on his own paper.)
  3. **Group.** Finally, read the rough draft to a revision group for feedback. Each student should read his paper while the others listen and offer possible revising and editing suggestions. (The author will determine whether to make corrections from the revision group's suggestions.)

SPECIAL INSTRUCTIONS FOR FINAL PAPER (Step 5 in the writing process):
- Write your final paper, using the Final Paper Checklist in Reference 53 on page 70.
- Staple your writing papers in this order: the final paper on top, the rough draft in the middle, and the prewriting map on the bottom. Place the stapled papers in the Final Paper folder.

>>>>>>>>>>>>>> **Student Tip...**

1. Be tactful and helpful in your comments during revising and editing time. The purpose of any suggestion should be to improve the writer's rough draft.

2. As you make your final corrections, you have the choice of accepting or rejecting any suggestions made by your partners or your revision group.

3. Study Vocabulary Words and Analogies 5–8 for the chapter test in the next lesson.

4. If you need to improve your handwriting, refer to the Resource Tools Section on pages 529–530 for information on writing legibly.

Chapter 3 Writing Evaluation Guide

Name:_____ Date:_____

ROUGH DRAFT CHECK

_____ 1. Did you write your rough draft in pencil?

_____ 2. Did you write the correct headings on the first seven lines of your paper?

_____ 3. Did you use extra wide margins and skip every other line?

_____ 4. Did you write a title at the end of your rough draft?

_____ 5. Did you place your edited rough draft in your Rough Draft folder?

REVISING CHECK

_____ 6. Did you identify the purpose, type of writing, and audience?

_____ 7. Did you check for a topic, topic sentence, and sentences supporting the topic?

_____ 8. Did you check sentences for the right order, and did you combine, rearrange, or delete sentences when necessary?

_____ 9. Did you check for a variety of simple, compound, and complex sentences?

_____ 10. Did you check for any left out, repeated, or unnecessary words?

_____ 11. Did you check for the best choice of words by replacing or deleting unclear words?

_____ 12. Did you check the content for interest and creativity?

_____ 13. Did you check the voice to make sure the writing says what you want it to say?

EDITING CHECK

_____ 14. Did you indent each paragraph?

_____ 15. Did you put an end mark at the end of every sentence?

_____ 16. Did you capitalize the first word of every sentence?

_____ 17. Did you check for all other capitalization mistakes?

_____ 18. Did you check for all punctuation mistakes? (commas, periods, apostrophes, quotation marks, underlining)

_____ 19. Did you check for misspelled words and for incorrect homonym choices?

_____ 20. Did you check for incorrect spellings of plural and possessive forms?

_____ 21. Did you check for correct construction and punctuation of your sentences?

_____ 22. Did you check for usage mistakes? (subject/verb agreement, a/an choices, contractions, verb tenses, pronoun/antecedent agreement, pronoun cases, degrees of adjectives, double negatives, etc.)

_____ 23. Did you put your revised and edited paper in the Rough Draft folder?

FINAL PAPER CHECK

_____ 24. Did you write the final paper in pencil?

_____ 25. Did you center the title on the top line and center your name under the title?

_____ 26. Did you skip a line before starting the writing assignment?

_____ 27. Did you single-space, use wide margins, and write the final paper neatly?

_____ 28. Did you staple your papers in this order: final paper on top, rough draft in the middle, and prewriting map on the bottom? Did you put them in the Final Paper folder?

START LESSON 11

Lesson 11

You will

- hand in WA 6 for grading.
- respond to oral review questions.
- take Chapter 3 Test.

CHAPTER TEST

It is time to evaluate your knowledge of the skills you have learned in this chapter. Your teacher will give you the Chapter 3 Test to help you assess your progress.

Writing Time

Hand It In: **WRITING ASSIGNMENT 6**

Get your stapled papers for Writing Assignment 6 from your Final Paper folder. Check to make sure they are in the correct order: the final paper on top, the rough draft in the middle, and the prewriting map on the bottom. Hand them in to your teacher.

LISTENING AND SPEAKING:

Oral Review Questions

Discuss It:

1. What is the word that connects its object to some other word in the sentence?
2. What is a noun or pronoun after a preposition called?
3. What begins with a preposition and ends with an object of a preposition?
4. What kind of noun means only one?
5. What kind of noun means more than one?
6. What kind of noun is not specific and is not capitalized?
7. What kind of noun is specific and is always capitalized?
8. What is another name for the subject and all the words that modify it?
9. What is another name for the verb and all the words that modify it?
10. What is another name for the subject noun or pronoun?
11. What is another name for the verb?
12. What are words called that sound alike but have different meanings and spellings?
13. Which point of view uses the pronouns I, we, me, us, my, our, and mine?
14. Which point of view uses the pronouns he, she, it, they, their, and them?
15. Are the verbs is, was, has, and does singular or plural verb forms?
16. Are the verbs sings, drives, and walks singular or plural verb forms?
17. Are the verbs are, were, have, and do singular or plural verb forms?
18. What type of writing is used to inform, to give facts, to give directions, to explain, or to define something?

>>>>>>>>>>>>> Student Tip...

For information about test-taking strategies, refer to the Resource Tools Section on page 528.

English Made Easy

LISTENING AND SPEAKING:
Vocabulary & Analogy Time

Learn It: Recite the new vocabulary and analogy words.

Reference 71	Vocabulary & Analogy Words

Word: embellish (em bĕl'ĭsh)
 Definition: to add details to make beautiful
 Synonym: enhance   **Antonym:** mar
 Sentence: The artist embellished his design with pearls.

Analogy: lamb : sheep :: calf : cow
 Progression relationship: Just as a **lamb** becomes a **sheep**, a **calf** becomes a **cow**.

Vocabulary Card 9: Record the vocabulary information above and write your own sentence, using the new word.

Analogy Card 9: Record the analogy information and write your own analogy, using the same relationship as the analogy above.

Jingle Time

Recite It: Recite the new jingles.

♪ **Jingle 13   The Pronoun Jingle**

These little pronouns,
Hangin' around,
Can take the place
Of any of the nouns.

With a smile and a nod
And a twinkle of the eye,
Give those pronouns
A big high five! Yeah!

♪ **Jingle 14   The Subject Pronoun Jingle**

There are seven subject pronouns
That are easy as can be.
SUBJECT PRONOUNS!
I and **We**,
He and **She**,
It and **They** and **You**.
Those are the subject pronouns!

♪ **Jingle 15   The Possessive Pronoun Jingle**

There are seven possessive pronouns
That are easy as can be.
POSSESSIVE PRONOUNS!
My and **Our**,
His and **Her**,
Its and **Their** and **Your**.
Those are possessive pronouns!

Lesson 1
You will
- study new vocabulary; make card 9; write own sentence using the vocabulary word.
- analyze new analogy; make card 9; write own analogy.
- recite new jingles (Pronoun, Subject Pronoun, Possessive Pronoun).
- identify pronouns, subject pronouns, understood subject pronouns, and possessive pronoun adjectives.
- classify Introductory Sentences.
- do a Skill Builder to identify pronouns.
- recognize pronouns as a part of speech.
- write in your journal.

Apply It: These Introductory Sentences are used to apply the new grammar concepts taught below. Classify these sentences orally with your teacher.

Introductory Sentences	Chapter 4: Lesson 1

1. _____ They yelled desperately for the neighborhood police!
2. _____ Walk very cautiously through the dark woods at night.
3. _____ We traveled slowly along the icy roads in our new truck.

Learn It: PRONOUNS AND SUBJECT PRONOUNS

 | **Reference 72** | **Pronouns & Subject Pronouns** |

1. A **pronoun** may take the place of any noun in a sentence. A pronoun may stand for a person, place, thing, or idea.
2. A **subject pronoun** takes the place of a noun that is used as the subject of a sentence.
3. The subject pronouns are *I, we, he, she, it, they,* and *you.* Use the Subject Pronoun Jingle to remember these subject pronouns.
4. To find a subject pronoun, ask the subject question *who* or *what.*
5. A *subject pronoun* is labeled with the abbreviation **SP.**

Learn It: UNDERSTOOD SUBJECT PRONOUNS

 | **Reference 73** | **Understood Subject Pronouns** |

1. A sentence has an **understood subject** when someone gives a command or makes a request and leaves the subject unwritten or unspoken. The unspoken subject will always be the pronoun **you.**
2. When a sentence has an understood subject and gives a command or makes a request, it is called an imperative sentence. It ends with a period and always has the word *you* understood, not expressed, as the subject. (**Example:** Close the door.)
3. When you classify sentences, the understood subject pronoun *you* is always written in **parentheses** at the beginning of the sentence with the label **SP** beside it: **(You) SP.**
4. Whenever you read **(You) SP**, you will say, "*You – understood subject pronoun.*"
5. In the example, *Close the door,* who is being commanded to close the door? Someone is being commanded to close the door even though the name of that person is not mentioned. The person receiving the command is the understood subject pronoun, **YOU.**

Learn It: **POSSESSIVE PRONOUNS**

 Reference 74 **Possessive Pronouns**

1. A **possessive pronoun** takes the place of a possessive noun, but a possessive pronoun does not use an apostrophe to make it possessive.
2. The possessive pronouns are *my, our, his, her, its, their,* and *your.*
   Use the Possessive Pronoun Jingle to remember these pronouns.
3. A possessive pronoun has two jobs: to show ownership or possession and to modify like an adjective.
4. A possessive pronoun's part of speech is an adjective.
5. When a possessive pronoun is classified, it is labeled as a possessive pronoun adjective in order to recognize both jobs. A **possessive pronoun adjective** is labeled with the abbreviation **PPA**.
   For the abbreviation **PPA**, say, *"Possessive pronoun adjective."*
6. Include possessive pronoun adjectives when you are asked to identify pronouns, possessives, or adjectives.
7. To find a possessive pronoun adjective, ask *"whose"* before the noun. (**Example:** Whose book? **his - PPA**)

Apply It: **A SKILL BUILDER FOR A NOUN CHECK WITH PRONOUNS**
Using the sentences just classified, do a Skill Builder orally with your teacher. The example below shows you what to do with pronouns in a Noun Check.

LISTENING AND SPEAKING:

FOR A NOUN CHECK WITH PRONOUNS

Circle the nouns in a Noun Check.

Sentence 1: Subject Pronoun **they**, *no, it is a pronoun;*
   Object of the Preposition (police) *yes, it is a noun.*

Sentence 2: Understood Subject Pronoun **you**, *no, it is a pronoun;*
   Object of the Preposition (woods) *yes, it is a noun;*
   Object of the Preposition (night) *yes, it is a noun.*

Sentence 3: Subject Pronoun **we**, *no, it is a pronoun;*
   Object of the Preposition (roads) *yes, it is a noun;*
   Object of the Preposition (truck) *yes, it is a noun.*

JOURNAL WRITING 7

Write an entry in your journal. Use Reference 9 on page 12 for ideas.

Learn It: **ADDING THE PRONOUN TO THE PARTS OF SPEECH**

A pronoun is a part of speech. You have learned six of the eight parts of speech. What are these six parts of speech?

START LESSON 2

Lesson 2

You will

- study new vocabulary; make card 10; write own sentence using the vocabulary word.
- analyze new analogy; make card 10; write own analogy.
- practice Jingles 13–15; recite new jingle (Conjunction).
- identify conjunctions and compound parts.
- classify Introductory Sentences.
- do a Skill Builder.
- recognize conjunctions as a part of speech.
- identify simple sentences, fragments, run-on sentences, and compound parts.
- do Classroom Practice 15.
  - read and discuss Discovery Time.

LISTENING AND SPEAKING:
Vocabulary & Analogy Time

Learn It: Recite the new vocabulary and analogy words.

📖 * Reference 75	Vocabulary & Analogy Words

Word: efface (ĭ-fās')
   Definition: to remove
   Synonym: erase   **Antonym:** create
   Sentence: An evening tide will efface the footprints in the sand.

Analogy: bee : hive :: bat : cave
   Purpose or use relationship: Just as a **bee** lives in a **hive**, a **bat** lives in a **cave**.

Vocabulary Card 10: Record the vocabulary information above and write your own sentence, using the new word.

Analogy Card 10: Record the analogy information and write your own analogy, using the same relationship as the analogy above.

Jingle Time

Recite It: 1. Practice Jingles 13–15 in the Jingle Section on pages 509–510.
              2. Recite the new jingle.

♪ Jingle 16	The Conjunction Sound-Off Jingle

Conjunctions are a part of speech.
   Conjunctions are a part of speech.
They join words or sentences; it's quite a feat!
   They join words or sentences; it's quite a feat!
Sound off! Conjunctions!   **Sound off! AND, OR, BUT!**
There are many conjunctions, but three stand out.
   There are many conjunctions, but three stand out.
Put your hands together and give a shout!
   Put your hands together and give a shout!
Sound off! Conjunctions!   **Sound off! AND, OR, BUT!**
     Sound off! Conjunctions!   **Sound off! AND, OR, BUT!**

Apply It: These Introductory Sentences are used to apply the new grammar concepts taught below. Classify these sentences orally with your teacher.

Introductory Sentences	Chapter 4: Lesson 2

1. _____ Several frisky little squirrels frolicked playfully and scampered around until dark.
2. _____ You and Lindsey whispered too often during our library time!
3. _____ Look at the horrible damage in our neighborhood after the tornado!

Learn It: COORDINATE CONJUNCTIONS AND COMPOUND PARTS

Reference 76 — Coordinate Conjunctions and Compound Parts

1. A **conjunction** is a word that joins words or groups of words together.
2. Conjunctions that join things of the same kind or of equal importance (like two subjects, two verbs, or two simple sentences) are called **coordinate conjunctions**.
3. The three most common coordinate conjunctions are **and**, **or**, and **but**. There are no questions used to find coordinate conjunctions; therefore, these conjunctions should be memorized.
4. A *coordinate conjunction* is labeled with the abbreviation **C**.
5. When words or groups of words in a sentence are joined by a coordinate conjunction, the parts that are joined are called **compound parts**. There are many parts of a sentence that can be **compound**. However, compound subjects and compound verbs are the most common.
6. The label **C** is also used to identify compound parts when it is used in front of regular labels. Examples of compound labels are **CSN, CSP, CV, CAdj, CAdv, COP**, etc. To classify a compound part, always say the word *compound* first. For example, read the label **CSN** as "*Compound Subject Noun.*"

>>>>>>>> Student Tip...

Swing your right hand to your chest and say **and**. Keeping your right hand at your chest, swing your left hand to your chest and say **or**. Then, swing both hands horizontally and say **but**. Repeat the chant and motions several times.

Discuss It:

1. What abbreviation is used for a compound subject noun?
2. What abbreviation is used for a compound subject pronoun?
3. What abbreviation is used for a compound verb?
4. What abbreviation is used for a compound adjective?
5. What abbreviation is used for a compound adverb?
6. What abbreviation is used for a compound object of the preposition?

FOR A nOUn CHECK WITH PRONOUNS

Using the sentences just classified, do a Skill Builder orally with your teacher.

Sentence 1: Subject noun (squirrels) *yes, it is a noun;.*
Object of the preposition (dark) *yes, it is a noun.*

Sentence 2: Compound subject pronoun **you**, *no, it is a pronoun;*
Compound subject noun (Lindsey) *yes, it is a noun;*
Object of the preposition (time) *yes, it is a noun.*

Sentence 3: Understood subject pronoun **you**, *no, it is a pronoun;*
Object of the preposition (damage) *yes, it is a noun;*
Object of the preposition (neighborhood) *yes, it is a noun;*
Object of the preposition (tornado) *yes, it is a noun.*

Learn It: ADDING THE CONJUNCTION TO THE PARTS OF SPEECH

A conjunction is a part of speech. You have learned seven of the eight parts of speech. What are these seven parts of speech?

Learn It: SIMPLE SENTENCES, SENTENCE FRAGMENTS,
RUN-ONS, AND COMPOUND PARTS

Reference 77	Simple Sentences, Fragments, Run-ons, and Compound Parts

1. A **simple sentence** must have three core parts to be complete: a subject, a verb, and a complete thought. A simple sentence is independent and can stand alone. The label for a *simple sentence* is the letter **S**.
   Example: *Red clover grows by the side of the road.*

2. A sentence **fragment** is an incomplete sentence. A fragment is missing one or more of the core sentence parts (subject, verb, or complete thought). The label for a *fragment* is the letter **F**.
   Example: *Grows by the side of the road.*

3. A **run-on sentence** is two sentences written together as one sentence without correct punctuation.
   Example: *Red clover grows by the side of the road it is a beautiful ground cover.*

4. A simple sentence may also have **compound parts**. Compound parts are usually joined by the conjunction **and**. When it is used in front of regular labels, the label **C** is used to identify compound parts. Here are the meanings and labels of several compound parts: **CS**—*compound subject;* **CV**—*compound verb;* **SCS**—*simple sentence with a compound subject;* **SCV**—*simple sentence with a compound verb.*

Part 1: The examples below show how each sentence is identified by the label in parentheses.

1. The two dogs barked at the squirrels. (**S**)
2. The two red birds in the tree. (**F**)
3. My mom and dad drove to Texas. (**SCS**)
4. Laura sang and danced in the play. (**SCV**)

Part 2: Correct each sentence fragment by adding the part in parentheses that is underlined.

1. At the edge of the pond for a drink of water.
   (subject part, predicate part, <u>both the subject and predicate</u>, sense)
   Example: *The thirsty lion stood fearlessly at the edge of the pond for a drink of water.*

Continued on next page. >>>

Reference 77 continued from previous page.

2. A pack of hungry wolves. (subject part, <u>predicate part</u>, both the subject and predicate, sense)
   Example: A pack of hungry wolves growled ferociously at the startled deer.
3. Was running toward the burning house.
   (<u>subject part</u>, predicate part, both the subject and predicate, sense)
   Example: The frantic father was running toward the burning house.
4. As I walked happily in the park. (subject part, predicate part, both the subject and predicate, <u>sense</u>)
   Example: Delete **As**. I walked happily in the park.

Part 3: Use a slash to separate each run-on sentence below.
Then, correct each run-on sentence by rewriting it as indicated by the labels in parentheses at the end of the sentence.

1. The baby birds were chirping / they were hungry. (**S, S**)
   The baby birds were chirping. They were hungry.
2. The milk is in the refrigerator / the butter is in the refrigerator. (**SCS**)
   The milk and butter are in the refrigerator.
3. The lifeguard jumped up / he dove into the pool. (**SCV**)
   The lifeguard jumped up and dove into the pool.

Part 4: Identify each type of sentence by writing the correct label in the blank. (**Labels: S, F, SCS, SCV**)

   S   1. Jimmy went to the party.   **SCV** 3. They jogged and walked down the trail.
   F   2. As Jimmy went to the party.   **SCS** 4. The boys and girls ran outside.

Classroom Practice 15

It is time to practice the skills you are learning. You will use the classroom practice on the next page to apply these skills.

ENRICHMENT:

(Portuguese) 1480-1521— Ferdinand Magellan was the first person to sail around the world. He proved that the planet earth is round and that all the oceans are connected. Magellan also named the Pacific Ocean for its calm waters.

Discovery Questions:
- **What do you think it was like to be an explorer in Magellan's time?**
- **What dangers and hardships would you have faced?**

Are you interested in learning more about Ferdinand Magellan?

1. You may explore this topic further by using the resources listed below.
   Computer resources: Internet, encyclopedia software
   Library resources: encyclopedias, books, magazines, newspapers
   Home/community resources: books, interviews, newspapers, magazines
2. A Discovery Share Time is provided in Lesson 7 if you wish to share your investigation results. You may share orally, or you may prepare a written report. You will put your written report in a class booklet titled "Notable People in History." This booklet will be placed in the class library for everyone to enjoy.

Classroom Practice 15

Name:_____ Date:_____

GRAMMAR

▶ **Exercise 1:** Classify each sentence. Underline the complete subject once and the complete predicate twice.

1. _____ Study for your French test with Patrick and Susan after school today.

2. _____ Larry and I worked on my research report yesterday.

SKILLS

▶ **Exercise 2:** Identify each type of sentence by writing the correct label in the blank. (**Labels: S, F, SCS, SCV**)

_____ 1. He and she rode to town with me.

_____ 2. After the students sat down.

_____ 3. Tiny gnats flew around my face and annoyed me.

_____ 4. Peanuts and pecans make good snacks.

_____ 5. Climb to the top of the tower and look over the city at night.

_____ 6. The old fox walked wearily down the dark road in search of easy food.

_____ 7. My brother's package arrived late and did not have a return address.

_____ 8. After the pie was eaten.

_____ 9. The flour, sugar, and milk for the recipe are on the counter.

▶ **Exercise 3:** Use a slash to separate the two complete thoughts in each run-on sentence. Correct the run-on sentences as indicated by the labels in parentheses at the end of each sentence.

1. The farmer plowed the fields the farmer planted his crops. (**SCV**)

_____

2. My mother cooked our family a Thanksgiving meal my sister helped Mother cook. (**SCS**)

_____

3. The left-over roast is in the refrigerator the left-over apple pie is in the refrigerator. (**SCS**)

_____

4. Grandfather jumped up he walked quickly to the door. (**SCV**)

_____

EDITING

▶ **Exercise 4:** Correct each mistake. **Editing Guide: End Marks: 3   Capitals: 8   Commas: 2   Homonyms: 7   Periods: 1   Underlining: 1   Misspelled Words: 1**

did you reed white fang a classick bye jack london in you're forth-grade class last year

i red it and made a book report on it mrs smith had us reed a knew book this year

English Made Easy

LISTENING AND SPEAKING:
 ### Vocabulary & Analogy Time

Learn It: Recite the new vocabulary and analogy words.

Lesson 3

You will
- study new vocabulary; make card 11; write own sentence using the vocabulary word.
- analyze new analogy; make card 11; write own analogy.
- practice Jingles 13-16.
- classify Practice Sentences.
- do a Skill Builder.
- identify a/an choices and contractions.
- do Classroom Practice 16.
- write in your journal.
- read and discuss Discovery·Time.

Reference 78	Vocabulary & Analogy Words

Word: placid (plăs'ĭd)
  Definition: pleasantly calm or unruffled
  Synonym: peaceful   **Antonym:** turbulent
  Sentence: The placid lake lay hidden deep in the woods.

Analogy: tadpole : frog :: boy : man
  Progression relationship: Just as a **tadpole** is a **young frog**, a **boy** is a **young man**.

Vocabulary Card 11: Record the vocabulary information above and write your own sentence, using the new word.

Analogy Card 11: Record the analogy information and write your own analogy, using the same relationship as the analogy above.

 ### Jingle Time

Recite It: Practice Jingles 13–16 in the Jingle Section on pages 509–510.

 ### Grammar Time

Apply It: Classify the Practice Sentences orally with your teacher.

Practice Sentences	Chapter 4: Lesson 3

1. _____ Maneuver carefully through the tall rows of golden cornstalks in our garden.

2. _____ They believed in freedom of religion for all citizens.

3. _____ Fuzzy black mold and green slime grew inside the carved pumpkin on the porch of their house!

LISTENING AND SPEAKING:

Using the sentences just classified, do a Skill Builder orally with your teacher.
1. **Identify the nouns in a Noun Check.**
2. **Identify the nouns as singular or plural.**
3. **Identify the nouns as common or proper.**
4. **Identify the complete subject and the complete predicate.**
5. **Identify the simple subject and the simple predicate.**
6. **Do a Vocabulary Check.**

Learn It: A/AN CHOICES

📖	**Reference 79**	**Choosing A or An**

RULE 1: Use the word **a** when the next word begins with a consonant sound. (**Example: a g**olden apricot.)

RULE 2: Use the word **an** when the next word begins with a vowel sound. (**Example: an a**pricot.)

Directions: Write **a** or **an** in the blanks.
1. Would you like ___*an*___ apple?
2. Would you like ___*a*___ red apple?
3. We saw ___*a*___ pumpkin.
4. We saw ___*an*___ orange pumpkin.

Learn It: CONTRACTIONS

📖	**Reference 80**	**Contraction Chart**

A **contraction** is two words combined into one. The new word always has an apostrophe that takes the place of the letter(s) that has (have) been left out. Sometimes, contractions may be confused with pronouns because they sound alike. Study the spellings of all contractions.

AM
I'm . . . . I am

IS
isn't . . . . is not
he's . . . . he is
she's . . . . she is
it's. . . . . it is
who's . . . . who is
that's. . . . . that is
what's . . . . what is
there's . . . . there is

ARE
aren't . . . . are not
you're. . . . . you are
we're . . . . we are
they're . . . . they are

HAS
hasn't . . . . has not
he's . . . . he has
she's . . . . she has

HAVE
haven't . . . . have not
I've. . . . . I have
you've . . . . you have
we've. . . . . we have
they've . . . . they have

HAD
hadn't. . . . . had not
I'd. . . . . I had
you'd . . . . you had
we'd . . . . we had
they'd. . . . . they had

CAN
can't. . . . . cannot

COULD
couldn't . . . . . could not

WOULD
wouldn't . . . . . would not
I'd. . . . . I would
he'd . . . . he would
she'd . . . . she would
you'd . . . . you would
we'd. . . . . we would
they'd . . . . . . they would

SHOULD
shouldn't . . . . should not

Continued on next page. >>>

Reference 80 continued from previous page.

WAS, WERE	DO, DOES, DID	WILL, SHALL
wasn't............. was not	don't.............do not	won't .... will not
weren't .... were not	doesn't ....does not	I'll .... I will, I shall
	didn't ....did not	he'll..........he will, he shall
		she'll.........she will, she shall
		you'll.........you will, you shall
		we'll .... we will, we shall
		they'll........they will, they shall

Contractions That May Be Confused With Pronouns

Contractions:

it's ....(it is) .... *It's cute.*
you're ..... (you are).... *You're right.*
they're .... (they are)... *They're gone.*
who's ...... (who is)..... *Who's going?*

Pronouns:

its ....(owns) ...... *its tail*
your ....(owns) ...... *your car*
their ....(owns) ...... *their house*
whose .....(owns) ...... *whose cat*

LET

let's..........let us

Classroom Practice 16

It is time to practice the skills you are learning. You will use the classroom practice on the next page to apply these skills.

ENRICHMENT:

Discovery Time

(English) 1564-1616— William Shakespeare is considered by critics to be the greatest playwright of all time. Some of his most famous works include *Romeo and Juliet*, *A Midsummer Night's Dream*, *Julius Caesar*, *Hamlet*, *Macbeth*, and *As You Like It*. Shakespeare wrote nearly all his plays between 1590 and 1611.

Discovery Questions:

- How many plays a year did Shakespeare average during his working life?
- What do you think is the hardest part about being a writer?
- Do you want to be a writer?
- What kind of stories would you write?

Are you interested in learning more about William Shakespeare?

1. You may explore this topic further by using the resources listed below.
   Computer resources: Internet, encyclopedia software
   Library resources: encyclopedias, books, magazines, newspapers
   Home/community resources: books, interviews, newspapers, magazines

2. A Discovery Share Time is provided in Lesson 7 if you wish to share your investigation results. You may share orally, or you may prepare a written report. You will put your written report in a class booklet titled "Notable People in History." This booklet will be placed in the class library for everyone to enjoy.

Student Tip...

Make two sets of cards. On the first set, write the contractions. On the second set, write the words from which each contraction was made. Practice matching the contraction cards to the word cards. Find a partner and practice matching the word cards to the contraction cards.

JOURNAL WRITING 8

Write an entry in your journal. Use Reference 9 on page 12 for ideas.

Classroom Practice 16

Name:_____ Date:_____

GRAMMAR

▶ **Exercise 1:** Classify each sentence. Underline the complete subject once and the complete predicate twice.

1. _____ Talk to my parents about my permission slip and my ticket for the concert.

2. _____ Tom and Kay worked hard for their college degrees from our local college.

SKILLS

▶ **Exercise 2:** Write either the contraction or the contraction words in the blanks.

1. do not _____   2. let's _____   3. does not _____   4. I've _____

▶ **Exercise 3:** Write **a** or **an** in the blanks.

1. We found _____ ant and _____ beetle.   2. I ate _____ cherry tart and _____ apple pie at the picnic.

▶ **Exercise 4:** Identify each type of sentence by writing the correct label in the blank. (**Labels: S, F, SCS, SCV**)

_____ 1. Cheetahs and zebras are my favorite animals.
_____ 2. Our neighbor's dog chewed the paper and scattered it around the yard.
_____ 3. As soon as the director raised his hands.
_____ 4. Jarrod's more experienced crew built the house in record time.
_____ 5. Mrs. Garner graded our papers and put them in our folders.
_____ 6. The two girls and their friends shopped at the mall.
_____ 7. Derek and I rode to town with Mr. Poole after school.
_____ 8. The mail carrier did not deliver Dad's overnight package to our house today.

▶ **Exercise 5:** Use a slash to separate the two complete thoughts in each run-on sentence.
Correct the run-on sentences as indicated by the labels in parentheses at the end of each sentence.

1. The students were yawning they were bored. (**S, S**)

_____

2. The seamstress worked at home her husband worked at home. (**SCS**)

_____

3. The audience stood up they cheered for the cast. (**SCV**)

_____

EDITING

▶ **Exercise 6:** Correct each mistake. **Editing Guide: End Marks: 6   Capitals: 12   Commas: 2   Apostrophes: 1   Homonyms: 5   A/An: 2   Subject-Verb Agreement: 4   Periods: 1   Misspelled Words: 2**

patty and i sea mr perry hour sixth-grade english techer at meadowlark mall in an baby store

we giggel at the look on his face and walks over he tell us that he are buying an baby gift for his

wife we lead him too the write area and then says farewell we look back hes still standing their

LISTENING AND SPEAKING:
Vocabulary & Analogy Time

START LESSON 4

Learn It: Recite the new vocabulary and analogy words.

📖 Reference 81	Vocabulary & Analogy Words

Word: preliminary (prĭ lĭm' ənĕr' ē)
  Definition: coming before; leading up to
  Synonym: preceding   **Antonym:** concluding
  Sentence: I had a preliminary interview for the job today.

Analogy: new : knew :: night : knight
  Homonym relationship: Just as **new** sounds the same as **knew**, **night** sounds the same as **knight**.

Vocabulary Card 12: Record the vocabulary information above and write your own sentence, using the new word.

Analogy Card 12: Record the analogy information and write your own analogy, using the same relationship as the analogy above.

Lesson 4

You will

- study new vocabulary; make card 12; write own sentence using the vocabulary word.
- analyze new analogy; make card 12; write own analogy.
- practice Jingles 5–11.
- classify Practice Sentences.
- do a Skill Builder.
- do Classroom Practice 17.
- read and discuss Discovery Time.
- do a homework assignment.
- do Home Connection activity.

Jingle Time

Recite It: Practice Jingles 5–11 in the Jingle Section on pages 507–508.

Grammar Time

Apply It: Classify the Practice Sentences orally with your teacher.

Practice Sentences	Chapter 4: Lesson 4

1. _____ The frightened toddler in the blue pajamas cried pitifully for his mother during the thunderstorm.

2. _____ He laughed and joked happily with his cousins during the commercial break.

3. _____ Sing softly to the children after their bedtime story.

LISTENING AND SPEAKING:

 Skill Builder

Using the sentences just classified, do a Skill Builder orally with your teacher.

1. **Identify the nouns in a Noun Check.**
2. **Identify the nouns as singular or plural.**
3. **Identify the nouns as common or proper.**
4. **Identify the complete subject and the complete predicate.**
5. **Identify the simple subject and the simple predicate.**
6. **Do a Vocabulary Check.**

 Classroom Practice 17

It is time to practice the skills you are learning. You will use the classroom practice on the next page to apply these skills.

ENRICHMENT:

 **Discovery Time**

(English) 1642-1727— Sir Isaac Newton discovered gravity and the three laws of motion. He also invented the reflecting telescope and calculus and designed a scientific method for performing experiments.

Discovery Questions:
- **What do you think it was like to be a scientist in Newton's time?**
- **Do you think Newton had books or other scientists to help him?**
- **What would Newton think if he could see all the equipment that scientists use today?**

Are you interested in learning more about Sir Isaac Newton?

1. You may explore this topic further by using the resources listed below.
   Computer resources: Internet, encyclopedia software
   Library resources: encyclopedias, books, magazines, newspapers
   Home/community resources: books, interviews, newspapers, magazines

2. A Discovery Share Time is provided in Lesson 7 if you wish to share your investigation results. You may share orally, or you may prepare a written report. You will put your written report in a class booklet titled "Notable People in History." This booklet will be placed in the class library for everyone to enjoy.

Classroom Practice 17

Name:_____ Date:_____

GRAMMAR

▶ **Exercise 1:** Classify each sentence. Underline the complete subject once and the complete predicate twice.

1. _____ The frightened little girl and her mother called frantically to the firemen!

2. _____ Look at this gorgeous view and beautiful sunset in the Grand Canyon!

SKILLS

▶ **Exercise 2:** Write **a** or **an** in the blanks.

I ate _____ banana and _____ orange for dessert.

▶ **Exercise 3:** Write the contraction in the blank.

1. did not _____   2. I am _____

▶ **Exercise 4:** Identify each type of sentence by writing the correct label in the blank. (**Labels: S, F, SCS, SCV**)

_____   1. Chase and Cooper invited me to dinner.
_____   2. Shady and cool spot on the lawn.
_____   3. We watched a scary movie last night and were not able to sleep.
_____   4. After school on Friday, you and I are going out for dinner.
_____   5. Celia grabbed her book bag and dashed out the door.
_____   6. During the half-time show at the ballgame on Saturday night.
_____   7. The icicle melted slowly and dripped steadily throughout the day.

▶ **Exercise 5:** Use a slash to separate the two complete thoughts in each run-on sentence.
Correct the run-on sentences as indicated by the labels in parentheses at the end of each sentence.

1. The baby kangaroos hopped around they chewed on tender leaves. (**SCV**)

_____

2. Tate mowed the grass Charlie mowed with him. (**SCS**)

_____

3. The hard rain drenched the backyard it also drowned the flowers. (**SCV**)

_____

EDITING

▶ **Exercise 6:** Correct each mistake. **Editing Guide: End Marks: 2   Capitals: 15   Commas: 2   Homonyms: 2**
Subject-Verb Agreement: 3   Underlining: 1   Misspelled Words: 2

in my favorite book where the red fern grows billy and his courageous pups lives and

grows up in the ozark mountains and has many adventures i bought many copies of this book

fore memers of the walker middle school student council too sell for our fund-raiser in september

 **Homework 2**

Complete this homework assignment on notebook paper.

1. Write a Practice Sentence, using the following set of labels. You may expand the sentence by adding more labels.
   A Adj SN V Adv P A OP

2. Write the names of the seven parts of speech you have studied so far.
   1. _____ 2._____ 3. _____ 4. _____
   5._____ 6. _____ 7. _____

3. Number your paper 1–10. Write the correct contraction for each set of words. Write answers only.

   1. who is _____   5. will not _____   9. they had _____
   2. they are _____   6. has not _____   10. we will _____
   3. it is _____   7. you have _____
   4. you are _____   8. she would _____

4. Number your paper 1–4. Write **a** or **an** for each sentence.

   1. He gave _____ oral test.   2. She gave _____ written test.   3. _____ hour   4. _____ planet

5. Number your paper 1–4. Identify each type of sentence by writing the correct label (**S, F, SCS,** or **SCV**) beside each number.

   _____ 1. Jessie ate breakfast with Mom and Dad.   _____ 3. My dog and cat ran into the kitchen.
   _____ 2. I rode and camped along the trail.   _____ 4. Under the Christmas tree.

6. Rewrite and correct each sentence fragment by adding the part in parentheses that is underlined.

   1. Around the flagpole in the schoolyard.   (subject part, predicate part, <u>both the subject and predicate</u>, sense)
   2. A tiny bead from her necklace.   (subject part, <u>predicate part</u>, both the subject and predicate, sense)
   3. Slithered silently in the underbrush.   (<u>subject part</u>, predicate part, both the subject and predicate, sense)
   4. Since you arrived early.   (subject part, predicate part, both the subject and predicate, <u>sense</u>)

Home Connection

Family Activity for Pronouns

1. Have a contest with family members or friends to see who can go the longest without using any pronouns. Down the left side of a sheet of paper, make a list of the pronouns that are used in the pronoun jingles on page 109. For an hour, do not use any pronouns in your conversations. Keep the list with you at all times. Every time you forget and say a pronoun, place a tally mark beside that pronoun. At the end of an hour, add up the number of times that you used pronouns. Which pronouns did you use most? Discuss the importance of pronouns in communication.

2. Expand the game to several hours on a weekend or all weekend. You could include relatives, guests, or friends in this activity.

Family Activity for Vocabulary and Analogies

Divide into family teams. The first team will use vocabulary and analogy cards 5–8 to ask questions about the information on their cards. The second team will use vocabulary and analogy cards 9–12 to ask questions about the information on their cards.

For vocabulary words:
- What is the definition of the word?
- Name a synonym and antonym for the word?
- Create a new sentence using the word.
- Find the word in another source (dictionary, newspaper, magazine, advertisement, etc.)

For analogies:
- What is the answer to the analogy?
- What is the relationship of the analogy?
- Make another analogy with the same relationship.
- Make another analogy with a different relationship.

English Made Easy

Grammar Time

Apply It: Classify the Practice Sentences orally with your teacher.

Practice Sentences	Chapter 4: Lesson 5

1. _____ Twenty huge elephants inside the circus arena balanced precariously on their hind feet!

2. _____ Jessie and Eric searched extensively and carefully for their poor lost puppy!

3. _____ We arrived too late for her graduation party at the Lexington Hotel in Memphis.

Chapter Checkup 18

It is time for a checkup of the skills you have learned in this chapter. You will use the chapter checkup on the next page to evaluate your progress.

ENRICHMENT:

Discovery Time

(American) 1731-1806— Benjamin Banneker was the first African American to write an almanac. *Banneker's Almanac* contained an ephemeris (an astrological chart) that he compiled. Banneker devised an irrigation system for his family farm at the age of 15. In 1980, the U.S. Postal Service issued a postage stamp in Banneker's honor.

Discovery Questions:
- **How long did Banneker's wooden striking clock work?**
- **What would you have invented during Banneker's time?**
- **Explain how your invention would have helped people?**
- **What would you have had available to help you?**

(American) 1735-1818— Paul Revere is best remembered for his midnight ride to warn the colonists about the approaching British army. Revere also drew political cartoons and was a silversmith by trade.

Discovery Questions:
- **Which poet made Paul Revere famous with his poem, "Paul Revere's Ride," in 1860?**
- **What dangers and hardships do you think you would have faced if you had lived during colonial times?**

Are you interested in learning more about Benjamin Banneker or Paul Revere?

1. You may explore these topics further by using the resources listed below.
   Computer resources: Internet, encyclopedia software
   Library resources: encyclopedias, books, magazines, newspapers
   Home/community resources: books, interviews, newspapers, magazines

2. A Discovery Share Time is provided in Lesson 7 if you wish to share your investigation results. You may share orally, or you may prepare a written report. You will put your written report in a class booklet titled "Notable People in History." This booklet will be placed in the class library for everyone to enjoy.

START LESSON 5

Lesson 5

You will
- classify Practice Sentences.
- do Chapter Checkup 18.
- write in your journal.
- read and discuss Discovery Time.

JOURNAL WRITING 9

JOURNAL

Write an entry in your journal. Use Reference 9 on page 12 for ideas.

Chapter 4 Checkup 18

Name:_____ Date:_____

GRAMMAR

▶ **Exercise 1:** Classify each sentence. Underline the complete subject once and the complete predicate twice.

1. _____ Go quickly to the hardware store for plumbing putty and three copper pipes.

2. _____ Hannah and Sarina waved to their friends from the top of the escalator.

3. _____ The smell of the hot cinnamon rolls drifted from our sidewalk café yesterday.

SKILLS

▶ **Exercise 2:** Write **a** or **an** in the blanks.

I like _____ onion with _____ grilled steak.

▶ **Exercise 3:** Write the contraction in the blank.

1. they have _____   2. are not _____

▶ **Exercise 4:** Identify each type of sentence by writing the correct label in the blank. (**Labels: S, F, SCS, SCV**)

_____ 1. Barely missed the car's fender.
_____ 2. During the evenings, my parents would take long walks along the beach.
_____ 3. Our uncle made puppets and sold them at the fair.
_____ 4. She and I ran to my neighbor's house down the street.
_____ 5. Larry and the neighborhood boys loaded up the camping equipment.
_____ 6. We clapped our hands and danced to the rhythm of the music.

▶ **Exercise 5:** Use a slash to separate the two complete thoughts in each run-on sentence. Correct the run-on sentences as indicated by the labels in parentheses at the end of each sentence.

1. My sister cleaned her room today my brother cleaned his room today. (**SCS**)

_____

2. My dad cooked the pizza he also cleaned the kitchen. (**SCV**)

_____

3. The student raised his hand he waited patiently for permission to speak. (**SCV**)

_____

EDITING

▶ **Exercise 6:** Correct each mistake. **Editing Guide: End Marks: 7   Capitals: 13   Apostrophes: 2   Homonyms: 2   A/An: 1   Subject-Verb Agreement: 5   Misspelled Words: 2**

the stormy weather makes kevins homework even harder too do he sit at the computer and stare at the blank screen his expostory essay on the french revolution are due on thersday in world history ll he tap lightly on the keys and tries to think where he should begin a unexpected surge of electricity leave the computer screen blank kevin chuckles too himself he is suddenly very glad he hasnt written his essay

English Made Easy

Writing Time

Write It: **WRITING ASSIGNMENT 7**

Lesson 6

You will

- conference with teacher about WA 6.
- write a creative writing piece for WA 7.

Writing Assignment ⑦: Creative Expressions

> **Purpose:** To entertain
>
> **Type of Writing:** Creative
>
> **Audience:** Classmates, family, or friends

Choose one of the writing topics below:

1. If you could have an exceptional talent, what would it be? How would you use it?

2. What does it take to be a hero? Whom do you consider a hero? Why?

3. Write a poem about a hero, an exceptional talent, or a topic of your choice.

Special Instructions:

1. A prewriting map is not required for this creative-writing assignment.

2. Follow the Rough Draft Checklist in Reference 46 on page 61.

3. Put your creative-writing paper in your Rough Draft folder when you have finished.

Note: Reference 54 on page 71 gives the steps in the writing process and the location of all the writing checklists.

 **Student Tip...**

> **For more information about writing poetry, look at Chapter 18, pages 465–482.**

Conference Time

Discuss It: **TEACHER-STUDENT CONFERENCES FOR WRITING ASSIGNMENT 6**

Meet with your teacher to discuss Writing Assignment 6.
After the conference, place this group of papers in your Publishing folder.

START LESSON 7

Lesson 7

You will

- publish WA 6.
- participate in Discovery Share Time.

 Publishing Time

Publish It: **WRITING ASSIGNMENT 6**

Choose a publishing form and publish Writing Assignment 6. After rewriting your paper for publication, give the stapled papers (evaluation guide, graded final paper, rough draft, and prewriting map) to your teacher to be placed in your Writing Portfolio.

Reference 66	Publishing Checklist for Step 6 in the Writing Process

The sixth step in the writing process is called publishing. Publishing is sharing your writing with others. With so many forms of publishing available, finding a match for every project and personality is easy. At times, a written work is best read aloud. Other times, the biggest impact is made when a written work is read silently. You can also use media sources to enhance any publication.

SPECIAL INSTRUCTIONS FOR PUBLISHING:

- Rewrite the graded paper in ink or type it on a computer, correcting any marked errors.
  (Do not display or publish papers that have marked errors or grades on them.)
- Give your teacher the set of stapled papers to place in your Writing Portfolio.
  (Stapled papers: evaluation guide, graded final paper, rough draft, and prewriting map.)
- Select a publishing form from the list below and publish your rewritten paper.

  1. Have classmates, family members, neighbors, or others read your writing at school or home.
  2. Share your writing with others during a Share Time. *(Refer to Reference 67 on page 99 for sharing guidelines.)*
  3. Display your writing on a bulletin board or wall.
  4. Put your writing in the classroom library or in the school library for checkout.
  5. Send your writing as a letter or an e-mail to a friend or relative.
  6. Frame your writing by gluing it on colored construction paper and decorating it.
  7. Make a book of your writing for your classroom, your family, or others.
  8. Illustrate your writing and give it to others to read.
  9. Dramatize your writing in the form of a play, puppet show, or radio broadcast.
  10. Send your writing to be placed in a waiting room (doctor, veterinarian, dentist, etc.), senior-citizen center, or a nursing home.
  11. Send your writing to a school newspaper, local newspaper, or a magazine for publication.
  12. Make a videotape, cassette tape, or slide presentation of your writing.
  13. Choose another publishing form that is not listed.

LISTENING AND SPEAKING:

 **Discovery Share Time**

If you have chosen to investigate a historical figure introduced in Chapter 3 or Chapter 4, you now have the opportunity to share your results in one of the following ways:

1. You may relate your information orally.
2. You may read a written report.
3. You may place your report in the booklet without reading it aloud.

After share time, all written reports should be turned in to be placed in the class booklet titled "Notable People in History." You are encouraged to check out this class booklet so you can enjoy the reports again.

LISTENING AND SPEAKING:

Jingle Time

Recite It: Practice Jingle 2 in the Jingle Section on page 506.

GRAMMAR & WRITING CONNECTION:
Practice and Revised Sentences

Apply It: BUILDING AND EXPANDING SENTENCES

Lesson 8

You will
- practice Jingle 2.
- do Classroom Practice 19.
- write an independent expository paragraph (WA 8).

Reference 82	A Guide for Using Pronouns and Conjunctions to Build & Expand Sentences

1. **SP (subject pronoun)** Sing or recite the Subject Pronoun Jingle to help you think of a pronoun that you want to use as the subject. Write the subject pronoun you have chosen for your sentence.

2. **PPA (possessive pronoun adjective)** Sing or recite the Possessive Pronoun Jingle to help you think of a possessive pronoun that you want to use. Choose the possessive pronoun that makes the best sense in your sentence. Write the possessive pronoun you have chosen for your sentence. Repeat this step for each possessive pronoun adjective you add to the sentence.

3. **C (conjunction)** Sing or recite the Conjunction Jingle. Choose one of the three coordinate conjunctions (*and, but, or*) that makes sense in your sentence. Make sure the conjunction connects the compound parts in your sentence. Write the conjunction you have chosen for your sentence. Repeat this step for each conjunction you add to the sentence.

Classroom Practice 19

It is time to practice the skills you are learning. You will use the classroom practice on page 131 to apply these skills.

>>>>>>>>> **Student Tip...**

Use your vocabulary words in your Practice and Revised Sentences. Use a thesaurus, synonym-antonym book, or a dictionary to help you develop your writing vocabulary.

Student Note: The conjunction allows any part of speech to be compound, including the core parts, Sn/SP V.

Write It: WRITING ASSIGNMENT 8

As you write a rough draft for your independent writing assignment, you will do two of the six steps in the writing process: prewriting and rough draft.

Writing Assignment 8

Purpose: To inform

Type of Writing: Three-point expository paragraph

Audience: Classmates

Writing topics: Favorite heroes
Favorite rides at the fair
Favorite sports
(Brainstorm for other ideas, individually or in groups.)

Special Instructions:

1. Follow the Prewriting and Rough Draft Checklists in References 44 and 46 on pages 57, 61.

2. Use References 38–43 on pages 53–56 to help you write your expository paragraph.

3. Use standard, time-order, or transition writing form. See Reference 69, page 103.

4. Write in first or third person. See Reference 70, page 104.
(First-person pronouns: *I, me, my, mine, we, us, our, and ours.*)
(Third-person pronouns: *he, his, him, she, her, hers, it, its, they, their, theirs,* and *them.*)

Note: Reference 54 on page 71 gives the steps in the writing process and the location of all the writing checklists.

Student Note: Some of your writing pieces will be selected for revision and editing later in the school year.

Classroom Practice 19

Name: _____ Date: _____

INDEPENDENT PRACTICE & REVISED SENTENCES

1. Write a Practice Sentence according to the labels you choose.
Use **SN/SP V** as your main labels. You may use the other labels in any order and as many times as you wish in order to make a Practice Sentence.
Chapter 4 labels for a Practice Sentence: **SN/SP**, V, Adj, Adv, A, P, OP, PPA, C

2. Write a Revised Sentence. Use the following revision strategies: *synonym (syn)*, *antonym (ant)*, *word change (wc)*, *added word (add)*, *deleted word (delete)*, or *no change (nc)*. Under each word, write the abbreviation of the revision strategy you use.

Labels:

Practice:

Revised:

Strategies:

Labels:

Practice:

Revised:

Strategies:

Labels:

Practice:

Revised:

Strategies:

Lesson 9

You will

- practice Jingle 12.
- read and discuss changing plural categories to singular points in your writing.
- read and discuss the parts of a three-paragraph expository essay.
- plan and write rough draft for expository essay (WA 9).

LISTENING AND SPEAKING:

Recite It: Practice Jingle 12 in the Jingle Section on page 509.

>>>> Student Tip...

Reviewing the transition words will help you apply them in your writing.

Learn It: CHANGING PLURAL CATEGORIES TO SINGULAR POINTS

📖 **Reference 83**   **Changing Plural Categories to Singular Points**

When you have a topic such as *My favorite animals*, you will usually name your favorite animals by categories, or groups, like kittens, monkeys, and horses. These categories, **kittens**, **monkeys**, and **horses**, are plural. When this happens, you need to change the plural categories to singular points as you write each point sentence.

CHANGING FROM PLURAL CATEGORIES TO SINGULAR POINTS
(First Person)

Topic: My favorite animals

Categories: 1. lemurs   2. prairie dogs   3. flamingos

    I have **several** favorite **animals** I enjoy seeing whenever I go to the zoo. The **animals** that I especially love to see **are lemurs, prairie dogs**, and **flamingos**. My first favorite **animal is** the **lemur**. I think lemurs are unique because they are similar to monkeys but have a fox-like face, large eyes, and a bushy tail. My second favorite zoo **animal is** the **prairie dog**. I find these short, bushy animals very interesting because they have a sophisticated language that they use to warn other prairie dogs of an approaching predator. My third favorite zoo **animal is** the **flamingo**. How these large tropical birds stand on one leg and are able to bend their legs backwards amazes me. I delight in watching my favorite animals, and they are on my "must see" list every time I visit the zoo.

CHANGING FROM PLURAL CATEGORIES TO SINGULAR POINTS
(Third Person)

Topic: Favorite animals

Categories: 1. lemurs   2. prairie dogs   3. flamingos

    Logan has several favorite **animals he** enjoys seeing whenever he goes to the zoo. The **animals** that he especially loves to see are **lemurs, prairie dogs**, and **flamingos**. Logan's first favorite **animal is** the **lemur**. Logan thinks lemurs are unique because they are similar to monkeys but have a fox-like face, large eyes, and a bushy tail. His second favorite zoo **animal is** the **prairie dog**. Logan finds these short, bushy animals very interesting because they have a sophisticated language that they use to warn other prairie dogs of an approaching predator. His third favorite zoo **animal is** the **flamingo**. How these large tropical birds stand on one leg and are able to bend their legs backwards amazes Logan. Logan delights in watching his favorite animals, and they are on his "must see" list every time he visits the zoo.

Learn It: WRITING AN ESSAY

When you write several paragraphs about a certain topic, it is called an essay.
The **essay** is a written discussion of one idea and is made up of several paragraphs.
An interesting fact is that the word *essay* comes from the French word *essai*,
meaning "a trial" or "a try."

Learn It: WRITING A THREE-PARAGRAPH EXPOSITORY ESSAY

Expository essays give facts, directions, explain ideas, or define words, just like expository paragraphs. Any time you do an expository writing, whether it is an essay or a paragraph, you will have three parts: the **Introduction**, the **Body**, and the **Conclusion**.

The three parts will always be written in that order. Although a title will be the first item appearing at the top of your essay, you will not write the title until you have finished writing the essay. In effect, the title will become the fourth part of a three-paragraph essay. In a three-paragraph essay, there will be three paragraphs. The introduction forms the first paragraph, the body forms the second paragraph, and the conclusion forms the third paragraph of the essay.

Compare It:

As you study the two outlines below, notice that there are more sentences in the introduction and conclusion of the essay. In addition, the second paragraph of the essay, which is the body, contains all the points and supporting sentences.

 Reference 84 | **Outlines for the Three-Point Paragraph and the Three-Paragraph Essay**

Outline of a Three-Point Paragraph

Paragraph
  A. Topic and number sentence
  B. Three-point sentence
  C. **First-point** sentence
  D. **Supporting** sentence for the first point
  E. **Second-point** sentence
  F. **Supporting** sentence for the second point
  G. **Third-point** sentence
  H. **Supporting** sentence for the third point
  I. Concluding general sentence

Title

Outline of a Three-Paragraph Essay

1. **Paragraph 1**—Introduction
  A. Topic and number sentence
  B. Extra-information sentence
  C. Three-point sentence
2. **Paragraph 2**—Body
  A. First-point sentence
  B. One or two supporting sentences for the first point
  C. Second-point sentence
  D. One or two supporting sentences for the second point
  E. Third-point sentence
  F. One or two supporting sentences for the third point
3. **Paragraph 3**—Conclusion
  A. Concluding general sentence
  B. Concluding three-point sentence
4. **Title**

Learn It: **WRITING THE INTRODUCTION**
FOR A THREE-PARAGRAPH EXPOSITORY ESSAY

The introduction forms the first paragraph. Two or three sentences make up the introduction. The first sentence in the introduction is called the **topic and number sentence**. The second sentence is the **extra-information sentence**, and the third sentence is called the **three-point sentence**.

Reference 85 | **Writing the Introduction for a Three-Paragraph Expository Essay**

LIST THREE POINTS ABOUT THE TOPIC.

Select three points to list about the topic. 1. **lemurs**   2. **prairie dogs**   3. **flamingos**

THE INTRODUCTION
Paragraph 1

Writing Topic: Favorite animals

Sentence 1 – Topic and Number Sentence:

To write the topic sentence, use some or all of the words in your topic and add a general or specific number word that tells the number of points that will be discussed.

> **General number words:** *several, many, some,* etc.
> **Specific number words:** *two, three, four,* etc.

In the sample sentence below, words from the topic *(favorite animals)* are used, and the general number word *(several)* is used instead of a specific number word.

> **I have several favorite animals I enjoy seeing whenever I go to the zoo.**

Sentence 2 – Extra-Information Sentence(s):

Sometimes, you need one or two extra sentences that will add information about the topic or embellish it. This sentence(s) is usually optional and can clarify, explain, define, or just be an extra interesting comment.

> **Every time I visit, I spend most of my time watching my favorite animals.**

Sentence 3 – Three-Point Sentence:

This sentence names the three points to be discussed in the order that you will present them in the body of your paper. You can list the points with or without the specific number in front. In the sample sentence, the points, *lemurs, prairie dogs, and flamingos,* are named without using the specific number *three*.

> **The animals that I especially love to see are lemurs, prairie dogs, and flamingos.**

Learn It: **WRITING THE BODY**
FOR A THREE-PARAGRAPH EXPOSITORY ESSAY

The body contains one paragraph. Notice that the three points and the supporting sentences for the three points form this paragraph.

Reference 86 | **Writing the Body for a Three-Paragraph Expository Essay**

THE BODY
Paragraph 2

Sentence 4 – First Point:

Write a sentence stating your first point.

> **My first favorite animal is the lemur.**

Continued on next page. >>>

Reference 86 continued from previous page.

Sentences 5–6 – Supporting Sentence(s):
Write one or more sentences that give more information about your first point.

> I think lemurs are unique because they are similar to monkeys but have a fox-like face, large eyes, and a bushy tail. The manner in which lemurs move sets me laughing nearly every time I visit the zoo.

Sentence 7 – Second Point:
Write a sentence stating your second point.

> My second favorite zoo animal is the prairie dog.

Sentences 8–9 – Supporting Sentence(s):
Write one or more sentences that give more information about your second point.

> I find these short, bushy animals very interesting because they have a sophisticated language that they use to warn other prairie dogs of an approaching predator. After they give their warning call, they bob up and down with excitement before quickly disappearing into their burrows.

Sentence 10 – Third Point:
Write a sentence stating your third point.

> My third favorite zoo animal is the flamingo.

Sentences 11–12 – Supporting Sentence(s):
Write one or more sentences that give more information about your third point.

> How these large tropical birds stand on one leg and are able to bend their legs backwards amazes me. Their bright pink feathers, which appear to be painted, intrigue me as well.

Learn It: WRITING THE CONCLUSION
FOR A THREE-PARAGRAPH EXPOSITORY ESSAY

The conclusion forms the third paragraph. The conclusion should tie all the important points together with a restatement of the main idea and your final comments on it.

Two sentences make up the conclusion. The first sentence in the conclusion is called the **concluding general sentence**, and the second sentence is the **concluding three-point sentence**.

Reference 87 — **Writing the Conclusion for a Three-Paragraph Expository Essay**

THE CONCLUSION
Paragraph 3

Sentence 13 – Concluding General Sentence:
Read the topic sentence again and then rewrite it, using some of the same words. The concluding general sentence is meant to be general in nature and restates the topic sentence. In the sample sentence, the word *animals* is used instead of the particular points, *lemurs*, *prairie dogs*, and *flamingos*.

> I delight in watching my favorite animals, and they are on my "must see" list every time I visit the zoo.

Sentence 14 – Concluding Three-Point Sentence:
Read the introductory three-point sentence again and then rewrite it, using some of the same words. The concluding three-point sentence restates the three-point sentence, listing the particular points and bringing the writing to a close. In the sample sentence, the particular points, *lemurs*, *prairie dogs*, and *flamingos*, are named, along with another closing thought.

> Even though I enjoy seeing the other animals, I think lemurs, prairie dogs, and flamingos stand head and shoulders above the rest.

Continued on next page. >>>

Reference 87 continued from previous page.

WRITING THE TITLE

Since there are many possibilities for titles, look at the topic and the three points listed about the topic. Use some of the words in the topic and write a phrase to tell what your essay is about. Your title can be short or long. Capitalize the first, last, and important words in your title.

Title: My Favorite Zoo Animals

Sample Three-Paragraph Essay

My Favorite Zoo Animals

I have several favorite animals I enjoy seeing whenever I go to the zoo. Every time I visit, I spend most of my time watching and learning about my favorite animals. The animals that I especially love to see are lemurs, prairie dogs, and flamingos.

My first favorite animal is the lemur. I think lemurs are unique because they are similar to monkeys but have a fox-like face, large eyes, and a bushy tail. The manner in which lemurs move sets me laughing nearly every time I visit the zoo. My second favorite zoo animal is the prairie dog. I find these short, bushy animals very interesting because they have a sophisticated language that they use to warn other prairie dogs of an approaching predator. After they give their warning call, they bob up and down with excitement before quickly disappearing into their burrows. My third favorite zoo animal is the flamingo. How these large tropical birds stand on one leg and are able to bend their legs backwards amazes me. Their bright pink feathers, which appear to be painted, intrigue me as well.

I delight in watching my favorite animals, and they are on my "must see" list every time I visit the zoo. Even though I enjoy seeing the other animals, I think lemurs, prairie dogs, and flamingos stand head and shoulders above the rest.

Write It: **WRITING ASSIGNMENT 9**

As you write a rough draft for your guided writing assignment, you will do two of the six steps in the writing process: prewriting and rough draft.

Writing Assignment ⑨

Purpose: To inform

Type of Writing: Three-paragraph expository essay

Audience: Classmates or family

Writing Topic: Favorite Animals

Special Instructions:

1. Follow the Prewriting and Rough Draft Checklists in References 44 and 46 on pages 57, 61.

2. Use Reference 83 on page 132 to help you change plural categories to singular points.

3. Use References 84–87 on pages 133–135 to help you write a three-paragraph expository essay.

4. Use standard, time-order, or transition writing form. See Reference 69, page 103.

5. Write in first or third person. See Reference 70, page 104.
   (First-person pronouns: *I, me, my, mine, we, us, our,* and *ours.*)
   (Third-person pronouns: *he, his, him, she, her, hers, it, its, they, their, theirs,* and *them.*)

Note: Reference 54 on page 71 gives the steps in the writing process and the location of all the writing checklists.

English Made Easy

Writing Time

Apply It: REVISE, EDIT, AND WRITE A FINAL PAPER

Following the schedule below, you will revise and edit Writing Assignment 9. Then, you will write a final paper. Use the Chapter 4 Writing Evaluation Guide on the next page to check your final paper one last time.

Lesson 10

You will
- revise, edit, and write a final paper for WA 9.

Reference 52   **Revising & Editing Schedule and Writing a Final Paper**

SPECIAL INSTRUCTIONS FOR REVISING AND EDITING (Steps 3-4 in the writing process):

- Use the Revising and Editing Checklists in References 48 and 50 as you revise and edit your rough draft.
- Follow the revising and editing schedule below as directed by your teacher.

   1. **Individual.** First, read your rough draft to yourself. Use the Revising Checklist in Reference 48 on page 64. Go through your paper, checking each item on the list and making revisions to your rough draft. Then, use the Editing Checklist in Reference 50 on pages 66. Go through your paper again, checking each item on the list and editing your rough draft.

   2. **Partner.** Next, get with your editing partner. Work together on each partner's rough draft, one paper at a time. Read each rough draft aloud and revise and edit it together, using the Revising and Editing Checklists. (The author of the paper should be the one to make the corrections on his own paper.)

   3. **Group.** Finally, read the rough draft to a revision group for feedback. Each student should read his paper while the others listen and offer possible revising and editing suggestions. (The author will determine whether to make corrections from the revision group's suggestions.)

SPECIAL INSTRUCTIONS FOR FINAL PAPER (Step 5 in the writing process):

- Write your final paper, using the Final Paper Checklist in Reference 53 on page 70.
- Staple your writing papers in this order: the final paper on top, the rough draft in the middle, and the prewriting map on the bottom. Place the stapled papers in the Final Paper folder.

>>>>>>>>>> Student Tip...

1. Be tactful and helpful in your comments during revising and editing time. The purpose of any suggestion should be to improve the writer's rough draft.

2. As you make your final corrections, you have the choice of accepting or rejecting any suggestions made by your partners or your revision group.

3. Study Vocabulary Words and Analogies 9–12 for the chapter test in the next lesson.

4. If you need to improve your handwriting, refer to the Resource Tools Section on pages 529–530 for information on writing legibly.

Chapter 4 Writing Evaluation Guide

Name:_____ Date:_____

ROUGH DRAFT CHECK

_____ 1. Did you write your rough draft in pencil?

_____ 2. Did you write the correct headings on the first seven lines of your paper?

_____ 3. Did you use extra wide margins and skip every other line?

_____ 4. Did you write a title at the end of your rough draft?

_____ 5. Did you place your edited rough draft in your Rough Draft folder?

REVISING CHECK

_____ 6. Did you identify the purpose, type of writing, and audience?

_____ 7. Did you check for a topic, topic sentence, and sentences supporting the topic?

_____ 8. Did you check sentences for the right order, and did you combine, rearrange, or delete sentences when necessary?

_____ 9. Did you check for a variety of simple, compound, and complex sentences?

_____ 10. Did you check for any left out, repeated, or unnecessary words?

_____ 11. Did you check for the best choice of words by replacing or deleting unclear words?

_____ 12. Did you check the content for interest and creativity?

_____ 13. Did you check the voice to make sure the writing says what you want it to say?

EDITING CHECK

_____ 14. Did you indent each paragraph?

_____ 15. Did you put an end mark at the end of every sentence?

_____ 16. Did you capitalize the first word of every sentence?

_____ 17. Did you check for all other capitalization mistakes?

_____ 18. Did you check for all punctuation mistakes?
   (commas, periods, apostrophes, quotation marks, underlining)

_____ 19. Did you check for misspelled words and for incorrect homonym choices?

_____ 20. Did you check for incorrect spellings of plural and possessive forms?

_____ 21. Did you check for correct construction and punctuation of your sentences?

_____ 22. Did you check for usage mistakes? *(subject/verb agreement, a/an choices, contractions, verb tenses, pronoun/antecedent agreement, pronoun cases, degrees of adjectives, double negatives, etc.)*

_____ 23. Did you put your revised and edited paper in the Rough Draft folder?

FINAL PAPER CHECK

_____ 24. Did you write the final paper in pencil?

_____ 25. Did you center the title on the top line and center your name under the title?

_____ 26. Did you skip a line before starting the writing assignment?

_____ 27. Did you single-space, use wide margins, and write the final paper neatly?

_____ 28. Did you staple your papers in this order: final paper on top, rough draft in the middle, and prewriting map on the bottom? Did you put them in the Final Paper folder?

START LESSON 11

Lesson 11

You will
- hand in WA 9 for grading.
- respond to oral review questions.
- take Chapter 4 Test.

CHAPTER TEST

It is time to evaluate your knowledge of the skills you have learned in this chapter. Your teacher will give you the Chapter 4 Test to help you assess your progress.

Hand It In: **WRITING ASSIGNMENT 9**

Get your stapled papers for Writing Assignment 9 from your Final Paper folder. Check to make sure they are in the correct order: the final paper on top, the rough draft in the middle, and the prewriting map on the bottom. Hand them in to your teacher.

LISTENING AND SPEAKING:

Discuss It:

1. What are the seven subject pronouns?

2. What are the seven possessive pronouns?

3. What is the definition for a pronoun?

4. What are the three most common coordinate conjunctions?

5. What is the understood subject pronoun?

6. What is the End Mark Flow for the imperative sentence?

7. What are the seven parts of speech you have learned so far?

8. When you use the article **a**, should the next word begin with a consonant or vowel sound?

9. When you use the article **an**, should the next word begin with a consonant or vowel sound?

10. What punctuation is used in a contraction to show that letters have been left out?

11. What are the five core parts of a simple sentence?

12. What is an incomplete sentence called?

13. What is a written discussion of one topic that is made up of several paragraphs?

14. What type of writing is used when your purpose is to inform, to give facts, to give directions, to explain, or to define something?

>>>>>>>>>>>>>> **Student Tip...**

For information about test-taking strategies, refer to the Resource Tools Section on page 528.

Review It: **GOALS**

Review the goals you wrote in your Goal Booklet at the beginning of the school year. Discuss your progress with your teacher or a student partner. Then, write a paragraph in your Goal Booklet that tells how well you are meeting your short-term goals. Give examples that support your evaluation of your progress. Next, write another paragraph to evaluate your long-term goals. Tell whether you want to change them or keep them the same. Give reasons to support either choice. Finally, return your Goal Booklet to your teacher when you have finished.

CHAPTER 5

START LESSON 1

Lesson 1

You will

- study new vocabulary; make card 13; write own sentence using the vocabulary word.
- analyze new analogy; make card 13; write own analogy.
- recite a new jingle (23 Helping Verbs).
- identify helping verbs, the NOT adverb, adverb exception, and natural and inverted order.
- classify Introductory Sentences.
- do a Skill Builder.
- write in your journal.

LISTENING AND SPEAKING:
 Vocabulary & Analogy Time

Learn It: Recite the new vocabulary and analogy words.

Reference 88	Vocabulary & Analogy Words

Word: vague (vāg)
    Definition: not clearly defined or understood
    Synonym: obscure   **Antonym:** clear
    Sentence: An eyewitness could only offer vague information.

Analogy: hoarse : horse :: here : hear
    Homonym relationship: Just as **hoarse** sounds the same as **horse**, **here** sounds the same as **hear**.

Vocabulary Card 13: Record the vocabulary information above and write your own sentence, using the new word.

Analogy Card 13: Record the analogy information and write your own analogy, using the same relationship as the analogy above.

 *Jingle Time*

Recite It: Recite the new jingle.

♪ Jingle 17	The **23** Helping Verbs of the Mean, Lean, Verb Machine Jingle

These twenty-three helping verbs
Will be on my test.
I've gotta remember them so I can do my best.
I'll start out with eight and finish with fifteen.
Just call me the mean, lean, verb machine.

There are the eight **be** verbs
That are easy as can be.
    am, is, are - was and were
    am, is, are - was and were
    am, is, are - was and were
    be, being, and been

All together now, the eight **be** verbs:
am, is, are - was and were - be, being, and been
am, is, are - was and were - be, being, and been
am, is, are - was and were - be, being, and been

There are twenty-three helping verbs,
And I've recited eight.
That leaves fifteen more that I must relate.
Knowing all these verbs will save my grade.
The mean, lean, verb machine is here to stay.
    has, have, and **had - do, does,** and **did**
    has, have, and **had - do, does,** and **did**
    might, must, and **may -**
    might, must, and **may**
    can and **could - would** and **should**
    can and **could - would** and **should**
    shall and **will - shall** and **will**
    has, have, and **had - do, does,** and **did**
    might, must, and **may**
    can and **could, would** and **should**
    shall and **will**
In record time, I did this drill.
I'm the mean, lean, verb machine — STILL!

English Made Easy

Grammar Time

Apply It: These Introductory Sentences are used to apply the new grammar concepts taught below. Classify these sentences orally with your teacher.

Introductory Sentences	Chapter 5: Lesson 1

1. _____ My sister and her husband have been looking for a new house in a quiet neighborhood.

2. _____ Becky did not drive across the flooded highway after the big rain yesterday.

3. _____ The enthusiastic young lawyer often spoke very passionately about his beliefs.

4. _____ Did she complain to her doctor about the sharp pains in her feet?

Learn It: HELPING VERBS

Reference 89   Helping Verbs

1. When two or more verbs make up the simple predicate of a sentence, the verbs in front of the main verb are known as the **helping verbs**. Helping verbs are also called **auxiliary verbs**. Together, the main verb and the helping verbs are called the **verb phrase**.

2. When directions are given to underline the verb, or simple predicate, the helping verb and the main verb are underlined because they are both part of the verb phrase. In the following sentence, the phrase *is running* makes up the verb phrase, and both verbs should be underlined:
    Your neighbor *is running* in the marathon.

3. A *helping verb* is labeled with the abbreviation **HV**. If you are labeling the verb phrase, *is running*, you would label the *helping verb* is with the abbreviation **HV** and the *main verb* running with the abbreviation **V**.

                    HV   V
    Example: Your neighbor is running in the marathon.

4. When a sentence *begins with a helping verb and asks a question*, it is called an **interrogative** sentence and is labeled with the abbreviation **Int**.

            HV PPA   SN   V   P A   OP
    Example: Is your neighbor running (in the marathon)? *Int*

Learn It: NOT ADVERB

Reference 90   The NOT Adverb

Sometimes, the helping verb can be split from the main verb by the adverb *NOT*. Even though the word *NOT* is an adverb, it is often confused as part of a verb phrase. The word *NOT* is an adverb telling *how*. Most negative words are adverbs telling *how* or *to what extent*.

  Example: We did not yell for the opposing team.

        (We did yell how? **not - adverb**)

Learn It: ADVERB EXCEPTION

📖 Reference 91 — **Adverb Exception**

An **adverb exception** occurs when an adverb comes immediately before the verb in a sentence. To add a check for an adverb exception to the Question and Answer Flow, ask,

"Is there an adverb exception?"

1. If there is not an adverb before the verb, answer, **"No,"** and the dividing line is not changed.
   Standard: The young soldiers / advanced swiftly.

2. If there is an adverb before the verb, answer, **"Yes - change the line,"** and the dividing line is moved in front of the adverb. Now, the adverb is the first word in the predicate.
   Adverb Exception: The young soldiers / swiftly advanced.

Note: If there is an adverb between the helping verb and the main verb, it is **not** an adverb exception.
   Standard: The young soldiers / are swiftly advancing.

Learn It: NATURAL AND INVERTED WORD ORDER

📖 Reference 92 — **Natural and Inverted Word Order**

A **Natural-Order** sentence has all subject parts before the verb and all predicate parts starting with the verb.

The word **inverted** means to reverse the position of something. Therefore, **Inverted Word Order** in a sentence means that some of the predicate words are located at the beginning of the complete subject, and the rest of the predicate words are located after the verb.

There are three ways a sentence can have inverted word order. An inverted-order sentence can have an **adverb**, a **helping verb**, or a **prepositional phrase** at the beginning of the sentence. Even though these words are located at the beginning of the complete subject, they modify the verb and are considered part of the predicate. These predicate words in the subject are inverted parts and cause the sentence to have an inverted word order. Using this inverted order in your writing is a way to give your sentences more variety.

1. **An adverb at the beginning of a sentence modifies the verb.**
   Inverted Order: Yesterday, we / went to the school play.

   Natural Order: We / went to the school play yesterday.

2. **A helping verb at the beginning of a sentence is part of the verb. It usually forms a question.**
   Inverted Order: Are you / going to the game?

   Natural Order: You / are going to the game.

3. **A prepositional phrase at the beginning of a sentence modifies the verb.**
   Inverted Order: After the exciting homecoming game, all the fans / went to the victory celebration.

   Natural Order: All the fans / went to the victory celebration after the exciting homecoming game.

To add an inverted-order check to the Question and Answer Flow, ask,

"Is this sentence in a natural or inverted order?"

1. If there are no predicate words at the beginning of the complete subject, answer, **"Natural - No change."**
   Natural Order: Our family / went to a nice restaurant before the movie.

2. If there are predicate words at the beginning of the complete subject, answer, **"Inverted - underline the subject parts once and the predicate parts twice."**
   Inverted Order: Before the movie, our family / went to a nice restaurant.

LISTENING AND SPEAKING:

Skill Builder

Using the sentences just classified, do a Skill Builder orally with your teacher.

1. Identify the nouns in a Noun Check.
2. Identify the nouns as singular or plural.
3. Identify the nouns as common or proper.
4. Identify the complete subject and the complete predicate.
5. Identify the simple subject and the simple predicate.
6. Do a Vocabulary Check.

JOURNAL WRITING 10

Write an entry in your journal. Use Reference 9 on page 12 for ideas.

START LESSON 2

Lesson 2

You will

- study new vocabulary; make card 14; write own sentence using the vocabulary word.
- analyze new analogy; make card 14; write own analogy.
- practice Jingle 17.
- classify Practice Sentences.
- do a Skill Builder.
- identify compound sentences, comma splices, run-on sentences, coordinating conjunctions, and connective adverbs.
- do Classroom Practice 20.
- read and discuss Discovery Time.

LISTENING AND SPEAKING:

Vocabulary & Analogy Time

Learn It: Recite the new vocabulary and analogy words.

Reference 93	Vocabulary & Analogy Words

Word: callous (kăl'əs)
  Definition: without feeling
  Synonym: insensitive   **Antonym:** compassionate
  Sentence: His callous remark offended his friend.

Analogy: hot : cold :: ease : difficulty
  Antonym relationship: Just as **hot** is the opposite of **cold**,
                    ease is the opposite of **difficulty**.

Vocabulary Card 14: Record the vocabulary information above and write your own sentence, using the new word.

    Analogy Card 14: Record the analogy information and write your own analogy, using the same relationship as the analogy above.

Jingle Time

Recite It: Practice Jingle 17 in the Jingle Section on page 510.

Grammar Time

Apply It: Classify the Practice Sentences orally with your teacher.

Practice Sentences	Chapter 5: Lesson 2

1. _____ During their expedition, the explorers could not adjust to the high altitude of the mountain.

2. _____ Dana and I eagerly traveled around the world for our interviews with world leaders.

3. _____ Did Leo and Tyler dig for clams on the beach in Georgia during their spring break?

LISTENING AND SPEAKING:

Skill Builder

Using the sentences just classified, do a Skill Builder orally with your teacher.

1. **Identify the nouns in a Noun Check.**
2. **Identify the nouns as singular or plural.**
3. **Identify the nouns as common or proper.**
4. **Identify the complete subject and the complete predicate.**
5. **Identify the simple subject and the simple predicate.**
6. **Do a Vocabulary Check.**

Learn It: COORDINATE CONJUNCTIONS AND CONNECTIVE ADVERBS

 Reference 94 | **Coordinate Conjunctions and Connective Adverbs**

COORDINATE CONJUNCTIONS

Conjunctions join words or groups of words together. Conjunctions that join things of equal importance are called **coordinate**, or **coordinating conjunctions**. There are seven coordinate conjunctions: **and, or, but, nor, yet, for,** and **so**. The seven coordinate conjunctions and how they are used are listed below.

Add information	Show contrast or choice	Show logic or result
, and	, but	, for
, nor	, or	, so (as a result of)
	, yet	so (that)—no comma

CONNECTIVE ADVERBS

When an adverb is used to connect sentences, it is called a **connective adverb**. Connective adverbs are often used as transition words between ideas. A connective adverb always uses two punctuation marks: a semicolon before it and a comma after it. A connective adverb is also called a **conjunctive adverb**. Some of the connective adverbs and how they are used are listed below.

Add information	Show contrast or choice	Show logic or result
; also,	; however,	; accordingly,
; besides,	; nevertheless,	; consequently,
; furthermore,	; otherwise,	; hence,
; likewise,		; so,
; moreover,		; therefore,
		; thus,

Learn It: COMPOUND SENTENCE

 Reference 95 | **The Compound Sentence**

The word **compound** means two. A **compound sentence** is the result of two simple sentences being joined together. The abbreviation for a *compound sentence* is **CD**. To make a *compound sentence*, join two simple sentences in one of the ways listed below. The information in parentheses at the end of each sentence shows how the *compound sentence* was made.

Continued on next page. >>>

Reference 95 continued from previous page.

1. **Compound sentence:** Use a comma and a coordinate conjunction.
    Example: I looked for my keys, but I could not find them. (CD, but)

2. **Compound sentence:** Use a semicolon, a connective adverb, and a comma.
    Example: I looked for my keys; however, I could not find them. (CD; however,)

3. **Compound sentence:** Use a semicolon only.
    Example: I looked for my keys; I could not find them. (CD;)

Compound sentences should be closely related in thought and importance.
    Correct: I looked for my keys, but I could not find them.

    Incorrect: I looked for my keys, but I failed my science test today.

›››››››››››› Student Tip...

Use the following information as a visual aid to help you construct compound sentences.
Simple Sentence + Simple Sentence = Compound Sentence
Joining two simple sentences in one of the following ways forms a compound sentence.
1. Two simple sentences joined by a comma and a conjunction.
    _____, and _____.
2. Two simple sentences joined by a semicolon, a connective adverb, and a comma.
    _____; therefore, _____.
3. Two simple sentences joined by a semicolon.
    _____; _____.

Learn It: COMMA SPLICES AND RUN-ON SENTENCES

Reference 96 — Comma Splices and Run-on Sentences

Two common mistakes are often made when joining simple sentences together to make a compound sentence. The first mistake is called a **comma splice**. The second mistake is called a **run-on sentence**.

1. A *comma splice occurs* when simple sentences are connected with a comma but without a conjunction.
    Incorrect: I looked for my keys, I could not find them.
To correct a comma splice, put a coordinate conjunction after the comma.
    Correct: I looked for my keys, but I could not find them.

2. A *run-on sentence occurs* in one of two ways.
    a. When the simple sentences are written together with a conjunction but without a comma.
       Incorrect: I looked for my keys but I could not find them.
    b. When the simple sentences are written together as one sentence without a comma or a conjunction.
       Incorrect: I looked for my keys I could not find them.

Use one of three strategies *to correct a run-on sentence*.

1. Put a comma and a coordinate conjunction between the two simple sentences.
    Correct: I looked for my keys, but I could not find them.

2. Put a semicolon, a connective adverb, and a comma between the two simple sentences.
    Correct: I looked for my keys; however, I could not find them.

3. Put a semicolon between the two simple sentences.
    Correct: I looked for my keys; I could not find them.

>>>>>>>>>> **Student Tip...**

> There are two times when you should put a comma in front of the conjunction and:
> 1. When you have three or more items in a series.
> 2. When you are connecting two simple sentences using and as a coordinate conjunction to make a compound sentence.

Learn It: CORRECTING RUN-ON SENTENCES

 Reference 97 — **Using Compound Sentences to Correct Run-On Sentences**

Use a slash to separate each run-on sentence below. Then, correct each run-on sentence by rewriting it as indicated by the labels in parentheses at the end of the sentence. **Example:** (**CD, but**) means to write a **compound sentence**, using a **comma** and the conjunction **but**.

PRACTICE EXAMPLES

1. Marty enjoyed the movie / he didn't like the popcorn.   (**CD, but**)
   Marty enjoyed the movie, but he didn't like the popcorn.

2. The young man began work at 5:00 each morning / he went to bed early at night.   (**CD; therefore,**)
   The young man began work at 5:00 each morning; therefore, he went to bed early at night.

3. I work out every day / exercise makes me feel great!   (**CD;**)
   I work out every day; exercise makes me feel great!

Learn It: IDENTIFYING TYPES OF SENTENCES

 Reference 98 — **Identifying S, F, SCS, SCV, and CD**

Directions: Identify each type of sentence by writing the correct label in the blank. (**Labels: S, F, SCS, SCV, CD**).

_CD_ 1. Samuel squinted at the computer screen; however, he could not see the symbols clearly.

SCS 2. Margaret and Tommy walk two miles together every day.

_F_ 3. Participated in basketball, football, and track.

_CD_ 4. We ate cheese and crackers for a snack, but we did not eat cookies.

SCV 5. My mother baked bread and muffins and boiled shrimp for our supper.

_S_ 6. The snowstorm dumped three feet of snow on our small town.

 Classroom Practice 20

It is time to practice the skills you are learning. You will use the classroom practice on page 149 to apply these skills.

ENRICHMENT:

(Scottish) 1736-1819— James Watt perfected the steam engine and coined the term "horsepower," which he used to calculate what companies saved by using his steam engine.

Discovery Questions:
- **What electrical unit was named in Watt's honor?**
- **What affect do you think the steam engine had on the way people worked and traveled?**
- **What inventions affect the way people work and travel today?**

Are you interested in learning more about James Watt?

1. You may explore this topic further by using the resources listed below.
   Computer resources: Internet, encyclopedia software
   Library resources: encyclopedias, books, magazines, newspapers
   Home/community resources: books, interviews, newspapers, magazines

2. A Discovery Share Time is provided in Lesson 7 if you wish to share your investigation results. You may share orally, or you may prepare a written report. You will put your written report in a class booklet titled "Notable People in History." This booklet will be placed in the class library for everyone to enjoy.

Classroom Practice 20

Name:_____ Date:_____

GRAMMAR

▶ **Exercise 1:** Classify each sentence.

1. _____ Yesterday, Eddie and his brother did not arrive at the coliseum in time for the concert.

2. _____ A huge riot suddenly erupted in the city streets of Italy after the chaotic soccer match!

SKILLS

▶ **Exercise 2:** Identify each type of sentence by writing the correct label in the blank. (**Labels: S, F, SCS, SCV, CD**)

_____ 1. Scrubbing the hideous stain on the floor.
_____ 2. The scent of fresh fudge filled the air, and it was mouthwatering.
_____ 3. The leaves and stems were wilted from the intense heat.
_____ 4. Emma dribbled around the guard and shot the ball.
_____ 5. It was cold outside; I wore my heavy coat.
_____ 6. The waitress brought our food orders and refilled our drinks.
_____ 7. Darren kicked the football, but he missed the field goal.
_____ 8. The team was finally defeated; therefore, they were no longer the champions.
_____ 9. Pine cones and acorns littered our front yard.

▶ **Exercise 3:** Use a slash to separate each run-on sentence below. Then, correct the run-on sentences by rewriting them as indicated by the labels in parentheses at the end of each sentence.

1. The sky was cloudy it did not rain. (**CD; however,**)
_____

2. The competition was fierce everyone kept a positive attitude. (**CD, yet**)
_____

3. Jackson and Mariana are leaving before noon I am leaving with them. (**SCS**)
_____

4. The lecture was long I took detailed notes until the end. (**CD, but**)
_____

5. Reggie washed his car Saturday afternoon He also waxed it. (**SCV**)
_____

EDITING

▶ **Exercise 4:** Correct each mistake. **Editing Guide: End Marks: 6   Capitals: 6   Commas: 4   Apostrophes: 1   Homonyms: 4   A/An: 2   Subject-Verb Agreement: 5   Misspelled Words: 1**

judy digs threw her purse in an panic but she cant find her keys she look in the

car and in the driveway but her keys are not their judy is getting hot so she take off her

coat suddenly she hear her keys rattling in her coat pocket they has been there the hole time

she breathes an sigh of releaf and head happily two her car

SHURLEY ENGLISH

START LESSON 3

Lesson 3

You will

- study new vocabulary; make card 15; write own sentence using the vocabulary word.
- analyze new analogy; make card 15; write own analogy.
- practice Jingles 13–17.
- classify Practice Sentences.
- do a Skill Builder.
- do Classroom Practice 21.
- write in your journal.
- read and discuss Discovery Time.

LISTENING AND SPEAKING:

Vocabulary & Analogy Time

Learn It: Recite the new vocabulary and analogy words.

Reference 99	Vocabulary & Analogy Words

Word: buoyant (boi'ənt)
  Definition: able to float
  Synonym: unsinkable   **Antonym:** sinkable
  Sentence: The buoyant raft drifted out to sea.

Analogy: star : constellation :: ship : fleet
  Part-to-whole relationship: Just as a **star** is part of a **constellation**, a **ship** is part of a **fleet**.

Vocabulary Card 15: Record the vocabulary information above and write your own sentence, using the new word.

Analogy Card 15: Record the analogy information and write your own analogy, using the same relationship as the analogy above.

Jingle Time

Recite It: Practice Jingles 13–17 in the Jingle Section on pages 509–510.

Grammar Time

Apply It: Classify the Practice Sentences orally with your teacher.

Practice Sentences	Chapter 5: Lesson 3

1. _____ During the party, her prized dolls proudly sat on the shelf in their evening gowns.

2. _____ The monkeys at the zoo scattered in all directions and screamed at Antonio and Frank.

3. _____ Stand on top of the bleachers for a better view of the game.

LISTENING AND SPEAKING:

Skill Builder

Using the sentences just classified, do a Skill Builder orally with your teacher.

1. Identify the nouns in a Noun Check.
2. Identify the nouns as singular or plural.
3. Identify the nouns as common or proper.
4. Identify the complete subject and the complete predicate.
5. Identify the simple subject and the simple predicate.
6. Do a Vocabulary Check.

Classroom Practice 21

It is time to practice the skills you are learning. You will use the classroom practice on the next page to apply these skills.

ENRICHMENT:

Discovery Time

(American) 1743-1826— Thomas Jefferson was the third president of the United States. He was also a farmer, lawyer, architect, inventor, naturalist, philosopher, and scientist.

Discovery Questions:
- What famous statement did Jefferson write that is found in the Declaration of Independence?
- What do you think Thomas Jefferson would say about our government today?
- What do you like most about Thomas Jefferson?

Are you interested in learning more about Thomas Jefferson?

1. You may explore this topic further by using the resources listed below.
   Computer resources: Internet, encyclopedia software
   Library resources: encyclopedias, books, magazines, newspapers
   Home/community resources: books, interviews, newspapers, magazines

2. A Discovery Share Time is provided in Lesson 7 if you wish to share your investigation results. You may share orally, or you may prepare a written report. You will put your written report in a class booklet titled "Notable People in History." This booklet will be placed in the class library for everyone to enjoy.

JOURNAL WRITING 11

Write an entry in your journal. Use Reference 9 on page 12 for ideas.

Classroom Practice 21

Name:_____ Date:_____

GRAMMAR

▶ **Exercise 1:** Classify each sentence.

1. _____ Did Eddie and Bo travel to the East by train for their vacation?

2. _____ Yesterday, the pilot of the huge jet finally landed safely with two damaged engines!

SKILLS

▶ **Exercise 2:** Identify each type of sentence by writing the correct label in the blank. (**Labels: S, F, SCS, SCV, CD**)

_____ 1. The tiny feather drifted slowly and landed on the ground.

_____ 2. Dad watched television; Mom read a book.

_____ 3. Our dog and cat pawed at the back door.

_____ 4. Crammed into the crowded elevator.

_____ 5. Anne vacuumed the carpet, and Lydia dusted the furniture.

▶ **Exercise 3:** Use a slash to separate each run-on sentence below. Then, correct the run-on sentences by rewriting them as indicated by the labels in parentheses at the end of each sentence.

1. The eager boy fished with his father they caught no fish. (**CD, but**)

   _____

2. The eager boy fished with his father they caught no fish. (**CD; however,**)

   _____

3. The eager boy talked with his father he fished with his father. (**SCV**)

   _____

4. The eager boy fished with his father they caught no fish. (**CD;**)

   _____

5. The boy was fishing with his father the girl was fishing with her father. (**SCS**)

   _____

EDITING

▶ **Exercise 4:** Correct each mistake. **Editing Guide: End Marks: 5   Capitals: 5   Commas: 2   Homonyms: 2   A/An: 1**
   Subject-Verb Agreement: 6   Misspelled Words: 1

jill suddenly hear a unhappy howl she look out the window and see her hunting dog

all tangled up again his chain is in one huge not and he cannot reach his water he are looking

toward the door with sorrowful eyes jill untangle him and he lick her hand and wags his tale

English Made Easy

LISTENING AND SPEAKING:
Vocabulary & Analogy Time

Learn It: Recite the new vocabulary and analogy words.

📖 Reference 100	Vocabulary & Analogy Words

Word: hindrance (hĭn'drəns)
   Definition: something that prevents
   Synonym: obstacle   **Antonym:** aid
   Sentence: The detour was a hindrance to their travel.

Analogy: flake : snow :: drop : rain
   Part-to-whole relationship: Just as **flake** is a part of **snow**,
                                    drop is a part of **rain**.

Vocabulary Card 16: Record the vocabulary information above and write your own
                        sentence, using the new word.
Analogy Card 16: Record the analogy information and write your own analogy,
                      using the same relationship as the analogy above.

Jingle Time

Recite It: Practice Jingles 3–11 in the Jingle Section on pages 507–508.

Grammar Time

Apply It: Classify the Practice Sentences orally with your teacher.

Practice Sentences	Chapter 5: Lesson 4

1. _____ The homecoming queen and her court smiled and waved at
   the crowd during halftime.

2. _____ Fly to Europe immediately for a special meeting with the
   president of the company.

3. _____ Did the bank employees at the downtown branch vote
   unanimously for a Christmas banquet?

Lesson 4
You will
- study new vocabulary; make card 16; write own sentence using the vocabulary word.
- analyze new analogy; make card 16; write own analogy.
- practice Jingles 3–11.
- classify Practice Sentences.
- do a Skill Builder.
- do Classroom Practice 22.
- read and discuss Discovery Time.
- do a homework assignment.
- do Home Connection activity.

LISTENING AND SPEAKING:

Skill Builder

Using the sentences just classified, do a Skill Builder orally with your teacher.

1. **Identify the nouns in a Noun Check.**
2. **Identify the nouns as singular or plural.**
3. **Identify the nouns as common or proper.**
4. **Identify the complete subject and the complete predicate.**
5. **Identify the simple subject and the simple predicate.**
6. **Do a Vocabulary Check.**

Classroom Practice 22

It is time to practice the skills you are learning. You will use the classroom practice on the next page to apply these skills.

ENRICHMENT:

Discovery Time

(Austrian) 1756-1791— Wolfgang Amadeus Mozart is considered one of the greatest musical geniuses of all time. He was composing and performing music by the age of six. In the 35 short years that he lived, his contributions to classical music included 16 operas, 41 symphonies, 25 string quartets, 19 masses, 27 piano concerts, and 5 violin concerts.

Discovery Questions:
- **What was the name given to Mozart when he was baptized?**
- **How did Mozart's music affect the musical world?**
- **How is Mozart's music different from music today?**
- **Do you like classical music?**
- **Do you like Mozart's music?**

Are you interested in learning more about Wolfgang Amadeus Mozart?

1. You may explore this topic further by using the resources listed below.
   Computer resources: Internet, encyclopedia software
   Library resources: encyclopedias, books, magazines, newspapers
   Home/community resources: books, interviews, newspapers, magazines

2. A Discovery Share Time is provided in Lesson 7 if you wish to share your investigation results. You may share orally, or you may prepare a written report. You will put your written report in a class booklet titled "Notable People in History." This booklet will be placed in the class library for everyone to enjoy.

Classroom Practice 22

Name:_____ Date:_____

GRAMMAR

▶ **Exercise 1:** Classify each sentence.

1. _____ At noon, the signal light at the intersection was not working.

2. _____ Melinda and Marie sing beautifully with the grace and style of concert performers.

▶ **Exercise 2:** List the seven parts of speech you have studied so far.

1. _____ 2._____ 3._____ 4._____ 5._____ 6._____ 7._____

SKILLS

▶ **Exercise 3:** Identify each type of sentence by writing the correct label in the blank. (**Labels: S, F, SCS, SCV, CD**)

_____ 1. Our knives and forks are packed away.
_____ 2. Had long, curly hair with a red bow to match her red dress.
_____ 3. Claire poured the milk in a large glass, and Lori drank it.
_____ 4. My brothers went to the library but did not get any books.
_____ 5. The homework was hard; however, I did it.

▶ **Exercise 4:** Use a slash to separate each run-on sentence below. Then, correct the run-on sentences by rewriting them as indicated by the labels in parentheses at the end of each sentence.

1. You must answer the phone you will miss your call. (**CD; otherwise,**)

_____

2. You must answer the phone you will miss your call. (**CD, or**)

_____

3. Answer the phone take a message. (**SCV**)

_____

4. Carla will answer the phone Amelia will answer the phone. (**SCS**)

_____

5. The mountain climber struggled he made it to the top. (**CD, but**)

_____

6. Kerri is at band practice until 6:00 Terri is at band practice until 6:00. (**SCS**)

_____

EDITING

▶ **Exercise 5:** Correct each mistake. **Editing Guide: End Marks: 4   Capitals: 10   Commas: 3   Homonyms: 3   Subject-Verb Agreement: 1   Misspelled Words: 2**

i made eggs and biscuits four jermaine and reggie this morning they was tasty in fact

jermaine ate fore eggs and reggie ate to after breckfast the boys left for school at dover collage

Homework 3

Complete this homework assignment on notebook paper.

1. Copy the sentence below. Classify the sentence, using the Question and Answer Flow, as you label each part.

_____ Fly to Europe immediately for a special meeting with the president of the company.

2. Use the four ways listed below to correct the run-on sentence.
   Jared washed the car Simon helped him.

   1. CD, and   (Key: **Jared washed the car, and Simon helped him.**)
   2. CD; furthermore,   (Key: **Jared washed the car; furthermore, Simon helped him.**)
   3. CD;   (Key: **Jared washed the car; Simon helped him.**)
   4. SCS   (Key: **Jared and Simon washed the car.**)

3. Number your paper 1–5. Identify each type of sentence by writing the correct label.
   (**Labels: S, F, SCS, SCV, CD**)

   _____ 1. Our cookies and milk are on the table in the kitchen.

   _____ 2. In the corner by the mop and broom.

   _____ 3. Carey baked a cake for the party, and Michael made the decorations.

   _____ 4. Peggy mopped and waxed the floor in the den.

   _____ 5. The semester exam was hard; however, I passed it.

4. Write three compound sentences. For the first sentence, connect the two sentences with a comma and a conjunction (**and, but, or**). For the second sentence, connect the two sentences with a semicolon, connective adverb, and comma. For the third sentence, connect the two sentences with a semicolon only. Double-check each sentence for correct punctuation.

Home Connection

Family Activity for Helping Verbs

1. In a newspaper or magazine article, underline the helping verbs and circle the main verbs.

2. Pretend your family has formed a band, and the band is performing the Helping Verb Jingle at a jingle concert. Each member must devise a homemade instrument to play. Practice at least three times before the concert. Invite friends and relatives to the performance. For more fun, add other jingles and individual performances to the concert. Make and illustrate programs for the concert, listing the time, place, performers, and sponsors. Video the concert to show those who could not attend. Write an article for the local newspaper about the jingle concert.

Family Activity for Vocabulary and Analogies

Divide into family teams. The first team will use vocabulary and analogy cards 9–12 to ask questions about the information on their cards. The second team will use vocabulary and analogy cards 13–16 to ask questions about the information on their cards.

For vocabulary words:
- What is the definition of the word?
- Name a synonym and antonym for the word.
- Create a new sentence using the word.
- Find the word in another source (dictionary, newspaper, magazine, advertisement, etc.)

For analogies:
- What is the answer to the analogy?
- What is the relationship of the analogy?
- Make another analogy with the same relationship.
- Make another analogy with a different relationship.

English Made Easy

LISTENING AND SPEAKING:

Grammar Time

Apply It: Classify the Practice Sentences orally with your teacher.

Practice Sentences	Chapter 5: Lesson 5

1. _____ Groundhogs and chipmunks scampered over the rocks and hurried to their homes before dark!

2. _____ Were the castaways stranded on a deserted island for several months?

3. _____ Yesterday, Maggie did not work through the test with speed and confidence.

Chapter Checkup 23

It is time for a checkup of the skills you have learned in this chapter. You will use the chapter checkup on the next page to evaluate your progress.

ENRICHMENT:

Discovery Time

(American) 1758-1843— Noah Webster is famous for his *American Dictionary of the English Language*, which has become the standard dictionary of the English language.

Discovery Questions:
- **How long did it take Webster to write his dictionary?**
- **Do you think you could devote your life to an endeavor such as this?**
- **Why was Webster's dictionary so important?**

(American) 1765-1825— Eli Whitney invented the cotton gin and created a new design for a musket that could be manufactured in bulk by specially designed machinery. Previously, no two muskets were alike because they were built by hand. With this idea, Whitney gave birth to the concept of mass production of interchangeable parts and the assembly line.

Discovery Questions:
- **How did Whitney's inventions change the United States?**

Are you interested in learning more about Noah Webster or Eli Whitney?

1. You may explore these topics further by using the resources listed below.
   Computer resources: Internet, encyclopedia software
   Library resources: encyclopedias, books, magazines, newspapers
   Home/community resources: books, interviews, newspapers, magazines

2. A Discovery Share Time is provided in Lesson 7 if you wish to share your investigation results. You may share orally, or you may prepare a written report. You will put your written report in a class booklet titled "Notable People in History." This booklet will be placed in the class library for everyone to enjoy.

START LESSON 5

Lesson 5

You will
- classify Practice Sentences.
- do Chapter Checkup 23.
- write in your journal.
- read and discuss Discovery Time.

JOURNAL WRITING 12

Write an entry in your journal. Use Reference 9 on page 12 for ideas.

Chapter 5 Checkup 23

Name:_____ Date:_____

GRAMMAR

▶ **Exercise 1:** Classify each sentence.

1. _____ The skydiver did not hesitate for a second during his first jump!

2. _____ During the summer, Joan and Dana frequently jogged around the track.

3. _____ Will you come to the school play with Sam and me on Saturday?

SKILLS

▶ **Exercise 2:** Identify each type of sentence by writing the correct label in the blank. (**Labels: S, F, SCS, SCV, CD**)

_____ 1. The Halloween candy on sale in the stores.
_____ 2. I jog in the mornings; my sister jogs in the evenings.
_____ 3. We yelled and cheered with the cheerleaders throughout the game.
_____ 4. My alarm did not go off; otherwise, I would have been on time.
_____ 5. Waves crashed against the rocks and rolled back out to sea.
_____ 6. We play in the sand along the beach near our home.
_____ 7. The rooster and two hens pecked for insects in the yard.
_____ 8. Sam must finish his chores, or he cannot go to the movie tonight.

▶ **Exercise 3:** Use a slash to separate each run-on sentence below. Then, correct the run-on sentences by rewriting them as indicated by the labels in parentheses at the end of each sentence.

1. The artist painted a picture he cleaned his brushes. (**CD, and**)

_____

2. The artist painted several pictures his student painted several pictures. (**SCS**)

_____

3. The artist painted a picture he cleaned his brushes. (**SCV**)

_____

4. The students had much work to do they went to recess. (**CD; however,**)

_____

5. The newborn colt struggled to his feet he was still wobbly. (**CD, but**)

_____

EDITING

▶ **Exercise 4:** Correct each mistake. **Editing Guide: End Marks: 3   Capitals: 11   Commas: 1   Homonyms: 4   Subject-Verb Agreement: 2   Misspelled Words: 1**

doug and i arrives on a plain from houston inn time four the annual maple syrup festival in

rutland vermont the hole town turns out for this delishous celebration doug and i loves the food

English Made Easy

Writing Time

Write It: WRITING ASSIGNMENT 10

Writing Assignment [10]: Creative Expressions

Purpose: To entertain

Type of Writing: Creative

Audience: Classmates, friends, or family members

Choose one of the writing topics below.

1. If you could live anywhere, where would you live? Why? Would your life be better? How do you know?

2. There have been many inventions. Is there anything left to invent? What would you invent and how would it be used?

3. Write a poem about inventions or about a topic of your choice.

Special Instructions:

1. A prewriting map is not required for this creative-writing assignment.

2. Follow the Rough Draft Checklist in Reference 46 on page 61.

3. Put your creative-writing paper in your Rough Draft folder when you have finished.

Note: Reference 54 on page 71 gives the steps in the writing process and the location of all the writing checklists.

Lesson 6

You will

- conference with teacher about WA 9.

- write a creative writing piece for WA 10.

 Student Tip...

> For more information about writing poetry, look at Chapter 18 on pages 465–482.

Conference Time

Discuss It: TEACHER-STUDENT CONFERENCES FOR WRITING ASSIGNMENT 9

Meet with your teacher to discuss Writing Assignment 9.
After the conference, place this group of papers in your Publishing folder.

START LESSON 7

Lesson 7

You will

- publish WA 9.
- participate in Discovery Share Time.
- do Across the Curriculum activity.

Publishing Time

Publish It: **WRITING ASSIGNMENT 9**

Choose a publishing form and publish Writing Assignment 9. After rewriting your paper for publication, give the stapled papers (evaluation guide, graded final paper, rough draft, and prewriting map) to your teacher to be placed in your Writing Portfolio.

Reference 66	**Publishing Checklist for Step 6 in the Writing Process**

The sixth step in the writing process is called publishing. Publishing is sharing your writing with others. With so many forms of publishing available, finding a match for every project and personality is easy.

At times, a written work is best read aloud. Other times, the biggest impact is made when a written work is read silently. You can also use media sources to enhance any publication.

SPECIAL INSTRUCTIONS FOR PUBLISHING:

- Rewrite the graded paper in ink or type it on a computer, correcting any marked errors. *(Do not display or publish papers that have marked errors or grades on them.)*
- Give your teacher the set of stapled papers to place in your Writing Portfolio. *(Stapled papers: evaluation guide, graded final paper, rough draft, and prewriting map.)*
- Select a publishing form from the list below and publish your rewritten paper.
    1. Have classmates, family members, neighbors, or others read your writing at school or home.
    2. Share your writing with others during a Share Time. *(Refer to Reference 67 on page 99 for sharing guidelines.)*
    3. Display your writing on a bulletin board or wall.
    4. Put your writing in the classroom library or in the school library for checkout.
    5. Send your writing as a letter or an e-mail to a friend or relative.
    6. Frame your writing by gluing it on colored construction paper and decorating it.
    7. Make a book of your writing for your classroom, your family, or others.
    8. Illustrate your writing and give it to others to read.
    9. Dramatize your writing in the form of a play, puppet show, or radio broadcast.
    10. Send your writing to be placed in a waiting room (doctor, veterinarian, dentist, etc.), senior-citizen center, or a nursing home.
    11. Send your writing to a school newspaper, local newspaper, or a magazine for publication.
    12. Make a videotape, cassette tape, or slide presentation of your writing.
    13. Choose another publishing form that is not listed.

LISTENING AND SPEAKING:

If you have chosen to investigate a historical figure introduced in this chapter, you now have the opportunity to share your results in one of the following ways:

1. You may relate your information orally.

2. You may read a written report.

3. You may place your report in the booklet without reading it aloud.

After share time, all written reports should be turned in to be placed in the class booklet titled "Notable People in History." You are encouraged to check out this class booklet so you can enjoy the reports again.

Math Connection: Write your own math word problem. Use as many common and proper nouns as possible. Solve the word problem at the bottom of the paper and write the answer on the back. Next, exchange papers with a partner. Underline the common nouns once and circle the proper nouns. Read the math problems to each other and discuss the importance of nouns in math. Then, put all of the word problems together to make a math booklet for the class.

SHURLEY ENGLISH

Lesson 8

You will
- practice Jingle 2.
- do Classroom Practice 24.
- write an independent expository essay (WA 11).

LISTENING AND SPEAKING:

Jingle Time

Recite It: Practice Jingle 2 in the Jingle Section on page 506.

GRAMMAR & WRITING CONNECTION:
Practice and Revised Sentence

Apply It: BUILDING AND EXPANDING SENTENCES

Reference 101

A Guide for Using Helping Verbs and the Not Adverb to Build & Expand Sentences

1. **HV** (*helping verb*) Recite the Helping Verb Jingle to help you choose a helping verb for your sentence. You may use more than one helping verb with your main verb. Before you write your helping verb, make sure it makes sense in your sentence. Repeat this step for each helping verb you add to the sentence. If you write an interrogative sentence, put a question mark at the end.

2. Sometimes, the helping verb can be split from the main verb by the *NOT* adverb . Even though the word *not* is an adverb, it is often confused as part of a verb phrase. The word *NOT* is an adverb telling *how*. Most negative words are adverbs telling *how* or *to what extent*. If you choose to use the NOT adverb, write it in your sentence.

Student Tip...

Use your vocabulary words in your Practice and Revised Sentences. Use a thesaurus, synonym-antonym book, or a dictionary to help you develop your writing vocabulary.

✏ Classroom Practice 24

It is time to practice the skills you are learning. You will use the classroom practice on the next page to apply these skills.

Writing Time

Write It: WRITING ASSIGNMENT 11

As you write a rough draft for your independent writing assignment, you will do two of the six steps in the writing process: prewriting and rough draft.

Writing Assignment 11

Purpose: To inform
Type of Writing: Three-paragraph expository essay
Audience: Classmates
Writing Topics: Reasons for Having a Good/Bad Day
Least Favorite Chores/Subjects/Foods
Favorite Eating Places
(Brainstorm for other ideas, individually or in groups.)

Special Instructions:
1. Follow the Prewriting and Rough Draft Checklists in References 44 and 46 on pages 57, 61.
2. Use References 83–87 on pages 132–135 to help you write a three-paragraph expository essay.
3. Use standard, time-order, or transition writing form. See Reference 69, page 103.
4. Write in first or third person. See Reference 70, page 104.
(First-person pronouns: *I, me, my, mine, we, us, our, and ours.*)
(Third-person pronouns: *he, his, him, she, her, hers, it, its, they, their, theirs,* and *them.*)
Note: Reference 54 on page 71 gives the steps in the writing process and the location of all the writing checklists.

Student Note:
Some of your writing pieces will be selected for revision and editing later in the school year.

Classroom Practice 24

INDEPENDENT PRACTICE & REVISED SENTENCES

1. Write a Practice Sentence according to the labels you choose.
   Use **SN/SP V** as your main labels. You may use the other labels in any order and as many times as you wish in order to make a Practice Sentence.
   Chapter 5 labels for a Practice Sentence: **SN/SP, V**, Adj, Adv, A, P, OP, PPA, C, HV

2. Write a Revised Sentence. Use the following revision strategies: *synonym (syn), antonym (ant), word change (wc), added word (add), deleted word (delete),* or *no change (nc)*. Under each word, write the abbreviation of the revision strategy you use.

Labels:

Practice:

Revised:

Strategies:

Labels:

Practice:

Revised:

Strategies:

Labels:

Practice:

Revised:

Strategies:

START LESSON 9

Lesson 9

You will

- practice Jingle 12.
- read and discuss a five-paragraph essay.
- plan and write rough draft for expository essay (WA 12).

LISTENING AND SPEAKING:

Jingle Time

Recite It: Practice Jingle 12 in the Jingle Section on page 509.

>>>> Student Tip...

> Reviewing the transition words will help you apply them in your writing.

Writing Time

Compare It:

As you compare the paragraph and the essay below, notice the similarities and the differences.

 Reference 102 — **Comparing a Three-Point Paragraph and a Three-Paragraph Essay**

THREE-POINT EXPOSITORY PARAGRAPH

Topic: Favorite animals

Three points: 1. **lemurs** 2. **prairie dogs** 3. **flamingos**

I have several favorite animals I enjoy seeing whenever I go to the zoo. The animals that I especially love to see are lemurs, prairie dogs, and flamingos. My first favorite animal is the lemur. I think lemurs are unique because they are similar to monkeys but have a fox-like face, large eyes, and a bushy tail. My second favorite zoo animal is the prairie dog. I find these short, bushy animals very interesting because they have a sophisticated language that they use to warn other prairie dogs of an approaching predator. My third favorite zoo animal is the flamingo. How these large tropical birds stand on one leg and are able to bend their legs backwards amazes me. I delight in watching my favorite animals, and they are on my "must see" list every time I visit the zoo.

THREE-PARAGRAPH EXPOSITORY ESSAY

Topic: Favorite animals

Three points: 1. **lemurs** 2. **prairie dogs** 3. **flamingos**

My Favorite Zoo Animals

I have several favorite animals I enjoy seeing whenever I go to the zoo. Every time I visit, I spend most of my time watching and learning about my favorite animals. The animals that I especially love to see are lemurs, prairie dogs, and flamingos.

My first favorite animal is the lemur. I think lemurs are unique because they are similar to monkeys but have a fox-like face, large eyes, and a bushy tail. The eerie, fast manner in which lemurs move sets me laughing nearly every time I visit the zoo. My second favorite zoo animal is the prairie dog. I find these short, bushy animals very interesting because they have a sophisticated language that they use to warn other prairie dogs of an approaching predator. After they give their warning call, they bob up and down with excitement before quickly disappearing into their burrows. My third favorite zoo animal is the flamingo. How these large tropical birds stand on one leg and are able to bend their legs backwards amazes me. Their bright pink feathers, which appear to be painted, intrigue me as well.

I delight in watching my favorite animals, and they are on my "must see" list every time I visit the zoo. Even though I enjoy seeing the other animals, I think lemurs, prairie dogs, and flamingos stand head and shoulders above the rest.

Compare It:

As you study the two outlines below, notice that the introduction and conclusion are the same for both essays. In the body of the three-paragraph essay, all the points and their supporting sentences are in one paragraph. However, the body of the five-paragraph essay has three paragraphs. In the body of the five-paragraph essay, each point and its supporting sentences are a separate paragraph.

Reference 103 — **Outlines for the Three-Paragraph Essay and the Five-Paragraph Essay**

Outline of a Three-Paragraph Essay

1. **Paragraph 1 - Introduction**
   A. Topic and number sentence
   B. Extra-information sentence(s)
   C. Three-point sentence

2. **Paragraph 2 - Body**
   A. **First-point** sentence
   B. One or more **supporting** sentences for the first point
   C. **Second-point** sentence
   D. One or more **supporting** sentences for the second point
   E. **Third-point** sentence
   F. One or more **supporting** sentences for the third point

3. **Paragraph 3 - Conclusion**
   A. Concluding general sentence
   B. Concluding three-point sentence

4. **Title**

Outline of a Five-Paragraph Essay

1. **Paragraph 1 - Introduction**
   A. Topic and number sentence
   B. Extra-information sentence(s)
   C. Three-point sentence

2. **Paragraph 2 - First Point (Body)**
   A. **First-point** sentence
   B. Two or more **supporting** sentences for the first point

3. **Paragraph 3 - Second Point (Body)**
   A. **Second-point** sentence
   B. Two or more **supporting** sentences for the second point

4. **Paragraph 4 - Third Point (Body)**
   A. **Third-point** sentence
   B. Two or more **supporting** sentences for the third point

5. **Paragraph 5 - Conclusion**
   A. Concluding general sentence
   B. Concluding three-point sentence

6. **Title**

Review It: PARTS OF A FIVE-PARAGRAPH ESSAY

You have learned that an essay has three main parts: **introduction**, **body**, and **conclusion**. The five-paragraph essay has these same main parts. The **introduction** is the first paragraph, the **body** includes the second, third, and fourth paragraphs, and the **conclusion** is the fifth paragraph of the essay. The title will be the fourth part of a five-paragraph essay. In a five-paragraph essay, there will be five paragraphs.

Learn It: WRITING THE INTRODUCTION FOR A FIVE-PARAGRAPH EXPOSITORY ESSAY

Three or more sentences make up the introduction. The first sentence in the introduction is called the **topic and number sentence**. The second sentence is the **extra-information sentence**, and the third sentence is called the **three-point sentence**.

Continued on next page. >>>

Reference 104

Writing the Introduction for a Five-Paragraph Expository Essay

LIST THREE POINTS ABOUT THE TOPIC.

Select three points to list about the topic. 1. **lemurs**   2. **prairie dogs**   3. **flamingos**

THE INTRODUCTION
Paragraph 1

Writing Topic: Favorite animals

Sentence 1 – Topic and Number Sentence:

To write the topic sentence, use some or all of the words in your topic and add a general or specific number word that tells the number of points that will be discussed.

> **General number words:** *several, many, some,* etc.
> **Specific number words:** *two, three, four,* etc.

In the sample sentence below, words from the topic *(favorite animals)* are used, and the general number word *(several)* is used instead of a specific number word.

> **I have several favorite animals I enjoy seeing whenever I go to the zoo.**

Sentence 2 – Extra-Information Sentence:

Sometimes, you need one or more extra sentences that will add information about the topic or embellish it. This sentence is usually optional and can clarify, explain, define, or just be an extra interesting comment.

> **Every time I visit, I spend most of my time watching my favorite animals.**

Sentence 3 – Three-Point Sentence:

This sentence names the three points to be discussed in the order that you will present them in the body of your paper. You can list the points with or without the specific number in front. In the sample sentence, the points, *lemurs, prairie dogs, and flamingos*, are named without using the specific number *three*.

> **The animals that I especially love to see are lemurs, prairie dogs, and flamingos.**

Learn It: **WRITING THE BODY**
FOR A FIVE-PARAGRAPH EXPOSITORY ESSAY

The body contains three paragraphs. Each of the three points forms a new paragraph. After the sentence for each point is written, notice that there are at least two or more supporting sentences that are added.

Reference 105

Writing the Body for a Five-Paragraph Expository Essay

THE BODY
Paragraph 2

Sentence 4 – First Point:

Write a sentence stating your first point.

> **My first favorite animal is the lemur.**

Sentences 5–7 – Supporting Sentences:

Write two or more sentences that give additional information about your first point.

> **I think lemurs are unique because they are similar to monkeys but have a fox-like face, large eyes, and a bushy tail. The manner in which lemurs move sets me laughing nearly every time I visit the zoo. In fact, they are called lemurs, which means "ghost," because they move so silently at night.**

Continued on next page. >>>

Reference 105 continued from previous page.

Paragraph 3

Sentence 8 – Second Point:
Write a sentence stating your second point.

My second favorite zoo animal is the prairie dog.

Sentences 9–11 – Supporting Sentences:
Write two or more sentences that give additional information about your second point.

I find these short, bushy animals very interesting because they have a sophisticated language that they use to warn other prairie dogs of an approaching predator. After they give their warning call, they bob up and down with excitement before quickly disappearing into their burrows. In my opinion, prairie dogs have a fantastic "neighborhood watch" program.

Paragraph 4

Sentence 12 – Third Point:
Write a sentence stating your third point.

My third favorite zoo animal is the flamingo.

Sentences 13–16 – Supporting Sentences:
Write two or more sentences that give additional information about your third point.

How these large tropical birds stand on one leg and are able to bend their legs backwards amazes me. Their bright pink feathers, which appear to be painted, intrigue me as well. I am surprised that flamingos fly mainly at night and can reach up to thirty-seven miles per hour! I think that their pink feathers, long skinny necks and legs, and dignified manner make them look like royal sentinels.

Learn It: **WRITING THE CONCLUSION FOR A FIVE-PARAGRAPH EXPOSITORY ESSAY**

The conclusion forms the fifth paragraph. The closing paragraph, or conclusion, should tie all the important points together with a restatement of the main idea and your final comments on it. Two sentences make up the conclusion. The first sentence in the conclusion is called the **concluding general sentence** and the second sentence is the **concluding three-point sentence**.

Reference 106 | **Writing the Conclusion for a Five-Paragraph Expository Essay**

THE CONCLUSION
Paragraph 5

Sentence 17 – Concluding General Sentence:
Read the topic sentence again and then rewrite it, using some of the same words. The Concluding General Sentence is meant to be general in nature and restates the topic sentence. In the sample sentence, the word, *animals*, is used instead of the particular points, *lemurs, prairie dogs,* and *flamingos.*

I delight in watching my favorite animals, and they are on my "must see" list every time I visit the zoo.

Sentence 18 – Concluding Three-Point Sentence:
Read the introductory three-point sentence again and then rewrite it, using some of the same words. The Concluding Three-Point Sentence restates the three-point sentence, listing the particular points and bringing the writing to a close. In the sample sentence, the particular points, lemurs, prairie dogs, and flamingos, are named, along with another closing thought.

Even though I enjoy seeing the other animals, I think lemurs, prairie dogs, and flamingos stand head and shoulders above the rest.

Continued on next page. >>>

Reference 106 continued from previous page.

WRITING THE TITLE
Since there are many possibilities for titles, look at the topic and the three points listed about the topic. Use some of the words in the topic and write a phrase to tell what your paragraph is about. Your title can be short or long. Capitalize the first, last, and important words in your title.

Title: My Favorite Zoo Animals

Sample Five-Paragraph Essay

My Favorite Zoo Animals

I have several favorite animals I enjoy seeing whenever I go to the zoo. Every time I visit, I spend most of my time watching and learning about my favorite animals. The animals that I especially love to see are lemurs, prairie dogs, and flamingos.

My first favorite animal is the lemur. I think lemurs are unique because they are similar to monkeys but have a fox-like face, large eyes, and a bushy tail. The manner in which lemurs move sets me laughing nearly every time I visit the zoo. In fact, they are called lemurs, which means "ghost," because they move so silently at night.

My second favorite zoo animal is the prairie dog. I find these short, bushy animals very interesting because they have a sophisticated language that they use to warn other prairie dogs of an approaching predator. After they give their warning call, they bob up and down with excitement before quickly disappearing into their burrows. In my opinion, prairie dogs have a fantastic "neighborhood watch" program.

My third favorite zoo animal is the flamingo. How these large tropical birds stand on one leg and are able to bend their legs backwards amazes me. Their bright pink feathers, which appear to be painted, intrigue me as well. I am surprised that flamingos fly mainly at night and can reach up to thirty-seven miles per hour! I think that their pink feathers, long skinny necks and legs, and dignified manner make them look like royal sentinels.

I delight in watching my favorite animals, and they are on my "must see" list every time I visit the zoo. Even though I enjoy seeing the other animals, I think lemurs, prairie dogs, and flamingos stand head and shoulders above the rest.

Write It: WRITING ASSIGNMENT 12
As you write a rough draft for your guided writing assignment, you will do two of the six steps in the writing process: prewriting and rough draft.

Writing Assignment 12

Purpose: To inform
Type of Writing: Five-paragraph expository essay
Audience: Classmates
Writing Topics: Things I Have Learned
Things Money Can't Buy
Favorite Movie(s)/Song(s)/Book(s)/Relative(s)
(Brainstorm for other ideas, individually or in groups.)

Special Instructions:
1. Follow the Prewriting and Rough Draft Checklists in References 44 and 46 on pages 57, 61.
2. Use References 103–106 on pages 165–168 to help you write your five-paragraph expository essay.
3. Use standard, time-order, or transition writing form. See Reference 69, page 103.
4. Write in first or third person. See Reference 70, page 104.
(First-person pronouns: *I, me, my, mine, we, us, our, and ours.*)
(Third-person pronouns: *he, his, him, she, her, hers, it, its, they, their, theirs,* and *them.*)

Note: Reference 54 on page 71 gives the steps in the writing process and the location of all the writing checklists.

Writing Time

Apply It: **REVISE, EDIT, AND WRITE A FINAL PAPER**

Following the schedule below, you will revise and edit Writing Assignment 12. Then, you will write a final paper. Use the Chapter 5 Writing Evaluation Guide on the next page to check your final paper one last time.

 Reference 52 — **Revising & Editing Schedule and Writing a Final Paper**

SPECIAL INSTRUCTIONS FOR REVISING AND EDITING (Steps 3-4 in the writing process):

• Use the Revising and Editing Checklists in References 48 and 50 as you revise and edit your rough draft.

• Follow the revising and editing schedule below as directed by your teacher.

   1. **Individual.** First, read your rough draft to yourself. Use the Revising Checklist in Reference 48 on page 64. Go through your paper, checking each item on the list and making revisions to your rough draft. Then, use the Editing Checklist in Reference 50 on page 66. Go through your paper again, checking each item on the list and editing your rough draft.

   2. **Partner.** Next, get with your editing partner. Work together on each partner's rough draft, one paper at a time. Read each rough draft aloud and revise and edit it together, using the Revising and Editing Checklists. (The author of the paper should be the one to make the corrections on his own paper.)

   3. **Group.** Finally, read the rough draft to a revision group for feedback. Each student should read his paper while the others listen and offer possible revising and editing suggestions. (The author will determine whether to make corrections from the revision group's suggestions.)

SPECIAL INSTRUCTIONS FOR FINAL PAPER (Step 5 in the writing process):

• Write your final paper, using the Final Paper Checklist in Reference 53 on page 70.

• Staple your writing papers in this order: the final paper on top, the rough draft in the middle, and the prewriting map on the bottom. Place the stapled papers in the Final Paper folder.

>>>>>>>>>> Student Tip...

1. Be tactful and helpful in your comments during revising and editing time. The purpose of any suggestion should be to improve the writer's rough draft.

2. As you make your final corrections, you have the choice of accepting or rejecting any suggestions made by your partners or your revision group.

3. Study Vocabulary Words and Analogies 13–16 for the chapter test in the next lesson.

4. If you need to improve your handwriting, refer to the Resource Tools Section on pages 524–530 for information on writing legibly.

SHURLEY ENGLISH

Chapter 5 Writing Evaluation Guide

Name:_____ Date:_____

ROUGH DRAFT CHECK

_____ 1. Did you write your rough draft in pencil?

_____ 2. Did you write the correct headings on the first seven lines of your paper?

_____ 3. Did you use extra wide margins and skip every other line?

_____ 4. Did you write a title at the end of your rough draft?

_____ 5. Did you place your edited rough draft in your Rough Draft folder?

REVISING CHECK

_____ 6. Did you identify the purpose, type of writing, and audience?

_____ 7. Did you check for a topic, topic sentence, and sentences supporting the topic?

_____ 8. Did you check sentences for the right order, and did you combine, rearrange, or delete sentences when necessary?

_____ 9. Did you check for a variety of simple, compound, and complex sentences?

_____ 10. Did you check for any left out, repeated, or unnecessary words?

_____ 11. Did you check for the best choice of words by replacing or deleting unclear words?

_____ 12. Did you check the content for interest and creativity?

_____ 13. Did you check the voice to make sure the writing says what you want it to say?

EDITING CHECK

_____ 14. Did you indent each paragraph?

_____ 15. Did you put an end mark at the end of every sentence?

_____ 16. Did you capitalize the first word of every sentence?

_____ 17. Did you check for all other capitalization mistakes?

_____ 18. Did you check for all punctuation mistakes?
         (commas, periods, apostrophes, quotation marks, underlining)

_____ 19. Did you check for misspelled words and for incorrect homonym choices?

_____ 20. Did you check for incorrect spellings of plural and possessive forms?

_____ 21. Did you check for correct construction and punctuation of your sentences?

_____ 22. Did you check for usage mistakes? _(subject/verb agreement, a/an choices, contractions, verb tenses, pronoun/antecedent agreement, pronoun cases, degrees of adjectives, double negatives, etc.)_

_____ 23. Did you put your revised and edited paper in the Rough Draft folder?

FINAL PAPER CHECK

_____ 24. Did you write the final paper in pencil?

_____ 25. Did you center the title on the top line and center your name under the title?

_____ 26. Did you skip a line before starting the writing assignment?

_____ 27. Did you single-space, use wide margins, and write the final paper neatly?

_____ 28. Did you staple your papers in this order: final paper on top, rough draft in the middle, and prewriting map on the bottom? Did you put them in the Final Paper folder?

Hand It In: WRITING ASSIGNMENT 12

Get your stapled papers for Writing Assignment 12 from your Final Paper folder. Check to make sure they are in the correct order: the final paper on top, the rough draft in the middle, and the prewriting map on the bottom. Hand them in to your teacher.

LISTENING AND SPEAKING:

Discuss It:

1. What are the eight be verbs?

2. What are verbs called that are used with a main verb?

3. What is it called when a helping verb and a main verb are used together?

4. What is it called when an adverb comes immediately before the verb?

5. What type of sentence has all subject parts first and all predicate parts after the verb?

6. What type of sentence has predicate words at the beginning of the sentence?

7. What are the three ways to form an inverted-order sentence?

8. What type of sentence is made by joining two sentences together correctly?

9. What are the three ways to write a compound sentence?

10. What are two run-on sentence mistakes?

11. What do you call a group of sentences that is written about one particular subject?

12. What do you call the sentence that tells what a paragraph is about?

13. What is a written discussion of one idea that is made up of several paragraphs?

14. What type of writing is used when your purpose is to inform, to give facts, to give directions, to explain, or to define something?

>>>>>>>>>>>>>> **Student Tip...**

For information about test-taking strategies, refer to the Resource Tools Section on page 528.

START LESSON 11

Lesson 11

You will
- hand in WA 12 for grading.
- respond to oral review questions.
- take Chapter 5 Test.

CHAPTER TEST

It is time to evaluate your knowledge of the skills you have learned in this chapter. Your teacher will give you the Chapter 5 Test to help you assess your progress.

CHAPTER 6

START LESSON 1

Lesson 1

You will

- study new vocabulary; make card 17; write own sentence using the vocabulary word.
- analyze new analogy; make card 17; write own analogy.
- recite new jingles (Interjection, Possessive Noun).
- identify interjections and possessive nouns.
- classify Introductory Sentences.
- do a Skill Builder to identify possessive nouns.
- recognize interjections as a part of speech.
- identify all eight parts of speech.
- write in your journal.
- read and discuss Discovery Time.

LISTENING AND SPEAKING:
Vocabulary & Analogy Time

Learn It: Recite the new vocabulary and analogy words.

Reference 107	**Vocabulary & Analogy Words**

Word: valiant (văl'yənt)
  Definition: showing bravery
  Synonym: courageous   **Antonym:** cowardly
  Sentence: The valiant firemen rescued the family from the fire.

Analogy: racket : tennis :: club : golf
  Purpose or use relationship: Just as a **racket** is used to play **tennis**, a **club** is used to play **golf**.

Vocabulary Card 17: Record the vocabulary information above and write your own sentence, using the new word.

Analogy Card 17: Record the analogy information and write your own analogy, using the same relationship as the analogy above.

Jingle Time

Recite It: Recite the new jingles.

♪ Jingle 18	**The Interjection Jingle**

Oh, Interjection, Interjection, Interjection, who are you?
  I'm a part of speech through and through.
Well, Interjection, Interjection, Interjection, what do you do?
  I show strong or mild emotion; need a review?
Oh, Interjection, Interjection, I still don't have a clue.
  I show strong emotion, like Wow! Great! or Yahoo!
  I show mild emotion, like Oh, Yes, Fine, or Toodle-oo.
Well, Interjection, Interjection, you really know how to groove!
  That's because I'm a part of speech through and through!

♪ Jingle 19	**The Possessive Noun Jingle**

A possessive noun just can't be beat.
It shows ownership, and that is neat.
Add an apostrophe to show possession.
This is a great ownership lesson.
Adjective is its part of speech.
Ask **WHOSE** to find it as you speak.
Whose house? Tommy's house.
Possessive Noun Adjective!

 Grammar Time

Apply It: These Introductory Sentences are used to apply the new grammar concepts taught below. Classify these sentences orally with your teacher.

Introductory Sentences — Chapter 6: Lesson 1

1. _____ Look! Those determined salmon fight and struggle vigorously upstream against the current!

2. _____ Lawanda's car sputtered and clanged noisily on the way to the mechanic's shop.

3. _____ Oh, no! Don and Alvada stumbled and fell down the steep ravine during their hike yesterday!

Learn It: INTERJECTIONS

Reference 108 — Interjections

1. An **interjection** is one or more words used to express mild or strong emotion.

2. An interjection is usually located at the beginning of a sentence and is separated from the rest of the sentence with a punctuation mark.

3. A mild interjection is followed by a comma or a period; a strong interjection is followed by an exclamation point.

4. There are no questions to ask to find interjections. Interjections are not connected grammatically to the rest of the sentence. For this reason, interjections are not underlined as subject parts or predicate parts. Likewise, interjections should not be considered when deciding whether a sentence is declarative, interrogative, exclamatory, or imperative.

5. An *interjection* is labeled with the abbreviation **I**.

Learn It: POSSESSIVE NOUNS

Reference 109 — Possessive Nouns

1. A **possessive noun** is the name of a person, place, or thing that owns something.

2. A possessive noun will always have an apostrophe after it. It will have either an *apostrophe* before the *s* ('s) or an *apostrophe* after the *s* (s'). The apostrophe makes a noun show ownership. (*Kim's car*)

3. A possessive noun has two jobs: to show ownership or possession and to modify like an adjective.

4. A possessive noun's part of speech is an adjective.

5. When a possessive noun is classified, it is labeled as a possessive noun adjective to recognize both jobs. A *possessive noun adjective* is labeled with the abbreviation **PNA**. For the abbreviation **PNA**, say, "*possessive noun adjective.*"

6. Include possessive nouns when you are asked to identify possessive nouns or adjectives.

7. To find a possessive noun, begin with the question *whose.* (Whose car? **Kim's - PNA**)

Since you use the whose question to find a possessive noun and a possessive pronoun, you must remember one important fact about each one in order to tell them apart. All possessive nouns have an apostrophe at the end. You can remember the possessive pronouns by reciting the Possessive Pronoun Jingle.

Learn It: **A SKILL BUILDER FOR A NOUN CHECK
WITH POSSESSIVE NOUNS**

The example below shows you what to do with possessive nouns when you are identifying nouns for a Noun Check.

LISTENING AND SPEAKING:

FOR A noun CHECK WITH POSSESSIVE nouns

Circle the nouns in a Noun Check.

Sentence 1: Subject Noun (salmon) *yes, it is a noun;*
Object of the Preposition (current) *yes, it is a noun.*

Sentence 2: Subject Noun (car) *yes, it is a noun;*
Object of the Preposition (way) *yes, it is a noun;*
Object of the Preposition (shop) *yes, it is a noun.*

Sentence 3: Compound Subject Noun (Don) *yes, it is a noun;*
Compound Subject Noun (Alvada) *yes, it is a noun;*
Object of the Preposition (ravine) *yes, it is a noun;*
Object of the Preposition (hike) *yes, it is a noun.*

Are there any possessive nouns in the sentences? **(Yes)**
Name them. **(Lawanda's and mechanic's)**

What part of speech is a possessive noun? **(adjective)**

JOURNAL WRITING **13**

Write an entry in your journal. Use Reference 9 on page 12 for ideas.

Learn It: **ADDING THE INTERJECTION TO THE PARTS OF SPEECH**

An interjection is a part of speech. You have now learned the eight parts of speech. What are the eight parts of speech?

ENRICHMENT:

(German) 1770-1827— Ludwig van Beethoven composed some of the most influential pieces of music ever written. His music was full of passion and emotion, leading the way into the Classical Era of music. Beethoven was also admired for his brilliant improvisations. Beethoven would compose entire symphonies in his head, hearing the part for every instrument before he wrote the first note on paper. Beethoven lost his hearing around 1819, but he continued to compose and direct music.

Discovery Questions:
• At what age did Beethoven begin giving public performances?
• Would you like to have Beethoven direct your band? Explain.
• How do you think Beethoven would fit into the world today?

Are you interested in learning more about Ludwig van Beethoven?

1. You may explore this topic further by using the resources listed below.
   Computer resources: Internet, encyclopedia software
   Library resources: encyclopedias, books, magazines, newspapers
   Home/community resources: books, interviews, newspapers, magazines

2. A Discovery Share Time is provided in Lesson 7 if you wish to share your investigation results. You may share orally, or you may prepare a written report. You will put your written report in a class booklet titled "Notable People in History." This booklet will be placed in the class library for everyone to enjoy.

English Made Easy

LISTENING AND SPEAKING:

Vocabulary & Analogy Time

Learn It: Recite the new vocabulary and analogy words.

📖 Reference 110	Vocabulary & Analogy Words

Word: prevalent (prĕv'ə lənt)
  Definition: widely practiced
  Synonym: common   **Antonym:** rare
  Sentence: Owning a computer is quite prevalent today.

Analogy: arid : dry :: moist : wet
  Synonym relationship: Just as **arid** means nearly the same as **dry**, **moist** means nearly the same as **wet**.

Vocabulary Card 18: Record the vocabulary information above and write your own sentence, using the new word.

Analogy Card 18: Record the analogy information and write your own analogy, using the same relationship as the analogy above.

Jingle Time

Recite It: 1. Practice Jingles 18–19 in the Jingle Section on page 511.
  2. Recite the new jingle.

♪ Jingle 20	The Eight Parts of Speech Jingle

Want to know how to write?
Use the eight parts of speech.
They're dynamite!

Nouns, **V**erbs, and **P**ronouns.
They rule!
They're called the **NVP's**, and they're really cool!
The **Double A's** are on the move.
Adjectives and **A**dverbs help you to groove.
Next come the **PIC's**, and then we're done.
They're **P**reposition, **I**nterjection, and **C**onjunction!

All together now.
The eight parts of speech, abbreviations, please.
NVP—AA—and—**PIC**!

Lesson 2
You will
- study new vocabulary; make card 18; write own sentence using the vocabulary word.
- analyze new analogy; make card 18; write own analogy.
- practice Jingles 18–19; recite new jingle (8 Parts of Speech).
- classify Practice Sentences.
- do a Skill Builder.
- identify clauses, subordinate conjunctions, and complex sentences.
- review eight parts of speech and types of sentences.
- do Classroom Practice 25.
- read and discuss Discovery Time.

Apply It: Classify the Practice Sentences orally with your teacher.

Practice Sentences	Chapter 6: Lesson 2

1. _____ Listen carefully to the supervisor's instructions for the new computers.
2. _____ Did Mother's kitchen curtains above the sink swirl wildly around in the brisk breeze?
3. _____ Whew! My slippery angelfish flopped out of my hand and landed in the kitchen sink.

LISTENING AND SPEAKING:

Using the sentences just classified, do a Skill Builder orally with your teacher.

1. **Identify the nouns in a Noun Check.**
2. **Identify the nouns as singular or plural.**
3. **Identify the nouns as common or proper.**
4. **Identify the complete subject and the complete predicate.**
5. **Identify the simple subject and the simple predicate.**
6. **Do a Vocabulary Check.**

Review It: **THE EIGHT PARTS OF SPEECH**

You have learned a jingle to help you remember the eight parts of speech.
What are the eight parts of speech? Recite the jingle for the eight parts of speech.

Learn It: **CLAUSES AND SUBORDINATE CONJUNCTIONS**

📖 Reference 111	**Clauses and Subordinate Conjunctions**

CLAUSES

A **clause** is a group of words that has a subject and a verb. There are two kinds of clauses: independent and subordinate. An **independent clause** has a subject and a verb and expresses a complete thought. An independent clause is also called a simple sentence.

    Independent clause: The bell rang for class.

A **subordinate** (or **dependent**) **clause** has a subject and a verb but does not express a complete thought because it begins with a subordinate conjunction. Since it does not express a complete thought, it is a fragment and cannot stand alone.

    Subordinate clause: <u>When</u> the bell rang for class.

Continued on next page. >>>

Reference 111 continued from previous page.

SUBORDINATE CONJUNCTIONS

The word **subordinate** means "to place below another in rank or importance." When a subordinate conjunction is added to the beginning of a simple sentence, that sentence becomes a fragment because it no longer expresses a complete thought. This fragment is called a subordinate (or dependent) clause and is unequal to an independent clause. To use a subordinate clause correctly, the subordinate clause must be connected to an independent clause. A **subordinate conjunction** is the word that makes a clause subordinate and, at the same time, connects it to an independent clause.

Some of the most common subordinate conjunctions are listed below.

after	because	except	so that	though	when
although	before	if	than	unless	where
as, or as soon as	even though	since	that	until	while

Learn It: COMPLEX SENTENCES

 Reference 112   The Complex Sentence

A **complex sentence** is the result of two clauses, a <u>subordinate</u> (or dependent) clause and an <u>independent</u> clause being joined together. The abbreviation for a *complex sentence* is **CX**. Remember that a subordinate clause must be joined to an independent clause in order to complete its meaning. To make a complex sentence, combine a subordinate clause and an independent clause in one of the two ways listed below.

1. If the subordinate clause comes first, a comma is required between the clauses.
   Complex sentence: <u>**When** the bell rang for class</u>, the students took their seats.

2. If the subordinate clause comes last, a comma is normally not required between the clauses.
   Complex sentence: The students took their seats <u>**when** the bell rang for class.</u>

A REVIEW

1. To make a complex sentence, join an independent clause and a subordinate clause together.

2. An independent clause can be made subordinate (dependent) by simply adding a subordinate conjunction to the beginning of that clause. (**The bell rang: As** the bell rang, **Before** the bell rang, **After** the bell rang.)

3. A subordinate (or dependent) clause can be made independent by removing the subordinate conjunction at the beginning of the clause. (**As** the bell rang, **Before** the bell rang, **After** the bell rang: **The bell rang.**)

PRACTICE EXERCISE

Below is a set of run-on sentences. First, use a slash between the two simple sentences. Next, follow the set of directions given in parentheses to make complex sentences. The abbreviation (**CX**) tells you to make a complex sentence. The words **when** and **after** tell you which subordinate conjunction to use. The numbers (**1**) or (**2**) tell you whether to put the subordinate conjunction at the beginning of the first clause (**1**) or the second clause (**2**).

Example 1: the bell rang for class / the students took their seats. (**CX, when**) (**1**)
When the bell rang for class, the students took their seats.

Example 2: the students took their seats / the bell rang for class. (**CX, after**) (**2**)
The students took their seats **after** the bell rang for class.

SHURLEY ENGLISH

>>>>>>>>>>>> **Student Tip...**

Use the following information as a visual aid to help you construct complex sentences.

Subordinate clause + Independent clause = Complex sentence
Independent clause + Subordinate clause = Complex sentence

A complex sentence is formed when a subordinate clause is joined to an independent clause.
A complex sentence can be punctuated in one of two ways.

1. A comma is needed when the subordinate clause comes first.
   (Subordinate Conjunction) _____ , _____ .

2. A comma is usually not needed when the independent clause comes first.
   _____ (subordinate conjunction) _____ .

Review It: TYPES OF SENTENCES

The sentence chart will help you to identify each type of sentence quickly.

Reference 113	A Review of the Types of Sentences
F.............. A fragment	does not contain a subject. (*Ran through the tall grass.*) does not contain a verb. (*The wind in the trees.*) has a subject and a verb but does not make sense. (*Until the lightning and thunder ceased.*)
S.............. A simple sentence (or independent sentence)	has a subject, a verb, and makes sense. (*Dogs barked.*)
SCS......... A simple sentence with a compound subject	has multiple subjects connected by a conjunction but only one verb. (*The fierce **lions** and enormous **elephants** performed amazingly well.*)
SCV........ A simple sentence with a compound verb	has multiple verbs connected by a conjunction but only one subject. (*The crowd **clapped** and **cheered** for the performers.*)
CD........... A compound sentence	is two independent sentences joined 1. by a comma and a conjunction. (*I ate fish, **and** Joe ate shrimp.*) 2. by a semicolon, connective adverb, comma. (*I ate fish; **however,** Joe ate shrimp.*) 3. by a semicolon only. (*I ate fish; Joe ate shrimp.*)
CX........... A complex sentence	is an independent clause joined with a subordinate clause. 1. (*I bought popcorn before the movie started.*) 2. (*Before the movie started, I bought popcorn.*)

IDENTIFYING THE TYPES OF SENTENCES

Identify each type of sentence by writing the correct label in the blank. (**Labels: S, F, SCS, SCV, CD, CX**)

    F   1. After the puppies played in the front yard.

    S   2. We ran quickly after our puppies in the front yard.

  SCS   3. After school, my sister and brother played with the puppies.

  SCV   4. My dad smiled at the puppies and talked to them.

  CD   5. My sister played with the black puppy, and my brother played with the brown puppy.

  CX   6. When you call them, the puppies will come to you.

  CX   7. The puppies will come to you when you call them.

Classroom Practice 25

It is time to practice the skills you are learning. You will use the classroom practice on the next page to apply these skills.

ENRICHMENT:

(Native American Cherokee) 1776-1843— Sequoyah, a Cherokee silversmith, published the first Native American newspaper, the *Cherokee Phoenix*, which is still printed today. He spent twelve years creating an alphabet for his people. He was raised in Tennessee by his Cherokee mother and never learned to speak, read, or write English.

Discovery Questions:
• **What do you think Sequoyah was like?**

Discovery Activity:

• **Work with friends to create your own alphabet without using the English letters.**

Are you interested in learning more about Sequoyah?

1. You may explore this topic further by using the resources listed below.
   Computer resources: Internet, encyclopedia software
   Library resources: encyclopedias, books, magazines, newspapers
   Home/community resources: books, interviews, newspapers, magazines

2. A Discovery Share Time is provided in Lesson 7 if you wish to share your investigation results. You may share orally, or you may prepare a written report. You will put your written report in a class booklet titled "Notable People in History." This booklet will be placed in the class library for everyone to enjoy.

SHURLEY ENGLISH

Classroom Practice 25

Name:_____ Date:_____

GRAMMAR

▶ **Exercise 1:** Classify each sentence.

1. _____ Oh, no! Yesterday, my oldest brother ran into Mr. Cobb's mailbox with Mom's new car!

2. _____ Jennifer and I worked yesterday on our science project for Mr. Smith's biology class.

SKILLS

▶ **Exercise 2:** Use a slash to separate each run-on sentence below. Then, correct the run-on sentences by rewriting them as indicated by the labels in parentheses at the end of each sentence.

1. Mother turned the key the car started. (**CX, when**) **(1)**

_____

2. Mother turned the key the car started. (**CX, until**) **(2)**

_____

3. Mother turned the key the car would not start. (**CX, even though**) **(1)**

_____

4. The sun rose again the farmers were busy with chores. (**CX, before**) **(1)**

_____

5. The little boy smiled the clown gave him a balloon. (**CX, after**) **(2)**

_____

▶ **Exercise 3:** Identify each type of sentence by writing the correct label in the blank. (**Labels: S, F, SCS, SCV, CD, CX**)

_____ 1. As soon as I arrived, I began looking for my friends.
_____ 2. Our dog jumped and scratched at the door.
_____ 3. Racing from door to door with the good news.
_____ 4. The Christmas presents were piled around the tree.
_____ 5. I called, yet my friend did not answer the phone.
_____ 6. During the movie, Chris and Doug ate popcorn.
_____ 7. Since I do not have a bicycle, I usually walk to school.
_____ 8. When I get finished, I can go home.
_____ 9. The cold, blustery wind whipped around us and froze our cheeks.

EDITING

▶ **Exercise 4:** Correct each mistake. **Editing Guide: End Marks: 3 Capitals: 9 Commas: 2 Apostrophes: 2 Homonyms: 2 Subject-Verb Agreement: 4 Periods: 2 Misspelled Words: 1**

as they complete there tour of washington d c warrens family pause on the steps of the

lincoln memorial for won last picture his mom gets everyones attention and snap the picture on

the count of three mom warn everyone not to move becuz she want another shot

LISTENING AND SPEAKING:
Vocabulary & Analogy Time

Learn It: Recite the new vocabulary and analogy words.

Reference 114	Vocabulary & Analogy Words

Word: validate (văl'ĭdāt')
  Definition: to confirm truth or fact
  Synonym: verify   **Antonym:** refute
  Sentence: The scientist validated his findings with careful documentation.

Analogy: waist : waste :: hair : hare
  Homonym relationship: Just as **waist** sounds like **waste**,
                                                hair sounds like **hare**.

Vocabulary Card 19: Record the vocabulary information above and write your own
                                    sentence, using the new word.

Analogy Card 19: Record the analogy information and write your own analogy,
                                using the same relationship as the analogy above.

Lesson 3

You will

- study new vocabulary; make card 19; write own sentence using the vocabulary word.
- analyze new analogy; make card 19; write own analogy.
- practice Jingles 13–20.
- classify Practice Sentences.
- do a Skill Builder.
- do Classroom Practice 26.
- write in your journal.
- read and discuss Discovery Time.

Jingle Time

Recite It: Practice Jingles 13–20 in the Jingle Section on pages 509–511.

Grammar Time

Apply It: Classify the Practice Sentences orally with your teacher.

Practice Sentences	Chapter 6: Lesson 3

1. _____ Mother's new little kitten loudly hissed and slapped at my older brother and his friend.

2. _____ Oh, no! That frightened horse ran away with its rider during our annual holiday parade!

3. _____ Dress lightly but warmly for the long hike to the wildlife preserve in our national park.

LISTENING AND SPEAKING:

Skill Builder

Using the sentences just classified, do a Skill Builder orally with your teacher.

1. **Identify the nouns in a Noun Check.**
2. **Identify the nouns as singular or plural.**
3. **Identify the nouns as common or proper.**
4. **Identify the complete subject and the complete predicate.**
5. **Identify the simple subject and the simple predicate.**
6. **Do a Vocabulary Check.**

JOURNAL WRITING 14

Write an entry in your journal. Use Reference 9 on page 12 for ideas.

Classroom Practice 26

It is time to practice the skills you are learning. You will use the classroom practice on the next page to apply these skills.

ENRICHMENT:

Discovery Time

(American) 1791-1872— Samuel Morse improved the telegraph and developed the Morse code, which used the pulses of electricity and an alphabetic code to convey information over wires. Morse was also a well-known portrait artist in his later years.

Discovery Questions:
- **What was the first message flashed over Morse's telegraph wire?**
- **How did Morse's work affect America?**

Discovery Activity:
- **Use the Morse code to send a message to a friend.**

Are you interested in learning more about Samuel Morse?

1. You may explore this topic further by using the resources listed below.
   Computer resources: Internet, encyclopedia software
   Library resources: encyclopedias, books, magazines, newspapers
   Home/community resources: books, interviews, newspapers, magazines

2. A Discovery Share Time is provided in Lesson 7 if you wish to share your investigation results. You may share orally, or you may prepare a written report. You will put your written report in a class booklet titled "Notable People in History." This booklet will be placed in the class library for everyone to enjoy.

Classroom Practice 26

Name:_____ Date:_____

GRAMMAR

▶ **Exercise 1:** Classify each sentence.

1. _____ Yikes! My paper and pencil flew across the aisle and landed at Ms. Simpson's feet!

2. _____ She and he talked excitedly to their friends during the morning break.

SKILLS

▶ **Exercise 2:** Identify each type of sentence by writing the correct label in the blank. (**Labels: S, F, SCS, SCV, CD, CX**)

_____ 1. I love to dance; I take lessons in jazz and tap.
_____ 2. In the spring, Crystal and Kate will play softball.
_____ 3. Gathered her books and supplies.
_____ 4. When the bell rang, the students left.
_____ 5. The snow melted when the sun came out.
_____ 6. You cannot go with us to the museum; unfortunately, you forgot your permission slip.
_____ 7. At lunch, teachers and students chatter noisily in the cafeteria.
_____ 8. The shiniest red sports car in the parking lot.
_____ 9. Before the comedian finished his joke, the crowd erupted with laughter.
_____ 10. The young mother and her two children waited patiently at the checkout.

▶ **Exercise 3:** Use a slash to separate each run-on sentence below. Then, correct the run-on sentences by rewriting them as indicated by the labels in parentheses at the end of each sentence.

1. The water was calm we walked along the beach. (**CX, as**) (**2**)

_____

2. Tom was tired he enjoyed the game. (**CX, although**) (**1**)

_____

3. Anna can draw well she entered an art contest. (**CX, since**) (**1**)

_____

4. I always eat popcorn I am upset. (**CX, when**) (**2**)

_____

5. I will go to the concert you will go with me. (**CX, if**) (**2**)

_____

EDITING

▶ **Exercise 4:** Correct each mistake. **Editing Guide: End Marks: 5   Capitals: 11   Commas: 2   Apostrophes: 1**
Homonyms: 2   A/An: 2   Subject-Verb Agreement: 2   Misspelled Words: 2

raymond julias brother graduated from ohio state university with an dagree in nurseing in

may he have had fifteen job offers in too weeks most employers offers him an bonus four

signing with them he is getting more job offers every day i wish i had his problem

START LESSON 4

Lesson 4

You will

- study new vocabulary; make card 20; write own sentence using the vocabulary word.
- analyze new analogy; make card 20; write own analogy.
- practice Jingles 3–11.
- classify Practice Sentences.
- do a Skill Builder.
- do Classroom Practice 27.
- read and discuss Discovery Time.
- do a homework assignment.
- do Home Connection activity.

LISTENING AND SPEAKING:

Vocabulary & Analogy Time

Learn It: Recite the new vocabulary and analogy words.

Reference 115	Vocabulary & Analogy Words

Word: reticent (rĕt'ĭsənt)
  Definition: reluctant to talk; reserved
  Synonym: hesitant   **Antonym:** talkative
  Sentence: Chip was reticent to tell his father that he failed his driver's test.

Analogy: bud : flower :: caterpillar : butterfly
  Progression relationship: Just as a **bud** develops into a **flower**, a **caterpillar** develops into a **butterfly**.

Vocabulary Card 20: Record the vocabulary information above and write your own sentence, using the new word.

Analogy Card 20: Record the analogy information and write your own analogy, using the same relationship as the analogy above.

Jingle Time

Recite It: Practice Jingles 3–11 in the Jingle Section on pages 507–508.

Grammar Time

Apply It: Classify the Practice Sentences orally with your teacher.

Practice Sentences	Chapter 6: Lesson 4

1. _____ Has Jose been studying diligently in the gym before basketball practice?
2. _____ Rats! After dark, we literally could not see down the eerie corridors of Jacob's haunted castle.
3. _____ Brrr! Jonathan and Devon stood at the corner in the extreme cold and waited for their bus.

Learn It: **A SKILL BUILDER FOR A VERB CHANT**

A verb chant will now be added to the Skill Builder. The verb chart you will use is located in Reference 116. As you can see, two of the verb forms use helping verbs with the main verbs. Only the helping verbs listed in a column can be used with the main verbs in that column. The verb chart shows only a partial listing of regular and irregular verbs, but you can add others. You will learn more about these verbs in Chapters 7 and 8.

Reference 116 — Verb Chart for Principal Parts

Principal Parts of Irregular Verbs

PRESENT	PAST	PAST PARTICIPLE		PRESENT PARTICIPLE	
become	became	(**has**, have, had)	become	(am, **is**, are, was, were)	becoming
begin	began	(**has**, have, had)	begun	(am, **is**, are, was, were)	beginning
blow	blew	(**has**, have, had)	blown	(am, **is**, are, was, were)	blowing
break	broke	(**has**, have, had)	broken	(am, **is**, are, was, were)	breaking
bring	brought	(**has**, have, had)	brought	(am, **is**, are, was, were)	bringing
buy	bought	(**has**, have, had)	bought	(am, **is**, are, was, were)	buying
choose	chose	(**has**, have, had)	chosen	(am, **is**, are, was, were)	choosing
come	came	(**has**, have, had)	come	(am, **is**, are, was, were)	coming
cut	cut	(**has**, have, had)	cut	(am, **is**, are, was, were)	cutting
do	did	(**has**, have, had)	done	(am, **is**, are, was, were)	doing
drink	drank	(**has**, have, had)	drunk	(am, **is**, are, was, were)	drinking
drive	drove	(**has**, have, had)	driven	(am, **is**, are, was, were)	driving
eat	ate	(**has**, have, had)	eaten	(am, **is**, are, was, were)	eating
fall	fell	(**has**, have, had)	fallen	(am, **is**, are, was, were)	falling
fly	flew	(**has**, have, had)	flown	(am, **is**, are, was, were)	flying
freeze	froze	(**has**, have, had)	frozen	(am, **is**, are, was, were)	freezing
get	got	(**has**, have, had)	gotten	(am, **is**, are, was, were)	getting
give	gave	(**has**, have, had)	given	(am, **is**, are, was, were)	giving
go	went	(**has**, have, had)	gone	(am, **is**, are, was, were)	going
grow	grew	(**has**, have, had)	grown	(am, **is**, are, was, were)	growing
know	knew	(**has**, have, had)	known	(am, **is**, are, was, were)	knowing
lay	laid	(**has**, have, had)	laid	(am, **is**, are, was, were)	laying
lie	lay	(**has**, have, had)	lain	(am, **is**, are, was, were)	lying
lose	lost	(**has**, have, had)	lost	(am, **is**, are, was, were)	losing
make	made	(**has**, have, had)	made	(am, **is**, are, was, were)	making
ride	rode	(**has**, have, had)	ridden	(am, **is**, are, was, were)	riding
ring	rang	(**has**, have, had)	rung	(am, **is**, are, was, were)	ringing
rise	rose	(**has**, have, had)	risen	(am, **is**, are, was, were)	rising
run	ran	(**has**, have, had)	run	(am, **is**, are, was, were)	running
say	said	(**has**, have, had)	said	(am, **is**, are, was, were)	saying
see	saw	(**has**, have, had)	seen	(am, **is**, are, was, were)	seeing
sell	sold	(**has**, have, had)	sold	(am, **is**, are, was, were)	selling
sing	sang	(**has**, have, had)	sung	(am, **is**, are, was, were)	singing
sink	sank	(**has**, have, had)	sunk	(am, **is**, are, was, were)	sinking
set	set	(**has**, have, had)	set	(am, **is**, are, was, were)	setting
shoot	shot	(**has**, have, had)	shot	(am, **is**, are, was, were)	shooting
sit	sat	(**has**, have, had)	sat	(am, **is**, are, was, were)	sitting
speak	spoke	(**has**, have, had)	spoken	(am, **is**, are, was, were)	speaking
swim	swam	(**has**, have, had)	swum	(am, **is**, are, was, were)	swimming
take	took	(**has**, have, had)	taken	(am, **is**, are, was, were)	taking
teach	taught	(**has**, have, had)	taught	(am, **is**, are, was, were)	teaching
tell	told	(**has**, have, had)	told	(am, **is**, are, was, were)	telling
throw	threw	(**has**, have, had)	thrown	(am, **is**, are, was, were)	throwing
wear	wore	(**has**, have, had)	worn	(am, **is**, are, was, were)	wearing
write	wrote	(**has**, have, had)	written	(am, **is**, are, was, were)	writing

Principal Parts of Regular Verbs

PRESENT	PAST	PAST PARTICIPLE		PRESENT PARTICIPLE	
call	called	(**has**, have, had)	called	(am, **is**, are, was, were)	calling
cry	cried	(**has**, have, had)	cried	(am, **is**, are, was, were)	crying
hop	hopped	(**has**, have, had)	hopped	(am, **is**, are, was, were)	hopping
play	played	(**has**, have, had)	played	(am, **is**, are, was, were)	playing

Student Tip...

Recite a set of five verbs in Reference 118 in a lively manner:
Follow the example below.

Say: (become)	(became)	(has become)	(is becoming)
Say: (begin)	(began)	(has begun)	(is beginning)
Say: (blow)	(blew)	(has blown)	(is blowing)
Say: (break)	(broke)	(has broken)	(is breaking)
Say: (bring)	(brought)	(has brought)	(is bringing)

Classroom Practice 27

It is time to practice the skills you are learning. You will use the classroom practice on the next page to apply these skills.

ENRICHMENT:

Discovery Time

(French) 1809-1852— Louis Braille created the Braille printing system of reading for the blind. He was blinded at the age of three in an accident while he was playing with tools in his father's harness shop. Braille excelled in a school for the blind and eventually became a teacher for the blind. The idea for his system originated when a soldier came to the school to demonstrate the army's "night writing" code, but this code was very complicated. Using a system of raised dots, Braille designed a simple alphabet for blind people.

Discovery Questions:
- What tool caused Braille's blindness and was also used by Braille to make the raised dots for his alphabet?
- How important is Braille to a blind person?

Discovery Activity:
- Check out a book written in Braille to see if you can feel the pattern of the dots enough to read them.

Are you interested in learning more about Louis Braille?

1. You may explore this topic further by using the resources listed below.
   Computer resources: Internet, encyclopedia software
   Library resources: encyclopedias, books, magazines, newspapers
   Home/community resources: books, interviews, newspapers, magazines

2. A Discovery Share Time is provided in Lesson 7 if you wish to share your investigation results. You may share orally, or you may prepare a written report. You will put your written report in a class booklet titled "Notable People in History." This booklet will be placed in the class library for everyone to enjoy.

Classroom Practice 27

Name:_____ Date:_____

GRAMMAR

▸ **Exercise 1:** Classify each sentence.

1. _____ The new advisor quietly waited outside the President's office.

2. _____ Wow! Look at the enormous tires on Jeremy's new truck!

SKILLS

▸ **Exercise 2:** Use a slash to separate each run-on sentence below. Then, correct the run-on sentences by rewriting them as indicated by the labels in parentheses at the end of each sentence.

1. We did not go to bed the movie was over. (**CX, until**) (**2**)

   _____

2. I watch scary movies I have trouble going to sleep. (**CX, whenever**) (**1**)

   _____

3. Jennifer was not allowed to have dessert she ate her vegetables. (**CX, until**) (**2**)

   _____

4. The girl was laughing no one seemed to notice. (**CX, although**) (**1**)

   _____

5. You must clean your room I will pay your allowance. (**CX, before**) (**2**)

   _____

▸ **Exercise 3:** Identify each type of sentence by writing the correct label in the blank. (**Labels: S, F, SCS, SCV, CD, CX**)

_____ 1. You left your bicycle out in the rain; consequently, it rusted.
_____ 2. I love to read, and I go to the library at least twice a week.
_____ 3. During the musical, Jan and Joe sang a duet.
_____ 4. During the summer, when the games were over.
_____ 5. When I heard the noise, I ran to the window.
_____ 6. The ice melted after the sun came out.
_____ 7. My sisters waved good-bye and left for the concert.
_____ 8. Since I do not drive a car, I usually walk or ride a bus.
_____ 9. Eat balanced meals every day, and you will be healthier.
_____ 10. The salesman walked to the door and rang the doorbell.

EDITING

▸ **Exercise 4:** Correct each mistake. **Editing Guide: End Marks: 2   Capitals: 13   Commas: 3   Apostrophes: 1**
Homonyms: 1   Subject-Verb Agreement: 2   Periods: 1   Misspelled Words: 2

did you no that sir arthur conan doyles famous detective character sherlock holmes were

inspired by his medacal school professor dr joseph bell dad have all the sherlock holmes storys

 **Homework 4**

Complete this homework assignment on notebook paper.

1. Copy the sentence below. Classify the sentence, using the Question and Answer Flow, as you label each part.

_____ Oh, no! The grandchildren are jumping on Nana's bed after thirty minutes

of running and playing.

2. Correct the run-on sentences on notebook paper by rewriting them as indicated by the labels in parentheses at the end of each sentence.

1. JoAnn got sick she went to the doctor. (**CX, when**) (1)

_____

2. I worked two jobs I needed the money. (**CX, because**) (2)

_____

3. You cannot pass this test you do not study. (**CX, if**) (2)

_____

4. The storm hit we took cover. (**CX, before**) (1)

_____

3. Write two complex sentences on notebook paper. For the first complex sentence, write the subordinate clause first and write the independent clause last. For the second complex sentence, write the independent clause first and write the subordinate clause last. Punctuate each complex sentence correctly.

Home Connection

Family Activity for Possessive Nouns

Divide into two teams. One team will write a set of directions, using prepositional phrases instead of possessive nouns. See the example below.

Directions to the **house of Martha:**
Go two blocks from school toward the **office of the mayor**. Turn right at the intersection next to the **playground of the children**. When you pass the library, turn to your left. The **house of Martha** is the second white house on the left. You will see the **motorcycle of her brother** in the front yard. Cross the street carefully to the **house of Martha**. Please do not walk on the **lawn of the neighbors**.

The second team will rewrite the directions, using possessive nouns as shown in the example below.

Directions to **Martha's house:**
Go two blocks from school toward the **mayor's office**. Turn right at the intersection next to the **children's playground**. When you pass the library, turn to your left. **Martha's house** is the second white house on the left. You will see her **brother's motorcycle** in the front yard. Cross the street carefully to **Martha's house**. Please do not walk on the **neighbor's lawn**.

After both teams have finished, each team will read its paragraph aloud. Discuss the importance of possessive nouns in everyday conversation. Then, the teams will exchange members and/or jobs and complete another set of directions.

Family Activity for Vocabulary and Analogies

Divide into family teams. The first team will use vocabulary and analogy cards 13–16 to ask questions about the information on their cards. The second team will use vocabulary and analogy cards 17–20 to ask questions about the information on their cards.

English Made Easy

Grammar Time

Apply It: Classify the Practice Sentences orally with your teacher.

Practice Sentences	Chapter 6: Lesson 5

1. _____ Yesterday, a cute little yellow car was completely stopped in the middle of the road!
2. _____ Quietly sit at the desk behind Jeff for the final examination.
3. _____ Yea! We proudly cheered for the boys and girls in the district's spelling competition.

Chapter Checkup 28

It is time for a checkup of the skills you have learned in this chapter. You will use the chapter checkup on the next page to evaluate your progress.

ENRICHMENT:

Discovery Time

(American) 1813-1906— Joseph Glidden invented barbed wire. Before Glidden's invention, farmers had no way to prevent cattle, sheep, or horses from grazing on their crops, and ranchers had no way to prevent their herds from roaming away. Glidden's barbed wire opened up the plains for large-acreage crop planting and contributed to the end of the cowboy era during which herds had been rounded-up for inspection, branding, and shipping to market.

Discovery Questions:
- **How do you think the farmers felt about barbed wire?**
- **How do you think the cowboys felt about barbed wire?**
- **How do you feel about barbed wire?**

(American) 1815-1902— Elizabeth Cady Stanton was the daughter of a U.S. congressman and spent her adult life fighting for the abolition of slavery and for women's rights. Her efforts were responsible for introducing a constitutional amendment for women's suffrage.

Discovery Questions:
- **Which amendment guarantees women the right to vote?**
- **Would you exercise your right to vote?**
- **Do you think this right is important?**

Are you interested in learning more about Joseph Glidden or Elizabeth Cady Stanton?

1. You may explore these topics further by using the resources listed below.
   Computer resources: Internet, encyclopedia software
   Library resources: encyclopedias, books, magazines, newspapers
   Home/community resources: books, interviews, newspapers, magazines

2. A Discovery Share Time is provided in Lesson 7 if you wish to share your investigation results. You may share orally, or you may prepare a written report. You will put your written report in a class booklet titled "Notable People in History." This booklet will be placed in the class library for everyone to enjoy.

START LESSON 5

Lesson 5

You will
- classify Practice Sentences.
- do Chapter Checkup 28.
- write in your journal.
- read and discuss Discovery Time.

JOURNAL WRITING 15

Write an entry in your journal. Use Reference 9 on page 12 for ideas.

Chapter 6 Checkup 28

Name:_____ Date:_____

GRAMMAR

▶ **Exercise 1:** Classify each sentence.

1. _____ Dan's three fishing buddies idly sat in their boat for a relaxing day at the lake.

2. _____ Mercy! All the newborn babies in the nursery cried loudly throughout the night!

3. _____ Did the alumni of our college meet and talk together after the football game?

SKILLS

▶ **Exercise 2:** Identify each type of sentence by writing the correct label in the blank. (**Labels: S, F, SCS, SCV, CD, CX**)

_____ 1. The wind whistled and howled during the night.
_____ 2. The glass door at the theatre's entrance.
_____ 3. A summer thunderstorm can be quite scary.
_____ 4. When Kyle finished his project, he treated himself to a movie.
_____ 5. Sports are fun, but they can be dangerous.
_____ 6. He didn't stop until he crossed the finish line.
_____ 7. Adam and Allison are planning a June wedding in England.
_____ 8. We like our new camera; however, it was expensive.

▶ **Exercise 3:** Use a slash to separate each run-on sentence below. Then, correct the run-on sentences by rewriting them as indicated by the labels in parentheses at the end of each sentence.

1. The road was bumpy I drove slowly. (**CX, because**) (1)

_____

2. The lights went out Kristi turned on the flashlight. (**CX, after**) (1)

_____

3. I like to read I go to bed. (**CX, before**) (2)

_____

4. Dale jumped he heard a loud noise. (**CX, when**) (2)

_____

EDITING

▶ **Exercise 4:** Correct each mistake. **Editing Guide: End Marks: 3   Capitals: 9   Commas: 1   Apostrophes: 2   Homonyms: 2   A/An: 1   Subject-Verb Agreement: 1   Periods: 2   Misspelled Words: 1**

ella didnt finish her homework for mr browns algebra class because back-to-back episodes

of her favorite show were on last night after she recieved an note too her parents from

mr brown she decided her priorities was not in order she knew their would be no tv tonight

Writing Time

Write It: WRITING ASSIGNMENT 13

Writing Assignment 13 : Creative Expressions

Purpose: To entertain

Type of Writing: Creative

Audience: Classmates or family members

Writing prompt: The secretary for the President of the United States was placing an important call to the President's most trusted advisor. By mistake, you received that phone call, and you just happened to be an expert on the matter the President wished to discuss. Write the telephone conversation between the President and you. You are to present the problem, the solution, and convince the President that you are right.

Special Instructions:

1. Write a response to the writing prompt above.

2. A prewriting map is not required for this creative-writing assignment.

3. Follow the Rough Draft Checklist in Reference 46 on page 61.

4. Put your creative-writing paper in your Rough Draft folder when you have finished.

Note: Reference 54 on page 71 gives the steps in the writing process and the location of all the writing checklists.

 Conference Time

Discuss It: TEACHER-STUDENT CONFERENCES
FOR WRITING ASSIGNMENT 12

Meet with your teacher to discuss Writing Assignment 12.
After the conference, place this group of papers in your Publishing folder.

START LESSON 7

Lesson 7

You will

- publish WA 12.
- participate in Discovery Share Time.
- do Across the Curriculum activity.

Publishing Time

Publish It: **WRITING ASSIGNMENT 12**

Choose a publishing form and publish Writing Assignment 12. After rewriting your paper for publication, give the stapled papers (evaluation guide, graded final paper, rough draft, and prewriting map) to your teacher to be placed in your Writing Portfolio.

Reference 66	Publishing Checklist for Step 6 in the Writing Process

The sixth step in the writing process is called publishing. Publishing is sharing your writing with others. With so many forms of publishing available, finding a match for every project and personality is easy.

At times, a written work is best read aloud. Other times, the biggest impact is made when a written work is read silently. You can also use media sources to enhance any publication.

SPECIAL INSTRUCTIONS FOR PUBLISHING:

- Rewrite the graded paper in ink or type it on a computer, correcting any marked errors. *(Do not display or publish papers that have marked errors or grades on them.)*
- Give your teacher the set of stapled papers to place in your Writing Portfolio. *(Stapled papers: evaluation guide, graded final paper, rough draft, and prewriting map.)*
- Select a publishing form from the list below and publish your rewritten paper.
    1. Have classmates, family members, neighbors, or others read your writing at school or home.
    2. Share your writing with others during a Share Time. *(Refer to Reference 67 on page 99 for sharing guidelines.)*
    3. Display your writing on a bulletin board or wall.
    4. Put your writing in the classroom library or in the school library for checkout.
    5. Send your writing as a letter or an e-mail to a friend or relative.
    6. Frame your writing by gluing it on colored construction paper and decorating it.
    7. Make a book of your writing for your classroom, your family, or others.
    8. Illustrate your writing and give it to others to read.
    9. Dramatize your writing in the form of a play, puppet show, or radio broadcast.
    10. Send your writing to be placed in a waiting room (doctor, veterinarian, dentist, etc.), senior-citizen center, or a nursing home.
    11. Send your writing to a school newspaper, local newspaper, or a magazine for publication.
    12. Make a videotape, cassette tape, or slide presentation of your writing.
    13. Choose another publishing form that is not listed.

LISTENING AND SPEAKING:

Discovery Share Time

If you have chosen to investigate a historical figure introduced in this chapter, you now have the opportunity to share your results in one of the following ways:

1. You may relate your information orally.
2. You may read a written report.
3. You may place your report in the booklet without reading it aloud.

After share time, all written reports should be turned in to be placed in the class booklet titled "Notable People in History." You are encouraged to check out this class booklet so you can enjoy the reports again.

Across the Curriculum

Language Development Connection: Divide into groups of five and sit in circles. One student in each group is designated as the leader and will stand outside the circle. The leader will give each person in the group one index card marked with the word *interrogative, declarative, imperative,* or *exclamatory*. The students in the group will pass the index cards around the circle until the leader says, "Stop!" Then, the leader will ask one student at a time to make up the kind of sentence listed on his card. Repeat the game until every person in the group has had a chance to be the leader.

Challenge: The leader will suggest a topic, such as *horses*, that everyone in the group must use as he/she makes up original sentences.

Chapter 6

START LESSON 8

Lesson 8

You will

- practice Jingle 2.
- do Classroom Practice 29.
- write an independent expository essay (WA 14).

LISTENING AND SPEAKING:

Jingle Time

Recite It: Practice Jingle 2 in the Jingle Section on page 506.

GRAMMAR & WRITING CONNECTION:
Practice and Revised Sentence

Apply It: BUILDING AND EXPANDING SENTENCES

Reference 117 — **A Guide for Using Possessive Nouns and Interjections to Build & Expand Sentences**

1. **PNA (possessive noun adjective)** Think of a possessive noun that answers the question "whose." The possessive noun should make sense in your sentence. Write the apostrophe correctly as you write the possessive noun adjective you have chosen for your sentence. Repeat this step for each possessive noun adjective you add to the sentence.

2. **I (interjection)** Choose an interjection that makes the best sense in your sentence. Make sure you punctuate the interjection with an exclamation point or a comma. Write the interjection you have chosen for your sentence.

Student Tip...

Use your vocabulary words in your Practice and Revised Sentences. Use a thesaurus, synonym-antonym book, or a dictionary to help you develop your writing vocabulary.

Classroom Practice 29

It is time to practice the skills you are learning. You will use the classroom practice on the next page to apply these skills.

Writing Time

Write It: WRITING ASSIGNMENT 14

As you write a rough draft for your independent writing assignment, you will do two of the six steps in the writing process: prewriting and rough draft.

Writing Assignment 14

Purpose: To inform
Type of Writing: Five-paragraph expository essay
Audience: Classmates or friends
Writing Topics: Things I Like to Do With My Friend(s)
Dangers of Sunburn/Smoking/Extreme Sports
Least Favorite Clothes/Car(s)/Song(s)/Book(s)
(Brainstorm for other ideas, individually or in groups.)

Special Instructions:

1. Follow the Prewriting and Rough Draft Checklists in References 44 and 46 on pages 57, 61.
2. Use References 103–106 on pages 165–168 to help you write your expository essay.
3. Use standard, time-order, or transition writing form. See Reference 69 on page 103.
4. Write in first or third person. See Reference 70 on page 104.
   (First-person pronouns: *I, me, my, mine, we, us, our, and ours.*)
   (Third-person pronouns: *he, his, him, she, her, hers, it, its, they, their, theirs, and them.*)

Note: Reference 54 on page 71 gives the steps in the writing process and the location of all the writing checklists.

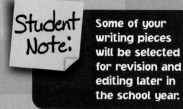
Student Note: Some of your writing pieces will be selected for revision and editing later in the school year.

Classroom Practice 29

Name: _____   Date: _____

INDEPENDENT PRACTICE & REVISED SENTENCES

1. Write a Practice Sentence according to the labels you choose.
Use **SN/SP V** as your main labels. You may use the other labels in any order and as many times as you wish in order to make a Practice Sentence.
Chapter 6 labels for a Practice Sentence: **SN/SP, V,** Adj, Adv, A, P, OP, PPA, C, HV, I, PNA

2. Write a Revised Sentence. Use the following revision strategies: *synonym (syn), antonym (ant), word change (wc), added word (add), deleted word (delete), or no change (nc).* Under each word, write the abbreviation of the revision strategy you use.

Labels:

Practice:

Revised:

Strategies:

Labels:

Practice:

Revised:

Strategies:

Labels:

Practice:

Revised:

Strategies:

SHURLEY ENGLISH

Lesson 9

You will

- practice Jingle 12.
- read and discuss a persuasive paragraph and three-paragraph essay.
- plan and write rough draft for persuasive essay (WA 15).

LISTENING AND SPEAKING:

Recite It: Practice Jingle 12 in the Jingle Section on page 509.

>>>> **Student Tip...**

> Reviewing the transition words will help you apply them in your writing.

Learn It: **PERSUASIVE WRITING**

You have been studying expository writing. Now, you will learn about persuasive writing. As you study persuasive writing, try to answer the following questions.

What does persuasion mean?

How is persuasive writing organized?

How is persuasive writing different from expository writing?

🖉 Reference 118   Persuasive Writing

Persuasion is getting other people to see things your way. When you write a persuasive paragraph or essay, you are encouraging, or **persuading**, your audience to take a certain action or to feel the same way you do. Persuasive writing expresses an opinion and tries to convince the reader that this opinion is correct. An opinion is a belief or feeling that cannot be proven. It is a personal judgment. A fact is a statement that can be proved as true. Persuasive writing uses facts to support opinions of the writer.

As the writer, you must make the issue clear and present facts and reasons that strongly support your opinion. It is VERY important to consider who your audience is and to use arguments that will appeal to that audience. You would not use the same kind of argument to persuade your five-year-old sister to tell you where she hid your skates that you would use to persuade your parents to allow you to have friends over.

The three-point writing format is one of the best ways to present your persuasive argument because it gives you an organized way of stating your opinion and supporting it. The persuasive-writing format is the same as the expository-writing format. They both use the three-point organization. The differences between persuasive and expository writing are your purpose for writing and the wording of your sentences.

In persuasive writing, the topic sentence is an opinion statement. In addition, all the points and supporting sentences are persuasive in nature and are intended to back up the opinion statement. Persuasive writing states your opinion and backs it up with supporting facts that try to convince your reader to agree with you.

There are certain words that signal when a writer is expressing an opinion. Opinion Words: think, believe, feel, hope, seem, best, better, worse, worst, probably, excellent, terrible, should, love, hate, etc.

Learn It: **WRITING A PERSUASIVE PARAGRAPH**

Any time you do persuasive writing, whether it is a paragraph or an essay, you will have three parts: the **introduction**, the **body**, and the **conclusion**. The three parts will always be written in that order. Although a title will be the first item appearing at the top of a paragraph or essay, you will not finalize the title until you have finished writing the persuasive piece. The title becomes the fourth part of a paragraph or essay.

As you study the persuasive paragraph, you should notice that most of the sentences used in a persuasive paragraph are opinion statements. Factual statements are used to support opinion statements.

Reference 119 — Writing a Persuasive Paragraph

Writing Topic: **Improving school lunches.**

Sentence 1 – **Topic Sentence:**
State your opinion in the topic sentence.

> **Along with the regular lunch line, our lunchroom needs an a-la-carte line in which students pay for each item separately.**

Sentence 2 – **General Number Sentence:**
You will use a general number word and restate the main idea in the topic sentence.

> **There are several reasons why we need an a-la-carte line.**

Sentence 3 – **First Point:**
You will give your first reason to support your opinion.

> **The first reason we need an a-la-carte line is to provide more interesting choices for lunch.**

Sentence 4 – **Supporting Sentence(s):**
You will give an example that supports and explains your first point. Write one or two sentences.

> **Schools that have a-la-carte lines serve such popular items as pizza, hamburgers, sandwiches, soup, salad, and fruit.**

Sentence 5 – **Second Point:**
You will give your second reason to support your opinion.

> **The second reason we need an a-la-carte line is to avoid wasting food.**

Sentence 6 – **Supporting Sentence(s):**
You will give an example that supports and explains your second point. Write one or two sentences.

> **Many students who buy hot lunches simply throw away most of the food because they do not want but one or two items on their tray.**

Sentence 7 – **Third Point:**
You will give your third reason to support your opinion.

> **The third reason we need an a-la-carte line is to give students practice in making decisions.**

Sentence 8 – **Supporting Sentence(s):**
You will give an example that supports and explains your third point. Write one or two sentences.

> **If students are taught how to make healthy food choices at school and at home, they will learn to be selective and make better choices at the food line.**

Sentence 9 – **First Concluding Sentence:**
The first concluding sentence is a restatement sentence that forcefully restates your original opinion in the topic sentence and usually starts with the words, *In conclusion*.

> **In conclusion, we need an a-la-carte line at our school.**

Sentence 10 – **Final Concluding Sentence:**
This sentence summarizes one or more of the reasons stated.

> **Not only would it provide an opportunity for more food selections, but this added lunch feature would prevent waste and promote wiser consumer participation.**

WRITING THE TITLE

The Title. Since there are many possibilities for titles, look at the topic and the three points listed about the topic. Use some of the words in the topic and write a phrase to tell what your paragraph is about. Your title can be short or long. Capitalize the first, last, and important words in your title.

Title: Spicing Up School Lunches

Continued on next page. >>>

Reference 119 continued from previous page.

Spicing Up School Lunches

Along with the regular lunch line, our lunchroom needs an a-la-carte line in which students pay for each item separately. There are several reasons why we need an a-la-carte line. The first reason we need an a-la-carte line is to provide more interesting choices for lunch. Schools that have a-la-carte lines serve such popular items as pizza, hamburgers, sandwiches, soup, salad, and fruit. The second reason we need an a-la-carte line is to avoid wasting food. Many students who buy hot lunches simply throw away most of the food because they do not want but one or two items on their tray. The third reason we need an a-la-carte line is to give students practice in making decisions. If students are taught how to make healthy food choices at school and at home, they will learn to be selective and make better choices at the food line. In conclusion, we need an a-la-carte line at our school. Not only would it provide an opportunity for more food selections, but this added lunch feature would prevent waste and promote wiser consumer participation.

Compare It:

As you study the two outlines below, notice that there are more sentences in the introduction and conclusion for the essay. Also, note that in the essay, the second paragraph contains all the points and supporting sentences.

 Reference 120 | ## Outlines for the Persuasive Paragraph and the Three-Paragraph Persuasive Essay

Guidelines for a Persuasive Paragraph

Paragraph

A. **Topic** sentence (opinion statement)

B. **General number** sentence

C. **First-point** persuasive sentence

D. One or two **supporting** sentences for the first point

E. **Second-point** persuasive sentence

F. One or two **supporting** sentences for the second point

G. **Third-point** persuasive sentence

H. One or two **supporting** sentences for the third point

I. **First concluding** sentence (Restate topic idea)

J. **Final concluding** sentence (Summarize reasons)

Title

Guidelines for a Three-Paragraph Persuasive Essay

1. **Paragraph 1**—Introduction

   A. **Topic** sentence (opinion statement)

   B. **Reason** sentence

   C. **General number** sentence

2. **Paragraph 2**—Body

   A. **First-point** persuasive sentence

   B. One or two **supporting** sentences for the first point

   C. **Second-point** persuasive sentence

   D. One or two **supporting** sentences for the second point

   E. **Third-point** persuasive sentence

   F. One or two **supporting** sentences for the third point

3. **Paragraph 3**—Conclusion

   A. **First concluding** sentence (Restate topic idea)

   B. **Final concluding** sentence (Summarize reasons)

4. **Title**

Learn It: WRITING THE INTRODUCTION FOR A THREE-PARAGRAPH PERSUASIVE ESSAY

The organization of a three-paragraph persuasive essay has three parts: the introduction forms the first paragraph, the body forms the second paragraph, and the conclusion forms the third paragraph.

Three sentences make up the introduction. The first sentence is the **topic sentence**. The second sentence is the added sentence that gives a **reason** why the topic sentence is true. The third sentence in the introduction is called a **general number sentence**. This is the sentence you will add when writing any persuasive essay. It gives a general or specific number of points (reasons or proofs) that will be mentioned to prove the topic sentence. You will NOT list your three points as you usually do in the expository three-point writing you have studied.

Reference 121 — Writing the Introduction for a Three-Paragraph Persuasive Essay

THE INTRODUCTION
Paragraph 1

Writing Topic: **Improving School Lunches**

Sentence 1 – Topic Sentence:
State your opinion in the topic sentence.
> **Along with the regular lunch line, our lunchroom needs an a-la-carte line in which students pay for each item separately.**

Sentence 2 – Reason Sentence:
You will give a general reason why you think the topic sentence is true.
> **An a-la-carte line would be popular with both students and teachers.**

Sentence 3 – General Number Sentence:
You will use a general number word and restate the main idea in the topic sentence.
> **There are several reasons why we need an a-la-carte line.**

Learn It: **WRITING THE BODY FOR A THREE-PARAGRAPH PERSUASIVE ESSAY**

After the introduction, you are ready to write the body. The body of a three-paragraph essay contains one paragraph. This paragraph lists each of the three persuasive points. Also, notice that each of the three main points has one or two supporting sentences.

Reference 122 — Writing the Body for a Three-Paragraph Persuasive Essay

THE BODY
Paragraph 2

Sentence 4 – First Point:
You will give your first reason to support your opinion.
> **The first reason we need an a-la-carte line is to provide more interesting choices for lunch.**

Sentences 5–6 – Supporting Sentence(s):
You will give an example that supports and explains your first point. Write one or more sentences.
> **Schools that have a-la-carte lines serve such popular items as pizza, hamburgers, sandwiches, soup, salad, and fruit. More students and teachers would actually eat lunch if they had these choices.**

Continued on next page. >>>

Reference 122 continued from previous page.

Sentence 7 – Second Point:
You will give your second reason to support your opinion.

> **The second reason we need an a-la-carte line is to avoid wasting food.**

Sentences 8–9 – Supporting Sentence(s):
You will give an example that supports and explains your second point. Write one or more sentences.

> **Many students who buy hot lunches simply throw away most of the food because they do not want but one or two items on their tray. With an a-la-carte line, students purchase only what they want to eat, and there is no waste.**

Sentence 10 – Third Point:
You will give your third reason to support your opinion.

> **The third reason we need an a-la-carte line is to give students practice in making decisions.**

Sentences 11–12 – Supporting Sentence(s):
You will give an example that supports and explains your third point. Write one or more sentences.

> **If students are taught how to make healthy food choices at school and at home, they will learn to be selective and make better choices at the food line. Learning to make good choices in school will help students become wiser consumers as adults.**

Learn It: **WRITING THE CONCLUSION FOR A THREE-PARAGRAPH PERSUASIVE ESSAY**

The conclusion forms the third paragraph. The closing paragraph, or conclusion, should tie all the important points together with a restatement of the main idea and your final comments.

Two sentences make up the conclusion. The first sentence in the conclusion is called the **first concluding sentence**. To write this sentence, you should refer to the third sentence in the introduction. Using the general or specific number and topic as stated in that introductory sentence, you can write a similar concluding sentence. The **final concluding sentences** summarize one or more of the reasons stated.

Reference 123 — Writing the Conclusion for a Three-Paragraph Persuasive Essay

THE CONCLUSION
Paragraph 3

Sentence 13 – First Concluding Sentence:
The first concluding sentence is a restatement sentence that forcefully restates your original opinion in the topic sentence and usually starts with the words, *In conclusion*. Write one sentence.

> **In conclusion, we need an a-la-carte line at our school.**

Sentences 14–15 – Final Concluding Sentence(s):
These final sentences summarize one or more of the reasons stated. Write one or two sentences.

> **Not only would it provide an opportunity for more food selections, but this added lunch feature would prevent waste and promote wiser consumer participation. Adding an a-la-cart line at our school would help students make healthy choices and would be a wise decision by our school board.**

WRITING THE TITLE
Since there are many possibilities for titles, look at the topic and the three points listed about the topic. Use some of the words in the topic and write a phrase to tell what your paragraph is about. Your title can be short or long. Capitalize the first, last, and important words in your title.

Title: Spicing Up School Lunches

Continued on next page. >>>

Reference 123 continued from previous page.

A Sample Three-Paragraph Persuasive Essay

Spicing Up School Lunches

Along with the regular lunch line, our lunchroom needs an a-la-carte line in which students pay for each item separately. An a-la-carte line would be popular with both students and teachers. There are several reasons why we need an a-la-carte line.

The first reason we need an a-la-carte line is to provide more interesting choices for lunch. Schools that have a-la-carte lines serve such popular items as pizza, hamburgers, sandwiches, soup, salad, and fruit. More students and teachers would actually eat lunch if they had these choices. The second reason we need an a-la-carte line is to avoid wasting food. Many students who buy hot lunches simply throw away most of the food because they do not want but one or two items on their tray. With an a-la-carte line, students purchase only what they want to eat, and there is no waste. The third reason we need an a-la-carte line is to give students practice in making decisions. If students are taught how to make healthy food choices at school and at home, they will learn to be selective and make better choices at the food line. Learning to make good choices in school will help students become wiser consumers as adults.

In conclusion, we need an a-la-carte line at our school. Not only would it provide an opportunity for more food selections, but this added lunch feature would prevent waste and promote wiser consumer participation. Adding an a-la-cart line at our school would help students make healthy choices and would be a wise decision by our school board.

Writing Time

Write It: **WRITING ASSIGNMENT 15**

As you write a rough draft for your guided writing assignment, you will do two of the six steps in the writing process: prewriting and rough draft.

Writing Assignment 15

Purpose: To persuade

Type of Writing: Three-paragraph persuasive essay

Audience: Classmates

Writing Topics: Reasons why hunter education is important
Why we need a family vacation/new car
Why a computer/an allowance is important
(Brainstorm for other ideas, individually or in groups.)

Special Instructions:

1. Follow the Prewriting and Rough Draft Checklists in References 44 and 46 on pages 57, 61.

2. Use References 118–123 on pages 196–201 to help you write your persuasive essay.

3. Use standard, time-order, or transition writing form. See Reference 69 on page 103.

4. Write in first or third person. See Reference 70 on page 104.
   (First-person pronouns: *I, me, my, mine, we, us, our,* and *ours*.)
   (Third-person pronouns: *he, his, him, she, her, hers, it, its, they, their, theirs,* and *them*.)

Note: Reference 54 on page 71 gives the steps in the writing process and the location of all the writing checklists.

START LESSON 10

Writing Time

Lesson 10

You will

- revise, edit, and write a final paper for WA 15.

Apply It: **REVISE, EDIT, AND WRITE A FINAL PAPER**

Following the schedule below, you will revise and edit Writing Assignment 15. Then, you will write a final paper. Use the Chapter 6 Writing Evaluation Guide on the next page to check your final paper one last time.

Reference 52 | **Revising & Editing Schedule and Writing a Final Paper**

SPECIAL INSTRUCTIONS FOR REVISING AND EDITING (Steps 3-4 in the writing process):

- Use the Revising and Editing Checklists in References 48 and 50 as you revise and edit your rough draft.
- Follow the revising and editing schedule below as directed by your teacher.

　1. **Individual.** First, read your rough draft to yourself. Use the Revising Checklist in Reference 48 on page 64. Go through your paper, checking each item on the list and making revisions to your rough draft. Then, use the Editing Checklist in Reference 50 on pages 66–67. Go through your paper again, checking each item on the list and editing your rough draft.

　2. **Partner.** Next, get with your editing partner. Work together on each partner's rough draft, one paper at a time. Read each rough draft aloud and revise and edit it together, using the Revising and Editing Checklists. (The author of the paper should be the one to make the corrections on his own paper.)

　3. **Group.** Finally, read the rough draft to a revision group for feedback. Each student should read his paper while the others listen and offer possible revising and editing suggestions. (The author will determine whether to make corrections from the revision group's suggestions.)

SPECIAL INSTRUCTIONS FOR FINAL PAPER (Step 5 in the writing process):

- Write your final paper, using the Final Paper Checklist in Reference 53 on page 70.
- Staple your writing papers in this order: the final paper on top, the rough draft in the middle, and the prewriting map on the bottom. Place the stapled papers in the Final Paper folder.

>>>>>>>>>>>>> **Student Tip...**

　1. Be tactful and helpful in your comments during revising and editing time. The purpose of any suggestion should be to improve the writer's rough draft.

　2. As you make your final corrections, you have the choice of accepting or rejecting any suggestions made by your partners or your revision group.

　3. Study Vocabulary Words and Analogies 17–20 for the chapter test in the next lesson.

　4. If you need to improve your handwriting, refer to the Resource Tools Section on pages 529–530 for information on writing legibly.

Chapter 6 Writing Evaluation Guide

Name:_____ Date:_____

ROUGH DRAFT CHECK

_____ 1. Did you write your rough draft in pencil?

_____ 2. Did you write the correct headings on the first seven lines of your paper?

_____ 3. Did you use extra wide margins and skip every other line?

_____ 4. Did you write a title at the end of your rough draft?

_____ 5. Did you place your edited rough draft in your Rough Draft folder?

REVISING CHECK

_____ 6. Did you identify the purpose, type of writing, and audience?

_____ 7. Did you check for a topic, topic sentence, and sentences supporting the topic?

_____ 8. Did you check sentences for the right order, and did you combine, rearrange, or delete sentences when necessary?

_____ 9. Did you check for a variety of simple, compound, and complex sentences?

_____ 10. Did you check for any left out, repeated, or unnecessary words?

_____ 11. Did you check for the best choice of words by replacing or deleting unclear words?

_____ 12. Did you check the content for interest and creativity?

_____ 13. Did you check the voice to make sure the writing says what you want it to say?

EDITING CHECK

_____ 14. Did you indent each paragraph?

_____ 15. Did you put an end mark at the end of every sentence?

_____ 16. Did you capitalize the first word of every sentence?

_____ 17. Did you check for all other capitalization mistakes?

_____ 18. Did you check for all punctuation mistakes?
(commas, periods, apostrophes, quotation marks, underlining)

_____ 19. Did you check for misspelled words and for incorrect homonym choices?

_____ 20. Did you check for incorrect spellings of plural and possessive forms?

_____ 21. Did you check for correct construction and punctuation of your sentences?

_____ 22. Did you check for usage mistakes? *(subject/verb agreement, a/an choices, contractions, verb tenses, pronoun/antecedent agreement, pronoun cases, degrees of adjectives, double negatives, etc.)*

_____ 23. Did you put your revised and edited paper in the Rough Draft folder?

FINAL PAPER CHECK

_____ 24. Did you write the final paper in pencil?

_____ 25. Did you center the title on the top line and center your name under the title?

_____ 26. Did you skip a line before starting the writing assignment?

_____ 27. Did you single-space, use wide margins, and write the final paper neatly?

_____ 28. Did you staple your papers in this order: final paper on top, rough draft in the middle, and prewriting map on the bottom? Did you put them in the Final Paper folder?

START LESSON 11

Lesson 11

You will

- hand in WA 15 for grading.
- respond to
  oral review questions.
- take Chapter 6 Test.

CHAPTER TEST

It is time to evaluate your knowledge of the skills you have learned in this chapter. Your teacher will give you the Chapter 6 Test to help you assess your progress.

Writing Time

Hand It In: **WRITING ASSIGNMENT 15**

Get your stapled papers for Writing Assignment 15 from your Final Paper folder. Check to make sure they are in the correct order: the final paper on top, the rough draft in the middle, and the prewriting map on the bottom. Hand them in to your teacher.

LISTENING AND SPEAKING:

Oral Review Questions

Discuss It:

1. What are the eight parts of speech?

2. What part of speech is used to show emotion?

3. What is the name of a noun that shows ownership and modifies like an adjective?

4. What are the two jobs of a possessive noun?

5. What punctuation mark is used to show that a noun is possessive?

6. What are the four kinds of sentences?

7. What is the End Mark Flow for the declarative sentence?

8. What is the End Mark Flow for the imperative sentence?

9. What is the End Mark Flow for the exclamatory sentence?

10. What is the End Mark Flow for the interrogative sentence?

11. What type of clause has a subject and verb but does not express a complete thought?

12. What two types of clauses make up a complex sentence?

13. What type of conjunction is used in a complex sentence?

14. What type of writing is used when your purpose is to express an opinion and to convince the reader that this opinion is correct?

>>>>>>>>>>>>> **Student Tip...**

For information about test-taking strategies, refer to the Resource Tools Section on page 528.

English Made Easy

LISTENING AND SPEAKING:
Vocabulary & Analogy Time

Learn It: Recite the new vocabulary and analogy words.

Reference 124	Vocabulary & Analogy Words

Word: adversary (ăd'vər sĕr'ē)
   Definition: a person that opposes or resists
   Synonym: enemy   **Antonym:** ally
   Sentence: His adversary fought to defeat him.

Analogy: Thanksgiving : holiday :: cumulus : cloud
   Type or kind relationship: Just as **Thanksgiving** is a type of **holiday**, **cumulus** is a type of **cloud**.

Vocabulary Card 21: Record the vocabulary information above and write your own sentence, using the new word.

Analogy Card 21: Record the analogy information and write your own analogy, using the same relationship as the analogy above.

Jingle Time

Recite It: Recite the new jingle.

♪ Jingle 21	The Direct Object Jingle

A **direct object** is a NOUN or a PRO,
      Is a noun or a pro, is a noun or a pro.
A **direct object** completes the meaning,
      Completes the meaning of the sentence.
A **direct object** follows the verb,
      Follows the **verb-transitive**.
To find a direct object,
      Ask *WHAT* or *WHOM*
      Ask *WHAT* or *WHOM* after the verb.

Lesson 1

You will

- study new vocabulary; make card 21; write own sentence using the vocabulary word.
- analyze new analogy; make card 21; write own analogy.
- recite new jingle (Direct Object).
- identify direct object, transitive verb, and Pattern 2.
- classify Introductory Sentences.
- do a Skill Builder to identify a direct object.
- write in your journal.

Apply It: These Introductory Sentences are used to apply the new grammar concepts taught below. Classify these sentences orally with your teacher.

Introductory Sentences	Chapter 7: Lesson 1

1. _____ I found a recipe.
2. _____ Yesterday, my aunt found a recipe for peach preserves on the Internet.
3. _____ Oh my! That extremely destructive storm in December disrupted power in Grandmother's neighborhood for two weeks!

Learn It: **DIRECT OBJECTS AND TRANSITIVE VERBS**

A Pattern 1 sentence has only one noun and an action verb as its main parts. The new sentence pattern, Pattern 2, has two nouns and an action verb as the sentence core.

Reference 125 · Direct Object, Verb-transitive, and Pattern 2

1. A **direct object** is a noun or a pronoun.

2. A direct object completes the meaning of a sentence and is located in the predicate.

3. To find the direct object, ask *WHAT* or *WHOM* after the verb. Ask *WHAT* when the direct object is a place, thing, or idea. Ask *WHOM* when the direct object is a person.

4. A direct object must be someone or something different from the subject noun. The direct object receives the action of the verb.

5. A direct object is labeled with the abbreviation **DO**.

6. In a sentence containing a direct object, the verb is transitive. A **transitive-verb** is an action verb that tells what the subject does, and it is followed by a direct object. The transitive verb transfers the action from the subject to the direct object. The *transitive verb* is labeled **V-t** and can be called **verb-transitive**.

7. A Pattern 2 sentence has a subject noun, transitive verb, and direct object as its core. A Pattern 2 sentence is labeled **SN V-t DO P2**. A Pattern 2 sentence has two noun jobs in its core: the subject noun and the direct-object noun. *If the subject is a pronoun, it is labeled as a subject pronoun in the sentence, but the pattern is still identified as **SN V-t DO P2**.*

8. **A review:**
   Pattern 1 is **SN V**. It has a noun-verb (**N V**) core.
   Pattern 2 is **SN V-t DO**. It has a noun-verb-noun (**N V N**) core.

The location of each noun determines its job in a sentence. Only certain noun jobs form the pattern parts of a sentence. For each pattern, the order of the core nouns does not change. A noun that is an object of the preposition is not part of a sentence pattern.

Continued on next page. >>>

Reference 125 continued from previous page.

Question and Answer Flow for the Practice Sentence, Adding Direct Objects

Practice Sentence: Alex bought a truck.

1. Who bought a truck? **Alex - SN**
2. What is being said about Alex? **Alex bought - V**
3. Alex bought what? **truck - verify the noun**
4. Does truck mean the same thing as Alex? **No.**
5. **Truck - DO**   (Say: *Truck - direct object.*)
6. **Bought - V-t**   (Say: *Bought - verb-transitive.*)
7. **A - A**
8. **SN V-t DO P2**   (Say: *subject noun, verb-transitive, direct object, Pattern 2.*)
9. Skill Check

10. Verb-transitive - check again
    (This check is to make sure the "t" is added to the verb.)
11. No prepositional phrases
12. **Period, statement, declarative sentence**
13. Go back to the verb. Divide the complete subject from the complete predicate.
14. Is there an adverb exception? **No.**
15. Is this sentence in a natural or inverted order? **Natural - no change.**

```
             SN    V-t  A DO
  SN  V-t     Alex / bought a truck. D
  DO  P2
```

Discuss It:

1. What is the pattern in a Pattern 2 sentence?

2. What are the core parts of a Pattern 2 sentence?

3. What parts of speech are used in a Pattern 2 sentence?

Learn It: A SKILL BUILDER FOR A NOUN CHECK WITH DIRECT OBJECTS

The example below shows you what to do with direct objects when you are identifying nouns for a Noun Check.

LISTENING AND SPEAKING:

FOR A NOUN CHECK WITH DIRECT OBJECTS

Sentence 1: Subject Pronoun *I, no, it is a pronoun;*
Direct Object recipe *yes, it is a noun.*

Sentence 2: Subject Noun aunt *yes, it is a noun;*
Direct Object recipe *yes, it is a noun;*
Object of the Preposition preserves *yes, it is a noun;*
Object of the Preposition Internet *yes, it is a noun.*

Sentence 3: Subject Noun storm *yes, it is a noun;*
Object of the Preposition December *yes, it is a noun;*
Direct Object power *yes, it is a noun;*
Object of the Preposition neighborhood *yes, it is a noun;*
Object of the Preposition weeks *yes, it is a noun.*

JOURNAL WRITING 16

Write an entry in your journal. Use Reference 9 on page 12 for ideas.

START LESSON 2

Lesson 2

You will

- study new vocabulary; make card 22; write own sentence using the vocabulary word.
- analyze new analogy; make card 22; write own analogy.
- practice Jingle 21.
- classify Practice Sentences.
- do a Skill Builder.
- identify verb tenses and regular/irregular verbs.
- do Classroom Practice 30.
- read and discuss Discovery Time.

LISTENING AND SPEAKING:

Vocabulary & Analogy Time

Learn It: Recite the new vocabulary and analogy words.

📖 Reference 126	Vocabulary & Analogy Words

Word: lavish (lăv'ĭsh)

  Definition: using or giving in great amounts
  Synonym: extravagant   **Antonym:** modest
  Sentence: They had a lavish Christmas this year.

Analogy: wood : plank :: cotton : cloth

  Purpose or use relationship: Just as **wood** is used to make **planks**, **cotton** is used to make **cloth**.

Vocabulary Card 22: Record the vocabulary information above and write your own sentence, using the new word.

Analogy Card 22: Record the analogy information and write your own analogy, using the same relationship as the analogy above.

Jingle Time

Recite It: Practice Jingle 21 in the Jingle Section on page 512.

Grammar Time

Apply It: Classify the Practice Sentences orally with your teacher.

Practice Sentences	Chapter 7: Lesson 2

1. _____ Plant several dogwood trees in your front yard before spring.

2. _____ During the evening show, Elliot and I watched with admiration the incredible acrobatic performers.

3. _____ Did Grandfather taste Jeffie's chocolate dessert during Thanksgiving dinner with his family?

LISTENING AND SPEAKING:

Using the sentences just classified, do a Skill Builder orally with your teacher.

1. **Identify the nouns in a Noun Check.**
2. **Identify the nouns as singular or plural.**
3. **Identify the nouns as common or proper.**
4. **Identify the complete subject and the complete predicate.**
5. **Identify the simple subject and the simple predicate.**
6. **Do a Vocabulary Check.**
7. **Do a Verb Chant.**

Learn It: SIMPLE VERB TENSES

 Reference 127 **Simple Verb Tenses**

Verbs are time-telling words. They not only tell of an action, but they also tell the time of the action. The time of the action is called the tense of the verb. The word *tense* means *time*.

There are three basic verb tenses that show when an action takes place: **present tense**, **past tense**, and **future tense**. These tenses are known as the **simple verb tenses**. When you are writing paragraphs, you should use verbs that are in the same tense.

1. The **present tense** shows that something is happening now, in the present. Present tense verbs can be singular or plural. Singular present tense verbs end in -**s**. Plural present tense verbs have **no** -**s** added.

Present Tense with a Singular Subject	Present Tense with a Plural Subject
The man <u>races</u>. The man <u>swims</u>.	The men <u>race</u>. The men <u>swim</u>.

2. The **simple past** tense shows that something has happened at some time in the past. Most past tense verbs end in -**ed** or have a middle vowel change. Past tense verbs are the same for singular or plural subjects.

Past Tense with a Singular Subject	Past Tense with a Plural Subject
The man <u>raced</u>. The man <u>swam</u>.	The men <u>raced</u>. The men <u>swam</u>.

3. The **future tense** shows that something will happen at some time in the future. Future tense verbs use the helping verb *will* or *shall* before the main verb. Future tense verbs are the same for singular or plural subjects.

Future Tense with a Singular Subject	Future Tense with a Plural Subject
The man <u>will race</u>. The man <u>will swim</u>.	The men <u>will race</u>. The men <u>will swim</u>.

Present Tense	Past Tense	Future Tense
Ends with -**s** or has **no** -**s** ending.	Ends with -**ed** or has a middle vowel change.	Has the helping verb **will** or **shall** before the main verb.
1. He <u>walks</u> to the gym.	3. He <u>walked</u> to the gym.	5. He <u>will walk</u> to the gym.
2. He <u>drives</u> to the gym.	4. He <u>drove</u> to the gym.	6. He <u>will drive</u> to the gym.

SHURLEY ENGLISH

Learn It: REGULAR AND IRREGULAR VERBS

 Reference 128 **Regular and Irregular Verbs**

Verbs are divided into two groups: regular and irregular.

Regular Verbs:

A verb is **regular** if you make the main verb past tense by **adding -ed** to the end. Most verbs are regular verbs because you add letters to the end of the verbs to make them past tense.

(**Examples:** want and want**ed**, jump and jump**ed**, laugh and laugh**ed**)

Irregular Verbs:

A verb is **irregular** if you make the main verb past tense by **changing a vowel in the middle of the word.** Irregular verbs do not form their past tense by adding letters to the end of a verb. They form their past tense by making a new verb with the vowel change.

(**Examples:** bec**o**me and bec**a**me, fr**ee**ze and fr**o**ze, t**e**ll and t**o**ld)

To decide if a verb is regular or irregular, remember these three things:

1. Look only at the main verb.

2. If the main verb is made past tense by **adding** an -ed, -d, or -t ending, it is a regular verb.
   (**Exception:** The verbs *pay/paid, say/said,* and *lay/laid* are irregular.)

3. If the main verb is made past tense by a **middle vowel change**, it is an irregular verb.
   (**Exception:** Verbs whose principal parts are all the same—*cost, has cost, will cost*—are also irregular.)

Some of the most common irregular verbs are listed on the irregular verb chart located in Reference 116 on page 185. Refer to this chart whenever necessary.

Exercise: Write the past-tense form. Then, Write **R** for regular or **I** for irregular.

1. dance..... *R*   **Past tense:** *danced*   3. write......... *I*   **Past tense:** *wrote*   5. drive......... *I*   **Past tense:** *drove*

2. grow......... *I*   **Past tense:** *grew*   4. try............. *R*   **Past tense:** *tried*   6. deal......... *R*   **Past tense:** *dealt*

>>>>>>>>>>>> **Student Tip...**

Consult a dictionary if you are in doubt about the spelling of regular or irregular verb forms.

>>>>>>>>>>>>>>>>>>>> **Student Tip...**

Use the following examples to study the different ways irregular verbs change forms.

1. The past-tense form shows a middle vowel spelling change.
   Examples: s**i**ng/s**a**ng/s**u**ng, beg**i**n/beg**a**n/beg**u**n, s**e**ll/s**o**ld/s**o**ld

2. The past-tense form shows a change when it ends in -**ought**.
   Examples: bring/br**ought**, buy/b**ought**

3. The past-tense form shows a change when it ends in -**t**.
   Examples: feel/fel**t**, send/sen**t**

4. The past participle shows a change when it ends in -**n** or -**en**.
   Examples: blow/blew/blow**n**, choose/chose/chose**n**

5. Exception: The past-tense form of a small number of verbs is irregular when ending in -**d**.
   Examples: have/ha**d**, say/sai**d**, pay/pai**d**, lay/lai**d**

6. Exception: The same form is used for the present tense and the past tense.
   Examples: bet, cost, cut, hit, hurt, let, put, or shut.

✏ Classroom Practice 30

It is time to practice the skills you are learning. You will use the classroom practice on the next page to apply these skills.

ENRICHMENT:

Discovery Time

(American) 1826-1854— Stephen Collins Foster was the first composer of distinctly American songs and the first professional songwriter in the United States. Foster wrote most of the lyrics for his songs. His songs are known for their simple harmonies and touching melodies. He wrote a total of 285 songs and musical works. His most popular songs include "Oh! Susanna," "Camptown Races," "My Old Kentucky Home," and "Jeanie with the Light Brown Hair."

Discovery Questions:
- How many of Foster's songs do you know?
- Which songs do you like the best?
- Do you think it is easy to be a songwriter?

Discovery Activity:
- Write a song just for fun.

Are you interested in learning more about Stephen Collins Foster?

1. You may explore this topic further by using the resources listed below.
   Computer resources: Internet, encyclopedia software
   Library resources: encyclopedias, books, magazines, newspapers
   Home/community resources: books, interviews, newspapers, magazines

2. A Discovery Share Time is provided in Lesson 7 if you wish to share your investigation results. You may share orally, or you may prepare a written report. You will put your written report in a class booklet titled *"Notable People in History."* This booklet will be placed in the class library for everyone to enjoy.

Classroom Practice 30

Name:_____ Date:_____

GRAMMAR

▶ **Exercise 1:** Classify each sentence.

1. _____ Wow! He gave an outstanding speech!

2. _____ After school, Terrance and I played a quick game of basketball before dinner.

▶ **Exercise 2:** Use sentence 2 and complete the table below.

List the Noun Used	List the Noun Job	Singular or Plural	Common or Proper	Simple Subject	Simple Predicate

SKILLS

▶ **Exercise 3:** (1) Underline the verb or verb phrase. (2) Identify the verb tense by writing **1** for present tense, **2** for past tense, or **3** for future tense. (3) Write the past-tense form. (4) Write **R** for Regular or **I** for Irregular.

	Verb Tense	Main Verb Past Tense Form	R or I
1. My sister swims every weekend.			
2. We laughed at his funny jokes.			
3. The small boy ran after the bus.			
4. My parents go to town on Monday nights.			
5. The pitcher throws the ball fast.			
6. I washed the dog last Saturday.			
7. I will leave soon for the grocery store.			
8. We walk a mile every day.			
9. The fireworks will begin at eight o'clock.			
10. Colorful leaves rustle in the chilly autumn wind.			

EDITING

▶ **Exercise 4:** Correct each mistake. **Editing Guide: End Marks:** 3 **Capitals:** 9 **Commas:** 3 **Apostrophes:** 3 **Homonyms:** 3 **A/An:** 1 **Subject-Verb Agreement:** 3 **Underlining:** 1 **Misspelled Words:** 1

matthew climb into his mothers lap for story time he listen attentively as his mothers

soft voise flows threw the words of hans christian andersens fairy tail the ugly duckling

soon his eyes become heavy with sleep and he drift away into an world full of fairy tails

LISTENING AND SPEAKING:
Vocabulary & Analogy Time

Learn It: Recite the new vocabulary and analogy words.

Reference 129	Vocabulary & Analogy Words

Word: stagnant (stăg′nənt)
  Definition: foul from not flowing
  Synonym: stale   **Antonym:** fresh
  Sentence: The stagnant water in the pool smelled rotten.

Analogy: ring : rang :: grow : grew
  Grammatical relationship: Just as **ring** is the present tense of **rang**,
  grow is the present tense of **grew**.

Vocabulary Card 23: Record the vocabulary information above and write your own
  sentence, using the new word.

Analogy Card 23: Record the analogy information and write your own analogy,
  using the same relationship as the analogy above.

Jingle Time

Recite It: Practice Jingles 13–21 in the Jingle Section on pages 509–512.

Grammar Time

Apply It: Classify the Practice Sentences orally with your teacher.

Practice Sentences	Chapter 7: Lesson 3

1. _____ Anna enthusiastically played the piano and the saxophone
   during our recent talent contest.

2. _____ Good grief! Yesterday, the lions and tigers at the zoo terrified
   the timid kindergarten students!

3. _____ After the frost, the busy farmers quickly harvested the rice crop
   in their fields.

Lesson 3
You will

- study new vocabulary; make card 23; write own sentence using the vocabulary word.
- analyze new analogy; make card 23; write own analogy.
- practice Jingles 13–21.
- classify Practice Sentences.
- do a Skill Builder.
- identify tenses of helping verbs.
- do Classroom Practice 31.
- write in your journal.
- read and discuss Discovery Time.

LISTENING AND SPEAKING:

Skill Builder

Using the sentences just classified, do a Skill Builder orally with your teacher.

1. **Identify the nouns in a Noun Check.**
2. **Identify the nouns as singular or plural.**
3. **Identify the nouns as common or proper.**
4. **Identify the complete subject and the complete predicate.**
5. **Identify the simple subject and the simple predicate.**
6. **Do a Vocabulary Check.**
7. **Do a Verb Chant.**

Skill Time

Learn It: TENSES OF HELPING VERBS

Reference 130   Tenses of Helping Verbs

If there is only a main verb in a sentence, the tense is determined by the main verb and will be either present tense or past tense.

If there is a helping verb with a main verb, the tense of both verbs is determined by the helping verb, not the main verb. If there is more than one helping verb, the tense is determined by the first helping verb.

Since the helping verb determines the tense, it is important to learn the tenses of the 14 helping verbs you will be using. You should memorize the list below so you will never have trouble with tenses.

Present-tense helping verbs: am, is, are, has, have, do, does

Past-tense helping verbs: was, were, had, did, been

Future-tense helping verbs: will, shall

Some present-tense helping verbs keep verb phrases in present tense even though the main verbs have a past-tense form. *Has* and *have* are the two present-tense helping verbs used most often with past-tense main verbs. When *has* and *have* are used with a past-tense main verb, it describes an action that began in the past and continues into the present or that occurred in the recent past. (*He has taken his pills today.*)

Example 1: (1) Underline the verb or verb phrase.
(2) Identify the verb tense by writing **1** for present tense, **2** for past tense, or **3** for future tense.
(3) Write the past-tense form.
(4) Write **R** for Regular or **I** for Irregular.

	Verb Tense	Main Verb Past Tense Form	R or I
1. The student <u>gives</u> his speech.	1	gave	I
2. The detective <u>had</u> <u>tried</u> the wrong door.	2	tried	R
3. The man <u>will</u> <u>wait</u> for his change.	3	waited	R

Example 2: List the present-tense and past-tense helping verbs in the blanks below.

Present Tense	1. am	2. is	3. are	4. has	5. have	6. do	7. does
Past Tense	1. was	2. were	3. had	4. did	5. been		

Classroom Practice 31

It is time to practice the skills you are learning. You will use the classroom practice on the next page to apply these skills.

>>>>>>>>>> **Student Tip...**

Verb-Tense Game:
Write each of the present-, past-, and future-tense helping verbs on the front of index cards. On the back of the cards, write either present, past, or future tense for each helping verb. (Make several sets of cards.)

Present-tense helping verbs: **am, is, are, has, have, do, does**

Past-tense helping verbs: **was, were, had, did, been**

Future-tense helping verbs: **will, shall**

Divide into several groups with three or four students in each group. Give each group a set of cards. Have the "dealer" in each group place a card on the desk, "verb side" up. The first person in the group to name the tense gets to keep the card. Continue until all the cards have been played. Rotate until each student has had a turn to be the dealer.

ENRICHMENT:

Discovery Time

(Native American Sioux) 1831–1890— Sitting Bull (Tatanka Iyotanka) was a Native American Lakota Sioux chief and medicine man. He killed his first buffalo at ten and went to battle at age 14. Sitting Bull was respected for his courage and wisdom. Sitting Bull defeated General George Armstrong Custer and his soldiers at the Battle of Little Big Horn. In 1881, Sitting Bull was the last Sioux chief to surrender to the U.S. Army.

Discovery Questions:
- When and where did the Battle of Little Big Horn take place?
- What do you think it was like to be a Sioux chief?
- What responsibilities would he have had?

Discovery Activity:
- Illustrate one of the following: Chief Sitting Bull, an Indian village, a frontier fort, General George Custer, or the Battle of Little Big Horn.

Are you interested in learning more about Chief Sitting Bull?

1. You may explore this topic further by using the resources listed below.
   Computer resources: Internet, encyclopedia software
   Library resources: encyclopedias, books, magazines, newspapers
   Home/community resources: books, interviews, newspapers, magazines

2. A Discovery Share Time is provided in Lesson 7 if you wish to share your investigation results. You may share orally, or you may prepare a written report. You will put your written report in a class booklet titled *"Notable People in History."* This booklet will be placed in the class library for everyone to enjoy.

JOURNAL WRITING 17

Write an entry in your journal. Use Reference 9 on page 12 for ideas.

Classroom Practice 31

Name:_____ Date:_____

GRAMMAR

▶ **Exercise 1:** Classify each sentence.

1. _____ Give an explanation and an apology to Mom and Dad for your absence during dinner.

2. _____ He and she have not sent their vacation photographs to their friends in Utah and Ohio.

▶ **Exercise 2:** Use sentence 2 above and complete the table below.

List the Noun Used	List the Noun Job	Singular or Plural	Common or Proper	Simple Subject	Simple Predicate

SKILLS

▶ **Exercise 3:** (1) Underline the verb or verb phrase. (2) Identify the verb tense by writing **1** for present tense, **2** for past tense, or **3** for future tense. (3) Write the past-tense form. (4) Write **R** for Regular or **I** for Irregular.

	Verb Tense	Main Verb Past Tense Form	R or I
1. The judges will choose the winner tonight.			
2. Our pool needed chemicals.			
3. Aunt Sue makes delicious peanut brittle.			
4. Sandy had given many haircuts to ladies.			
5. The rude boy has argued with everyone.			

▶ **Exercise 4:** List the present-tense and past-tense helping verbs.

Present Tense	1.	2.	3.	4.	5.	6.	7.
Past Tense	1.	2.	3.	4.	5.		

EDITING

▶ **Exercise 5:** Correct each mistake. **Editing Guide: End Marks: 4   Capitals: 8   Commas: 5   Apostrophes: 1   Homonyms: 3   Subject-Verb Agreement: 3   Misspelled Words: 1**

mother always fixes uncle leos favorite dessert for christmas dinner he are her only brother

she and her five sisters prepares turkey ham dressing saleds homemade rolls and desserts

four our annual christmas gathering even hour neighbors comes to hour feast

English Made Easy

LISTENING AND SPEAKING:
Vocabulary & Analogy Time

Learn It: Recite the new vocabulary and analogy words.

Reference 131	Vocabulary & Analogy Words

Word: petty (pĕt'ē)
  Definition: having little or no importance
  Synonym: trivial   **Antonym:** significant
  Sentence: The boys' petty arguments drove their mom crazy.

Analogy: ring : finger :: bracelet : wrist
  Purpose or use relationship: Just as a **ring** goes on a **finger**,
                                     a **bracelet** goes on a **wrist**.

Vocabulary Card 24: Record the vocabulary information above and write your own
                           sentence, using the new word.
Analogy Card 24: Record the analogy information and write your own analogy,
                        using the same relationship as the analogy above.

Jingle Time

Recite It: Practice Jingles 3–11 in the Jingle Section on pages 507–508.

Grammar Time

Apply It: Classify the Practice Sentences orally with your teacher.

Practice Sentences	Chapter 7: Lesson 4

1. _____ Sheets of plastic covered the broken windows of the old, dilapidated house.
2. _____ Did the foul ball hit a transformer in the adjacent field during Anthony's baseball game?
3. _____ Levi's more experienced team very quickly assembled the parts of their huge model airplane.

Lesson 4

You will
- study new vocabulary; make card 24; write own sentence using the vocabulary word.
- analyze new analogy; make card 24; write own analogy.
- practice Jingles 3–11.
- classify Practice Sentences.
- do a Skill Builder.
- do Classroom Practice 32.
- read and discuss Discovery Time.
- do a homework assignment.
- do Home Connection activity.

SHURLEY ENGLISH

Skill Builder

Using the Practice Sentences just classified, do a Skill Builder orally with your teacher.
1. Identify the nouns in a Noun Check.
2. Identify the nouns as singular or plural.
3. Identify the nouns as common or proper.
4. Identify the complete subject and the complete predicate.
5. Identify the simple subject and the simple predicate.
6. Do a Vocabulary Check.
7. Do a Verb Chant.

Classroom Practice 32

It is time to practice the skills you are learning. You will use the classroom practice on the next page to apply these skills.

->>>> Student Tip...

Play the verb-tense game from Lesson 3 again. The directions are reprinted below for your convenience.

Write each of the present-, past-, and future-tense helping verbs on the front of index cards. On the back of the cards, write either present, past, or future tense for each helping verb. (Make several sets of cards.)

Present-tense helping verbs: **am, is, are, has, have, do, does**

Past-tense helping verbs: **was, were, had, did, been**

Future-tense helping verbs: **will, shall**

Divide into several groups with three or four students in each group. Give each group a set of cards. Have the "dealer" in each group place a card on the desk, "verb side" up. The first person in the group to name the tense gets to keep the card. Continue until all the cards have been played. Rotate until each student has had a turn to be the dealer.

ENRICHMENT:

Discovery Time

(American) 1831-1888— **John S. Pemberton** was the creator of *Coca-Cola*. Pemberton, a pharmacist in Atlanta, Georgia, originally marketed his cola drink as a tonic for common ailments. Pemberton's mixture contained the coca plant that was advertised as a stimulant, an aid to digestion, and a life-extender. In addition to this ingredient, Pemberton added the cola nut, which was thought to have medicinal properties. Later, he joined with businessman, Frank Robinson, who named the drink *Coca-Cola*, using the two main ingredients, coca and cola.

Discovery Questions: • Why did Pemberton and his immediate family never profit from his invention?

Discovery Activity:
• Invite a guest speaker to speak to your class about his/her successful company in your town.

Are you interested in learning more about John S. Pemberton or the history of Coca-Cola?

1. You may explore this topic further by using the resources listed below.
   Computer resources: Internet, encyclopedia software
   Library resources: encyclopedias, books, magazines, newspapers
   Home/community resources: books, interviews, newspapers, magazines

2. A Discovery Share Time is provided in Lesson 7 if you wish to share your investigation results. You may share orally, or you may prepare a written report. You will put your written report in a class booklet titled "*Notable People in History.*" This booklet will be placed in the class library for everyone to enjoy.

Classroom Practice 32

Name:_____ Date:_____

GRAMMAR

▶ **Exercise 1:** Classify each sentence.

1. _____ Suddenly, the heavyweight boxer in the ring threw a knockout punch at his opponent!

2. _____ Darcy and I checked the prices and availability of the new computer games today.

SKILLS

▶ **Exercise 2:** (1) Underline the verb or verb phrase. (2) Identify the verb tense by writing **1** for present tense, **2** for past tense, or **3** for future tense. (3) Write the past-tense form. (4) Write **R** for Regular or **I** for Irregular.

	Verb Tense	Main Verb Past Tense Form	R or I
1. We are picking tomatoes in your garden.			
2. The puppy napped in a corner of the room.			
3. Will Bobby catch the ball on first base?			
4. The butcher will slice you a thick steak.			
5. The baby goat has been sleeping in the hay.			
6. Our truck will be sold at the auction.			
7. The artist paints one picture every week.			
8. Were you watching those children in the pool?			
9. Have you studied your science lesson?			
10. The author was writing about a boy and his dog.			

▶ **Exercise 3:** List the present-tense and past-tense helping verbs below.

Present Tense	1.	2.	3.	4.	5.	6.	7.
Past Tense	1.	2.	3.	4.	5.		

EDITING

▶ **Exercise 4:** Correct each mistake. **Editing Guide: End Marks: 5   Capitals: 13   Commas: 1   Apostrophes: 1
Homonyms: 5   A/An: 2   Subject-Verb Agreement: 6   Periods: 2   Misspelled Words: 1**

tony stare longingly through the window at jaspers pet store he wants sew much too take an

puppy home but he nose that his family are not allowed to have pets in the apartment he is

about two leave when mr jasper knock on the window and motion for tony too come in tony

is thrilled when mr jasper offer him an job tony promise to be the best employee ever

Homework 5

Complete this homework assignment on notebook paper.

1. Write the **helping verbs** for each verb tense listed.

   Present Tense: _____, _____, _____, _____, _____, _____, _____

   Past Tense: _____, _____, _____, _____, _____

   Future tense: _____, _____

2. Number your paper 1–8. For each sentence, do four things. (1) Write the verb or verb phrase. (2) Identify the verb tense by writing **1** for present tense, **2** for past tense, or **3** for future tense. (3) Write the past-tense form. (4) Write **R** for Regular or **I** for Irregular.

	Verb Tense	Main Verb Past Tense Form	R or I
1. Our paints are drying in the sun.			
2. Dad's shoes were thrown under the bed.			
3. The thirsty players will drink several quarts of water.			
4. My mother's favorite vase had been broken.			
5. David and Bill pick oranges every summer.			
6. What will we eat for dinner on Friday?			
7. We are writing our reports.			
8. Her pencil was moving quickly across the page.			

Home Connection

Family Activity for Direct Objects

Have each family member (or team) choose a different historical figure from the Discovery Time list in the Resource Tools section of the Student Textbook. Look up information about the historical figure in books, encyclopedias, or on the Internet. On one side of an index card, write at least five sentences with direct objects that give clues to the identity of the person chosen. Put the most revealing clues last. Write the mystery person's name on the opposite side of the index card. Read the clues, one at a time, to a member of the family. In order for a family member to guess the mystery person's name, he must first identify the direct-object word in the clue sentence that is read. See how many clues have to be read before the mystery person can be identified. The person or team that is the first to guess the correct historical figure is the winner.

Example: Clues with direct objects for Leonardo da Vinci:
    He designed **battleships**.
    He performed **autopsies** on corpses.
    He painted famous **pictures**.
    He painted the "**Last Supper**."
    He painted the "**Mona Lisa**."

Family Activity for Vocabulary and Analogies

Divide into family teams. The first team will use vocabulary and analogy cards 17–20 to ask questions about the information on their cards. The second team will use vocabulary and analogy cards 21–24 to ask questions about the information on their cards.

For vocabulary words:
- What is the definition of the word?
- Name a synonym and antonym for the word.
- Create a new sentence using the word.
- Find the word in another source (dictionary, newspaper, magazine, advertisement, etc.)

For analogies:
- What is the answer to the analogy?
- What is the relationship of the analogy?
- Make another analogy with the same relationship.
- Make another analogy with a different relationship.

Apply It: Classify the Practice Sentences orally with your teacher.

Practice Sentences	Chapter 7: Lesson 5

1. _____ Piles of snow near Lake Erie covered the highways outside Cleveland in January.

2. _____ Ugh! For breakfast, my brother and sister put mustard on their scrambled eggs and bacon!

3. _____ Repair and restore your antique Hopi jewelry and pottery for the display at the new library.

Chapter Checkup 33

It is time for a checkup of the skills you have learned in this chapter. You will use the chapter checkup on the next page to evaluate your progress.

ENRICHMENT:

Discovery Time

(Swedish) 1833-1896— Alfred Nobel invented and accumulated a huge fortune from the manufacturing of explosives and ammunition, but, amazingly enough, he was more of a pacifist and hoped that his inventions would end wars. When he died, he left most of his fortune in a trust to establish the Nobel Prizes.

Discovery Questions:
- What are the Nobel Prizes?
- What could you do to win the Nobel prize?

(American) 1833-1916— Sally Tompkins ran a private hospital in Richmond, Virginia, during the American Civil War. During the four years her hospital was in operation, it cared for more than a thousand patients, of whom only 73 died. This was the best record of any hospital during the war. She was the only woman to hold military rank in the Confederate army. After the war, she continued her philanthropic activities until her family fortune was spent. She died in 1916 and was buried in Virginia with military honors.

Discovery Questions:
- At what rank was Tompkins commissioned in the Confederate army?
- Why do you think Sally Tompkins was so successful in saving lives?
- What would she think of our hospitals today?
- Do you think she would change anything?

Are you interested in learning more about Alfred Nobel or Sally Tompkins?

1. You may explore these topics further by using the resources listed below.
   Computer resources: Internet, encyclopedia software
   Library resources: encyclopedias, books, magazines, newspapers
   Home/community resources: books, interviews, newspapers, magazines
2. A Discovery Share Time is provided in Lesson 7 if you wish to share your investigation results. You may share orally, or you may prepare a written report. You will put your written report in a class booklet titled *"Notable People in History."* This booklet will be placed in the class library for everyone to enjoy.

Lesson 5

You will
- classify Practice Sentences.
- do Chapter Checkup 33.
- write in their journal.
- read and discuss Discovery Time.

JOURNAL WRITING 18

Write an entry in your journal. Use Reference 9 on page 12 for ideas.

Chapter 7 Checkup 33

Name:_____ Date:_____

GRAMMAR

▶ **Exercise 1:** Classify each sentence.

1. _____ Send an e-mail to Aunt Natalie and Uncle Drew about our family's Christmas party.

2. _____ Mercy! That large herd of cattle trampled and destroyed those young saplings!

3. _____ Are the old machines in the clothing factory finally showing signs of extreme wear?

SKILLS

▶ **Exercise 2:** (1) Underline the verb or verb phrase. (2) Identify the verb tense by writing **1** for present tense, **2** for past tense, or **3** for future tense. (3) Write the past-tense form. (4) Write **R** for Regular or **I** for Irregular.

	Verb Tense	Main Verb Past Tense Form	R or I
1. Our family leaves for California on Saturday.			
2. Traffic moved carefully through the construction zone.			
3. The carpenter carries his tools with him.			
4. The birds are flying over the lake.			
5. The pitcher throws the ball hard and fast.			
6. Our dogs have eaten all their food.			
7. I see three kittens in the basket.			
8. Mom has cooked my favorite meal.			
9. The wind will blow hard from the north.			
10. My sisters had practiced ballet today.			

▶ **Exercise 3:** List the present-tense and past-tense helping verbs below.

Present Tense	1.	2.	3.	4.	5.	6.	7.
Past Tense	1.	2.	3.	4.	5.		

EDITING

▶ **Exercise 4:** Correct each mistake. **Editing Guide: End Marks: 4 Capitals: 18 Commas: 3 Quotation Marks: 2 Apostrophes: 1 Subject-Verb Agreement: 3 Misspelled Words: 1**

harriets favorite christmas carol is silver bells by jay livingston and ray evans harriet play

this song and other holiday favorates at the carter rest home on christmas eve the residents and

staff sings as harriet plays before harriet leaves she give gifts candy and cards to everyone

Writing Time

Write It: WRITING ASSIGNMENT 16

Lesson 6

You will
- conference with teacher about WA 15.
- write a creative writing piece for WA 16.

Writing Assignment 16 : Creative Expressions

Purpose: To persuade

Type of Writing: Creative/persuasive

Audience: Parents

Writing Prompt: Most of your friends receive a weekly allowance for doing various jobs at home. You do not get an allowance but would like to convince your parents to give you one for the chores you do. Explain why you need an allowance, what chores you will do, and how much money you feel is reasonable. Then, tell how you would approach your parents for an allowance.

Special Instructions:

1. Write a response to the writing prompt above.

2. A prewriting map is not required for this creative-writing assignment.

3. Follow the Rough Draft Checklist in Reference 46 on page 61.

4. Put your creative-writing paper in your Rough Draft folder when you have finished.

Note: Reference 54 on page 71 lists the steps in the writing process and the location of all the writing checklists.

Conference Time

Discuss It: TEACHER-STUDENT CONFERENCES
FOR WRITING ASSIGNMENT 15

Meet with your teacher to discuss Writing Assignment 15.
After the conference, place this group of papers in your Publishing folder.

Lesson 7

You will

- publish WA 15.
- participate in Discovery Share Time.
- do Across the Curriculum activity.

 Publishing Time

Publish It: **WRITING ASSIGNMENT 15**

Choose a publishing form and publish Writing Assignment 15. After rewriting your paper for publication, give the stapled papers (evaluation guide, graded final paper, rough draft, and prewriting map) to your teacher to be placed in your Writing Portfolio.

Reference 66	**Publishing Checklist for Step 6 in the Writing Process**

The sixth step in the writing process is called publishing. Publishing is sharing your writing with others. With so many forms of publishing available, finding a match for every project and personality is easy.

At times, a written work is best read aloud. Other times, the biggest impact is made when a written work is read silently. You can also use media sources to enhance any publication.

SPECIAL INSTRUCTIONS FOR PUBLISHING:

- Rewrite the graded paper in ink or type it on a computer, correcting any marked errors. *(Do not display or publish papers that have marked errors or grades on them.)*
- Give your teacher the set of stapled papers to place in your Writing Portfolio. *(Stapled papers: evaluation guide, graded final paper, rough draft, and prewriting map.)*
- Select a publishing form from the list below and publish your rewritten paper.
    1. Have classmates, family members, neighbors, or others read your writing at school or home.
    2. Share your writing with others during a Share Time. *(Refer to Reference 67 on page 99 for sharing guidelines.)*
    3. Display your writing on a bulletin board or wall.
    4. Put your writing in the classroom library or in the school library for checkout.
    5. Send your writing as a letter or an e-mail to a friend or relative.
    6. Frame your writing by gluing it on colored construction paper and decorating it.
    7. Make a book of your writing for your classroom, your family, or others.
    8. Illustrate your writing and give it to others to read.
    9. Dramatize your writing in the form of a play, puppet show, or radio broadcast.
    10. Send your writing to be placed in a waiting room (doctor, veterinarian, dentist, etc.), senior-citizen center, or a nursing home.
    11. Send your writing to a school newspaper, local newspaper, or a magazine for publication.
    12. Make a videotape, cassette tape, or slide presentation of your writing.
    13. Choose another publishing form that is not listed.

LISTENING AND SPEAKING:

Discovery Share Time

If you have chosen to investigate a historical figure introduced in this chapter, you now have the opportunity to share your results in one of the following ways:

1. You may relate your information orally.
2. You may read a written report.
3. You may place your report in the booklet without reading it aloud.

After share time, all written reports should be turned in to be placed in the class booklet titled "Notable People in History." You are encouraged to check out this class booklet so you can enjoy the reports again.

Across the Curriculum

Literature Connection: Divide into small groups. Select a short story from your reading book, a book from the library, or a children's book. At the top of a sheet of paper, make one column titled "Regular Verbs" and one column titled "Irregular Verbs." List the verbs in the story under either the "Regular Verbs" column or the "Irregular Verbs" column. Discuss which type of verb is used most often. Recite as many irregular verbs as you can. Check the Irregular Chart for some of the irregular verbs. Discuss the importance of different verbs in other subjects.

Lesson 8

You will

- practice Jingle 21.
- do Classroom Practice 34.
- write an independent persuasive essay (WA 17).

LISTENING AND SPEAKING:

Recite It: Practice Jingle 21 in the Jingle Section on page 512.

GRAMMAR & WRITING CONNECTION:
Practice and Revised Sentence

Apply It: BUILDING AND EXPANDING SENTENCES

Reference 132	A Guide for Using a Pattern 2 Core (Sn V-t DO) to Build and Expand Sentences

1. **SN** or **SP** (**subject**) Think of a noun or pronoun that you want to use as the subject. Write the noun or pronoun you have chosen as the subject of your sentence.

2. **V-t** (**transitive verb**) The transitive verb tells what the subject does, and it is followed by a direct object. First, choose a verb for your sentence. Then, after you have chosen a direct object, verify that the verb is transitive and keep it as the verb of your Pattern 2 core.

3. **DO** (**direct object**) The direct object is a noun or pronoun after the verb that answers the question *whom* or *what*. The direct object receives the action of a transitive verb and does not mean the same thing as the subject. To help you think of a **direct object**, ask the question *WHAT* or *WHOM* after the verb. Write the direct object you have chosen in the predicate part of your sentence.

>>>>>>>>>>>>> Student Tip...

Use your vocabulary words in your Practice and Revised Sentences. Use a thesaurus, synonym-antonym book, or a dictionary to help you develop your writing vocabulary.

Classroom Practice 34

It is time to practice the skills you are learning. You will use the classroom practice on the next page to apply these skills.

Writing Time

Write It: **WRITING ASSIGNMENT 17**

As you write a rough draft for your independent writing assignment, you will do two of the six steps in the writing process: prewriting and rough draft.

Writing Assignment [17]

Purpose: To persuade

Type of Writing: Three-paragraph persuasive essay

Audience: Classmates

Writing Topics: Reasons people should visit my state/city/school
Why I need a pet/a job/an education
Benefits of playing a musical instrument/a sport/games
(Brainstorm for other ideas, individually or in groups.)

Special Instructions:

1. Follow the Prewriting and Rough Draft Checklists in References 44 and 46 on pages 57, 61.

2. Use References 118–123 on pages 196–200 to help you write your persuasive essay.

3. Use standard, time-order, or transition writing form. See Reference 69, page 103.

4. Write in first or third person. See Reference 70, page 104.
   (First-person pronouns: *I, me, my, mine, we, us, our,* and *ours.*)
   (Third-person pronouns: *he, his, him, she, her, hers, it, its, they, their, theirs,* and *them.*)

Note: Reference 54 on page 71 lists the steps in the writing process and the location of all the writing checklists.

Student Note: **Some of your writing pieces will be selected for revision and editing later in the school year.**

SHURLEY ENGLISH

Classroom Practice 34

Name: _____   Date: _____

INDEPENDENT PRACTICE & REVISED SENTENCES

1. Write a Practice Sentence according to the labels you choose.
Use **SN/SP V-t DO** as your main labels. You may use the other labels in any order and as many times as you wish in order to make a Practice Sentence.
Chapter 7 labels for a Practice Sentence: **SN/SP, V-t, DO**, Adj, Adv, A, P, OP, PPA, C, HV, I, PNA

2. Write a Revised Sentence. Use the following revision strategies: *synonym (syn), antonym (ant), word change (wc), added word (add), deleted word (delete),* or *no change (nc).* Under each word, write the abbreviation of the revision strategy you use.

Labels:

Practice:

Revised:

Strategies:

Labels:

Practice:

Revised:

Strategies:

Labels:

Practice:

Revised:

Strategies:

LISTENING AND SPEAKING:

Jingle Time

Recite It: Practice Jingle 12 in the Jingle Section on page 509.

>>>>> **Student Tip...**

Reviewing the transition words will help you apply them in your writing.

Writing Time

Learn It: **WRITING A FIVE-PARAGRAPH PERSUASIVE ESSAY**

As you learned earlier, a **persuasive essay** expresses an opinion and tries to convince the reader that this opinion is correct. Any time you do persuasive writing, whether it is a three- or five-paragraph essay, you will have three parts: the **introduction**, the **body**, and the **conclusion**. The three parts will always be written in that order.

In a five-paragraph essay, there will be five paragraphs. The introduction forms the first paragraph; the body forms the second, third, and fourth paragraphs; and the conclusion forms the fifth paragraph of the essay. Although a title will be the first item appearing at the top of your essay, you will not finalize the title until you have finished writing the essay.

Learn It: **WRITING THE INTRODUCTION**
FOR A FIVE-PARAGRAPH PERSUASIVE ESSAY

The introduction forms the first paragraph. Notice that the words *In fact* have been added to the beginning of the second sentence in the introduction. The transitional words *In fact* are needed to help the sentences "flow together." Three sentences make up the introduction.

Reference 133	**Writing the Introduction for a Five-Paragraph Persuasive Essay**

THE INTRODUCTION
Paragraph 1

Writing Topic: Improving School Lunches

Sentence 1 – Topic Sentence:
State your opinion in the topic sentence.
> **Along with the regular lunch line, our lunchroom needs an a-la-carte line in which students pay for each item separately.**

Sentence 2 – Reason Sentence:
Give a general reason why you think the topic sentence is true.
> **In fact, an a-la-carte line would be popular with both students and teachers.**

Sentence 3 – General Number Sentence:
Use a general number word and restate the main idea in the topic sentence.
> **There are several reasons why we need an a-la-carte line.**

START LESSON 9

Lesson 9

You will
- practice Jingle 12.
- read and discuss a persuasive five-paragraph essay.
- plan and write rough draft for persuasive essay (WA 18).

Learn It: **WRITING THE BODY**
FOR A FIVE-PARAGRAPH PERSUASIVE ESSAY

After the introduction, you are ready to write the body. The body of a five-paragraph essay contains three paragraphs. Each of the three persuasive points forms a new paragraph. Also, notice that each of the three paragraphs has two or more supporting sentences.

Reference 134 | **Writing the Body for a Five-Paragraph Persuasive Essay**

THE BODY
Paragraph 2

Sentence 4 – First Point:
Give your first reason to support your opinion.

The first reason we need an a-la-carte line is to provide more interesting choices for lunch.

Sentences 5–8 – Supporting Sentences:
Give an example that supports and explains your first point. Write two or more supporting sentences.

Schools that have a-la-carte lines serve such popular items as pizza, hamburgers, sandwiches, soup, salad, and fruit. More students and teachers would actually eat lunch if they had these choices. With an increase in people eating lunch, the extra food line is more than justified. Expanding the food choices would make happier students and teachers.

Paragraph 3

Sentence 9 – Second Point:
Give your second reason to support your opinion.

The second reason we need an a-la-carte line is to avoid wasting food.

Sentences 10–11 – Supporting Sentences:
Give an example that supports and explains your second point. Write two or more supporting sentences.

Many students who buy hot lunches simply throw away most of the food because they do not want but one or two items on their tray. With an a-la-carte line, students purchase only what they want to eat, and there is no waste.

Paragraph 4

Sentence 12 – Third Point:
Give your third reason to support your opinion.

The third reason we need an a-la-carte line is to give students practice in making decisions.

Sentences 13–15 – Supporting Sentences:
Give an example that supports and explains your third point. Write two or more sentences.

If students are taught how to make healthy food choices at school and at home, they will learn to be selective and make better choices at the food line. Learning to make good choices in school will help students become wiser consumers as adults. Teaching students to make good choices makes this one of the best investments our school board could make.

Learn It: WRITING THE CONCLUSION
FOR A FIVE-PARAGRAPH PERSUASIVE ESSAY

The conclusion forms the fifth paragraph of a five-paragraph essay. The closing paragraph, or conclusion, should tie all the important points together with a restatement of the main idea and your final comments on it.

Two or more sentences make up the conclusion. The first sentence in the conclusion is called the **first concluding sentence**. To write this sentence, you should refer to the third sentence in the introduction. Using the general or specific number and topic as stated in that introductory sentence, you can write a similar concluding sentence. The **final concluding sentences** summarize one or more of the reasons stated.

| Reference 135 | Writing the Conclusion for a Five-Paragraph Persuasive Essay |

THE CONCLUSION
Paragraph 5

Sentence 16 – First Concluding Sentence:
The first concluding sentence is a restatement sentence that forcefully restates your original opinion in the topic sentence and usually starts with the words, *in conclusion*. Write one sentence.

> **In conclusion, we need an a-la-carte line at our school.**

Sentences 17–18 – Final Concluding Sentences:
These final sentences summarize one or more of the reasons stated. Write one or two sentences.

> **Not only would it provide an opportunity for more food selections, but this added lunch feature would prevent waste and promote wiser consumer participation. Adding an a-la-cart line at our school would help students make healthy choices and would be a wise decision by our school board.**

WRITING THE TITLE
Since there are many possibilities for titles, look at the topic and the three points listed about the topic. Use some of the words in the topic and write a phrase to tell what your paragraph is about. Your title can be short or long. Capitalize the first, last, and important words in your title.

Title: Spicing Up School Lunches

Sample Five-Paragraph Persuasive Essay

Spicing Up School Lunches

Along with the regular lunch line, our lunchroom needs an a-la-carte line in which students pay for each item separately. In fact, an a-la-carte line would be popular with both students and teachers. There are several reasons why we need an a-la-carte line.

The first reason we need an a-la-carte line is to provide more interesting choices for lunch. Schools that have a-la-carte lines serve such popular items as pizza, hamburgers, sandwiches, soup, salad, and fruit. More students and teachers would actually eat lunch if they had these choices. **The a-la-carte line would increase the number of people eating lunch each day, which would more than justify this added lunch feature. The expanded food choices would also make happier students and teachers.**

The second reason we need an a-la-carte line is to avoid wasting food. Many students who buy hot lunches simply throw away most of the food because they do not want but one or two items on their tray. With an a-la-carte line, students purchase only what they want to eat, and there is no waste.

The third reason we need an a-la-carte line is to give students practice in making decisions. If students are taught how to make healthy food choices at school and at home, they will learn to be selective and make better choices at the food line. Learning to make good choices in school will help students become wiser consumers as adults. **Giving students a chance to make healthy food choices makes this one of the best investments our school board could make.**

In conclusion, we need an a-la-carte line at our school. Not only would it provide an opportunity for more food selections, but this added lunch feature would prevent waste and promote wiser consumer participation. Adding an a-la-cart line at our school would help students make healthy choices and would be a wise decision by our school board.

Write It: WRITING ASSIGNMENT 18

As you write a rough draft for your guided writing assignment, you will do two of the six steps in the writing process: prewriting and rough draft.

Writing Assignment 18

Purpose: To persuade

Type of Writing: Five-paragraph persuasive essay

Audience: Classmates

Writing Topics: Why we need a swimming pool/new house
Why recess/fire drills/setting goals is/are important
Why cheating/lying doesn't pay
(Brainstorm for other ideas, individually or in groups.)

Special Instructions:

1. Expand your three-paragraph persuasive essay from Writing Assignment 15 to a five-paragraph persuasive essay or choose a new topic from the ones listed above.

2. Follow the Prewriting and Rough Draft Checklists in References 44 and 46 on pages 57, 61.

3. Use References 133–135 on pages 229–231 to help you write your persuasive essay.

4. Use standard, time-order, or transition writing form. Use Reference 69, page 103.

5. Write in first or third person. Use Reference 70, page 104.
(First-person pronouns: *I, me, my, mine, we, us, our, and ours.*)
(Third-person pronouns: *he, his, him, she, her, hers, it, its, they, their, theirs,* and *them.*)

Note: Reference 54 on page 71 gives the steps in the writing process and the location of all the writing checklists.

START LESSON 10

Lesson 10

You will
- revise, edit, and write a final paper for WA 18.

Apply It: **REVISE, EDIT, AND WRITE A FINAL PAPER**

Following the schedule below, you will revise and edit Writing Assignment 18. Then, you will write a final paper. Use the Chapter 7 Writing Evaluation Guide on the next page to check your final paper one last time.

| Reference 52 | Revising & Editing Schedule and Writing a Final Paper |

SPECIAL INSTRUCTIONS FOR REVISING AND EDITING (Steps 3-4 in the writing process):

- Use the Revising and Editing Checklists in References 48 and 50 as you revise and edit your rough draft.
- Follow the revising and editing schedule below as directed by your teacher.
    1. **Individual.** First, read your rough draft to yourself. Use the Revising Checklist in Reference 48 on page 64. Go through your paper, checking each item on the list and making revisions to your rough draft. Then, use the Editing Checklist in Reference 50 on page 66. Go through your paper again, checking each item on the list and editing your rough draft.
    2. **Partner.** Next, get with your editing partner. Work together on each partner's rough draft, one paper at a time. Read each rough draft aloud and revise and edit it together, using the Revising and Editing Checklists. (The author of the paper should be the one to make the corrections on his own paper.)
    3. **Group.** Finally, read the rough draft to a revision group for feedback. Each student should read his paper while the others listen and offer possible revising and editing suggestions. (The author will determine whether to make corrections from the revision group's suggestions.)

SPECIAL INSTRUCTIONS FOR FINAL PAPER (Step 5 in the writing process):

- Write your final paper, using the Final Paper Checklist in Reference 53 on page 70.
- Staple your writing papers in this order: the final paper on top, the rough draft in the middle, and the prewriting map on the bottom. Place the stapled papers in the Final Paper folder.

>>>>>>>>> Student Tip...

1. Be tactful and helpful in your comments during revising and editing time. The purpose of any suggestion should be to improve the writer's rough draft.

2. As you make your final corrections, you have the choice of accepting or rejecting any suggestions made by your partners or your revision group.

3. Study Vocabulary Words and Analogies 21–24 for the chapter test in the next lesson.

4. If you need to improve your handwriting, refer to the Resource Tools Section on pages 529–530 for information on writing legibly.

SHURLEY ENGLISH

Chapter 7 Writing Evaluation Guide

Name:_____ Date:_____

ROUGH DRAFT CHECK

_____ 1. Did you write your rough draft in pencil?

_____ 2. Did you write the correct headings on the first seven lines of your paper?

_____ 3. Did you use extra wide margins and skip every other line?

_____ 4. Did you write a title at the end of your rough draft?

_____ 5. Did you place your edited rough draft in your Rough Draft folder?

REVISING CHECK

_____ 6. Did you identify the purpose, type of writing, and audience?

_____ 7. Did you check for a topic, topic sentence, and sentences supporting the topic?

_____ 8. Did you check sentences for the right order, and did you combine, rearrange, or delete sentences when necessary?

_____ 9. Did you check for a variety of simple, compound, and complex sentences?

_____ 10. Did you check for any left out, repeated, or unnecessary words?

_____ 11. Did you check for the best choice of words by replacing or deleting unclear words?

_____ 12. Did you check the content for interest and creativity?

_____ 13. Did you check the voice to make sure the writing says what you want it to say?

EDITING CHECK

_____ 14. Did you indent each paragraph?

_____ 15. Did you put an end mark at the end of every sentence?

_____ 16. Did you capitalize the first word of every sentence?

_____ 17. Did you check for all other capitalization mistakes?

_____ 18. Did you check for all punctuation mistakes?
(*commas, periods, apostrophes, quotation marks, underlining*)

_____ 19. Did you check for misspelled words and for incorrect homonym choices?

_____ 20. Did you check for incorrect spellings of plural and possessive forms?

_____ 21. Did you check for correct construction and punctuation of your sentences?

_____ 22. Did you check for usage mistakes? (*subject/verb agreement, a/an choices, contractions, verb tenses, pronoun/antecedent agreement, pronoun cases, degrees of adjectives, double negatives, etc.*)

_____ 23. Did you put your revised and edited paper in the Rough Draft folder?

FINAL PAPER CHECK

_____ 24. Did you write the final paper in pencil?

_____ 25. Did you center the title on the top line and center your name under the title?

_____ 26. Did you skip a line before starting the writing assignment?

_____ 27. Did you single-space, use wide margins, and write the final paper neatly?

_____ 28. Did you staple your papers in this order: final paper on top, rough draft in the middle, and prewriting map on the bottom? Did you put them in the Final Paper folder?

Writing Time

Hand It In: **WRITING ASSIGNMENT 18**

Get your stapled papers for Writing Assignment 18 from your Final Paper folder. Check to make sure they are in the correct order: the final paper on top, the rough draft in the middle, and the prewriting map on the bottom. Hand them in to your teacher.

LISTENING AND SPEAKING:

Oral Review Questions

Discuss It:

1. What word receives the action of the verb and answers the question what or whom?

2. What type of verb is used with a direct object?

3. What are the core parts of a Pattern 2 sentence?

4. What kind of verb makes the past tense by adding -ed, -d, or -t to the main verb?

5. What kind of verb makes the past tense by a vowel-spelling change?

6. What are the three simple verb tenses?

7. If there is a helping verb and main verb, which verb determines the tense?

8. What are the seven present-tense helping verbs?

9. What are the five past-tense helping verbs?

10. What are the two future-tense helping verbs?

11. What type of writing is used when your purpose is to express an opinion and to convince the reader that this opinion is correct?

12. What type of writing is used when your purpose is to inform, to give facts, to give directions, to explain, or to define something?

>>>>>>>>>>>>>>> **Student Tip...**

For information about test-taking strategies, refer to the Resource Tools Section on page 528.

Chapter 7

START LESSON 11

Lesson 11

You will

• hand in WA 18 for grading.

• respond to oral review questions.

• take Chapter 7 Test.

CHAPTER TEST

It is time to evaluate your knowledge of the skills you have learned in this chapter. Your teacher will give you the Chapter 7 Test to help you assess your progress.

START LESSON 1

Lesson 1

You will

- study new vocabulary;
  make card 25;
  write own sentence using
  the vocabulary word.
- analyze new analogy;
  make card 25;
  write own analogy.
- recite new jingle
  (Object Pronoun).
- identify object pronouns
  and Mixed Patterns 1-2.
- classify Introductory
  Sentences.
- do a Skill Builder to
  identify object pronouns.
- change verb tenses
  in paragraphs.
- do Classroom Practice 35.
- write in your journal.
- read and discuss
  Discovery Time.

LISTENING AND SPEAKING:
Vocabulary & Analogy Time

Learn It: Recite the new vocabulary and analogy words.

Reference 136	Vocabulary & Analogy Words

Word: precipice (prĕs'ə pĭs)
  Definition: a steep or overhanging place
  Synonym: cliff   **Antonym:** valley
  Sentence: A deer stood on a precipice overlooking the valley.

Analogy: knob : door :: headlight : car
  Part-to-whole relationship: Just as a **knob** is part of a **door**,
  a **headlight** is part of a **car**.

Vocabulary Card 25: Record the vocabulary information above and write your own
sentence, using the new word.

Analogy Card 25: Record the analogy information and write your own analogy,
using the same relationship as the analogy above.

Jingle Time

Recite It: Recite the new jingle.

♪ Jingle 22	The Object Pronoun Jingle

There are seven object pronouns
That are easy as can be.
OBJECT PRONOUNS!
Me and **us**,
Him and **her**,
It and **them** and **you**.
Those are the object pronouns.

Grammar Time

Apply It: These Introductory Sentences are used to apply the new grammar
concepts taught below. Classify these sentences orally with your teacher.

Introductory Sentences	Chapter 8: Lesson 1

1. _____ Tomorrow, my mother and father are taking me to the Alamo
in historic San Antonio.

2. _____ Does the outlaw in the movie saunter downtown for a gunfight
with the sheriff at sundown?

3. _____ We did not get a postcard or a souvenir for her during our
travels to Egypt and Africa.

English Made Easy

Learn It: OBJECT PRONOUNS

What are the names of the two types of pronouns you have studied? The new type of pronoun you will learn is called the object pronoun. Recite the jingles to help you remember the different types of pronouns.

Reference 137 Object Pronouns

1. **Object pronouns** are used as *objects* of prepositions, direct *objects*, and indirect *objects*. Did you notice that all of these jobs have the word *object* in them?

2. The object pronouns are listed in your Object Pronoun Jingle: **me, us, him, her, it, them,** and **you.**

3. An object pronoun does not have an object pronoun label. An *object pronoun* keeps the **OP, DO,** or **IO** label that names its job.

OP	DO	IO

Example 1: David gave the ball to *him*. **Example 2:** The reporter interviewed *us*. **Example 3:** Mom made *me* a cake.

Other object pronouns can be substituted for the object pronouns in the examples in Reference 137.

David gave the ball **to me, to us, to her, to them,** or **to you.**

The reporter interviewed **me, him, her, them,** or **you.**

Mom made **us, him, her, them,** or **you** a cake.

Learn It: MIXED GRAMMAR PATTERNS 1–2

The sentences classified in this chapter will be Patterns 1 and 2. They are called **Mixed Patterns** because there are two different patterns from which to choose. Be alert to the parts of speech and where they are located in each sentence. Use the sentence cores to determine the patterns of the sentences.

Learn It: A SKILL BUILDER FOR A NOUN CHECK WITH OBJECT PRONOUNS

The example below shows you what to do with object pronouns when you are identifying nouns for a Noun Check.

LISTENING AND SPEAKING:

FOR A NOUN CHECK WITH OBJECT PRONOUNS

Circle the nouns in a Noun Check.

Sentence 1: Compound Subject Noun (mother) *yes, it is a noun;*
Compound Subject Noun (father) *yes, it is a noun;*
Direct Object **me**, *no, it is a pronoun;*
Object of the Preposition (Alamo) *yes, it is a noun;*
Object of the Preposition (San Antonio) *yes, it is a noun.*

Sentence 2: Subject Noun (outlaw) *yes, it is a noun;*
Object of the Preposition (movie) *yes, it is a noun;*
Object of the Preposition (gunfight) *yes, it is a noun;*
Object of the Preposition (sheriff) *yes, it is a noun;*
Object of the Preposition (sundown) *yes, it is a noun.*

Continued on next page. >>>

Continued from previous page.

Sentence 3: Subject Pronoun **we**, *no, it is a pronoun;*
Compound Direct Object (postcard) *yes, it is a noun;*
Compound Direct Object (souvenir) *yes, it is a noun;*
Object of the Preposition **her**, *no, it is a pronoun;*
Object of the Preposition (travels) *yes, it is a noun;*
Compound Object of the Preposition (Egypt) *yes, it is a noun;*
Compound Object of the Preposition (Africa) *yes, it is a noun.*

Learn It: **CHANGING VERBS TO DIFFERENT TENSES IN PARAGRAPHS**

Reference 138 — Changing Present Tense to Past Tense in Paragraphs

It is very important to study verb tenses because they tell the reader the time period in which an event takes place. If your tense is not consistent, it makes it difficult for your reader to know the time of an event. It takes knowledge and practice to work well with verb tenses. To check the tense of your writing, you must check each verb to make sure it is written in the tense you have chosen. It helps to read a paragraph aloud so you can train your ear to hear the tense of the verbs.

Paragraph 1: Present Tense

Mama **goes** to the barn and **begins** milking Bossie. Bossie **kicks** over the milk pail. The warm milk **spills** on the ground. Mama **talks** angrily to Bossie, but Bossie **does** not **listen**. She just **rolls** her eyes at Mama. Finally, Mama **stands** up and **calls** for Papa. Papa **knows** the problem. He **whispers** in Bossie's ear as he **pets** her. Then, he **sits** down and **milks** her without any trouble. Bossie just **grins** at Mama.

To Check the Verb Tense

To make sure each verb in Paragraph 1 is written in the present tense, identify each verb and check for present tense. You must make sure there are no past-tense forms mixed with your present-tense verbs. It is best to separate the verbs from the paragraph so that you can check each verb individually. (*goes, begins, kicks, spills, talks, does listen, rolls, stands, calls, knows, whispers, pets, sits, milks, grins*)

To Change the Verb Tense

If you want to change a present-tense paragraph to a past-tense paragraph, you must change each verb to past tense, one at a time. Again, it is best to separate the verbs from the paragraph so that you can check each verb individually. (*goes-went, begins-began, kicks-kicked, spills-spilled, talks-talked, does-did listen, rolls-rolled, stands-stood, calls-called, knows-knew, whispers-whispered, pets-petted, sits-sat, milks-milked, grins-grinned*)

Paragraph 2: Past Tense

Mama **went** to the barn and **began** milking Bossie. Bossie **kicked** over the milk pail. The warm milk **spilled** on the ground. Mama **talked** angrily to Bossie, but Bossie **did** not **listen**. She just **rolled** her eyes at Mama. Finally, Mama **stood** up and **called** for Papa. Papa **knew** the problem. He **whispered** in Bossie's ear as he **petted** her. Then, he **sat** down and **milked** her without any trouble. Bossie just **grinned** at Mama.

Classroom Practice 35

It is time to practice the skills you are learning. You will use the classroom practice on the next page to apply these skills.

ENRICHMENT:

JOURNAL WRITING 19

Write an entry in your journal. Use Reference 9 on page 12 for ideas.

(French) 1834-1904—Frederic Auguste Bartholdi was a French sculptor who designed the Statue of Liberty. The statue was titled, "Liberty Enlightening the World" and was given to the United States in 1885 by France in recognition of the friendship between the two countries during the American Revolution. The statue and pedestal cost about $500,000. The American poet, Emma Lazarus, wrote the poem that is on the pedestal. The poem is a sonnet and is titled "The New Colossus."

> *Not like the brazen giant of Greek fame,*
> *With conquering limbs astride from land to land;*
> *Here at our sea-washed, sunset gates shall stand*
> *A mighty woman with a torch, whose flame*
> *Is the imprisoned lightning, and her name*
> *Mother of Exiles. From her beacon-hand*
> *Glows world-wide welcome; her mild eyes command*
> *The air-bridged harbor that twin cities frame.*
> *"Keep, ancient lands, your storied pomp!" cries she*
> *With silent lips. "Give me your tired, your poor,*
> *Your huddled masses yearning to breathe free,*
> *The wretched refuse of your teeming shore.*
> *Send these, the homeless, tempest-tossed to me,*
> *I lift my lamp beside the golden door!"*

Discovery Questions:

- How tall is the Statue of Liberty from the ground to the tip of the torch?
- How many steps are there to the crown?
- Have you ever visited the Statue of Liberty?
- What does the Statue of Liberty mean to you?

Are you interested in learning more about Frederic Auguste Bartholdi or the Statue of Liberty?

1. You may explore this topic further by using the resources listed below.
   Computer resources: Internet, encyclopedia software
   Library resources: encyclopedias, books, magazines, newspapers
   Home/community resources: books, interviews, newspapers, magazines

2. A Discovery Share Time is provided in Lesson 7 if you wish to share your investigation results. You may share orally, or you may prepare a written report. You will put your written report in a class booklet titled "Notable People in History." This booklet will be placed in the class library for everyone to enjoy.

SHURLEY ENGLISH

Classroom Practice 35

Name:_____ Date:_____

GRAMMAR

▶ **Exercise 1:** Classify each sentence.

1. _____ Did Grandfather send his collection of rare stamps to several museums for display?

2. _____ My mom and dad were cheering loudly for us during our soccer game today!

SKILLS

▶ **Exercise 2:** Change the underlined present-tense verbs in Paragraph 1 to past-tense verbs in Paragraph 2.

Paragraph 1: Present Tense

     My brother **is** a student of the martial arts. He **loves** it and **practices** all the time. He **shouts** and **kicks** his bare foot high in the air. I **shout** at him to stop, but he **goes** right on. I **glare** at him and his black belt. This constant practice **has** to stop! I **kick** my chair out of the way and **jump** in front of him. I **wave** my arms, **grunt** loudly, and **shuffle** my feet. I **hold** my funny-looking stance in front of him. I **dare** him to practice one more time in front of me. He **grins** at me and **bows**. Then, he **walks** out and **leaves** me in peace.

Paragraph 2: Past Tense

     My brother _____ a student of the martial arts. He _____ it and _____ all the time. He _____ and _____ his bare foot high in the air. I _____ at him to stop, but he _____ right on. I _____ at him and his black belt. This constant practice _____ to stop! I _____ my chair out of the way and _____ in front of him. I _____ my arms, _____ loudly, and _____ my feet. I _____ my funny-looking stance in front of him. I _____ him to practice one more time in front of me. He _____ at me and _____ . Then, he _____ out and _____ me in peace.

EDITING

▶ **Exercise 3:** Correct each mistake. **Editing Guide: End Marks: 7 Capitals: 10 Commas: 5 Apostrophes: 1 Homonyms: 4 A/An: 1 Subject-Verb Agreement: 7 Periods: 2 Misspelled Words: 1**

elaine gracefully walk across the stage in her shimmering gown she nervously grip the

microphone but her smile never fade the music begins to play over the speakers elaine weights

fore her cue and she begin to sing her voice flows beautifuly threw the song and she smile

as she completes the final verse she nose that she have finished an magical performance

mr and mrs harris elaines parents claps and cheer louder than anyone in the big auditorium

English Made Easy

LISTENING AND SPEAKING:
Vocabulary & Analogy Time

Lesson 2

You will

- study new vocabulary; make card 26; write own sentence using the vocabulary word.
- analyze new analogy; make card 26; write own analogy.
- practice Jingle 22.
- classify Practice Sentences.
- do a Skill Builder.
- change mixed tenses to one tense in paragraphs.
- do Classroom Practice 36.
- read and discuss Discovery Time.

Learn It: Recite the new vocabulary and analogy words.

Reference 139	Vocabulary & Analogy Words

Word: impudent (ĭm'pyə dənt)
   Definition: to be disrespectful of others
   Synonym: rude   **Antonym:** polite
   Sentence: The impudent cashier made two other workers angry.

Analogy: boat : coat :: single : jingle
   Rhyming relationship: Just as **boat** rhymes with **coat**, **single** rhymes with **jingle.**

Vocabulary Card 26: Record the vocabulary information above and write your own sentence, using the new word.

Analogy Card 26: Record the analogy information and write your own analogy, using the same relationship as the analogy above.

Jingle Time

Recite It: Practice Jingle 22 in the Jingle Section on page 512.

Grammar Time

Apply It: Classify the Practice Sentences orally with your teacher.

Practice Sentences	Chapter 8: Lesson 2

1. _____ Is the thunderstorm in our county producing hail and high winds?
2. _____ The huge waves rolled along the surface, crashed against the rocks, and slid back into the sea.
3. _____ Rain, cold temperatures, and fog always dampen my spirits on dreary winter days.

LISTENING AND SPEAKING:

Using the sentences just classified, do a Skill Builder orally with your teacher.

1. **Identify the nouns in a Noun Check.**
2. **Identify the nouns as singular or plural.**
3. **Identify the nouns as common or proper.**
4. **Identify the complete subject and the complete predicate.**
5. **Identify the simple subject and the simple predicate.**
6. **Do a Vocabulary Check.**
7. **Do a Verb Chant.**

Learn It: CHANGING MIXED TENSES
TO PAST OR PRESENT TENSE IN A PARAGRAPH

Reference 140	Changing Mixed Tenses to Past or Present Tense in a Paragraph

In writing, one of the most common mistakes made is mixing present-tense and past-tense verbs. Mixing verb tenses can make your writing awkward and confusing to your reader.

Mixed Tenses: We **yelled** and **scream** for our team and **go** home happy after we **won**.

In this sentence, *yelled* and *won* are past tense, and *scream* and *go* are present tense. The shift from past to present and back to past leaves your reader wondering about the time these actions take place. To make your writing clear and effective, choose a verb tense for your writing and stick to it.

Past Tense: We **yelled** and **screamed** for our team and **went** home happy after we **won**.

Present Tense: We **yell** and **scream** for our team and **go** home happy after we **win**.

Change the underlined mixed-tense verbs in Paragraph 1 to <u>past-tense</u> verbs in Paragraph 2 and to <u>present-tense</u> verbs in Paragraph 3.

Paragraph 1: Mixed Tenses

    I **did** not **understand** my neighbor. His yard **is** okay, but it never **grew** very much unless it **rained** a lot. Ultimately, he **decides** to sod his yard. The sod **looked** like squares of carpet. He **places** them carefully in front of his house. Afterward, he **waters** and **fertilized** his lawn quite often. His beautiful lawn now **had** growing pains. It **grew** too well, and he **had** to mow it twice a week. That **is** his problem, right? Wrong! Before long, my dad **bought** sod for our "okay" yard. Who **had** to mow it twice a week? Me!

Continued on next page. >>>

Reference 140 continued from previous page.

Paragraph 2: Past Tense

I <u>did</u> not <u>understand</u> my neighbor. His yard <u>was</u> okay, but it never <u>grew</u> very much unless it <u>rained</u> a lot. Ultimately, he <u>decided</u> to sod his yard. The sod <u>looked</u> like squares of carpet. He <u>placed</u> them carefully in front of his house. Afterward, he <u>watered</u> and <u>fertilized</u> his lawn quite often. His beautiful lawn now <u>had</u> growing pains. It <u>grew</u> too well, and he <u>had</u> to mow it twice a week. That <u>was</u> his problem, right? Wrong! Before long, my dad <u>bought</u> sod for our "okay" yard. Who <u>had</u> to mow it twice a week? Me!

Paragraph 3: Present Tense

I <u>do</u> not <u>understand</u> my neighbor. His yard <u>is</u> okay, but it never <u>grows</u> very much unless it <u>rains</u> a lot. Ultimately, he <u>decides</u> to sod his yard. The sod <u>looks</u> like squares of carpet. He <u>places</u> them carefully in front of his house. Afterward, he <u>waters</u> and <u>fertilizes</u> his lawn quite often. His beautiful lawn now <u>has</u> growing pains. It <u>grows</u> too well, and he <u>has</u> to mow it twice a week. That <u>is</u> his problem, right? Wrong! Before long, my dad <u>buys</u> sod for our "okay" yard. Who <u>has</u> to mow it twice a week? Me!

 Classroom Practice 36

It is time to practice the skills you are learning. You will use the classroom practice on the next page to apply these skills.

ENRICHMENT:

(American) 1835-1910— Mark Twain was known for his humorous, often satirical writing that exposed hypocrisy and corruption in the small-town life of America. "Mark Twain" was the pseudonym used by Samuel Langhorne Clemens. A pseudonym is a fictitious name used by an author to conceal his identity. His most famous works include *The Adventures of Tom Sawyer*, *The Adventures of Huckleberry Finn*, and *The Prince and the Pauper*.

Discovery Questions:
- On the Mississippi River, what did the river term "mark twain" mean?
- Have you read any of Mark Twain's books?
  Can you name the ones you have read?
  Which book did you like the best? Explain.
- Do you think it is hard or easy to be a writer?

Discovery Activity:
- Write a paragraph or short story and share it with a friend.
- What was your purpose for writing?
  Did you achieve that purpose?

Are you interested in learning more about Mark Twain?

1. You may explore this topic further by using the resources listed below.
   Computer resources: Internet, encyclopedia software
   Library resources: encyclopedias, books, magazines, newspapers
   Home/community resources: books, interviews, newspapers, magazines

2. A Discovery Share Time is provided in Lesson 7 if you wish to share your investigation results. You may share orally, or you may prepare a written report. You will put your written report in a class booklet titled "Notable People in History." This booklet will be placed in the class library for everyone to enjoy.

Classroom Practice 36

Name:_____ Date:_____

GRAMMAR

▶ **Exercise 1:** Classify each sentence.

1. _____ Are you introducing them at the wedding rehearsal tonight?

2. _____ Shhh! The baby is finally sleeping after a long afternoon of fretting and crying!

SKILLS

▶ **Exercise 2:** Change the underlined mixed-tense verbs in Paragraph 1 to **present-tense verbs** in Paragraph 2.

Paragraph 1: Mixed Tenses

   Today **is** the first time I **had flown**, and I **was** very anxious. The airport **is** busy, and people **rushed** to get to their planes on time. On board, I **found** my assigned seat and **buckle** up as the flight attendant **demonstrates** the use of the oxygen masks. We **taxied** on the runway, **pause**, and then **raced** toward the sky. I **lost** my stomach as the wheels **bump** farewell to the earth. My clammy hands **unclench** slowly, and I gradually **relaxed**. I **grin** broadly as the refreshment cart **rattled** up the aisle. The snack **kept** my mind busy, and I **did** not **think** about flying.

Paragraph 2: Present Tense

   Today _____ the first time I _____ _____, and I _____ very anxious. The airport _____ busy, and people _____ to get to their planes on time. On board, I _____ my assigned seat and _____ up as the flight attendant _____ the use of the oxygen masks. We _____ on the runway, _____, and then _____ toward the sky. I _____ my stomach as the wheels _____ farewell to the earth. My clammy hands _____ slowly, and I gradually _____. I _____ broadly as the refreshment cart _____ up the aisle. The snack _____ my mind busy, and I _____ not _____ about flying.

EDITING

▶ **Exercise 3:** Correct each mistake. **Editing Guide: End Marks: 6 Capitals: 9 Commas: 4 Apostrophes: 2 Homonyms: 7 A/An: 3 Subject-Verb Agreement: 6 Misspelled Words: 1**

   the omelet sizzle on the stove as kristi pour a glass of orange juice elizabeth her sister

arrange the plate and silverware on the trey and she neatly folds a cloth napkin kristi place

an vase containing an single read rose in the corner of the tray the girls beams as they hand the

trey too they're dad he smile and balances the tray with both hands dad winks at his daughers

and he leads the weigh into there mothers bedroom for an mothers day surprise

English Made Easy

LISTENING AND SPEAKING:

Vocabulary & Analogy Time

Learn It: Recite the new vocabulary and analogy words.

📖 Reference 141	Vocabulary & Analogy Words

Word: minimum (mĭn'ə məm)
   Definition: the smallest amount allowable
   Synonym: least   **Antonym:** most
   Sentence: The minimum voting age is eighteen.

Analogy: dark : night :: rough : sandpaper
   Descriptive or characteristic relationship: Just as **dark** describes **night**, **rough** describes **sandpaper**.

Vocabulary Card 27: Record the vocabulary information above and write your own sentence, using the new word.

Analogy Card 27: Record the analogy information and write your own analogy, using the same relationship as the analogy above.

Lesson 3

You will
- study new vocabulary; make card 27; write own sentence using the vocabulary word.
- analyze new analogy; make card 27; write own analogy.
- practice Jingles 13–22.
- classify Practice Sentences.
- do a Skill Builder.
- identify principal parts of verbs.
- do Classroom Practice 37.
- write in your journal.
- read and discuss Discovery Time.

Jingle Time

Recite It: Practice Jingles 13–22 in the Jingle Section on pages 509–512.

Grammar Time

Apply It: Classify the Practice Sentences orally with your teacher.

Practice Sentences	Chapter 8: Lesson 3

1. _____ Alas! An enormous deer demolished my new truck on the way to the airport yesterday!
2. _____ Have Curtis and Derek entered the chess tournaments in Springfield and St. Louis?
3. _____ The hummingbird's nest in the apple tree is dangling and swaying in the breeze.

LISTENING AND SPEAKING:

Using the sentences just classified, do a Skill Builder orally with your teacher.

1. **Identify the nouns in a Noun Check.**
2. **Identify the nouns as singular or plural.**
3. **Identify the nouns as common or proper.**
4. **Identify the complete subject and the complete predicate.**
5. **Identify the simple subject and the simple predicate.**
6. **Do a Vocabulary Check.**
7. **Do a Verb Chant.**

Learn It: PRINCIPAL PARTS OF VERBS

Reference 142 — Principal Parts of Verbs

Every main verb has four principal parts, or forms. The four principal parts of main verbs are called **present**, **past**, **past participle**, and **present participle**. All forms of a main verb are made by using one of the four principal parts. The names of the four principal parts are the same for regular and irregular verbs.

1. The **PRESENT** (principal part) has a present-tense main verb and no helping verb.
   (**Regular:** I <u>walk</u>. He <u>walks</u>. We <u>walk</u>.) (**Irregular:** I <u>eat</u>. He <u>eats</u>. We <u>eat</u>.)

2. The **PAST** (principal part) has a past-tense main verb and no helping verb.
   (**Regular:** I <u>walked</u>. He <u>walked</u>. We <u>walked</u>.) (**Irregular:** I <u>ate</u>. He <u>ate</u>. We <u>ate</u>.)

3. The **PAST PARTICIPLE** (principal part) has a main verb (past-participle form) and one of these helping verbs: *has, have,* or *had.*
   (**Regular:** I have <u>walked</u>. He has <u>walked</u>. We have <u>walked</u>. She had <u>walked</u>.)
   (**Irregular:** I have <u>eaten</u>. He has <u>eaten</u>. We have <u>eaten</u>. She had <u>eaten</u>.)

4. The **PRESENT PARTICIPLE** (principal part) has a main verb ending in -ing (present-participle form) and one of these helping verbs: *am, is, are, was,* or *were.*
   (**Regular:** I am <u>walking</u>. He is <u>walking</u>. We are <u>walking</u>. She was <u>walking</u>. They were <u>walking</u>.)
   (**Irregular:** I am <u>eating</u>. He is <u>eating</u>. We are <u>eating</u>. She was <u>eating</u>. They were <u>eating</u>.)

The **four principal parts** of the regular verb *walk*: **walk(s), walked, (has) walked, (is) walking**

The **four principal parts** of the irregular verb *eat*: **eat(s), ate, (has) eaten, (is) eating**

The present and past principal parts have no helping verbs. The principal parts for present participles and past participles <u>always</u> have helping verbs. Study the examples below and use the Verb Chart in Reference 116 on page 185 to help you learn the four principal parts of some regular and irregular main verbs.

	PRESENT	PAST	PAST PARTICIPLE		PRESENT PARTICIPLE	
IRREGULAR:	begin	began	(has, have, had)	begun	(am, is, are, was, were)	beginning
IRREGULAR:	break	broke	(has, have, had)	broken	(am, is, are, was, were)	breaking
REGULAR:	call	called	(has, have, had)	called	(am, is, are, was, were)	calling
REGULAR:	dance	danced	(has, have, had)	danced	(am, is, are, was, were)	dancing

English Made Easy

Classroom Practice 37

It is time to practice the skills you are learning. You will use the classroom practice on the next page to apply these skills.

JOURNAL WRITING 20

Write an entry in your journal. Use Reference 9 on page 12 for ideas.

ENRICHMENT:

Discovery Time

(Scottish American) 1847-1922— Alexander Graham Bell invented the telephone. Bell became interested in the transmission of sound as a speech teacher of deaf students. Bell studied and experimented in such varied areas as aviation, sheep-breeding, water distillation, artificial respiration, and communication. Bell had 18 patents in his name alone and 12 patents with colleagues.

Discovery Questions:

- **What do you think it was like to be an inventor during Bell's time?**
- **What hardships do you think he encountered?**

Are you interested in learning more about Alexander Graham Bell?

1. You may explore this topic further by using the resources listed below.
   Computer resources: Internet, encyclopedia software
   Library resources: encyclopedias, books, magazines, newspapers
   Home/community resources: books, interviews, newspapers, magazines

2. A Discovery Share Time is provided in Lesson 7 if you wish to share your investigation results. You may share orally, or you may prepare a written report. You will put your written report in a class booklet titled "Notable People in History." This booklet will be placed in the class library for everyone to enjoy.

Classroom Practice 37

Name:_____ Date:_____

GRAMMAR

▶ **Exercise 1:** Classify each sentence.

1. _____ After dinner, Dad and my baby brother laughed and played in the hammock.

2. _____ The very swift planes certainly exceeded the speed of sound during their flights.

SKILLS

▶ **Exercise 2:** Write the four principal parts of the following verbs: **choose** and **jump**.

PRESENT	PAST	PAST PARTICIPLE	PRESENT PARTICIPLE
1._____	3._____	5. **(has)** _____	7. **(is)** _____
2._____	4._____	6. **(has)** _____	8. **(is)** _____

▶ **Exercise 3:** Change the underlined mixed-tense verbs in Paragraph 1 to present-tense verbs in Paragraph 2.

Paragraph 1: Mixed Tenses

My dad **was** a big lovable bear this morning. He **comes** into the kitchen and **gave** our mom a big bear hug while she **made** breakfast. Then, he **roams** through the house and **growled** at us kids to get up. While we **ate** breakfast, he **tells** us the latest jokes and **laughed** louder than anyone else. Then, he **gave** us a list of chores to do and **cautions** us to finish them. After he **leaves** the house, we **heard** our beloved bear around the trash cans. We **looked** at each other and **race** to the window. We **sighed** with relief. Our bear **is** only **taking** out the garbage!

Paragraph 2: Present Tense

My dad _____ a big lovable bear this morning. He _____ into the kitchen and _____ our mom a big bear hug while she _____ breakfast. Then, he _____ through the house and _____ at us kids to get up. While we _____ breakfast, he _____ us the latest jokes and _____ louder than anyone else. Then, he _____ us a list of chores to do and _____ us to finish them. After he _____ the house, we _____ our beloved bear around the trash cans. We _____ at each other and _____ to the window. We _____ with relief. Our bear _____ only _____ out the garbage!

EDITING

▶ **Exercise 4:** Correct each mistake. **Editing Guide: End Marks: 5   Capitals: 12   Commas: 2   Apostrophes: 1   Homonyms: 2   A/An: 2   Subject-Verb Agreement: 6   Misspelled Words: 3**

aunt sally gather fresh honey from her behives every morning i loves too watch from aunt

sallys kitchen window as the bees buzz angerly around her like an dark cloud they swarms

around and threatens her with there nasty stings thankfully she always wear protective clotheing

and an netted hood i help aunt sally bottle her honey and uncle lester sell the honey in town

English Made Easy

LISTENING AND SPEAKING:
Vocabulary & Analogy Time

Learn It: Recite the new vocabulary and analogy words.

Reference 143	Vocabulary & Analogy Words

Word: motive (mō'tǐv)
> **Definition:** purpose for acting
> **Synonym:** reason   **Antonym:** deterrent
> **Sentence:** His motive for working was a good paycheck.

Analogy: book : chapter :: movie : scene
> **Part-to-whole relationship:** Just as a **book** is made up of **chapters**, a **movie** is made up of **scenes**.

Vocabulary Card 28: Record the vocabulary information above and write your own sentence, using the new word.

Analogy Card 28: Record the analogy information and write your own analogy, using the same relationship as the analogy above.

Jingle Time

Recite It: Practice Jingles 3–11 in the Jingle Section on pages 507–508.

Grammar Time

Apply It: Classify the Practice Sentences orally with your teacher.

Practice Sentences	Chapter 8: Lesson 4

1. _____ Libby's open box of cereal tipped over and spilled onto the floor in front of her mother!

2. _____ Finally, the conscientious technician repaired and upgraded my computer for me.

3. _____ Mrs. Howard did not approve of Henry's lackluster performance on the science test.

START LESSON 4

Lesson 4

You will
- study new vocabulary; make card 28; write own sentence using the vocabulary word.
- analyze new analogy; make card 28; write own analogy.
- practice Jingles 3–11.
- classify Practice Sentences.
- do Classroom Practice 38.
- read and discuss Discovery Time.
- do a homework assignment.
- do Home Connection activity.

Classroom Practice 38

It is time to practice the skills you are learning. You will use the classroom practice on the next page to apply these skills.

ENRICHMENT:

(American) 1847-1931— **Thomas Edison's** most famous inventions include the light bulb, an electric generating system, a vote counter, the phonograph, the alkaline battery, the carbon telephone transmitter, and the first talking motion pictures. Edison is known as one of the most productive inventors of practical electrical devices in history. Edison paved the way into the future with his inventions. When he died at 84, Edison had patented 1,093 inventions.

Discovery Questions:
• How has Edison's inventions affected the way we live today?
• What would your life be like without his inventions?

Are you interested in learning more about Thomas Edison?

1. You may explore this topic further by using the resources listed below.
   Computer resources: Internet, encyclopedia software
   Library resources: encyclopedias, books, magazines, newspapers
   Home/community resources: books, interviews, newspapers, magazines

2. A Discovery Share Time is provided in Lesson 7 if you wish to share your investigation results. You may share orally, or you may prepare a written report. You will put your written report in a class booklet titled "Notable People in History." This booklet will be placed in the class library for everyone to enjoy.

Classroom Practice 38

Name:_____ Date:_____

GRAMMAR

▶ **Exercise 1:** Classify each sentence.

1. _____ Call me for an appointment at your earliest convenience.

2. _____ Would you study with me after school for the English and math exams?

SKILLS

▶ **Exercise 2:** Write the four principal parts of the following verbs: **throw** and **whisper**.

PRESENT	PAST	PAST PARTICIPLE	PRESENT PARTICIPLE
1. _____	3. _____	5. **(has)** _____	7. **(is)** _____
2. _____	4. _____	6. **(has)** _____	8. **(is)** _____

▶ **Exercise 3:** Change the underlined mixed-tense verbs in Paragraph 1 to past-tense verbs in Paragraph 2.

Paragraph 1: Mixed Tenses

Blinky **was** my beloved computer. He **helps** me when I **check** my homework. I **am** tired tonight, so I **program** Blinky to work my math problems. When my mom **looks** over them, she **told** me all my problems **are** wrong! My mouth **dropped** open. I **march** back into my room and **glare** at Blinky. I **tapped** my fingers angrily beside Blinky's keyboard. I finally **decide** to check Blinky's command system. Then, I **groan** loudly. It **isn't** Blinky's fault after all. It **is** Dad's fault. He **had programmed** Blinky not to do my homework.

Paragraph 2: Past Tense

Blinky _____ my beloved computer. He _____ me when I _____ my homework. I _____ tired tonight, so I _____ Blinky to work my math problems. When my mom _____ over them, she _____ me all my problems _____ wrong! My mouth _____ open. I _____ back into my room and _____ at Blinky. I _____ my fingers angrily beside Blinky's keyboard. I finally _____ to check Blinky's command system. Then, I _____ loudly. It _____ Blinky's fault after all. It _____ Dad's fault. He _____ _____ Blinky not to do my homework.

EDITING

▶ **Exercise 4:** Correct each mistake in the present-tense paragraph. **Editing Guide: End Marks: 6   Capitals: 6   Commas: 7   Apostrophes: 1   Homonyms: 3   Verb Tense: 6   Misspelled Words: 2**

agnes my calico cat loved to look out the window doug my brother loved to pull her tale

as she sits on the window sill and stared outside agnes should be my brothers cat becaus she

pouts when he was not around she looks fore him every day after school and she was never

disapointed doug comes in sneaked up behind her and pulls her tail what a pear of comedians

SHURLEY ENGLISH

🏠 Homework 6

Complete this homework assignment on notebook paper.

1. Number your paper 1–3. Write Present Tense beside Number 1 and list the present-tense helping verbs. Write Past Tense beside Number 2 and list the past-tense helping verbs. Write Future Tense beside Number 3 and list the future-tense helping verbs.

   Present Tense: _____, _____, _____, _____, _____, _____, _____

   Past Tense: _____, _____, _____, _____, _____, _____

   Future tense: _____, _____

2. Number your paper 1–7. For each sentence, do four things. (1) Write the verb or verb phrase. (2) Identify the verb tense by writing **1** for present tense, **2** for past tense, or **3** for future tense. (3) Write the past-tense form. (4) Write **R** for Regular or **I** for Irregular.

	Verb Tense	Main Verb Past Tense Form	R or I
1. Those mice chew holes in our flour sacks.			
2. We were planning a vacation this summer.			
3. The manager gave us some free popcorn.			
4. My dad sells insurance for a big company.			
5. The windows will rattle during a severe thunderstorm.			
6. Two birds fly to the big oak tree in our yard.			
7. Did you eat the peaches?			

3. Write a Practice Sentence, using the labels below. You may expand the sentence by adding more labels.
   SN V-t A DO P A OP

Home Connection

Family Activity for Irregular Verbs

1. Complete the rhymes below with the correct form of each irregular verb in parentheses. (Note: There is one rhyme that does not need to be changed because it already has the correct verb forms.)

   Yesterday, my sister (tear) the beautiful new dress she (wear).   _____/_____

   I was (tell) that the car was (sell).   _____/_____

   We (fight) over the cookies he (bring).   _____/_____

   My new parakeet always (sing) every time the doorbell (ring).   _____/_____

   If he does not (choose) the right answer, his team will (lose).   _____/_____

   The nest was (make), and the eggs were (lay).   _____/_____

2. Divide into two teams. Both teams will make up rhymes that are similar to the ones above. As each team reads its rhymes, the other team tells the correct verb forms.

3. Divide into teams and divide the irregular-verb chart (Reference 116 on page 185) into as many sections as teams. Each team, using its designated verb section, will recite a present-tense verb, and the other team(s) must respond by reciting the verb forms for the past tense, present participle, and past participle.

Answers for number 1: tore-wore, told-sold, fought-bought, sings-rings, choose-lose, made-laid

English Made Easy

LISTENING AND SPEAKING:

Grammar Time

Apply It: Classify the Practice Sentences orally with your teacher.

Practice Sentences	Chapter 8: Lesson 5

1. _____ The conscientious monitor always checks the signatures of the teachers on all hall passes.

2. _____ The bright ray from the huge spotlight is shining upward in a vertical column of colored light.

3. _____ Before the party, Mollie's mother baked and decorated the birthday cake very professionally.

Chapter Checkup 39

It is time for a checkup of the skills you have learned in this chapter. You will use the chapter checkup on the next page to evaluate your progress.

ENRICHMENT:

Discovery Time

(American) 1854–1932— John Philip Sousa is known as the "March King" because he composed so many marches during his career. His father apprenticed him to the U. S. Marine Band when he tried to join a circus band at the age of 13. Sousa wrote 135 band marches. The most popular are "Semper Fidelis" and "The Stars and Stripes Forever." Sousa composed music he heard in his head and did not use an instrument to help him. In addition to his marches, Sousa wrote operettas, arranged music for other bands, and wrote several novels and an autobiography.

Discovery Questions:
- **What instrument was named after Sousa?**
- **Which musical instruments do you like? Explain.**

Are you interested in learning more about John Phillip Sousa?

1. You may explore this topic further by using the resources listed below.
   Computer resources: Internet, encyclopedia software
   Library resources: encyclopedias, books, magazines, newspapers
   Home/community resources: books, interviews, newspapers, magazines

2. A Discovery Share Time is provided in Lesson 7 if you wish to share your investigation results. You may share orally, or you may prepare a written report. You will put your written report in a class booklet titled "Notable People in History." This booklet will be placed in the class library for everyone to enjoy.

Lesson 5

You will
- classify Practice Sentences.
- do Chapter Checkup 39.
- write in your journal.
- read and discuss Discovery Time.

JOURNAL WRITING 21

Write an entry in your journal. Use Reference 9 on page 12 for ideas.

Chapter 8 Checkup 39

Name:_____ Date:_____

GRAMMAR

▶ **Exercise 1:** Classify each sentence.

1. _____ Ouch! I bumped my elbow on the edge of that table in the back of the room!

2. _____ Yesterday, a family of wild bears slowly lumbered to their cave for the winter.

3. _____ Did my picky little brother eat one raisin from the middle of his oatmeal cookie?

SKILLS

▶ **Exercise 2:** Write the four principal parts of the following verbs: **take** and **laugh**.

PRESENT	PAST	PAST PARTICIPLE	PRESENT PARTICIPLE
1. _____	3. _____	5. (**has**) _____	7. (**is**) _____
2. _____	4. _____	6. (**has**) _____	8. (**is**) _____

▶ **Exercise 3:** Change the underlined mixed-tense verbs in Paragraph 1 to past-tense verbs in Paragraph 2.

Paragraph 1: Mixed Tenses

Chores always **send** me into orbit! They **spoil** a perfect day. My mom **told** me that chores **develop** responsibility. My dad **tells** me that they **build** character, and my little brother **tells** me that he **is** too young for chores. Of course, I **argue** with my mom, **sigh** at my dad, and **glare** at my little brother. However, my mom **has** the perfect solution. She **waved** my allowance in front of my nose. It **is** funny how my chores suddenly **became** more bearable. I **agree** with my mom, **nod** at my dad, but still **glared** at my little brother.

Paragraph 2: Past Tense

Chores always _____ me into orbit! They _____ a perfect day. My mom _____ me that chores _____ responsibility. My dad _____ me that they _____ character, and my little brother _____ me that he _____ too young for chores. Of course, I _____ with my mom, _____ at my dad, and _____ at my little brother. However, my mom _____ the perfect solution. She _____ my allowance in front of my nose. It _____ funny how my chores suddenly _____ more bearable. I _____ with my mom, _____ at my dad, but still _____ at my little brother.

EDITING

▶ **Exercise 4:** Correct each mistake. **Editing Guide: End Marks: 3   Capitals: 6   Commas: 2   Apostrophes: 1   Subject-Verb Agreement: 1   Periods: 1   Misspelled Words: 1**

ms turleys science class made a miniature rocket and they launched it yesterday a parent

filmed it and the students watched it on tv during class today the launch were truly spectackular

English Made Easy

Writing Time

Write It: WRITING ASSIGNMENT 19

Writing Assignment [19]: Creative Expressions

Purpose: To entertain
Type of Writing: Creative
Audience: Classmates, relatives, or friends

Choose one of the writing topics below.

1. If you had no electricity or running water, how would you survive?
2. If you were given five million dollars, what would you do with it?
3. Write a poem about difficult times or good times or about a topic of your choice.

Special Instructions:

1. A prewriting map is not required for this creative-writing assignment.
2. Follow the Rough Draft Checklist in Reference 46 on page 61.
3. Put your creative-writing paper in your Rough Draft folder when you have finished

Note: Reference 54 on page 71 gives the steps in the writing process and the location of all the writing checklists..

 **Student Tip...**

> For more information about writing poetry, look at Chapter 18 on pages 465–482.

Conference Time

Discuss It: TEACHER-STUDENT CONFERENCES
FOR WRITING ASSIGNMENT 18

Meet with your teacher to discuss Writing Assignment 18.
After the conference, place this group of papers in your Publishing folder.

Lesson 6

You will

- conference with teacher about WA 18.
- write a creative writing piece for WA 19.

Chapter 8

START LESSON 7

Lesson 7

You will
- publish WA 18.
- participate in Discovery Share Time.
- write an independent persuasive essay (WA 20).

Publishing Time

Publish It: **WRITING ASSIGNMENT 18**

Choose a publishing form and publish Writing Assignment 18. After rewriting your paper for publication, give the stapled papers (evaluation guide, graded final paper, rough draft, and prewriting map) to your teacher to be placed in your Writing Portfolio.

Reference 66	Publishing Checklist for Step 6 in the Writing Process

The sixth step in the writing process is called publishing. Publishing is sharing your writing with others. With so many forms of publishing available, finding a match for every project and personality is easy.

At times, a written work is best read aloud. Other times, the biggest impact is made when a written work is read silently. You can also use media sources to enhance any publication.

SPECIAL INSTRUCTIONS FOR PUBLISHING:

- Rewrite the graded paper in ink or type it on a computer, correcting any marked errors. *(Do not display or publish papers that have marked errors or grades on them.)*
- Give your teacher the set of stapled papers to place in your Writing Portfolio. *(Stapled papers: evaluation guide, graded final paper, rough draft, and prewriting map.)*
- Select a publishing form from the list below and publish your rewritten paper.
  1. Have classmates, family members, neighbors, or others read your writing at school or home.
  2. Share your writing with others during a Share Time. *(Refer to Reference 67 on page 99 for sharing guidelines.)*
  3. Display your writing on a bulletin board or wall.
  4. Put your writing in the classroom library or in the school library for checkout.
  5. Send your writing as a letter or an e-mail to a friend or relative.
  6. Frame your writing by gluing it on colored construction paper and decorating it.
  7. Make a book of your writing for your classroom, your family, or others.
  8. Illustrate your writing and give it to others to read.
  9. Dramatize your writing in the form of a play, puppet show, or radio broadcast.
  10. Send your writing to be placed in a waiting room (doctor, veterinarian, dentist, etc.), senior-citizen center, or a nursing home.
  11. Send your writing to a school newspaper, local newspaper, or a magazine for publication.
  12. Make a videotape, cassette tape, or slide presentation of your writing.
  13. Choose another publishing form that is not listed.

LISTENING AND SPEAKING:

If you have chosen to investigate a historical figure introduced in this chapter, you now have the opportunity to share your results in one of the following ways:

1. You may relate your information orally.
2. You may read a written report.
3. You may place your report in the booklet without reading it aloud.

After share time, all written reports should be turned in to be placed in the class booklet titled "Notable People in History." You are encouraged to check out this class booklet so you can enjoy the reports again.

Writing Time

Write It: **WRITING ASSIGNMENT 20**

As you write a rough draft for your independent writing assignment, you will do two of the six steps in the writing process: prewriting and rough draft.

Writing Assignment [20]

Purpose: To persuade

Type of Writing: Five-paragraph persuasive essay

Audience: Classmates

Writing Topics: Why teenagers should have limited/unlimited phone privileges
The importance of exercise/laughter/doctors
Why everyone needs to learn to swim/cook/read
(Brainstorm for other ideas, individually or in groups.)

Special Instructions:

1. Follow the Prewriting and Rough Draft Checklists in References 44 and 46 on pages 57, 61.

2. Use References 133–135 on pages 229–231 to help you write your persuasive essay.

3. Use standard, time-order, or transition writing form. See Reference 69 on page 103.

4. Write in first or third person. See Reference 70 on page 104.
   (First-person pronouns: *I, me, my, mine, we, us, our,* and *ours.*)
   (Third-person pronouns: *he, his, him, she, her, hers, it, its, they, their, theirs,* and *them.*)

Note: Reference 54 on page 71 gives the steps in the writing process and the location of all the writing checklists.

 Student Note:

Some of your writing pieces will be selected for revision and editing later in the school year.

START LESSON 8

Lesson 8

You will
- practice Jingle 12.
- read and discuss descriptive paragraphs.
- plan and write rough draft for descriptive paragraph (WA 21).

>>> **Student Tip...**

Reviewing the transition words will help you apply them in your writing.

LISTENING AND SPEAKING:

Recite It: Practice Jingle 12 in the Jingle Section on page 509.

Learn It: DESCRIPTIVE WRITING

An artist paints a picture on canvas with paint. A descriptive writer paints a picture on paper with words. Both the artist and writer must select what they will include in their picture.

Reference 144   Descriptive Writing

Descriptive writing shows the reader what is being described. It does not just tell him about it. Descriptive writing paints a picture on paper with words. Even though you can use description in expository, narrative, and persuasive writing, sometimes you are asked to write only a descriptive piece of writing. Then, you must understand that a descriptive paragraph gives a detailed picture of a person, place, thing, or idea.

A descriptive paragraph will usually start with an overall impression of what you are describing. That will be your topic sentence. Then, you will add supporting sentences that give details about the topic. To make a description clear and vivid, these detail sentences should include as much information as possible about how the topic looks, sounds, feels, tastes, or smells. The sensory details that you include will depend on what you are describing. Since all the senses are not significant in all situations, the following guidelines about descriptive writing will give you the types of details that you should consider when you are describing certain topics.

Descriptive Guidelines

WHEN DESCRIBING PEOPLE

Use these types of details:
1. Appearance, walk, voice, mannerisms, gestures, personality traits
2. Any special situations related to the person being described
3. Striking details that make that person stand out

WHEN DESCRIBING PLACES

Use these types of details:
1. Sensory details that create a clear picture of the place's physical features (colors, textures, sights, shapes, age, sounds, smells, and feelings)
2. Unusual or unique features
3. Special circumstances related to the place
4. Why the place is special

WHEN DESCRIBING ANIMALS, PLANTS, OR OBJECTS

Use these types of details:
1. Sensory details that create a clear picture of the animal, plant, or object's physical features (colors, textures, sights, shapes, age, sounds, smells, and feelings)
2. Unusual or unique features
3. Special situations related to the animal, plant, or object
4. Why the animal, plant, or object is special

WHEN DESCRIBING NATURE

Use these types of details:
1. Special features of the season or scene
2. Sensory details that create a clear picture of the scene (colors, textures, sights, sounds, smells, and feelings)
3. Any plants, insects, birds, or other animals in the scene
4. Any special conditions related to the scene

Continued on next page. >>>

Reference 144 continued from previous page.

WHEN DESCRIBING AN INCIDENT OR EVENT

Use these types of details:

1. The order in which things happen
2. Facts that help the action move along smoothly from a beginning to an ending
3. Any of the who, what, when, where, why, and how questions
4. Sensory details that create a clear picture of the incident or event (sights, sounds, smells, and feelings)

WHEN DESCRIBING A FEELING

Use these types of details:

1. The cause of this feeling or emotion
2. Physical signs that occur as a result of this feeling (smile, frown, tears, hugs, sobs, laughter, red face)
3. Figurative language for comparison (similes, metaphors, personification)

Learn It: WRITING A DESCRIPTIVE PARAGRAPH

 Reference 145 | **Writing a Descriptive Paragraph**

Writing Topic: A drive through the park

Sentence 1 – Topic Sentence:
Introduces what is being described.

> **My family and I love to drive through Yellowstone National Park on sunny days.**

Following Sentences – Body of Paragraph:
Uses some of the descriptive details in Reference 144.

> **While riding comfortably in our family car, we especially like to tour the geyser basins. We go to see the hot springs filled with bubbling pools of mud called the Fountain Paint Pots. Everyone can hear the sound of the bubbling mud and smell warm dirt and clay wafting through the air. We even notice that the mud has various colors due to the minerals in the clay. As we travel to the Great Fountain Geyser, we can see the powerful bursts of water spouting 200 feet above its pool. It sounds just like a cannon exploding when it erupts! Grand Prismatic Spring is the largest hot spring in Yellowstone. Its pool has a deep blue center, ringed with pink. We look at the small plants called algae that give the spring its color. It's absolutely spectacular to see. Of course, Old Faithful is the most famous geyser in the park. Steam and boiling water erupt from Old Faithful on an average of every 73 minutes; so, we wait in the warm sunshine with many other spectators to watch it blow.**

Last Sentence – Concluding Sentence:
Restates or relates back to the topic sentence.

> **My parents and I learn more each time we drive through the scenic Yellowstone National Park to view the geyser basins.**

A Sample Descriptive Paragraph

A Drive Through Yellowstone National Park

My family and I love to drive through Yellowstone National Park on sunny days. While riding comfortably in our family car, we especially like to tour the geyser basins. We go to see the hot springs filled with bubbling pools of mud called the Fountain Paint Pots. Everyone can hear the sound of the bubbling mud and smell warm dirt and clay wafting through the air. We even notice that the mud has various colors due to the minerals in the clay. As we travel to the Great Fountain Geyser, we can see the powerful bursts of water spouting 200 feet above its pool. It sounds just like a cannon exploding when it erupts! Grand Prismatic Spring is the largest hot spring in Yellowstone. Its pool has a deep blue center, ringed with pink. We look at the small plants called algae that give the spring its color. It's absolutely spectacular to see. Of course, Old Faithful is the most famous geyser in the park. Steam and boiling water erupt from Old Faithful on an average of every 73 minutes; so, we wait in the warm sunshine with many other spectators to watch it blow. My parents and I learn more each time we drive through the scenic Yellowstone National Park to view the geyser basins.

Discuss It:

The example shows how the writer followed the Descriptive Writing Guidelines to write a descriptive paragraph.

　1. What is the writing topic?

　2. What title did the author decide to use?

　3. What is being described in the topic sentence?

　4. In the body of the descriptive paragraph, the writer uses sights and sounds to describe his drive through Yellowstone National Park. What are some of the examples of what he sees and hears?

　5. Which sentence do you think is the most descriptive?

　6. Compare the topic sentence to the concluding sentence. How do they relate to each other?

Write It: WRITING ASSIGNMENT 21

As you write a rough draft for your guided writing assignment, you will do two of the six steps in the writing process: prewriting (descriptive guidelines) and rough draft.

Writing Assignment [21]

　　　　　　Purpose: To describe
　　Type of Writing: Descriptive paragraph
　　　　　Audience: Classmates
　Writing Topics: An amazing winter/summer day
　　　　　　　　　Funny haircut(s)
　　　　　　　　　An unusual family car/room/activity
　　　　　　　　　(Brainstorm for other ideas, individually or in groups.)

Special Instructions:

1. Follow the Prewriting and Rough Draft Checklists in References 44 and 46 on pages 57, 61.

2. Make a prewriting map using the descriptive guidelines in References 144–145 on pages 258–259 to help you write your descriptive paragraph.

3. Write in first or third person. See Reference 70, page 104.
　(First-person pronouns: *I, me, my, mine, we, us, our,* and *ours.*)
　(Third-person pronouns: *he, his, him, she, her, hers, it, its, they, their, theirs,* and *them.*)

Note: Reference 54 on page 71 gives the steps in the writing process and the location of all the writing checklists.

Writing Time

Apply It: **REVISE, EDIT, AND WRITE A FINAL PAPER**

Following the schedule below, you will revise and edit Writing Assignment 21. Then, you will write a final paper. Use the Chapter 8 Writing Evaluation Guide on the next page to check your final paper one last time.

 Reference 52 | **Revising & Editing Schedule and Writing a Final Paper**

SPECIAL INSTRUCTIONS FOR REVISING AND EDITING (Steps 3-4 in the writing process):

• Use the Revising and Editing Checklists in References 48 and 50 as you revise and edit your rough draft.

• Follow the revising and editing schedule below as directed by your teacher.

1. **Individual.** First, read your rough draft to yourself. Use the Revising Checklist in Reference 48 on page 64. Go through your paper, checking each item on the list and making revisions to your rough draft. Then, use the Editing Checklist in Reference 50 on page 66. Go through your paper again, checking each item on the list and editing your rough draft.

2. **Partner.** Next, get with your editing partner. Work together on each partner's rough draft, one paper at a time. Read each rough draft aloud and revise and edit it together, using the Revising and Editing Checklists. (The author of the paper should be the one to make the corrections on his own paper.)

3. **Group.** Finally, read the rough draft to a revision group for feedback. Each student should read his paper while the others listen and offer possible revising and editing suggestions. (The author will determine whether to make corrections from the revision group's suggestions.)

SPECIAL INSTRUCTIONS FOR FINAL PAPER (Step 5 in the writing process):

• Write your final paper, using the Final Paper Checklist in Reference 53 on page 70.

• Staple your writing papers in this order: the final paper on top, the rough draft in the middle, and the prewriting map on the bottom. Place the stapled papers in the Final Paper folder.

>>>>>>>>> **Student Tip...**

1. Be tactful and helpful in your comments during revising and editing time. The purpose of any suggestion should be to improve the writer's rough draft.

2. As you make your final corrections, you have the choice of accepting or rejecting any suggestions made by your partners or your revision group.

3. Study Vocabulary Words and Analogies 25–28 for the chapter test in the next lesson.

4. If you need to improve your handwriting, refer to the Resource Tools Section on pages 529–530 for information on writing legibly.

Chapter 8 Writing Evaluation Guide

Name:_____ Date:_____

ROUGH DRAFT CHECK

_____ 1. Did you write your rough draft in pencil?

_____ 2. Did you write the correct headings on the first seven lines of your paper?

_____ 3. Did you use extra wide margins and skip every other line?

_____ 4. Did you write a title at the end of your rough draft?

_____ 5. Did you place your edited rough draft in your Rough Draft folder?

REVISING CHECK

_____ 6. Did you identify the purpose, type of writing, and audience?

_____ 7. Did you check for a topic, topic sentence, and sentences supporting the topic?

_____ 8. Did you check sentences for the right order, and did you combine, rearrange, or delete sentences when necessary?

_____ 9. Did you check for a variety of simple, compound, and complex sentences?

_____ 10. Did you check for any left out, repeated, or unnecessary words?

_____ 11. Did you check for the best choice of words by replacing or deleting unclear words?

_____ 12. Did you check the content for interest and creativity?

_____ 13. Did you check the voice to make sure the writing says what you want it to say?

EDITING CHECK

_____ 14. Did you indent each paragraph?

_____ 15. Did you put an end mark at the end of every sentence?

_____ 16. Did you capitalize the first word of every sentence?

_____ 17. Did you check for all other capitalization mistakes?

_____ 18. Did you check for all punctuation mistakes?
(*commas, periods, apostrophes, quotation marks, underlining*)

_____ 19. Did you check for misspelled words and for incorrect homonym choices?

_____ 20. Did you check for incorrect spellings of plural and possessive forms?

_____ 21. Did you check for correct construction and punctuation of your sentences?

_____ 22. Did you check for usage mistakes? (*subject/verb agreement, a/an choices, contractions, verb tenses, pronoun/antecedent agreement, pronoun cases, degrees of adjectives, double negatives, etc.*)

_____ 23. Did you put your revised and edited paper in the Rough Draft folder?

FINAL PAPER CHECK

_____ 24. Did you write the final paper in pencil?

_____ 25. Did you center the title on the top line and center your name under the title?

_____ 26. Did you skip a line before starting the writing assignment?

_____ 27. Did you single-space, use wide margins, and write the final paper neatly?

_____ 28. Did you staple your papers in this order: final paper on top, rough draft in the middle, and prewriting map on the bottom? Did you put them in the Final Paper folder?

Writing Time

Chapter 8

START LESSON 10

Lesson 10

You will
- hand in WA 21 for grading.
- respond to oral review questions.
- take Chapter 8 Test.
- discuss and evaluate goals.
- write a paragraph in your goal booklet.

Hand It In: **WRITING ASSIGNMENT 21**

Get your stapled papers for Writing Assignment 21 from your Final Paper folder. Check to make sure they are in the correct order: the final paper on top, the rough draft in the middle, and the prewriting map (Descriptive Outline) on the bottom. Hand them in to your teacher.

LISTENING AND SPEAKING:

Oral Review Questions

CHAPTER TEST

It is time to evaluate your knowledge of the skills you have learned in this chapter. Your teacher will give you the Chapter 8 Test to help you assess your progress.

Discuss It:

1. What are the seven object pronouns?
2. What are the core parts of a Pattern 2 sentence?
3. What kind of verb makes the past tense by adding -ed to the main verb?
4. What kind of verb makes the past tense by a vowel-spelling change?
5. What are the three simple verb tenses?
6. If there is a helping verb and main verb, which verb determines the tense?
7. What are the seven present-tense helping verbs?
8. What are the five past-tense helping verbs?
9. What are the two future-tense helping verbs?
10. Name the four principal parts of a verb?
11. Which two principal parts have helping verbs?
12. Which two principal parts do not have helping verbs?
13. What type of writing is used when your purpose is to paint a picture with words?
14. What type of writing is used when your purpose is to express an opinion and to convince the reader that this opinion is correct?
15. What type of writing is used when your purpose is to inform, to give facts, to give directions, to explain, or to define something?

>>>>>>>>>>>>>>> **Student Tip...**

For information about test-taking strategies, refer to the Resource Tools Section on page 528.

Review It: **GOALS**

Review the goals you wrote in your Goal Booklet at the beginning of the school year. Discuss your progress with your teacher or a student partner. Then, write a paragraph in your Goal Booklet that tells how well you are meeting your short-term goals. Give examples that support your evaluation of your progress. Next, write another paragraph to evaluate your long-term goals. Tell whether you want to change them or keep them the same. Give reasons to support either choice. Finally, return your Goal Booklet to your teacher when you have finished.

Lesson 1

You will

- study new vocabulary; make card 29; write own sentence using the vocabulary word.
- analyze new analogy; make card 29; write own analogy.
- recite new jingle (Indirect Object).
- identify indirect objects and Pattern 3.
- classify Introductory Sentences.
- do a Skill Builder to identify indirect objects.
- write in your journal.

LISTENING AND SPEAKING:

 Vocabulary & Analogy Time

Learn It: Recite the new vocabulary and analogy words.

📖	Reference 146	**Vocabulary & Analogy Words**

Word: comprise (kəm prīz')
  Definition: to include or contain
  Synonym: consists   **Antonym:** excludes
  Sentence: The dessert is comprised of sugar, milk, and eggs.

Analogy: colt : horse :: acorn : tree
  Progression relationship: Just as a **colt** grows into a **horse**, an **acorn** grows into a **tree**.

Vocabulary Card 29: Record the vocabulary information above and write your own sentence, using the new word.

Analogy Card 29: Record the analogy information and write your own analogy, using the same relationship as the analogy above.

 **Jingle Time**

Recite It: Recite the new jingle.

♪	Jingle 23	**The Indirect Object Jingle**

Indirect, oh, indirect, oh, indirect object.
Give me that indirect, oh, indirect, oh, indirect object.

An indirect object is a NOUN or a PRONOUN
That receives what the direct, the direct object names.
An indirect object is found between the **verb**, **verb-transitive**,
And the **direct object**.

      To find the indirect object,   *(sha-bop)*
      Ask **TO WHOM** or **FOR WHOM**   *(sha-bop)*
      After the direct object.   *(sha-bop)*

An indirect, indirect, indirect, indirect, yeah!
An **INDIRECT OBJECT!**

    Just give me that indirect, oh, indirect, oh, indirect object.
    Give me that indirect, oh, indirect, oh, indirect object.
    Give me that object, oh, indirect, oh, indirect object.

An **INDIRECT OBJECT!**

Grammar Time

Apply It: These Introductory Sentences are used to apply the new grammar concepts taught below. Classify these sentences orally with your teacher.

Introductory Sentences	Chapter 9: Lesson 1

1. _____ Grandmother made me a cake.

2. _____ Yesterday, our devoted grandmother carefully made Curtis and me a chocolate birthday cake.

3. _____ Ha! As a funny joke, Marcie and I gave Tracy an empty gift-wrapped box!

Learn It: **INDIRECT OBJECTS**

A Pattern 1 sentence has only one noun and an action verb as the sentence core. A Pattern 2 sentence has two nouns and an action verb as the sentence core. The new sentence pattern, Pattern 3, has three nouns and an action verb as the sentence core.

Reference 147   Indirect Object and Pattern 3

1. An **indirect object** is a noun or pronoun.

2. An indirect object receives what the direct object names. The indirect object tells *to whom* or *for whom or to what or for what* the action is done. It does not receive the action of the verb.

3. An indirect object is located between the verb-transitive and the direct object.

4. To find an indirect object, ask TO WHOM or FOR WHOM, TO WHAT or FOR WHAT after the direct object. Use WHOM when the indirect object is a person. Use WHAT when the indirect object is a place, thing, or idea.

5. An *indirect object* is labeled with the abbreviation **IO**.

6. A Pattern 3 sentence has a subject noun, transitive verb, indirect object, and a direct object as its core. A Pattern 3 sentence is labeled **SN V-t IO DO P3**. A Pattern 3 sentence has three noun jobs in its pattern: the subject noun, the indirect-object noun, and the direct-object noun. *(If the subject is a subject pronoun, it is labeled as a pronoun in the sentence, but the pattern is still identified as SN V-t IO DO P3.)*

7. **A review:**
   <u>Pattern 1</u> is **SN V.** It has a noun-verb (**N V**) core.
   <u>Pattern 2</u> is **SN V-t DO.** It has a noun-verb-noun (**N V N**) core.
   <u>Pattern 3</u> is **SN V-t IO DO.** It has a noun-verb-noun-noun (**N V N N**) core.

   The location of each noun determines its job in a sentence. Only certain noun jobs form the pattern parts of a sentence. For each pattern, the order of the core nouns does not change. A noun that is an object of the preposition is not part of a sentence pattern.

Continued on next page. >>>

Reference 147 continued from previous page.

Question and Answer Flow for the Practice Sentence, adding Indirect Objects

Practice Sentence: Alex bought me a truck.

1. Who bought me a truck? **Alex - SN**
2. What is being said about Alex? **Alex bought - V**
3. Alex bought what? **truck - verify the noun**
4. Does truck mean the same thing as Alex? **No.**
5. **Truck - DO**
6. **Bought - V-t**
7. Alex bought truck for whom? **me - IO** (Say: *me - indirect object.*)
8. **A - A**

9. **SN V-t IO DO P3** (Say: *subject noun, verb-transitive, indirect object, direct object, Pattern 3.*)
10. Skill Check
11. Verb-transitive - check again
12. No prepositional phrases
13. **Period, statement, declarative sentence**
14. Go back to the verb. Divide the complete subject from the complete predicate.
15. Is there an adverb exception? **No.**
16. Is this sentence in a natural or inverted order? **Natural - no change.**

```
          SN      V-t IO A DO
 SN  V-t    Alex / bought me a truck. D
 IO DO P3
```

Discuss It:

1. What is the pattern in a Pattern 3 sentence?
2. What are the core parts of a Pattern 3 sentence?
3. What parts of speech are used in a Pattern 3 sentence?

Learn It: **A SKILL BUILDER FOR A NOUN CHECK WITH INDIRECT OBJECTS**

The example below shows you what to do with indirect objects when you are identifying nouns for a Noun Check

LISTENING AND SPEAKING:

WITH INDIRECT OBJECTS.

Circle the nouns for a Noun Check.

Sentence 1: Subject Noun (grandmother) *yes, it is a noun;*
Indirect Object me, *no, it is a pronoun;*
Direct Object (cake) *yes, it is a noun.*

Sentence 2: Subject Noun (grandmother) *yes, it is a noun;*
Compound Indirect Object (Curtis) *yes, it is a noun;*
Compound Indirect Object me, *no, it is a pronoun;*
Direct Object (cake) *yes, it is a noun.*

Sentence 3: Object of the Preposition (joke) *yes, it is a noun;*
Compound Subject Noun (Marcie) *yes, it is a noun;*
Compound Subject Pronoun I, *no, it is a pronoun;*
Indirect Object (Tracy) *yes, it is a noun;*
Direct Object (box) *yes, it is a noun.*

JOURNAL WRITING 22

Write an entry in your journal. Use Reference 9 on page 12 for ideas.

English Made Easy

LISTENING AND SPEAKING:

Vocabulary & Analogy Time

Learn It: Recite the new vocabulary and analogy words.

 | **Reference 148** | **Vocabulary & Analogy Words**

Word: edifice (ĕd'ə fĭs)
   Definition: a large, imposing structure
   Synonym: building   **Antonym:** hut
   Sentence: The towering edifice had stately marble columns.

Analogy: pull : tug :: push : shove
   Synonym relationship: Just as **pull** means nearly the same as **tug**, **push** means nearly the same as **shove**.

Vocabulary Card 30: Record the vocabulary information above and write your own sentence, using the new word.

Analogy Card 30: Record the analogy information and write your own analogy, using the same relationship as the analogy above.

Jingle Time

Recite It: Practice Jingle 23 in the Jingle Section on page 512.

Grammar Time

Apply It: Classify the Practice Sentences orally with your teacher.

Practice Sentences	Chapter 9: Lesson 2

1. _____ Over the intercom, the co-pilot gave us a weather report for Amsterdam and Copenhagen.

2. _____ Did Jack's dad buy him that cool yellow motorcycle from the advertisement in the newspaper?

3. _____ My boss and his wife gave their esteemed friend an engraved watch for his retirement gift.

Lesson 2

You will

- study new vocabulary; make card 30; write own sentence using the vocabulary word.
- analyze new analogy; make card 30; write own analogy.
- practice Jingle 23.
- classify Practice Sentences.
- do a Skill Builder.
- identify and punctuate quotations (beginning, ending, and split).
- do Classroom Practice 40.
- read and discuss Discovery Time.

LISTENING AND SPEAKING:

Using the sentences just classified, do a Skill Builder orally with your teacher.

1. **Identify the nouns in a Noun Check.**
2. **Identify the nouns as singular or plural.**
3. **Identify the nouns as common or proper.**
4. **Identify the complete subject and the complete predicate.**
5. **Identify the simple subject and the simple predicate.**
6. **Do a Vocabulary Check.**
7. **Do a Verb Chant.**

Compare It:

The following stories have the same topic, but they are written differently. Tell which story you enjoyed more, Story 1 or Story 2.

STORY 1

Carla could hardly believe she was not watching the noon news when the meteorologist dialed her number, hoping to give away a jackpot of seven hundred dollars. She was so upset because she did not know the count or amount. Any other day she would have been tuned in, but today she was having lunch guests. She was in the kitchen preparing tuna salad when the phone rang.

It is safe to say that Carla will never forgive herself. She has watched the noon news almost without fail for years. And the day her number was called was one of the rare occasions her TV was not turned on.

STORY 2

"No! No! No!" Carla screamed. "You can't do this to me! Any other day I would have been watching, but today I was in the kitchen making tuna salad for lunch guests. I can't believe this!" Carla wailed miserably to the meteorologist. He patiently listened to her wail. Carla did not know the count and amount that would have made her the winner of Tuesday's seven-hundred-dollar jackpot. She continued to wail miserably.

The meteorologist tried to console her, but no amount of talking could lessen her devastation. Finally, he said, "You will receive a consolation prize. Have a good day."

"The man wants me to have a good day," Carla said disgustedly as she looked at the phone in her hand. "I'll never have a good day again! All I'll ever have is an expensive $700 tuna salad!"

Learn It: **BEGINNING QUOTES**

Quotations help build pictures for readers as a story unfolds. Writers use three types of quotations: the beginning quote, the end quote, and the split quote.

Reference 149   Rules for Punctuating Beginning Quotes

Quotations are words spoken by someone, and quotation marks are used to set off the spoken words. The words set off by quotation marks are called a **direct quotation. Explanatory words** are the words that explain who is talking, but they are not part of the actual quote.

When writers use quotations in a story, it is called **dialogue**, or **conversation**. Dialogue helps move the plot along and helps the reader to understand the characters.

There are special rules for punctuating quotations. You will use five rules to punctuate a beginning quote. Each rule tells you how to punctuate a specific part of the sample sentence below. Before you begin, read the sample sentence aloud.

Sample Sentence: the boys and i are going hunting on friday with b j moss my dad said

RULE 1: Underline **end explanatory words** and place a period at the end of the explanatory words. If the quote is at the beginning of the sentence, the explanatory words are at the end. (*Explanatory words are the words that explain who is talking but which are not part of the actual quote.*)

Following Rule 1, the explanatory words are underlined, and a period is placed at the end of the explanatory words in the sample sentence below.

1. the boys and i are going hunting on friday with b j moss **my dad said.**

RULE 2: Place quotation marks at the beginning and end of what is said. For a beginning quote, put a comma, question mark, or exclamation point (no period) after the last word of the quote but in front of the quotation mark. Use a comma if the quote is a statement; use a question mark if the quote is a question; use an exclamation point if the quote is an exclamation and shows strong feeling.

Following Rule 2, quotation marks are placed at the beginning and end of what is said in the sample sentence below. A comma is placed at the end of the quote but in front of the quotation mark.

2. **"**the boys and i are going hunting on friday with b j moss**,"** my dad said.

RULE 3: Capitalize the beginning of a quote and any proper nouns or the pronoun *I*.

Following Rule 3, the beginning of the quote is capitalized, the proper nouns are capitalized, and the pronoun I is capitalized in the sample sentence below. The noun, dad, is not capitalized because it has a possessive pronoun in front of it.

3. **"T**he boys and **I** are going hunting on **F**riday with **B J M**oss," my dad said.

RULE 4: Punctuate the rest of the sentence by checking for any apostrophes, periods, or commas that may be needed within the sentence.

Following Rule 4, the rest of the sentence is checked for any words needing apostrophes, periods, or commas within the sample sentence below.

4. "The boys and I are going hunting on Friday with B**.** J**.** Moss," my dad said.

RULE 5: Use the **beginning quotation pattern** to check the punctuation of a beginning quote.

Beginning Quotation Pattern: "C (quote) (**,!?**)**"** (explanatory words) (**.**)

Translation of the Beginning Quotation Pattern: beginning quotation marks, capital letter to begin the quote, the quote itself, choices for an end mark (**,!?**), ending quotation marks,

Corrected Sentence: "The boys and I are going hunting on Friday with B. J. Moss," my dad said.

Learn It: ENDING QUOTES

Reference 150 — Rules for Punctuating Ending Quotes

You will use five rules to punctuate an ending quote. Each rule tells you how to punctuate a specific part of the sample sentence below. Before you begin, read the sample sentence aloud.

Sample Sentence: my dad said the boys and i are going hunting on friday with b j moss

RULE 1: Underline **beginning explanatory words** and place a comma at the end of the explanatory words. If the quote is at the end of the sentence, the explanatory words are at the beginning. (*Explanatory words are the words that explain who is talking but which are not part of the actual quote.*)

Following Rule 1, the explanatory words are underlined, and a comma is placed at the end of the explanatory words in the sample sentence below.

1. <u>my dad said,</u> the boys and i are going hunting on friday with b j moss

RULE 2: Place quotation marks at the beginning and end of what is said. For an end quote, put an end-mark punctuation (no comma) after the quote but in front of the quotation mark. Use a period if the quote is a statement; use a question mark if the quote is a question; use an exclamation point if the quote is an exclamation and shows excitement or strong feeling.

Following Rule 2, quotation marks are placed at the beginning and end of what is said in the sample sentence below. A period is placed at the end of the quote but in front of the quotation mark.

2. <u>my dad said,</u> **"**the boys and i are going hunting on friday with b j moss.**"**

RULE 3: **Capitalize** the first word of the explanatory words, the first word of the quote, and any proper nouns or the pronoun I.

Following Rule 3, the first word of the explanatory words is capitalized, the beginning of the quote is capitalized, the proper nouns are capitalized, and the pronoun I is capitalized in the sample sentence below. The noun, *dad*, is not capitalized because it has a possessive pronoun in front of it.

3. <u>My dad said,</u> "The boys and I are going hunting on Friday with **B J M**oss."

RULE 4: **Punctuate** the rest of the sentence by checking for any apostrophes, periods, or commas that may be needed.

Following Rule 4, the rest of the sentence is checked for any words needing apostrophes, periods, or commas.

4. <u>My dad said,</u> "The boys and I are going hunting on Friday with B. J. Moss."

RULE 5: Use the **ending quotation pattern** to check the punctuation of an end quote.

Ending Quotation Pattern: C (<u>explanatory words</u>) (**,**) **"**C (quote) (**.!?**)**"**

Translation of the Ending Quotation Pattern: capital letter to begin the explanatory words, the explanatory words, comma, beginning quotation marks, capital letter to begin the quote, the quote itself, choices for an end mark (.!?), ending quotation marks.

Corrected Sentence: <u>My dad said,</u> "The boys and I are going hunting on Friday with B. J. Moss."

English Made Easy

Learn It: SPLIT QUOTES

Reference 151 — Rules for Punctuating Split Quotes

When one sentence has a quote that is split by explanatory words, it is called a **split quotation**. You will use the five rules below to punctuate a split quote. Each rule tells you how to punctuate a specific part of the sample sentence below. Before you begin, read the sample sentence aloud.

Sample Sentence: the boys and i my dad said are going hunting on friday with b j moss

RULE 1: Underline the **middle explanatory words** and place a comma at the end of the explanatory words. If the quote is split, the explanatory words are in the middle of the sentence. (*Explanatory words are the words that explain who is talking but which are not part of the actual quote.*)

Following Rule 1, the explanatory words are underlined, and a comma is placed at the end of the explanatory words in the sample sentence below.

1. the boys and i **my dad said,** are going hunting on friday with b j moss

RULE 2: **For the first part of a split quote**, place quotation marks at the beginning and end of the first part of what is said. Put a comma after the last word of the first part of the quote but in front of the quotation mark.

For the second part of a split quote, place quotation marks at the beginning and end of the second part of what is said. Put an end-mark punctuation (no comma) after the quote but in front of the quotation mark. Use a period if the quote is a statement; use a question mark if the quote is a question; use an exclamation point if the quote is an exclamation and shows excitement or strong feeling.

Following Rule 2, quotation marks are placed at the beginning and end of what is said in the sample sentence below. A comma is placed at the end of the first part of the quote but in front of the quotation mark. For this example, the end mark is a period and is placed at the end of the second part of the quote but in front of the quotation mark.

2. "the boys and i," my dad said, "are going hunting on friday with b j moss."

RULE 3: **Capitalize** the beginning of the quote and any proper nouns or the pronoun I.

Following Rule 3, the beginning of the quote is capitalized, the proper nouns are capitalized, and the pronoun I is capitalized in the sample sentence below. The noun, *dad*, is not capitalized because it has a possessive pronoun in front of it.

3. "The boys and I," my dad said, "are going hunting on Friday with B J Moss."

RULE 4: **Punctuate** the rest of the sentence by checking for any apostrophes, periods, or commas that may be needed.

Following Rule 4, the rest of the sentence is checked for any words needing apostrophes, periods, or commas.

4. "The boys and I," my dad said, "are going hunting on Friday with B. J. Moss."

RULE 5: Use the **split quotation pattern** to check the punctuation of a split quote.

Split Quotation Pattern:
"C (first part of the quote) **(,)"** c (explanatory words) **(,)** **"c** (second part of the quote) **(.!?)"**

Translation of the Split Quotation Pattern: beginning quotation marks, capital letter to begin the quote, first part of the split quote, comma, ending quotation marks, lowercase letter unless there is a proper noun, explanatory words, comma, beginning quotation marks for the second part of the split quote, lowercase letter unless there is a proper noun, second part of the split quote, choices for an end mark (.!?), ending quotation marks.

Corrected Sentence: "**The boys and I**," my dad said, "**are going hunting on Friday with B. J. Moss.**"

Note: When consecutive sentences are part of a quotation, you do not have a split quotation.

Example: "The boys and I are going hunting on Friday," my dad said. "I think they need the experience."

Classroom Practice 40

It is time to practice the skills you are learning. You will use the classroom practice on the next page to apply these skills.

Student Note: Anytime the word "exclaimed" is used in explanatory words, the end mark for the quote should be an exclamation point, not a period.

ENRICHMENT:

(American) 1856-1915— **Booker T. Washington** organized a vocational school for African Americans that eventually became Tuskegee University. He advocated the advancement of black communities through education and economic improvement. Booker T. Washington was the first African American whose face appeared on a postage stamp. In 1946, his image appeared on a fifty-cent piece.

Discovery Questions:
- Washington acted as an advisor to which two U.S. Presidents?
- Why do you think Booker T. Washington was a strong advocate for education?
- If you could interview Washington, what questions would you ask him?

Are you interested in learning more about Booker T. Washington?

1. You may explore this topic further by using the resources listed below.
   Computer resources: Internet, encyclopedia software
   Library resources: encyclopedias, books, magazines, newspapers
   Home/community resources: books, interviews, newspapers, magazines

2. A Discovery Share Time is provided in Lesson 7 if you wish to share your investigation results. You may share orally, or you may prepare a written report. You will put your written report in a class booklet titled "Notable People in History." This booklet will be placed in the class library for everyone to enjoy.

Classroom Practice 40

Name:_____ Date:_____

GRAMMAR

▶ **Exercise 1:** Classify each sentence.

1. _____ Golly! That loud dynamite blast gave me a huge scare during lunchtime!

2. _____ Today, the patrolman gave Jared a warning ticket for speeding in a school zone.

SKILLS & EDITING

▶ **Exercise 2:** Punctuate the sentences below. **Editing Guide: End Marks: 8 Capitals: 23 Commas: 6 Quotation Marks: 12 Underlined Explanatory Words: 4 Apostrophes: 4 Periods: 4**

1. jeremy could you order pizza for ms smiths class courtney asked

2. courtney asked jeremy could you order pizza for ms smiths class

3. jeremy courtney asked could you order pizza for ms smiths class

4. jeremy could you order pizza for ms smiths class courtney asked her students won the math contest at riverdale middle school they are going to celebrate with a pizza party

SKILLS & EDITING

▶ **Exercise 3:** Punctuate the sentences below. **Editing Guide: End Marks: 7 Capitals: 37 Commas: 4 Quotation Marks: 10 Underlined Explanatory Words: 4 Apostrophes: 1**

1. travis exclaimed darren and i are going to palm springs to the jefferson golf tournament

2. darren and i are going to palm springs to the jefferson golf tournament exclaimed travis

3. darren and i travis exclaimed are going to palm springs to the jefferson golf tournament

4. travis exclaimed darren and i are going to palm springs to the jefferson golf tournament do you think danny and leroy can go with us its three weeks from saturday

START LESSON 3

Lesson 3

You will

- study new vocabulary; make card 31; write own sentence using the vocabulary word.
- analyze new analogy; make card 31; write own analogy.
- practice Jingles 13-23.
- classify Practice Sentences.
- do a Skill Builder.
- identify other quotation rules.
- do Classroom Practice 41.
- write in your journal.
- read and discuss Discovery Time.

LISTENING AND SPEAKING:

Learn It: Recite the new vocabulary and analogy words.

📖 * Reference 152	Vocabulary & Analogy Words

Word: vagrant (vā'grənt)
    Definition: a person who has no job or home
    Synonym: vagabond   **Antonym:** homebody
    Sentence: The vagrant spent the night in a shelter.

Analogy: old : new :: antique : modern
    Antonym relationship: Just as **old** is the opposite of **new**,
                  antique is the opposite of **modern**.

Vocabulary Card 31: Record the vocabulary information above and write your own sentence, using the new word.

Analogy Card 31: Record the analogy information and write your own analogy, using the same relationship as the analogy above.

Recite It: Practice Jingles 13–23 in the Jingle Section on pages 509–512.

Grammar Time

Apply It: Classify the Practice Sentences orally with your teacher.

Practice Sentences	Chapter 9: Lesson 3

1. _____ The talented artist painted us a picture of our school's mascot on the gym floor.

2. _____ Give him a glass of buttermilk in the early morning and late afternoon.

3. _____ The local florist sent us a vase of roses for our anniversary.

Skill Builder

Using the sentences just classified, do a Skill Builder orally with your teacher.

1. **Identify the nouns in a Noun Check.**
2. **Identify the nouns as singular or plural.**
3. **Identify the nouns as common or proper.**
4. **Identify the complete subject and the complete predicate.**
5. **Identify the simple subject and the simple predicate.**
6. **Do a Vocabulary Check.**
7. **Do a Verb Chant.**

Learn It: OTHER QUOTATION RULES

Reference 153   Other Quotation Rules

1. Longer Quotes

A. The examples below show how to punctuate quotations with more than one sentence.

> Mom said, "We are having a family reunion on Saturday. All our relatives will be there. I hope you and your family can come."

> "We are having a family reunion on Saturday. All our relatives will be there. I hope you and your family can come," said Mom.

> "We are having a family reunion on Saturday," said Mom. "All our relatives will be there. I hope you and your family can come."

B. When a speaker has a lengthy quote that is longer than one paragraph, quotation marks are used at the beginning of each paragraph but only at the end of the last paragraph of that speaker's quote. Then, when the speaker changes, a new paragraph is started with another set of quotation marks.

> Lucy told her parents, "I am turning over a new leaf. I want more responsibility and more respect. I am a changed person.   } speaker begins

> "In fact, I will prove how sincere I am. I will give you a written list of all the changes I am willing to make."   } same speaker continues and ends

> "This should be good," said Dad. "How long is your list?"   } new speaker begins and ends

2. A Quote Within a Quote

Single quotation marks are used to punctuate a quotation within a quotation.

> My sister asked, "Did you hear Mom say, 'Let's go shopping'?"

3. Quotation Marks to Punctuate Titles

Quotation marks are used to punctuate titles of songs, short stories, poems, articles, essays, radio and television programs, short plays, and book chapters. (*Capitalize the first word, last word, and every word in between except for articles, short prepositions, and short conjunctions.*)

> I can recite several stanzas of "Paul Revere's Ride."

4. Direct Quotations, Indirect Quotations, and Statements

A. A direct quotation occurs when you show exactly what someone says by using quotation marks.

> **Direct quotation:** Roger said, "I want a big glass of tea."

B. An indirect quotation occurs when you describe what someone says without using his exact words.

> **Indirect quotation:** Roger said he wanted a big glass of tea.

C. A statement occurs when no speaker is mentioned and no quotation is used.

> **Statement:** Roger wants a big glass of tea.

Classroom Practice 41

It is time to practice the skills you are learning. You will use the classroom practice on the next page to apply these skills.

ENRICHMENT:

(British) 1859-1930— Sir Arthur Conan Doyle was a British physician, writer, and war correspondent. He used his experiences from his travels around the world in his stories. Doyle is well known as the creator of Sherlock Holmes. Doyle modeled this famous detective character after one of his teachers in medical school, Dr. Joseph Bell. Doyle wrote a number of novels and nonfictional works, but none was as famous as his *Sherlock Holmes* series.

Discovery Questions:
• **Have you read any of the *Sherlock Holmes* stories?**
  Can you name the ones you have read?
• **Who is your favorite author? Explain.**

Are you interested in learning more about Sir Arthur Conan Doyle?

1. You may explore this topic further by using the resources listed below.
   Computer resources: Internet, encyclopedia software
   Library resources: encyclopedias, books, magazines, newspapers
   Home/community resources: books, interviews, newspapers, magazines

2. A Discovery Share Time is provided in Lesson 7 if you wish to share your investigation results. You may share orally, or you may prepare a written report. You will put your written report in a class booklet titled "Notable People in History." This booklet will be placed in the class library for everyone to enjoy.

JOURNAL WRITING 23

Write an entry in your journal. Use Reference 9 on page 12 for ideas.

Classroom Practice 41

Name:_____ Date:_____

GRAMMAR

▶ **Exercise 1:** Classify each sentence.

1. _____ Give Kerry and Lana several questions for their interview with the new mayor.

2. _____ The terrific salesman in the electronics store gave us a fantastic deal on a computer.

SKILLS & EDITING

▶ **Exercise 2:** Punctuate the story below. **Editing Guide: End Marks: 15 Capitals: 24 Commas: 9 Quotation Marks: 16 Underlined Explanatory Words: 8 Apostrophes: 2**

jean i went fishing yesterday henry said

jean asked did you catch anything

yes i caught a fish so big that i couldnt get him into the boat exclaimed henry

wow what happened then asked jean excitedly

that big fish pulled me overboard henry declared loudly

well did you have to swim jean wanted to know

henry laughed hysterically and said no i landed on his back and we went on a wild ride

jean glared at henry and muttered you got that stupid tale out of a book i knew you

didnt make up a story that good by yourself which book did you read

START LESSON 4

Lesson 4

You will
- study new vocabulary; make card 32; write own sentence using the vocabulary word.
- analyze new analogy; make card 32; write own analogy.
- practice Jingles 3–11.
- classify Practice Sentences.
- do a Skill Builder.
- do Classroom Practice 42.
- read and discuss Discovery Time.
- do a homework assignment.
- do Home Connection activity.

LISTENING AND SPEAKING:

Vocabulary & Analogy Time

Learn It: Recite the new vocabulary and analogy words.

Reference 154	Vocabulary & Analogy Words

Word: constrain (kən strān')
    Definition: to force by imposing limits
    Synonym: confine   **Antonym:** free
    Sentence: The small pot constrained the plant's growth.

Analogy: birds : migrate :: bears : hibernate
    Descriptive or characteristic relationship: Just as **birds migrate,**
                                   bears hibernate.

Vocabulary Card 32: Record the vocabulary information above and write your own sentence, using the new word.

Analogy Card 32: Record the analogy information and write your own analogy, using the same relationship as the analogy above.

Jingle Time

Recite It: Practice Jingles 3–11 in the Jingle Section on pages 507–508.

Grammar Time

Apply It: Classify the Practice Sentences orally with your teacher.

Practice Sentences	Chapter 9: Lesson 4

1. _____ Before lunch, I quickly handed Mr. Boyd's class five questions for their quiz.

2. _____ Mail me several pictures from Europe during your two-week cruise in the Mediterranean.

3. _____ Today, our teacher taught us an important lesson about manners and respect.

Skill Builder

Using the sentences just classified, do a Skill Builder orally with your teacher.

1. Identify the nouns in a Noun Check.
2. Identify the nouns as singular or plural.
3. Identify the nouns as common or proper.
4. Identify the complete subject and the complete predicate.
5. Identify the simple subject and the simple predicate.
6. Do a Vocabulary Check.
7. Do a Verb Chant.

Classroom Practice 42

It is time to practice the skills you are learning. You will use the classroom practice on the next page to apply these skills.

ENRICHMENT:

Discovery Time

(American) 1860-1935— Jane Addams founded the Hull House, which became the most famous social facility in the United States, in the slums of Chicago. The Hull House fed the hungry and offered medical care, child care, legal aid, and language classes for immigrants. Her work with the poor inspired her to push for laws to protect immigrants, to mandate schooling for children, to limit working hours, and to provide industrial safety. She was the first American woman to receive the Nobel Peace Prize.

Discovery Questions:
- How did Jane's father influence her life?
- If you could invite Jane Addams as a speaker at your school or neighborhood, what do you think she would say?
- Do you know anyone like Jane Addams? What has this person done to help others?

Are you interested in learning more about Jane Addams?

1. You may explore this topic further by using the resources listed below.
   Computer resources: Internet, encyclopedia software
   Library resources: encyclopedias, books, magazines, newspapers
   Home / community resources: books, interviews, newspapers, magazines

2. A Discovery Share Time is provided in Lesson 7 if you wish to share your investigation results. You may share orally, or you may prepare a written report. You will put your written report in a class booklet titled "Notable People in History." This booklet will be placed in the class library for everyone to enjoy.

SHURLEY ENGLISH

Classroom Practice 42

Name:_____ Date:_____

GRAMMAR

▶ **Exercise 1:** Classify each sentence.

1. _____ Quick! Give me my camera for an exceptional shot of the koalas in the trees!

2. _____ As a reward, Mom and Dad opened me an account at our bank yesterday.

SKILLS & EDITING

▶ **Exercise 2:** Punctuate the sentences below. **Editing Guide: End Marks: 5 Capitals: 14 Commas: 9 Quotation Marks: 12 Underlined Explanatory Words: 4 Apostrophes: 1**

1. mom said joe i want you to do the dishes tonight

2. joe i want you to do the dishes tonight mom said

3. joe mom said i want you to do the dishes tonight

4. joe i want you to do the dishes tonight said mom i have a meeting after dinner

   and i wont get back in time to do them

SKILLS & EDITING

▶ **Exercise 3:** Punctuate the sentences below. **Editing Guide: End Marks: 6 Capitals: 16 Commas: 8 Quotation Marks: 6 Underlined Explanatory Words: 2 Apostrophes: 2**

1. joe i want you to do the dishes tonight said mom because i have a meeting

   after dinner it will be late when i get back and i wont have time to do them

2. mom said joe i want you to do the dishes tonight because i have a meeting after dinner

   it will be late when i get back and i wont have time to do them your grandmother will be

   here soon and you can show her your new game you also have snacks in the refrigerator

Homework 7

Complete this homework assignment on notebook paper.

1. Copy the sentence below. Classify the sentence, using the Question and Answer Flow, as you label each part.

    _____ Today, our teacher taught us an important lesson about manners and respect.

2. Rewrite the sentences below, using the Quotation Rules to help you capitalize and punctuate each sentence correctly. Underline the explanatory words.

   1. tommy explained sadly rabbits are eating my dads vegetables

   2. rabbits are eating my dads vegetables tommy explained sadly

   3. rabbits tommy explained sadly are eating my dads vegetables

   4. rabbits are eating my dads vegetables tommy explained sadly now my dad says that

      he is going to turn the garden over to them

Home Connection

Family Activity for Quotations

1. Find a familiar short story that contains dialogue (such as *Beauty and the Beast, The Lion King,* or *Winnie the Pooh*). First, read the story aloud for enjoyment. Then, rewrite a section of the story with no dialogue. Discuss the difference dialogue makes in stories.

2. Read a short story with dialogue to a partner. The partner must stand up when a quotation is started and sit down when it is finished.

3. Make up a short story about an amusing family event. Use dialogue and punctuate quotations correctly.

Family Activity for Vocabulary and Analogies

Divide into family teams. The first team will use vocabulary and analogy cards 25–28 to ask questions about the information on their cards. The second team will use vocabulary and analogy cards 29–32 to ask questions about the information on their cards.

For vocabulary words:
- What is the definition of the word?
- Name a synonym and antonym for the word.
- Create a new sentence using the word.
- Find the word in another source (dictionary, newspaper, magazine, advertisement, etc.)

For analogies:
- What is the answer to the analogy?
- What is the relationship of the analogy?
- Make another analogy with the same relationship.
- Make another analogy with a different relationship.

START LESSON 5

Lesson 5

You will
- classify Practice Sentences.
- do Chapter Checkup 43.
- write in your journal.
- read and discuss Discovery Time.

LISTENING AND SPEAKING:

Grammar Time

Apply It: Classify the Practice Sentences orally with your teacher.

Practice Sentences	Chapter 9: Lesson 5

1. _____ Has Patricia sent you many unusual stamps for your extraordinary collection?
2. _____ The fathers and their sons built the children a playhouse between the slides and the swings.
3. _____ For Mom's birthday present, little Tyler and his brother made her a mud pie with berries on top.

JOURNAL WRITING 24

Write an entry in your journal. Use Reference 9 on page 12 for ideas.

Chapter Checkup 43

It is time for a checkup of the skills you have learned in this chapter. You will use the chapter checkup on the next page to evaluate your progress.

ENRICHMENT:

Discovery Time

(American) 1863-1947— Henry Ford created his first automobile, the "Quadricycle," in Michigan in 1896. The vehicle was a buggy frame mounted on four bicycle wheels. He founded the Ford Motor Company in 1903 and produced the Model T in 1908. By 1916, Ford was building more than 500,000 cars annually. He used standardized, interchangeable parts and assembly-line techniques to increase production. He also raised wages to keep a stable work force.

Discovery Questions:
- **What was the selling price of a Ford car in 1916?**
  Compare new car prices today to the car prices in 1916.
- **The Ford Motor Company is over 100 years old.**
  What do you think it takes to keep a company in business for 100 years?

Discovery Activity:
- **Invite someone from a local car dealership to speak to your class.**

(American) 1864-1943— George Washington Carver was an agricultural scientist who revolutionized agriculture in the Southern United States. He received his Bachelor of Science degree in 1894, becoming the first African American to graduate from Iowa State University. While at Tuskegee Institute, Carver developed over 300 uses for peanuts, sweet potatoes, soybeans, and the by-products of these crops. He taught farmers the advantages of diversifying their crops to help enrich the soil and to reduce economic dependency on one kind of crop.

Discovery Questions:
- **After studying Carver, what impresses you most about him?**
- **What questions would you like to ask Carver?**

Are you interested in learning more about Henry Ford or George Washington Carver?
1. You may explore these topics further by using the resources listed below.
   Computer resources: Internet, encyclopedia software
   Library resources: encyclopedias, books, magazines, newspapers
   Home/community resources: books, interviews, newspapers, magazines
2. A Discovery Share Time is provided in Lesson 7 if you wish to share your investigation results. You may share orally, or you may prepare a written report. You will put your written report in a class booklet titled "Notable People in History." This booklet will be placed in the class library for everyone to enjoy.

Chapter 9 Checkup 43

Name:_____ Date:_____

GRAMMAR

▶ **Exercise 1:** Classify each sentence.

1. _____ Pass me the salt and pepper for my baked potato and sliced tomatoes.

2. _____ Mercy! I have not written you a letter in a long time!

3. _____ The proud firemen showed the reporter their new fire equipment from the city.

SKILLS & EDITING

▶ **Exercise 2:** Part 1. Punctuate the story below. **Editing Guide: End Marks: 4 Capitals: 6 Commas: 6**
Quotation Marks: 8 Homonyms: 5 Misspelled Words: 2

dad it is just to hot outside too work in the garden dave grumbled as he

grudgeingly picked up the garden tools and followed his father too the garden besides

dave continued to much sun is definately bad for your health dave emphasized

what he just said by squinting at the bright son and by wiping his brow with his sleeve

actually you could get a sunstroke he said lamely as he worked beside his father

SKILLS & EDITING

▶ **Exercise 3:** Part 2. Punctuate the rest of the story below. **Editing Guide: End Marks: 5 Capitals: 11 Commas: 11**
Quotation Marks: 14 Apostrophes: 4 Homonyms: 3

his fathers eyes danced with laughter as he said i think thats called a

heatstroke dave

sunstroke—heatstroke it doesnt matter dave said it all amounts too a garden stroke

well his father replied i thought you might enjoy going too the lake after we

have finished but it looks like you might be to stroked out

you know dad dave blurted if we work faster well get less sun

START LESSON 6

Lesson 6

You will

- conference with teacher about WA 21.
- write a creative writing piece for WA 22.

Writing Time

Write It: **WRITING ASSIGNMENT 22**

Writing Assignment 22: Creative Expressions

Purpose: To entertain

Type of Writing: Creative

Audience: Classmates, family, or friends

Choose one of the writing prompts below.

1. You have just discovered that your pet can talk. Write a conversation that you think will take place between you and your pet (or favorite animal).

2. What do you think you will be doing by the time you are twenty-one? Thirty-one?

3. Write a poem about pets or about a topic of your choice.

Special Instructions:

1. A prewriting map is not required for this creative-writing assignment.

2. Follow the Rough Draft Checklist in Reference 46 on page 61.

3. Put your creative-writing paper in your Rough Draft folder when you have finished.

Note: Reference 54 on page 71 gives the steps in the writing process and the location of all the writing checklists.

>>>>>>>>>>>>>>>>>>>>>>>> Student Tip...

> For more information about writing poetry, look at Chapter 18, pages 465–482.

Conference Time

Discuss It: **TEACHER-STUDENT CONFERENCES FOR WRITING ASSIGNMENT 21**

Meet with your teacher to discuss Writing Assignment 21.
After the conference, place this group of papers in your Publishing folder.

Publishing Time

Publish It: WRITING ASSIGNMENT 21

Choose a publishing form and publish Writing Assignment 21. After rewriting your paper for publication, give the stapled papers (evaluation guide, graded final paper, rough draft, and prewriting map) to your teacher to be placed in your Writing Portfolio.

START LESSON 7

Lesson 7

You will
- publish WA 21.
- participate in Discovery Share Time.
- do Across the Curriculum activity.

Reference 66	Publishing Checklist for Step 6 in the Writing Process

The sixth step in the writing process is called publishing. Publishing is sharing your writing with others. With so many forms of publishing available, finding a match for every project and personality is easy.

At times, a written work is best read aloud. Other times, the biggest impact is made when a written work is read silently. You can also use media sources to enhance any publication.

SPECIAL INSTRUCTIONS FOR PUBLISHING:

- Rewrite the graded paper in ink or type it on a computer, correcting any marked errors. *(Do not display or publish papers that have marked errors or grades on them.)*
- Give your teacher the set of stapled papers to place in your Writing Portfolio. *(Stapled papers: evaluation guide, graded final paper, rough draft, and prewriting map.)*
- Select a publishing form from the list below and publish your rewritten paper.
    1. Have classmates, family members, neighbors, or others read your writing at school or home.
    2. Share your writing with others during a Share Time. *(Refer to Reference 67 on page 99 for sharing guidelines.)*
    3. Display your writing on a bulletin board or wall.
    4. Put your writing in the classroom library or in the school library for checkout.
    5. Send your writing as a letter or an e-mail to a friend or relative.
    6. Frame your writing by gluing it on colored construction paper and decorating it.
    7. Make a book of your writing for your classroom, your family, or others.
    8. Illustrate your writing and give it to others to read.
    9. Dramatize your writing in the form of a play, puppet show, or radio broadcast.
    10. Send your writing to be placed in a waiting room (doctor, veterinarian, dentist, etc.), senior-citizen center, or a nursing home.
    11. Send your writing to a school newspaper, local newspaper, or a magazine for publication.
    12. Make a videotape, cassette tape, or slide presentation of your writing.
    13. Choose another publishing form that is not listed.

LISTENING AND SPEAKING:

 Discovery Share Time

If you have chosen to investigate a historical figure introduced in this chapter, you now have the opportunity to share your results in one of the following ways:

1. You may relate your information orally.

2. You may read a written report.

3. You may place your report in the booklet without reading it aloud.

After share time, all written reports should be turned in to be placed in the class booklet titled "Notable People in History." You are encouraged to check out this class booklet so you can enjoy the reports again.

 Across the Curriculum

Art Connection: Look in the library for a picture of an art piece such as a painting or sculpture that you like. Write a paragraph describing the art piece. Use the Descriptive Writing Guidelines to help you. Read your descriptive paragraph in a cooperative-learning group. You might also show the picture or make a sketch of the item you describe. Then, take your description home to share with family members.

English Made Easy

LISTENING AND SPEAKING:

 Jingle Time

Recite It: Practice Jingle 23 in the Jingle Section on page 512.

GRAMMAR & WRITING CONNECTION:
Practice and Revised Sentences

Apply It: **BUILDING AND EXPANDING SENTENCES**

Lesson 8

You will
- practice Jingle 23.
- do Classroom Practice 44.
- write an independent descriptive paragraph (WA 23).

Reference 155	A Guide for Using a Pattern 3 Core (SN V-t IO DO) to Build & Expand Sentences

1. **SN or SP (subject)** Think of a noun or pronoun that you want to use as the *subject*. Write the noun or pronoun you have chosen as the *subject* of your sentence.

2. **V-t (transitive-verb)** The *transitive-verb* does two things. It tells what the subject does, and it is followed by a direct object. First, choose a verb for your sentence. Then, after you have chosen a direct object, verify that the verb is transitive and keep it as the verb of your Pattern 3 core.

3. **DO (direct object)** The *direct object* is a noun or pronoun after the verb that answers the question *what* or *whom*. The *direct object* receives the action of a transitive verb and does not mean the same thing as the subject. To help you think of a *direct object*, ask the question WHAT or WHOM after the verb. Write the direct object you have chosen.

4. **IO (indirect object)** An *indirect object* receives what the direct object names. The indirect object tells *to whom* or *for whom* the action is done. It does not receive the action of the verb. To help you think of an *indirect object*, ask the question TO WHOM or FOR WHOM, TO WHAT or FOR WHAT after the direct object. Write the indirect object you have chosen. The indirect object will always be located between the verb and direct object.

>>> **Student Tip...**

Use your vocabulary words in your Practice and Revised Sentences. Use a thesaurus, synonym-antonym book, or a dictionary to help you develop your writing vocabulary.

Classroom Practice 44

It is time to practice the skills you are learning. You will use the classroom practice on the next page to apply these skills.

Write It: **WRITING ASSIGNMENT 23**

As you write a rough draft for your independent writing assignment, you will do two of the six steps in the writing process: prewriting and rough draft.

Writing Assignment ⟨23⟩

Purpose: To describe

Type of Writing: Descriptive paragraph

Audience: Classmates

Writing Topics: My old tennis shoes/the wildest shirt (family member) ever wore
A circus performer/fire fighter/dessert/park
My neighbor's yard/house/dog
(Brainstorm for other ideas, individually or in groups.)

Special Instructions:

1. Follow the Prewriting and Rough Draft Checklists in References 44 and 46 on pages 57, 61.

2. Make a prewriting map using the descriptive guidelines in References 144–145 on pages 258–259 to help you write your descriptive paragraph.

3. Write in first or third person. See Reference 70 on page 104.
   (First-person pronouns: *I, me, my, mine, we, us, our,* and *ours.*)
   (Third-person pronouns: *he, his, him, she, her, hers, it, its, they, their, theirs,* and *them.*)

Note: Reference 54 on page 71 gives the steps in the writing process and the location of all the writing checklists.

Student Note: Some of your writing pieces will be selected for revision and editing later in the school year.

Classroom Practice 44

Name: _____   Date: _____

INDEPENDENT PRACTICE & REVISED SENTENCES

1. Write a Practice Sentence according to the labels you choose.
Use **SN/SP V-t IO DO** as your main labels. You may use the other labels in any order and as many times as you wish in order to make a Practice Sentence. **Chapter 9 labels for a Practice Sentence: SN/SP, V-t, IO, DO,** Adj, Adv, A, P, OP, PPA, C, HV, I, PNA

2. Write a Revised Sentence. Use the following revision strategies: *synonym (syn), antonym (ant), word change (wc), added word (add), deleted word (delete),* or *no change (nc).* Under each word, write the abbreviation of the revision strategy you use.

Labels:

Practice:

Revised:

Strategies:

Labels:

Practice:

Revised:

Strategies:

Labels:

Practice:

Revised:

Strategies:

Chapter 9

START LESSON 9

Lesson 9

You will

- practice Jingle 12.
- read and discuss narrative writing and story elements outline.
- plan and write rough draft for narrative with dialogue (WA 24).

LISTENING AND SPEAKING:

Recite It: Practice Jingle 12 in the Jingle Section on page 509.

>>>> Student Tip...

Reviewing the transition words will help you apply them in your writing.

Learn It: STORY ELEMENTS FOR A NARRATIVE WITH DIALOGUE

  Reference 156   **Story Elements for a Narrative With Dialogue**

Narrative writing is simply the telling of a story. When you compose stories, you are actually writing what professional writers call narratives, or short stories. Short stories have certain characteristics that make them different from other types of writing. These characteristics are known as story elements.

Writers use five story elements. The story elements are **main idea, setting, characters, plot,** and **ending**. Narrative writing skills are developed through the use of these elements. A Story Elements Outline will help you keep your writing focused, and it will help you choose details and events that support the main idea of your story. Narrative writing has a beginning, middle, and end, and it can be written with or without dialogue (quotations).

STORY ELEMENTS OUTLINE

1. Main Idea:
Tell the problem or situation that needs a solution.
Laura planned to go to a swimming party but was grounded because of a messy room.

2. Setting:
Tell when and where the story takes place, either clearly stated or implied.
When – The story takes place in the summertime. Where – The story takes place at Laura's house.

3. Characters:
Tell whom or what the story is about.
The main characters are Laura, her mother, and her younger brother, Tommy.

4. Plot:
Tell what the characters in the story do and what happens to them.
The story is about a girl who pays her younger brother to clean her room so she can go to a swimming party.

5. Ending:
Use a strong ending that will bring the story to a close.
The story ends with Laura getting tricked by her younger brother.

Continued on next page. >>>

Reference 156 continued from previous page.

Example of Narrative Writing With Dialogue

Why Can't "Growing Up" Be Easy?

My friends and I had been planning tonight's swimming party for weeks. But, my mom wouldn't let me do anything until my room was spic and span. I couldn't talk on the phone, see my friends, or leave the house. Mom had been after me for days, but I saw no reason to be "Ms. Clean." Anyway, there was nothing wrong with my room. I sort of liked having everything out where I could get to it easily. Mom was just unfair! All she could say was, "Laura, you're grounded until this room is cleaned up, and that means today!"

"She treats me like a baby!" I wailed. "How am I going to get ready to go to the party and clean up this dumb room?" Then, I spotted my brother standing in the doorway. "Tommy," I coaxed, "you don't mind helping me out, do you?" As Tommy started backing away, I added, "I'll pay you five dollars if it passes Mom's inspection!"

Later, as Mom walked around my room, shaking her head in disbelief, I smiled smugly and handed my brother his well-earned five dollars. He grinned and took off without a backward glance. I followed Mom around as she gave my room the white-glove treatment. I had my bag slung over my shoulder, ready to leave as soon as she gave the sign. Mom was telling me how pleased she was when she opened my closet door. My mouth fell open, and my eyes bugged out as everything I owned came crashing into the middle of my room. I just stood glued to the spot and stared at the biggest mess in the world. In total distress, I knotted my fists, threw back my head, and screamed, "Tommeeeeeee!"

There is another special element that makes narrative writing especially interesting, and that is conversation. Another word for conversation is **dialogue**. Writers use dialogue, or conversation, in their short stories because it helps move the plot along, and it helps the reader understand the characters better. Writers like to use dialogue because it "shows" instead of "tells" in narratives. Dialogue "shows" what a character is like. A character's personal quotations show the readers a great deal about the character.

Review It: MAIN PUNCTUATION RULES TO OBSERVE WITH DIALOGUE

1. Dialogue is always placed INSIDE quotation marks. This placement will separate dialogue from any explanatory words or other words that develop the plot of the story.

2. Periods, commas, question marks, and exclamation points that punctuate dialogue always go INSIDE the quotation marks. You should follow the rules that you have already learned for punctuating quotations.

3. If more than one character is speaking, you must indent and create a new paragraph each time the speaker changes.

Write It: **WRITING ASSIGNMENT 24**

As you write a rough draft for your guided writing assignment, you will do two of the six steps in the writing process: prewriting (the Story Elements Outline) and rough draft.

Writing Assignment 24

Purpose: To tell a story

Type of Writing: Narrative

Audience: Classmates

Writing Topics: A day in the life of a frog/tree/pet
The time (Name) got lost/won a contest
My happiest/saddest/funniest day
(Brainstorm for other ideas, individually or in groups.)

Special Instructions:

1. Follow the Prewriting and Rough Draft Checklists in References 44 and 46 on pages 57, 61.

2. Make a Story Elements Outline instead of a prewriting map. See Reference 156 on page 290.

3. Use Reference 156 to help you write your narrative.

4. Write your narrative with dialogue. Use the review below and References 149–151 and 153 on pages 269–271, 275 to help you punctuate quotations.

   • Dialogue is always placed INSIDE quotation marks. This placement will separate dialogue from any explanatory words or other words that develop the plot of the story.

   • Periods, commas, question marks, and exclamation points that punctuate dialogue always go INSIDE the quotation marks.

   • If more than one character is speaking, you must indent and create a new paragraph each time the speaker changes.

5. Write in first or third person. See Reference 70 on page 104.
   (First-person pronouns: *I, me, my, mine, we, us, our,* and *ours.*)
   (Third-person pronouns: *he, his, him, she, her, hers, it, its, they, their, theirs,* and *them.*)

Note: Reference 54 on page 71 gives the steps in the writing process and the location of all the writing checklists.

Writing Time

Apply It: **REVISE, EDIT, AND WRITE A FINAL PAPER**

Following the schedule below, you will revise and edit Writing Assignment 24. Then, you will write a final paper. Use the Chapter 9 Writing Evaluation Guide on the next page to check your final paper one last time.

Lesson 10

You will
- revise, edit, and write a final paper for WA 24.

✎* **Reference 52** **Revising & Editing Schedule and Writing a Final Paper**

SPECIAL INSTRUCTIONS FOR REVISING AND EDITING (Steps 3-4 in the writing process):
- Use the Revising and Editing Checklists in References 48 and 50 as you revise and edit your rough draft.
- Follow the revising and editing schedule below as directed by your teacher.
    1. **Individual.** First, read your rough draft to yourself. Use the Revising Checklist in Reference 48 on page 64. Go through your paper, checking each item on the list and making revisions to your rough draft. Then, use the Editing Checklist in Reference 50 on page 66. Go through your paper again, checking each item on the list and editing your rough draft.
    2. **Partner.** Next, get with your editing partner. Work together on each partner's rough draft, one paper at a time. Read each rough draft aloud and revise and edit it together, using the Revising and Editing Checklists. (The author of the paper should be the one to make the corrections on his own paper.)
    3. **Group.** Finally, read the rough draft to a revision group for feedback. Each student should read his paper while the others listen and offer possible revising and editing suggestions. (The author will determine whether to make corrections from the revision group's suggestions.)

SPECIAL INSTRUCTIONS FOR FINAL PAPER (Step 5 in the writing process):
- Write your final paper, using the Final Paper Checklist in Reference 53 on page 70.
- Staple your writing papers in this order: the final paper on top, the rough draft in the middle, and the prewriting map on the bottom. Place the stapled papers in the Final Paper folder.

>>>>>>>>>> **Student Tip...**

1. Be tactful and helpful in your comments during revising and editing time. The purpose of any suggestion should be to improve the writer's rough draft.

2. As you make your final corrections, you have the choice of accepting or rejecting any suggestions made by your partners or your revision group.

3. Study Vocabulary Words and Analogies 29-32 for the chapter test in the next lesson.

4. If you need to improve your handwriting, refer to the Resource Tools Section on pages 529-530 for information on writing legibly.

Chapter 9 Writing Evaluation Guide

Name:_____ Date:_____

ROUGH DRAFT CHECK

_____ 1. Did you write your rough draft in pencil?

_____ 2. Did you write the correct headings on the first seven lines of your paper?

_____ 3. Did you use extra wide margins and skip every other line?

_____ 4. Did you write a title at the end of your rough draft?

_____ 5. Did you place your edited rough draft in your Rough Draft folder?

REVISING CHECK

_____ 6. Did you identify the purpose, type of writing, and audience?

_____ 7. Did you check for a topic, topic sentence, and sentences supporting the topic?

_____ 8. Did you check sentences for the right order, and did you combine, rearrange, or delete sentences when necessary?

_____ 9. Did you check for a variety of simple, compound, and complex sentences?

_____ 10. Did you check for any left out, repeated, or unnecessary words?

_____ 11. Did you check for the best choice of words by replacing or deleting unclear words?

_____ 12. Did you check the content for interest and creativity?

_____ 13. Did you check the voice to make sure the writing says what you want it to say?

EDITING CHECK

_____ 14. Did you indent each paragraph?

_____ 15. Did you put an end mark at the end of every sentence?

_____ 16. Did you capitalize the first word of every sentence?

_____ 17. Did you check for all other capitalization mistakes?

_____ 18. Did you check for all punctuation mistakes?
(commas, periods, apostrophes, quotation marks, underlining)

_____ 19. Did you check for misspelled words and for incorrect homonym choices?

_____ 20. Did you check for incorrect spellings of plural and possessive forms?

_____ 21. Did you check for correct construction and punctuation of your sentences?

_____ 22. Did you check for usage mistakes? *(subject/verb agreement, a/an choices, contractions, verb tenses, pronoun/antecedent agreement, pronoun cases, degrees of adjectives, double negatives, etc.)*

_____ 23. Did you put your revised and edited paper in the Rough Draft folder?

FINAL PAPER CHECK

_____ 24. Did you write the final paper in pencil?

_____ 25. Did you center the title on the top line and center your name under the title?

_____ 26. Did you skip a line before starting the writing assignment?

_____ 27. Did you single-space, use wide margins, and write the final paper neatly?

_____ 28. Did you staple your papers in this order: final paper on top, rough draft in the middle, and prewriting map on the bottom? Did you put them in the Final Paper folder?

Writing Time

Hand It In: **WRITING ASSIGNMENT 24**

Get your stapled papers for Writing Assignment 24 from your Final Paper folder. Check to make sure they are in the correct order: the final paper on top, the rough draft in the middle, and the prewriting map on the bottom. Hand them in to your teacher.

LISTENING AND SPEAKING:

Discuss It:

1. What word receives what the direct object names?
2. What type of verb is used with an indirect object?
3. What are the core parts of a Pattern 3 sentence?
4. What are the core parts of a Pattern 2 sentence?
5. What are the core parts of a Pattern 1 sentence?
6. What punctuation is used to set off the exact words that are spoken by someone?
7. In writing, what is dialogue?
8. What is another name for dialogue?
9. What are the three types of quotes?
10. What are the End Mark choices for a beginning quote?
11. What are the End Mark choices for an end quote?
12. What type of writing is used when your purpose is to tell a story?
13. What type of writing is used when your purpose is to paint a picture with words?
14. What type of writing is used when your purpose is to express an opinion and to convince the reader that this opinion is correct?
15. What type of writing is used when your purpose is to inform, to give facts, to give directions, to explain, or to define something?

>>>>>>>>>>>>>>> Student Tip...

For information about test-taking strategies, refer to the Resource Tools Section on page 528.

Lesson 11

You will

- hand in WA 24 for grading.
- respond to oral review questions.
- take Chapter 9 Test.

CHAPTER TEST

It is time to evaluate your knowledge of the skills you have learned in this chapter. Your teacher will give you the Chapter 9 Test to help you assess your progress.

Lesson 1

You will

- study new vocabulary;
  make card 33;
  write own sentence using
  the vocabulary word.
- analyze new analogy;
  make card 33;
  write own analogy.
- practice Jingles 18–23.
- identify Mixed Patterns 1–3.
- classify Introductory
  Sentences.
- do a Skill Builder.
- write in your journal.
- read and discuss
  Discovery Time.

LISTENING AND SPEAKING:

Vocabulary & Analogy Time

Learn It: Recite the new vocabulary and analogy words.

Reference 157	Vocabulary & Analogy Words

Word: maximum (măk'sə məm)
  Definition: the greatest amount possible
  Synonym: most   **Antonym:** least
  Sentence: The plane flew at maximum speed.

Analogy: jacket : clothing :: drill : tool
  Type or kind relationship: Just as a **jacket** is a type of **clothing**,
                        a **drill** is a type of **tool**.

Vocabulary Card 33: Record the vocabulary information above and write your own
                  sentence, using the new word.
Analogy Card 33: Record the analogy information and write your own analogy,
                  using the same relationship as the analogy above.

Jingle Time

Recite It: Practice Jingles 18–23 in the Jingle Section on pages 511–512.

Grammar Time

Apply It: These Introductory Sentences are used to apply the new grammar
concepts taught below. Classify these sentences orally with your teacher.

Introductory Sentences	Chapter 10: Lesson 1

1. _____ In the middle of the afternoon, I always eat a
   chocolate bar for energy.
2. _____ Yesterday, the impudent little boy defiantly gave his mom
   fits at the store.
3. _____ The massive and destructive mudslides were caused
   by the torrential rains.

Learn It: MIXED GRAMMAR PATTERNS 1–3

The sentences classified in this chapter will be Patterns 1–3. They are called
Mixed Patterns because there are three different patterns from which to choose.
Be alert to the parts of speech and where they are located in each sentence.
Use the sentence cores to help determine the patterns of the sentences.

 Skill Builder

Using the sentences just classified, do a Skill Builder orally with your teacher.

1. **Identify the nouns in a Noun Check.**
2. **Identify the nouns as singular or plural.**
3. **Identify the nouns as common or proper.**
4. **Identify the complete subject and the complete predicate.**
5. **Identify the simple subject and the simple predicate.**
6. **Do a Vocabulary Check.**
7. **Do a Verb Chant.**

ENRICHMENT:

 **Discovery Time**

(British) 1865-1936— **Rudyard Kipling** was one of the greatest British short-story writers. He was also the first English author to receive a Nobel Prize in literature. Born in Bombay, India, he used his boyhood experiences there to write *Kim*, which is regarded as his best long narrative. Some of his most popular novels were *The Jungle Book*, *The Second Jungle Book*, and *Captains Courageous*.

Discovery Questions:
- **What do you think it was like for Kipling to grow up in India?**
- **Why is it important for a writer to draw from personal experiences or experiences of others when writing a story?**
- **What experiences have you had that would help you write good stories?**

Are you interested in learning more about Rudyard Kipling?

1. You may explore this topic further by using the resources listed below.
   Computer resources: Internet, encyclopedia software
   Library resources: encyclopedias, books, magazines, newspapers
   Home/community resources: books, interviews, newspapers, magazines

2. A Discovery Share Time is provided in Lesson 8 if you wish to share your investigation results. You may share orally, or you may prepare a written report. You will put your written report in a class booklet titled "Notable People in History." This booklet will be placed in the class library for everyone to enjoy.

JOURNAL WRITING 25

Write an entry in your journal. Use Reference 9 on page 12 for ideas.

START LESSON 2

Lesson 2

You will

- study new vocabulary; make card 34; write own sentence using the vocabulary word.
- analyze new analogy; make card 34; write own analogy.
- practice Jingles 13-17.
- classify Practice Sentences.
- do a Skill Builder.
- identify ten spelling rules for the plurals of nouns.
- make a spelling rule book.
- do Classroom Practice 45.
- read and discuss Discovery Time.

LISTENING AND SPEAKING:

Vocabulary & Analogy Time

Learn It: Recite the new vocabulary and analogy words.

📖 Reference 158	Vocabulary & Analogy Words

Word: impeccable (ĭm pĕk' ə bəl)
    Definition: having no flaws; free from fault
    Synonym: perfect   **Antonym:** defective
    Sentence: My dad speaks impeccable Italian.

Analogy: chameleon : coloring :: skunk : odor
Purpose or use relationship: Just as a **chameleon** uses **coloring** for protection, a **skunk** uses **odor** for protection.

Vocabulary Card 34: Record the vocabulary information above and write your own sentence, using the new word.

Analogy Card 34: Record the analogy information and write your own analogy, using the same relationship as the analogy above.

Jingle Time

Recite It: Practice Jingles 13–17 in the Jingle Section on pages 509–510.

Grammar Time

Apply It: Classify the Practice Sentences orally with your teacher.

Practice Sentences	Chapter 10: Lesson 2

1. _____ For Julie's wedding, the seamstress made her a gown from the most exquisite silk material.
2. _____ Did the dark, ominous clouds hover threateningly over the small town?
3. _____ Mercy! The gigantic apes in the jungle hungrily ate the food from the scientists' camp!

Skill Builder

Using the sentences just classified, do a Skill Builder orally with your teacher.

1. **Identify the nouns in a Noun Check.**
2. **Identify the nouns as singular or plural.**
3. **Identify the nouns as common or proper.**
4. **Identify the complete subject and the complete predicate.**
5. **Identify the simple subject and the simple predicate.**
6. **Do a Vocabulary Check.**
7. **Do a Verb Chant.**

Skill Time

Learn It: RULES FOR MAKING NOUNS PLURAL

This list of rules will help you form the plurals of nouns correctly.

 Reference 159 | **Rules for Making Nouns Plural**

Nouns are regular or irregular according to how they are made plural. **A regular noun is made plural by adding -s or -es to the end of the word.** Use Rules 1–8 below for making regular nouns plural.

Irregular nouns are made plural in ways other than adding -s or -es. The following lists of irregular nouns should be memorized. Use Rules 9–10 below for making irregular nouns plural.

- Some irregular nouns are made plural by a complete spelling change. **(Rule 9)**

| **Singular:** | child | foot | goose | man | mouse | ox | tooth | woman |
| **Plural:** | children | feet | geese | men | mice | oxen | teeth | women |

- Other irregular nouns are spelled the same for both singular and plural. **(Rule 10)**

Singular/Plural: aircraft, deer, fish, fowl, headquarters, moose, salmon, series, sheep, scissors, species, and trout.

RULES FOR MAKING REGULAR NOUNS PLURAL	**Add -s to nouns with these special endings:**
Add -s to nouns without special endings.	6. *f* or *ff*.
1. most singular nouns.	7. a vowel plus *o*.
	8. a vowel plus *y*.
Add -es to nouns with these special endings:	**RULES FOR MAKING IRREGULAR NOUNS PLURAL**
2. *ch, sh, z, s, ss, x*.	9. Change the spelling completely for the plural form.
3. a consonant plus *o*.	10. Spell the same for both the singular and plural form.
4. a consonant plus *y*, change y to i before adding **es**.	
5. *f* or *fe*, change f or fe to v before adding **es**.	

Continued on next page. >>>

Reference 159 continued from previous page.

Directions: For each noun, write the rule number and the plural form that follows the rule. Some nouns have two acceptable plural forms, but you should use the plural spellings that can be verified by these rules.

	Rule	Plural Form		Rule	Plural Form
1. pencil	1	pencils	6. roof	6	roofs
2. recess	2	recesses	7. patio	7	patios
3. tomato	3	tomatoes	8. alley	8	alleys
4. penny	4	pennies	9. child	9	children
5. calf	5	calves	10. deer	10	deer

Discuss It:

Look at the word **pencil**. What is the rule number that tells you what to do when you want to make most singular nouns plural? What does Rule 1 tell you to do to make **pencil** plural? How do you spell the plural of **pencil**?

Look at the word **recess**. What are the two letters at the end of **recess**? What is the number of the rule that tells you what to do when you have **ss** at the end of a word? What does Rule 2 tell you to do to make **recess** plural? How do you spell the plural of **recess**?

Look at the words **tomato** and **penny**. Is the letter before the **o** in **tomato** a consonant or a vowel? What rule number is used for a consonant plus **o**? What does Rule 3 tell you to do to make **tomato** plural? How do you spell the plural of **tomato**?

Is the letter before the **y** in **penny** a consonant or vowel? What rule number is used for a consonant plus **y**? What does Rule 4 tell you to do to make **penny** plural? How do you spell the plural of **penny**?

Look at the words **calf** and **roof**. What is the letter at the end of each of these words? What two rules deal with the letter **f**? By just reading these two rules, can you tell how to make **roof** and **calf** plural? Words that end only in **f**, like **calf** and **roof**, must be looked up in the dictionary or memorized if you do not already know how to form their plurals.

Look at the words **patio** and **alley**. Is the letter before the **o** in **patio** a consonant or a vowel? What rule number is used for a vowel plus **o**? What does Rule 7 tell you to do to make **patio** plural? How do you spell the plural of **patio**? Is the letter before the **y** in **alley** a consonant or vowel? What rule number is used for a vowel plus **y**? What does Rule 8 tell you to do to make **alley** plural? How do you spell the plural of **alley**?

Look at the words **child** and **deer**. What rule number is used in making **child** plural? What does Rule 9 tell you to do to make **child** plural? How do you spell the plural of **child**? Since these words are irregular nouns, they must be memorized or looked up in the dictionary if you do not already know how to form their plurals. A list of the most common words that fit this rule is provided in the reference. You should memorize this list.

What rule number is used in making **deer** plural? What does Rule 10 tell you to do to make **deer** plural? How do you spell the plural of **deer**? A list of the most common words that fit this rule is provided in the reference. You should memorize this list.

Classroom Practice 45

It is time to practice the skills you are learning. You will use the classroom practice on the next page to apply these skills.

Student Activity

How to make a spelling rule book.

1. Write the title of each spelling rule at the top of lined notebook paper (one sheet per rule).

2. On each page, make two columns. Write **singular** at the top of the first column and **plural** at the top of the second column.

3. Use a folder or two sheets of construction paper as the cover of your book. Write the book title **My Spelling Rule Book** and your name on the front cover.

4. Put the pages in order according to the rule numbers. Staple the pages on the left-hand side if you do not use a folder with brads.

5. Illustrate the cover page. (*Suggestions: rulers, books, pencils, pictures of singular and plural nouns, etc.*)

6. During your study of singular and plural nouns, write the singular and plural forms for the nouns you have learned on the appropriate rule page.

7. At various times, get into small groups to compare and expand lists. You can also quiz fellow group members on plural spellings and the spelling rules.

ENRICHMENT:

(American) 1867-1957— Laura Ingalls Wilder is best known for a series of historical novels for children, known as the *Little House* books. The *Little House* series, based on Wilder's life, gives a detailed and realistic portrayal of pioneer family life. The television series, "Little House on the Prairie," during the 1970s and 1980s, was based on Wilder's *Little House* books. The last five *Little House* books, beginning with *On the Banks of Plum Creek*, were recipients of the Newberry Award.

Discovery Questions: • What do you think it was like for children growing up during the pioneer days?

Discovery Activities:

• Name as many books in the *Little House* series as you can find.

• Write a book report on your favorite Laura Ingalls Wilder book.

Are you interested in learning more about Laura Ingalls Wilder or the Little House series?

1. You may explore this topic further by using the resources listed below.
   Computer resources: Internet, encyclopedia software
   Library resources: encyclopedias, books, magazines, newspapers
   Home / community resources: books, interviews, newspapers, magazines

2. A Discovery Share Time is provided in Lesson 8 if you wish to share your investigation results. You may share orally, or you may prepare a written report. You will put your written report in a class booklet titled "Notable People in History." This booklet will be placed in the class library for everyone to enjoy.

Classroom Practice 45

Name:_____ Date:_____

GRAMMAR

▶ **Exercise 1:** Classify each sentence.

1. _____ Did the boys and girls quietly listen to the librarian's story?

2. _____ During science class, the teacher showed Jeff a diagram of the human heart.

SKILLS

▶ **Exercise 2:** For each noun, write the rule number and the plural form that follows the rule. Some nouns have two acceptable plural forms, but you should use the plural spellings that can be verified by these rules.

RULES FOR MAKING REGULAR NOUNS PLURAL	Add -s to nouns with these special endings:
Add -s to nouns without special endings.	6. *f* or *ff*.
1. most singular nouns.	7. a vowel plus *o*.
Add -es to nouns with these special endings:	8. a vowel plus *y*.
2. *ch, sh, z, s, ss, x*.	**RULES FOR MAKING IRREGULAR NOUNS PLURAL**
3. a consonant plus *o*.	9. Change the spelling completely
4. a consonant plus *y*,	for the plural form.
change **y** to **i** before adding **es**.	10. Spell the same for both the singular
5. *f* or *fe*, change **f** or **fe** to **v** before adding **es**.	and plural form.

	Rule	Plural Form		Rule	Plural Form
1. kite			11. woman		
2. try			12. video		
3. guess			13. half		
4. foot			14. chimney		
5. tooth			15. knife		
6. pulley			16. proof		
7. mystery			17. deer		
8. series			18. brush		
9. touch			19. radio		
10. cliff			20. veto		

EDITING

▶ **Exercise 3:** Punctuate the Kay and Robert story, "Brotherless." (Part 1 of 5)
Editing Guide: End Marks: 6   Capitals: 7   Commas: 2   Quotation Marks: 6   Apostrophes: 1

kay looked at her brother and shook her head what did i do to deserve a brother like you

she asked irritably

i have to admit robert replied with a wide smile that you are ONE lucky girl i guess you know

that most girls would love to have a brother like me roberts blue eyes sparkled as he teased

his twin sister

English Made Easy

LISTENING AND SPEAKING:
Vocabulary & Analogy Time

Learn It: Recite the new vocabulary and analogy words.

📖 Reference 160	Vocabulary & Analogy Words

Word: persevere (pûr'sə vîr')
  Definition: not giving up during difficulty
  Synonym: endure   **Antonym:** quit
  Sentence: He persevered during the long winter.

Analogy: freeze : froze :: bring : brought
Grammatical relationship: Just as **freeze** is the present tense of **froze**,
                  bring is the present tense of **brought**.

Vocabulary Card 35: Record the vocabulary information above and write your own
                sentence, using the new word.
   Analogy Card 35: Record the analogy information and write your own analogy,
                using the same relationship as the analogy above.

Jingle Time

Recite It: Practice Jingles 8–11 in the Jingle Section on page 508.

Grammar Time

Apply It: Classify the Practice Sentences orally with your teacher.

Practice Sentences	Chapter 10: Lesson 3

1. _____ The shy little girl in the red dress was standing behind her
        mother and would not speak to the teacher.
2. _____ During the holidays, the florist down the street stocks priceless
        collectibles from Europe.
3. _____ Sarah eagerly showed me her notes from the lecture on
        Egyptian history.

START LESSON 3

Lesson 3

You will

- study new vocabulary; make card 35; write own sentence using the vocabulary word.
- analyze new analogy; make card 35; write own analogy.
- practice Jingles 8–11.
- classify Practice Sentences.
- do a Skill Builder.
- do Classroom Practice 46.
- write in your journal.
- read and discuss Discovery Time.

SHURLEY ENGLISH

LISTENING AND SPEAKING:

Skill Builder

Using the sentences just classified, do a Skill Builder orally with your teacher.

1. **Identify the nouns in a Noun Check.**
2. **Identify the nouns as singular or plural.**
3. **Identify the nouns as common or proper.**
4. **Identify the complete subject and the complete predicate.**
5. **Identify the simple subject and the simple predicate.**
6. **Do a Vocabulary Check.**
7. **Do a Verb Chant.**

JOURNAL WRITING 26

Write an entry in your journal. Use Reference 9 on page 12 for ideas.

Classroom Practice 46

It is time to practice the skills you are learning. You will use the classroom practice on the next page to apply these skills.

ENRICHMENT:

Discovery Time

(American) Wilbur Wright (1867-1912) and Orville Wright (1871-1948) were brothers who invented the first airplane. The brothers used the profits from their print shop and their bicycle operation to fund their aeronautical experiments. Orville and Wilbur made aviation history when they became the first persons to fly a powered aircraft near Kitty Hawk, North Carolina. Orville flew the aircraft first, staying in the air for 12 seconds. Later, on the same day, Wilbur flew the aircraft for 59 seconds. In 1908, the Wright brothers signed a contract for the sale of an airplane to the U.S. Army and to France.

Discovery Questions: • **What do you think it is like to be the first person to invent or design something that significantly affects the future?**

Discovery Activity:
• **Make a collage of inventions that have made a major impact in the world.**

Are you interested in learning more about Wilbur and Orville Wright?

1. You may explore this topic further by using the resources listed below.
   Computer resources: Internet, encyclopedia software
   Library resources: encyclopedias, books, magazines, newspapers
   Home/community resources: books, interviews, newspapers, magazines
2. A Discovery Share Time is provided in Lesson 8 if you wish to share your investigation results. You may share orally, or you may prepare a written report. You will put your written report in a class booklet titled "Notable People in History." This booklet will be placed in the class library for everyone to enjoy.

Homework 8

On notebook paper, number 1–12. For each noun, write the rule number and the plural form that follows the rule. If a noun has two acceptable plural forms, use the plural spelling that can be verified by these rules.

RULES FOR MAKING REGULAR NOUNS PLURAL

Add -s to nouns without special endings.
1. most singular nouns.

Add -es to nouns with these special endings:
2. *ch, sh, z, s, ss, x.*
3. a consonant plus *o.*
4. a consonant plus *y,*
   change **y** to **i** before adding **es.**
5. *f* or *fe,* change **f** or **fe** to **v** before adding **es.**

Add -s to nouns with these special endings:
6. *f* or *ff.*
7. a vowel plus *o.*
8. a vowel plus *y.*

RULES FOR MAKING IRREGULAR NOUNS PLURAL
9. Change the spelling completely for the plural form.
10. Spell the same for both the singular and plural form.

	Rule	Plural Form		Rule	Plural Form
1. lullaby			7. volcano		
2. video			8. shelf		
3. valley			9. goose		
4. belief			10. tax		
5. potato			11. elf		
6. pulley			12. child		

Home Connection

Family Activity for Vocabulary and Analogies

Divide into family teams. The first team will use vocabulary and analogy cards 29–32 to ask questions about the information on their cards. The second team will use vocabulary and analogy cards 33–36 to ask questions about the information on their cards.

Family Activity for Plurals of Nouns

Write the plurals of the nouns in the blanks. Then, circle them in the word search below. Words may appear across or down.

calf _____

child _____

church _____

deer _____

dog _____

family _____

fly _____

potato _____

radio _____

roof _____

```
Q E R H Y G H C P M S W A U V
W X F J A S D C O F G F L Y S
O R A D I O S H T U M P T E F
Z K M O Q D F U A T D E E R O
F U I G B X V R T J W Q A O T
P O L E L R E C O V Z C A O Q
L A I S U Y E H E Y C A L F S
T V E H F L I E S C G L J E Z
L O S F E N G S A U T V C S R
D B O T T E N U S T S E H I L
S R E O T A B R O O F S I M A
Z G C H I L D R E N H O L R P
E A R A S R A D I O E S D Y N
A D O G S T O R N G A T S O R
```

Puzzle Answers: calf/calves child/children church/churches deer/deer dog/dogs family/families fly/flies potato/potatoes radio/radios roof/roofs

End of
Lesson 4

START LESSON 5

Lesson 5

You will

- classify Practice Sentences.
- do Chapter Checkup 48.
- write in your journal.
- read and discuss Discovery Time.

JOURNAL WRITING 27

Write an entry in your journal. Use Reference 9 on page 12 for ideas.

LISTENING AND SPEAKING:

Grammar Time

Apply It: Classify the Practice Sentences orally with your teacher.

Practice Sentences	Chapter 10: Lesson 5

1. _____ Wow! That racecar veered suddenly from its course and crashed into a bale of hay!
2. _____ Bring a pencil and a sheet of paper to class tomorrow for your final exam.
3. _____ Did your dad really build you that soapbox car for the derby?

Chapter Checkup 48

It is time for a checkup of the skills you have learned in this chapter. You will use the chapter checkup on the next page to evaluate your progress.

ENRICHMENT:

Discovery Time

(Italian) 1874-1937— Guglielmo Marconi is known as the father of the radio. He produced and detected radio waves over long distances. Marconi worked on the development of short-wave wireless communication and obtained a patent for the wireless telegraph in 1897. He opened the first radio factory in England in 1898. In 1909, he received the Nobel Prize for physics, along with Ferdinand Braun. Marconi's work became the basis of nearly all modern long-distance radio transmissions.

Discovery Questions:
- How often do you listen to the radio? What kind of radio programs do you enjoy?

Discovery Activity:
- Invite a local ham-radio operator to speak to your class.

Are you interested in learning more about Guglielmo Marconi?

1. You may explore this topic further by using the resources listed below.
   Computer resources: Internet, encyclopedia software
   Library resources: encyclopedias, books, magazines, newspapers
   Home/community resources: books, interviews, newspapers, magazines
2. A Discovery Share Time is provided in Lesson 8 if you wish to share your investigation results. You may share orally, or you may prepare a written report. You will put your written report in a class booklet titled "Notable People in History." This booklet will be placed in the class library for everyone to enjoy.

Chapter 10 Checkup 48

Name:_____ Date:_____

GRAMMAR

▶ **Exercise 1:** Classify each sentence.

1. _____ Take the overflowing trash from the birthday party to the incinerator.

2. _____ Were the potted plants in the sunroom watered today?

3. _____ Can you give me directions to the downtown conservatory?

SKILLS

▶ **Exercise 2:** For each noun, write the rule number and the plural form that follows the rule. Some nouns have two acceptable plural forms, but you should use the plural spellings that can be verified by these rules.

RULES FOR MAKING REGULAR NOUNS PLURAL

Add -s to nouns without special endings.
  1. most singular nouns.

Add -es to nouns with these special endings:
  2. *ch*, *sh*, *z*, *s*, *ss*, *x*.
  3. a consonant plus *o*.
  4. a consonant plus *y*,
     change **y** to **i** before adding **es**.
  5. *f* or *fe*, change **f** or **fe** to **v** before adding **es**.

Add -s to nouns with these special endings:
  6. *f* or *ff*.
  7. a vowel plus *o*.
  8. a vowel plus *y*.

RULES FOR MAKING IRREGULAR NOUNS PLURAL
  9. Change the spelling completely
     for the plural form.
  10. Spell the same for both the singular
     and plural form.

	Rule	Plural Form		Rule	Plural Form
1. tragedy			10. class		
2. dinosaur			11. pulley		
3. roof			12. clock		
4. woman			13. video		
5. radio			14. foot		
6. series			15. tornado		
7. boundary			16. tax		
8. journey			17. half		
9. cliff			18. calf		

EDITING

▶ **Exercise 3:** Punctuate the Kay and Robert story, "Brotherless." (Part 4 of 5)
  Editing Guide: End Marks: 7   Capitals: 10   Commas: 5   Quotation Marks: 8   Apostrophes: 1

robert chuckled as he eyed his sister with respect kay ive decided to move on with my life he

said besides i know that it is to your advantage to have a brother robert declared airily having

a brother means that there are always boys around making goo-goo eyes at you

oh my have we increased our vocabulary since we discovered the dictionary retorted kay

START LESSON 6

Lesson 6

You will

- read and discuss fiction, nonfiction, autobiography, and biography.
- read and discuss card catalog and how to find fiction books in the library.
- read and discuss how to write a fiction book review.
- write a fiction book review for WA 25.

Literature Time

Learn It: TWO KINDS OF BOOKS

 Reference 162 | **Two Kinds of Books**

When you go to the library to check out a book, you need to know which books are available and how to find them. There are two large categories of books, fiction and nonfiction.

1. FICTION

Fiction books contain stories about people, places, or things that are not true even though the author may use ideas based on real people or events. Fiction writers use their imagination and make up stories for the reader's enjoyment. There are several types of fictional writings. Some of these include fables, myths, novels, plays, science fiction, short stories, horror stories, and mysteries. Fiction books are grouped together in a special section of the library and are arranged alphabetically by the author's last name.

2. NONFICTION

Nonfiction books contain factual information and stories that are true. You can find a nonfiction book on just about any subject. Nonfiction books have been written about plants, animals, oceans, planets, space, countries, history, and all kinds of other topics. In most libraries, these nonfiction books are grouped together in numerical order, according to a call number. A call number is the number that is seen on the spine of all nonfiction books.

Autobiographies and biographies are special types of nonfiction writings. An autobiography tells about the writer's own life. In a biography, on the other hand, a writer writes about another person's life. Details and facts are true and cannot be changed or embellished. Even though autobiographies and biographies are nonfiction, they are not arranged by call numbers like other nonfiction books. Instead, they are grouped together by the last name of the person about whom they are written.

Learn It: THE CARD CATALOG

Reference 163 | **Card Catalogs**

The **card catalog** is an index to the books in a library. A book is listed in the card catalog in three ways—by author, by title, and by subject. An electronic or traditional card catalog can help you find any book in the library.

A computerized card catalog is an electronic file where you can search by author, title, or subject to find the same information that you would get by searching for a card in the traditional card catalog. Many community libraries have websites that offer access to the card catalog from home. After the book's title, the author's name, or the subject of the book has been entered in an electronic card catalog, the computer will search its library database for your request. The information you requested will be displayed on a computer screen if it is available in that particular library. You can print or copy the information received to help you find the book.

A traditional card catalog is a file of cards, arranged alphabetically, that is usually placed in the drawers of a card catalog cabinet. Labels on the drawers tell which cards are in each drawer. The catalog cards contain information about every book and nearly all the other materials located in the library.

Continued on next page. >>>

Reference 163 continued from previous page.

CARD CATALOG CARDS

The card catalog has three kinds of cards for every book: an **author card**, a **title card**, and a **subject card**. All three kinds of cards are arranged alphabetically by the word(s) on the top line. All three kinds of cards give the name of the book, the name of the author, and the call number of the book. They also give the place and date of publication, the publisher, the number of pages in the book, and other important information. The main difference in the cards is how the information is arranged.

Author cards have the name of the author of the book on the top line, and they are filed alphabetically by the author's last name. **Title cards** have the title of the book on the top line, and they are filed alphabetically by the first word of the title (except for *A*, *An*, or *The*). **Subject cards** have the subject of the book on the top line, and they are filed alphabetically by the first word of the subject (except for *A*, *An*, or *The*).

Author Card	Title Card	Subject Card

586.3
Author: Pacton, James R.
   Title: <u>Science for Kids and Parents</u>
     III. by Charles Finley
     Children's Press, Chicago
     (c1990) 116p.
	586.3
	   Title: <u>Science for Kids and Parents</u>
	Author: Pacton, James R.
	     III. by Charles Finley
	     Children's Press, Chicago
	     (c1990) 116p.
		586.3
		Subject: Science Projects
		Author: Pacton, James R.
		   Title: <u>Science for Kids and Parents</u>
		     III. by Charles Finley
		     Children's Press, Chicago
		     (c1990) 116p.

Learn It: **FINDING FICTION BOOKS IN THE LIBRARY**

Reference 164 **How to Find Fiction Books in the Library**

To find out if a library has a certain fiction book, look in the card catalog for the title card of that book. If you don't know the title but know the author, look for the author card. If you don't know the title or the author, look under the subject of the book. Also, look under the subject if you are interested in finding several books about your topic. Sometimes, fiction books are not classified by subject like other books. You must then look for the title or author of the book.

After you find the card for the book you want in the card catalog, you must know how to find the book. Fiction books are arranged on the shelves in **alphabetical order** according to the **authors' last name**; therefore, a fiction book can be located only if you know the author's last name.

If you look on the spine of a fiction book, you will see only a letter(s). This is the first letter in the author's last name, and all three catalog cards will have the first letter of the author's last name in the top left corner of each card. Be sure to write the author's last name and the book title down on paper before you look for the book.

When you go to the library shelf, look at the letter printed on the spines of the books until you find the same letter(s) on the book that you copied from the catalog card. If two authors have the same last name, their books are arranged in alphabetical order according to the authors' first names. If there are two or more books by the same author, they are arranged in alphabetical order by titles.

Learn It: **WRITING A BOOK REVIEW FOR A FICTION BOOK**

Reference 165 **Writing a Book Review for a Fiction Book**

Writing a book review gives you an opportunity to tell what a book is about and what you think about the book. The things you share in your review could influence others as they decide whether or not to read the book. Therefore, it is important that you consider carefully the information and opinion you share. Use the following guidelines to help you decide what to include in a book review for a **fiction book**.

Continued on next page. >>>

Reference 165 continued from previous page.

1. List the title and author.

2. Tell the type of book: Fiction.

3. Write an introductory paragraph to describe the main character(s) and the problem he/she/they faced. In the second paragraph, write a short version (summary) of the main events in the story. In the third paragraph, tell how the problem was resolved and/or how the story ended.

4. In the last paragraph, give your opinion of the book. In this paragraph, tell why you liked or disliked the book.

The example below shows one way to write a book review for a fiction book.

<u>Shiloh</u>

by Phyllis Reynolds Naylor

Fiction Book

There are three main characters in this story. Marty Preston is a tender-hearted boy who loves animals. Judd Travers is Marty's neighbor, and he is mean to his hunting dogs. Shiloh is one of Mr. Travers's hunting dogs that has been beaten and starved. Marty is upset that Shiloh is being mistreated and wants to help him.

Marty finds Shiloh and hides him so Judd Travers cannot harm him again. Marty learns to love Shiloh and is devoted to him. He is torn between keeping Shiloh and telling Mr. Travers the truth. Finally, Marty confesses to Mr. Travers and offers him a deal.

In the end, Marty offers to work for Mr. Travers. In return, Mr. Travers gives Shiloh to Marty.

I liked the book a lot because it showed how loyalty and honesty gave Marty the courage to stand up for what he believed and to protect the dog he loved. Marty's devotion to Shiloh gave him the strength to do what was right.

Student Tip...

For additional information and activities about fiction and nonfiction books, the library, and the card catalog, refer to Study Skills in the Resource Tools Section on pages 532–533.

Write It: **WRITING ASSIGNMENT 25**

Even though this writing assignment for a book review of a fiction book is given today, your book review is not due until Lesson 6 of Chapter 11.

Writing Assignment 25: Fiction Book-Review

Purpose: To provide information about events or persons in a book and to express an opinion

Type of Writing: Book review of a fiction book

Audience: Classmates, family, or friends

Writing Topics: Choose a fiction book.

Special Instructions:

1. Choose a fiction book about which to write a book review.

2. Use References 162–165 on pages 312–314 to guide you in writing a book review of a fiction book of your choice.

3. Write a rough draft; then, revise and edit it. Next, write a final paper of your book review during a study time or outside of class.

4. Finish Book Review 25 by Lesson 6 of Chapter 11 and give it to your teacher.

5. Keep your book review in the Final Paper folder if you finish early.

English Made Easy

Reading Time

Read It: **FICTION BOOK**

Use this reading time to read the fiction book you have selected for a book review. When you finish your book, you may begin working on your book review assignment, Writing Assignment 25.

Conference Time

Discuss It: **TEACHER-STUDENT CONFERENCES FOR WRITING ASSIGNMENT 24**

Meet with your teacher to discuss Writing Assignment 24.
After the conference, place this group of papers in your Publishing folder.

>>>>>>>>>>>>>>>>>>>> **Student Tip...**

To review the information about fiction book reviews, look at pages 313-314.

Across the Curriculum

Social Studies Connection: Write a narrative based on an important event in history. Use dialogue in your narrative, if appropriate. You might also illustrate your narrative with drawings or pictures. Read your narrative in a cooperative-learning group.

Lesson 7

You will

- conference with teacher about WA 24.
- read a fiction book.
- do Across the Curriculum activity.

Chapter 10

START LESSON 8

Lesson 8

You will

- publish WA 24.
- participate in Discovery Share Time.
- write an independent narrative with dialogue (WA 26).

Publishing Time

Publish It: **WRITING ASSIGNMENT 24**

Choose a publishing form and publish Writing Assignment 24. After rewriting your paper for publication, give the stapled papers (evaluation guide, graded final paper, rough draft, and Story Elements Outline) to your teacher to be placed in your Writing Portfolio.

	Reference 66	Publishing Checklist for Step 6 in the Writing Process

The sixth step in the writing process is called publishing. Publishing is sharing your writing with others. With so many forms of publishing available, finding a match for every project and personality is easy.

At times, a written work is best read aloud. Other times, the biggest impact is made when a written work is read silently. You can also use media sources to enhance any publication.

SPECIAL INSTRUCTIONS FOR PUBLISHING:

- Rewrite the graded paper in ink or type it on a computer, correcting any marked errors. *(Do not display or publish papers that have marked errors or grades on them.)*
- Give your teacher the set of stapled papers to place in your Writing Portfolio. *(Stapled papers: evaluation guide, graded final paper, rough draft, and prewriting map.)*
- Select a publishing form from the list below and publish your rewritten paper.
  1. Have classmates, family members, neighbors, or others read your writing at school or home.
  2. Share your writing with others during a Share Time. *(Refer to Reference 67 on page 99 for sharing guidelines.)*
  3. Display your writing on a bulletin board or wall.
  4. Put your writing in the classroom library or in the school library for checkout.
  5. Send your writing as a letter or an e-mail to a friend or relative.
  6. Frame your writing by gluing it on colored construction paper and decorating it.
  7. Make a book of your writing for your classroom, your family, or others.
  8. Illustrate your writing and give it to others to read.
  9. Dramatize your writing in the form of a play, puppet show, or radio broadcast.
  10. Send your writing to be placed in a waiting room (doctor, veterinarian, dentist, etc.), senior-citizen center, or a nursing home.
  11. Send your writing to a school newspaper, local newspaper, or a magazine for publication.
  12. Make a videotape, cassette tape, or slide presentation of your writing.
  13. Choose another publishing form that is not listed.

LISTENING AND SPEAKING:

Discovery Share Time

If you have chosen to investigate a historical figure introduced in this chapter, you now have the opportunity to share your results in one of the following ways:

1. You may relate your information orally.
2. You may read a written report.
3. You may place your report in the booklet without reading it aloud.

After share time, all written reports should be turned in to be placed in the class booklet titled "Notable People in History." You are encouraged to check out this class booklet so you can enjoy the reports again.

Writing Time

Write It: WRITING ASSIGNMENT 26

As you write a rough draft for your independent writing assignment, you will do two of the six steps in the writing process: prewriting (the Story Elements Outline) and rough draft.

Writing Assignment 26

Purpose: To tell a story

Type of Writing: Narrative

Audience: Classmates, relatives, or friends

Writing Topics: The hardest/easiest thing I've ever done
The big game/a surprise/an overnight stay
Getting caught/the most memorable birthday party
(Brainstorm for other ideas, individually or in groups.)

Special Instructions:

1. Follow the Prewriting and Rough Draft Checklists in References 44 and 46 on pages 57, 61.

2. Use Reference 156 on page 290 to help you write your narrative. Make a Story Elements Outline instead of a prewriting map.

3. Write your narrative with dialogue.

4. Write in first or third person. See Reference 70 on page 104.
(First-person pronouns: *I, me, my, mine, we, us, our, and ours.*)
(Third-person pronouns: *he, his, him, she, her, hers, it, its, they, their, theirs,* and *them.*)

Note: Reference 54 on page 71 gives the steps in the writing process and the location of all the writing checklists.

Student Note: Some of your writing pieces will be selected for revision and editing later in the school year.

START LESSON 9

Lesson 9

You will

- practice Jingle 12.
- read and discuss a narrative essay without dialogue.
- plan and write rough draft for narrative without dialogue (WA 27).

>>> **Student Tip...**

Reviewing the transition words will help you apply them in your writing.

LISTENING AND SPEAKING:

Recite It: Practice Jingle 12 in the Jingle Section on page 509.

Learn It: **NARRATIVE WRITING WITHOUT DIALOGUE**

Some narratives are written without dialogue. The Story Elements Outline is still used because it keeps your writing focused and helps you choose details and events that support the main idea of your story.

Reference 166 | **Story Elements for a Narrative Without Dialogue**

STORY ELEMENTS OUTLINE

1. Main Idea:
Tell the problem or situation that needs a solution.

Barry put a toad in Jenny's backpack, and she wanted to get even.

2. Setting:
Tell when and where the story takes place, either clearly stated or implied.

When: **The story takes place during warm weather, when toads are out.**
Where: **The story takes place in a city park and a city library.**

3. Characters:
Tell whom or what the story is about.

The main characters are Barry and his friend, Jenny.

4. Plot:
Tell what the characters in the story do and what happens to them.

The story is about a boy named Barry who slips a toad into the backpack of his friend, Jenny, on their way to the library. She discovers the toad in the library and retaliates by dropping the toad down Barry's shirt.

5. Ending:
Use a strong ending that will bring the story to a close.

Jenny evens the score and earns Barry's respect and admiration.

Example of Narrative Writing Without Dialogue

Getting Toad-ally Even

On their way to the city library, Barry and his friend, Jenny, cut through the park. Suddenly, Barry spied a toad. He looked at Jenny, who was just a few steps ahead of him. Chuckling to himself, he picked up the toad and quietly slipped it into Jenny's backpack. She was blissfully unaware of his mischief and continued on ahead.

As Jenny settled down to study at the library, she reached inside her backpack to get her notebook and pencil. Instantly, she felt something cold and let out a loud scream. The librarian scowled disapprovingly, and everyone stared as Jenny knocked her bag off the table, sending papers and books onto the floor.

Continued on next page. >>>

Reference 166 continued from previous page.

> Barry was doubled over, trying to hold his laughter to a whisper. Jenny glared at him. She knew he was the culprit. Her mind raced. How could she get even? She smiled sweetly at Barry as she picked up her stuff. Then, she turned her back to him, gritted her teeth, and retrieved the cold little critter from her backpack to even the score.
>
> Barry was holding his breath and trying to calm down from his laugh-attack. When Barry turned his head, Jenny quickly dropped the warty toad down the front of his shirt. Barry hollered, tossing books and leaping about like someone dancing a jig. Now, Jenny was doubled over with laughter. Suddenly, she spied the librarian heading their way. Grabbing Barry, she pushed him toward the door.
>
> On their way home, the two friends hooted loudly as they relived the toad episode. After Barry waved goodbye to Jenny, he shook his head in admiration. He still could not believe Jenny had actually picked up that toad!

Write It: WRITING ASSIGNMENT 27

As you write a rough draft for your guided writing assignment, you will do two of the six steps in the writing process: prewriting (the Story Elements Outline) and rough draft.

Writing Assignment 27

Purpose: To tell a story

Type of Writing: Narrative

Audience: Classmates, relatives, or friends

Writing Topics: Wild ride
Stage fright
Adopting a stray animal
The mystery gift
(Brainstorm for other ideas, individually or in groups.)

Special Instructions:

1. Follow the Prewriting and Rough Draft Checklists in References 44 and 46 on pages 57, 61.

2. Use Reference 166 on page 318 to help you write your narrative. Make a Story Elements Outline instead of a prewriting map.

3. Write your narrative without dialogue.

4. Write in first or third person. See Reference 70 on page 104.
(First-person pronouns: *I, me, my, mine, we, us, our,* and *ours.*)
(Third-person pronouns: *he, his, him, she, her, hers, it, its, they, their, theirs,* and *them.*)

Note: Reference 54 on page 71 gives the steps in the writing process and the location of all the writing checklists.

START LESSON 10

Lesson 10

You will
- revise, edit, and write a final paper for WA 27.

Apply It: **REVISE, EDIT, AND WRITE A FINAL PAPER**
Following the schedule below, you will revise and edit Writing Assignment 27. Then, you will write a final paper. Use the Chapter 10 Writing Evaluation Guide on the next page to check your final paper one last time.

| Reference 52 | Revising & Editing Schedule and Writing a Final Paper |

SPECIAL INSTRUCTIONS FOR REVISING AND EDITING (Steps 3-4 in the writing process):
- Use the Revising and Editing Checklists in References 48 and 50 as you revise and edit your rough draft.
- Follow the revising and editing schedule below as directed by your teacher.
  1. **Individual.** First, read your rough draft to yourself. Use the Revising Checklist in Reference 48 on page 64. Go through your paper, checking each item on the list and making revisions to your rough draft. Then, use the Editing Checklist in Reference 50 on page 67. Go through your paper again, checking each item on the list and editing your rough draft.
  2. **Partner.** Next, get with your editing partner. Work together on each partner's rough draft, one paper at a time. Read each rough draft aloud and revise and edit it together, using the Revising and Editing Checklists. (The author of the paper should be the one to make the corrections on his own paper.)
  3. **Group.** Finally, read the rough draft to a revision group for feedback. Each student should read his paper while the others listen and offer possible revising and editing suggestions. (The author will determine whether to make corrections from the revision group's suggestions.)

SPECIAL INSTRUCTIONS FOR FINAL PAPER (Step 5 in the writing process):
- Write your final paper, using the Final Paper Checklist in Reference 53 on page 70.
- Staple your writing papers in this order: the final paper on top, the rough draft in the middle, and the prewriting map on the bottom. Place the stapled papers in the Final Paper folder.

>>>>>>>>>>>>> **Student Tip...**

1. Be tactful and helpful in your comments during revising and editing time. The purpose of any suggestion should be to improve the writer's rough draft.

2. As you make your final corrections, you have the choice of accepting or rejecting any suggestions made by your partners or your revision group.

3. Study Vocabulary Words and Analogies 33–36 for the chapter test in the next lesson.

4. If you need to improve your handwriting, refer to the Resource Tools Section on pages 529–530 for information on writing legibly.

Chapter 10 Writing Evaluation Guide

Name:_____ Date:_____

ROUGH DRAFT CHECK

_____ 1. Did you write your rough draft in pencil?

_____ 2. Did you write the correct headings on the first seven lines of your paper?

_____ 3. Did you use extra wide margins and skip every other line?

_____ 4. Did you write a title at the end of your rough draft?

_____ 5. Did you place your edited rough draft in your Rough Draft folder?

REVISING CHECK

_____ 6. Did you identify the purpose, type of writing, and audience?

_____ 7. Did you check for a topic, topic sentence, and sentences supporting the topic?

_____ 8. Did you check sentences for the right order, and did you combine, rearrange, or delete sentences when necessary?

_____ 9. Did you check for a variety of simple, compound, and complex sentences?

_____ 10. Did you check for any left out, repeated, or unnecessary words?

_____ 11. Did you check for the best choice of words by replacing or deleting unclear words?

_____ 12. Did you check the content for interest and creativity?

_____ 13. Did you check the voice to make sure the writing says what you want it to say?

EDITING CHECK

_____ 14. Did you indent each paragraph?

_____ 15. Did you put an end mark at the end of every sentence?

_____ 16. Did you capitalize the first word of every sentence?

_____ 17. Did you check for all other capitalization mistakes?

_____ 18. Did you check for all punctuation mistakes?
(commas, periods, apostrophes, quotation marks, underlining)

_____ 19. Did you check for misspelled words and for incorrect homonym choices?

_____ 20. Did you check for incorrect spellings of plural and possessive forms?

_____ 21. Did you check for correct construction and punctuation of your sentences?

_____ 22. Did you check for usage mistakes? (subject/verb agreement, a/an choices, contractions, verb tenses, pronoun/antecedent agreement, pronoun cases, degrees of adjectives, double negatives, etc.)

_____ 23. Did you put your revised and edited paper in the Rough Draft folder?

FINAL PAPER CHECK

_____ 24. Did you write the final paper in pencil?

_____ 25. Did you center the title on the top line and center your name under the title?

_____ 26. Did you skip a line before starting the writing assignment?

_____ 27. Did you single-space, use wide margins, and write the final paper neatly?

_____ 28. Did you staple your papers in this order: final paper on top, rough draft in the middle, and prewriting map on the bottom? Did you put them in the Final Paper folder?

START LESSON 11

Lesson 11

You will

- hand in WA 27 for grading.
- respond to oral review questions.
- take Chapter 10 Test.

CHAPTER TEST

It is time to evaluate your knowledge of the skills you have learned in this chapter. Your teacher will give you the Chapter 10 Test to help you assess your progress.

Writing Time

Hand It In: **WRITING ASSIGNMENT 27**

Get your stapled papers for Writing Assignment 27 from your Final Paper folder. Check to make sure they are in the correct order: the final paper on top, the rough draft in the middle, and the Story Elements Outline on the bottom. Hand them in to your teacher.

LISTENING AND SPEAKING:
Oral Review Questions

Discuss It:

1. What are the core parts of a Pattern 3 sentence?
2. What are the core parts of a Pattern 2 sentence?
3. What are the core parts of a Pattern 1 sentence?
4. When do you use quotations?
5. What are the three types of quotes?
6. What are the End Mark choices for a beginning quote?
7. What are the End Mark choices for an end quote?
8. What do explanatory words do in dialogue?
9. What kinds of books contain stories and information that are true?
10. What kinds of books contain stories that are not true?
11. Name two different types of nonfiction writing?
12. What is an autobiography?
13. What is a biography?
14. How are fiction books arranged in the library?
15. How are nonfiction books arranged in the library?
16. What type of writing is used when your purpose is to tell a story?
17. What type of writing is used when your purpose is to paint a picture with words?
18. What type of writing is used when your purpose is to express an opinion and to convince the reader that this opinion is correct?
19. What type of writing is used when your purpose is to inform, to give facts, to give directions, to explain, or to define something?

>>>>>>>>>>>>>>>>>>>>>>>>> **Student Tip...**

For information about test-taking strategies, refer to the Resource Tools Section on page 528.

English Made Easy

LISTENING AND SPEAKING:
Vocabulary & Analogy Time

Learn It: Recite the new vocabulary and analogy words.

📖 **Reference 167** | **Vocabulary & Analogy Words**

Word: inclement (ĭnklĕm'ənt)
  Definition: severe; rough; threatening
  Synonym: stormy   **Antonym:** balmy
  Sentence: He could not fly because of the inclement weather.

Analogy: run : ran :: sit : sat
Grammatical relationship: Just as **run** is the present tense of **ran**,
                sit is the present tense of **sat**.

Vocabulary Card 37: Record the vocabulary information above and write your own
                sentence, using the new word.
Analogy Card 37: Record the analogy information and write your own analogy,
                using the same relationship as the analogy above.

Jingle Time

Recite It: Recite the new jingle.

♪ **Jingle 24**   **The Predicate Noun Jingle**

A predicate, predicate noun
Is a special, special noun
In the predicate, predicate, predicate
That means the **same as the subject**,
The simple, simple subject.
A predicate, predicate noun
Follows after a linking verb.

To locate a predicate noun,
Ask **WHAT** or **WHO** after the verb
And verify the answer.
Verify that the noun in the predicate
Means the **same thing as the subject**,
The simple, simple subject.

Grammar Time

Apply It: These Introductory Sentences are used to apply the new grammar
concepts taught. Classify these sentences orally with your teacher.

Introductory Sentences | **Chapter 11: Lesson 1**

1. _____ Roses are flowers.
2. _____ Roses are the most popular flowers for anniversaries.
3. _____ *Macbeth* is the title of a well-known Shakespearean play.

Lesson 1

You will
- study new vocabulary; make card 37; write own sentence using the vocabulary word.
- analyze new analogy; make card 37; write own analogy.
- recite new jingle (Predicate Noun).
- identify predicate noun, linking verb, and Pattern 4.
- classify Introductory Sentences.
- do a Skill Builder to identify predicate nouns.
- write in your journal.

Learn It: PREDICATE NOUNS AND LINKING VERBS

Earlier, you learned that nouns can have different jobs, or functions, in a sentence. You have already studied four of these jobs. A noun can be a subject, an object of a preposition, an indirect object, or a direct object. You have also learned that not all nouns are part of a sentence pattern.

You have been studying Patterns 1–3. A Pattern 1 sentence has only one noun and an action verb as the sentence core. A Pattern 2 sentence has two nouns and an action verb as the sentence core. A Pattern 3 sentence has three nouns and an action verb as the sentence core. Now, we will learn a new sentence pattern. The new sentence pattern, Pattern 4, has two nouns and a linking verb as the sentence core.

Reference 168 — Predicate Noun or Pronoun, Linking Verb, and Pattern 4

1. A **predicate noun** is located in the predicate and means the same thing as the simple subject.

2. A predicate noun is located after a linking verb.

3. A *predicate noun* is labeled with the abbreviation **PrN**.

4. A predicate pronoun can take the place of a predicate noun. Label a *predicate pronoun* as **PrP**.

5. A predicate noun or pronoun is also known as a **predicate nominative**.

6. To find a predicate noun or pronoun, ask WHAT or WHO after the verb.

7. A **linking verb** is a verb that expresses a state of **being** instead of **action**. A linking verb states that someone or something exists. It shows no action. A linking verb links, or connects, the subject to a predicate noun or pronoun that means the same thing. A *linking verb* is labeled with the abbreviation **LV**. (**Common linking verbs:** *am, is, are, was, were, being, been, appear, become, feel, grow, look, remain, seem, smell, sound,* and *taste*.)

8. A Pattern 4 sentence has a subject noun, linking verb, and predicate noun as its core. A Pattern 4 sentence is labeled **SN LV PrN P4**. A Pattern 4 sentence has two noun jobs in its core: the subject noun and the predicate noun. (*If the subject is a pronoun, it is labeled as a subject pronoun in the sentence, but the pattern is still identified as **SN LV PrN P4**.*)

9. **A review:**
   Pattern 1 is **SN V**. It has a noun-verb (**N V**) core.
   Pattern 2 is **SN V-t DO**. It has a noun-verb-noun (**N V N**) core.
   Pattern 3 is **SN V-t IO DO**. It has a noun-verb-noun-noun (**N V N N**) core.
   Pattern 4 is **SN LV PrN**. It has a noun-linking verb-noun (**N LV N**) core.

The location of each noun determines its job in a sentence. Only certain noun jobs form the pattern parts of a sentence. For each pattern, the order of the core nouns does not change. A noun that is an object of the preposition is not part of a sentence pattern.

Question and Answer Flow for the Practice Sentence, adding Predicate Nouns

Practice Sentence: Dad is an excellent carpenter.

1. Who is an excellent carpenter? **Dad - SN**
2. What is being said about Dad? **Dad is - V**
3. Dad is what? **carpenter - verify the noun**
4. Does carpenter mean the same thing as Dad? **Yes.**
5. Carpenter - **PrN** (Say: *Carpenter - predicate noun.*)
6. Is - **LV** (Say: *Is - linking verb.*)
7. What kind of carpenter? **excellent - Adj**
8. **An - A**
9. **SN LV PrN P4** (Say: *subject noun, linking verb, predicate noun, Pattern 4.*)
10. Skill Check
11. Linking verb - check again
12. No prepositional phrases
13. **Period, statement, declarative sentence**
14. Go back to the verb. Divide the complete subject from the complete predicate.
15. Is there an adverb exception? **No.**
16. Is this sentence in a natural or inverted order? **Natural - no change.**

```
        SN   LV A  Adj    PrN
 SN LV   Dad / is an excellent carpenter. D
 PrN P4
```

Dicuss It: **PREDICATE NOUNS AND LINKING VERBS**

1. What is the pattern in a Pattern 4 sentence?
2. What are the core parts of a Pattern 4 sentence?
3. What parts of speech are used in a Pattern 4 sentence?

Learn It: **A SKILL BUILDER FOR A NOUN CHECK WITH PREDICATE NOUNS**

The example below shows you what to do with predicate nouns when you are identifying nouns for a Noun Check.

LISTENING AND SPEAKING:

FOR A noun CHECK WITH PREDICATE nouns

Circle the nouns for a Noun Check.

Sentence 1: Subject Noun (roses) *yes, it is a noun;*
Predicate Noun (flowers) *yes, it is a noun.*

Sentence 2: Subject Noun (roses) *yes, it is a noun;*
Predicate Noun (flowers) *yes, it is a noun;*
Object of the Preposition (anniversaries) *yes, it is a noun.*

Sentence 3: Subject Noun (Macbeth) *yes, it is a noun;*
Predicate Noun (title) *yes, it is a noun;*
Object of the Preposition (play) *yes, it is a noun.*

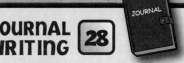

JOURNAL WRITING 28

Write an entry in your journal. Use Reference 9 on page 12 for ideas.

START LESSON 2

Lesson 2

You will

- study new vocabulary; make card 38; write own sentence using the vocabulary word.
- analyze new analogy; make card 38; write own analogy.
- practice Jingle 24.
- classify Practice Sentences.
- do a Skill Builder.
- identify how to make nouns possessive.
- do Classroom Practice 49.
- read and discuss Discovery Time.

LISTENING AND SPEAKING:
Vocabulary & Analogy Time

Learn It: Recite the new vocabulary and analogy words.

Reference 169	Vocabulary & Analogy Words

Word: feasible (fē′ zə bəl)
  Definition: capable of being done
  Synonym: attainable   **Antonym:** impossible
  Sentence: The plans for the new library were feasible.

Analogy: their : they're :: your : you're
Homonym relationship: Just as the word **their** sounds like the word **they're** but has a different spelling and meaning, the word **your** sounds like the word **you're** but has a different spelling and meaning.

Vocabulary Card 38: Record the vocabulary information above and write your own sentence, using the new word.

Analogy Card 38: Record the analogy information and write your own analogy, using the same relationship as the analogy above.

Jingle Time

Recite It: Practice Jingle 24 in the Jingle Section on page 512.

Grammar Time

Apply It: Classify the Practice Sentences orally with your teacher.

Practice Sentences	Chapter 11: Lesson 2

1. _____ The two states against the proposal are Alaska and Arizona.
2. _____ In our barn, the mice are friends with the cats.
3. _____ My uncle is a steamboat pilot on the Mississippi River.

English Made Easy

Skill Builder

Using the sentences just classified, do a Skill Builder orally with your teacher.
1. **Identify the nouns in a Noun Check.**
2. **Identify the nouns as singular or plural.**
3. **Identify the nouns as common or proper.**
4. **Identify the complete subject and the complete predicate.**
5. **Identify the simple subject and the simple predicate.**
6. **Do a Vocabulary Check.**
7. **Do a Verb Chant.**

Skill Time

Learn It: **RULES FOR MAKING NOUNS POSSESSIVE**

In order to form nouns that show ownership (possessive nouns), you must first decide if the noun is singular or plural before you add the apostrophe. After you know whether a noun is singular or plural, you can then use three rules to help you decide how to make the noun possessive.

Reference 170 — Rules for Making Nouns Possessive

A **possessive noun** is the name of a person, place, or thing that owns something. A possessive noun will always have an **apostrophe** after it. It will have either an *apostrophe* before the *s* (*'s*) or an *apostrophe* after the *s* (*s'*). The apostrophe makes a noun show ownership (*Jackie's coat*). Follow the rules below to make nouns possessive.

RULE 1: boy's	RULE 2: boys'	RULE 3: men's
For a singular noun — add ('s)	For a plural noun that ends in s — add (')	For a plural noun that does not end in s — add ('s)

Directions: For Part A, underline each noun to be made possessive. Write **S** for singular or **P** for plural, the rule number, and the possessive form. **For Part B**, write the singular possessive and plural possessive of each noun.

Part A	S-P	Rule	Possessive Form	Part B	Singular Poss	Plural Poss
1. <u>girl</u> ring	S	1	girl's	5. boss	boss's	bosses'
2. <u>writers</u> pens	P	2	writers'	6. women	woman's	women's
3. <u>children</u> sleds	P	3	children's	7. wife	wife's	wives'
4. <u>cow</u> hooves	S	1	cow's	8. Smith	Smith's	Smiths'

Discuss It: **RULES FOR MAKING NOUNS POSSESSIVE**

Look at Number 1 under Part A.
1. Which noun should be made possessive, girl or ring?
2. Is the word girl singular or plural?
3. Which rule is used to make the word girl possessive?

Continued on next page. >>>

4. What is Rule 1?

5. How do you spell the possessive form of girl?

(Continue Numbers 2–4 under Part A)

Look at Number 5 under Part B.

1. Is the word boss singular or plural?

2. Which rule is used to make the word boss possessive?

3. What is Rule 1?

4. How do you spell the possessive form of the word boss?

5. What is the plural spelling of boss?

6. Which rule is used to make the word boss possessive?

7. What is Rule 2?

8. How do you spell the possessive form of the word bosses?

(Continue Numbers 6–8 under Part B)

✏ Classroom Practice 49

It is time to practice the skills you are learning. You will use the classroom practice on the next page to apply these skills.

ENRICHMENT:

Discovery Time

(American) 1876-1916— Jack London is best known for his novels *The Call of the Wild*, *White Fang*, and *The Sea-Wolf*. "Jack London" is the pen name (pseudonym) used by the American novelist and short-story writer John Griffith London. He quit school at 14 and saw much of the United States as a hobo, riding on freight trains. He eventually finished high school and entered college, but quit after a year and joined the Klondike gold rush of 1897. He started writing at the age of 19. *The Son of the Wolf*, his first published collection of short stories, was about the Klondike. He wrote over 50 books of fiction and nonfiction in 17 years.

Discovery Questions:
- **How did London's personal experience influence his stories?**
- **Have you read any of Jack London's books? Can you name the ones you have read?**

Are you interested in learning more about Jack London?

1. You may explore this topic further by using the resources listed below.
   Computer resources: Internet, encyclopedia software
   Library resources: encyclopedias, books, magazines, newspapers
   Home/community resources: books, interviews, newspapers, magazines

2. A Discovery Share Time is provided in Lesson 8 if you wish to share your investigation results. You may share orally, or you may prepare a written report. You will put your written report in a class booklet titled "Notable People in History." This booklet will be placed in the class library for everyone to enjoy.

Classroom Practice 49

Name:_____ Date:_____

GRAMMAR

▶ **Exercise 1:** Classify each sentence.

1. _____ The large stone in her ring is an expensive diamond.

2. _____ Tooth enamel is the hardest substance in the human body.

SKILLS

▶ **Exercise 2: For Part A**, underline each noun to be made possessive. Write **S** for singular or **P** for plural, the rule number, and the possessive form. **For Part B**, write the singular possessive and plural possessive of each noun.

RULE 1: boy's	RULE 2: boys'	RULE 3: men's
For a singular noun — add ('s)	For a plural noun that ends in s — add (')	For a plural noun that does not end in s — add ('s)

Part A	S-P	Rule	Possessive Form	Part B	Singular Poss	Plural Poss
1. dog bone				10. boss		
2. children toys				11. man		
3. Smiths phones				12. giraffe		
4. monkeys food				13. mother		
5. Thomas foot				14. child		
6. agent badge				15. books		
7. Dennis letter				16. wife		
8. cats paws				17. son		
9. tractor tires				18. wolf		

EDITING

▶ **Exercise 3:** Punctuate the Kay and Robert story, "Pass the Salt." (Part 1 of 5) Editing Guide: **End Marks: 8 Capitals: 13 Commas: 4 Quotation Marks: 4 Single Quotes: 2 Apostrophes: 1 Homonyms: 1**

the stillness at the table was electrifying brother and sister glared at each other as kay

slowly repeated pass the salt i need the salt i dont care how you do it i just want you to

pass the stupid salt

robert was going to do know such thing his mischievous eyes twinkled as he watched

his serious-minded sister work herself up until she was boiling he replied sweetly

you have to say i love you robert

START LESSON 3

Lesson 3

You will

- study new vocabulary; make card 39; write own sentence using the vocabulary word.
- analyze new analogy; make card 39; write own analogy.
- practice Jingles 20–24.
- classify Practice Sentences.
- do a Skill Builder.
- identify pronoun cases.
- do Classroom Practice 50.
- write in your journal.
- read and discuss Discovery Time.

LISTENING AND SPEAKING:
Vocabulary & Analogy Time

Learn It: Recite the new vocabulary and analogy words.

📖 Reference 171	Vocabulary & Analogy Words

Word: elusive (ĭlōō'sĭv)
  Definition: hard to catch
  Synonym: evasive   **Antonym:** forthright
  Sentence: An elusive burglar disappeared into the night.

Analogy: miniature : small :: colossal : huge
Synonym relationship: Just as **miniature** means nearly the same as **small**, **colossal** means nearly the same as **huge**.

Vocabulary Card 39: Record the vocabulary information above and write your own sentence, using the new word.

Analogy Card 39: Record the analogy information and write your own analogy, using the same relationship as the analogy above.

Jingle Time

Recite It: Practice Jingles 20–24 in the Jingle Section on pages 511–512.

Grammar Time

Apply It: Classify the Practice Sentences orally with your teacher.

Practice Sentences	Chapter 11: Lesson 3

1. _____ Hunter orange is my brother's favorite color.
2. _____ The temperature of the water was thirty-nine degrees.
3. _____ Everyone at the party was a suspect after the theft of the diamond ring!

Skill Builder

Using the sentences just classified, do a Skill Builder orally with your teacher.

1. **Identify the nouns in a Noun Check.**
2. **Identify the nouns as singular or plural.**
3. **Identify the nouns as common or proper.**
4. **Identify the complete subject and the complete predicate.**
5. **Identify the simple subject and the simple predicate.**
6. **Do a Vocabulary Check.**
7. **Do a Verb Chant.**

Skill Time

Learn It: PRONOUN CASES

| Reference 172 | Subjective, Objective, and Possessive Pronoun Cases |

Personal pronouns can function in any of the ways in which nouns function: as subjects, predicate nouns, and as objects. Nouns do not change forms in the different jobs. However, most pronouns change forms according to how they are used in a sentence. A pronoun's form and how it is used are known as its **case**. Understanding pronoun cases will help you choose pronouns correctly.

> **Incorrect:** Tom and **him** gave the key to **he** and I.
> **Correct:** Tom and **he** gave the key to **him** and **me**.

PRONOUN CASES

1. **Subjective Case:** Pronouns that are used as <u>subjects</u> or <u>predicate pronouns</u> are in the subjective (sometimes called nominative) case. (***He*** *went home. This is* ***he***.)

    Subjective Case Pronouns: I, we, he, she, it, they, and **you.**

2. **Objective Case:** Pronouns that are used as <u>objects</u> are in the objective case: <u>objects</u> of prepositions, direct <u>objects</u>, or indirect <u>objects</u>. (*Jan gave* ***us*** *a present from* ***him*** *and* ***her***. *Jay found* ***me*** *in the gym.*)

    Objective Case Pronouns: me, us, him, her, it, them, and **you.**

3. **Possessive Case:** Pronouns that are used <u>to show ownership</u> are in the possessive case. Unlike nouns, pronouns are not made possessive by using an apostrophe.

    Possessive Case Pronouns: my, our, his, her, its, their, and **your.**

Use these steps to help you choose the correct pronoun and pronoun case.

- Identify the job for the pronoun choices in parentheses by deciding if the pronoun is used as a subject, object of the preposition, a direct object, indirect object, or predicate pronoun.

- If the pronoun is used as a subject or as a predicate pronoun, it is in the subjective (nominative) case. Write **S** in the blank for subjective case. Recite the Subject Pronoun Jingle. Look at the two pronouns in parentheses. Underline the one that was recited in the jingle.

- If the pronoun is used as an object of the preposition, a direct object, or an indirect object, it is in the objective case. Write **O** in the blank for objective case. Recite the Object Pronoun Jingle. Look at the two pronouns in parentheses. Underline the one that was recited in the jingle.

Continued on next page. >>>

Reference 172 continued from previous page.

Directions: Write **S** for subjective, **O** for objective, or **P** for possessive in the blank. Underline the correct pronoun in parentheses.

S	1. (She, Her) and (I, me) are riding with Tim.	O	4. Lynn gave (he and I, him and me) an invitation.
P	2. (Me, My) friend borrowed (he, his) pen.	P	5. We picked (us, our) mother a bouquet of flowers.
O	3. Susan will listen to Pam and (I, me).	S	6. The comedians are Dad and (her, she).

 Classroom Practice 50

It is time to practice the skills you are learning. You will use the classroom practice on the next page to apply these skills.

JOURNAL WRITING 29

Write an entry in your journal. Use Reference 9 on page 12 for ideas.

ENRICHMENT:

 **Discovery Time**

(American) 1877-1963— Garrett A. Morgan's inventions made the lives of other people safer and more convenient. As a young man, he invented a zig-zag stitching attachment for sewing machines, which he used in his clothing manufacturing company. His most famous invention was the Morgan traffic signal, for which he obtained the patent in America, Great Britain, and Canada. In 1916, Morgan received national attention when he used his invention, the gas mask, to rescue several men trapped during an underground explosion. The Morgan gas mask was later used by fire departments across the country and by the U.S. Army during World War I.

Discovery Questions:
- **How many inventions can you name that have made the lives of people safer and more convenient?**
- **Sometimes, inventions are a result of a need or problem. Can you think of a need or a problem that an invention would help solve?**
- **What would this invention be called? How would it work?**

Are you interested in learning more about Garrett A. Morgan?

1. You may explore this topic further by using the resources listed below.
   Computer resources: Internet, encyclopedia software
   Library resources: encyclopedias, books, magazines, newspapers
   Home/community resources: books, interviews, newspapers, magazines

2. A Discovery Share Time is provided in Lesson 8 if you wish to share your investigation results. You may share orally, or you may prepare a written report. You will put your written report in a class booklet titled "Notable People in History." This booklet will be placed in the class library for everyone to enjoy.

Classroom Practice 50

Name:_____ Date:_____

GRAMMAR

▶ **Exercise 1:** Classify each sentence.

1. _____ In the evenings, my father is the manager at the theater in town.

2. _____ His speech was an informative message about the extinction of many species.

SKILLS

▶ **Exercise 2: For Part A**, underline each noun to be made possessive. Write **S** for singular or **P** for plural, the rule number, and the possessive form. **For Part B**, write the singular possessive and plural possessive of each noun.

RULE 1: boy's	RULE 2: boys'	RULE 3: men's
For a singular noun — add ('s)	For a plural noun that ends in s — add (')	For a plural noun that does not end in s — add ('s)

Part A	S-P	Rule	Possessive Form	Part B	Singular Poss	Plural Poss
1. mayor agenda				10. wife		
2. Russ dad				11. eagle		
3. donkeys ears				12. turkey		
4. Joneses toys				13. louse		
5. computer virus				14. radio		
6. women forum				15. child		
7. farmers crops				16. calf		
8. river current				17. cloud		
9. men clothes				18. church		

▶ **Exercise 3:** Identify the pronoun case by writing **S** for subjective or **O** for objective in the blank. Underline the correct pronoun in parentheses.

1. Save a place for Dan and (I, me).	5. Can you go with Bill and (I, me)?
2. The fishermen were Stan and (I, me).	6. (They, Them) are good scissors.
3. Mom made Jon and (I, me) a cake.	7. (We, Us) girls couldn't see the kite.
4. Dave and (he, him) mowed yards.	8. Buy a ticket from (we, us) girls.

EDITING

▶ **Exercise 4:** Punctuate the Kay and Robert story, "Pass the Salt." (Part 2 of 5) **Editing Guide: End Marks: 8 Capitals: 14 Commas: 4 Quotation Marks: 4 Single Quotes: 2 Apostrophes: 2 Homonyms: 2 Periods: 1**

kay eyed her brother angrily this was going to far her voice snapped as she said you are

really the pits who do you think you are mr big shot

im your brother im the one who has too pass the salt you are my sister you are the one who

has to say i love you robert

START LESSON 4

Lesson 4

You will

- study new vocabulary; make card 40; write own sentence using the vocabulary word.
- analyze new analogy; make card 40; write own analogy.
- recite new jingle (The Noun Job).
- classify Practice Sentences.
- identify noun jobs.
- do a Skill Builder to identify noun jobs.
- do Classroom Practice 51.
- read and discuss Discovery Time.
- do a homework assignment.
- do Home Connection activity.

LISTENING AND SPEAKING:
Vocabulary & Analogy Time

Learn It: Recite the new vocabulary and analogy words.

Reference 173	Vocabulary & Analogy Words

Word: pursue (pər sōō')
   Definition: to chase or seek
   Synonym: hunt   **Antonym:** flee
   Sentence: The dogs pursued the rabbit.

Analogy: lemon : sour :: ice : cold
Descriptive or characteristic relationship: Just as **lemons** can be described as **sour, ice** can be described as **cold**.

Vocabulary Card 40: Record the vocabulary information above and write your own sentence, using the new word.

Analogy Card 40: Record the analogy information and write your own analogy, using the same relationship as the analogy above.

Jingle Time

Recite It: Recite the new jingle.

♪ Jingle 25	The Noun Job Jingle

Nouns will give you a run for your money.
They do so many jobs
That it's not even funny.
A noun—person, place, thing, or idea—
is very appealing!
But it's the noun job *(noun job)*
That is so revealing!

To find the nouns in a sentence,
Go to their jobs *(go to their jobs)*
Nouns can do objective jobs *(objective jobs)*
They're the **IO** *(IO)*, **DO** *(DO)*, and **OP** jobs *(OP jobs)*.
And nouns can do subjective jobs *(subjective jobs)*.
They're the **SN** *(SN)* and **PrN** jobs *(PrN jobs)*.
Jobs. Jobs. Noun Jobs! Yeah!

Grammar Time

Apply It: These Practice Sentences are used to apply grammar concepts taught. Classify these sentences orally with your teacher.

Practice Sentences	Chapter 11: Lesson 4

1. _____ The sheriff's badge is a symbol of his authority in his county.
2. _____ That crooked road is a steep and dangerous passage through the mountains.
3. _____ The unusually colorful rug on the floor is a valued family heirloom.

 Skill Time

Learn It: NOUN JOBS

📖 **Reference 174** | **Noun Jobs**

Every word in a sentence has a job. A word's position and function in a sentence determine its job. Nouns are the only part of speech that can be used in different jobs and still be identified as a noun. If you can recognize noun jobs in a sentence, you will identify nouns more accurately.

In the sentences below, the word *football* is used in several noun-job positions and in one adjective position. You must always look at the position of a word instead of its meaning to determine if it is a noun. For example, *kitchen* is an adjective in Sentence 3, and *football* is an adjective in Sentence 6.

1. Nouns have many jobs in a sentence. These jobs include the following: **subject, object of the preposition, direct object, indirect object,** and **predicate noun.**

2. These jobs give nouns specific identification to show their function in a sentence. It is easier to find nouns in a sentence if you look at the noun-job positions.

3. The noun jobs can be divided into **subjective jobs** (subject noun and predicate noun) and **objective jobs** (object of the preposition, direct object, and indirect object). The possessive form of a noun functions as an adjective and is not considered a noun job.

The examples below demonstrate the importance of looking at noun jobs to help identify nouns.

1. **The football was kicked hard.** Look at the noun jobs: **SN, OP, DO, IO, PrN.** *Football is a noun that is used as a subject.*

2. **Scott saved his money for a football.** Look at the noun jobs: **SN, OP, DO, IO, PrN.** *Scott is a noun in the SN job position. Money is a noun in the DO position. Football is a noun in the OP position.*

3. **Tom threw the football through the kitchen window.** Look at the noun jobs: **SN, OP, DO, IO, PrN.** *Tom is a noun in the SN job position. Football is a noun in the DO position. Window is a noun in the OP position. Kitchen is an adjective. An adjective is not a noun job.*

4. **Jeffery threw Randy the football during practice.** Look at the noun jobs: **SN, OP, DO, IO, PrN.** *Jeffery is a noun in the SN job position. Randy is a noun in the IO position. Football is a noun in the DO position. Practice is a noun in the OP position.*

5. **His favorite gift was a football from his uncle.** Look at the noun jobs: **SN, OP, DO, IO, PrN.** *Gift is a noun in the SN job position. Football is a noun in the PrN position. Uncle is a noun in the OP position.*

6. **Sam and Joe went to the football game.** Look at the noun jobs: **SN, OP, DO, IO, PrN.** *Sam and Joe are nouns in the SN job position. Game is a noun in the OP position. Football is an adjective. An adjective is not a noun job.*

Learn It: **A SKILL BUILDER FOR A NOUN JOB CHECK**

The example below shows you how to identify nouns and their jobs in a Noun Job Check.

LISTENING AND SPEAKING:

FOR A noun JOB CHECK

Identify the nouns and their jobs in a Noun Job Check.

Sentence 1: **badge** - Subject Noun
symbol – Predicate Noun
authority - Object of the Preposition
county - Object of the Preposition

Sentence 2: **road** - Subject Noun
passage – Predicate Noun
mountains - Object of the Preposition

Sentence 3: **rug** - Subject Noun
floor - Object of the Preposition
heirloom – Predicate Noun

▷▷▷▷▷▷ Student Tip...

1. Finding a noun is easier if you know the noun job. The nouns below are just nouns until you label each noun with a special name that identifies its job.

noun	noun	noun	noun	noun
girls	girls	girls	girls	girls
SN	OP	DO	IO	PrN

SN
The **girls** were laughing.   I tiptoed behind the *OP* **girls**.   I surprised the *DO* **girls**.

IO *DO*
I gave the **girls** a big **scare**.   The *SN* **winners** were the *PrN* **girls**.

2. As you review each pattern, notice how the Shurley patterns relate to the traditional patterns.

	Pattern 1	OP	Pattern 2	Pattern 3	Pattern 4
Traditional	N V	N	N V N	N V N N	N LV N
Shurley	SN V	OP	SN V-t DO	SN V-t IO DO	SN LV PrN

✏ Classroom Practice 51

It is time to practice the skills you are learning. You will use the classroom practice on the next page to apply these skills.

ENRICHMENT:

Discovery Time

(German American) 1879-1955— Albert Einstein discovered the theory of relativity, $E=mc^2$, in 1905. He did not receive a Nobel Prize for his theory of relativity because the ideas he presented were still very controversial during his lifetime. However, in 1921, he received the Nobel Prize in physics for his work on the photoelectric effect. Einstein was a pacifist and left Germany for the United States following Hitler's rise to power. In the United States, Einstein taught mathematics at Princeton University and continued working on various scientific experiments.

Discovery Questions:
- **After researching Einstein, what did you find most interesting about him?**
- **What do you think Einstein was like?**

Are you interested in learning more about Albert Einstein?

1. You may explore this topic further by using the resources listed below.
   Computer resources: Internet, encyclopedia software
   Library resources: encyclopedias, books, magazines, newspapers
   Home/community resources: books, interviews, newspapers, magazines

2. A Discovery Share Time is provided in Lesson 8 if you wish to share your investigation results. You may share orally, or you may prepare a written report. You will put your written report in a class booklet titled "Notable People in History." This booklet will be placed in the class library for everyone to enjoy.

Classroom Practice 51

Name:_____ Date:_____

GRAMMAR

▶ **Exercise 1:** Classify each sentence.

1. _____ The flowerbed in my neighbor's yard is a beautiful arrangement of different blossoms.

2. _____ Life, liberty, and the pursuit of happiness are the foundations of our great nation.

SKILLS

▶ **Exercise 2: For Part A**, underline each noun to be made possessive. Write **S** for singular or **P** for plural, the rule number, and the possessive form. **For Part B**, write the singular possessive and plural possessive of each noun.

RULE 1: boy's	RULE 2: boys'	RULE 3: men's
For a singular noun — add ('s)	For a plural noun that ends in s — add (')	For a plural noun that does not end in s — add ('s)

Part A	S-P	Rule	Possessive Form	Part B	Singular Poss	Plural Poss
1. volcano steam				8. meteor		
2. parrots feet				9. child		
3. burglar wrists				10. loaf		
4. circle diameter				11. thief		
5. barbers chairs				12. turkey		
6. mice footprints				13. box		
7. Ross grandma				14. grass		

▶ **Exercise 3:** Identify the pronoun case by writing **S** for subjective or **O** for objective in the blank. Underline the correct pronoun in parentheses.

1. (We, Us) boys heard a loud noise.	5. For (they, them), I will buy a ticket.
2. Buy (he and I, him and me) a pizza.	6. (We, Us) voted for Joyce for president.
3. He took (we, us) girls to a game.	7. Joan's mom saw (I, me) at the mall.
4. Please loan (I, me) your keys.	8. My uncle's only child is (she, her).

EDITING

▶ **Exercise 4:** Punctuate the Kay and Robert story, "Pass the Salt." (Part 3 of 5) **Editing Guide: End Marks: 10 Capitals: 13   Commas: 6   Quotation Marks: 8   Apostrophes: 3   Misspelled Words: 1**

oh brother why do sisters have brothers i just dont understand you why are you making

such a big issue out of such a little thing as passing the salt kay fumed as she watched the fun

her brother was having then her anger faded and her eyes sparkled she stifled a gigle as

she said i cant say it i just cant

sure you can said robert merrily take a deep breath and start with the word i

Homework 9

Complete this homework assignment on notebook paper.

1. Number your paper 1–12. **For Part A**, write each noun to be made possessive. Write **S** for singular or **P** for plural, the rule number, and the possessive form. **For Part B**, write the singular possessive and plural possessive of each noun.

RULE 1: boy's	RULE 2: boys'	RULE 3: men's
For a singular noun — add ('s)	For a plural noun that ends in s — add (')	For a plural noun that does not end in s — add ('s)

Part A	S-P	Rule	Possessive Form	Part B	Singular Poss	Plural Poss
1. girl hairdo				7. knife		
2. Carlos sister				8. potato		
3. trains whistles				9. woman		
4. men boots				10. mice		
5. trees limbs				11. child		
6. truck tires				12. ax		

2. Number your paper 1–4. Identify the pronoun case by writing **S** for subjective case or **O** for objective case beside the number. Then, write the correct pronoun within the parentheses.

1. The dog bit (I, me) on the ankle.	3. Do you want (he and I, him and me) on your team?
2. The leader is obviously (he, him).	4. My dad helped (they, them) bale hay yesterday.

Home Connection

Family Activity for Vocabulary and Analogies

Divide into family teams. The first team will use vocabulary and analogy cards 33–36 to ask questions about the information on their cards. The second team will use vocabulary and analogy cards 37–40 to ask questions about the information on their cards.

Family Activity for Linking Verbs

Get three sheets of colored paper. You will need two sheets of one color and one sheet of a second color. Cut each page lengthwise into five long strips. Write the subject nouns and predicate nouns from the list below on the strips that are the same color. Write the linking verbs from the list on the other-colored strips.

Choose a subject noun, a linking verb, and a predicate noun that make sense together. Fasten the ends of the subject-noun strip together to form a paper link. Do the same with the predicate-noun strip. Now, loop the linking-verb strip to connect the subject-noun and predicate-noun strips. Fasten the ends of the linking-verb strip together. Your sentence chain should follow this order: subject noun, linking verb, and predicate noun.

Subject Nouns

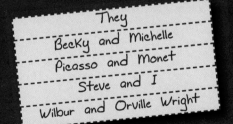

They
Becky and Michelle
Picasso and Monet
Steve and I
Wilbur and Orville Wright

Linking Verbs

are
are
were
are
were

Predicate Nouns

sisters
co-workers
artists
friends
inventors

START LESSON 5

Lesson 5

You will
- classify Practice Sentences.
- do Chapter Checkup 52.
- write in your journal.
- read and discuss Discovery Time.

JOURNAL WRITING 30

Write an entry in your journal. Use Reference 9 on page 12 for ideas.

LISTENING AND SPEAKING:

Apply It: Classify the Practice Sentences orally with your teacher.

Practice Sentences	Chapter 11: Lesson 5

1. _____ Beef exports are Argentina's most valuable export commodity.
2. _____ Without a doubt, Silas Marner was a miser.
3. _____ Comets are bright heavenly bodies with long, glowing tails.

Chapter Checkup 52

It is time for a checkup of the skills you have learned in this chapter. You will use the chapter checkup on the next page to evaluate your progress.

ENRICHMENT:

(American) 1880–1968— Helen Keller was 19 months old when she had a severe illness that left her blind and deaf. Keller's teacher and constant companion, Anne Sullivan, first taught her how to spell words with her hands. Keller learned to read five different languages in Braille. She graduated with honors from Radcliffe College. She helped found the American Foundation for the Blind and raised more money for the foundation than any other person. Her first book, *The Story of My Life*, was translated into 50 different languages.

Discovery Questions:
- **Keller was awarded the highest honor that an American civilian can receive. What was the award called?**
- **What do you think about Helen Keller?**
- **What traits helped Helen Keller accomplish so much during her life?**

(American) 1886–1956— Clarence Birdseye was a pioneer of the frozen food industry. He started out working for the government as a naturalist. Birdseye observed people in Labrador freezing their food in the winter. This inspired Birdseye to develop the process of "quick freezing" food to retain the taste and nutrients. Next, he created the concept of putting his frozen food in packages that could be sold directly to the consumers. Birdseye also introduced the refrigerated display case and created the single-unit bulb for display lighting. He designed heat lamps for keeping food warm and developed the freeze-drying process.

Discovery Questions:
- **How many foreign and U.S. patents were granted to Birdseye?**
- **What do you think of Birdseye's inventions?**
- **What would life be like without Birdseye's inventions?**
- **What inspires a person to invent something?**

Are you interested in learning more about Helen Keller or Clarence Birdseye?

1. You may explore these topics further by using the resources listed below.
   Computer resources: Internet, encyclopedia software
   Library resources: encyclopedias, books, magazines, newspapers
   Home/community resources: books, interviews, newspapers, magazines

2. A Discovery Share Time is provided in Lesson 8 if you wish to share your investigation results. You may share orally, or you may prepare a written report. You will put your written report in a class booklet titled "Notable People in History." This booklet will be placed in the class library for everyone to enjoy.

Chapter 11 Checkup 52

Name:_____ Date:_____

GRAMMAR

▶ **Exercise 1:** Classify each sentence.

1. _____ Today is the first anniversary of our company's grand opening.

2. _____ During the war, my sister was the first female pilot in the military.

3. _____ The mink is a slender, aggressive, water-loving member of the weasel family.

SKILLS

▶ **Exercise 2: For Part A**, underline each noun to be made possessive. Write **S** for singular or **P** for plural, the rule number, and the possessive form. **For Part B**, write the singular possessive and plural possessive of each noun.

RULE 1: boy's	RULE 2: boys'	RULE 3: men's
For a singular noun — add ('s)	For a plural noun that ends in s — add (')	For a plural noun that does not end in s — add ('s)

Part A	S-P	Rule	Possessive Form	Part B	Singular Poss	Plural Poss
1. rabbit ears				9. shelf		
2. women hats				10. ox		
3. serpent venom				11. tomato		
4. widows sons				12. wolf		
5. Wes mentor				13. comb		
6. donkeys tails				14. child		
7. firemen boots				15. parent		
8. soldiers rifles				16. mouse		

▶ **Exercise 3:** Identify the pronoun case by writing **S** for subjective or **O** for objective in the blank. Underline the correct pronoun in parentheses.

1. I talked to (he, him) earlier today.	5. (He, Him) looked at a new truck today.
2. Jo is going with (she, her) to the dance.	6. The attorney gave advice to (they, them).
3. Yes, this is (she, her).	7. (We, Us) made oatmeal cookies yesterday.
4. Most of the class voted for (he, him).	8. Aunt Sue bought (I, me) a new pair of shoes.

EDITING

▶ **Exercise 4:** Punctuate the Kay and Robert story, "Pass the Salt." (Part 4 of 5) **Editing Guide: End Marks: 5 Capitals: 10 Commas: 5 Quotation Marks: 4 Apostrophes: 1 Homonyms: 1 Periods: 1 Misspelled Words: 1**

kay tossed her head and said airily why should i this hole conversation has goten out

of hand ill just get the salt myself kay walked to the end of the table picked up the salt and

turned to her brother i love you mr big shot she said sweetly

START LESSON 6

Lesson 6

You will

- hand in WA 25.
- read and discuss the parts of a nonfiction book and how to find a nonfiction book in the library.
- read and discuss how to write a nonfiction book review.
- write a nonfiction book review for WA 28.

 Literature Time

Hand It In: WRITING ASSIGNMENT 25

Get the book review for your fiction book ready to hand in when your teacher asks for it. Your review will be given back to you for sharing in Chapter 12.

Learn It: PARTS OF A NONFICTION BOOK

> **Reference 175**   **Parts of a Nonfiction Book**
>
> A **nonfiction book** can be divided into three parts: the front, the body, and the back. Any time you use a nonfiction book to help you with an assignment, you must understand how to use that book efficiently. Knowing the parts of a book will help you make full use of the special features that are frequently found in nonfiction books.
>
> **THE FRONT OF A BOOK**
> **1. Title Page**
> This page has the full title of the book, the author's name, the illustrator's name, the name of the publishing company, and the city where the book was published.
> **2. Copyright Page**
> This page is right after the title page and tells the year in which the book was published and who owns the copyright. If the book has an ISBN (International Standard Book Number), it is listed here.
> **3. Preface** (also called **introduction**)
> If a book has this page, it will come before the table of contents and will usually tell you briefly why the book was written and what it is about.
> **4. Table of Contents**
> This section lists the major divisions of the book by units or chapters and tells their beginning page numbers.
>
> **THE BODY OF A BOOK**
> **5. Body**
> This is the main section, or text, of the book.
>
> **THE BACK OF A BOOK**
> **6. Appendix**
> This section includes extra informative material such as maps, charts, tables, diagrams, and letters. It is always wise to find out what is in the appendix, since it may contain supplementary material that you could otherwise find only by going to the library.
> **7. Glossary**
> This section is like a dictionary and gives the meanings of some of the important words in the book.
> **8. Bibliography**
> This section includes a list of sources used by the author. It could serve as a guide for further reading on a topic.
> **9. Index**
> This will probably be your most useful section. The purpose of the index is to help you quickly locate information about the topics in the book. It contains an alphabetical list of specific topics and tells the page on which that information can be found. It is similar to the table of contents, but it is much more detailed.

Learn It: HOW TO FIND NONFICTION BOOKS IN THE LIBRARY

Reference 176   How to Find Nonfiction Books in the Library

To find out if a library has a certain nonfiction book, look in the card catalog for the title card of that book. If you don't know the title but do know the author, look for the author card. If you don't know the title or the author, look under the subject of the book. Also, look under the subject if you are interested in finding several books about your topic.

After you find the card in the card catalog, you must find the book on the library shelves. Nonfiction books are arranged on the shelves in **numerical order** according to a **call number**. A *call number* is the number on the spine of all nonfiction books.

The **Dewey Decimal System** is the means of identifying nonfiction books by number. All nonfiction books are given a *call number*, which will identify where they are located on the shelf. All three catalog cards for a book will have the same call number in the top left corner.

Be sure to write the call number down on paper before you look for the book. When you go to the library shelf, look at the call numbers printed on the spines of the books until you find the same number you copied from the catalog card.

Note: Individual biographies and autobiographies are arranged alphabetically on a separate shelf by the last name of the person about whom they are written.

Learn It: WRITING A BOOK REVIEW FOR A NONFICTION BOOK

Reference 177   Writing a Book Review for a Nonfiction Book

A book review gives you an opportunity to tell what a book is about and what you think about the book. The following guidelines will help you know what to include in a book review for a nonfiction book.

BOOK REVIEW FOR A NONFICTION BOOK

1. List the title and author.
2. Tell the type of book: **Nonfiction**.
3. Write an introductory paragraph to tell what the book is about (the topic), and list one, two, or three major facts that you will discuss. In the body of the review, write about each fact you have listed in the introductory paragraph and provide supporting details.
4. In the last paragraph, give your opinion of the book. In this paragraph, tell why you liked or disliked the book. The example below shows you one way to write a nonfiction book review.

<u>The Indianapolis 500: Speedway to Fame</u>
by Larry Bortstein
Nonfiction Book

America's most famous auto race, the Indianapolis 500, has two very important parts. The first part is the trial run, and the second part is the official race.

The trial run begins several weeks before the actual race day. Each time the car is taken onto the track for a test run, the driver is alert for any signs of trouble. At the end of each day, when the car returns to "Gasoline Alley," the crew makes adjustments and replaces parts by completely overhauling the engine.

On the day of the official race, the driver arrives in his protective gear, and the crew checks the car one last time. Then, the cars line up for the start of the race. Once the race has begun, each driver's focus is the finish line. The prize money, the thrill of the sport, and the glory that comes with winning America's most famous auto race are the key factors motivating the drivers and crews in every Indianapolis 500 race.

This book is fascinating, especially if you like racing. Even if racing isn't your favorite sport, you will find this book quite enjoyable.

Continued on next page. >>>

Reference 177 continued from previous page.

BOOK REVIEW FOR AN AUTOBIOGRAPHY OR BIOGRAPHY

1. List the title and author.
2. Tell the type of book: **Autobiography**.
3. Write an introductory paragraph to tell who the book is about, and list one, two, or three major facts or events that you will present. In the body of the review, write about each fact or event you have listed in the introductory paragraph and provide supporting details.
4. In the last paragraph, give your opinion of the book. In this paragraph, tell why you liked or disliked the book. The example below shows you one way to write an autobiographical book review.

<u>The Story of My Life</u>
by Helen Keller
Autobiography

In this amazing autobiography, Helen Keller tells how she overcame her handicaps and emerged from the darkness of being deaf, blind, and mute. With the help of her teacher, Anne Sullivan, Helen learned to communicate by associating objects with finger signals, by learning to read, and by learning to speak.

Helen Keller lost her sight and hearing after a high fever when she was only nineteen months old. She was forced to live in a dark and silent world with crude signs and gestures as her only means of communication.

Her life changed abruptly with the arrival of her teacher, Anne Sullivan. Anne Sullivan first taught Helen how to associate objects with words spelled out by finger signals on her palm. This technique opened a new world of communication to Helen. Next, Helen learned to read. As soon as Helen could spell, Anne gave her slips of cardboard on which were printed words in raised letters. A few years later, she learned Braille. Finally, Helen started the slow and very challenging process of learning to speak. She would feel the position of her teacher's tongue and lips and, then, imitate every motion. Helen's first spoken words were "It is warm."

I found this autobiography to be one of the best that I have read. The devotion, courage, and determination of both Helen Keller and Anne Sullivan were inspiring. I would recommend this book to anyone looking for a story that goes beyond uplifting.

Writing Time

Write It: WRITING ASSIGNMENT 28

Even though this writing assignment for a book review of a nonfiction book is given today, it is not due until Lesson 4 of Chapter 12.

Writing Assignment 28 : Nonfiction Book-Review

Purpose: To provide information about events or persons in a book and to express an opinion

Type of Writing: Biography/autobiography/nonfiction book review

Audience: Classmates, family, or friends

Writing Topics: Choose a biography/autobiography/nonfiction book.

Special Instructions:

1. Choose a biography/autobiography/nonfiction book about which to write a book review.

2. Use References 175–177 on pages 342–344 to guide you in writing a book review of a biography/autobiography/nonfiction book of your choice.

3. Write a rough draft; then, revise and edit it. Next, write a final paper for your book review during a study time or outside of class.

4. Finish Book Review 28 by Lesson 4 of Chapter 12 and give it to your teacher.

5. Keep your book review in the Final Paper folder if you finish early.

>>>>>>>>>>>>>>>>>>>>>>> Student Tip...

For additional information and activities about nonfiction books, the table of contents, and the index, refer to Study Skills in the Resource Tools Section on pages 532 –536.

START LESSON 7

Lesson 7

You will

- conference with teacher about WA 27.
- read nonfiction book during conferences.

Reading Time

Read It: **NONFICTION BOOK**

Use this reading time to read the fiction book you have selected for a book review. When you finish your book, you may begin working on your book review assignment, Writing Assignment 28.

Conference Time

Discuss It: **TEACHER-STUDENT CONFERENCES FOR WRITING ASSIGNMENT 27**

Meet with your teacher to discuss Writing Assignment 27.
After the conference, place this group of papers in your Publishing folder.

Publishing Time

Publish It: WRITING ASSIGNMENT 27

Choose a publishing form and publish Writing Assignment 27. After rewriting your paper for publication, give the stapled papers (evaluation guide, graded final paper, rough draft, and story elements outline) to your teacher to be placed in your Writing Portfolio.

START LESSON 8

Lesson 8

You will
- publish WA 27.
- participate in Discovery Share Time.
- do Across the Curriculum activity.

Reference 66	Publishing Checklist for Step 6 in the Writing Process

The sixth step in the writing process is called publishing. Publishing is sharing your writing with others. With so many forms of publishing available, finding a match for every project and personality is easy.

At times, a written work is best read aloud. Other times, the biggest impact is made when a written work is read silently. You can also use media sources to enhance any publication.

SPECIAL INSTRUCTIONS FOR PUBLISHING:

- Rewrite the graded paper in ink or type it on a computer, correcting any marked errors. *(Do not display or publish papers that have marked errors or grades on them.)*
- Give your teacher the set of stapled papers to place in your Writing Portfolio. *(Stapled papers: evaluation guide, graded final paper, rough draft, and prewriting map.)*
- Select a publishing form from the list below and publish your rewritten paper.
    1. Have classmates, family members, neighbors, or others read your writing at school or home.
    2. Share your writing with others during a Share Time. *(Refer to Reference 67 on page 99 for sharing guidelines.)*
    3. Display your writing on a bulletin board or wall.
    4. Put your writing in the classroom library or in the school library for checkout.
    5. Send your writing as a letter or an e-mail to a friend or relative.
    6. Frame your writing by gluing it on colored construction paper and decorating it.
    7. Make a book of your writing for your classroom, your family, or others.
    8. Illustrate your writing and give it to others to read.
    9. Dramatize your writing in the form of a play, puppet show, or radio broadcast.
    10. Send your writing to be placed in a waiting room (doctor, veterinarian, dentist, etc.), senior-citizen center, or a nursing home.
    11. Send your writing to a school newspaper, local newspaper, or a magazine for publication.
    12. Make a videotape, cassette tape, or slide presentation of your writing.
    13. Choose another publishing form that is not listed.

LISTENING AND SPEAKING:

Discovery Share Time

If you have chosen to investigate a historical figure introduced in this chapter, you now have the opportunity to share your results in one of the following ways:

1. You may relate your information orally.

2. You may read a written report.

3. You may place your report in the booklet without reading it aloud.

After share time, all written reports should be turned in to be placed in the class booklet titled "Notable People in History." You are encouraged to check out this class booklet so you can enjoy the reports again.

Across the Curriculum

Language Development Connection: Divide into small groups. Work together with members of the group to write all of the be verbs on index cards: *am, is, are, was, were, be, being,* and *been*. Put the cards in a basket. Each person in the group will draw a card from the basket and use the verb correctly in a sentence. A main verb and/or additional auxiliary verbs must be used with be, being, and been. The verbs am, is, are, was, and were can be used alone or with other helping verbs. Discuss how action verbs and linking verbs influence writing. What type of verb do you use most often in your writing? Why?

Social Studies Connection: Write a narrative based on a current event. Read your narrative in a cooperative-learning group. You might also want to illustrate your story.

LISTENING AND SPEAKING:
Jingle Time

START LESSON 9

Lesson 9
You will
- practice Jingles 24-25.
- do Classroom Practice 53.
- write an independent narrative without dialogue (WA 29).

Recite It: Practice Jingles 24–25 in the Jingle Section on pages 512–513.

GRAMMAR & WRITING CONNECTION:
Practice and Revised Sentences

Apply It: **BUILDING AND EXPANDING SENTENCES**

Reference 178	A Guide for Using a Pattern 4 Core (Sn LV Prn) to Build & Expand Sentences

1. **SN or SP (subject)** Think of a noun or pronoun that you want to use as the *subject*. Write the noun or pronoun you have chosen as the *subject* of your sentence.
2. **LV (linking verb)** A *linking verb* links the subject with a word in the predicate. You may choose a linking verb from this list: *am, is, are, was, were, be, being, been, appear, become, feel, grow, look, remain, seem, smell, sound, stay,* and *taste*. First, choose a verb for your sentence. Then, wait until you have chosen a predicate noun to verify that it is a linking verb. If the verb is verified as linking, keep it as the verb of your Pattern 4 core.
3. **PrN (predicate noun)** The *predicate noun* is a noun or pronoun after the verb that renames and means the same thing as the subject. To help you think of a *predicate noun*, ask the question WHAT or WHO after the verb. Check to make sure it renames the subject of the sentence. Write the predicate noun you have chosen in the predicate part of your sentence.

Classroom Practice 53
It is time to practice the skills you are learning. You will use the classroom practice on the next page to apply these skills.

Student Tip...

Use your vocabulary words in your Practice and Revised Sentences. Use a thesaurus, synonym-antonym book, or a dictionary to help you develop your writing vocabulary.

Writing Time

Write It: **WRITING ASSIGNMENT 29**

As you write a rough draft for your independent writing assignment, you will do two of the six steps in the writing process: prewriting (the story elements outline) and rough draft.

Writing Assignment 29

Purpose: To tell a story
Type of Writing: Narrative
Audience: Classmates, family, or friends
Writing Topics: A favorite family story
Traveling days/Camping trip
The longest day/night
(Brainstorm for other ideas, individually or in groups.)

Special Instructions:
1. Follow the Prewriting and Rough Draft Checklists in References 44 and 46 on pages 57, 61.
2. Make a story elements outline instead of a prewriting map. See Reference 166 on page 318.
3. Use Reference 166 to help you write your narrative.
4. Write your narrative without dialogue.
5. Write in first or third person. See Reference 70, page 104.
(First-person pronouns: *I, me, my, mine, we, us, our,* and *ours.*)
(Third-person pronouns: *he, his, him, she, her, hers, it, its, they, their, theirs,* and *them.*)
Note: Reference 54 on page 71 gives the steps in the writing process and the location of all the writing checklists.

Student Note:

Some of your writing pieces will be selected for revision and editing later in the school year.

SHURLEY ENGLISH

Classroom Practice 53

Name: _____ Date: _____

INDEPENDENT PRACTICE & REVISED SENTENCES

1. Write a Practice Sentence according to the labels you choose.
Use **SN/SP LV PrN** as your main labels. You may use the other labels in any order and as many times as you wish in order to make a Practice Sentence.
Chapter 11 labels for a Practice Sentence: **SN/SP, LV, PrN**, Adj, Adv, A, P, OP, PPA, C, HV, I, PNA

2. Write a Revised Sentence. Use the following revision strategies: *synonym (syn), antonym (ant), word change (wc), added word (add), deleted word (delete),* or *no change (nc)*. Under each word, write the abbreviation of the revision strategy you use.

Labels:

Practice:

Revised:

Strategies:

Labels:

Practice:

Revised:

Strategies:

Labels:

Practice:

Revised:

Strategies:

LISTENING AND SPEAKING:

Jingle Time

Recite It: Practice Jingle 12 in the Jingle Section on page 509.

>>>>> **Student Tip...**

> Reviewing the transition words will help you apply them in your writing.

Writing Time

Learn It: WRITING A COMPARISON-CONTRAST ESSAY

Lesson 10

You will
- practice Jingle 12.
- read and discuss a comparison/contrast essay.
- plan and write rough draft for comparison/contrast essay (WA 30).

Reference 179   Writing a Comparison-Contrast Essay

When you **compare** subjects, you tell how they are alike.

When you **contrast** subjects, you tell how they are different.

First, you must choose two subjects that can be easily compared and contrasted. Next, you should make a pre-writing map. For this type of writing, make a Venn diagram by drawing two large overlapping circles. Show how the subjects are alike and how they are different by writing the differences in the outer circles and the similarities in the inner circle. Make sure the differences are balanced. This means that for every fact you list about the first subject, you must list a contrasting fact for the second subject. *(See the Venn diagram.)* Brainstorm for details to compare and contrast. Ideas could include the following: size, shape, color, texture, behavior, purpose, location, degree of importance, unusual facts, accomplishments, etc.

The transitional words and phrases that are used to **compare** subjects include the following:
    also, and, another, as, besides, furthermore, in addition, like, likewise, same, similarly, too, which, etc.

The transitional words and phrases that are used to **contrast** subjects include the following:
    although, but, different, even though, however, in contrast, in other ways, on the other hand, otherwise, still, while, yet, etc.

A comparison-contrast essay has four parts.

1. Write an **introduction**. The introduction should name the subjects you will compare and contrast. Keep the interest high by asking a question, by stating an interesting or unusual fact, or by citing an incident.

2. Write a **paragraph of comparison** that tells how the two subjects are similar. Use the similarities listed in the inner section of the Venn diagram to help you write the sentences for this paragraph.

3. Write a **paragraph of contrast** that tells how the two subjects are different. Use the differences listed in the outer sections of the Venn diagram to help you write the sentences for this paragraph.

4. Write a **conclusion**. The conclusion should include a summary of your ideas. It can also include what you think about the likeness and differences and/or a final comment that ties your ideas together and draws the writing to a close. Use the following words to help you write a conclusion: *all in all, as a result, finally, in conclusion, in summary, last, therefore, to sum it up.*

Continued on next page. >>>

Reference 179 continued from previous page.

Example of a Venn Diagram

Unique to Football

played outdoors
oval ball
11 players on the field
heavy contact
grassy field
slow-paced

Similarities of Both

team sports
rectangular playing area
ball
2 teams
offense and defense
anyone can play
spectator support

Unique to Basketball

played indoors
round ball
5 players on the court
light to medium contact
wooden court
fast-paced

I love basketball, and my brother loves football. We eat, drink, sleep, and breathe our sports. One day, arguing, as usual, over whose sport was the best, our mom became the referee. She told us to list what each sport had in common and what was different about each one. As we compared our lists, my brother and I looked at each other in surprise. We could not believe our sports had so much in common.

In fact, football and basketball are alike in many ways. The most obvious similarities are the rectangular playing area, a ball, and two teams. Both sports are team sports, and winning depends on every member of the team working together as a unit. Both sports have an offense to score points and a defense to keep the other team from scoring. In both sports, the team with the most points at the end of a certain time period wins the game. Both sports can be played casually in neighborhoods and in civic groups, or, more seriously, in schools, colleges, and professional organizations. Finally, both sports have cheerleaders and widespread fan support.

On the other hand, football and basketball are very different sports. Football is usually played outdoors on a grassy field with an oval-shaped ball. Basketball, however, is usually played indoors on a wooden court with a round ball. Football has eleven players on the field for each team, but basketball has only five players on the court for each team. Football is a heavy-contact sport in which players wear special equipment to protect themselves from injury. In contrast, basketball is a light-contact sport because excessive contact results in a foul. Also, basketball is a faster-paced game than football because the rules allow the ball to change from one team to the other team more frequently.

All in all, my brother and I both gained a new respect for each other's favorite sport. We had never paid attention to the finer points of the two sports. We also gained a new respect for our mom. It turned out that she was a pretty smart referee after all.

Write It: **WRITING ASSIGNMENT 30**

As you write a rough draft for your independent writing assignment, you will do two of the six steps in the writing process: prewriting (Venn diagram) and rough draft.

Writing Assignment 30

Purpose: To show how subjects are alike and how they are different

Type of Writing: Comparison-contrast

Audience: Family, friends, or school librarian

Writing Topics: Two eating places
School library and city/county library
Hurricanes and tornadoes
Bus and subway
(Brainstorm for other ideas, individually or in groups.)

Special Instructions:

1. Follow the Prewriting and Rough Draft Checklists in References 44 and 46 on pages 57, 61.

2. Make a Venn diagram instead of a prewriting map. Use Reference 179 on page 351 to help you write your comparison-contrast essay.

3. Use standard, time-order, or transition writing form. See Reference 69 page 103.

4. Write in first or third person. See Reference 70 on page 104.
(First-person pronouns: *I, me, my, mine, we, us, our,* and *ours.*)
(Third-person pronouns: *he, his, him, she, her, hers, it, its, they, their, theirs,* and *them.*)

Note: Reference 54 on page 71 gives the steps in the writing process and the location of all the writing checklists.

START LESSON 11

Writing Time

Lesson 11

You will

• revise, edit, and write a final paper for WA 30.

Apply It: **REVISE, EDIT, AND WRITE A FINAL PAPER**

Following the schedule below, you will revise and edit Writing Assignment 30. Then, you will write a final paper. Use the Chapter 11 Writing Evaluation Guide on the next page to check your final paper one last time.

Reference 52 | **Revising & Editing Schedule and Writing a Final Paper**

SPECIAL INSTRUCTIONS FOR REVISING AND EDITING (Steps 3-4 in the writing process):

• Use the Revising and Editing Checklists in References 48 and 50 as you revise and edit your rough draft.

• Follow the revising and editing schedule below as directed by your teacher.

1. **Individual.** First, read your rough draft to yourself. Use the Revising Checklist in Reference 48 on page 64. Go through your paper, checking each item on the list and making revisions to your rough draft. Then, use the Editing Checklist in Reference 50 on pages 66. Go through your paper again, checking each item on the list and editing your rough draft.

2. **Partner.** Next, get with your editing partner. Work together on each partner's rough draft, one paper at a time. Read each rough draft aloud and revise and edit it together, using the Revising and Editing Checklists. (The author of the paper should be the one to make the corrections on his own paper.)

3. **Group.** Finally, read the rough draft to a revision group for feedback. Each student should read his paper while the others listen and offer possible revising and editing suggestions. (The author will determine whether to make corrections from the revision group's suggestions.)

SPECIAL INSTRUCTIONS FOR FINAL PAPER (Step 5 in the writing process):

• Write your final paper, using the Final Paper Checklist in Reference 53 on page 70.

• Staple your writing papers in this order: the final paper on top, the rough draft in the middle, and the prewriting map on the bottom. Place the stapled papers in the Final Paper folder.

>>>>>>>>>>>>> **Student Tip...**

1. Be tactful and helpful in your comments during revising and editing time. The purpose of any suggestion should be to improve the writer's rough draft.

2. As you make your final corrections, you have the choice of accepting or rejecting any suggestions made by your partners or your revision group.

3. Study Vocabulary Words and Analogies 37–40 for the chapter test in the next lesson.

4. If you need to improve your handwriting, refer to the Resource Tools Section on pages 529–530 for information on writing legibly.

Chapter 11 Writing Evaluation Guide

Name:_____ Date:_____

ROUGH DRAFT CHECK

_____ 1. Did you write your rough draft in pencil?

_____ 2. Did you write the correct headings on the first seven lines of your paper?

_____ 3. Did you use extra wide margins and skip every other line?

_____ 4. Did you write a title at the end of your rough draft?

_____ 5. Did you place your edited rough draft in your Rough Draft folder?

REVISING CHECK

_____ 6. Did you identify the purpose, type of writing, and audience?

_____ 7. Did you check for a topic, topic sentence, and sentences supporting the topic?

_____ 8. Did you check sentences for the right order, and did you combine, rearrange, or delete sentences when necessary?

_____ 9. Did you check for a variety of simple, compound, and complex sentences?

_____ 10. Did you check for any left out, repeated, or unnecessary words?

_____ 11. Did you check for the best choice of words by replacing or deleting unclear words?

_____ 12. Did you check the content for interest and creativity?

_____ 13. Did you check the voice to make sure the writing says what you want it to say?

EDITING CHECK

_____ 14. Did you indent each paragraph?

_____ 15. Did you put an end mark at the end of every sentence?

_____ 16. Did you capitalize the first word of every sentence?

_____ 17. Did you check for all other capitalization mistakes?

_____ 18. Did you check for all punctuation mistakes?
(commas, periods, apostrophes, quotation marks, underlining)

_____ 19. Did you check for misspelled words and for incorrect homonym choices?

_____ 20. Did you check for incorrect spellings of plural and possessive forms?

_____ 21. Did you check for correct construction and punctuation of your sentences?

_____ 22. Did you check for usage mistakes? *(subject/verb agreement, a/an choices, contractions, verb tenses, pronoun/antecedent agreement, pronoun cases, degrees of adjectives, double negatives, etc.)*

_____ 23. Did you put your revised and edited paper in the Rough Draft folder?

FINAL PAPER CHECK

_____ 24. Did you write the final paper in pencil?

_____ 25. Did you center the title on the top line and center your name under the title?

_____ 26. Did you skip a line before starting the writing assignment?

_____ 27. Did you single-space, use wide margins, and write the final paper neatly?

_____ 28. Did you staple your papers in this order: final paper on top, rough draft in the middle, and prewriting map on the bottom? Did you put them in the Final Paper folder?

START LESSON 12

Lesson 12

You will

- hand in WA 30 for grading.
- respond to oral review questions.
- take Chapter 11 Test.

CHAPTER TEST

It is time to evaluate your knowledge of the skills you have learned in this chapter. Your teacher will give you the Chapter 11 Test to help you assess your progress.

Writing Time

Hand It In: **WRITING ASSIGNMENT 30**

Get your stapled papers for Writing Assignment 30 from your Final Paper folder. Check to make sure they are in the correct order: the final paper on top, the rough draft in the middle, and the prewriting map on the bottom. Hand them in to your teacher.

LISTENING AND SPEAKING:
Oral Review Questions

Discuss It:

1. What word in the predicate means the same thing as the subject?
2. What is another name for a predicate noun?
3. What type of verb is used with a predicate noun?
4. What are the core parts of a Pattern 4 sentence?
5. What are the core parts of a Pattern 3 sentence?
6. What are the core parts of a Pattern 2 sentence?
7. What are the core parts of a Pattern 1 sentence?
8. What are the subjective-case pronouns?
9. How are subjective pronouns used?
10. What are the objective-case pronouns?
11. How are objective pronouns used?
12. What are the possessive-case pronouns?
13. How are possessive pronouns used?
14. What type of writing is used when your purpose is to show similarities and differences?
15. What type of writing is used when your purpose is to tell a story?
16. What type of writing is used when your purpose is to paint a picture with words?
17. What type of writing is used when your purpose is to express an opinion and to convince the reader that this opinion is correct?
18. What type of writing is used when your purpose is to inform, to give facts, to give directions, to explain, or to define something?

>>>>>>>>>>>>>>>>>>>>>>>>>>>> **Student Tip...**

For information about test-taking strategies, refer to the Resource Tools Section on page 528.

English Made Easy

Student Note: Beginning with this chapter, you will no longer have Vocabulary and Analogy Time. You will work word analogies independently during practice and test times. This will develop your ability to analyze word relationships on your own.

LISTENING AND SPEAKING:

Lesson 1

You will
- identify Mixed Patterns 1–4.
- classify Introductory Sentences.
- do a Skill Builder.
- identify pronoun and antecedent agreement.
- do Classroom Practice 54.
- write in your journal.
- read and discuss Discovery Time.

Apply It: These Introductory Sentences are used to apply the new grammar concepts taught below. Classify these sentences orally with your teacher.

Introductory Sentences	Chapter 12: Lesson 1

1. _____ Mow the yard after school tomorrow.
2. _____ That song was the opening number for our band concert on Friday.
3. _____ Over the holidays, Sidney gave them a wild ride in his new convertible.
4. _____ Her nimble fingers stitched on the heirloom quilt for many hours.

Learn It: MIXED GRAMMAR PATTERNS 1–4

The sentences classified in this chapter will be Patterns 1–4. They are called **Mixed Patterns** because there are four different patterns from which to choose. Be alert to the parts of speech and where they are located in each sentence. Use the sentence cores to help determine the pattern of the sentences.

Using the sentences just classified, do a Skill Builder orally with your teacher.

1. **Identify the nouns in a Noun Check.**
2. **Identify the nouns as singular or plural.**
3. **Identify the nouns as common or proper.**
4. **Identify the complete subject and the complete predicate.**
5. **Identify the simple subject and the simple predicate.**
6. **Do a Vocabulary Check.**
7. **Do a Verb Chant.**

SHURLEY ENGLISH

Learn It: PERSONAL PRONOUNS AND THEIR ANTECEDENTS

Reference 180 — Personal Pronouns and Their Antecedents

The most common pronouns are known as personal pronouns. A personal pronoun refers to the one speaking (first person), the one spoken to (second person), or the one spoken about (third person).

Any time a personal pronoun is used in a sentence, it refers to a noun. The noun to which a pronoun refers is called the **antecedent** of that pronoun. The antecedent can come before a pronoun or even in a preceding sentence.

　　　antecedent　pronoun　　　　　　　antecedent　pronoun　pronoun
　1. The **boy** loved **his** new computer.　2. The **boy** smiled. **He** loved **his** new computer.

Since antecedents determine the pronouns used, it is important for the pronoun to agree with the antecedent in number (singular/plural) and gender (male/female). See the two rules below for number and gender.

1. Number: Decide if the antecedent is singular or plural; choose the pronoun that agrees in number.

If the antecedent is singular, the pronoun must be singular. (For the antecedent **man**, use **he, him, his**.)

If the antecedent is plural, the pronoun must be plural. (For the antecedent **men**, use **they, them, their**.)

2. Gender: Decide if the antecedent is male or female; choose the pronoun that agrees in gender.

If the antecedent is masculine, the pronoun must be of masculine gender. (antecedent **boy**—pronoun **he**)

If the antecedent is feminine, the pronoun must be of feminine gender. (antecedent **girl**—pronoun **she**)

If the gender of the antecedent is not specified, the general rule is to use the masculine form of the pronoun. (For the antecedent **musician, pilot, doctor, nurse**, etc., use the pronouns **he, him, his**, etc.)

If the antecedent is not a person and is neither masculine nor feminine, the pronoun must be of neuter gender. (antecedent **book**—pronoun **if**) The plural pronouns *they* and *them* also show neuter gender. (The **logs** were very dry. **They** quickly burned in the fireplace.)

Examples of Pronoun-Antecedent Agreement

　　　　antecedent　　pronoun　　　　　　antecedent　　pronoun　　pronoun
Incorrect: 1a. The **boy** loved **their** new computer.　2a. The **boy** smiled. **She** loved **her** new computer.

　　　　antecedent　　pronoun　　　　　　antecedent　　pronoun　pronoun
Correct: 1b. The **boy** loved **his** new computer.　2b. The **boy** smiled. **He** loved **his** new computer.

PRACTICE FOR PRONOUN-ANTECEDENT AGREEMENT

Complete the table. Then, underline the correct pronoun in the parentheses that agrees with its antecedent.

Pronoun-Antecedent Agreement	Antecedent	S or P	Pronoun S or P
1. The puppies barked at (its, <u>their</u>) mother.	puppies	P	P
2. The chairman was in (<u>his</u>, their) meeting.	chairman	S	S
3. Every student needs (<u>his</u>, their) books today.	student	S	S

English Made Easy

Classroom Practice 54

It is time to practice the skills you are learning. You will use the classroom practice on the next page to apply these skills.

ENRICHMENT:

JOURNAL WRITING 31

Write an entry in your journal. Use Reference 9 on page 12 for ideas.

(Scottish) 1888-1946—John Logie Baird invented television, radar, and fiber optics. He demonstrated the televising of moving objects in 1926. In 1938, he demonstrated color television and completed research on stereoscopic (three dimensional) television in 1946. Before he died, he was drafting plans for high-resolution television. World technology would not catch up with him until 1990, when the Japanese introduced high-resolution TV.

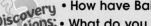

Discovery Questions:
- How have Baird's inventions influenced today's technology?
- What do you think about John Baird?
- What do you think it is like to be an inventor?

Are you interested in learning more about John Baird?

1. You may explore this topic further by using the resources listed below.
   Computer resources: Internet, encyclopedia software
   Library resources: encyclopedias, books, magazines, newspapers
   Home/community resources: books, interviews, newspapers, magazines

2. A Discovery Share Time is provided in Lesson 7 if you wish to share your investigation results. You may share orally, or you may prepare a written report. You will put your written report in a class booklet titled "Notable People in History." This booklet will be placed in the class library for everyone to enjoy.

Classroom Practice 54

Name:_____ Date:_____

GRAMMAR

▶ **Exercise 1:** Classify each sentence.

1. _____ In December, my little brother was an angel in the play at school.

2. _____ Our parents gave my sister an expensive present for her college graduation.

3. _____ Yikes! Those gophers dug a maze of tunnels in Mr. Hoodwink's big hayfield!

4. _____ Give me the key to your car.

SKILLS

▶ **Exercise 2:** Complete the table. Then, underline the pronoun in parentheses that agrees with its antecedent.

Pronoun-Antecedent Agreement	Antecedent	S or P	Pronoun S or P
1. The winner of the scholarship is (I, me).			
2. The kittens played with (his, their) toys.			
3. The customer signed (his, their) name in ink.			
4. Cindy filled (her, their) grocery basket full.			
5. The calf jumped out of (its, their) stall.			
6. The janitor misplaced (his, their) mop.			
7. The men were in (his, their) meeting.			
8. She made dresses and sold (it, them).			

▶ **Exercise 3:** Write the letter of the word that best completes the analogy.

dentist : teeth :: mechanic : ___   a. wrench   b. screwdriver   c. garage   d. engines

EDITING

▶ **Exercise 4:** Punctuate the Kay and Robert story, "The Cinnamon Rolls." (Part 1 of 5)
   Editing Guide: End Marks: 5   Capitals: 9   Commas: 1   Quotation Marks: 8   Apostrophes: 3   Homonyms: 1

   i cant believe you ate four cinnamon rolls during lunch exclaimed kay youre probably

going to throw up during pe

   i will not robert replied you are just mad because i wouldnt give you won of my

cinnamon rolls

English Made Easy

LISTENING AND SPEAKING:

Grammar Time

Lesson 2

You will
- classify Practice Sentences.
- do a Skill Builder.
- identify indefinite pronouns.
- do Classroom Practice 55.
- read and discuss Discovery Time.

Apply It: Classify the Practice Sentences orally with your teacher.

Practice Sentences	Chapter 12: Lesson 2

1. _____ The stalactite in the cave almost touched the ground.
2. _____ The temperamental dog in the fenced yard continuously barked at the neighbor's puppy!
3. _____ The handsome gentleman in the black suit and tie is he.

Skill Builder

Using the sentences just classified, do a Skill Builder orally with your teacher.

1. **Identify the nouns in a Noun Check.**
2. **Identify the nouns as singular or plural.**
3. **Identify the nouns as common or proper.**
4. **Identify the complete subject and the complete predicate.**
5. **Identify the simple subject and the simple predicate.**
6. **Do a Vocabulary Check.**
7. **Do a Verb Chant.**

Skill Time

Learn It: INDEFINITE PRONOUNS

 Reference 181 **Indefinite Pronouns**

Indefinite means not definite or not specific. A pronoun that does not refer to a definite person, place, or thing is called an **indefinite pronoun**. In order to prevent problems in subject-verb agreement and in pronoun-antecedent agreement, it is important to know which indefinite pronouns are always singular, which indefinite pronouns are always plural, and which indefinite pronouns can be either singular or plural.

1. INDEFINITE PRONOUNS THAT ARE ALWAYS SINGULAR:

end in -**one**	*(anyone, everyone, someone, no one)*
end in -**body**	*(anybody, everybody, somebody, nobody)*
end in -**thing**	*(anything, everything, something)*
imply **one** or **nothing**	*(one, each, either, neither, nothing, another)*

Subject-verb agreement. Singular indefinite subject pronouns use singular verbs.

> **Example: Everyone** in the class **wants** a ticket.

Continued on next page. >>>

Reference 181 continued from previous page.

Pronoun-antecedent agreement. When singular indefinite pronouns are antecedents, use singular personal pronouns for agreement. Since gender is not specified, the general rule is to use the masculine form or rewrite the sentence.

> **Examples: Everyone** did **his** homework. **Everyone** did the homework assigned.

2. INDEFINITE PRONOUNS THAT ARE ALWAYS PLURAL:

both, few, many, others, several

Subject-verb agreement. Plural indefinite subject pronouns use plural verbs.

> **Example: Several** in the class **want** tickets.

Pronoun-antecedent agreement. When plural indefinite pronouns are antecedents, use plural personal pronouns for agreement.

> **Example: Many** should complete **their** assignment.

3. INDEFINITE PRONOUNS THAT CAN BE EITHER SINGULAR OR PLURAL:

all, most, none, some, any, half

If a prepositional phrase follows any of the indefinite pronouns in this third group, the object of the preposition determines whether the indefinite pronoun is singular or plural.

> **Example of *singular* object of the preposition: Some** (of the **trash**) **is** gone.

> **Example of *plural* object of the preposition: Some** (of the **gems**) **are** missing.

If these indefinite pronouns are used alone, they are usually considered plural. Only the "either singular or plural" pronouns depend on prepositional phrases to determine whether they are singular or plural.

> **Example of *no* prepositional phrase: Some are** shivering from the cold.

4. WAYS INDEFINITE PRONOUNS CAN BE USED

Indefinite pronouns can be used as subjects or objects, but if an indefinite word is used as an adjective, then it is not an indefinite pronoun.

> **Example of an indefinite <u>pronoun</u> used as a *subject*: Many** wait for the storm to pass.

> **Example of an indefinite <u>pronoun</u> used as an *object*:** The doctor helps **many** of the citizens.

> **Example of an indefinite <u>word</u> used as an *adjective*: Many** boys are in line.

Directions: Complete the table. Then, underline the correct verb. **N/Pro** means to identify the subject as a noun or pronoun. Use **S** for singular and **P** for plural.

Subject-Verb Agreement	Subject	N/Pro	S or P	Verb S or P
1. Everybody in the class (<u>likes</u>, like) pepperoni pizza.	Everybody	Pro	S	S
2. Your keys (was, <u>were</u>) on the table.	Keys	N	P	P
3. All of your keys (is, <u>are</u>) on the table.	All	Pro	P	P

Classroom Practice 55

It is time to practice the skills you are learning. You will use the classroom practice on the next page to apply these skills.

ENRICHMENT:

(Russian American) 1888-1989 — Irving Berlin wrote about 1,500 songs. His songs helped define American music for much of the century. He wrote humorous songs, romantic ballads, and songs for musicals and films. Berlin's song "White Christmas" won the Academy Award for the Best Song of the Year in 1942. Other famous songs include "There's No Business Like Show Business," "God Bless America," "Easter Parade," and "Anything You Can Do, I Can Do Better."

 Discovery Questions:
• What do you think it was like to be a composer and song writer?
• Do you like Berlin's type of music? Explain.

Discovery Activity:

- Make a list of Berlin's most popular songs.
- Interview grandparents and find out if they remember any of Berlin's songs?

Are you interested in learning more about Irving Berlin?

1. You may explore this topic further by using the resources listed below.
   Computer resources: Internet, encyclopedia software
   Library resources: encyclopedias, books, magazines, newspapers
   Home/community resources: books, interviews, newspapers, magazines

2. A Discovery Share Time is provided in Lesson 7 if you wish to share your investigation results. You may share orally, or you may prepare a written report. You will put your written report in a class booklet titled "Notable People in History." This booklet will be placed in the class library for everyone to enjoy.

Classroom Practice 55

Name:_____ Date:_____

GRAMMAR

▶ **Exercise 1:** Classify each sentence.

1. _____ The shade from the maple tree is a cool and welcome relief.

2. _____ Eventually, the fat, hairy caterpillars will turn into beautiful butterflies.

SKILLS

▶ **Exercise 2:** Complete the table. Then, underline the pronoun in parentheses that agrees with its antecedent.

Pronoun-Antecedent Agreement	Antecedent	S or P	Pronoun S or P
1. The nurses checked (her, their) patients.			
2. Dad had pie for (his, their) birthday treat.			
3. Everybody heard (his, their) own name called.			
4. Anyone can buy (his, their) own football jacket.			
5. Several ate (his, their) lunches in the park.			

▶ **Exercise 3:** Complete the table and underline the correct verb. **N/Pro** means to identify the subject as a noun or pronoun. Use **S** for singular and **P** for plural.

Subject-Verb Agreement	Subject	N/Pro	S or P	Verb S or P
1. Either of the two choices (is, are) fine.				
2. Two sacks of money (was, were) found today.				
3. A sack of money (was, were) found today.				
4. Everything (don't, doesn't) go up to the attic.				
5. All of the band members (feel, feels) proud.				

▶ **Exercise 4:** Identify these indefinite pronouns as singular (**S**), plural (**P**), or either (**E**) singular or plural.
  1. ____ nobody   2. ____ some   3. ____ each   4. ____ few   5. ____ everyone

EDITING

▶ **Exercise 5:** Punctuate the Kay and Robert story, "The Cinnamon Rolls." (Part 2 of 5)
  Editing Guide: End Marks: 6   Capitals: 7   Commas: 3   Quotation Marks: 4   Homonyms: 1   Misspelled Words: 2

kay was getting irritated you really have a lot of nerve she snapped you begged for my

cinnamon roll until i gave it to you then you sweet-talked two more girls out of there

cinnamon rolls that made three and your cinnamon roll made four the least you coud

have done was to give my cinamon roll back to me

LISTENING AND SPEAKING:

Recite It: Practice Jingles 20–25 in the Jingle Section on pages 511–513.

Apply It: Classify the Practice Sentences orally with your teacher.

Practice Sentences	Chapter 12: Lesson 3
1. _____ Yesterday, you should have prepared for inclement weather.	
2. _____ In April, our accountant saved us thousands of dollars on our taxes.	
3. _____ The day before my birthday is Thanksgiving.	

Using the sentences just classified, do a Skill Builder orally with your teacher.

1. **Identify the nouns in a Noun Check.**
2. **Identify the nouns as singular or plural.**
3. **Identify the nouns as common or proper.**
4. **Identify the complete subject and the complete predicate.**
5. **Identify the simple subject and the simple predicate.**
6. **Do a Vocabulary Check.**
7. **Do a Verb Chant.**

Lesson 3

You will

- practice Jingles 20–25.
- classify Practice Sentences.
- do a Skill Builder.
- do Classroom Practice 56.
- write in your journal.
- read and discuss Discovery Time.

Classroom Practice 56

It is time to practice the skills you are learning. You will use the classroom practice on the next page to apply these skills.

JOURNAL WRITING 32

Write an entry in your journal. Use Reference 9 on page 12 for ideas.

ENRICHMENT:
Discovery Time

(Irish English) 1898–1963—**C. S. Lewis** is most famous for his children's series, *The Chronicles of Narnia*, which includes seven allegorical tales, the most popular being *The Lion, the Witch, and the Wardrobe*. He was a professor of literature at the University of Cambridge.

Discovery Questions:
- Which C. S. Lewis book was first made into a movie?
- Do you like fantasy stories? Explain.

Discovery Activities:
- Name as many books as you can in *The Chronicles of Narnia* series.
- Write a book report on your favorite C. S. Lewis book.
- Write a fantasy story of your own.

Are you interested in learning more about C. S. Lewis?

1. You may explore this topic further by using the resources listed below.
   Computer resources: Internet, encyclopedia software
   Library resources: encyclopedias, books, magazines, newspapers
   Home/community resources: books, interviews, newspapers, magazines

2. A Discovery Share Time is provided in Lesson 7 if you wish to share your investigation results. You may share orally, or you may prepare a written report. You will put your written report in a class booklet titled "Notable People in History." This booklet will be placed in the class library for everyone to enjoy.

Classroom Practice 56

Name:_____ Date:_____

GRAMMAR

▶ **Exercise 1:** Classify each sentence.

1. _____ Are the grapevines used for wreaths and decorations after the harvest?

2. _____ After the tornado, the retired electrician offered the people his services

for a very small fee.

SKILLS

▶ **Exercise 2:** Complete the table. Then, underline the pronoun in parentheses that agrees with its antecedent.

Pronoun-Antecedent Agreement	Antecedent	S or P	Pronoun S or P
1. Everybody sits in (his, their) assigned seat.			
2. The acrobats stood on (his, their) heads.			
3. Many took cushions for (his, their) comfort.			
4. Somebody on our street sold (his, their) car.			
5. Everyone recognized (his, their) name.			

▶ **Exercise 3:** Complete the table and underline the correct verb. **N/Pro** means to identify the subject as a noun or pronoun. Use **S** for singular and **P** for plural.

Subject-Verb Agreement	Subject	N/Pro	S or P	Verb S or P
1. Some of the banks (was, were) closed.				
2. Nobody in our office (has, have) the flu.				
3. A bouquet of roses (grace, graces) our table.				
4. None of the winners (is, are) qualified.				
5. He and she (go, goes) swimming every day.				

▶ **Exercise 4:** Identify these indefinite pronouns as singular (**S**), plural (**P**), or either (**E**) singular or plural.
1. ____ any   2. ____ everything   3. ____ either   4. ____ someone   5. ____ both

EDITING

▶ **Exercise 5:** Punctuate the Kay and Robert story, "The Cinnamon Rolls." (Part 3 of 5) **Editing Guide: End Marks: 3 Capitals: 5   Commas: 2   Quotation Marks: 2   Apostrophes: 2   Homonyms: 1   Misspelled Words: 1**

robert tried not to smile as he said kay i had already eaten your cinamon roll and my

cinnamon roll i just couldnt hand you won of the girls cinnamon rolls with them watching

that would show lack of appreciation

START LESSON 4

Lesson 4

You will

- hand in WA 28.
- classify Practice Sentences.
- do Chapter Checkup 57.
- write in your journal.
- read and discuss Discovery Time.

JOURNAL WRITING 32

Write an entry in your journal. Use Reference 9 on page 12 for ideas.

Hand It In: **WRITING ASSIGNMENT 28**

Get the book review for your nonfiction book ready to hand in when your teacher asks for it. Your review will be given back to you for sharing in the next lesson.

LISTENING AND SPEAKING:

Apply It: Classify the Practice Sentences orally with your teacher.

Practice Sentences	Chapter 12: Lesson 4

1. _____ During the night, the strong front did not bring a lot of rain to our area.
2. _____ Chocolate fudge and sugar cookies are delicious Christmas desserts.
3. _____ The talented artist skillfully painted Grandmother a picture of her family homestead.

Chapter Checkup 57

It is time for a checkup of the skills you have learned in this chapter. You will use the chapter checkup on the next page to evaluate your progress.

ENRICHMENT:

Discovery Time

(American) 1902-1984— Ray Kroc was the founder of McDonald's. As a distributor of milk-shake mixers, Kroc visited a restaurant in San Bernardino, California, that was owned by brothers, Maurice and Richard McDonald. They used an assembly-line format to prepare and sell a large volume of hamburgers, French fries, and milk shakes. Kroc decided to set up a chain of drive-in restaurants based on the McDonald brothers' format. Kroc agreed to pay the brothers 0.5 percent of gross receipts (total sales). The first McDonald's restaurant opened in 1955 in Des Plaines, Illinois. Currently, there are over 30,000 McDonald's restaurants worldwide.

Discovery Questions:
- What do you think it was like to start and run a successful business during the 1950s?
- Why did the McDonald's type of restaurant succeed?

Discovery Activity:
- Invite a business person to speak to your class. Prepare good questions to ask your speaker.

(American) 1908-1988— Louis L'Amour was a popular American writer of Western fiction. Although his early works were written to entertain readers, they also offered facts about history and life in the Old West. L'Amour was the first novelist awarded a Congressional gold medal, and in 1984 he received the Presidential Medal of Freedom. L'Amour published over 100 novels, short-story collections, poems, and pieces of nonfiction. Among his most popular books are *Hondo* and the *Sackett* series.

Discovery Questions:
- What do you think it was like to be a writer of Western fiction?
- What do you think of Louis L'Amour?
- Have you read any of L'Amour's books? Which ones have you read?

Are you interested in learning more about Ray Kroc or the McDonald's restaurants, or more about Louis L'Amour?

1. You may explore these topics further by using the resources listed below.
   Computer resources: Internet, encyclopedia software
   Library resources: encyclopedias, books, magazines, newspapers
   Home/community resources: books, interviews, newspapers, magazines
2. A Discovery Share Time is provided in Lesson 7 if you wish to share your investigation results. You may share orally, or you may prepare a written report. You will put your written report in a class booklet titled "Notable People in History." This booklet will be placed in the class library for everyone to enjoy.

Chapter 12 Checkup 57

Name:_____ Date:_____

GRAMMAR

▶ **Exercise 1:** Classify each sentence.

1. _____ Yesterday, Mom sent the water department a check for her monthly bill.

2. _____ The two horses beside the rail are strong competitors for the title.

3. _____ Drive quickly to the corner store for the ingredients in this new recipe.

SKILLS

▶ **Exercise 2:** Complete the table. Then, underline the pronoun in parentheses that agrees with its antecedent.

Pronoun-Antecedent Agreement	Antecedent	S or P	Pronoun S or P
1. All of the employees raised (his, their) hands.			
2. Did somebody lose (his, their) jacket?			
3. Pam bought (her, their) favorite movie.			
4. Several of the men voiced (his, their) opinions.			
5. Several fans cheered for (his, their) team.			

▶ **Exercise 3:** Complete the table. Then, underline the correct verb. **N/Pro** means to identify the subject as a noun or pronoun. Use **S** for singular and **P** for plural.

Subject-Verb Agreement	Subject	N/Pro	S or P	Verb S or P
1. All of the pie (was, were) gone by noon.				
2. Many of today's patients (has, have) the flu.				
3. Steve and Sue (isn't, aren't) related.				
4. Most of the invited guests (was, were) there.				
5. No one (was, were) absent on the first day.				

▶ **Exercise 4:** Identify these indefinite pronouns as singular (**S**), plural (**P**), or either (**E**) singular or plural.
1. ___ several   2. ___ half   3. ___ anything   4. ___ everybody   5. ___ everyone

EDITING

▶ **Exercise 5:** Punctuate the Kay and Robert story, "The Cinnamon Rolls." (Part 4 of 5) **Editing Guide: End Marks: 7 Capitals: 13   Commas: 7   Quotation Marks: 10   Apostrophes: 1   Homonyms: 1   Misspelled Words: 1**

lack of appreciation for whom kay howled i will never help you out again you moocher

now kay soothed robert dont get to upset remember i am your favorit brother

kay rolled her eyes and snorted ha robert orliss barfield you are my only brother

Publishing Time

START LESSON 5

Lesson 5

You will

- share book reviews.
- choose a book to be read in the next lesson.

Share It: **BOOK REVIEWS, WRITING ASSIGNMENTS 25 AND 28**

Look over Writing Assignments 25 and 28 after your teacher returns them. Prepare to share your reviews in cooperative-learning groups.

You will be assigned to two different groups. Share the fiction book review from Writing Assignment 25 in your first cooperative-learning group. After this group has finished sharing, each of you will pass your book review around so everyone in your group can record the title and author of each book in his journal. Under each book title, add a brief comment to help you remember whether you would like to read that particular book.

In your second group, you will share the nonfiction book review from Writing Assignment 28, following the same procedure of sharing and recording. Your teacher will tell you when to change groups.

Choose It: **A FICTION OR NONFICTION BOOK**

Choose a fiction or nonfiction book to read for enjoyment and have it ready to read during Conference Time in the next lesson.

START LESSON 6

Lesson 6

You will

- conference with teacher about WA 30.
- read a book.
- do student reading activity.

Reading Time

Read It: **FICTION OR NONFICTION BOOK**

Use your reading time to read the fiction or nonfiction book you selected in the previous lesson. This book is for enjoyment, and there is no book review required.

Conference Time

Discuss It: **TEACHER-STUDENT CONFERENCES FOR WRITING ASSIGNMENT 30**

Meet with your teacher to discuss Writing Assignment 30.
After the conference, place this group of papers in your Publishing folder.

>>>>>>>>>>>>> **Student Tip...**

Form an after-school book club. A book club is a small group of students who are reading the same book and meet together to talk about the book. Meet at different times to read and discuss the book with each other. Talk about the different characters and the plot. Keep a notebook and record your opinion and the comments from the other members.

Student Reading Activity

1. Write a poem to describe a character in the book you are reading. To find information on poems, study the different types of poems in Chapter 18 on pages 465–482. Share your poem with friends and family.

2. Write a different ending for the book you are reading. Think about how your ending compares with the book ending. Write the comparison in your journal.

Publishing Time

Publish It: WRITING ASSIGNMENT 30

Choose a publishing form and publish Writing Assignment 30. After rewriting your paper for publication, give the stapled papers (evaluation guide, graded final paper, rough draft, and prewriting map) to your teacher to be placed in your Writing Portfolio.

Lesson 7

You will

- publish WA 30.
- participate in Discovery Share Time.
- write an independent comparison/contrast essay (WA 31).

Reference 66	Publishing Checklist for Step 6 in the Writing Process

The sixth step in the writing process is called publishing. Publishing is sharing your writing with others. With so many forms of publishing available, finding a match for every project and personality is easy.

At times, a written work is best read aloud. Other times, the biggest impact is made when a written work is read silently. You can also use media sources to enhance any publication.

SPECIAL INSTRUCTIONS FOR PUBLISHING:

- Rewrite the graded paper in ink or type it on a computer, correcting any marked errors. *(Do not display or publish papers that have marked errors or grades on them.)*
- Give your teacher the set of stapled papers to place in your Writing Portfolio. *(Stapled papers: evaluation guide, graded final paper, rough draft, and prewriting map.)*
- Select a publishing form from the list below and publish your rewritten paper.

  1. Have classmates, family members, neighbors, or others read your writing at school or home.
  2. Share your writing with others during a Share Time.
     (Refer to Reference 67 on page 99 for sharing guidelines.)
  3. Display your writing on a bulletin board or wall.
  4. Put your writing in the classroom library or in the school library for checkout.
  5. Send your writing as a letter or an e-mail to a friend or relative.
  6. Frame your writing by gluing it on colored construction paper and decorating it.
  7. Make a book of your writing for your classroom, your family, or others.
  8. Illustrate your writing and give it to others to read.
  9. Dramatize your writing in the form of a play, puppet show, or radio broadcast.
  10. Send your writing to be placed in a waiting room (doctor, veterinarian, dentist, etc.), senior-citizen center, or a nursing home.
  11. Send your writing to a school newspaper, local newspaper, or a magazine for publication.
  12. Make a videotape, cassette tape, or slide presentation of your writing.
  13. Choose another publishing form that is not listed.

LISTENING AND SPEAKING:

Discovery Share Time

If you have chosen to investigate a historical figure introduced in this chapter, you now have the opportunity to share your results in one of the following ways:

1. You may relate your information orally.

2. You may read a written report.

3. You may place your report in the booklet without reading it aloud.

After share time, all written reports should be turned in to be placed in the class booklet titled "Notable People in History." You are encouraged to check out this class booklet so you can enjoy the reports again.

Write It: WRITING ASSIGNMENT 31

As you write a rough draft for your guided writing assignment, you will do two of the six steps in the writing process: prewriting and rough draft.

Writing Assignment 31

Purpose: To show how subjects are alike and how they are different

Type of Writing: Comparison-contrast

Audience: Classmates, parents, or friends

Writing Topics: Large city and small town
Book and movie
Something old and something new
(Brainstorm for other ideas, individually or in groups.)

Special Instructions:

1. Follow the Prewriting and Rough Draft Checklists in References 44 and 46 on pages 57, 61.

2. Make a Venn diagram instead of a prewriting map. Use Reference 179 on page 351 to help you write your comparison-contrast essay.

3. Use standard, time-order, or transition writing form. See Reference 69 on page 103.

4. Write in first or third person. See Reference 70 on page 104.
   (First-person pronouns: *I, me, my, mine, we, us, our,* and *ours.*)
   (Third-person pronouns: *he, his, him, she, her, hers, it, its, they, their, theirs,* and *them.*)

Note: Reference 54 on page 71 gives the steps in the writing process and the location of all the writing checklists.

LISTENING AND SPEAKING:

Lesson 8

You will
- practice Jingle 12.
- read and discuss tall tales.
- plan and write rough draft for tall tale (WA 32).

Recite It: Practice Jingle 12 in the Jingle Section on page 509.

>>>>> Student Tip...

> Reviewing the transition words will help you apply them in your writing.

Writing Time

Learn It: WRITING TALL TALES

A **tall tale** is a humorous story that uses fabrication (a big lie), a surprise, something funny, something clever, something unexpected, or something that leaves the reader guessing to make it an unbelievable tale.

| Reference 182 | Writing a Tall Tale |

A **tall tale** is a humorous story that makes use of exaggeration, but it also includes believable events and situations. A tall tale is a story that "stretches" people, places, or events into unbelievable proportions. Pecos Bill's roping a tornado is an example of a tall tale. The story of Paul Bunyan, the giant lumberjack, and his blue ox, Babe, is also a tall tale.

A tall tale may take on different forms, but every tall tale is a "far-fetched" story that is hard to believe. It usually takes something believable, such as a man fishing, and "stretches" the story into an unbelievable tale. Although you know the story is "stretched," you still find it fun to read or hear. The speech in a tall tale is almost always colloquial, or informal, and characters speak in dialect. The way characters speak is very much a part of the charm of the story. The guidelines below will help you write a tall tale.

1. Make a Story Elements Outline for your tall tale.
2. Choose a believable story and "stretch" the story to make it unbelievable in some way.
3. Tell the story in the order that you want the events to happen.
4. Use the following list of words for the purpose of exaggeration: *extraordinary, never before, unbelievable, outlandish, worst, biggest, horrendous, million, faster than, impossible, tremendous, meanest, longest, heaviest, terrible, cleverest, most unexpected, strangest, etc.*
5. Use colloquial, or informal, speech for your characters.
6. Think of a title that will tell what your story is about. The title is usually written after the story is finished.

Example of a Tall Tale

THE BIG ONE

One time, back when we wuz youngens, me and my best friend, Garland Kennedy, wuz fishin' down on the Blue Pie River. It wuz a perty slow day for ketchin' fish, and both of us jes 'bout fell asleep in Garland's lil' ole fishin' boat.

All of a sudden, somethin' struck my line, pullin' th' cork right near under. Me and Garland woke up fast, and I got me a firm grip on my fishin' pole. Land sakes! This had to be th' biggest fish I ever hooked in all my fishin' days!

Next thing I knowed, that there fish wuz head'n straight toward our boat! That's when we found out it weren't no fish a'tall. It wuz a big, ugly ole gran'daddy gator! An' let me tell you, he shore wuz mad! But me an' that gator had no notion of turnin' loose. So we both dug in, an' th' battle begun.

Continued on next page. >>>

Reference 182 continued from previous page.

I tugged an' tugged one way, and that gator tugged an' tugged th' other way. Then, that gator got a' idee in his ornery head. He circled our boat, tryin' to tangle my line. Then, he jes headed upriver, pullin' me and Garland right along. As that gator gained speed, I wuz pulled half outa th' boat, holdin' on to that there fishing pole fer dear life. Garland weren't no help a'tall. He jes' held on and yelled like a wild man.

That gator pulled me and Garland all the way to Frisbee, ten miles upriver 'GAINST th' current. As the town folks looked on, he jes' walked out on dry land an' pulled us a good fifty feet to th' top of th' riverbank. Then, that ornery ole gator jest spit out my bait. He turned 'round an' gave me and Garland a long, uppity stare, and then, he ambled right back down th' riverbank and into th' river. Yep! Me and Garland learnt our lesson. We ain't never fished in th' Blue Pie River since that day!

Write It: WRITING ASSIGNMENT 32

As you write a rough draft for your independent writing assignment, you will do two of the six steps in the writing process: prewriting (the story elements outline) and rough draft.

Writing Assignment [32]

Purpose: To tell a story
Type of Writing: Tall tale (narrative)
Audience: Classmates, parents, or friends
Writing Topics: The worst flood/drought ever
The computer whiz/dummy
The longest/shortest game
(Brainstorm for other ideas, individually or in groups.)

Special Instructions:

1. Use Reference 182 to help you write your tall-tale narrative.

2. Make a story elements outline instead of a prewriting checklist. See References 156 and 166 on pages 290, 318.)

3. Write your tall tale with or without dialogue.

4. You will rewrite your tall tale in Lesson 8 of Chapter 13. You will share it in Lessons 9 and 10. If you wish, you may dress the part of a character in your tall tale, make and show illustrations, or just do a dramatic reading. Keep this in mind as you write your tall tale.

5. Write in first or third person. See Reference 70 on page 104.
(First-person pronouns: *I, me, my, mine, we, us, our,* and *ours.*)
(Third-person pronouns: *he, his, him, she, her, hers, it, its, they, their, theirs,* and *them.*)

Note: Reference 54 on page 71 gives the steps in the writing process and the location of all the writing checklists.

>>>>>>>>>>> Student Tip...

Check out a collection of tall tales from the school and/or city library to read and enjoy. Pick a few to read aloud to your friends or family.

Writing Time

Lesson 9

You will
- revise, edit, and write a final paper for WA 32.

Apply It: **REVISE, EDIT, AND WRITE A FINAL PAPER**

Following the schedule below, you will revise and edit Writing Assignment 32. Then, you will write a final paper. Use the Chapter 12 Writing Evaluation Guide on the next page to check your final paper one last time.

Reference 52 — Revising & Editing Schedule and Writing a Final Paper

SPECIAL INSTRUCTIONS FOR REVISING AND EDITING (Steps 3-4 in the writing process):

- Use the Revising and Editing Checklists in References 48 and 50 as you revise and edit your rough draft.
- Follow the revising and editing schedule below as directed by your teacher.
  1. **Individual.** First, read your rough draft to yourself. Use the Revising Checklist in Reference 48 on page 64. Go through your paper, checking each item on the list and making revisions to your rough draft. Then, use the Editing Checklist in Reference 50 on page 66. Go through your paper again, checking each item on the list and editing your rough draft.
  2. **Partner.** Next, get with your editing partner. Work together on each partner's rough draft, one paper at a time. Read each rough draft aloud and revise and edit it together, using the Revising and Editing Checklists. (The author of the paper should be the one to make the corrections on his own paper.)
  3. **Group.** Finally, read the rough draft to a revision group for feedback. Each student should read his paper while the others listen and offer possible revising and editing suggestions. (The author will determine whether to make corrections from the revision group's suggestions.)

SPECIAL INSTRUCTIONS FOR FINAL PAPER (Step 5 in the writing process):

- Write your final paper, using the Final Paper Checklist in Reference 53 on page 70.
- Staple your writing papers in this order: the final paper on top, the rough draft in the middle, and the prewriting map on the bottom. Place the stapled papers in the Final Paper folder.

>>>>>>>>>> **Student Tip...**

1. Be tactful and helpful in your comments during revising and editing time. The purpose of any suggestion should be to improve the writer's rough draft.

2. As you make your final corrections, you have the choice of accepting or rejecting any suggestions made by your partners or your revision group.

3. If you need to improve your handwriting, refer to the Resource Tools Section on pages 529–530 for information on writing legibly.

Chapter 12 Writing Evaluation Guide

Name:_____ Date:_____

ROUGH DRAFT CHECK

_____ 1. Did you write your rough draft in pencil?

_____ 2. Did you write the correct headings on the first seven lines of your paper?

_____ 3. Did you use extra wide margins and skip every other line?

_____ 4. Did you write a title at the end of your rough draft?

_____ 5. Did you place your edited rough draft in your Rough Draft folder?

REVISING CHECK

_____ 6. Did you identify the purpose, type of writing, and audience?

_____ 7. Did you check for a topic, topic sentence, and sentences supporting the topic?

_____ 8. Did you check sentences for the right order, and did you combine, rearrange, or delete sentences when necessary?

_____ 9. Did you check for a variety of simple, compound, and complex sentences?

_____ 10. Did you check for any left out, repeated, or unnecessary words?

_____ 11. Did you check for the best choice of words by replacing or deleting unclear words?

_____ 12. Did you check the content for interest and creativity?

_____ 13. Did you check the voice to make sure the writing says what you want it to say?

EDITING CHECK

_____ 14. Did you indent each paragraph?

_____ 15. Did you put an end mark at the end of every sentence?

_____ 16. Did you capitalize the first word of every sentence?

_____ 17. Did you check for all other capitalization mistakes?

_____ 18. Did you check for all punctuation mistakes?
(commas, periods, apostrophes, quotation marks, underlining)

_____ 19. Did you check for misspelled words and for incorrect homonym choices?

_____ 20. Did you check for incorrect spellings of plural and possessive forms?

_____ 21. Did you check for correct construction and punctuation of your sentences?

_____ 22. Did you check for usage mistakes? (subject/verb agreement, a/an choices, contractions, verb tenses, pronoun/antecedent agreement, pronoun cases, degrees of adjectives, double negatives, etc.)

_____ 23. Did you put your revised and edited paper in the Rough Draft folder?

FINAL PAPER CHECK

_____ 24. Did you write the final paper in pencil?

_____ 25. Did you center the title on the top line and center your name under the title?

_____ 26. Did you skip a line before starting the writing assignment?

_____ 27. Did you single-space, use wide margins, and write the final paper neatly?

_____ 28. Did you staple your papers in this order: final paper on top, rough draft in the middle, and prewriting map on the bottom? Did you put them in the Final Paper folder?

Writing Time

Hand It In: WRITING ASSIGNMENT 32

Get your stapled papers for Writing Assignment 32 from your Final Paper folder. Check to make sure they are in the correct order: the final paper on top, the rough draft in the middle, and the Story Elements Outline on the bottom. Hand them in to your teacher.

LISTENING AND SPEAKING:

Oral Review Questions

Discuss It:

1. What is an antecedent?
2. True or False. A pronoun should agree with the antecedent in number and gender.
3. True or False. A pronoun that does not refer to a definite person, place, or thing is called an indefinite pronoun.
4. Name the five plural indefinite pronouns.
5. Name the six indefinite pronouns that can be either singular or plural.
6. Name the seventeen singular indefinite pronouns.
7. What are the core parts of a Pattern 4 sentence?
8. What are the seven subjective-case pronouns?
9. How are subjective pronouns used?
10. What are the seven objective-case pronouns?
11. How are objective pronouns used?
12. What are the seven most common possessive-case pronouns?
13. How are possessive pronouns used?
14. What type of writing is a humorous story that makes use of exaggeration?
15. What type of writing is used when your purpose is to show similarities and differences?

>>>>>>>>>>>>>>>>>>>>> **Student Tip...**

For information about test-taking strategies, refer to the Resource Tools Section on page 528.

Review It: GOALS

Review the goals you wrote in your Goal Booklet at the beginning of the school year. Discuss your progress with your teacher or a student partner. Then, write a paragraph in your Goal Booklet that tells how well you are meeting your short-term goals. Give examples that support your evaluation of your progress. Next, write another paragraph to evaluate your long-term goals. Tell whether you want to change them or keep them the same. Give reasons to support either choice. Finally, return your Goal Booklet to your teacher when you have finished.

START LESSON 10

Lesson 10

You will

- hand in WA 32 for grading.
- respond to oral review questions.
- take Chapter 12 Test.
- discuss and evaluate goals.
- write a paragraph in your goal booklet.

CHAPTER TEST

It is time to evaluate your knowledge of the skills you have learned in this chapter. Your teacher will give you the Chapter 12 Test to help you assess your progress.

Lesson 1

You will

- recite new jingle (Predicate Adjective).
- identify predicate adjectives and Pattern 5.
- classify Introductory Sentences.
- do a Skill Builder to identify predicate adjectives.
- write in your journal.

LISTENING AND SPEAKING:

Jingle Time

Recite It: Recite the new jingle.

> ♪ **Jingle 26** **The Predicate Adjective Jingle**
>
> A predicate, predicate, predicate adjective
> Is a special, special adjective
> In the predicate, predicate, predicate
> That modifies, modifies, **modifies**
> The simple, simple **subject**.
>
> A predicate, predicate, predicate adjective
> Follows after a linking verb.
> To find a predicate adjective,
> Ask **WHAT KIND** of subject and verify the answer.
> Verify that the adjective in the predicate
> Modifies, modifies, **modifies**
> The simple, simple **subject**.

Grammar Time

Apply It: These Introductory Sentences are used to apply the new grammar concepts taught below. Classify these sentences orally with your teacher.

Introductory Sentences	Chapter 13: Lesson 1
1. _____ The popcorn is salty.	
2. _____ Phooey! The popcorn from the concession stand is too salty!	
3. _____ The chocolate cake was rich, moist, and delicious.	

Learn It: **PREDICATE ADJECTIVE**

You have studied five jobs of nouns: subject, object of a preposition, indirect object, direct object, and predicate noun. You have learned that certain nouns form parts of different sentence patterns, and you have learned that these patterns have either action verbs or linking verbs. The new sentence pattern, Pattern 5, has an adjective as one of its pattern parts.

> 📖 **Reference 183** **Predicate Adjective and Pattern 5**
>
> 1. A **predicate adjective** is an adjective that is located in the predicate and modifies the simple subject.
> 2. A predicate adjective is located after a linking verb. A linking verb links, or connects, the subject and the predicate adjective.
> 3. A predicate adjective tells **what kind** of subject.

Continued on next page. >>>

Reference 183 continued from previous page.

4. To find the predicate adjective, ask WHAT KIND OF SUBJECT after the verb.
5. A *predicate adjective* is labeled with the abbreviation **PA**.
6. A Pattern 5 sentence has a subject noun, linking verb, and predicate adjective as its core. A Pattern 5 is labeled **SN LV PA P5**. A Pattern 5 sentence has one noun job and one adjective job in its core: the subject noun and the predicate adjective. *(If the subject is a pronoun, it is labeled as a subject pronoun in the sentence, but the pattern is still identified as **SN LV PA P5**.)*
7. A review:
   Pattern 1 is **SN V**. It has a noun-verb (**N V**) core.
   Pattern 2 is **SN V-t DO**. It has a noun-verb-noun (**N V N**) core.
   Pattern 3 is **SN V-t IO DO**. It has a noun-verb-noun-noun (**N V N N**) core.
   Pattern 4 is **SN LV PrN**. It has a noun-linking verb-noun (**N LV N**) core.
   Pattern 5 is **SN LV PA**. It has a noun-linking verb-adjective (**N LV Adj**) core.

   In Patterns 1-4, adjectives are not part of the pattern core. However, in Pattern 5, an adjective is part of the pattern core because it is located in the predicate and modifies the subject.

Question and Answer Flow for the Practice Sentence, adding Predicate Adjectives

Practice Sentence: Her new dress is absolutely gorgeous!

1. What is absolutely gorgeous? **dress - SN**	10. Skill Check
2. What is being said about dress? **dress is - V**	11. Linking verb - check again
3. Dress is what? **gorgeous - verify the adjective**	12. No prepositional phrases
4. What kind of dress? **gorgeous - PA** (Say: *gorgeous - predicate adjective.*)	13. **Exclamation point, strong feeling, exclamatory sentence**
5. Is - LV	14. Go back to the verb. Divide the complete subject from the complete predicate.
6. How gorgeous? **absolutely - Adv**	15. Is there an adverb exception? **No.**
7. What kind of dress? **new - Adj**	16. Is this sentence in a natural or inverted order?
8. Whose dress? **her - PPA**	**Natural - no change.**
9. **SN LV PA P5** (Say: *subject noun, linking verb, predicate adjective, Pattern 5.*)	

```
      PPA Adj  SN   LV   Adv      PA
SN LV
_____   Her new dress / is absolutely gorgeous!  E
PA P5
```

Discuss It:

1. What is the pattern in a Pattern 5 sentence?
2. What are the core parts of a Pattern 5 sentence?
3. What parts of speech are used in a Pattern 5 sentence?

Learn It: **A SKILL BUILDER FOR A NOUN CHECK WITH PREDICATE ADJECTIVES**

The example below shows you what to do with predicate adjectives when you are identifying nouns for a Noun Check.

Skill Builder

FOR A NOUN CHECK WITH PREDICATE ADJECTIVES

Circle the nouns for a Noun Check.

Sentence 1: Subject Noun (popcorn) *yes, it is a noun.*

Sentence 2: Subject Noun (popcorn) *yes, it is a noun;*
Object of the Preposition (stand) *yes, it is a noun.*

Sentence 3: Subject Noun (cake) *yes, it is a noun.*

JOURNAL WRITING 34

Write an entry in your journal. Use Reference 9 on page 12 for ideas.

START LESSON 2

Lesson 2

You will

- practice Jingle 26.
- classify Practice Sentences.
- do a Skill Builder.
- identify degrees of comparison of adjectives.
- do Classroom Practice 58.
- read and discuss Discovery Time.

LISTENING AND SPEAKING:

Jingle Time

Recite It: Practice Jingle 26 in the Jingle Section on page 513.

Grammar Time

Apply It: Classify the Practice Sentences orally with your teacher.

Practice Sentences	Chapter 13: Lesson 2
1. _____ The president of the company was apprehensive about the new advertising campaign.	
2. _____ Beth and Carla were very upset about their geography test scores!	
3. _____ The old receipt was torn and barely legible.	

Skill Builder

Using the sentences just classified, do a Skill Builder orally with your teacher.

1. Identify the nouns in a Noun Check.
2. Identify the nouns as singular or plural.
3. Identify the nouns as common or proper.
4. Identify the complete subject and the complete predicate.
5. Identify the simple subject and the simple predicate.
6. Do a Vocabulary Check.
7. Do a Verb Chant.

Skill Time

Learn It: DEGREES OF COMPARISON OF ADJECTIVES

📖 Reference 184 — Degrees of Comparison of Adjectives

When adjectives are describing one noun, they are usually in a simple form, as indicated in Rule 1 below. However, when adjectives are used to compare two or more nouns, they change to comparative or superlative forms, as in Rule 2 and Rule 3 below. **Simple, comparative, and superlative forms of adjectives are called degrees of comparison.** Study the rules below to help you understand the degrees of comparison.

> **RULE 1: Simple Form.** This is also known as the positive form. This form is the one used most often because it describes **ONE** person, place, or thing. Use the **Simple Form** when no comparison is being made.
>
> > **Simple Form: fast** (one syllable), **nervous** (two syllables), **good** (irregular)
>
> **RULE 2: Comparative Form.** Use the comparative form to compare **TWO** people, places, or things. **To make the comparative form, add *-er* or MORE to the simple form.** Use *-er* with one-syllable adjectives and some two-syllable adjectives. Use *more* with some two-syllable adjectives and all adjectives of three or more syllables.
>
> > **Comparative Form: faster** (one syllable), **more nervous** (two syllables), **better** (irregular)
>
> **RULE 3: Superlative Form.** The superlative form is used to compare **THREE** or more people, places, or things. **To make the superlative form, add *-est* or MOST to the simple form.** Use *-est* with one-syllable adjectives and some two-syllable adjectives. Use *most* with some two-syllable adjectives and all adjectives of three or more syllables.
>
> > **Superlative Form: fastest** (one syllable), **most nervous** (two syllables), **best** (irregular)

Most adjectives use regular forms in the comparative and superlative degrees, but some adjectives have irregular forms in the comparative and superlative degrees. You must memorize the irregular forms.

IRREGULAR ADJECTIVES MUST BE MEMORIZED

Simple	Comparative	Superlative
good	better	best
bad, ill	worse	worst
little (amount)	less or lesser	least
much, many	more	most

Avoid double comparisons. **Do not** use both *-er* and *more* or *-est* and *most* to form the comparative or superlative degrees. (**My car is** <u>more older</u> **than yours.**)

Classroom Practice 58

It is time to practice the skills you are learning. You will use the classroom practice on the next page to apply these skills.

Student Note: Look at the editing section at the bottom of the Classroom Practice 58. Starting with Classroom Practice 58, the editing section will give only a total number of mistakes. There will no longer be an editing guide for a detailed list of each kind of mistake.

ENRICHMENT:

Discovery Time

(French) 1910-1997— Jacques-Yves Cousteau was a pioneer in underwater research. He created and tested the first scuba-diving device, called an Aqua-Lung. While serving in the French navy, Cousteau began his underwater explorations. Cousteau was one of the first people to develop underwater color photography. He won an Academy Award for the best documentary film in 1956 for *The Silent World* and again in 1966 for *World Without Sun*.

Discovery Questions:
- What do you think it was like to be one of the first persons to do underwater research?
- What water activities appeal to you? Explain.
- What do you think about scuba diving?
- What do you think about photography?
- Do you know anyone who scuba dives or takes pictures as a hobby or as a profession?

Discovery Activity:
- Invite a photographer or a scuba diver to speak to your class. Prepare good questions to ask your speaker.

Are you interested in learning more about Jacques-Yves Cousteau?

1. You may explore this topic further by using the resources listed below.
   Computer resources: Internet, encyclopedia software
   Library resources: encyclopedias, books, magazines, newspapers
   Home/community resources: books, interviews, newspapers, magazines

2. A Discovery Share Time is provided in Lesson 8 if you wish to share your investigation results. You may share orally, or you may prepare a written report. You will put your written report in a class booklet titled "Notable People in History." This booklet will be placed in the class library for everyone to enjoy.

Classroom Practice 58

Name:_____ Date:_____

GRAMMAR

▶ **Exercise 1:** Classify each sentence.

1. _____ The college students were nervous during the final exams.

2. _____ The gravel road to my aunt's house in the mountains is very bumpy.

SKILLS

▶ **Exercise 2:** Write the different forms for the adjectives below.

RULE 1: Simple form	RULE 2: Comparative form (er, more)	RULE 3: Superlative form (est, most)

Simple Form	Comparative Form	Superlative Form
1.	better	
2. comfortable		
3.		funniest
4. helpful		
5.	finer	
6. dependable		
7.		worst
8.	more cheerful	

▶ **Exercise 3:** In each blank, write the correct form of the adjective in parentheses to complete the sentences.

1. Juan has completed the _____ part of his training. **(difficult)**

2. This gold is _____ than the gold in that necklace. **(fine)**

3. Kelly was a very _____ assistant for the program. **(helpful)**

4. The chocolate cookies were _____ than the sugar cookies. **(good)**

5. Of all the stories, yours is _____. **(good)**

▶ **Exercise 4:** Write the letter of the word that best completes each analogy.

1. **needle : sewing :: ____ : painting**   a. picture   b. artist   c. brush   d. gallery

2. **swim : swam :: go : ____**   a. walked   b. swum   c. going   d. went

EDITING

▶ **Exercise 5:** Correct the sentences below. (Total mistakes: 16)

our basketball team played well last night replied the coach too my dad they deserved

two win they played there best game of the season and i am very proud of them

START LESSON 3

Lesson 3

You will

- practice Jingles 20-26.
- classify Practice Sentences.
- do a Skill Builder.
- identify double negatives.
- do Classroom Practice 59.
- write in your journal.
- read and discuss Discovery Time.

LISTENING AND SPEAKING:

Recite It: Practice Jingles 20–26 in the Jingle Section on pages 511–513.

Apply It: Classify the Practice Sentences orally with your teacher.

Practice Sentences	Chapter 13: Lesson 3
1. _____ That Christmas tree at the mall was absolutely breathtaking!	
2. _____ During the move to our new house, my mother's antique china was chipped and broken.	
3. _____ The Christmas lights and decorations in our neighborhood look very festive.	

Using the sentences just classified, do a Skill Builder orally with your teacher.

1. **Identify the nouns in a Noun Check.**
2. **Identify the nouns as singular or plural.**
3. **Identify the nouns as common or proper.**
4. **Identify the complete subject and the complete predicate.**
5. **Identify the simple subject and the simple predicate.**
6. **Do a Vocabulary Check.**
7. **Do a Verb Chant.**

Learn It: DOUBLE NEGATIVES

 Reference 185 | **Double Negatives**

Double means TWO. Negative means NOT. You have a **double-negative** mistake when you use two negative words in the same sentence. Most negative words begin with the letter n. Other negative words do not begin with the letter n but are negative in meaning. There are also some prefixes that give words a negative meaning.

Negative Words that Begin with *N*			Other Negative Words	Negative Prefixes
• neither	• no	• no one	• barely	• dis
• not (n't)	• nowhere	• never	• hardly	• non
• nobody	• none	• nothing	• scarcely	• un

THREE WAYS TO CORRECT A DOUBLE NEGATIVE

RULE 1: **Change** the second negative to a positive:

Incorrect: Debbie **couldn't** find **nothing**. Correct: Debbie **couldn't** find **anything**.

RULE 2: **Take out** the negative part of a contraction:

Incorrect: Debbie **couldn't** find **nothing**. Correct: Debbie **could** find **nothing**.

RULE 3: **Remove** the first negative word (possibility of a verb change):

Incorrect: Debbie **didn't** say **nothing**. Correct: Debbie **said nothing**.

CHANGING NEGATIVE WORDS TO POSITIVE WORDS

1. Change *no* or *none* to *any*.
2. Change *nobody* to *anybody*.
3. Change *no one* to *anyone*.

4. Change *nothing* to *anything*.
5. Change *nowhere* to *anywhere*.
6. Change *never* to *ever*.

7. Change *neither* to *either*.
8. Remove the *n't* from a contraction.

Directions: Underline the negative words in each sentence. Rewrite each sentence and correct the double-negative mistake as indicated by the rule number at the end of the sentence.

He <u>doesn't</u> have <u>no</u> homework over the weekend. **(Rule 3)** *He has no homework over the weekend.*

I <u>can't</u> <u>hardly</u> wait for my birthday this year. **(Rule 2)** *I can hardly wait for my birthday this year.*

He <u>hasn't</u> done <u>nothing</u> about his problem. **(Rule 1)** *He hasn't done anything about his problem.*

Classroom Practice 59

It is time to practice the skills you are learning. You will use the classroom practice on the next page to apply these skills.

ENRICHMENT:

(American) 1918-1992— Sam Walton was the founder of Wal-Mart and Sam's Club. He earned a degree in economics from the University of Missouri. Walton began working for JC Penney and the Ben Franklin five-and-dime stores. He opened the first Wal-Mart store in Rogers, Arkansas, in 1962. He implemented such innovative ideas as offering name-brand items at low prices, giving stock options to employees, and decentralizing the distribution of products. Today, Wal-Mart Stores, incorporated, is based in Bentonville, Arkansas, and employs about 1.6 million people.

Discovery Questions:
- **Look up the word entrepreneur in the dictionary. What do you think it takes to become a successful entrepreneur?**
- **Would you want to run a business? Why or why not?**
- **If you could choose your profession now, what would it be? Explain.**

Are you interested in learning more about Sam Walton?

1. You may explore this topic further by using the resources listed below.
   Computer resources: Internet, encyclopedia software
   Library resources: encyclopedias, books, magazines, newspapers
   Home/community resources: books, interviews, newspapers, magazines

2. A Discovery Share Time is provided in Lesson 8 if you wish to share your investigation results. You may share orally, or you may prepare a written report. You will put your written report in a class booklet titled "Notable People in History." This booklet will be placed in the class library for everyone to enjoy.

Classroom Practice 59

Name:_____ Date:_____

GRAMMAR

▶ **Exercise 1:** Classify each sentence.

1. _____ During the wintry storm, the rough seas were impassable.

2. _____ The stairwell to the top of the lighthouse is too steep and narrow for many tourists.

SKILLS

▶ **Exercise 2:** Write the different forms for the adjectives below.

RULE 1: Simple form	RULE 2: Comparative form (er, more)	RULE 3: Superlative form (est, most)

Simple Form	Comparative Form	Superlative Form
1. beautiful		
2.	more restful	
3.		least

▶ **Exercise 3:** In each blank, write the correct form of the adjective in parentheses to complete the sentences.

1. Janice's cake is the _____ of the two. **(attractive)**

2. Fred's cold is _____ than Daniel's cold. **(bad)**

3. Susan is the _____ person in the world! **(lucky)**

▶ **Exercise 4:** Underline the negative words in each sentence. Rewrite each sentence and correct the double-negative mistake as indicated by the rule number in parentheses at the end of the sentence.

RULE 1: Change the second negative to a positive.	RULE 2: Take out the negative part of a contraction.	RULE 3: Remove the first negative word (verb change).

1. She couldn't find nothing. **(Rule 2)** _____

2. He doesn't have no money. **(Rule 3)** _____

3. They don't know nothing. **(Rule 1)** _____

4. There wasn't no time left. **(Rule 1)** _____

5. Doug hadn't never played tennis. **(Rule 2)** _____

▶ **Exercise 5:** Write the letter of the word that best completes each analogy.

1. **scatter : gather :: stale : ____**   a. old   b. bread   c. moldy   d. fresh

2. **ware : wear :: aisle : ____**   a. pew   b. theater   c. island   d. isle

EDITING

▶ **Exercise 6:** Correct the sentence below. (Total mistakes: 13)

you wont get a slice of chocolate cake mother said if you dont eat all you're vegtables

START LESSON 4

Lesson 4

You will
- practice Jingles 13-19.
- classify Practice Sentences.
- do Classroom Practice 60.
- read and discuss Discovery Time.
- do a homework assignment.
- do Home Connection activity.

LISTENING AND SPEAKING:

 **Jingle Time**

Recite It: Practice Jingles 13–19 in the Jingle Section on pages 509–511.

 **Grammar Time**

Apply It: Classify the Practice Sentences orally with your teacher.

Practice Sentences	Chapter 13: Lesson 4

1. _____ Our prom committee was very frugal with the funds for our prom expenses.
2. _____ The pipes in the bathroom of the old Victorian mansion were rusted and cracked.
3. _____ The pink roses in the crystal vase on the table are wilted.

 Classroom Practice 60

It is time to practice the skills you are learning. You will use the classroom practice on the next page to apply these skills.

ENRICHMENT:

 **Discovery Time**

(American) 1922-2000— Charles Schulz created the famous comic strip *Peanuts*. The main characters were Charlie Brown, Sally, Lucy, Linus, Schroeder, Snoopy, and Woodstock. The strip was originally titled *Li'l Folks*. The *Peanuts* comic strip was adapted to television and the stage. Schulz also wrote screenplays for two feature-length-animated films. In 1999, Schulz was diagnosed with cancer and decided he would retire. He died February 12, 2000, the night before his final comic strip was published.

Discovery Questions:
- **What do you think it would be like to be a famous artist?**
- **Do you like to draw or paint?**
- **What is your talent? Explain.**

Discovery Activities:
- **Find a *Peanuts* comic strip that you like.**
  Tape or glue it on cardboard and bring it to class to share with others.
- **Divide into small groups and make up a *Peanuts* comic strip. Share your creation with others.**

Are you interested in learning more about Charles Schulz?

1. You may explore this topic further by using the resources listed below.
   Computer resources: Internet, encyclopedia software
   Library resources: encyclopedias, books, magazines, newspapers
   Home/community resources: books, interviews, newspapers, magazines

2. A Discovery Share Time is provided in Lesson 8 if you wish to share your investigation results. You may share orally, or you may prepare a written report. You will put your written report in a class booklet titled "Notable People in History." This booklet will be placed in the class library for everyone to enjoy.

Classroom Practice 60

Name:_____ Date:_____

GRAMMAR

▶ **Exercise 1:** Classify each sentence.

1. _____ Several snakes in the exhibit at the local zoo are very poisonous!

2. _____ During her first performance at the circus, the baby elephant was shy and nervous.

SKILLS

▶ **Exercise 2:** Write the different forms for the adjectives below.

RULE 1: Simple form	RULE 2: Comparative form (er, more)	RULE 3: Superlative form (est, most)

Simple Form	Comparative Form	Superlative Form
1.	happier	
2. supportive		
3. bad		

▶ **Exercise 3:** In each blank, write the correct form of the adjective in parentheses to complete the sentences.

1. Dad's old recliner is _____ than the new rocking chair. **(comfortable)**

2. Sarah collected the _____ money for our carnival. **(many)**

3. Mr. Simmons was a very _____ coach. **(tough)**

4. My grandmother had the _____ lawn in her neighborhood. **(green)**

▶ **Exercise 4:** Underline the negative words in each sentence. Rewrite each sentence and correct the double-negative mistake as indicated by the rule number in parentheses at the end of the sentence.

RULE 1:	RULE 2:	RULE 3:
Change the second negative to a positive.	Take out the negative part of a contraction.	Remove the first negative word (verb change).

1. Sue didn't buy nothing for the party. **(Rule 3)** _____

2. Dad hasn't never worked late. **(Rule 2)** _____

3. I wouldn't buy nothing from him. **(Rule 1)** _____

4. She couldn't find no paper. **(Rule 3)** _____

5. We haven't had no breakfast. **(Rule 1)** _____

▶ **Exercise 5:** Write the letter of the word that best completes the analogy.

1. **playful : puppy :: ____ : movie**   a. theater   b. film   c. actor   d. entertaining

EDITING

▶ **Exercise 6:** Correct the sentence below. (Total mistakes: 15)

we wont get an good seat jennifer said if jeff and i dont leave write after school

Homework 10

Complete this homework assignment on notebook paper.

1. Number your paper 1–6. Write the correct form of the adjective listed in parentheses at the end of the sentence.

  1. My job is _____ than my sister's job. **(easy)**

  2. Austin Smith is _____ than his brother, Taylor. **(daring)**

  3. My brother has the _____ patience of anyone in our family. **(little)**

  4. Steak is _____ than hamburger. **(expensive)**

  5. My brother has the _____ handwriting of anyone. **(bad)**

  6. A cheetah is _____ than a horse. **(fast)**

2. Number your paper 1–4. Write the negative words in each sentence. Then, rewrite each sentence and correct the double-negative mistake as indicated by the rule number in parentheses at the end of the sentence.

RULE 1:	RULE 2:	RULE 3:
Change the second negative to a positive.	Take out the negative part of a contraction.	Remove the first negative word (verb change).

  1. My brother didn't say nothing. (**Rule 3**)

  2. Patty didn't bake no cookies. (**Rule 1**)

  3. Chris hadn't never worked in a factory. (**Rule 2**)

  4. Ann doesn't take no music lessons. (**Rule 1**)

Home Connection

Family Activity for Double Negatives

1. Pretend that you and your classmates have entered a poster contest for a stop-smoking campaign at your school. Below are some of the slogans with double negatives your classmates have written. Rewrite the slogans, correcting the errors. See how many ways each slogan can be corrected.

  Winners don't never smoke.

  Don't never say yes to cigarettes.

  I won't never smoke.

  Smoking never got no one nowhere.

  Smoking isn't no good.

  Lung cancer ain't no joke.

2. Write your own slogans about a subject of your choice.

3. Divide into family teams. Each team should write slogans with double-negative errors for another team to correct. After each team has corrected the other team's slogans, the teams could choose a way to illustrate or dramatize the corrected slogans.

LISTENING AND SPEAKING:
Grammar Time

Apply It: Classify the Practice Sentences orally with your teacher.

Practice Sentences	Chapter 13: Lesson 5

1. _____ The weather will be sunny and cool tomorrow.
2. _____ The parched leaves of my aunt's favorite plant were brown from lack of water.
3. _____ That ski trail is too rough and dangerous for beginners.

Chapter Checkup 61

It is time for a checkup of the skills you have learned in this chapter. You will use the Chapter Checkup on the next page to evaluate your progress.

ENRICHMENT:
Discovery Time

(American) 1929-1968— Martin Luther King, Jr. was a leader of the Civil Rights Movement in the United States. He is best remembered for his "I Have a Dream" speech that was delivered to civil rights marchers at the Lincoln Memorial in Washington, D. C. King won the Nobel Peace Prize in 1964 and was the first black American to be honored as *Time* magazine's Man of the Year.

Discovery Questions:
• In what year was the first national holiday observed for Martin Luther King, Jr.?
• Have you read the "I Have a Dream" speech? What points does King make in his speech?
• What do you think about this speech?

Discovery Activity:
• Write a speech on a topic about which you feel strongly.

(American) 1930— Sandra Day O'Connor was the first woman to be appointed an associate justice of the United States Supreme Court. Raised on an isolated cattle ranch in Arizona, she learned to drive, fire a rifle, and ride horses by the time she was eight years old. O'Connor received her law degree in 1952. Her political career started in 1965 as an assistant attorney general for Arizona. In 1981, President Reagan appointed O'Connor to the Supreme Court. As a Supreme Court justice, she was known for her meticulously researched opinions on the bench and her tendency to moderate an often-divided court. O'Connor retired from the Supreme Court in 2005.

Discovery Questions:
• What are your views about a judge's responsibilities?
• What political office would you like to hold?

Discovery Activity:
• Invite a lawyer, judge, or politician to speak to your class. Prepare good questions to ask your speaker.

Are you interested in learning more about Martin Luther King, Jr. or Sandra Day O'Connor?

1. You may explore these topics further by using the resources listed below.
   Computer resources: Internet, encyclopedia software
   Library resources: encyclopedias, books, magazines, newspapers
   Home/community resources: books, interviews, newspapers, magazines
2. A Discovery Share Time is provided in Lesson 8 if you wish to share your investigation results. You may share orally, or you may prepare a written report. You will put your written report in a class booklet titled "Notable People in History." This booklet will be placed in the class library for everyone to enjoy.

START LESSON 5

Lesson 5
You will
• classify Practice Sentences.
• do Chapter Checkup 61.
• write in your journal.
• read and discuss Discovery Time.

JOURNAL WRITING 36

Write an entry in your journal. Use Reference 9 on page 12 for ideas.

Chapter 13 Checkup 61

Name:_____ Date:_____

GRAMMAR

▶ **Exercise 1:** Classify each sentence.

1. _____ The water in the pot on the stove was warm.

2. _____ Warren was exhausted after his long flight from New York to Paris.

3. _____ During the outdoor concert, we were hot and miserable.

SKILLS

▶ **Exercise 2:** Write the different forms for the adjectives below.

RULE 1: Simple form	RULE 2: Comparative form (er, more)	RULE 3: Superlative form (est, most)

Simple Form	Comparative Form	Superlative Form
1.	drier	
2. interesting		
3. good		

▶ **Exercise 3:** In each blank, write the correct form of the adjective in parentheses to complete the sentences.

1. Did Andrew or Leroy do _____ work? **(good)**

2. These mountains look much _____ than the mountains at home. **(rocky)**

3. That was the _____ game the team had played all year. **(bad)**

4. On _____ days than this one, the skyscrapers can be seen. **(clear)**

▶ **Exercise 4:** Underline the negative words in each sentence. Rewrite each sentence and correct the double-negative mistake as indicated by the rule number in parentheses at the end of the sentence.

RULE 1: Change the second negative to a positive.	RULE 2: Take out the negative part of a contraction.	RULE 3: Remove the first negative word (verb change).

1. Mom hasn't never been sick. **(Rule 2)** _____

2. I didn't buy nothing. **(Rule 1)** _____

3. Matt doesn't need nothing. **(Rule 3)** _____

4. My dad hadn't never played cards. **(Rule 2)** _____

5. He didn't buy no new shoes. **(Rule 1)** _____

▶ **Exercise 5:** Write the letter of the word that best completes the analogy.

1. **oak** : ____ :: **bass** : **fish**   a. tree   b. maple   c. forest   d. acorn

EDITING

▶ **Exercise 6:** Correct the sentence below. (Total mistakes: 15)

mitch ill do your chores this weakend martha pleaded if youll take me too the mall

LISTENING AND SPEAKING:

 Jingle Time

Lesson 6

You will

- practice Jingle 26.
- do Classroom Practice 62.
- choose a book to read for enjoyment.
- do Across the Curriculum activity.

Recite It: Practice Jingle 26 in the Jingle Section on page 513.

GRAMMAR & WRITING CONNECTION:
Practice and Revised Sentence

Apply It: **BUILDING AND EXPANDING SENTENCES**

| Reference 186 | A Guide for Using a Pattern 5 Core (SN LV PA) to Build & Expand Sentences |

1. **SN** or **SP** (**subject**) Think of a noun or pronoun that you want to use as the *subject*. Write the noun or pronoun you have chosen as the *subject* of your sentence.

2. **LV** (**linking verb**) A *linking verb* links the subject with a word in the predicate. You may choose a linking verb from this list: *am, is, are, was, were, be, being, been, appear, become, feel, grow, look, remain, seem, smell, sound, stay,* and *taste.* First, choose a verb for your sentence. Then, wait until you have chosen a predicate adjective to verify that it is a linking verb. If the verb is verified as linking, keep it as the verb of your Pattern 5 core.

3. **PA** (**predicate adjective**) A *predicate adjective* is an adjective in the predicate that tells **what kind** of subject is in the sentence. To find a predicate adjective, ask the question WHAT KIND of subject after the verb. Check to make sure the predicate adjective describes the subject. Write the predicate adjective you have chosen in the predicate part of your sentence.

Classroom Practice 62

It is time to practice the skills you are learning. You will use the classroom practice on the next page to apply these skills.

Student Tip...

Use your vocabulary words in your Practice and Revised Sentences. Use a thesaurus, synonym-antonym book, or a dictionary to help you develop your writing vocabulary.

Choose It: **A FICTION OR NONFICTION BOOK**

Choose a fiction or nonfiction book to read for enjoyment and have it ready to read during Reading Time in the next lesson.

 **Across the Curriculum**

Drama/Social Studies Connection: Divide into small groups. Select a historical event from your social studies book. Write a short play, using the historical figures and events from your book. Use your imagination and the information from your book to write the dialogue for your play. When you write a play, you do not use quotation marks. On the left side of your paper, write the character's name, followed by a colon. Then, write the words that are spoken after the character's name. Start a new line each time the dialogue changes from one character to another.

Additional instructions, or cues, for the actors are always written in parentheses and italicized. These instructions tell the actor where to stand, when to leave the stage, and what type of voice inflections to use: soft, loud, irritable, proud, etc.

Classroom Practice 62

Name: _____ Date: _____

INDEPENDENT PRACTICE & REVISED SENTENCES

1. Write a Practice Sentence according to the labels you choose.
Use **SN/SP LV PA** as your main labels. You may use the other labels in any order and as many times as you wish in order to make a Practice Sentence.
Chapter 13 labels for a Practice Sentence: **SN/SP, LV, PA**, Adj, Adv, A, P, OP, PPA, C, HV, I, PNA

2. Write a Revised Sentence. Use the following revision strategies: *synonym (syn), antonym (ant), word change (wc), added word (add), deleted word (delete), or no change (nc)*. Under each word, write the abbreviation of the revision strategy you use.

Labels:

Practice:

Revised:

Strategies:

Labels:

Practice:

Revised:

Strategies:

Labels:

Practice:

Revised:

Strategies:

English Made Easy

Reading Time

Read It: A FICTION OR NONFICTION BOOK

Use your reading time to read the fiction or nonfiction book you selected in the previous lesson. This book is for enjoyment, and there is no book review required.

Conference Time

Discuss It: TEACHER-STUDENT CONFERENCES FOR WRITING ASSIGNMENT 32

Meet with your teacher to discuss Writing Assignment 32.
After the conference, place this group of papers in your Publishing folder.

START LESSON 7

Lesson 7

You will
- conference with teacher about WA 32.
- read a book.

START LESSON 8

Lesson 8

You will

- participate in Discovery Share Time.
- read and discuss guidelines for dramatic presentations.
- begin publishing WA 32 by rewriting your tall tale.

LISTENING AND SPEAKING:

Discovery Share Time

If you have chosen to investigate a historical figure introduced in this chapter, you now have the opportunity to share your results in one of the following ways:

1. You may relate your information orally.
2. You may read a written report.
3. You may place your report in the booklet without reading it aloud.

After share time, all written reports should be turned in to be placed in the class booklet titled "Notable People in History." You are encouraged to check out this class booklet so you can enjoy the reports again.

Publishing Time

Learn It: **DRAMATIC PRESENTATIONS OF TALL TALES**

You will publish your tall tale by presenting it to the class in a dramatic presentation. Your teacher will give you a presentation schedule to follow. If you are in Group 1, you will share in Lesson 9. If you are in Group 2, you will share in Lesson 10. Use the guidelines below as you prepare for your presentation.

Reference 187 — Guidelines for Dramatic Presentations

1. Your teacher will post a presentation schedule.

2. Stay seated until the current presenter has finished.

3. When it is your turn, go to the designated area. Make all preparations necessary for your presentation before you begin.

4. Introduce yourself and your presentation. Be sure to say your first and last name. Here are two examples.

   Say: "**Hello, my name is (***your first and last name***). The title of my story is (***the title of your story***).**"

   Say: "**(***the title of your story***) by (***your first and last name***).**"

5. Read clearly, slowly, and loudly enough for everyone to hear. Read with expression. Do not be afraid to raise your voice and read with feeling. Look at your audience from time to time.

6. If you make a mistake, correct it or ignore it and keep going. Most people do not notice minor mistakes if the speaker recovers quickly and smoothly. It takes practice to become a calm and fluent speaker.

7. You are part of the audience when you are not presenting. You must be as quiet as possible and give the speaker your full attention. Show appreciation by clapping after the speaker has finished.

8. The information in the Share Time Guidelines applies to all presentations. If you need to review this information, look at Reference 67 on page 399.

Review It:

| Reference 67 | **Share Time Guidelines** |

Speaker Presentation

1. Have your paper ready to read when called upon.
2. Tell the title of your writing selection.
3. Tell the purpose and type of writing used.

PRESENTATION TIPS:

4. Stand with your feet flat on the floor and your shoulders straight. Do not shift your weight as you stand.
5. Hold your paper about chin high to help you project your voice to your audience.
6. Make sure you do not read too fast.
7. Read in a clear voice that can be heard so that your audience does not have to strain to hear you.
8. Change your voice tone for different characters or for different parts of the writing selection.

Audience Response

1. Look at the speaker.
2. Turn your body toward the speaker.
3. Listen attentively. Do not let your thoughts wander.
4. Do not make distracting noises as you listen.
5. Do not make distracting motions as you listen.
6. Show interest in what the speaker is saying.
7. Silently summarize what the speaker is saying. Take notes if necessary.
8. Ask questions about anything that is not clear.
9. Show appreciation by clapping after the speaker has finished.

Write It: **REWRITE WRITING ASSIGNMENT 32, TALL TALE**

Correct any errors in your tall tale before you rewrite it in ink or type it on a computer. After rewriting your paper for publication, give the stapled papers (evaluation guide, graded final paper, rough draft, and Story Elements Outline) to your teacher to be placed in your Writing Portfolio.

>>>>>>>>>> **Student Tip...**

1. Dress the part of a character in your tall tale or make and use illustrations.
2. Take your rewritten tall tale home to practice before your presentation.

START LESSON 9

Lesson 9

You will

- review guidelines for dramatic presentations.
- continue publishing WA 32 by sharing your tall tale in a dramatic presentation.

Publishing Time

Publish It: **WRITING ASSIGNMENT 32**

Review the Guidelines for Dramatic Presentations. If you are in Group 1, you will share your tall tale today. If you are in Group 2, you will share during the next lesson. Use the Share Time Guidelines as presentations are made. After each presentation, you should write the title of the tall tale and the student author in your journal.

| Reference 187 | Guidelines for Dramatic Presentations |

1. Your teacher will post a presentation schedule.
2. Stay seated until the current presenter has finished.
3. When it is your turn, go to the designated area. Make all preparations necessary for your presentation before you begin.
4. Introduce yourself and your presentation. Be sure to say your first and last name. Here are two examples.

   Say: "**Hello, my name is** *(your first and last name)*. **The title of my story is** *(the title of your story)*."

   Say: "*(the title of your story)* **by** *(your first and last name)*."
5. Read clearly, slowly, and loudly enough for everyone to hear. Read with expression. Do not be afraid to raise your voice and read with feeling. Look at your audience from time to time.
6. If you make a mistake, correct it or ignore it and keep going. Most people do not notice minor mistakes if the speaker recovers quickly and smoothly. It takes practice to become a calm and fluent speaker.
7. You are part of the audience when you are not presenting. You must be as quiet as possible and give the speaker your full attention. Show appreciation by clapping after the speaker has finished.
8. The information in the Share Time Guidelines applies to all presentations. If you need to review this information, look at Reference 67.

| Reference 67 | Share Time Guidelines |

Speaker Presentation

1. Have your paper ready to read when called upon.
2. Tell the title of your writing selection.
3. Tell the purpose and type of writing used.

PRESENTATION TIPS:

4. Stand with your feet flat on the floor and your shoulders straight. Do not shift your weight as you stand.
5. Hold your paper about chin high to help you project your voice to your audience.
6. Make sure you do not read too fast.
7. Read in a clear voice that can be heard so that your audience does not have to strain to hear you.
8. Change your voice tone for different characters or for different parts of the writing selection.

Audience Response

1. Look at the speaker.
2. Turn your body toward the speaker.
3. Listen attentively. Do not let your thoughts wander.
4. Do not make distracting noises as you listen.
5. Do not make distracting motions as you listen.
6. Show interest in what the speaker is saying.
7. Silently summarize what the speaker is saying. Take notes if necessary.
8. Ask questions about anything that is not clear.
9. Show appreciation by clapping after the speaker has finished.

English Made Easy

Publishing Time

Publish It: **WRITING ASSIGNMENT 32**

Review the Guidelines for Dramatic Presentations. If you are in Group 2, you will share your tall tale today. Use the Share Time Guidelines as presentations are made. After each presentation, you should write the title of the tall tale and the student author in your journal.

Lesson 10

You will

- review guidelines for dramatic presentations.
- finish publishing WA 32 by sharing your tall tale in a dramatic presentation.

Reference 187   Guidelines for Dramatic Presentations

1. Your teacher will post a presentation schedule.

2. Stay seated until the current presenter has finished.

3. When it is your turn, go to the designated area. Make all preparations necessary for your presentation before you begin.

4. Introduce yourself and your presentation. Be sure to say your first and last name. Here are two examples.

   Say: "**Hello, my name is (***your first and last name***). The title of my story is (***the title of your story***).**"

   Say: "(***the title of your story***) by (***your first and last name***)."

5. Read clearly, slowly, and loudly enough for everyone to hear. Read with expression. Do not be afraid to raise your voice and read with feeling. Look at your audience from time to time.

6. If you make a mistake, correct it or ignore it and keep going. Most people do not notice minor mistakes if the speaker recovers quickly and smoothly. It takes practice to become a calm and fluent speaker.

7. You are part of the audience when you are not presenting. You must be as quiet as possible and give the speaker your full attention. Show appreciation by clapping after the speaker has finished.

8. The information in the Share Time Guidelines applies to all presentations. If you need to review this information, look at Reference 67.

Reference 67   Share Time Guidelines

Speaker Presentation

1. Have your paper ready to read when called upon.

2. Tell the title of your writing selection.

3. Tell the purpose and type of writing used.

PRESENTATION TIPS:

4. Stand with your feet flat on the floor and your shoulders straight. Do not shift your weight as you stand.

5. Hold your paper about chin high to help you project your voice to your audience.

6. Make sure you do not read too fast.

7. Read in a clear voice that can be heard so that your audience does not have to strain to hear you.

8. Change your voice tone for different characters or for different parts of the writing selection.

Audience Response

1. Look at the speaker.

2. Turn your body toward the speaker.

3. Listen attentively. Do not let your thoughts wander.

4. Do not make distracting noises as you listen.

5. Do not make distracting motions as you listen.

6. Show interest in what the speaker is saying.

7. Silently summarize what the speaker is saying. Take notes if necessary.

8. Ask questions about anything that is not clear.

9. Show appreciation by clapping after the speaker has finished.

START LESSON 11

Lesson 11

You will

- read and discuss evaluations of dramatic presentations.
- write an evaluation of your own dramatic presentation and a classmate's presentation for WA 33.

Writing Time

Learn It: **EVALUATION OF DRAMATIC PRESENTATIONS**

Use the questions below to help you evaluate your dramatic presentation and the presentation of a classmate for Writing Assignment 33.

Reference 188 **Evaluation Prompts for Dramatic Presentations**

Choose the evaluation prompt below that describes your presentation. Write your answers and comments in complete sentences. Try to be as objective as possible. This evaluation will help you improve your next dramatic presentation.

Character Portrayal

1. Explain why you made the choice to do a character portrayal.

2. Which character did you choose to portray? Explain how you made your choice.

3. How did you look? (Describe your hair, face, and costume or outfit.)

4. Did you use any other props? If so, what were they? Did they add to your presentation? Did they distract from it?

5. Were you aware of nonverbal cues in your presentation? Did you hold your paper so that your face could be seen? Did you look at the audience from time to time? Did you use facial expressions and body gestures effectively? Did you move around or did you stand still?

Illustration

1. Explain why you made the choice to use illustrations for your presentation.

2. How did you illustrate your story? Did you use paint, markers, chalk, crayons, pencils, or other media? Were your illustrations easy for the audience to see? Did you use them effectively?

3. Did you use any other props? If so, what were they? Did they add to your presentation? Did they distract from it?

4. Were you aware of nonverbal cues in your presentation? Did you hold your paper so that your face could be seen? Did you look at the audience from time to time? Did you use facial expressions and body gestures effectively? Did you move around or did you stand still?

Reading Dramatization

1. Explain why you made the choice to do a dramatic reading of your story.

2. Were you aware of nonverbal cues in your presentation? Did you hold your paper so that your face could be seen? Did you look at the audience from time to time? Did you use facial expressions and body gestures effectively? Did you move around or did you stand still?

3. Did you speak clearly and loudly enough to be heard? Did you use inflections in your voice to make the characters come alive?

4. How could you enhance your presentation? What would you change and what would you not change?

Continued on next page. >>>

Reference 188 continued from previous page.

6. Did you speak clearly and loudly enough to be heard? Did you use inflections in your voice to make the characters come alive?	5. Did you speak clearly and loudly enough to be heard? Did you use inflections in your voice to make the characters come alive?	5. What is your honest opinion of your presentation? What were the strong points, and what areas needed improvement?
7. How could you enhance your presentation? What would you change and what would you not change?	6. How could you enhance your presentation? What would you change and what would you not change?	
8. What is your honest opinion of your presentation? What were the strong points, and what areas needed improvement?	7. What is your honest opinion of your presentation? What were the strong points, and what areas needed improvement?	

Write It: **WRITING ASSIGNMENT 33**

Write two evaluations in your journal. Evaluate your dramatic presentation and evaluate the presentation of one classmate.

Writing Assignment 33

1. **Personal Evaluation:** The evaluation of the dramatic presentation of your own tall tale will be written in your journal. At the top of the page, write today's date and the title of your presentation. Next, choose the evaluation prompt according to the way you made your presentation. *(Refer to Reference 188 on page 402 for the evaluation prompts.)* For example, if you portrayed a character, use the evaluation section under Character Portrayal. Write your answers and comments in complete sentences. Try to be as objective as possible.

2. **Evaluation of a Classmate:** At the top of another journal page, write today's date, the title, and the author of your favorite tall-tale presentation by another classmate. Use your list of titles and the names of the student authors to help you. Tell your favorite part of your classmate's tall tale. Try to include as many details as you can remember. End your evaluation by telling why you liked the presentation.

SHURLEY ENGLISH

Lesson 12

You will

- respond to oral review questions.
- take Chapter 12 Test.

CHAPTER TEST

It is time to evaluate your knowledge of the skills you have learned in this chapter. Your teacher will give you the Chapter 13 Test to help you assess your progress.

LISTENING AND SPEAKING:
Oral Review Questions

Discuss It:

1. What word in the predicate describes or tells what kind of subject?

2. What type of verb is used with a predicate adjective?

3. What are the core parts of a Pattern 5 sentence?

4. What are the core parts of a Pattern 4 sentence?

5. What are the core parts of a Pattern 3 sentence?

6. What are the core parts of a Pattern 2 sentence?

7. What are the core parts of a Pattern 1 sentence?

8. What are the three degrees of comparison for adjectives?

9. Which comparison form is used to compare three or more nouns?

10. What are the three degrees of the word happy?

11. What is it called when two negative words are used in a sentence?

12. Most negative words begin with which letter?

13. Name four negative words that begin with the letter **n**.

14. Name a negative word that does not begin with the letter **n**.

15. What type of writing is a humorous story that makes use of exaggeration?

Student Tip...

For information about test-taking strategies, refer to the Resource Tools Section on page 528.

LISTENING AND SPEAKING:
Grammar Time

Apply It: These Introductory Sentences are used to apply the new grammar concepts taught below. Classify these sentences orally with your teacher.

Introductory Sentences	Chapter 14: Lesson 1

1. _____ Ah! These hollow, uncooked noodles will make perfect beads for our necklaces!

2. _____ The viral outbreak in our school was highly contagious.

3. _____ The light from the moon and stars was shining brightly overhead during the cold winter night.

Lesson 1

You will
- identify Mixed Patterns 1–5.
- classify Introductory Sentences.
- read and discuss the parts of a friendly letter and a friendly letter envelope.
- read and discuss commonly used abbreviations.
- do Classroom Practice 63.
- write in your journal.
- read and discuss Discovery Time.

➡>>> Student Tip...

As you review each pattern, study how the Shurley patterns relate to the traditional patterns.					
	Pattern 1	Pattern 2	Pattern 3	Pattern 4	Pattern 5
Traditional	N V	N V N	N V N N	N LV N	N LV Adj
Shurley English	SN V	SN V-t DO	SN V-t IO DO	SN LV PrN	SN LV PA

Learn It: MIXED PATTERNS 1–5

The sentences classified in this chapter will be Patterns 1–5. They are called **Mixed Patterns** because there are five different patterns from which to choose. Use the sentence cores to help determine the pattern of the sentences.

Skill Time

Learn It: TIPS FOR WRITING A FRIENDLY LETTER

Reference 189	Tips for Writing Friendly Letters

Writing letters is a great way to preserve memories of people you care about and who care about you. A letter written to or received from friends or relatives is called a **friendly letter**. Follow the tips below to write a friendly letter.

Tip 1: Write as if you were talking to the person face-to-face. Share information about yourself and mutual friends. Tell stories, conversations, or jokes. Share photographs, articles, drawings, poems, etc. Avoid saying something about someone else that you'll be sorry for later.

Tip 2: If you are writing a return letter, be sure to answer any questions that were asked. Repeat the question so that your reader will know what you are writing about. (You asked about...)

Tip 3: End your letter in a positive way so that your reader will want to write a return letter.

SHURLEY ENGLISH

Learn It: **THE FIVE PARTS OF A FRIENDLY LETTER**
The language used in a friendly letter is conversational and informal.
Each part of a friendly letter has a specific place and purpose.

Reference 190 — The Five Parts of a Friendly Letter

1. Heading:
- Box or street address of writer
- City, state, zip code of writer
- Full date letter was written

2. Friendly Greeting or Salutation:
- Begins with *Dear*
- Names the person receiving the letter
- Has a comma after the person's name

3. Body:
- Tells the reason the letter is being written
- Can have one or more paragraphs
- Has indented paragraphs

4. Closing:
- Closes the letter with a personal phrase (*Your friend,*)
- Capitalizes only the first word
- Is followed by a comma

5. Signature:
- Tells who has written the letter
- Is usually signed in cursive
- Uses your first name only unless there is a question as to which friend or relative you are

EXAMPLE OF THE FRIENDLY LETTER

Friendly letter style:
The modified-block style is used in writing friendly letters. In the modified-block style, place the heading, closing, and signature in the middle of the page. Indent each paragraph and do not skip a line between paragraphs.

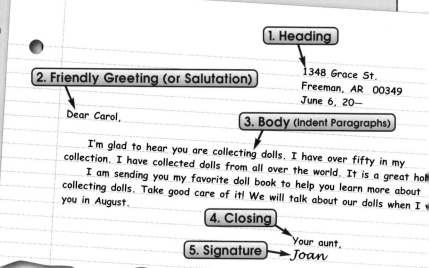

> **1. Heading**
> 1348 Grace St.
> Freeman, AR 00349
> June 6, 20—
>
> **2. Friendly Greeting (or Salutation)**
> Dear Carol,
>
> **3. Body (Indent Paragraphs)**
> I'm glad to hear you are collecting dolls. I have over fifty in my collection. I have collected dolls from all over the world. It is a great ho[...] I am sending you my favorite doll book to help you learn more about collecting dolls. Take good care of it! We will talk about our dolls when I [...] you in August.
>
> **4. Closing**
> Your aunt,
>
> **5. Signature**
> Joan

Learn It: **THE PARTS OF AN ENVELOPE**
Each part of an envelope for a friendly letter has a specific place and purpose.

Reference 191 — Envelope Parts for a Friendly Letter

The Return Address:
- Name of the person writing the letter
- Box or street address of the writer
- City, state, and zip code of the writer

The Mailing Address:
- Name of the person receiving the letter
- Street address of the person receiving the letter
- City, state, and zip code of the person receiving the letter

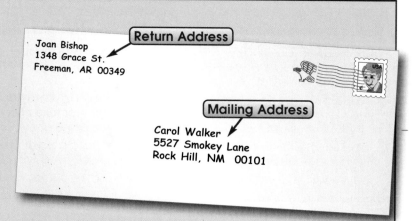

> **Return Address**
> Joan Bishop
> 1348 Grace St.
> Freeman, AR 00349
>
> **Mailing Address**
> Carol Walker
> 5527 Smokey Lane
> Rock Hill, NM 00101

Learn It: COMMONLY USED ABBREVIATIONS

Reference 192 — Commonly Used Abbreviations

Addresses

Apartment	Apt.
Avenue	Ave.
Building	Bldg.
Boulevard	Blvd.
Circle	Cir.
County	Co.
Court	Ct.
Drive	Dr.
Fort	Ft.
Headquarters	Hq.
Highway	Hwy.
Lane	Ln.
Mount	Mt.
Mountain	Mt./Mtn.
Parkway	Pkwy.
Place	Pl.
Point	Pt.
Post Office	P.O./PO
Road	Rd.
Route	Rt.
School	Sch.
Street	St.
Terrace	Ter./Terr.
University	Univ.

Math Abbreviations

foot	ft.
hour	hr.
inch	in.
mile	mi.
minute	min.
month	mo.
ounce	oz.
pint	pt.
pound	lb.
quart	qt.
second	sec.
week	wk.
yard	yd.
year	yr.

Titles

Attorney	Atty.
Doctor	Dr.
Governor	Gov.
Honorable	Hon.
Junior	Jr.
Manager	Mgr.
Miss/Mistress	Ms.
Mistress	Mrs.
Mister	Mr.
President	Pres.
Professor	Prof.
Representative	Rep.
Reverend	Rev.
Senator	Sen.
Senior	Sr.
Superintendent	Supt.

Business Titles

Company	Co.
Corporation	Corp.
Department	Dept.
Incorporated	Inc.

Military Titles

Admiral	Adm.
Captain	Capt.
Colonel	Col.
Commander	Cmdr.
Corporal	Cpl.
Ensign	Ens.
General	Gen.
Lieutenant	Lt.
Major	Maj.
Private	Pvt.
Sergeant	Sgt.
Specialist	Spec.

States and Postal Abbreviations

Alabama	AL	Montana	MT
Alaska	AK	Nebraska	NE
Arizona	AZ	Nevada	NV
Arkansas	AR	New Hampshire	NH
California	CA	New Jersey	NJ
Colorado	CO	New Mexico	NM
Connecticut	CT	New York	NY
Delaware	DE	North Carolina	NC
Florida	FL	North Dakota	ND
Georgia	GA	Ohio	OH
Hawaii	HI	Oklahoma	OK
Idaho	ID	Oregon	OR
Illinois	IL	Pennsylvania	PA
Indiana	IN	Rhode Island	RI
Iowa	IA	South Carolina	SC
Kansas	KS	South Dakota	SD
Kentucky	KY	Tennessee	TN
Louisiana	LA	Texas	TX
Maine	ME	Utah	UT
Maryland	MD	Vermont	VT
Massachusetts	MA	Virginia	VA
Michigan	MI	Washington	WA
Minnesota	MN	West Virginia	WV
Mississippi	MS	Wisconsin	WI
Missouri	MO	Wyoming	WY

Days

Monday	Mon.
Tuesday	Tues.
Wednesday	Wed.
Thursday	Thurs.
Friday	Fri.
Saturday	Sat.
Sunday	Sun.

Directions

North	N
South	S
East	E
West	W
Northeast	NE
Northwest	NW
Southeast	SE
Southwest	SW

Months

January	Jan.
February	Feb.
March	Mar.
April	Apr.
May	——
June	——
July	——
August	Aug.
September	Sept.
October	Oct.
November	Nov.
December	Dec.

Others

District of Columbia	D.C./DC
afternoon	p.m.
before noon	a.m.

JOURNAL WRITING 37

Write an entry in your journal. Use Reference 9 on page 12 for ideas.

Classroom Practice 63

It is time to practice the skills you are learning. You will use the classroom practice on the next page to apply these skills.

ENRICHMENT:

Discovery Time

(American) 1935— Loretta Lynn rose from poverty and established herself as one of the most popular and influential female singers and songwriters in country-western music. She was a pioneer in breaking through social barriers for women in the 1960s. Loretta used the lyrics of her songs to speak out about women's issues. Her song "Coal Miner's Daughter" was number one on the country charts in 1970. She was also the first female millionaire in country music. Loretta Lynn was inducted into the Country Music Hall of Fame in 1988.

Discovery Questions:
- What do you think it is like to be a famous singer?
- How do famous people influence the public?
- What would you do to let your voice be heard about social issues important to you?

Discovery Activity:
- Write a song, poem, or story about something important to you.

Are you interested in learning more about Loretta Lynn?

1. You may explore this topic further by using the resources listed below.
   Computer resources: Internet, encyclopedia software
   Library resources: encyclopedias, books, magazines, newspapers
   Home/community resources: books, interviews, newspapers, magazines

2. A Discovery Share Time is provided in Lesson 4 if you wish to share your investigation results. You may share orally, or you may prepare a written report. You will put your written report in a class booklet titled "Notable People in History." This booklet will be placed in the class library for everyone to enjoy.

Classroom Practice 63

Name:_____ Date:_____

GRAMMAR

▶ **Exercise 1:** Classify each sentence.

1. _____ The new battery-powered scooter is a fantastic innovation in personal transportation.

2. _____ The man stood on the corner and waited patiently for the next bus.

3. _____ Did you leave a tip on the table for that young waiter?

4. _____ The ruts in the dirt road were deep and treacherous after the downpour.

5. _____ Fax me a copy of the contract negotiations before our next meeting.

SKILLS

▶ **Exercise 2:** Use the letter parts below to fill in the blanks of the friendly letter.

TITLE PARTS of a Friendly Letter: Closing   **Signature**   **Heading**   **Greeting**   **Body**

SAMPLE PARTS of a Friendly Letter: Brian   Dear Charles,   Dallas, TX 00267   Your pal,
October 10, 20—   19 Overland Trail   Last week my family and I went to a college football game. What a game! The home team won, and the fans went wild! I hope all the games are this exciting.

Friendly Letter

1. Title: _____

Sample: _____
_____
_____

2. Title: _____

Sample: _____

3. Title: _____

Sample: _____
_____

4. Title: _____

Sample: _____

5. Title: _____

Sample: _____

START LESSON 2

Lesson 2

You will

- practice Jingles 20-26.
- classify Practice Sentences.
- edit a friendly letter for rule numbers only.
- do Classroom Practice 64.
- read and discuss Discovery Time.
- do a homework assignment.
- do Home Connection activity.

LISTENING AND SPEAKING:

Recite It: Practice Jingles 20–26 in the Jingle Section on pages 511–513.

Apply It: Classify the Practice Sentences orally with your teacher.

Practice Sentences	Chapter 14: Lesson 2

1. _____ This meal is a wonderful example of exotic foods from countries around the world.
2. _____ The little children gleefully ran and played in the wet snow.
3. _____ Earlier, the professor gave the students a short review before the exam.

Learn It: EDITING A FRIENDLY LETTER, USING RULE NUMBERS

The friendly letter in Classroom Practice 64 has already been punctuated. Write the capitalization and punctuation rule numbers for each correction that appears in **bold** type. There are thirty-five rule numbers that you must write.

Classroom Practice 64

It is time to practice the skills you are learning. You will use the classroom practice on the next page to apply these skills.

ENRICHMENT:

(American) 1936— Marva Collins was a teacher in the public schools for over 16 years. Frustrated by the low standards of the Chicago schools, Collins opened her own school in 1975 in her home, naming it the "Westside Preparatory School." At the end of the first year, every student scored at least five grades higher on their standardized tests. Collins gained national attention when profiled by *Time* and *Newsweek* magazines and *60 Minutes* and *Good Morning America* television shows. Collins has also written several books on education and teaching. She has received several awards, including the prestigious Jefferson Award for the Greatest Public Service Benefiting the Disadvantaged.

Discovery Questions:
- Why do you need a good education?
- What are the distinguishing characteristics of a good teacher?
- Why is it important to have good role models, such as parents, teachers, and coaches?

Are you interested in learning more about Marva Collins?

1. You may explore this topic further by using the resources listed below.
   Computer resources: Internet, encyclopedia software
   Library resources: encyclopedias, books, magazines, newspapers
   Home/community resources: books, interviews, newspapers, magazines

2. A Discovery Share Time is provided in Lesson 4 if you wish to share your investigation results. You may share orally, or you may prepare a written report. You will put your written report in a class booklet titled "Notable People in History." This booklet will be placed in the class library for everyone to enjoy.

>>>>>>>>>>>> Student Tip...

Make sure you are aware of the homework note that tells you to bring an envelope from home for a letter-writing assignment in Lesson 6.

Classroom Practice 64

Name:_____ Date:_____

GRAMMAR

▶ **Exercise 1:** Classify each sentence.

1. _____ After his illness, Uncle Howard's handwriting was not legible.

2. _____ We did not swim in the ocean during our vacation.

3. _____ Did you change the password on your computer?

4. _____ Will you loan me your umbrella for my trip today?

5. _____ Carrots are an excellent source of vitamins.

SKILLS AND EDITING

▶ **Exercise 2:** Write the capitalization and punctuation rule numbers for each correction in **bold type**. Use References 11–13 on pages 13–16 to look up rule numbers. (Total rule numbers required: 35.)

700 **N**orth **M**ichigan **A**ve**.**

Lansing**,** **MI** 00333

June 28**,** 20—

Dear **P**atty**,**

    I broke my arm climbing a tree**.** **Dr. C**hapman**,** our family doctor**,** put a cast on my arm and told me not to climb trees until **I** get the cast off my arm**.** **T**his is going to be a dull summer**.** **I**'ll go to **T**exas in **J**uly to visit **G**randma**.** **W**rite soon**.**

Your cousin**,**

Susie

Homework 11

Complete the homework assignment on notebook paper. Choose one of the following writing prompts:

1. Write a friendly letter to the author of your favorite book.

2. Pretend you are writing a friendly letter to a pen pal in another country for the first time. You must tell your new pen pal some interesting things about yourself so that he or she can get to know you. Use a social studies book, the library, or the internet to help you pick the city and country where your imaginary friend lives.

Follow the friendly-letter form. Make up a reasonable name and address. You could research names from the country you choose. Even though this is a pretend pen pal, make sure you always use writing etiquette, or manners. This means you should not write anything that would embarrass your family, teacher, or school.

Note: For a letter-writing assignment in Lesson 6, you should bring an envelope from home. Also, bring the name and address of a friend or family member to whom you will write and mail your friendly letter.

Home Connection

Family Activity for the Friendly Letter

Glue the friendly letter below onto cardstock or construction paper. Cut the sections apart at the dotted lines and glue or write the number and the title for each friendly-letter part on the back of the corresponding strip.

Divide into teams. Time each team as members put the pieces of the friendly-letter puzzle together and identify each part. Check the correct answers with the number and title on the back of each piece. The team that completes the puzzle correctly in the shortest time is the winner.

Friendly Letter

Titles: | 1. Heading | 2. Greeting or Salutation | 3. Body | 4. Closing | 5. Signature |

109 Appaloosa Trail
Flagstaff, AZ 00088
April 12, 20——

Dear Jenny,

My mom and dad surprised me with the prettiest pony for my birthday! He's brown with white spots. I named him Comet. When you visit next summer, we'll go on a trail ride near the Grand Canyon.

Your friend,

Alice

5. Signature — Alice

4. Closing — Your friend,

3. Body — My mom and dad surprised me with the prettiest pony for my birthday! He's brown with white spots. I named him Comet. When you visit next summer, we'll go on a trail ride near the Grand Canyon.

2. Greeting or Salutation — Dear Jenny,

1. Heading — 109 Appaloosa Trail Flagstaff, AZ 00088 April 12, 20——

START LESSON 3

Lesson 3

You will

- practice Jingles 13-19.
- classify Practice Sentences.
- edit a friendly letter for corrections only.
- do Classroom Practice 65.
- write in your journal.
- read and discuss Discovery Time.

LISTENING AND SPEAKING:

Recite It: Practice Jingles 13–19 in the Jingle Section on pages 509–511.

Apply It: Classify the Practice Sentences orally with your teacher.

Practice Sentences	Chapter 14: Lesson 3
1. _____ At the end of the school program, my little niece blew her father a kiss!	
2. _____ Wow! Racecar is a palindrome.	
3. _____ The ducks on the lake were listless in the heat of the afternoon sun.	

Learn It: **EDITING A FRIENDLY LETTER, USING CORRECTIONS ONLY**

The friendly letter in Classroom Practice 65 has not been punctuated. Write capitalization corrections above the capitalization mistakes, and write the punctuation corrections where they belong in the letter. Look at the editing guide to find the total number of errors you need to correct.

Classroom Practice 65

It is time to practice the skills you are learning. You will use the classroom practice on the next page to apply these skills.

ENRICHMENT:

Discovery Time

(Native Americans) 1942-1945— Navajo code talkers were Native Americans who were recruited by the Marines to use their native language to transmit secure messages during World War II. The Navajos transmitted coded messages by telephone and radio, and the Japanese were never able to break the code. The Navajo code talkers could encode, transmit, and decode a three-line English message in twenty seconds. It would take machines 30 minutes to perform the same job. The Navajo language is an unwritten language that is very complex. It has no alphabet or symbols. A Marine officer said that Iwo Jima would never have been taken if it had not been for the Navajo code talkers.

Discovery Questions:
- What do you think it was like to be a Navajo code talker?
- If you could speak another language, what would it be and why?

Discovery Activity:
- Develop an original code to send a message to a friend.

JOURNAL WRITING 38

Write an entry in your journal. Use Reference 9 on page 12 for ideas.

(American) 1955— Bill Gates is the co-founder of the Microsoft Corporation, one of the world's largest personal-computer software companies. Gates wrote his first software program at the age of 13, and, in high school, he created a computerized payroll system. Gates, with his friend Paul Allen, created software for the IBM personal computer, released in 1981. Beginning in 1995, Gates produced Microsoft software for the Internet, developed the Windows operating system, and created Microsoft Network as a means of competing with other Internet providers. By 2005, Microsoft had revenues of over $39 billion and employed more than 61,000 people. By the end of 2005, the Bill and Melinda Gates Foundation had contributed more than $28 billion to philanthropic causes.

Discovery Questions:
- How has the computer revolutionized the way the world does business?
- Do you feel it is necessary to know how to use a computer? Explain.
- For what reasons do you use a computer? How much time do you spend on the computer?
- If your company made enough money, who would you help?

Are you interested in learning more about Navajo code talkers or Bill Gates?

1. You may explore these topics further by using the resources listed below.
   Computer resources: Internet, encyclopedia software
   Library resources: encyclopedias, books, magazines, newspapers
   Home/community resources: books, interviews, newspapers, magazines

2. A Discovery Share Time is provided in Lesson 4 if you wish to share your investigation results. You may share orally, or you may prepare a written report. You will put your written report in a class booklet titled "Notable People in History." This booklet will be placed in the class library for everyone to enjoy.

SHURLEY ENGLISH

Classroom Practice 65

Name:_____ Date:_____

GRAMMAR

▶ **Exercise 1:** Classify each sentence.

1. _____ For many people, baseball is a great American sport.

2. _____ Good grief! Do not give that strange dog a bath in my bathtub!

3. _____ The huge volcano in Hawaii violently erupted with an explosive boom!

4. _____ The ship's maiden voyage to Alaska was unforgettable.

5. _____ My friends did not see you at the band concert on Friday.

SKILLS AND EDITING

▶ **Exercise 2:** Write the capitalization and punctuation corrections only.
   Editing Guide: End marks: 4   Capitals: 24   Commas: 8   Apostrophes: 1   Periods: 4

549 caldwell place

philadelphia pa 00004

march 19 20—

dear meeka

   i am organizing a community clean-up project this april and i still need several volunteers

would you alice and jd be willing to help well meet at the corner of maple and east main

at 2:00 pm on saturday april 7 i hope to see you there

your favorite aunt

melinda

LISTENING AND SPEAKING:
Grammar Time

Lesson 4

You will
- classify Practice Sentences.
- read and discuss thank-you notes.
- write an independent thank-you note for WA 34.
- participate in Discovery Share Time.

Apply It: Classify the Practice Sentences orally with your teacher.

Practice Sentences	Chapter 14: Lesson 4

1. _____ Yesterday, the wind whipped furiously at the sheets on the clothesline.
2. _____ During the long route, the crowded city bus was uncomfortable for the passengers.
3. _____ Send the governor your application for a summer internship in his office.
4. _____ In the boy's imagination, the empty cardboard box was a fighter jet.
5. _____ The officer left a ticket on the windshield of the old, abandoned car.

Skill Time

Learn It: **WRITING THANK-YOU NOTES**

You usually write thank-you notes to thank someone for a gift or for doing something nice for you. In either case, a thank-you note should include at least three statements.

1. You should tell the person **what** you are thanking him/her for.
2. You should tell the person **how the gift was used** or **how it helped**.
3. You should tell the person **how much you appreciated the gift or action**.

A thank-you note should follow the same form as a friendly letter: heading, greeting, body, closing, and signature.

Reference 193	Thank-You Notes

For a Gift
What: Thank you for... (describe the gift)
Use: Tell how the gift is used.
Thanks: I appreciate your remembering me with this special gift.

For an Action
What: Thank you for... (tell action)
Helped: Tell how the action helped.
Thanks: I appreciate your thinking of me at this time.

Continued on next page. >>>

Reference 193 continued from previous page.

Example of a Gift Thank-You Note

608 Martin Street
Glenwood, TN 00016
August 30, 20—

Dear Janet,

Thank you for the new Nancy Drew book. That makes ten in my collection! I appreciate your thoughtful gift.

Your friend,
Jenny

Example of an Action Thank-You Note

456 Concord Street
East Plains, MD 00245
March 16, 20—

Dear John,

Thank you for helping with the Pick-Up-Litter Campaign. Our work was a huge success because of people like you. I appreciate your participation very much.

Your friend,
Sam

Write It: WRITING ASSIGNMENT 34

Write a thank-you note to a real or imaginary person. After your teacher has checked it, take it home to share with family members.

Writing Assignment 34

Purpose: To thank someone
Type of Writing: Thank-you note
Audience: Person who gave a gift

Special Instructions:

1. Think of a person who has done something nice for you or who has given you a gift (including the gift of time).

2. Write that person a thank-you note, using the information in Reference 193 on page 417 as a guide.

3. Write in first person. See Reference 70 on page 104.
   (First-person pronouns: *I, me, my, mine, we, us, our,* and *ours.*)

LISTENING AND SPEAKING:

If you have chosen to investigate a historical figure introduced in this chapter, you now have the opportunity to share your results in one of the following ways:

1. You may relate your information orally.
2. You may read a written report.
3. You may place your report in the booklet without reading it aloud.

After share time, all written reports should be turned in to be placed in the class booklet titled "Notable People in History." You are encouraged to check out this class booklet so you can enjoy the reports again.

English Made Easy

LISTENING AND SPEAKING:

Grammar Time

Apply It: Classify the Practice Sentences orally with your teacher.

Practice Sentences	Chapter 14: Lesson 5

1. _____ The courteous clerk sold me a new winter coat during the store's annual sale.
2. _____ The nurse injected me with a series of antibiotics at the doctor's office.
3. _____ My brother and his friends fish in the winter on the frozen lake behind Grandfather's house.

✏ Chapter Checkup 66

It is time for a checkup of the skills you have learned in this chapter. You will use the Chapter Checkup on the next page to evaluate your progress.

Student Note: Bring an envelope from home if you have not done so. You will use the envelope in the next lesson. Also, bring the name and address of a friend or family member to whom you will write.

START LESSON 5

Lesson 5

You will
- classify Practice Sentences.
- do Chapter Checkup 66.
- write in your journal.
- bring envelopes from home.

JOURNAL WRITING 39

Write an entry in your journal. Use Reference 9 on page 12 for ideas.

Chapter 14 Checkup 66

Name:_____   Date:_____

GRAMMAR

▶ **Exercise 1:** Classify each sentence.

1. _____ The advisor did not offer the media an explanation for the sudden change in policy.

2. _____ The caterpillar slowly inched up to the top of the large sunflower.

3. _____ Pam's impulsive shopping habits were a serious problem for her monthly budget.

4. _____ Pollen causes serious allergic reactions for some people.

5. _____ After the severe weather and rough waters, the sailors were sick at their stomachs.

SKILLS AND EDITING

▶ **Exercise 2:** Write the capitalization and punctuation corrections only.
  Editing Guide: End Marks: 6   Capitals: 21   Commas: 4   Apostrophes: 3

7005 shamrock lane

lincoln ne 00287

february 25 20—

dear uncle jim

    thank you for the computer you gave dad for christmas its so nice to have a computer around the house i hope youll understand about dad not getting to use it until his turn were all hooked on the computer we get our chores and homework done early so that we do not miss our turn on the computer see you on the Internet

your grateful nephew

computer kevin

English Made Easy

Writing Time

Write It: WRITING ASSIGNMENT 35

Writing Assignment [35]

Purpose: To write a letter
Type of Writing: Friendly letter
Audience: Family member or friend

Special Instructions:

1. Use References 189–192 on pages 405–407 to help you write your friendly letter.

2. Write a friendly letter to a family member or a friend.

3. Address an envelope for the friendly letter.

4. Revise and edit the friendly letter and envelope by yourself. Then, write a final copy. Write it neatly or type it on a computer.

5. Take the final copy of your letter home in the unsealed envelope. Mail the friendly letter after your parent has looked over the letter one last time.

>>>>>>>>>> **Student Tip...**

If you need to improve your handwriting, refer to the Resource Tools Section on pages 529–530 for information on writing legibly.

START LESSON 6

Lesson 6

You will

- write an independent friendly letter for WA 35.
- revise and edit WA 35.
- address an envelope for a friendly letter.

START LESSON 7

Lesson 7

You will

- respond to oral review questions.
- take Chapter 14 Test.

CHAPTER TEST

It is time to evaluate your knowledge of the skills you have learned in this chapter. Your teacher will give you the Chapter 14 Test to help you assess your progress.

LISTENING AND SPEAKING:
Oral Review Questions

Discuss It:

1. What kind of letter is written to or received from friends or relatives?

2. What are the five parts of a friendly letter?

3. What two kinds of addresses are used for an envelope?

4. What information is contained in the heading?

5. What punctuation mark is used after the greeting in a friendly letter?

6. Whose name appears in the greeting?

7. Why do you write a thank-you note?

8. What type of writing is used when your purpose is to inform, to give facts, to give directions, to explain, or to define something?

9. What type of writing is used when your purpose is to express an opinion and to convince the reader that this opinion is correct?

10. What type of writing is used when your purpose is to tell a story?

11. What type of writing is used when your purpose is to paint a picture with words?

12. What type of writing is used when your purpose is to show similarities and differences?

>>>>>>>>>>>>>>>>>>>>>>>>> **Student Tip...**

For information about test-taking strategies, refer to the Resource Tools Section on page 528.

LISTENING AND SPEAKING:
Grammar Time

Apply It: Classify the Practice Sentences orally with your teacher.

Practice Sentences	Chapter 15: Lesson 1

1. _____ Brooke and Dana's sister are frequent volunteers at the local library.

2. _____ After the party, we cleaned the kitchen and vacuumed the floor.

3. _____ The covered gazebo was cool and comfortable for the guests at our yearly cookout.

4. _____ Does your geography teacher always give your class daily homework assignments?

5. _____ Yikes! Danny's huge black python escaped from its cage and slithered across Mother's foot!

✎ Posttest

Take the posttest. After it has been checked, compare the Pretest with the Posttest to evaluate how much you have learned during the year.

Lesson 1

You will
- classify Practice Sentences.
- take Post Test.
- write in your journal.

JOURNAL WRITING 40

Write an entry in your journal. Use Reference 9 on page 12 for ideas.

START LESSON 2

Lesson 2

You will

- read and discuss four types of business letters.
- read and discuss the parts of a business letter and a business letter envelope.
- do Classroom Practice 67.

Skill Time

Learn It: THE FOUR TYPES OF BUSINESS LETTERS

Sometimes, you may need to write a letter to someone you do not know about something that is not personal in nature. This kind of letter is called a **business letter**. Even if you are not in business, there are several reasons why you may need to write a business letter.

Reference 194	Four Types of Business Letters

There are four common reasons to write business letters.
  1. If you need to send for information, write a letter of inquiry.
  2. If you want to order a product, write a letter of request or order.
  3. If you want to express an opinion, write a letter to an editor or official.
  4. If you want to complain about a product, write a letter of complaint.

Letter of Inquiry	Letter of Request or Order
1. Ask for information or answers to your questions.	1. Carefully and clearly describe the product.
2. Keep the letter short and to the point.	2. Keep the letter short and to the point.
3. Word the letter so that there can be no question as to what it is you need to know.	3. Include information on how and where the product should be shipped.
	4. Include information on how you will pay for the product.

Letter to an Editor or Official	Letter of Complaint About a Product
1. Clearly explain the problem or situation.	1. Carefully and clearly describe the product.
2. Offer your opinion of the cause and possible solutions.	2. Describe the problem and what may have caused it. (Don't spend too much time explaining how unhappy you are.)
3. Support your opinions with facts and examples.	3. Explain any action you have already taken to solve the problem.
4. Suggest ways to change or improve the situation.	4. End your letter with the action you would like the company to take to solve the problem.

Learn It: THE SIX PARTS OF A BUSINESS LETTER

Each part of a business letter has a specific place and purpose. The language used in a business letter is formal and to the point. Business people do not have time to read a "friendly" business letter.

Reference 195 **The Six Parts of a Business Letter**

1. Heading:
- Post office box or street address of writer
- City, state, zip code of writer
- Full date letter was written

2. Inside Address:
- Name of person or company receiving the letter (Place a person's title after his name. Separate the title from the name with a comma. If the title is long, place the title separately on the next line.)
- Post office box or street address of the company
- City, state, zip code of company

3. Salutation (Formal Greeting):
- Begins with *Dear*
- Names the person receiving the letter (For a specific person, use a greeting like Dear Mr. (*last name*) or Ms. (*last name*). For a letter addressed to a person by title, use Dear Sir, Dear Madam, or Dear (*Title*). For a company or organization, use Gentlemen or Dear Sirs.)
- Has a colon at the end of the greeting

4. Body:
- Tells the reason the letter is being written (The information should be clearly and briefly written.)
- Can have one or more paragraphs

5. Closing:
- Closes the letter with a formal phrase (*Very truly, Yours truly, Sincerely,* etc.)
- Capitalizes only the first word
- Is followed by a comma

6. Signature:
- Tells who wrote the letter
- Is usually signed in cursive and in ink
- Uses your first and last name (If you are typing your letter, skip four lines and type your full name. Then, sign your name in ink between the closing and typed name.)

Business letter styles: There are several letter styles that are used in business. Two popular styles are the full block and the modified block. In the full-block style, begin all lines at the left margin and skip a line between each paragraph. In the modified-block style, place the heading, closing, and signature in the middle of the page. Indent each paragraph and do not skip a line between paragraphs.

Review It: THE BUSINESS LETTER

1. A business letter has an inside address above the greeting that tells who is receiving the letter. The inside address saves companies or business people time because they do not have to read the entire letter in order to know which person in the company should receive the letter.

2. How you write the inside address will depend on what you know about the business or company that will receive the letter. If you know the name of a person in the company who can help you, you will use that person's name as part of the inside address. If you do not know the name of a person in the company who can help you, you will just use the name of the company.

3. Greetings in business letters are formal. This means that you use the title and last name of the person who is receiving the letter followed by a colon. If you do not know the name of the person receiving the letter, you should use **Sir** or **Madam**.

4. For the signature of a business letter, you should sign your first and last name in ink between the closing and typed name.

5. Two popular styles are usually used to write business letters. The full-block style is demonstrated in Reference 196, and the modified-block style is demonstrated in Reference 197.

Learn It: THE FULL-BLOCK BUSINESS LETTER
AND THE MODIFIED-BLOCK BUSINESS LETTER

Reference 196 **Example of the Full-Block Business Letter**

1. Heading

313 West Drive
Dover, TX 00123
May 2, 20—

2. Inside Address

Mr. Harold Dodd, Pilot
Dusty's Air Services
2312 Barton Blvd.
Glen, TX 00456

Dear Mr. Dodd: 3. Salutation (Formal Greeting)

4. Body (Space Between Paragraphs)

I need 200 acres of cotton sprayed for weed control. I am having significant problems with pigweed, nutsedge, and crabgrass.

Please let me know when you will be available this month. You can call me at this number anytime during the day: 000-001-1234. Thank you for your prompt response.

Sincerely yours, 5. Formal Closing

Tom Greene

Tom Greene 6. Signature

Reference 197   **Example of the Modified-Block Business Letter**

1. Heading

313 West Drive
Dover, TX 00123
May 2, 20—

2. Inside Address

Mr. Harold Dodd, Pilot
Dusty's Air Services
2312 Barton Blvd.
Glen, TX 00456

3. Salutation (Formal Greeting)   **4. Body (Indent Paragraphs)**

Dear Mr. Dodd:

   I need 200 acres of cotton sprayed for weed control. I am having significant problems with pigweed, nutsedge, and crabgrass.
   Please let me know when you will be available this month. You can call me at this number anytime during the day: 000-001-1234. Thank you for your prompt response.

5. Formal Closing → Sincerely yours,

6. Signature → Tom Greene

Learn It: ADDRESSING THE ENVELOPE FOR A BUSINESS LETTER

Reference 198 — Parts Of A Business Envelope

In order to address the envelope for your business letter correctly, you must know **how** and **where** to write the two addresses used for a business-letter envelope. The addresses of a business-letter envelope are similar to the addresses of a friendly-letter envelope. There are two differences, however, in the mailing address for the business envelope that you should remember.

1. You must put the name of the person within the company to whom you are writing and his title (if you know it) on the first line of the mailing address. If you do not know the name of the person who would handle your request or problem, write the name of the department (such as, SALES, SHIPPING, ACCOUNTING, etc.) on the first line of the mailing address. If you do not know the name of the person or the department, you may choose to leave the first line blank.

2. You must put the name of the company on the second line of the mailing address.

The Return Address:

- Name of the person writing the letter
- Box or street address of the writer
- City, state, and zip code of the writer

The Mailing Address:

- Name and title of the person receiving the letter
- Name of the company receiving the letter
- Street address of the company receiving the letter
- City, state, and zip code of the company receiving the letter

Tom Greene
313 West Drive
Dover, TX 00123

Return Address

Mailing Address

Mr. Harold Dodd, Pilot
Dusty's Air Services
2312 Barton Blvd.
Glen, TX 00456

Student Tip...

A two-letter abbreviation is used for states in most business letters. For a list of commonly used abbreviations, refer to Reference 192 on page 407.

Classroom Practice 67

It is time to practice the skills you are learning. You will use the classroom practice on the next page to apply these skills.

Classroom Practice 67

Name:_____ Date:_____

SKILLS

Use the letter parts below to fill in the blanks of the business letter.

TITLE PARTS of a Business Letter:

Closing	Signature	Heading
Salutation	Body	Inside Address

SAMPLE PARTS of a Business Letter:

Sincerely yours,   Ellen Warren   Mr. Frederick Rogers, Manager
                                        Blue Thumb, Inc.
Dear Mr. Rogers: 307 Elm Street   147 West Main Street
                    Marshall, AR 00033   East Port, NC 00049   October 11, 20—

I would like to order twelve packages of Royal Blue tulip bulbs from your current catalog. Enclosed is my check for $38.95. Please ship the bulbs by UPS.

Business Letter

1. Title: _____
_____
_____
_____

2. Title: _____
_____
_____
_____

3. Title: _____
_____

4. Title: _____
_____

5. Title: _____
_____

6. Title: _____

START LESSON 3

Lesson 3

You will

- edit a business letter using rule numbers.
- do Classroom Practice 68.
- do a homework assignment.
- do Home Connection activity.

>>> Student Note...

Make sure you are aware of the homework note that tells you to bring an envelope from home for a letter-writing assignment in Lesson 6.

Skill Time

Learn It: **EDITING A BUSINESS LETTER, USING RULE NUMBERS**

The business letter in Classroom Practice 68 has already been punctuated. Write the capitalization and punctuation rule numbers for each correction that appears in **bold** type. There are forty-two rule numbers that you must write.

Classroom Practice 68

It is time to practice the skills you are learning. You will use the classroom practice on the next page to apply these skills.

Classroom Practice 68

Name:_____ Date:_____

SKILLS AND EDITING

Write the capitalization and punctuation rule numbers for each correction in **bold type**.
Use References 11–13 on pages 13–16 to look up rule numbers. (Total rule numbers required: 42)

P.O. Box 94

Carlton **C**ity, **MT** 00017

January 18, 20—

Senator **L**arry **J. B**urns

978 **S**outh **A**venue

Lansing, **MI** 00029

Dear **S**enator **B**urns**:**

    I want to express my support for your bill on energy conservation in **M**aryland**,** **M**ichigan**,**

and **M**innesota**. T**hank you for all the progress you have made in these states.

Sincerely yours**,**

Jason **T. L**ong

Homework 12

Complete this homework assignment on notebook paper.

Write, revise, and edit a business letter to the Chamber of Commerce in a city you would like to visit. Ask for brochures and information about hotels, restaurants, unique attractions, and local history. Also, use the Internet, library, or telephone directories to find information that would help you. When you get a response, bring the information you receive to school and share it with your teacher and classmates. Use References 194–198.

Note: You should bring an envelope from home for a business-letter assignment in Lesson 6.

Home Connection

Family Activity for the Business Letter

Glue the business letter below onto cardstock or construction paper. Cut the sections apart at the dotted lines and glue or write the number and the title for each business-letter part on the back of the corresponding strip.

Divide into teams. Time each team as members put the pieces of the business-letter puzzle together and identify each part. Check the correct answers with the number and title on the back of each piece. The team that completes the puzzle correctly in the shortest time is the winner.

Business Letter

Titles:	1. Heading	2. Inside Address	3. Salutation	4. Body	5. Closing	6. Signature

14 Cliff Street
Salina, KS 00042
October 10, 20—

Salina City Council
102 Commerce Blvd.
Salina, KS 00042

Dear Council Members:

    The lack of a traffic light or a stop sign at the corner of Cliff and Cook Streets has created a dangerous situation for both motorists and pedestrians. Within the past three months, nine accidents have occurred.
    Since school children cross the street daily at this intersection on their way to and from Central Elementary, it is imperative that immediate action be taken to control traffic at this hazardous intersection.

Sincerely,

Peter Madison
Peter Madison

6. Signature
Peter Madison
Peter Madison

5. Closing
Sincerely,

4. Body
The lack of a traffic light or a stop sign at the corner of Cliff and Cook Streets has created a dangerous situation for both motorists and pedestrians. Within the past three months, nine accidents have occurred.
Since school children cross the street daily at this intersection on their way to and from Central Elementary, it is imperative that immediate action be taken to control traffic at this hazardous intersection.

3. Salutation
Dear Council Members:

2. Inside Address
Salina City Council
102 Commerce Blvd.
Salina, KS 00042

1. Heading
14 Cliff Street
Salina, KS 00042
October 10, 20—

Learn It: EDITING A BUSINESS LETTER, USING CORRECTIONS ONLY

The business letter in Classroom Practice 69 has not been punctuated. Write capitalization corrections above the capitalization mistakes, and write the punctuation corrections where they belong in the letter. Look at the editing guide to find the total number of mistakes you need to correct.

Classroom Practice 69

It is time to practice the skills you are learning. You will use the classroom practice on the next page to apply these skills.

Across the Curriculum

Social Studies Connection: Think about jobs people do. Select a job you would like. Write a paragraph that describes the job and tell why you would like it. Then, underline all the pronouns that you used in your paragraph. Share your paragraph with others.

Lesson 4

You will

- edit a business letter for corrections only.
- do Classroom Practice 69.
- do Across the Curriculum activity.

Classroom Practice 69

Name:_____ Date:_____

SKILLS AND EDITING

Write the capitalization and punctuation corrections only.

Editing Guide: End Marks: 4   Capitals: 34   Commas: 6   Colons: 1   Underlining: 3   Periods: 2

203 shady lane

shady city ut 00606

july 3 20—

magazine clearing house

fifth and broadway streets

new york city ny 00721

dear sirs

your list of magazines is impressive i want to order house and garden popular mechanics and popular science send the bill to the above address i am happy to do business with your company

sincerely yours

j p jones

START LESSON 5

Chapter Checkup 70

It is time for a checkup of the skills you have learned in this chapter. You will use the chapter checkup on the next page to evaluate your progress.

Student Note: Bring an envelope from home if you have not done so. You will use the envelope in the next lesson.

Lesson 5

You will
- do Chapter Checkup 70.
- write in your journal.
- bring envelopes from home.

JOURNAL WRITING [41]

Write an entry in your journal. Use Reference 9 on page 12 for ideas.

Chapter 15 Checkup 70

Name:_____ Date:_____

SKILLS AND EDITING

Write the capitalization and punctuation corrections only.
Editing Guide: End Marks: 3   Capitals: 35   Commas: 6   Apostrophes: 1   Colons: 1   Periods: 3

36 glendale cove

trenton nj 00056

march 30 20—

food magazine publications inc

ms nina freeman editor

701 copper cove

atlanta ga 00492

dear ms freeman

i would like to submit the enclosed recipe in your super summer salsa recipe contest my black bean salsa dip is made from an original spanish recipe that has been passed down through many generations of the martinez family i hope our familys favorite dip impresses your judges

sincerely

vanessa martinez

Writing Time

Write It: **WRITING ASSIGNMENT 36**

Writing Assignment 36

Purpose: To write a letter
Type of Writing: Business letter
Audience: Principal
Writing Topics: A Request to the Principal
Special Instructions:

1. Use References 194–198 on pages 424–428 to help you write your business letter.

2. Write a business letter to the principal of your school. The purpose of your business letter is to request something for the school or classroom, ask about something the students can do for the school or community, or choose a reason of your own. Before you begin your letter, make a list of the things you want to say.

3. Address an envelope for the business letter. Draw a stamp on the envelope in the correct position.

4. Revise and edit the business letter and envelope by yourself and then with an editing partner. Next, write a final copy. Write it neatly or type it on a computer.

5. Put your letter in the envelope but do not seal it until your teacher looks over it.

6. Mail the business letter to the principal via school mail.

>>>>>>>>>> Student Tip...

> If you need to improve your handwriting, refer to the Resource Tools Section on pages 529–530 for information on writing legibly.

Lesson 6
You will
- write a independent business letter for WA 36.
- revise and edit WA 36.
- address an envelope for a business letter.

SHURLEY ENGLISH

START LESSON 7

Lesson 7

You will
- respond to oral review questions.
- take Chapter 15 Test.

CHAPTER TEST

It is time to evaluate your knowledge of the skills you have learned in this chapter. Your teacher will give you the Chapter 15 Test to help you assess your progress.

LISTENING AND SPEAKING:

Oral Review Questions

Discuss It:

1. What kind of letter is written about something that is not personal in nature?

2. What are the four types of business letters?

3. What are the six parts of a business letter?

4. What information that is not contained in a friendly letter is added to the business letter?

5. What information is included in the inside address?

6. What two business letter styles were introduced?

7. Which style uses indented heading, closing, signature, and paragraphs?

8. What two kinds of addresses are used for a business envelope?

9. What extra information is added to the mailing addresses of the business envelope?

10. What punctuation mark is used after the greeting in a business letter?

11. If you do not know the name of the person receiving the business letter, what should be used in the greeting?

12. How should a business letter be signed?

>>>>>>>>>>>>>>>>>>>>>> **Student Tip...**

For information about test-taking strategies, refer to the Resource Tools Section on page 528.

Skill Time

Learn It: **FACT, OPINION, AND PROPAGANDA TECHNIQUES**

Reference 199 — Recognizing Fact and Opinion

You are bombarded daily with information from television, radio, movies, printed materials, and advertisements. This information is designed to attract your attention and influence your way of thinking. Some information is based on facts and can be checked for accuracy. Other information is based on opinion or other factors that cannot be proved or disproved. You must be able to tell the difference between fact and opinion in order to make an informed judgement about the information you are receiving.

A **fact** is a specific statement that can be looked up, measured, counted, or otherwise proved or disproved.

Example: John is six feet tall.
> (This is a statement that can be proved or disproved. Either John is six feet tall or he isn't. It can be proved or disproved by measuring John's height.)

An **opinion** is a belief, estimate, judgment, or feeling held by one or more people that cannot be proven. It is a personal judgment.

Example: John is a considerate young man.
> (This is a statement that cannot be proved or disproved. Each person has his own definition of **considerate**. Some people may think John considerate; others may not.)

Facts are statements that can be proved or disproved. Opinions are statements that cannot be proved or disproved. Opinions that are widely accepted often appear to be factual when they are not. Recognizing whether a statement is a fact or an opinion will help you make informed choices.

There are certain words that signal when a writer is expressing an opinion.
Opinion Words: *think, believe, feel, hope, seem, best, better, worse, worst, probably, excellent, terrible, should, love, hate, etc.*

Learn It: **PROPAGANDA**

Reference 200 — Propaganda

Propaganda is a form of language used to spread ideas or information in an attempt to change the opinions and actions of a group of people. Propaganda usually contains some accurate facts along with exaggerations and untruths.

The information that you see and hear on television, radio, newspapers, and magazines often leaves out facts or uses techniques to persuade you in a specific direction. You need to evaluate these techniques by asking questions and by thinking about the information first. Then, you can make better decisions.

Some propaganda techniques are listed on the next page. Learn to recognize and evaluate these techniques so they will not mislead you.

Continued on next page. >>>

Reference 200 continued from previous page.

COMMON PROPAGANDA TECHNIQUES

1. **Loaded Words.** This technique uses words that appeal to our emotions. Loaded words can give pleasant or unpleasant feelings, such as *new, best, exciting, tired, dull,* and *boring.* This technique is used to make us accept or reject something without examining the evidence.

   Example: You can buy the car of the future, the amazing Gazelle, at Winford Motors, the best place in town to shop for a car!

   To Evaluate: Leaving the loaded words out, what are the key facts?
   (The Gazelle can be bought at Winford Motors.)

2. **Important/Famous People.** This technique uses an important or famous person to recommend that you do, buy, or believe something. When a person that we admire is used to recommend something, we are likely to accept what is said. On the other hand, when a person that we do not admire is used to recommend something, we are more likely to question the dependability of the product or idea.

   Example: Improve your game! Use Sam Wood's Golf Clubs!

   To Evaluate: Is the famous person an expert on the product/idea advertised?
   (Is Sam Woods an expert golf player who uses the Sam Wood's Golf Clubs with great success?)

3. **Bandwagon.** This technique is used to make you feel that something is good because it is popular. It is also referred to as the everybody-does-it technique. The key approach is to make you feel left out if you don't join the crowd. Since no one wants to be left out, this technique can be quite successful.

   Example: We're having a factory blowout! All of your friends and neighbors have been here and have gone home with some great deals. Don't be left out!

   To Evaluate: If no one else was interested, would you still want this product or support this idea?
   (Do I really want or need what everyone else is buying or supporting?)

4. **Mudslinging.** This technique is used to indicate that something is wrong with the competition but gives no facts to support these claims. This technique uses a negative image in the hope that individuals will reject a person or an issue based on that negative image instead of looking at the facts. Mudslinging is a common technique used in political campaigns.

   Example: After the state tax scandal, can you really trust Jo Blue with your money? Vote for the man with values. Vote for Jay Sams, the candidate you can trust.

   To Evaluate: Check out what was claimed about both candidates or about both sides of an issue.
   (How was Jo Blue involved with the state tax scandal? What values do these candidates support?)

5. **Fact/Opinion.** A fact is often followed by a reasonable opinion that appears to be true. This technique is used in the hope that individuals will also accept the opinion as fact.

   Example: We've sold over a thousand printers. People trust us because we are the best!

   To Evaluate: Can every statement be checked to see if it is true? Do any of the statements use opinion words? Have any of the important facts been left out?
   (The first statement can be proven, true or false. The second statement uses the opinion word "best" and cannot be proven. An important fact about how long it took to sell a thousand printers has been left out.)

6. **Stereotyping.** This technique is used to give specific groups certain characteristics, images, or attitudes based on assumptions. Stereotyping implies that all members of a group are alike or believe the same way.

   Example: All business owners in your area support the new sales tax.

   To Evaluate: Is it correct to assume that everyone in a certain group believes the same way?
   (Do all the business owners in your area support the new sales tax?)

Classroom Practice 71

It is time to practice the skills you are learning. You will use the classroom practice on the next page to apply these skills.

English Made Easy

Classroom Practice 71

Name:_____ Date:_____

SKILLS

▶ **Exercise 1:** For each statement, write **O** (opinion) or **F** (fact) in the blank.

_____ 1. Americans traveling to England need a passport.

_____ 2. Traveling to England is an exciting experience.

_____ 3. Everyone should eat four servings of broccoli each day.

_____ 4. A carrot is a vegetable.

_____ 5. That was the best movie ever made about animals.

_____ 6. It took three years to make that movie.

▶ **Exercise 2:** Identify each of these sentences in terms of the propaganda technique it contains. **L** (loaded words), **I** (important/famous people), **B** (bandwagon), **M** (mudslinging), **S** (stereotyping), **F/O** (fact/opinion)

_____ 1. Brand X may not last. Buy Brand Y. It does not break!

_____ 2. His amazing body-building program created sharply chiseled arms and huge thighs.

_____ 3. Men are better drivers than women.

_____ 4. Everyone is moving to Wildwood Estates. Don't miss out on the best homes in town!

_____ 5. Cigarette smoke causes health problems. Everyone who smokes will get cancer.

_____ 6. Drink the power juice the Hawks used to win the national title. Drink Stamina!

▶ **Exercise 3:** Write **True** or **False** before each statement.

_____ 1. Opinions that are widely accepted are true.

_____ 2. Mudslinging is a form of propaganda.

_____ 3. A fact can be verified.

_____ 4. Propaganda is used to spread the truth.

_____ 5. Propaganda is an effort to change the opinions and actions of people.

_____ 6. Certain opinion words help identify opinion statements: hope, seem, best, think, etc.

▶ **Exercise 4:** Answer the questions below, using the information in the following article.

[1] A tornado-warning siren alerts people to approaching tornadoes and could save many lives. [2] Most surrounding towns have a warning system, and we need one, too! [3] This would provide advanced warning of tornadoes and high-intensity thunderstorms that damage our property and take the lives of our citizens. [4] The committee working against funding this warning system must not be concerned about saving property and lives. [5] Everyone who cares about our community will vote yes for the tax increase. You should vote yes, too. [6] Your vote will allow us to purchase this absolutely essential equipment.

By Mayor Jim Eddy

1. Who wrote this information? _____

2. What is the purpose? _____

3. Write the propaganda technique for each numbered sentence above.

(1) _____   (4) _____

(2) _____   (5) _____

(3) _____   (6) _____

START LESSON 2

Skill Time

Lesson 2

You will

- read and discuss different media sources.
- evaluate propaganda techniques in the media.
- do Classroom Practice 72.
- do student activity on media advertisement.

Learn It: **DIFFERENT MEDIA SOURCES**

Reference 201 — Propaganda and Mass Media

Newspapers, radio, television, billboards, magazines, and the Internet are types of **mass media**. Mass media use verbal and visual communication to send information to large numbers of people. Their purpose is to inform, educate, entertain, or persuade.

Different media use their own ways of presenting a message. They will use fact, opinion, and some or all of the propaganda techniques. Sometimes, the propaganda techniques will be so subtle that you have to read or listen very carefully to detect them. Other times, the propaganda techniques will be obvious. Even so, individuals can interpret the same media message in different ways.

Learn It: **EVALUATING PROPAGANDA IN THE DIFFERENT MEDIA SOURCES**

Reference 202 — Evaluating Propaganda Techniques in the Media

Look at and listen to the news, the stories, and the advertisements on television, radio, billboards, and the Internet and in newspapers and magazines. Use the questions below to help you evaluate the stories and the advertisements in the media.

1. Think about how the information is organized. Which stories appear first? Do you think they are the most important stories? How much time or space is devoted to each story? Does the newspaper or magazine include a large headline or photograph? Does the television program use visuals or video footage?

2. What is the purpose of the information? Does the information focus on a product, person, or idea? Decide whether it is intended to inform, persuade, advertise, or entertain. Ask yourself what the information wants you to think or do. How does it make you feel?

3. Can you tell if the information you read or hear is fair and truthful? Can you tell if the story is based on fact or opinion? Is there a way to verify the facts of the story?

4. Consider whether important information is missing. Does the story tell you all there is to know?

5. What kinds of commercials are shown during the program? What kinds of advertisements are in the newspapers and magazines or on the radio? Do you think any of the advertising companies influenced the story in any way?

6. Which propaganda techniques are used to attract your attention or to influence your way of thinking? Why do you think these techniques were chosen?

Classroom Practice 72

It is time to practice the skills you are learning. You will use the classroom practice on the next page to apply these skills.

Student Activity

1. Divide into five cooperative-learning groups. Each group should choose a product/person/idea to promote or a news story to publish. Select a media source for your advertisement/story (television, radio, newspaper, magazine, billboard, or Internet).

2. Make a presentation of your advertisement or story.

3. Discuss the purpose and success of each advertisement or story and the propaganda techniques used.

Classroom Practice 72

Name:_____ Date:_____

SKILLS

▶ **Exercise 1:** For each statement, write **O** (opinion) or **F** (fact) in the blank.

_____ 1. White City Bank is the most progressive bank in town.

_____ 2. White City Bank is building a new branch.

_____ 3. Having to pay a tax on groceries is unfair to people on a limited income.

_____ 4. The litter clean-up project is a great help to our community.

_____ 5. Rembrandt's painting hung in the museum for three weeks.

▶ **Exercise 2:** Identify each of these sentences in terms of the propaganda technique it contains. **L** (loaded words), **I** (important/famous people), **B** (bandwagon), **M** (mudslinging), **S** (stereotyping), **F/O** (fact/opinion)

_____ 1. Buy Anne's Pies. They are delicious, homemade, and mouth-watering good!

_____ 2. Attend the College of William and Mary, the alma mater of President John Tyler.

_____ 3. Invest in U.S. Savings Bonds; all of your neighbors have!

_____ 4. Will Adams make a good leader? He has been linked to unethical business practices.

_____ 5. If you are an American patriot, you will buy American-made products.

_____ 6. Hurricanes destroyed 50,000 homes last year. No one should live on the coast.

▶ **Exercise 3:** Write **True** or **False** before each statement.

_____ 1. Mass media are designed to reach large numbers of people.

_____ 2. Television, radio, and newspapers are types of mass media.

_____ 3. All people will interpret the same media message in the same way.

_____ 4. Certain opinion words help identify opinion statements: believe, feel, should, etc.

_____ 5. All propaganda techniques are subtle.

▶ **Exercise 4:** Answer the questions below, using the information in the following advertisement.

Buy your next sofa
at Barker's Furniture.

[1]*Most people do.*

Even the [2]Mayor of Baltimore, Joe Skillings, drove from three states away to purchase a leather sofa for the city library. Barker's foremost competitors have good prices, but [3]their merchandise is of inferior quality. Nobody wants to pay less for merchandise that will not hold up. [4]Even though Barker's competitors have lower prices, Barker's continues to outsell them.

Simply put, people buy from Barker's because Barker's can be trusted. Without a doubt, Barker's main competitor is a[5]fly-by-night outfit that will likely be out of business this time next year. [6]Smart shoppers know the difference between quality products and inferior ones.

BARKER'S
FURNITURE

4321 RHODE ROAD • SEIDY, IN 98765 • (555) 456-7890

1. What is the purpose?

_____

_____

_____

2. Write the propaganda technique for each numbered set of underlined words.

(1) _____

(2) _____

(3) _____

(4) _____

(5) _____

(6) _____

 Skill Time

START LESSON 3

Lesson 3

You will

- read and discuss reasons for reading.
- read and discuss how to read subject-matter (skim, question, read, scan).
- do Classroom Practice 73.
- do Across the Curriculum activity.

Learn It: **REASONS FOR READING AND READING SPEEDS**

Have you ever run out of time when doing an assignment that requires you to read information and look up answers to questions? Do you enjoy reading books for fun but dislike subjects in school like social studies, reading, and science because you get frustrated looking for answers to study questions?

Whether or not this describes you, everyone can use some tips to help save time when reading for information.

 Reference 203 | **Reasons for Reading and Reading Speeds**

Do you know that not all reading material should be read slowly and carefully? How fast or slowly you read should depend on your reason for reading.

REASONS FOR READING: **READING SPEED:**

1. **To enjoy** yourself . . . . **Read slowly** enough to absorb details and enjoy the author's style.

2. **To understand** main ideas and details . . . . **Read slowly** so you can stop and think about what is being said.

3. **To get an idea** about the topic . . . . **Read quickly**, looking for titles, topic headings, underlining, and words in bold type.

4. **To locate answers** to specific questions . . . **Read quickly**, looking for titles, topic headings, underlining, and words in bold type to find the key words in your question. Then, **read slowly** to find the answers to your specific questions.

Learn It: **STEPS FOR READING SUBJECT MATTER**

Remember that your purpose for reading will determine how quickly or slowly you read. When you have a reading assignment in a subject area like science or social studies, it is called **subject-matter** reading.

 Reference 204 | **Steps for Reading Subject Matter: Skim, Question, Read, Scan**

When you read **subject matter**, such as topics in the areas of science and social studies, *you should use a combination of reading speeds.* Your reading should be done in four steps.

Step 1.   **SKIM - read quickly to get a general idea of the article.**
Your purpose is to get an idea about the topic. This is called **skimming**. Look quickly over titles, topic headings, topic sentences of each paragraph, and underlined or in bold type.

Step 2.   **QUESTION - turn headings into questions to establish a purpose for reading.**
Some headings are written as questions. You have to turn other headings into **questions**. These heading questions will give you a reason for reading. You are more likely to pick out and remember the main facts when you are looking for answers to questions.

Step 3.   **READ - read slowly to find and understand details about topic headings.**
The purpose of this step is to **read the whole article slowly** enough to find answers to the questions you asked in the question step. Read carefully to understand and remember the main ideas and details of the article.

Continued on next page. >>>

Reference 204 continued from previous page.

Step 4. **SCAN – read quickly to locate specific answers to study questions.**
The purpose is to locate specific answers to study questions from your book or worksheet. This is called **scanning**. First, find the key words in your study questions. Then, quickly look over titles, topic headings, topic sentences, and underlined or in bold type to find the section that discusses your question. Finally, read that section carefully to find the answer.

DOLPHINS

SECTION 1 **Dolphins Are Sea Mammals.**

Dolphins are not fish, but they are in a group of animals called **mammals**. Unlike fish who breathe underwater with gills, dolphins have lungs and breathe air through an air hole at the top of their head. Just like you, they take a deep breath when they go underwater. Fish are hatched from soft eggs, but a dolphin is born live and must swim to the top of the water before it can breathe. In addition, dolphins don't have scales like fish, but their bodies are covered with skin that feels like soft rubber. To move forward, the dolphin's tail moves up and down instead of side-to-side like a fish.

SECTION 2 **Dolphins Are Whales.**

Dolphins are members of the whale family. Whales are divided into two groups according to the way they catch their food. One group, **baleen whales**, have no teeth but have bristly plates called baleen that filter small fish and **plankton** into the whale's open mouth as he swims around. These baleen whales are usually very large.

The other group of whales, **toothed whales**, have teeth that are used for catching their prey. They are smaller and quicker and must hunt for their food. Prey is caught one at a time and swallowed whole. Dolphins are toothed whales. They eat squid, crabs, and fish.

SECTION 3 **Dolphins Use Their Ears to See!**

Dolphins have a type of hearing called **echo location** that works like a radar system. They send out a high-pitched clicking sound that passes through the bump on their head called the **melon**. The melon is filled with oil which causes the clicking sound to get louder as it passes through. The sound travels out through the water, until it reaches an object. Then the clicking sound bounces off the object and comes back to the dolphin where it travels through his jawbone into his inner ear. The dolphin can tell many things about the object from the signals that have been bounced back. He can tell how far away the object is, what shape it is, what size it is, and even what it is made of.

SECTION 4 **Dolphins Are Intelligent.**

Many scientists believe dolphins are highly intelligent animals. Scientists have seen dolphins working together to help other dolphins who are sick. Dolphins are great imitators and can be taught games and tricks easily. Playful and friendly by nature, they have been known to make up games of their own when they are bored.

Discuss It: **THE SKIMMING STEP**

1. What is the first step of reading subject matter?

2. What is the purpose of skimming?

3. What is the reading speed for skimming?

4. What parts of an article do you skim?

Use the article about dolphins to practice skimming for the title, topic headings, topic sentences, and underlined or in bold type. Look at the article at the bottom of the reference.

1. What is the title of the article?

2. Find the topic headings. Where are they?

Continued on next page. >>>

3. Name them.

4. Where are the topic sentences for each paragraph?

5. Name the topic sentences for each paragraph.

6. What are the bold-type words in each section?

Skimming is used **before** you actually read an article. Skimming gives you a general idea of what you are about to read.

1. What is the article about?

2. Are dolphins fish?

3. Are dolphins whales?

4. What type of hearing do they have?

Discuss It: THE QUESTIONING STEP

In this step, change your topic headings into questions.

1. How would you turn the first topic heading into a question?

2. How would you turn the second topic heading into a question?

3. How would you turn the third topic heading into a question?

4. How would you turn the fourth topic heading into a question?

5. What is the purpose of the questioning step?

Discuss It: THE READING STEP

1. What is the third step of reading subject matter?

2. What is the purpose of the reading step?

3. What is the reading speed for the reading step?

4. What parts of an article do you read?

Now, slowly read the article about dolphins. Make a mental note of the details that will answer these questions as you read: *Why are dolphins sea mammals? What kind of whales are dolphins? How do dolphins use their ears to see? In what ways are dolphins intelligent?*

Discuss It: THE SCANNING PROCESS

1. What is the fourth step of reading subject matter?

2. What is the purpose of the scanning step?

3. What is the reading speed for the scanning step?

4. What procedures do you follow in the scanning step?

Apply It: THE SCANNING PROCESS

Sample Question: **"What is the purpose of the oil in the melon of a dolphin?"**

1. What is the key word in the sample question?

2. In what section do you find the answer?

3. What made it easy and fast for you to find the answer as you scanned?

4. What is the next step after you find the section?

5. What is the answer?

Continued on next page. >>>

Discuss It: **HOW TO READ SUBJECT MATTER MATERIAL**

1. What is Step 1?
2. What is Step 2?
3. What is Step 3?
4. What is Step 4?

Classroom Practice 73

It is time to practice the skills you are learning. You will use the classroom practice on the next page to apply these skills.

Science Connection: Divide into an even number of cooperative-learning groups and pair with another group. Read and write study questions from a science lesson in your textbook. Then, exchange your study questions with the other group. Use the four steps in Reference 204 to help your group find answers to the questions. Finally, participate in a class discussion about the advantages of using the steps to read and understand subject matter material.

Classroom Practice 73

Name:_____ Date:_____

SKILLS

▶ **Exercise 1:** Underline the key word in each question. The word *dolphin* cannot be used as a key word. Scan for the answers in the article in Reference 204. Write only the section number where you will find the answer.

Section:_____ 1. What is the melon?

Section:_____ 2. How do dolphins breathe?

Section:_____ 3. Which group of whales do dolphins belong to?

Section:_____ 4. How do dolphins use their ears?

Section:_____ 5. How do scientists know that dolphins are intelligent?

▶ **Exercise 2:** Using Reference 204, write the answers in the blanks below and put the numbers of the sections where the answers were found.

Section:_____ 1. Dolphins are not fish, but are in a group of animals called_____.

Section:_____ 2. Dolphins have a type of hearing called_____that works by bouncing "clicking sounds" off objects.

Section:_____ 3. _____have bristly plates used for straining_____ from the water.

Section:_____ 4. The oil-filled bump on a dolphin's head is called the_____.

Section:_____ 5. Whales that catch their prey one at a time and swallow it whole are called_____.

▶ **Exercise 3:** Using the article in Reference 204, write the answers in the blanks below and put the number of the section where it is found.

Section:_____ 1. Give three reasons why dolphins are different from fish.

1. _____

2. _____

3. _____

Section:_____ 2. Give two reasons why scientists believe dolphins are intelligent.

1. _____

2. _____

START LESSON 4

Lesson 4

You will
- read and discuss outlining.
- do Classroom Practice 74.

 Skill Time

Learn It: OUTLINES

📖 **Reference 205** | **Outlines**

Making an outline will give you a visual map of your report. There are two reasons to use an outline when you plan to write. First, outlining helps to put ideas and information in the correct order for writing. Second, outlining helps you remember information more easily and keeps you focused as you write.

There are two kinds of outlines: the **topic outline** and the **sentence outline**. In a *topic outline*, information is written in single words or phrases. In a *sentence outline*, information is written in complete sentences. Outlines have very rigid rules about how they are organized and formatted. Even though the topic outline and the sentence outline are formatted the same, you cannot mix the two styles by using phrases and complete sentences in the same outline. The topic outline is the easiest and most commonly used outline. Outlines have a vocabulary and set of rules that are unique to outlining and follow the same basic plan.

1. Write a TITLE.
- At first, your outline title should be the same or similar to your narrowed topic. This will help you stay focused on the main idea of your report. If you decide to change the title for your final paper, you must remember to change your outline title.
- Capitalization rules for titles are the same for outlines as for final papers: Capitalize the first word, the last word, and all important words in your title. Conjunctions, articles, and prepositions with fewer than five letters are not usually capitalized unless they are the first or last word. Titles for outlines are not underlined or placed in quotation marks unless the title is a quote.

2. Use Roman numerals to indicate the MAIN TOPICS. (I., II., III., IV.)
- Outlines must always have two or more Roman numerals. Never use just one. Each Roman numeral has a paragraph in the <u>body</u> of the report. *(Three Roman numerals indicate three paragraphs in the body. The Introduction and the Conclusion will each have a paragraph, but they do not have Roman numerals.)*
- Periods after the Roman numerals must be lined up, one under the other.
- Information following a Roman numeral is called the main topic and gives the main idea or the main point of each paragraph. It will be used to form the topic sentence of the paragraph.
- The first word in a main topic is always capitalized.

3. Use capital letters to indicate SUBTOPICS. (A., B., C., D.)
- An outline must always have two or more capital letters. If you only have one subtopic, do not put it in the outline. Each capital letter is indented under the first word of the main topic.
- Periods after the capital letters must be lined up, one under the other.
- Information beside a capital letter is called the subtopic and gives details that support the main topic, or main point, of the paragraph that is stated in the Roman numeral above it.
- The first word in a subtopic is always capitalized.

Continued on next page. >>>

Reference 205 continued from previous page.

4. Use Arabic numerals to indicate DETAILS. (1., 2., 3., 4.)

- Outlines must always have two or more Arabic numerals. If you only have one detail, do not put it in the outline. Each Arabic numeral is indented under the first word of the subtopic.
- Periods after the Arabic numerals must be lined up, one under the other.
- Information beside an Arabic numeral is called a detail and tells specific information about the subtopic of the paragraph that is stated in the capital letter above it.
- The first word in a detail is always capitalized.

5. Use these basic rules to punctuate an outline.

- You cannot have a **I.** without a **II.**, an **A.** without a **B.**, or a **1.** without a **2.** because outlining is a process of dividing. You cannot divide something into fewer than two parts.
- Put periods after Roman numerals, capital letters, Arabic numerals, and anything else that would require a period in a sentence.
- Capitalize the first word of each entry and any word that would be capitalized in a sentence.
- Follow the outline guide in Reference 206 to line up the parts of an outline correctly.

6. Use parallel form for outlines.

- All the main topics in an outline should be in parallel form. This means that all the main topics should begin in the same way: all nouns, all verbs, all noun phrases, all verb phrases, all prepositional phrases, etc. If necessary, change or rearrange the words of your outline so they are parallel. *(See Reference 207, number one, for examples of parallel form for main topics.)*
- All the subtopics under a specific Roman numeral must have the same parallel form, but these subtopics do not have to be in the same parallel form as the subtopics under another Roman numeral. For example, the subtopics under Roman numeral **I** must be parallel, and even though the subtopics under Roman numeral **II** must also be parallel, they do not have to be in the same form as the subtopics under Roman numeral **I**, etc. *(See Reference 207, number two, for examples of parallel form for subtopics.)*
- All the details under a specific letter must have the same parallel form, but these details do not have to be in the same form as the details under another letter. For example, the details under the letter **A** must be parallel, and even though the details under letter **B** must also be parallel, they do not have to be in the same parallel form as the details under letter **A**, etc. *(See Reference 207, number three, for examples of parallel form for details.)*

Learn It: **HOW THE OUTLINE RULES ARE APPLIED**

Reference 206   Outline Guide and Example

Notice that the introduction and the conclusion do not have Roman numerals. They are automatically the first and last paragraphs of a report. The outline applies only to the body of the report. Since main topics are identified by Roman numerals, the body of a report contains as many paragraphs as there are Roman numerals in the outline.

Continued on next page. >>>

Reference 206 continued from previous page.

A report written from this outline example will have three paragraphs in the body because there are three Roman numerals. There will be a total of five paragraphs after the introduction and conclusion paragraphs are added.

OUTLINE GUIDE	EXAMPLE
Topic: Chores	Chores at Home
Title	
Introduction	Introduction
I. Main Topic (First main point)	I. Inside chores
A. Subtopic (Supports first main point)	A. Keep bedroom neat
1. Details (Supports subtopic)	1. Bed
2. Details (Supports subtopic)	2. Clothes
3. Details (Supports subtopic)	3. Floor
B. Subtopic (Supports first main point)	B. Empty trash
1. Details (Supports subtopic)	1. Replace with new trash bag
2. Details (Supports subtopic)	2. Take trash to dumpster
C. Subtopic (Supports first main point)	C. Wash dishes
II. Main Topic (Second main point)	II. Outside chores
A. Subtopic (Supports second main point)	A. Yard work
B. Subtopic (Supports second main point)	B. Garden work
III. Main Topic (Third main point)	III. Miscellaneous chores
A. Subtopic (Supports third main point)	A. Garage
B. Subtopic (Supports third main point)	B. Shed
Conclusion	Conclusion

Learn It: **HOW THE OUTLINE RULES ARE APPLIED**

Reference 207 **Rules and Examples for Parallel Form in an Outline**

1. All the main topics in an outline should be in parallel form. This means that all the main topics should begin in the same way: all nouns, all verbs, all noun phrases, all verb phrases, all prepositional phrases, etc. If necessary, change or rearrange the words of your outline so they are parallel. It does not matter how a main topic begins; it is just important that all topics have the same form.

I. **Inside chores**	I. **My inside chores**
II. **Outside chores**	II. **My outside chores**
III. **Miscellaneous chores**	III. **My miscellaneous chores**

2. All the subtopics under a specific Roman numeral must have the same parallel form, but these subtopics do not have to be in the same parallel form as the subtopics under another Roman numeral. For example, the subtopics under Roman numeral **I** must be parallel, and even though the subtopics under Roman numeral **II** must also be parallel, they do not have to be in the same form as the subtopics under Roman numeral **I**, etc.

Parallel form, using verbs	Parallel form, using adjectives	Parallel form, using nouns
I. Inside chores	II. Outside chores	III. Miscellaneous chores
A. **Keep** bedroom clean	A. **Yard** work	A. **Garage**
B. **Empty** trash	B. **Garden** work	B. **Shed**
C. **Wash** dishes		

Continued on next page. >>>

Reference 207 continued from previous page.

3. All the details under a specific letter must have the same parallel form, but these details do not have to be in the same parallel form as the details under another letter. For example, the details under the letter **A** must be parallel, and even though the details under letter **B** must also be parallel, they do not have to be in the same form as the details under letter **A**, etc.

Parallel form, using nouns	Parallel form, using verbs
A. Keep bedroom clean	B. Empty trash
1. **Bed**	1. **Replace** with new trash bag
2. **Clothes**	2. **Take** trash to dumpster
3. **Floor**	

Classroom Practice 74

It is time to practice the skills you are learning. You will use the classroom practice on the next page to apply these skills.

SHURLEY ENGLISH

Classroom Practice 74

Name:_____ Date:_____

SKILLS

▶ **Exercise 1:** Copy the notes below into an outline. Use the correct outline form.
(The notes are in correct parallel form.)

NOTES:	OUTLINE:
Collecting shells	
Introduction	
searching for shells	
when to search	
what to take	
flashlight	
bag or bucket	
where to search	
clams in sand	
snails under rocks	
scallops in eelgrass	
cleaning shells	
boil for 5 to 10 minutes	
soak in alcohol	
pull out meat	
dry in sun	
displaying shells	
mounting	
labeling	
use scientific name	
tell where, when, and who found it	
Conclusion	

▶ **Exercise 2:** Place an **X** in front of those items that are parallel.

_____ 1. wingless insects _____ 2. aquatic insects _____ 3. flying insects _____ 4. insects that bite

English Made Easy

✏ Chapter Checkups 75 and 76

It is time for a checkup of the skills you have learned in this chapter. You will use the chapter checkups on the next two pages to evaluate your progress.

START LESSON 5

Lesson 5

You will

- do Chapter Checkups 75 and 76.
- write in your journal.

JOURNAL WRITING 42

Write an entry in your journal. Use Reference 9 on page 12 for ideas.

Chapter 16 Checkup 75

Name:_____ Date:_____

SKILLS

▶ **Exercise 1:** For each statement, write **O** (opinion) or **F** (fact) in the blank.

_____ 1. All college students will find a job after graduation.

_____ 2. The elm tree in our front yard is six feet high.

_____ 3. Everyone should eat six small meals each day.

_____ 4. Strawberry cobbler is the best dessert.

_____ 5. Bananas are fruit.

_____ 6. Aunt Martha is the best seamstress in town.

_____ 7. It took two weeks to make this dress.

▶ **Exercise 2:** Identify each of these sentences in terms of the propaganda technique it contains. **L** (loaded words), **I** (important/famous people), **B** (bandwagon), **M** (mudslinging), **S** (stereotyping), **F/O** (fact/opinion)

_____ 1. Don't be the only college student without a credit card. Apply today!

_____ 2. Seat belts have saved the lives of thousands of people. All cars should have seat belts.

_____ 3. Governor Monty Star buys his cars from Plush Motors. Drive away in a new car today!

_____ 4. Come by Sha's Shoes for fabulous bargains, lots of fun, and exciting bonus discounts.

_____ 5. Vote against incompetence in the mayor's office. Vote for honesty! Vote for Jan See.

_____ 6. Everyone who eats salad for lunch is healthy! Be healthy. Eat at the Salad Palace.

▶ **Exercise 3:** Answer the questions below, using the information in the following article.

[1]Every smart homeowner in our town owns a guard dog. [2]The crime rate on our block is very high. It is common sense to have some type of protection, and guard dogs are a logical choice. [3]German shepherds make great guard dogs because they are smarter and more aggressive than many other dogs. [4]Most other breeds can't do the job and cannot be trusted to protect you. [5]Most people in our town own a German shepherd, and you need to get one, too.

1. What is the purpose? _____

2. Write the propaganda technique for each numbered sentence above.

(1) _____   (4) _____

(2) _____   (5) _____

(3) _____

Chapter 16 Checkup 76

Name:_____ Date:_____

SKILLS

▶ **Exercise 1:** Put the notes into a two-point outline form. Wording must be changed for correct parallel form.

NOTES:	OUTLINE:
two types of trees	
deciduous trees	
leaves are shed in winter	
have broad, flat leaves	
have flowers	
evergreen trees	
keep leaves in winter	
have needle-shaped leaves	
cones	

▶ **Exercise 2:** Place an **X** in front of the items that are parallel.

_____ 1. the coastline of the Antarctic   _____ 3. on the slopes of the Andes

_____ 2. along the banks of the Amazon   _____ 4. at the bottom of the Atlantic

▶ **Exercise 3:** Write the correct word beside each definition. **Use these words: skim, question, read, scan.**

_____ 1. Process completed slowly to find and understand details about topic headings.

_____ 2. Process in which you change section headings to get a purpose for reading.

_____ 3. Process completed quickly to get a general idea of the article.

_____ 4. Process completed quickly to locate answers to specific questions.

▶ **Exercise 4:** Write **True** or **False** before each statement.

_____ 1. You are more likely to pick out and remember the main facts when you are looking for answers to specific questions.

_____ 2. How fast or slowly you read should not depend on your reason for reading.

_____ 3. Titles, topic headings, topic sentences for each paragraph, and underlining or boldface type are parts of an article that you would skim.

_____ 4. Skimming is the first step of subject matter reading.

_____ 5. Scanning is done slowly to get a general idea of the article.

_____ 6. You should read slowly to understand details.

_____ 7. Skimming is used after you actually read an article.

_____ 8. Turning topic headings into questions gives you a purpose for reading.

START LESSON 6

Lesson 6

You will

- respond to oral review questions.
- take Chapter 16 Test.
- discuss and evaluate goals.
- write a paragraph in your goal booklet.

CHAPTER TEST

It is time to evaluate your knowledge of the skills you have learned in this chapter. Your teacher will give you the Chapter 16 Test to help you assess your progress.

LISTENING AND SPEAKING:
Oral Review Questions

Discuss It:

1. What is a fact?

2. What is an opinion?

3. What is propaganda?

4. What are six propaganda techniques?

5. What are six media sources?

6. True or False. You read slowly for enjoyment.

7. True or False. You read quickly for understanding main ideas and details.

8. True or False. You read slowly to get an idea about the topic.

9. What is subject-matter reading?

10. What are the four steps to subject-matter reading?

11. What are the two kinds of outlines?

12. What are the parts of an outline?

13. How are the main topics designated in an outline?

14. How are the subtopics designated in an outline?

15. How are the details designated in an outline?

16. What is parallel form in an outline?

17. What is the parallel form for these examples?

Example 1:   A. *Rake* the leaves   B. *Mow* the yard   C. *Clean* the shed

Example 2:   A. *Air* pollution   B. *Land* pollution   C. *Water* pollution

Student Tip...

For information about test-taking strategies, refer to the Resource Tools Section on page 528.

Review It: GOALS

Review the goals you wrote in your Goal Booklet at the beginning of the school year. Discuss your progress with your teacher or a student partner. Then, write a paragraph in your Goal Booklet that tells how well you are meeting your short-term goals. Give examples that support your evaluation of your progress. Next, write another paragraph to evaluate your long-term goals. Tell whether you want to change them or keep them the same. Give reasons to support either choice. Finally, return your Goal Booklet to your teacher when you have finished.

English Made Easy

Writing Time

Apply It: REVISING, EDITING, AND WRITING A FINAL PAPER

Revise and edit Writing Assignment 20 from your Rough Draft folder. First, revise and edit your rough draft by yourself. Next, exchange papers with your editing partner. Then, make the final revisions and corrections to your rough draft as you write a final paper.

After you have finished your final paper, put it in your Final Paper folder. As you begin, refer to Reference 54. This reference will tell you where to find the Final Paper Checklist and will give you a visual check of all the steps you should have completed at this point. Make it a habit to review these steps mentally to make sure you do not miss a step in the writing process.

Lesson 1

You will

- revise and edit WA 20 independently.
- write a final paper for WA 20.
- write in your journal.

JOURNAL WRITING 43

Write an entry in your journal. Use Reference 9 on page 12 for ideas.

Reference 54	The Steps in the Writing Process

The steps below will take you through the writing process and will give you the location of each checklist.

1. **Prewriting.** Use the Prewriting Checklist to plan and organize your writing. See Reference 44 on page 57.

2. **Rough Draft.** Use the Rough Draft Checklist to set up and write the rough draft. See Reference 46 on page 61.

3. **Revising.** Use the Revising Checklist to revise the content of your writing. See Reference 48 on page 64.

4. **Editing.** Use the Editing Checklist to edit your writing for spelling, grammar, usage, capitalization, and punctuation mistakes. See Reference 50 on page 66.

5. **Final Paper.** Use the Final Paper Checklist to set up and write the final paper. See Reference 53 on page 70.

6. **Publishing.** Use the Publishing Checklist to choose a publishing form for sharing your writing with others. See Reference 66, page 98.

>>>>>>>> Student Tip...

If you need to improve your handwriting, refer to the Resource Tools Section on pages 529–530 for information on writing legibly.

Chapter 17

START LESSON 2

Lesson 2

You will

- revise and edit WA 26 or WA 29 with a partner.
- write a final paper for WA 26 or WA 29.
- write in your journal.

JOURNAL WRITING 44

Write an entry in your journal. Use Reference 9 on page 12 for ideas.

Writing Time

Apply It: REVISING, EDITING, AND WRITING A FINAL PAPER

Choose Writing Assignment 26 or 29 from your Rough Draft folder to revise and edit. First, revise and edit your rough draft by yourself. Next, exchange papers with your editing partner. Then, make the final revisions and corrections to your rough draft as you write a final paper. After you have finished your final paper, put it in your Final Paper folder.

As you begin, refer to Reference 54. This reference will tell you where to find the Final Paper Checklist and will give you a visual check of all the steps you should have completed at this point.

Reference 54	The Steps in the Writing Process

The steps below will take you through the writing process and will give you the location of each checklist.

1. **Prewriting.** Use the Prewriting Checklist to plan and organize your writing. See Reference 44 on page 57.

2. **Rough Draft.** Use the Rough Draft Checklist to set up and write the rough draft. See Reference 46 on page 61.

3. **Revising.** Use the Revising Checklist to revise the content of your writing. See Reference 48 on page 64.

4. **Editing.** Use the Editing Checklist to edit your writing for spelling, grammar, usage, capitalization, and punctuation mistakes. See Reference 50 on page 66.

5. **Final Paper.** Use the Final Paper Checklist to set up and write the final paper. See Reference 53 on page 70.

6. **Publishing.** Use the Publishing Checklist to choose a publishing form for sharing your writing with others. See Reference 66, page 98.

English Made Easy

Writing Time

Apply It: REVISING, EDITING, AND WRITING A FINAL PAPER

Select a creative writing assignment of your choice from your Rough Draft folder to revise and edit. Revise and edit your rough draft by yourself. Then, write a final paper. After you have finished your final paper, put it in your Final Paper folder.

As you begin, refer to Reference 54. This reference will tell you where to find the Final Paper Checklist and will give you a visual check of all the steps you should have completed at this point.

Lesson 3

You will

- revise and edit a selected creative writing assignment independently.
- write a final paper for the creative writing selection.
- write in your journal.

JOURNAL WRITING 45

Write an entry in your journal. Use Reference 9 on page 12 for ideas.

START LESSON 4

Lesson 4

You will

- revise and edit WA 23 or WA 31 with a partner.
- write a final paper for WA 23 or WA 31.
- write in your journal.

JOURNAL WRITING 46

Write an entry in your journal. Use Reference 9 on page 12 for ideas.

Writing Time

Apply It: **REVISING, EDITING, AND WRITING A FINAL PAPER**

Choose Writing Assignment 23 or 31 from your Rough Draft folder to revise and edit. First, revise and edit your rough draft by yourself. Next, exchange papers with your editing partner. Then, make the final revisions and corrections to your rough draft as you write a final paper. After you have finished your final paper, put it in your Final Paper folder.

As you begin, refer to Reference 54. This reference will tell you where to find the Final Paper Checklist and will give you a visual check of all the steps you should have completed at this point.

Reference 54	The Steps in the Writing Process

The steps below will take you through the writing process and will give you the location of each checklist.

1. **Prewriting.** Use the Prewriting Checklist to plan and organize your writing. See Reference 44 on page 57.

2. **Rough Draft.** Use the Rough Draft Checklist to set up and write the rough draft. See Reference 46 on page 61.

3. **Revising.** Use the Revising Checklist to revise the content of your writing. See Reference 48 on page 64.

4. **Editing.** Use the Editing Checklist to edit your writing for spelling, grammar, usage, capitalization, and punctuation mistakes. See Reference 50 on page 66.

5. **Final Paper.** Use the Final Paper Checklist to set up and write the final paper. See Reference 53 on page 70.

6. **Publishing.** Use the Publishing Checklist to choose a publishing form for sharing your writing with others. See Reference 66, page 98.

Plan It:

Your teacher will give you a presentation schedule to follow as you share a writing selection with your class in the next two lessons. If you are in Group 1, you will share in Lesson 5. If you are in Group 2, you will share in Lesson 6.

English Made Easy

START LESSON 5

Lesson 5
You will
- select a final paper and share it with classmates.

Publishing Time

Publish It: **SHARE A WRITING SELECTION**

Select a favorite writing piece from your Final Paper folder to share with your classmates on your presentation day. If you are in Group 1, you will share today. If you are in Group 2, you will share during the next lesson. Use the Share Time Guidelines as presentations are made.

Reference 67 — Share Time Guidelines

Speaker Presentation
1. Have your paper ready to read when called upon.
2. Tell the title of your writing selection.
3. Tell the purpose and type of writing used.

PRESENTATION TIPS:
4. Stand with your feet flat on the floor and your shoulders straight. Do not shift your weight as you stand.
5. Hold your paper about chin high to help you project your voice to your audience.
6. Make sure you do not read too fast.
7. Read in a clear voice that can be heard so that your audience does not have to strain to hear you.
8. Change your voice tone for different characters or for different parts of the writing selection.

Audience Response
1. Look at the speaker.
2. Turn your body toward the speaker.
3. Listen attentively. Do not let your thoughts wander.
4. Do not make distracting noises as you listen.
5. Do not make distracting motions as you listen.
6. Show interest in what the speaker is saying.
7. Silently summarize what the speaker is saying. Take notes if necessary.
8. Ask questions about anything that is not clear.
9. Show appreciation by clapping after the speaker has finished.

End of Lesson 5

START LESSON 6

Lesson 6
You will
- select a final paper and share it with classmates.

Publishing Time

Publish It: **SHARE A WRITING SELECTION**

If you are in Group 2, you will share your selected writing piece with your classmates today. Use the Share Time Guidelines as presentations are made.

Chapter 17 Writing Evaluation Guide

Name:_____ Date:_____

ROUGH DRAFT CHECK

_____ 1. Did you write your rough draft in pencil?

_____ 2. Did you write the correct headings on the first seven lines of your paper?

_____ 3. Did you use extra wide margins and skip every other line?

_____ 4. Did you write a title at the end of your rough draft?

_____ 5. Did you place your edited rough draft in your Rough Draft folder?

REVISING CHECK

_____ 6. Did you identify the purpose, type of writing, and audience?

_____ 7. Did you check for a topic, topic sentence, and sentences supporting the topic?

_____ 8. Did you check sentences for the right order, and did you combine, rearrange, or delete sentences when necessary?

_____ 9. Did you check for a variety of simple, compound, and complex sentences?

_____ 10. Did you check for any left out, repeated, or unnecessary words?

_____ 11. Did you check for the best choice of words by replacing or deleting unclear words?

_____ 12. Did you check the content for interest and creativity?

_____ 13. Did you check the voice to make sure the writing says what you want it to say?

EDITING CHECK

_____ 14. Did you indent each paragraph?

_____ 15. Did you put an end mark at the end of every sentence?

_____ 16. Did you capitalize the first word of every sentence?

_____ 17. Did you check for all other capitalization mistakes?

_____ 18. Did you check for all punctuation mistakes?
    (commas, periods, apostrophes, quotation marks, underlining)

_____ 19. Did you check for misspelled words and for incorrect homonym choices?

_____ 20. Did you check for incorrect spellings of plural and possessive forms?

_____ 21. Did you check for correct construction and punctuation of your sentences?

_____ 22. Did you check for usage mistakes? _(subject/verb agreement, a/an choices, contractions, verb tenses, pronoun/antecedent agreement, pronoun cases, degrees of adjectives, double negatives, etc.)_

_____ 23. Did you put your revised and edited paper in the Rough Draft folder?

FINAL PAPER CHECK

_____ 24. Did you write the final paper in pencil?

_____ 25. Did you center the title on the top line and center your name under the title?

_____ 26. Did you skip a line before starting the writing assignment?

_____ 27. Did you single-space, use wide margins, and write the final paper neatly?

_____ 28. Did you staple your papers in this order: final paper on top, rough draft in the middle, and prewriting map on the bottom? Did you put them in the Final Paper folder?

English Made Easy

Literature Time

Learn It: POETRY

Reference 208 Poetry

Artistic writing includes many literary genres—essays, poems, short stories, plays, etc. A **genre** identifies what type of writing a piece of literature is. One of the oldest forms of literature is poetry. Throughout history, people have used poetry to pass along news, create songs and stories, and record historical events.

Poetry is a very compact and focused form of writing that spurs the imagination and calls up sensory images and emotional responses. Poetry says a lot in a few words. It allows you to share your thoughts and feelings in a unique way. With its multiple images, poetry relates to the heart as well as to the mind. A poem is a delicate juggling act of rhythm, figurative language, and sometimes rhyme.

The poem, whether it rhymes or not, is probably the most artistic of all genres. The poem, as an art form, is both visual and auditory. Poetry looks different. Without reading words, you can look at a poem and know it is a poem by its appearance on the page. Most poetry is pleasing to the ear. You can hear a poem read aloud and know it is a poem because it sounds like one. A poem should be read aloud in order to be fully appreciated and enjoyed. By reading a poem silently, you miss its music and, perhaps, even its meaning.

Poetry often says things in a special way by using figurative language. **Figurative language** uses words to draw pictures of things being compared. There are three figures of speech that create images that compare one thing to another. They are *simile*, *metaphor*, and *personification*.

1. **Simile** compares two or more things by using the words *like* or *as*.
   Example: Jeff is **as** tall **as** a giraffe. She is **as** quiet **as** a mouse. My brother jumps **like** a frog.

2. **Metaphor** compares things by stating that one thing is something else. It uses linking verbs such as *am, is, are, was,* and *were.*
   Example: The **fog was a curtain** during the morning hours. The **soldiers were ants** marching in a row.

3. **Personification** compares things by giving human qualities to something nonhuman.
   Example: The **door eyed the visitor with contempt and refused to open**.

Poems sometimes contain sound devices. The four principal **sound devices** are *alliteration, assonance, repetition,* and *rhyme.*

1. **Alliteration** is the repetition of initial consonant sounds (at the beginning of words).
   Example: Five feathered fowls (**f sounds**)

2. **Assonance** is the repetition of internal vowel sounds (within words).
   Example: Long, low moan (**o sounds**)

3. **Repetition** refers to the repeating, or restating, of any words, phrases, or sentences. Words, phrases, or sentences can be repeated anywhere within the poem.

4. **Rhyme** is the sound-alike quality of words, regardless of their spellings (*do/few, made/paid*). Rhyme may be of two types: end rhymes and internal rhymes. End rhymes are rhymes at the end of lines whereas internal rhymes are rhymes within lines.

A poem will most often be organized into sections called **stanzas.**

Lesson 1

You will
- read and discuss the genre of poetry.
- read and analyze an Emily Dickinson poem.
- read and discuss a color poem.
- write a poem for WA 37.
- write a report on Emily Dickinson for Homework WA 38.

LISTENING AND SPEAKING:

Discuss It: POETRY

1. What genre of writing is one of the oldest forms of literature?
2. What is figurative language?
3. What are three figures of speech?
4. Which figure of speech uses the words **like** or **as** to make a comparison?
5. Which figure of speech makes a comparison by stating that one thing is something else?
6. Which figure of speech gives human qualities to something nonhuman?
7. What are four sound devices used in poetry?
8. Which sound device repeats beginning consonant sounds?
9. Which sound device repeats vowel sounds within words?
10. How are poems organized?

Read It:

📖 **Reference 209** **Emily Dickinson**

I'm Nobody

I'm nobody! Who are you?
Are you nobody, too?
Then there's a pair of us—don't tell!
They'd banish us, you know.

How dreary to be somebody!
How public like a frog
To tell your name the livelong day
To an admiring bog!

— Emily Dickinson

Discuss It: ANALYZING "I'M NOBODY"

1. In this poem, whom does Emily Dickinson celebrate?
2. According to the narrator, people who like to brag on themselves
   a. resemble a croaking frog.
   b. sound like passing freight trains.
   c. are a model for others.
3. Does the poem use figurative language?
4. Which line in the poem contains the figurative language?
5. Is the figurative language a simile, metaphor, or personification?
6. How do you know it is a simile?
7. Which sound devices are used?
8. What are some examples of rhyme?
9. What picture do you have of "a somebody" after reading the last stanza?
10. What does this poem mean to you?

Learn It: COLOR POEMS

✎* **Reference 210**   **Color Poems**

Directions: Pick a color as your title. Tell about your color in complete sentences. Your sentences do not have to rhyme.

Purple is...

Purple is a cluster of grapes.
Purple is a royal kingly robe.
It's plums and pens, and pretty paint.
It's pansies, violets, and eggplants.
Purple is an angry face.
Purple is the circus clown's hair.
Purple is a hard word to describe.

Yellow and the Senses

Yellow looks like daffodils.
Yellow smells like lemons.
Yellow tastes as good as a banana.
Yellow sounds like children laughing.
Yellow feels like warm sunshine.

Write It: WRITING ASSIGNMENT 37

Writing Assignment 〔37〕

Choose one of the options below about which to write your poem.

1. Emily Dickinson's poem, "I'm Nobody," is critical of people who advertise their importance. The second stanza could be rewritten in a number of ways, using an equally graphic comparison. Rewrite the second stanza. Use at least one simile or metaphor in your poem.

2. Write a companion piece to Emily Dickinson's poem. Instead of "I'm Nobody," title your poem, "I'm Somebody." Use at least one simile or metaphor in your poem.

3. Write a color poem, using similes or metaphors.

4. Make up a poem of your own. Use at least one simile or metaphor in your poem.

Activity:

Look up poems by poets Jack Prelutsky and Carl Sandburg. Pick out the poem you like the best. Why do you like this poem? What is your interpretation of the poem? Read and discuss it with a partner. What does your partner think about the poem?

Special Instructions:

1. Type this assignment on the computer or write it neatly on notebook paper.

2. Illustrate your poem with your own artwork, clip art, or magazine pictures.

3. Read your poem to a family member or a friend.

4. Give the finished poem to your teacher in the next lesson.

Write It: HOME WRITING ASSIGNMENT 38

Home Writing Assignment 38

Purpose: To inform

Type of Writing: Expository paragraph or essay

Audience: Classmates

Writing Topic: Emily Dickinson

Special Instructions:

1. You have been studying a poem by Emily Dickinson. Look up more information about her, using the Internet, a poetry reference, and/or an encyclopedia.

2. Write a paragraph or essay that includes the following information.
Introduction: Tell who Emily Dickinson was and what she did.
Body: Tell one or more important or unusual facts about Emily Dickinson's early life. Tell one or more important or unusual facts about Emily Dickinson's later life. Mention one or more important works written by Emily Dickinson.
Conclusion: Give a summation, or wrap-up, of what the paragraph/essay is about.

3. Type your paragraph or essay on the computer or write it neatly on notebook paper. Everyone's report will be compiled into a classroom booklet.

4. Use standard, time-order, or transition writing form. See Reference 69 on page 103.

5. Write in third person. See Reference 70 on page 104.

>>>>>>>>>>>> Student Tip...

If you need to improve your handwriting, refer to the Resource Tools Section on pages 524–530 for information on writing legibly.

Literature Time

Discuss It: WRITING ASSIGNMENT 38

What did you learn about Emily Dickinson in your writing assignment?

Did you discover anything about Emily Dickinson's life that could have influenced her to write "I'm Nobody"?

Give your report about Emily Dickinson to your teacher to be placed in a class booklet. This booklet will be available to you for checkout so you may enjoy the research that was done.

Share It: WRITING ASSIGNMENT 37

A poem should be read aloud in order to be fully appreciated and enjoyed. When listening to a poem, you are enjoying one of the oldest forms of literature. Reading poems aloud gives us a chance to hear their rhythms and understand their images. However, since poems are also a personal expression of your thoughts, you have several ways of sharing your poem.

1. You may share your poem aloud.
2. You may have your poem put in the class poetry booklet for everyone to read.
3. You may give your poem to your teacher.

If you do not want to display your poem in the class booklet, you must write "return" in the lower right corner of your paper. It will be returned in a few days. The poems in the class booklet will be returned before the end of the school year. This will give everyone a chance to read and enjoy the poems.

Lesson 2

You will

- discuss reports on Emily Dickinson.
- share reports and poems.

Chapter 18

START LESSON 3

Lesson 3

You will
- read and analyze an Eugene Field poem.
- read and discuss a parts-of-speech poem, a couplet, a triplet, and a quatrain.
- write a poem for WA 39.
- write a report on Eugene Field for Homework WA 40.

Literature Time

Read It:

Reference 211 — Eugene Field

Little Boy Blue

The little toy dog is covered with dust,
 But sturdy and staunch he stands;
The little toy soldier is red with rust,
 And his musket molds in his hands.
Time was when the little toy dog was new
 And the soldier was passing fair;
And that was the time when our Little Boy Blue
 Kissed them and put them there.

"Now don't you go till I come," he said,
 "And don't you make any noise!"
So toddling off to his trundle bed,
 He dreamt of the pretty toys;
And, as he was dreaming, an angel song
 Awakened our Little Boy Blue—
Oh! the years are many, the years are long,
 But the little toy friends are true!

Ay, faithful to Little Boy Blue they stand,
 Each in the same old place,
Awaiting the touch of a little hand,
 The smile of a little face;
And they wonder, as waiting the long years through,
 In the dust of that little chair,
What has become of our Little Boy Blue
 Since he kissed them and put them there.

—Eugene Field

LISTENING AND SPEAKING:

Discuss It: ANALYZING "LITTLE BOY BLUE"

1. What one word best describes the way his toy friends felt toward Little Boy Blue?
   a. abandoned
   b. faithful
   c. envious

2. What toys did Little Boy Blue tell to stay where they were until he returned?
   a. a teddy bear and a lion
   b. a truck and a school bus
   c. a soldier and a dog

3. Does "Little Boy Blue" use sound devices?

Continued on next page. >>>

4. Which sound devices are used?

5. What are some examples of alliteration?

6. What are some examples of repetition?

7. What are some examples of rhyme?

8. Does the poem use figurative language? Is the figurative language a simile, metaphor, or personification?

9. How do you know it is personification?

10. The phrase, "kissed them and put them there," is used in the eighth line as well as the twenty-fourth line, but each one evokes a different emotion. What are the differences in the two?

11. What does this poem mean to you?

Learn It: PARTS-OF-SPEECH, COUPLET, TRIPLET, AND QUATRAIN POEMS

Reference 212 — Parts-of-Speech, Couplet, Triplet, and Quatrain Poems

Parts-of-Speech Poem: Follow the directions and use the parts of speech listed to write this poem.

Line 1. Write your name. — Greg

Line 2. Write two adjectives that describe your personality. — Forgetful, happy

Line 3. Write four words that describe your appearance: adjective, noun, adjective, noun — Blue eyes, big smile

Line 4. Write five nouns naming things you enjoy. — Football, skateboard, stamps, friends, jokes

Line 5. Write any descriptive word you choose. — Likable

A **couplet** has two lines that rhyme. Some poems are written entirely in couplets. Other poems have only one couplet. Couplets are often silly and are usually about one subject.

While riding my bike, I had a wreck.
I scraped my knee and hurt my neck.

While riding my bike, I had a wreck.
I scraped my knee and hurt my neck.

I told my mom, and we had a talk.
Next time I think that I'll just walk.

A **triplet** has three lines that rhyme.

I ordered the rice stir-fried.
I put the hot sauce on the side.
I didn't want my taste buds mummified.

A **quatrain** is a four-line poem with at least two lines that rhyme. There are several rhyming schemes possible. For example, the first and second lines rhyme, and the third and fourth lines rhyme (aabb). Some other rhyming combinations include abab, abba, aaba, abcb, etc.

(aabb)
My dad, the golfer, tries a par three,
But instead, he hits a big oak tree.
He whacks that ball with all his might,
And this time, his ball sails out of sight!

(abcb)
I saw a silly yellow bird
who blinked and winked at me;
He hopped quite high from branch to branch
in our maple tree.

Write It: **WRITING ASSIGNMENT 39**

Writing Assignment 39

Choose one of the options below about which to write your poem.

1. Think of some remembrance that someone gave you, which simply collects dust now. Make a list of thoughts that cross your mind every time you see it, forgotten and ignored. Then, take items from your list to write your own poem of a special memory.

2. Write a parts-of-speech poem about a friend or yourself.

3. Write a couplet, triplet, or quatrain.

4. Make up a poem of your own.

Activity:

Look up poems by poets Rebecca Ives and Nikki Giovanni. Pick out the poem you like the best. Why do you like this poem? What is your interpretation of the poem? Read and discuss it with a partner. What does your partner think about the poem?

Special Instructions:

1. Type this assignment on the computer or write it neatly on notebook paper.

2. Illustrate your poem with your own artwork, clip art, or magazine pictures.

3. Read your poem to a family member or a friend.

4. Give the finished poem to your teacher in the next lesson.

Write It: **HOME WRITING ASSIGNMENT 40**

Home Writing Assignment 40

Purpose: To inform

Type of Writing: Expository paragraph or essay

Audience: Classmates

Writing Topic: Eugene Field

Special Instructions:

1. You have been studying a poem by Eugene Field. Look up more information about him, using the Internet, a poetry reference, and/or an encyclopedia.

2. Write a paragraph or essay that includes the following information.
   Introduction: Tell who Eugene Field was and what he did.
   Body: Tell one or more important or unusual facts about Eugene Field's early life. Tell one or more important or unusual facts about Eugene Field's later life. Mention one or more important works written by Eugene Field.
   Conclusion: Give a summation, or wrap-up, of what the paragraph/essay is about.

3. Type your paragraph or essay on the computer or write it neatly on notebook paper. Everyone's report will be compiled into a classroom booklet.

4. Use standard, time-order, or transition writing form. See Reference 69 on page 103.

5. Write in third person. See Reference 70 on page 104.

Literature Time

START LESSON 4

Lesson 4

You will
- discuss reports on Eugene Field.
- share reports and poems.

Discuss It: WRITING ASSIGNMENT 40

What did you learn about Eugene Field in your writing assignment?

Did you discover anything about Eugene Field's life that could have influenced him to write "Little Boy Blue"?

Give your report about Eugene Field to your teacher to be placed in a class booklet. This booklet will be available to you for checkout so you may enjoy the research that was done.

Share It: WRITING ASSIGNMENT 39

You have several ways of sharing your poem.

1. You may share your poem aloud.
2. You may have your poem put in the class poetry booklet for everyone to read.
3. You may give your poem to your teacher.

If you do not want to display your poem in the class booklet, you must write "return" in the lower right corner of your paper. It will be returned in a few days. The poems in the class booklet will be returned before the end of the school year. This will give everyone a chance to read and enjoy the poems.

START LESSON 5

Lesson 5

You will
- read and analyze a Robert Burns poem.
- read and discuss an acrostic poem and a haiku.
- write a poem for WA 41.
- write a report on Robert Burns for Homework WA 42.

Literature Time

Read It:

Reference 213 — Robert Burns

A Red, Red Rose

O my Luve's like a red, red rose
    That's newly sprung in June:
O my Luve's like the melodie
    That's sweetly play'd in tune!

As fair art thou, my bonnie lass,
    So deep in luve am I:
And I will luve thee still, my dear,
    Till a' the seas gang dry:

Till a' the seas gang dry, my dear,
    And the rocks melt wi' the sun;
I will luve thee still, my dear,
    While the sands o' life shall run.

And fare thee weel, my only Luve
    And fare thee weel awhile!
And I will come again, my Luve,
    Tho' it were ten thousand mile.

—*Robert Burns*

LISTENING AND SPEAKING:

Discuss It: ANALYZING "A RED, RED ROSE"

1. How widely separated are the lovers in this poem?
   a. two towns away
   b. ten thousand miles
   c. in the neighboring county

2. Which one of these choices does not reflect how long the narrator will love his bonnie lass?
   a. as long as the sands of life shall run
   b. until the earth and sky are one
   c. till all the seas go dry
   d. until the rocks melt with the sun

3. Notice the many words in this poem that are either spelled differently from words in modern English or that no longer exist in the language. Words that are no longer used in a language are called archaic words. What are the modern-day versions for these words: **luve, melodie, thou, gang, weel**?

4. What are the actual words for these contractions: **play'd, a', wi', o', tho'**?

Continued on next page. >>>

5. What are archaic words?

6. Does "A Red, Red Rose" use **sound devices**?

7. Which sound devices are used?

8. What are some examples of repetition?

9. What are some examples of rhyme?

10. Does the poem use **figurative language**?
    Is the figurative language a simile, metaphor, or personification?

11. Which verses contain the similes?

12. How do you know it is a simile?

13. What do you think is the meaning of the Scottish phrase "bonnie lass"?

14. Find three ways the poet describes how long he will love
    his bonnie lass?

15. What does this poem mean to you?

Learn It: ACROSTIC POETRY

Reference 214 | **Acrostic Poem**

In an **acrostic** poem, the letters that begin each line often spell the subject of the poem. To write an acrostic, think of a person (or thing) to describe. Write the letters of the name vertically. Beside each letter, write an adjective or short phrase that starts with that letter and describes the person or thing.

ACROSTIC POEM 1
B – blonde hair and blue eyes
I – intelligent and hard working
L – laughs a lot with friends
L – likes sports and music

ACROSTIC POEM 2
T – tasty with meat, lettuce, cheese, and hot sauce
A – always messy but great to eat
C – crunchy or soft shells
O – order as many as I can eat

Learn It: HAIKU POETRY

Reference 215 | **Haiku**

Haiku is a form of Japanese poetry. Historically, haiku reflected some subject of nature, but modern haiku is more inclusive and the subject matter is not restricted to nature. Most traditional haiku have the following characteristics.

- Haiku has only three lines.
- Haiku does not rhyme.
- Haiku describes a specific moment in time, using present-tense verbs.
- The whole haiku has a total of seventeen syllables.
- The first line has five syllables.
- The second line has seven syllables.
- The third line has five syllables.
- The haiku uses descriptive words and poetic imagery to create one clear image, or word picture. It freezes a moment in time. It does not matter whether or not a haiku uses complete sentences. Only the first word of a haiku may be capitalized, or the first word of each line may be capitalized. Put a period at the end of a haiku.

HAIKU 1
Temple bells die out.
The fragrant blossoms remain.
A perfect evening.
—*Basho*

HAIKU 2
The inviting beach
opens glistening white arms
and lures sun seekers.

Continued on next page. >>>

Reference 215 continued from previous page.

STEPS FOR WRITING HAIKU

1. Select something that appeals to you. Narrow your subject down to a specific idea about your subject. (Subject: *grandchild*   Specific idea: *the way a grandchild affects a grandmother*)

2. Write the subject down in noun form, possibly with an adjective or two. (*a grandchild*)
   Note: *Your haiku does not always have to start with a noun phrase. It can begin with an adjective, an adverb, or whatever YOU choose. Use words that tell about the specific idea you are trying to portray.*

3. Count the syllables to see if you have enough to meet the five-syllable requirement for your first line. (*a grand•child*) Since your first line needs to be five syllables, you are two syllables short.

4. If necessary, add another adjective or a verb that has the number of syllables you need for the first line to be complete. (*a•lit•tle grand•child*) Now you have the five syllables needed for your first line.

5. For the second line, think of something special about your subject. You might want to use a verb or two to tell the action or a few words to describe what is special about the subject. Try to use imagery or personification to create a vivid mental picture. Remember that you need seven syllables, and your end word should **not** rhyme with the end word in the first line. Add extra modifiers as needed to achieve the desired seven syllables. (*creep•ing and crawl•ing a•long*)

6. For the last line, try to give your haiku an effective conclusion by adding an unusual ending to the specific idea you have developed. Remember that you need five syllables and your words should **not** rhyme. (*steal•ing Grand•ma's heart*)

7. Check your completed haiku to be sure it has all nine characteristics of a haiku.

   A little grandchild,

   Creeping and crawling along

   Stealing Grandma's heart.

8. Decide how you want to capitalize the lines of your haiku. Put a period at the end of the last line and commas where they are needed. Title your three-line poem "Haiku."

Write It: **WRITING ASSIGNMENT 41**

Writing Assignment [41]

Choose one of the options below about which to write your poem.

1. No writing course would be complete without the opportunity to write a love poem. Love poems, especially, lend themselves to the use of comparisons. Notice that the word *like* signals the approach of a comparison. Remember that direct comparisons, signaled by *like* or *as*, are known as similes.

   In his celebration of love, Robert Burns says his love is "like a red, red rose/...newly sprung in June" and is "like the melodie/...sweetly play'd in tune."

   Write your own love poem. Consider these lines for starters. If one of them works as the opening line of your love poem, use it. If not, create your own line.

   My love is like a butterfly   My love is like a nighttime star

   My love is like a meteorite   My love is like a burning bush

   My love is like a missing tooth   My love is like a fiery coal

2. Write a haiku or an acrostic poem.

3. Make up a poem of your own.

Activity:

Look up poems by poets e.e. cummings and Barbara Juster Esbensen. Pick out the poem you like the best. Why do you like this poem? What is your interpretation of the poem? Read and discuss it with a partner. What does your partner think about the poem?

Special Instructions:

1. Type this assignment on the computer or write it neatly on notebook paper.

2. Illustrate your poem with your own artwork, clip art, or magazine pictures.

3. Read your poem to a family member or a friend.

4. Give the finished poem to your teacher in the next lesson.

Write It: HOME WRITING ASSIGNMENT 42

Home Writing Assignment 42

Purpose: To inform

Type of Writing: Expository paragraph or essay

Audience: Classmates

Writing Topic: Robert Burns

Special Instructions:

1. You have been studying a poem by Robert Burns. Look up more information about him, using the Internet, a poetry reference, and/or an encyclopedia.

2. Write a paragraph or essay that includes the following information.
   Introduction: Tell who Robert Burns was and what he did.
   Body: Tell one or more important or unusual facts about Robert Burns's early life. Tell one or more important or unusual facts about Robert Burns's later life. Mention one or more important works written by Robert Burns.
   Conclusion: Give a summation, or wrap-up, of what the paragraph/essay is about.

3. Type your paragraph or essay on the computer or write it neatly on notebook paper. Everyone's report will be compiled into a classroom booklet.

4. Use standard, time-order, or transition writing form. See Reference 69 on page 103.

5. Write in third person. See Reference 70 on page 104.

START LESSON 6

Lesson 6

You will

- discuss reports on Robert Burns.
- share reports and poems.

Literature Time

Discuss It: WRITING ASSIGNMENT 42

What did you learn about Robert Burns in your writing assignment?

Did you discover anything about Robert Burns's life that could have influenced him to write "A Red, Red Rose"?

Give your report about Robert Burns to your teacher to be placed in a class booklet. This booklet will be available to you for checkout so you may enjoy the research that was done.

Share It: WRITING ASSIGNMENT 41

You have several ways of sharing your poem.

1. You may share your poem aloud.
2. You may have your poem put in the class poetry booklet for everyone to read.
3. You may give your poem to your teacher.

If you do not want to display your poem in the class booklet, you must write "return" in the lower right corner of your paper. It will be returned in a few days. The poems in the class booklet will be returned before the end of the school year. This will give everyone a chance to read and enjoy the poems.

Literature Time

Read It:

Reference 216 Edgar Allan Poe

Annabel Lee

It was many and many a year ago,
    In a kingdom by the sea,
That a maiden there lived whom
you may know
    By the name of Annabel Lee;—
And this maiden she lived
with no other thought
    Than to love and be loved by me.

She was a child and I was a child,
    In this kingdom by the sea,
But we loved with a love that was more
than love—
    I and my Annabel Lee—
With a love that the winged seraphs
of Heaven
    Coveted her and me.

And this was the reason that, long ago,
    In this kingdom by the sea,
A wind blew out of a cloud by night
    Chilling my Annabel Lee;
So that her highborn kinsmen came
    And bore her away from me,
To shut her up in a sepulchre
    In this kingdom by the sea

The angels, not half so happy
in Heaven,
    Went envying her and me:—
Yes! that was the reason
(as all men know,
    In this kingdom by the sea)
That the wind came out of the cloud,
chilling
    And killing my Annabel Lee.

But our love it was stronger by far
than the love
    Of those who were older
    than we—
Of many far wiser than we—
    And neither the angels
    in Heaven above
Nor the demons down under the sea,
    Can ever dissever my soul from
    the soul
Of the beautiful Annabel Lee—

For the moon never beams
without bringing me dreams
    Of the beautiful Annabel Lee;
And the stars never rise but I see
the bright eyes
    Of the beautiful Annabel Lee;
And so, all the night-tide,
I lie down by the side
    Of my darling, my darling,
    my life and my bride,
In the sepulchre there by the sea—
    In her tomb by the sounding sea.

—Edgar Allan Poe

LISTENING AND SPEAKING:

Discuss It: ANALYZING "ANNABEL LEE"

1. Does "Annabel Lee" use **sound devices**?

2. Which sound devices are used?

3. What are some examples of alliteration?

4. What are some examples of assonance?

Continued on next page. >>>

Lesson 7

You will

- read and analyze an Edgar Allan Poe poem.
- read and discuss a diamante and a limerick.
- write a poem for WA 43.
- write a report on Edgar Allan Poe for Homework WA 44.

5. What are some examples of repetition?

6. What are some examples of rhyme?

7. Does the poem use figurative language? Is the figurative language a simile, metaphor, or personification?

8. How do you know it is personification?

9. How would Edgar Allan Poe's "Annabel Lee" read if the maiden's name were changed to one of these? Read the poem again, but this time, substitute one of the names below in place of Annabel Lee.

Celeste Henley	Marva-Jean Lincoln
Abigail Torrence	Lucille Draper

10. Why did a wind come and take the maiden away from the poet?

11. What does this poem mean to you?

Learn It: DIAMANTE AND LIMERICK POEMS

Reference 217 Diamante and Limerick Poems

A **diamante** *(dee-ah-mahn-tay)* poem is a diamond-shaped poem that tells about opposites. First, select two opposite nouns to describe. Then, follow the directions below to write each line.

Line 1. Write the first noun.

Line 2. Write two adjectives describing the first noun.

Line 3. Write three *ing* words that describe the first noun.

Line 4. Write two synonyms for the first noun.
Write two synonyms for the second (*opposite*) noun.

Line 5. Write three *ing* words describing the second noun.

Line 6. Write two adjectives describing the second noun.

Line 7. Write the second (*opposite*) noun.

Sunshine

happy and bright

smiling, laughing, talking

Sunrise, daytime, sunset, nighttime

depressing, frowning, crying

sad and lonely

Darkness

The **limerick** is a popular type of rhymed poem consisting of five lines. The poet Ogden Nash popularized it in the United States. The intent of the *limerick* is to evoke a smile or chuckle in the reader. Almost all *limericks* are humorous and are fun to write. The rules are simple. The first, second, and fifth lines contain three strong beats, or accents, and rhyme with each other. The third and fourth lines contain two strong beats, or accents, and rhyme with each other.

PRISCILLA LONG

Priscilla Long has one grand dream,

To marry the boy who brings ice cream.

She loves the taste

That expands her waist,

Especially strawberry supreme.

Writing Time

Write It: WRITING ASSIGNMENT 43

Writing Assignment 43

Choose one of the options below about which to write your poem.

1. Love poems are usually wrought with intense emotion, but poems about lost or stolen loves are even more intense. Write about a real or an imaginary lost love. Your goal is to leave the reader feeling emotionally drained after reading what you have written.

2. Write a diamante poem.

3. Write a limerick. Think of words that will make it funny.

4. Make up a poem of your own.

Activity:

Look up poems by poets Robert Louis Stevenson and Langston Hughes. Pick out the poem you like the best. Why do you like this poem? What is your interpretation of the poem? Read and discuss it with a partner. What does your partner think about the poem?

Special Instructions:

1. Type this assignment on the computer or write it neatly on notebook paper.

2. Illustrate your poem with your own artwork, clip art, or magazine pictures.

3. Read your poem to a family member or a friend.

4. Give the finished poem to your teacher in the next lesson.

Write It: HOME WRITING ASSIGNMENT 44

Home Writing Assignment 44

Purpose: To inform

Type of Writing: Expository paragraph or essay

Audience: Classmates

Writing Topic: Edgar Allan Poe

Special Instructions:

1. You have been studying a poem by Edgar Allan Poe. Look up more information about him, using the Internet, a poetry reference, and/or an encyclopedia.

2. Write a paragraph or essay that includes the following information.
   Introduction: Tell who Edgar Allan Poe was and what he did.
   Body: Tell one or more important or unusual facts about Edgar Allan Poe's early life. Tell one or more important or unusual facts about Edgar Allan Poe's later life. Mention one or more important works written by Edgar Allan Poe.
   Conclusion: Give a summation, or wrap-up, of what the paragraph/essay is about.

3. Type your paragraph or essay on the computer or write it neatly on notebook paper. Everyone's report will be compiled into a classroom booklet.

4. Use standard, time-order, or transition writing form. See Reference 69 on page 103.

5. Write in third person. See Reference 70 on page 104.

START LESSON 8

Lesson 8

You will

- discuss reports on Edgar Allen Poe.
- share reports and poems.
- do Across the Curriculum activity.

Literature Time

Discuss It: **WRITING ASSIGNMENT 44**

What did you learn about Edgar Allan Poe in your writing assignment?

Did you discover anything about Edgar Allan Poe's life that could have influenced him to write "Annabel Lee"?

Give your report about Edgar Allan Poe to your teacher to be placed in a class booklet. This booklet will be available to you for checkout so you may enjoy the research that was done.

Share It: **WRITING ASSIGNMENT 43**

You have several ways of sharing your poem.

1. You may share your poem aloud.
2. You may have your poem put in the class poetry booklet for everyone to read.
3. You may give your poem to your teacher.

If you do not want to display your poem in the class booklet, you must write "return" in the lower right corner of your paper. It will be returned in a few days. The poems in the class booklet will be returned before the end of the school year. This will give everyone a chance to read and enjoy the poems.

Across the Curriculum

Science/Math/Social Studies/Poetry/Music Connection: Get into small groups. Each group will select a paragraph in a science, math, or social studies book that contains several facts. Using the facts, write a poem. Use rhyme and rhythm in your poem. You can also use a musical tune from a song you know to help you write your poem. Recite, rap, or sing the poem for the other groups.

 Writing Time

Learn It: RESEARCH REPORT WRITING

Today, you will learn how to write a research report, using a five-paragraph format. There are certain steps you need to follow in order to make writing a report easy and interesting. In this chapter, you will learn the steps of writing a report. First, you will study references that cover the basic guidelines for each step. These are the same steps you will use when you write an independent report in the next chapter.

Reference 218	Steps for Writing a Research Report

When you are assigned a report, you will gather information about your topic. This search for information is called **research**. In doing this research, you will learn facts and details about a specific subject that you did not know before.

Then, you will organize these facts and details into a clear, well-written report. By writing a report, you are sharing with others the information you have learned.

There are twelve steps you will follow in order to research a topic and write a report.

Step 1: Select and narrow a topic.

Step 2: Select the main points.

Step 3: Select sources by skimming.

Step 4: Make a bibliography card for each source selected.

Step 5: Take notes on note cards.

Step 6: Organize note cards.

Step 7: Write an outline from the information on note cards.

Step 8: Write a rough draft, using the outline.

Step 9: Revise and edit the rough draft.

Step 10: Write the final outline.

Step 11: Write the final report from the revised and edited rough draft.

Step 12: Put the final report and all related research work in the correct order.

(**Note:** Write everything in pencil except your final outline and report.)

Lesson 1

You will

- read and discuss research report writing
- read and discuss The Topic Guide
- read and discuss Steps 1-2 in a research report:
  — Select and narrow a topic.
  — Select main points.

SHURLEY ENGLISH

Learn It: THE TOPIC GUIDE

 Reference 219 **The Topic Guide**

When you choose a topic, visualizing different topic areas can help. The Topic Guide provides different topic categories with main-point ideas for each one. It will help you choose and narrow a topic, select main points about a topic, and organize the information gathered about a topic.

For the body of your report, you may choose three different main points, or you may choose one point and expand it into three or more main points.

TOPIC CATEGORY FOR PEOPLE
Introduction: First paragraph
Body: Choose three or more main points
 1. Childhood
 2. Adult life
 3. People or events that influenced his/her life
 4. Accomplishments
 5. Characteristics
 6. Unusual/interesting facts
 7. Think of your own main point to fit the topic.
Conclusion: Last paragraph

TOPIC CATEGORY FOR ANIMALS
Introduction: First paragraph
Body: Choose three or more main points
 1. Habitat (where it lives)
 2. Physical characteristics (what it looks like)
 3. Usual and/or unusual behaviors
 4. What it eats and how it gets its food
 5. Enemies
 6. Interesting or little known facts
 7. Think of your own main point to fit the topic.
Conclusion: Last paragraph

TOPIC CATEGORY FOR THINGS
Introduction: First paragraph
Body: Choose three or more main points
 1. Physical appearance, makeup, or identification (size, shape, looks, texture, weight, color, etc.)
 2. Can it be classified into different groups?
 3. Important characteristics or uses
 4. Unusual and interesting facts
 5. Does it change with time?
 6. Think of your own main point to fit the topic.
Conclusion: Last paragraph

TOPIC CATEGORY FOR PLACES
Introduction: First paragraph
  Include the location. Is it real or imaginary?
Body: Choose three or more main points
 1. Famous landmarks
 2. Physical characteristics and climate
 3. History or interesting facts
 4. People and/or animals that live there
 5. Major industries, products, and services
 6. Think of your own main point to fit the topic.
Conclusion: Last paragraph

TOPIC CATEGORY FOR A PROCESS
A process is how something is done or made.
Introduction: First paragraph
  Identify the process.
  Identify why the process is necessary.
Body: Choose the main points
  List the steps you must take in order to complete the process in the most logical order.
Conclusion: Last paragraph

TOPIC CATEGORY FOR AN EVENT
Introduction: First paragraph
  What was the event?
  When and where did the event occur?
  Who or what was involved in the event?
Body: Choose three or more main points
 1. Reasons why the event occurred
 2. What was the effect of the event?
 3. Widespread importance of the event
 4. Think of your own main point to fit the topic.
Conclusion: Last paragraph

TOPIC CATEGORY FOR OPINIONS
To write an opinion research report, follow the five-paragraph-persuasive-essay outline.
Introduction: First paragraph
Body: Main points
 1. First point and supporting sentences
 2. Second point and supporting sentences
 3. Third point and supporting sentences
Conclusion: Last paragraph

TOPIC CATEGORY FOR IDEAS
Introduction: First paragraph
  Include facts and definitions.
Body: Main points
 1. Reasons
 2. Examples
 3. Think of your own main point to fit the topic.
Conclusion: Last paragraph

Learn It: STEP 1: SELECT AND NARROW A TOPIC

 Reference 220 **(Step 1) Select and Narrow a Topic**

In order to choose a topic, look over the topic categories in your Topic Guide in Reference 219. The topic categories are *people, things, animals, places, processes, events, opinions,* and *ideas*. Then, choose the topic category that you want to explore. As you can see, each topic category covers a large amount of information. This means the topics are too broad. When a topic is too broad, you need to narrow it. To narrow the topic means to reduce or limit it. No matter which topic category you choose, it must be narrowed. The scenario below shows one way a topic was narrowed.

First, the writer looked at all the topic categories in the Topic Guide and chose the category **People** for his broad writing topic. The writer knew the topic category he chose had to be narrowed. He thought about all the different kinds of people and decided that he wanted to know more about famous people in history. However, he knew that the narrowed topic, **Famous People in History**, was still too broad because there were too many people to write about. So, he chose one person in history, **Benjamin Franklin**, as his further narrowed topic. Now that the topic was narrowed to a specific person, the writer needed to narrow the topic one last time because the topic, **Benjamin Franklin**, was still too broad. Before the writer could select a final narrowed topic, he returned to the Topic Guide and chose the three main points he wanted to present in his report. The selection of these points helped the writer finalize his narrowed topic.

Topic Category: People

Narrowed Topic: Famous People in History

Further Narrowed Topic: Benjamin Franklin

Final Narrowed Topic: Some of Benjamin Franklin's Accomplishments

Learn It: STEP 2: SELECT THE MAIN POINTS

 Reference 221 **(Step 2) Select the Main Points**

To select the main points, look at the choices listed under the category selected in the Topic Guide. Choose three separate points, or choose one point and expand it into three points. The scenario below shows one way the main points were selected.

First, the writer looked at the seven main points listed in the Topic Guide under the category for **People**. Each point listed a specific area of a person's life. The writer could either choose three separate points, or he could choose only one and expand it into three points. The writer decided to use only one aspect of Benjamin Franklin's life, his **accomplishments**, and expand it into his three main points instead of choosing three separate points. The writer then made his final choice for a narrowed topic: **Benjamin Franklin's Accomplishments**.

Main Points:

1. 1st Accomplishment
2. 2nd Accomplishment
3. 3rd Accomplishment

The writer now has a final narrowed topic and has selected three main points for his report. His next step will be to look up information about Benjamin Franklin's accomplishments so he can determine which three accomplishments he wants to develop and support in the body of his report.

Your topic choices may go through many changes as you determine the direction of your report. If you cannot find enough interesting information about your final narrowed topic, go back to the Topic Guide and choose other points to write about. If you change your points, you must remember to change your final narrowed topic.

START LESSON 2

Lesson 2

You will

- read and discuss main sources used to research a topic
- read and discuss Steps 3-4 in a research report:
  - Select sources by skimming.
  - Make bibliography cards.
- write in your journal.

Writing Time

Learn It: **MAIN SOURCES USED TO RESEARCH A TOPIC**

There are four main sources that you have available when you research a topic for a report. They are encyclopedias, the Internet, books, and magazines.

Reference 222 | **Main Sources Used to Research a Topic**

AN ENCYCLOPEDIA SOURCE

Encyclopedias are always good sources for reports because they give you a general introduction to your topic, along with specific details. Encyclopedia articles on your narrowed topic are usually easy to find because they are listed alphabetically. However, if you cannot find your narrowed topic in an encyclopedia, you may need to look under a broader topic.

> **Example: Narrowed topic:** Woodpeckers; **Broader topic:** Birds

Before you leave your first encyclopedia article, check the end of that article for a list of related encyclopedia articles that also match your topic. This list will be helpful whether you use the first article or not. Always check the publication date when using an encyclopedia. Depending on the nature of the topic, material in an older encyclopedia could be outdated. Most current encyclopedias are also available in CD-ROM format in public libraries.

THE INTERNET AS A SOURCE

Most libraries provide access to the Internet through computers. Computers provide an excellent way for you to search for different types of information. If you have a computer and access to the Internet, you can do on-line searches to find information about a specific topic. To find information through an on-line search engine, type in a key word, phrase, or topic. If a key word is too general, it may provide a list of articles that is too broad for your topic. Check Internet sources carefully to make sure they are reliable. *(For example, is the site or author associated with a college, university, or other credible organization? Does the site include links to other reliable documents?)* As you find information you can use, write down the source of that information just as you would for a book. If possible, print the information. It is also a good idea to write the date on which you found the information since information on the Internet can change daily.

A BOOK SOURCE

Books can give details about your narrowed topic. Use the card catalog in the library to find books related to your topic. Then, use the book's index and table of contents to find the information you need. Review the table of contents to get an overall picture of what the book is about. If you see any chapter titles that relate to your topic, skim the pages in those chapters. Also, look in the index for information related to your topic. Then, look on the specific pages listed in the index to see if the information can be used. It is usually not necessary to read the whole book in order to locate specific information about your topic.

Continued on next page. >>>

Reference 222 continued from previous page.

A MAGAZINE SOURCE

Magazine articles can also give you details about your topic. Use the *Readers' Guide to Periodical Literature* to find magazine articles related to your topic. Magazine articles are listed alphabetically by topic and by author. Some entries have cross-references (marked *See* or *See also*) that will help you find related articles. Since periodical materials cannot be checked out, you may need to ask the librarian for assistance.

For more information about using an encyclopedia, the Internet, books, and magazines as sources for a report, see the Resource Tools Section on pages 532–536, 540.

Learn It: STEP 3: SELECT SOURCES BY SKIMMING

| Reference 223 | (Step 3) Select Sources by Skimming |

1. **Skimming** is reading only the key parts of a source to determine quickly if that source has information that will fit the narrowed topic and main points you have selected from the Topic Guide.
2. Skim key parts, such as titles, topic headings in bold type, first sentences of paragraphs, underlining, captions under pictures, text outlined by boxes, questions, and summaries.
3. The best way to skim several paragraphs in a longer article is to read all of the first paragraph because it usually contains a brief summary of the article. Then, read only the first sentence of each paragraph in the body of the article. This will give you a brief summary of each paragraph. Finally, read all of the last paragraph because it restates the most important points.
4. As you skim an article, consider these things: Does this information contain enough facts about your narrowed topic and main points? Is the information interesting enough to use in your report? Is the information presented clearly, and is it easy to understand?
5. Skimming a source will quickly help you decide if the source can be used. If the source has enough information about your narrowed topic and main points, then it **can be used**. If the source does not have enough information about your narrowed topic and main points, then it **should not be used**. If, after skimming several sources, you cannot find enough information about the final narrowed topic and main points, you need to go back to the Topic Guide and choose new main points. Be aware that this could change your final narrowed topic. If you still cannot find enough information, you may need to choose a different topic and select three or more main points for the new topic.

Learn It: STEP 4: MAKE BIBLIOGRAPHY CARDS

| Reference 224 | (Step 4) Make a Bibliography Card for Each Source Selected |

As soon as you decide to use an article in an encyclopedia, a book, the Internet, or a magazine, immediately make a bibliography card that records specific, detailed information about that source. You will later use your bibliography cards to make a bibliography page for your report.

The **bibliography** page gives credit to the sources actually used in your report and tells others where they can find information on your subject. This is done even if you have only one source. The directions below tell you how to record bibliographic information from each of the four types of sources. The examples show you how each card is arranged and punctuated.

• **Book:** To record a book source on your bibliography card, write the name of the author(s), the title of the book, the city where the book is published, the publisher, and the date of publication.

Continued on next page. >>>

Reference 224 continued from previous page.

- **Encyclopedia:** To record an encyclopedia source on your bibliography card, write the name of the author(s) (if given), the title of the article, the name of the encyclopedia, and the edition date of the encyclopedia.

- **Internet:** To record an Internet source on your bibliography card, write the name of the author(s) (if given), the title of the page or article, the name of the web site, the date posted/revised, and the name of the organization associated with the web site. Next, include the day, month, and year you looked up the information. Finally, write the electronic address.

- **Magazine:** To record a magazine source on your bibliography card, write the name of the author(s), the title of the article, the name of the magazine, the day, the month, and the year of publication, and the page number(s).

Bibliography Card (Book)	Bibliography Card (Internet)
Franklin, Benjamin. Benjamin Franklin's Wit and Wisdom (Americana Pocket Gift Edition). White Plains, New York: Peter Pauper Press, Inc., 1998.	"A Quick Biography of Benjamin Franklin." ushistory.org 1999/2004. The Independence Hall Association. 15 Sept. 2004. http://www.ushistory.org/franklin/facts

Bibliography Card (Encyclopedia)	Bibliography Card (Magazine)
"Ben Franklin." Compton's Encyclopedia & Fact-Index. 2004 ed.	Isaacson, Walter. "The Amazing Adventures of Ben Franklin." Time 7 July 2003: 70-71.

JOURNAL WRITING 47

Write an entry in your journal. Use Reference 9 on page 12 for ideas.

Student Tip...

1. Use colored index cards to record your bibliography sources. This makes it easy to distinguish them from the white note cards you will make in the next lesson.

2. For a review of the library, computer terminology, and the Internet, refer to the Resource Tools Section on pages 532–533, 540–543.

English Made Easy

Writing Time

Learn It: **STEP 5: TAKE NOTES**

Reference 225 — (Step 5) Take Notes

Notes are recorded information that is written in your own words by using words and phrases. Write your notes on note cards and use a different note card for each set of facts you record. Later, when you get to the outlining step of your report, it will be easier to shuffle and rearrange the order of your information by shifting the order of the cards. The directions below will guide you as you take notes.

1. INTRODUCTION

Write the word *Introduction-1* at the top of a note card. On the first **introduction** note card, write words or phrases that tell what your report is about. Write the word *Introduction-2* at the top of another note card. On the second **introduction** note card, list extra information or a definition that tells more about the topic.

2. BODY

Write a 1st and the first **main-point heading** at the top of several note cards. Write words or phrases that support your first main point on each of these cards. Write only one or two notes on each card.

Write a 2nd and the second **main-point heading** at the top of several note cards. Write words or phrases that support your second main point on each of these cards. Write only one or two notes on each card.

Write a 3rd and the third **main-point heading** at the top of several note cards. Write words or phrases that support your third main point on each of these cards. Write only one or two notes on each card.

3. CONCLUSION

Write the word *Conclusion-1* at the top of a note card. On the first **conclusion** note card, write words or phrases that describe your topic again. Write the word *Conclusion-2* at the top of another note card. On the second *Conclusion-2* note card, write supporting facts, opinions, or quotations that help you summarize the conclusions that you have drawn from your research.

Writing Notes

- As you take your notes, start at the beginning of the article and work to the end. If the information you are reading does not support a main point, keep moving through the source.

- Put the information you write on your note cards *in your own words*. Put only one note from a source on a note card.

- Write your notes in **phrases**, not complete sentences. A good way to do this is to read the information, set your source aside, and then write the information on your note cards as you remember it.

- At the bottom of every note card, write the author's last name and the page number where the information is found. You will use this information in the body of your report as you acknowledge your sources. If no author is given, write the name of the source and the page number.

Lesson 3

You will

- read and discuss Steps 5–6 in a research report:
  — Take notes.
  — Organize note cards.
- write in your journal.

Sample Note Cards

Introduction-1   1

contributed many things to colonial
America during life
accomplishments-publisher,
scientist/inventor, public servant

Compton's, p. 380

Introduction-2   2

"Wish not so much to live long,
as to live well."

Franklin, p. 4

1st Accomplishment - Publisher   3

published weekly newspaper,
Pennsylvania Gazette at age 22
paper became very popular

Compton's, p. 380

1st Accomplishment - Publisher   4

used editorials to accomplish changes
for public good in Philadelphia & all
of Pennsylvania

Compton's, p. 380

1st Accomplishment - Publisher   5

published Poor Richard's Almanac
over 10,000 copies a year
contained calendar, weather forecast,
jokes, original proverbs

Compton's, p. 381

1st Accomplishment - Publisher   6

Poor Richard's Almanac
featured fictional character named
Richard Saunders
almanac made Franklin famous for
humor and wisdom

Compton's, p. 381

1st Accomplishment - Publisher   7

became official printer for these
colonies: Pennsylvania, New Jersey,
Delaware, Maryland

Compton's, p. 381

2nd Accomplishment - Scientist/Inventor   8

retired from publishing to explore
science
wrote book about electricity that
is foundation of modern theories
of electricity

Compton's, p. 383

2nd Accomplishment - Scientist/Inventor   9

did experiments on electricity
discovered electricity in lightning
and invented lightning rod

Compton's, p. 383

2nd Accomplishment - Scientist/Inventor   10

invented Franklin stove that produced
more heat than fireplaces
used for over 100 years to heat
thousands of homes

Compton's, p. 382

2nd Accomplishment - Scientist/Inventor   11

invented bifocals

invented swim fins

"A Quick Biography," p. 3

3rd Accomplishment - Public Servant   12

as young publisher:
organized fund-raiser for first
hospital in America
formed Philadelphia's first volunteer
fire department

Compton's, p. 380

3rd Accomplishment - Public Servant   13

as young publisher:
organized first library in colonial
America

Compton's, p. 380

3rd Accomplishment - Public Servant   14

in later years: served as postmaster
general of colonies
set up postal system with fair
rates, weekly delivery

Compton's, p. 382

3rd Accomplishment - Public Servant   15

in later years:
helped write the Declaration of
Independence

Compton's, p. 384-385

3rd Accomplishment - Public Servant   16

in later years:
gained support for colonies as
ambassador to France during
Revolutionary War

Compton's, p. 384-385

Conclusion-1   17

one of greatest citizens
of colonial America
heralded throughout the world as
a champion of liberty

Compton's, p. 385

Conclusion-2   18

contributions had great effect on
America then and now

Compton's, p. 385

Learn It: STEP 6: ORGANIZE NOTE CARDS

Reference 227 — (Step 6) Organize Note Cards

Once you have finished your reading and note-taking, the next step is to organize the note cards. Follow the directions below to help you.

1. Since you have written the introduction, main points, and conclusion at the top of your note cards, most of your information is already organized.

2. Now, sort your note cards into piles according to the titles at the top of the note cards. You should have five piles: introduction, first main point, second main point, third main point, and conclusion.

3. Arrange the introduction note cards in the correct order for your report. Then, write *Paragraph 1* on the back of each card.

4. Next, decide if you want to keep the order of the main points that you have written on your note cards. Renumber and rearrange the cards, if necessary.

5. Arrange the note cards within each main point in a logical order for your report.

6. On the note cards for each main point, write *Paragraph 2* on the back of the first main-point cards, *Paragraph 3* on the back of the second main-point cards, and *Paragraph 4* on the back of the third main-point cards.

7. Arrange the conclusion note cards in the correct order for your report. Then, write *Paragraph 5* on the back of each card.

8. Finally, number all your note cards (1, 2, 3, 4, etc.) in the upper right hand corner to prevent them from getting out of order. Put the bibliography card(s) at the end.

9. Store all note cards in a plastic zip bag. You will use these note cards to complete **Step 7, Write an Outline**. You will hand in your note cards with your final report.

JOURNAL WRITING 48

Write an entry in your journal. Use Reference 9 on page 12 for ideas.

START LESSON 4

Writing Time

Lesson 4

You will

- read and discuss Step 7 in a research report:
  — Write an outline.

Learn It: **STEP 7: WRITE AN OUTLINE**

Once you have organized your note cards, you are ready to make an outline. Remember that an outline is your road map. You must constantly check your outline to make adjustments and to make sure you keep focused on the narrowed topic of your report.

Reference 228 (Step 7) Write an Outline

An **outline** is a concisely written list of the information on your note cards in the order it will be presented in your report. To make an outline for your report, you must use the note cards that you have already organized. You will put your notes from the note cards into correct outline form. Keep in mind that you may not use all of your notes as you make your outline. *(See References 206-207 on pages 451-452 for outline examples.)*

Use the information below to guide you as you make your outline.

1. **Title.** Write your outline title on the top line of your paper. It should be the same or similar to your narrowed topic.

2. **Details for the introduction.** Look at the notes on the note cards titled Introduction. Using these notes, write at least three phrases for the introductory paragraph. The first phrase will tell what your report is about. The other phrases will give extra information or a definition that tells more about the topic.

3. **Main Points.** Next, find the note cards titled *1st (main point)*, *2nd (main point)*, and *3rd (main point)*. Write the main points in parallel form on your outline. For the main points, put a Roman numeral beside each one, capitalize the first word, and skip several lines after each main point to give you room to write the rest of your outline.

4. **Subtopics or details for the first main point.** Look at the note cards titled *1st (main point)*. Write the notes that support the first main topic as subtopics A., B., C., etc. Under each subtopic, list any details from your notes that support it as 1., 2., 3. Write the subtopics (A., B., C.) and details (1., 2., 3.) in parallel form.

5. **Subtopics or details for the second main point.** Look at the note cards titled *2nd (main point)*. Write the notes that support the second main topic as subtopics A., B., C., etc. Under each subtopic, list any details from your notes that support it as 1., 2., 3. Write the subtopics (A., B., C.) and details (1., 2., 3.) in parallel form.

6. **Subtopics or details for the third main point.** Look at the note cards titled *3rd (main point)*. Write the notes that support the third main topic as subtopics A., B., C., etc. Under each subtopic, list any details from your notes that support it as 1., 2., 3. Write the subtopics (A., B., C.) and details (1., 2., 3.) in parallel form.

7. **Details for the conclusion.** Look at the notes on the note cards titled Conclusion. Using these notes, write at least two phrases for the concluding paragraph. The first phrase restates or supports the information in the introduction. The other phrases give supporting facts, opinions, or quotations to help summarize the conclusions you have drawn from your research.

Discuss It:

Sometimes, there is too much information on the note cards to include in your report. When that happens, you must decide which information you want to use and which you should discard. When you get ready to write your rough draft, you will write from your outline, not from your note cards.

Now, look at Reference 229. This is the report outline that was made from the notes about Benjamin Franklin. Some of the information on some of the note cards was left out when the outline was made. The information left out of the outline will not be used in the report. For example, none of the information on two cards was used. Can you find the two cards that were not used at all?

Also, on two of the note cards, only part of the information was left out of the outline. What detail was left out on note card 5? What detail was left out on note card 17? Since none of this information was put in the outline, it will not be mentioned in the report.

Continued on next page. >>>

Also, notice how the topics and subtopics on the outline have been lined up and how they have been made parallel. This is the standard outline form that you should follow every time you make an outline.

 Reference 229   Example of an Outline

Major Accomplishments of Benjamin Franklin
Introduction
    Made good contributions to American way of life
    Said, "Wish not so much to live long, as to live well"
    Accomplished much as a publisher, scientist/inventor, and public servant

I. Publisher
    A. Published weekly newspaper, <u>Pennsylvania Gazette</u>, at age 22
        1. Became popular
        2. Influenced people to establish public improvements in Philadelphia and all of Pennsylvania
    B. Published popular <u>Poor Richard's Almanac</u>
        1. Made Franklin famous for his humor and wisdom
        2. Featured fictional character, Richard Saunders
        3. Contained calendar, weather forecasts, jokes, original proverbs
II. Scientist/Inventor
    A. Retired from publishing to devote more time to science
    B. Conducted experiments and wrote important book on electricity
    C. Discovered electricity in lightning and invented lightning rod
    D. Invented Franklin stove
        1. Produced more heat in room than commonly used fireplace
        2. Used for over 100 years to heat thousands of homes
III. Public servant
    A. As a young publisher
        1. Helped establish first hospital in America
        2. Established first volunteer fire department
        3. Established first library in colonial America
    B. In later years
        1. Served as postmaster general of colonies and established system with fair rates and weekly mail delivery
        2. Helped write <u>Declaration of Independence</u>
        3. Served as ambassador to France to win support for colonies during Revolutionary War

Conclusion
    One of the greatest citizens of colonial America
    Contributions still being felt in America today

Lesson 5

You will

- read and discuss Step 8 in a research report:
  — Write a rough draft.

Writing Time

Write It: **STEP 8: WRITE A ROUGH DRAFT**

Reference 230 (Step 8) Write a Rough Draft

With your outline before you, you are ready to write your rough draft. There are several things you need to do to write the rough draft of your research report.

- Follow the order of your outline.
- If you decide to include another main topic or eliminate a main topic, stop and use your note cards to reorganize the outline.
- Remember, your outline is the "visual map" of your report. It will keep you going in the right direction. Keep it up-to-date.
- You should **use your own words in your report** as you present facts and give examples. This will make your paper special because no one writes quite like you.

1. Your report will be a five-paragraph report. You will have an introductory paragraph, three paragraphs in the body (a paragraph for each of the main points), and a concluding paragraph. Use a pencil and skip every other line on your notebook paper.

2. **Paragraph 1: Introduction.** Look at the introduction on your outline and write at least three sentences for the introductory paragraph. The first sentence is a topic sentence that tells what your report is about. Remember to indent this sentence because it is the first sentence of the paragraph. The next sentences give extra information, a definition, or a quotation that tells more about the topic.

3. **Paragraph 2: 1st Main Point.** Look at the first main point on your outline (Roman numeral I.) Write a topic sentence that states the first main point and that tells what the paragraph is about. Remember to indent this sentence because it is the first sentence of the paragraph. Then, using the subtopics and details in the outline, write complete sentences that support this main point. Make sure these sentences are arranged in the same order as they appear in the outline.

4. **Paragraph 3: 2nd Main Point.** Look at the second main point on your outline (Roman numeral II.) Write a topic sentence that states the second main point and that tells what the paragraph is about. Remember to indent this sentence because it is the first sentence of the paragraph. Then, using the subtopics and details in the outline, write complete sentences that support this main point. Make sure these sentences are arranged in the same order as they appear in the outline.

5. **Paragraph 4: 3rd Main Point.** Look at the third main point on your outline (Roman numeral III.) Write a topic sentence that states the third main point and that tells what the paragraph is about. Remember to indent this sentence because it is the first sentence of the paragraph. Then, using the subtopics and details in the outline, write complete sentences that support this main point. Make sure these sentences are arranged in the same order as they appear in the outline.

6. **Paragraph 5: Conclusion.** Look at the conclusion on your outline and write at least two sentences for the concluding paragraph. The first sentence is a concluding general statement that restates or supports the information in the introduction. Remember to indent this sentence because it is the first sentence of the paragraph. The next sentence or sentences use facts, opinions or quotations to summarize the conclusions that you have drawn from your research.

Continued on next page. >>>

7. **Title Page.** The title page will be the **first page** of your report. Make a title page, using the following information: Write neatly in ink. Skip three lines from the top line. On the fourth line, center and write the title of your report. Skip three more lines. Then, on the next line, center and write **By** (*your name*). Skip three more lines, and on the next line, center and write **For** (*your teacher's name*). On the next line, under the teacher's name, write the date the report is due.

8. **Bibliography Page or Works Cited Page.** At the end of your report, you will use your bibliography cards to list all the encyclopedias, books, articles, and Internet sources **that you actually used** to write your report. The bibliography will be the **last page** of your report. Write neatly in ink. On the top line, center and write **Bibliography**, skip two lines, then copy the information from your bibliography cards to your notebook paper.

   These entries should be listed in alphabetical order, according to the last name of the author. *(Note: In the example below, the article from the encyclopedia does not have an author listed. In this case, you should use the first word of the article title.)*

   Do not number the sources on the bibliography page. Use a "hanging indent" when an entry's information wraps to a second line. "Hanging indent" means to indent the information on the second and additional lines five to seven spaces.

9. **Citations Within Your Report.** Within the text of your report, you must acknowledge any paraphrased idea or quotation that you have borrowed from someone else. Even if you have summarized the information in your own words, you are still using another person's idea and must include a citation. The only information that does not have to be cited is your own personal opinion, original ideas, or well-known facts.

   To cite a source, place the author's last name and the page number where the information was found in parentheses at the end of each sentence. If several sentences in a row contain information from the same source, acknowledgement need only appear at the end of the last sentence.

   Example: (Compton's 381).

Example of a Bibliography Page

BIBLIOGRAPHY

"Ben Franklin." <u>Compton's Encyclopedia & Fact-Index</u>. 2004 ed.

Franklin, Benjamin. <u>Benjamin Franklin's Wit and Wisdom (Americana Pocket Gift Edition)</u>. White Plains, New York: Peter Pauper Press, Inc., 1998.

START LESSON 6

Lesson 6

You will

- read and discuss Steps 9-12 in a research report:
  - Revise and edit your rough draft.
  - Write final outline.
  - Write the final report.
  - Put final report and all related research work in the correct order.
- write in your journal.

 Writing Time

Write It: **STEP 9: REVISE AND EDIT THE ROUGH DRAFT**

Reference 231	(Step 9) Revise & Edit a Rough Draft

Revision and editing are part of the writing process. During the revision and editing time, use References 48 and 50 on pages 64, 66. As you revise and edit your paper, make sure you check for good organization, for clear and logical development of ideas, and for general statements supported by details and examples. After you revise and edit your rough draft, ask at least one more person to edit it. The final responsibility for revision and editing, however, is yours. A quick review is provided below to help you do a final proofreading of your report.

1. Is the first line of each paragraph indented?
2. Does your paper have an introduction, a body, and a conclusion?
3. Does each supporting sentence develop the main idea in each of the main-point paragraphs?
4. Do your main points and supporting sentences follow the order of your outline?
5. Have you capitalized and punctuated your sentences correctly?
6. Have you spelled each word correctly?
7. Have you read your report orally to see how it sounds?
8. Have you checked for sentence fragments and run-on sentences?
9. Are your sentences varied to avoid monotony?
10. Have you completed a title page, an outline, and a bibliography?

Learn It: **STEP 10: WRITE THE FINAL OUTLINE**

Reference 232	(Step 10) Write the Final Outline

Check over your first outline to see if there are any revisions necessary after writing and editing the rough draft of your report. Make any necessary changes. Then, write your final outline neatly in ink. Both outlines will be handed in with your final report.

Learn It: **STEP 11: WRITE THE FINAL REPORT**

Reference 233	(Step 11) Write the Final Report

Before you recopy your edited rough draft for your final paper, reread your report and make any necessary changes. Also, decide if you want to include illustrations or visual aids with your final report. If so, they must be completed at this time. Then, write your final report neatly. Finally, proofread your final paper again.

Discuss It:

Reference 234 — Example of a Final Report

Major Accomplishments of Benjamin Franklin

Benjamin Franklin, through hard-work and lifelong curiosity, contributed much to the American way of life. Franklin once said, "Wish not so much to live long, as to live well" (Franklin 4). He lived by this saying throughout his long and productive life. Benjamin Franklin accomplished many amazing things as a publisher, as an inventor, and as a public servant (Compton's 380).

At the age of twenty-two, Benjamin Franklin began his first career as a publisher. During this time, he published a weekly newspaper, the *Pennsylvania Gazette*. Franklin wrote articles in this popular newspaper that influenced people to make public improvements in Philadelphia and all of Pennsylvania (Compton's 380). Franklin also published the *Poor Richard's Almanac* with great success. In fact, this publication made Franklin famous for his humor and wisdom. It featured a fictional character named Richard Saunders and contained a calendar, weather forecasts, jokes, and original proverbs (Compton's 381).

Franklin's second career as a scientist and inventor began after he retired from the publishing business. This allowed him to devote more time to his scientific studies. Franklin conducted many experiments in electricity and wrote one of the most important early books on electricity. One of his inventions, the lightning rod, was made after his discovery of electricity in lightning (Compton's 383). Another invention, the Franklin stove, produced better heat in homes than the fireplace. Franklin stoves were used for over one hundred years to heat thousands of colonial homes (Compton's 382).

Franklin's third career as a public servant was established throughout his adult life. As a young publisher, Franklin was instrumental in establishing the first hospital, the first volunteer fire department, and the first library in colonial America (Compton's 380). In later years, Franklin served as postmaster general of the colonies. He developed an organized and fair postal system that delivered mail weekly instead of every two or three months (Compton's 382). Franklin was also one of the major authors of the Declaration of Independence and served as ambassador to France to win support for the colonies during the Revolutionary War (Compton's 384-385).

In conclusion, Benjamin Franklin was truly one of the greatest citizens of Colonial America for many reasons. His contributions as a publisher, an inventor, and a public servant are still being felt in America today (Compton's 385).

Learn It: **STEP 12: PUT THE FINAL REPORT AND ALL RELATED RESEARCH WORK IN THE CORRECT ORDER.**

Reference 235 — (Step 12) Put the Final Report and All Related Research Papers in the Correct Order

1. Title page (in ink or typed)
2. Final report (in ink or typed)
3. Illustrations and visual aids (optional)
4. Bibliography page (in ink or typed)
5. Final Outline (in ink or typed)
6. Rough draft (in pencil)
7. First outline (in pencil)
8. Note cards and bibliography cards (Put all cards in a plastic zip bag.)
9. Hand in final report and all related papers when your teacher calls for them.

JOURNAL WRITING 49

Write an entry in your journal. Use Reference 9 on page 12 for ideas.

START LESSON 7

Lesson 7

You will

- review Steps 1-12 in writing a research report.
- write an evaluation essay for WA 45.

Writing Time

Write It: **EVALUATING THE STEPS IN A RESEARCH REPORT**

Write an evaluation of the steps used in writing a report. Look at Writing Assignment 45. The writing prompt tells you the points to include in your evaluation.

Writing Assignment 45

Purpose: To evaluate the steps used in writing a research report

Type of Writing: Evaluation essay

Audience: Classmates or teacher

Writing Prompt:

Use at least three of the questions below to help you write your evaluation of the steps in a report.

1. Which steps did you find most useful and why?

2. Which steps did you find most difficult and why?

3. Would you add, delete, or change the order of any of the steps? Explain your reasoning.

4. Do you think you can write a report by following these steps? Why or why not?

Special Instructions:

1. Write in first person. See Reference 70 on page 104.
   (First-person pronouns: *I, me, my, mine, we, us, our, and ours.*)

2. Write in complete sentences.

3. Write your evaluation in paragraph form.

Note: Reference 218 on page 483 gives the steps for writing a research report.

Writing Time

Learn It: **SCHEDULE FOR AN INDEPENDENT RESEARCH REPORT**

Today, you will begin working on your independent research report. Look at Reference 236. This reference gives you the schedule you will follow as you work on your report.

This is Day 1, and you will do Steps 1–3. First, you must select and narrow a topic. Your topic choices are listed in Writing Assignment 46.

Lesson 1

You will

- read and discuss the schedule for writing an independent research report.
- apply Steps 1-3 for research report (WA 46):
  — Select and narrow a topic.
  — Select main points.
  — Select sources by skimming.

Reference 236 **Schedule for an Independent Research Report**

DAY 1 Use References 220-223 on pages 485-487.

Step 1: Select and narrow a topic.

Step 2: Select the main points.

Step 3: Select sources by skimming.

DAY 2 Use Reference 224 on page 487.

Step 4: Make a bibliography card for each source selected.

DAY 3 Use References 225-226 on pages 489-490.

Step 5: Take notes.

DAY 4 Use References 227-229 on pages 491-493.

Step 6: Organize note cards.

Step 7: Write a first-draft outline.

DAY 5 Use Reference 230 on page 494.

Step 8: Write a rough draft.

DAY 6 Use References 231-232 on page 496.

Step 9: Revise and edit the rough draft.

Step 10: Write the final outline.

DAY 7 Use References 233-235 on pages 496-497.

Step 11: Write the final report.

Step 12: Put the final report and all related research work in the correct order.

(**Note:** Make sure you write everything, except your final outline and report, in pencil.)

DAY 8 Share and Evaluate

DAY 9 Share and Evaluate

Write It: INDEPENDENT REPORT WRITING 46

Writing Assignment [46]

Purpose: To inform
Type of Writing: Independent report
Audience: Classmates

Choose and narrow one of the report topics below.

1. A city, state, or country
2. A famous person (scientist, inventor, entertainer, etc.)
3. A musical instrument (woodwind, brass, percussion, string, etc.)
4. An interesting or unusual animal
5. A famous American
6. A sport (a team sport or an individual sport)
7. A current event or issue

Special Instructions:

1. Use References 218–236 on pages 483–499 to help you write your independent report.
2. Use standard, time-order, or transition writing form. See Reference 69 on page 103.
3. Write in third person. See Reference 70 on page 104.
   (Third-person pronouns: *he, his, him, she, her, hers, it, its, they, their, theirs,* and *them.*)

End of
Lesson 1

START LESSON 2

Lesson 2

You will

- apply Step 4 for research report (WA 46):
  — Make a bibliography card for each source.

End of
Lesson 2

Write It: INDEPENDENT REPORT WRITING 46

Use the schedule in Reference 236 as you continue working on your independent report. This is Day 2, and you will do Step 4.

START LESSON 3

Lesson 3

You will

- apply Step 5 for research report (WA 46):
  — Take notes.

Write It: INDEPENDENT REPORT WRITING 46

Use the schedule in Reference 236 as you continue working on your independent report. This is Day 3, and you will do Step 5.

End of
Lesson 3

Write It: INDEPENDENT REPORT WRITING 46

Use the schedule in Reference 236 as you continue working on your independent report. This is Day 4, and you will do Steps 6–7.

START LESSON 4

Lesson 4

You will
- apply Steps 6–7 for research report (WA 46):
  — Organize note cards.
  — Write a first-draft outline.

End of Lesson 4

Write It: INDEPENDENT REPORT WRITING 46

Use the schedule in Reference 236 as you continue working on your independent report. This is Day 5, and you will do Step 8.

START LESSON 5

Lesson 5

You will
- apply Step 8 for research report (WA 46):
  — Write a rough draft.

End of Lesson 5

Write It: INDEPENDENT REPORT WRITING 46

Use the schedule in Reference 236 as you continue working on your independent report. This is Day 6, and you will do Steps 9–10.

START LESSON 6

Lesson 6

You will
- apply Steps 9–10 for research report (WA 46):
  — Revise and edit the rough draft.
  — Write the final outline.

End of Lesson 6

Write It: INDEPENDENT REPORT WRITING 46

Use the schedule in Reference 236 as you continue working on your independent report. This is Day 7, and you will do Steps 11–12.

Plan It:

Your teacher will give you a presentation schedule to follow as you share your research report with your class in the next two lessons. If you are in Group 1, you will share in Lesson 8. If you are in Group 2, you will share in Lesson 9.

START LESSON 7

Lesson 7

You will
- apply Steps 11–12 for research report (WA 46):
  — Write the final report.
  — Put the final report and all related research work in the correct order.

End of Lesson 7

START LESSON 8

Lesson 8

You will

- begin publishing WA 46 by sharing independent research reports.
- write an evaluation of a classmate's presentation for WA 47.
- write an evaluation of your own report presentation for WA 48.

Writing Time

Write It: **WRITING ASSIGNMENTS 47 AND 48**

Writing Assignment 47

You will choose a classmate's report for a commentary that you will write in your journal. A commentary is an essay that tells what you think about a person's work or presentation. At the top of a new journal page, write the date and title of your favorite presentation from today. Write a commentary that includes an introduction, a paragraph that tells why you liked the report, a paragraph that tells what you learned from it, and a conclusion.

Writing Assignment 48

Do this part only on the day you give your report. For your own report, write a commentary in your journal that includes the reasons why you liked your topic, some of the most interesting things you learned during your research, and an evaluation of your presentation.

Publishing Time

Publish It: **SHARE INDEPENDENT REPORTS**

Now, you will share your research report with your classmates. Students in Group 1 will share today, and students in Group 2 will share during the next lesson. Use the Share Time Guidelines as reports are shared.

Reference 67 **Share Time Guidelines**

Speaker Presentation

1. Have your paper ready to read when called upon.
2. Tell the title of your writing selection.
3. Tell the purpose and type of writing used.

PRESENTATION TIPS:

4. Stand with your feet flat on the floor and your shoulders straight. Do not shift your weight as you stand.
5. Hold your paper about chin high to help you project your voice to your audience.
6. Make sure you do not read too fast.
7. Read in a clear voice that can be heard so that your audience does not have to strain to hear you.
8. Change your voice tone for different characters or for different parts of the writing selection.

Audience Response

1. Look at the speaker.
2. Turn your body toward the speaker.
3. Listen attentively.
   Do not let your thoughts wander.
4. Do not make distracting noises as you listen.
5. Do not make distracting motions as you listen.
6. Show interest in what the speaker is saying.
7. Silently summarize what the speaker is saying. Take notes if necessary.
8. Ask questions about anything that is not clear.
9. Show appreciation by clapping after the speaker has finished.

Writing Time

Write It: WRITING ASSIGNMENTS 48 AND 49

Writing Assignment [48]

Do this part only on the day you give your report. For your own report, write a commentary in your journal that includes the reasons why you liked your topic, some of the most interesting things you learned during your research, and an evaluation of your presentation.

Writing Assignment [49]

You will choose a classmate's report for a commentary that you will write in your journal. A commentary is an essay that tells what you think about a person's work or presentation. At the top of a new journal page, write the date and title of your favorite presentation from today. Write a commentary that includes an introduction, a paragraph that tells why you liked the report, a paragraph that tells what you learned from it, and a conclusion.

Publishing Time

Publish It: SHARE INDEPENDENT REPORTS

If you are in Group 2, you will share your research report with your classmates today. Use the Share Time Guidelines as reports are shared.

Lesson 9

You will

- finish publishing WA 46 by sharing independent research reports.
- write an evaluation of your own report presentation for WA 48.
- write an evaluation of a different classmate's report presentation for WA 49.

Jingle Time

SHURLEY ENGLISH

Student Textbook

Level 6

SHURLEY ENGLISH

♪ **Jingle 1**   **The Study Skills Jingle**

Un-Quigley, Un-Quigley,
What are you going to do?
You've got a frown on your face,
And you're singing the blues!
You're not organized, Quigley;
You are not prepared.
You're not listening,
And your mind's not there.
You don't have plans, and you don't have goals.
Your homework's unfinished,
And you've been told.
You need to get your act together
'Cause you don't have a clue.
You've got the Study Skills Blues!

O-Quigley, O-Quigley,
Now, you see what to do.
You've got a smile on your face,
And you're lookin' cool!
You're so organized, Quigley;
You are so prepared.
You're listening carefully,
And your mind is there.
You've got plans, and you've got goals.
Your homework is finished;
You don't have to be told.
You've got your act together, Quigley,
'Cause you followed the clues.
And you're not singing the Study Skills Blues!

♪ **Jingle 2**   **The Sentence Jingle**

A sentence, sentence, sentence
Is complete, complete, complete
When five simple rules
It meets, meets, meets.

It has a subject, subject, subject
And a verb, verb, verb.
And it makes sense, sense, sense
With every word, word, word.

Add a capital letter
And a punctuation mark.
And now our sentence has all its parts!

But REMEMBER—
Subject and **verb** and **complete sense**,
With a **capital letter** and an **end mark**, too.
Our sentence is complete,
And now we're through!

English Made Easy

♪ Jingle 3 — The Noun Jingle

This is a noun jingle, my friend,
A noun jingle, my friend.
You can shake it to the left
And shake it to the right.
Find yourself a noun,
And then recite:

A noun names a person.
A noun names a thing.
A noun names a person,
Place, or thing,
And sometimes an idea.

Person, place, thing, idea!
Person, place, thing, idea!
So, shake it to the left,
And shake it to the right.
Find yourself a noun,
And feel just right!

♪ Jingle 4 — The Verb Jingle

A verb, a verb.
What is a verb?
Haven't you heard?
There are two kinds of verbs:
The **action verb**
And the **linking verb**.

The action verb
Shows a state of action,
Like **stand** and **sit** and **smile**.
The action verb is always in motion
Because it tells what the subject does.
*We **stand**! We **sit**! We **smile**!*

The linking verb shows a state of being,
Like **am**, **is**, **are**, **was**, and **were**,
Looks, **becomes**, **grows**, and **feels**.
The linking verb shows no action
Because it tells what the subject is.
*He **is** a clown. He **looks** funny.*

♪ Jingle 5 — The Adverb Jingle

An adverb modifies a verb, adjective, or another adverb.
An adverb asks, "HOW? WHEN? WHERE?"
To find an adverb: **Go,** (snap) **Ask,** (snap) **Get.** (snap)
But where do I **go**? *To a verb, adjective, or another adverb.*
What do I **ask**? HOW? WHEN? WHERE?
What do I **get**? An adverb, man. Cool!

♪ Jingle 6 — The Adjective Jingle

An adjective modifies a noun or a pronoun.
An adjective asks, "WHAT KIND?"
An adjective asks, "WHICH ONE?"
An adjective asks, "HOW MANY?"
To identify an adjective: **Go!** (stomp, stomp) **Ask!** (clap, clap) **Get!** (snap)
Where do I **go**? (stomp, stomp) To a noun or a pronoun.
What do I **ask**? (clap, clap) WHAT KIND? WHICH ONE? or HOW MANY?
What do I **get**? (snap, snap) An Adjective!

♪ Jingle 7 — The Article Adjective Jingle

We are the article adjectives,
Teeny, tiny adjectives.
A, AN, THE — A, AN, THE

We are called article adjectives and noun markers.
We are memorized and used every day.
So, if you spot us, you can mark us
With a capital A.

We are the article adjectives,
Teeny, tiny adjectives.
A, AN, THE — A, AN, THE

SHURLEY ENGLISH

♪ **Jingle 8** — **The Preposition Jingle**

A prep, prep, preposition
Is an extra-special word

That connects a
Noun, noun, noun

Or a pro, pro, pronoun
To the rest of the sentence.

♪ **Jingle 9** — **The Object of the Preposition Jingle**

An object of the preposition
Is a NOUN or PRONOUN.
An object of the preposition
Is a NOUN or PRONOUN

After the prep, prep, prep
After the prep, prep, prep
After the prep, prep, prep
That answers **WHAT** or **WHOM**.

♪ **Jingle 10** — **The Prepositional Phrase Jingle**

I've been working with prepositions
'Til I can work no more.
They're connecting their objects
To the rest of the sentence before.

When I put them all together,
The prep and its noun or pro,
I get a prepositional phrase
That could cause my mind to blow!

♪ **Jingle 11** — **The Preposition Flow Jingle**

1. Preposition, Preposition,
   Starting with an **A**:
   **aboard, about, above,
   across, after, against,
   along, among, around, as, at!**

2. Preposition, Preposition,
   Starting with a **B**:
   **before, behind, below,
   beneath, beside, between,
   beyond, but,** and **by!**

3. Preposition, Preposition,
   Starting with a **D**:
   **despite, down, during
   despite, down, during!**

4. Oh, Preposition,
   Please, don't go away.
   Go to the middle of the alphabet,
   And see just what we say.
   E and **F** and **I** and **L**
   And **N** and **O** and **P**:
   **except, for, from,
   in, inside, into, like,
   near, of, off, on, out,
   outside, over, past!**

5. Preposition, Preposition,
   Almost through.
   Start with **S** and end with **W**:
   **since, through,
   throughout, to, toward,
   under, underneath,
   until, up, upon,
   with, within, without!**

6. Preposition, Preposition,
   Easy as can be.
   We just recited
   All **fifty-one** of these!

♪ Jingle 12   The Transition Words Jingle

Aw, listen, comrades, and you shall hear
About transition words
That make your writing smooth and clear.

Transition words are connecting words.
You add them to the beginning
Of sentences and paragraphs
To keep your ideas spinning and give your writing flow.

These words can clarify, summarize, or emphasize,
Compare or contrast, inform or show time.
Learn them now, and your writing will shine!

Transition, Transition,
For words that **SHOW TIME**:
first, second, third, before, during, after,
next, then, and *finally.*

Transition, Transition,
For words that **INFORM**:
for example, for instance, in addition, as well,
also, next, another, along with, and *besides.*

Transition, Transition,
For words that **CONTRAST**:
although, even though, but, yet, still,
otherwise, however, and *on the other hand.*

Transition, Transition,
For words that **COMPARE**:
as, also, like, and *likewise.*

Transition, Transition,
For words that **CLARIFY**:
for example, for instance, and *in other words.*

Transition, Transition,
For words that **EMPHASIZE**:
truly, again, for this reason, and *in fact.*

Transition, Transition,
For words that **SUMMARIZE**:
therefore, in conclusion, in summary, and *finally,*
to sum it up, all in all, as a result, and *last.*

TRANSITION WORD

♪ Jingle 13   The Pronoun Jingle

These little pronouns,
Hangin' around,
Can take the place
Of any of the nouns.

With a smile and a nod
And a twinkle of the eye,
Give those pronouns
A big high five! Yeah!

SHURLEY ENGLISH

♪ Jingle 14 — The Subject Pronoun Jingle

There are seven subject pronouns
That are easy as can be.
SUBJECT PRONOUNS!
I and **We**,
He and **She**,
It and **They** and **You**.
Those are the subject pronouns!

♪ Jingle 15 — The Possessive Pronoun Jingle

There are seven possessive pronouns
That are easy as can be.
POSSESSIVE PRONOUNS!
My and **Our**,
His and **Her**,
Its and **Their** and **Your**.
Those are possessive pronouns!

♪ Jingle 16 — The Conjunction Sound-Off Jingle

Conjunctions are a part of speech.
Conjunctions are a part of speech.
They join words or sentences; it's quite a feat!
They join words or sentences; it's quite a feat!
Sound off! Conjunctions!   Sound off! AND, OR, BUT!
There are many conjunctions, but three stand out.
There are many conjunctions, but three stand out.
Put your hands together and give a shout!
Put your hands together and give a shout!
Sound off! Conjunctions!   Sound off! AND, OR, BUT!
Sound off! Conjunctions!   Sound off! AND, OR, BUT!

♪ Jingle 17 — The 23 Helping Verbs of the Mean, Lean, Verb Machine Jingle

These twenty-three helping verbs
Will be on my test.
I've gotta remember them so I can do my best.
I'll start out with eight and finish with fifteen.
Just call me the mean, lean, verb machine.

There are the eight *be* verbs
That are easy as can be.
   am, is, are   was and **were**
   am, is, are   was and **were**
   am, is, are   was and **were**
   be, being, and **been**

All together now, the eight *be* verbs:
am, is, are   was and **were   be, being,** and **been**
am, is, are   was and **were   be, being,** and **been**
am, is, are   was and **were   be, being,** and **been**

There are twenty-three helping verbs,
And I've recited eight.
That leaves fifteen more that I must relate.
Knowing all these verbs will save my grade.
The mean, lean, verb machine is here to stay.
   has, have, and **had   do, does,** and **did**
   has, have, and **had   do, does,** and **did**
   might, must, and **may**
   might, must, and **may**
   can and **could   would** and **should**
   can and **could   would** and **should**
   shall and **will   shall** and **will**
   has, have, and **had   do, does,** and **did**
   might, must, and **may**
   can and **could, would** and **should**
   shall and **will**
In record time, I did this drill.
I'm the mean, lean, verb machine — STILL!

♪ **Jingle 18** **The Interjection Jingle**

Oh, Interjection, Interjection, Interjection, who are you?
I'm a part of speech through and through.
Well, Interjection, Interjection, Interjection, what do you do?
I show strong or mild emotion; need a review?
Oh, Interjection, Interjection, I still don't have a clue.
*I show strong emotion, like **Wow! Great!** or **Yahoo!***
*I show mild emotion, like **Oh, Yes, Fine,** or **Toodle-oo.***
Well, Interjection, Interjection, you really know how to groove!
That's because I'm a part of speech through and through!

♪ **Jingle 19** **The Possessive Noun Jingle**

A possessive noun just can't be beat.
It shows ownership, and that is neat.
Add an apostrophe to show possession.
This is a great ownership lesson.
Adjective is its part of speech.
Ask **WHOSE** to find it as you speak.
Whose house? Tommy's house.
Possessive Noun Adjective!

♪ **Jingle 20** **The Eight Parts of Speech Jingle**

Want to know how to write?
Use the eight parts of speech.
They're dynamite!

Nouns, **V**erbs, and **P**ronouns.
They rule!
They're called the **NVP's**, and they're really cool!
The **Double A's** are on the move.
Adjectives and **A**dverbs help you to groove.
Next come the **PIC's**, and then we're done.
They're **P**reposition, **I**nterjection, and **C**onjunction!

All together now.
The eight parts of speech, abbreviations, please.
NVP—AA—and—**PIC**!

♪ Jingle 21 — The Direct Object Jingle

A **direct object** is a NOUN or a PRO,
  Is a noun or a pro, is a noun or a pro.
A **direct object** completes the meaning,
  Completes the meaning of the sentence.
A **direct object** follows the verb,
  Follows the **verb-transitive**.
To find a direct object,
  Ask **WHAT** or **WHOM**
  Ask **WHAT** or **WHOM**
 After the verb.

♪ Jingle 22 — The Object Pronoun Jingle

There are seven object pronouns
That are easy as can be.
OBJECT PRONOUNS!

Me and **Us**,
Him and **Her**,
It and **Them** and **You**.
Those are the object pronouns.

♪ Jingle 23 — The Indirect Object Jingle

Indirect, oh, indirect, oh, indirect object.
Give me that indirect, oh, indirect, oh, indirect object.

An indirect object is a NOUN or a PRONOUN
That receives what the direct, the direct object names.
An indirect object is found between the verb, **verb-transitive**,
And the direct object.
  To find the indirect object,   *(sha-bop)*
  Ask **TO WHOM** or **FOR WHOM**   *(sha-bop)*
  After the direct object.   *(sha-bop)*

An indirect, indirect, indirect, indirect, yeah!
An indirect object!
  Just give me that indirect, oh, indirect, oh, indirect object.
  Give me that indirect, oh, indirect, oh, indirect object.
  Give me that object, oh, indirect, oh, indirect object.
An INDIRECT OBJECT!

♪ Jingle 24 — The Predicate Noun Jingle

A predicate, predicate noun
Is a special, special noun
In the predicate, predicate, predicate
That means the **same as the subject**,
The simple, simple subject.

A predicate, predicate noun
Follows after a linking verb.
To locate a predicate noun,
Ask **WHAT** or **WHO** after the verb
And verify the answer.
Verify that the noun in the predicate
Means the **same thing as the subject**,
The simple, simple subject.

♪ Jingle 25 The Noun Job Jingle

Nouns will give you a run for your money.
They do so many jobs
That it's not even funny.
A noun—person, place, thing, or idea—
Is very appealing!
But it's the noun job (noun job)
That is so revealing!

To find the nouns in a sentence,
Go to their jobs (go to their jobs)
Nouns can do objective jobs (objective jobs)
They're the **IO** (IO), **DO** (DO), and **OP** jobs (OP jobs).
And nouns can do subjective jobs (subjective jobs).
They're the **SN** (SN) and **PrN** jobs (PrN jobs).
Jobs. Jobs. Noun Jobs! Yeah!

♪ Jingle 26 The Predicate Adjective Jingle

A predicate, predicate, predicate adjective
Is a special, special adjective
In the predicate, predicate, predicate
That modifies, modifies, **modifies**
The simple, simple **subject**.

A predicate, predicate, predicate adjective
Follows after a linking verb.
To find a predicate adjective,
Ask **WHAT KIND** of subject and verify the answer.
Verify that the adjective in the predicate
Modifies, modifies, modifies
The simple, simple subject.

Resource Tools

SHURLEY ENGLISH

SHURLEY ENGLISH

Resource Tool: Level 6 References

The following list provides a quick reference to the Reference Boxes used in Shurley English.

Resource Tools

SHURLEY ENGLISH

Student Textbook   **Level 6**

SHURLEY ENGLISH

Resource Tool: Level 6 References

The following list provides a quick reference to the Reference Boxes used in Shurley English.

English Made Easy

Resource Tool: Notable People in History for DISCOVERY TIME

Discovery Time provides an opportunity for you to investigate the theme from Level 6, which is historical time travel. During Discovery Time, you will learn interesting facts about notable people in history. After reviewing these facts, you may look for more information at the library, at home, or on the Internet. Reports written on any of these topics may be shared with classmates during Discovery Share Time. Use the information below to guide your exploration.

Page	Chapter	Lesson	Date	Historical Figure
82	3	2	1412-1431	**Joan of Arc**, a French woman and soldier
87	3	3	1400(?)-1468	**Johannes Gutenberg**, a German inventor
91	3	4	1452-1519	**Leonardo da Vinci**, an Italian artist and inventor
95	3	5	1475-1564	**Michelangelo**, an Italian painter, sculptor, architect, and poet
115	4	2	1480-1521	**Ferdinand Magellan**, Portuguese explorer
119	4	3	1564-1616	**William Shakespeare**, English playwright and poet
122	4	4	1642-1727	**Sir Isaac Newton**, English scientist and inventor
125	4	5	1731-1806	**Benjamin Banneker**, African-American mathematician, astronomer, inventor, and publisher
125	4	5	1735-1818	**Paul Revere**, American silversmith, engraver, and patriot
148	5	2	1736-1819	**James Watt**, Scottish scientist and businessman
151	5	3	1743-1826	**Thomas Jefferson**, America's third president
154	5	4	1756-1791	**Wolfgang Amadeus Mozart**, Austrian musician and composer
157	5	5	1758-1843	**Noah Webster**, American lexicographer, lawyer, teacher, grammarian, journalist, essayist, and lobbyist
157	5	5	1765-1825	**Eli Whitney**, American scientist and inventor
174	6	1	1770-1827	**Ludwig van Beethoven**, German musician and composer
179	6	2	1776-1843	**Sequoyah**, Native-American Cherokee
182	6	3	1791-1872	**Samuel Morse**, American artist, scientist, and inventor
186	6	4	1809-1852	**Louis Braille**, French educator and inventor
189	6	5	1813-1906	**Joseph Glidden**, American farmer and inventor
189	6	5	1815-1902	**Elizabeth Cady Stanton**, American advocate for women's rights
211	7	2	1826-1854	**Stephen Collins Foster**, American musician and composer
215	7	3	1831-1890	**Sitting Bull**, Native-American, chief of the Sioux
218	7	4	1831-1888	**John S. Pemberton**, American pharmacist and businessman
221	7	5	1833-1896	**Alfred Nobel**, Swedish chemist, inventor, and humanitarian
221	7	5	1833-1916	**Sally Tompkins**, American philanthropist
239	8	1	1834-1904	**Frederic-Auguste Bartholdi**, French sculptor
243	8	2	1835-1910	**Mark Twain**, American writer
247	8	3	1847-1922	**Alexander Graham Bell**, Scottish-American teacher, scientist, and inventor
250	8	4	1847-1931	**Thomas Edison**, American scientist and inventor
253	8	5	1854-1932	**John Philip Sousa**, American bandmaster and composer
272	9	2	1856-1915	**Booker T. Washington**, African-American advocate
276	9	3	1859-1930	**Sir Arthur Conan Doyle**, British physician and writer
279	9	4	1860-1935	**Jane Addams**, American philanthropist
282	9	5	1863-1947	**Henry Ford**, American inventor and automobile manufacturer
282	9	5	1864-1943	**George Washington Carver**, African-American scientist and educator
297	10	1	1865-1936	**Rudyard Kipling**, British writer
301	10	2	1867-1957	**Laura Ingalls Wilder**, American writer
304	10	3	1867-1912	**Wilbur Wright and Orville Wright** (1871-1948), American aviation pioneers
307	10	4	1867-1934	**Marie Curie**, Polish scientist
310	10	5	1874-1937	**Guglielmo Marconi**, Italian scientist and inventor
328	11	2	1876-1916	**Jack London**, American writer
332	11	3	1877-1963	**Garrett Morgan**, African-American businessman and inventor
337	11	4	1879-1955	**Albert Einstein**, German-American physicist

Continued on next page. >>>

Continued from previous page.

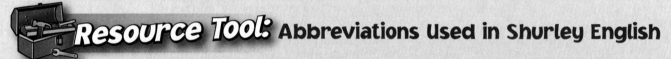

Resource Tool: Abbreviations Used in Shurley English

The following list provides a quick reference of the most commonly used abbreviations in Shurley English.

Abbreviation	Description
N	Noun
SN	Subject Noun
CSN	Compound Subject Noun
Pro	Pronoun
SP	Subject Pronoun
CSP	Compound Subject Pronoun
V	Verb
HV	Helping Verb
CV	Compound Verb
V-t	Verb-transitive
CV-t	Compound Verb-transitive
LV	Linking Verb
CLV	Compound Linking Verb
A	Article Adjective
Adj	Adjective
CAdj	Compound Adjective
Adv	Adverb
CAdv	Compound Adverb
P	Preposition
OP	Object of the Preposition
COP	Compound Object of the Preposition
PPA	Possessive Pronoun Adjective
PNA	Possessive Noun Adjective

Abbreviation	Description
C	Conjunction
I	Interjection
DO	Direct Object
CDO	Compound Direct Object
IO	Indirect Object
CIO	Compound Indirect Object
PrN	Predicate Noun
CPrN	Compound Predicate Noun
PA	Predicate Adjective
CPA	Compound Predicate Adjective

Sentences	
D	Declarative Sentence
E	Exclamatory Sentence
Int	Interrogative Sentence
Imp	Imperative Sentence
S	Simple Sentence
F	Fragment
SCS	Simple Sentence Compound Subject
SCV	Simple Sentence Compound Verb
CD	Compound Sentence
CX	Complex Sentence

Level 6 Patterns	
SN V P1	Subject Noun Verb Pattern 1
SN V-t DO P2	Subject Noun Verb-transitive Direct Object Pattern 2
SN V-t IO DO P3	Subject Noun Verb-transitive Indirect Object Direct Object Pattern 3
SN LV PrN P4	Subject Noun Linking Verb Predicate Noun Pattern 4
SN LV PA P5	Subject Noun Linking Verb Predicate Adjective Pattern 5

Resource Tool: Vocabulary

Prefixes

A **prefix** is a word part added to the beginning of a base word to change its meaning. Prefixes have meanings of their own. If you know the meanings of the prefix part and the base word, you can usually figure out the meaning of the new word that is made from combining the two parts. Some common prefixes are listed below to help you learn their meanings.

Prefix	Meaning	Examples
bi	two, twice	bilingual; bimonthly
dis, non, un	not, opposite of, without	distrust; nonfat; unhappy
im, in	not, in, into	impatient; incapable
inter	between, among	interstate; interact
mis	wrong, wrongly, badly	misbehave; mistake
post	after	posttest
pre	before	pretest
re	again, back	repay; return
sub	beneath, under	submarine; subway

Suffixes

A suffix is a word part added to the end of a base word to change its meaning. Suffixes have meanings of their own, too. If you know the meanings of the suffix part and the base word, you can usually figure out the meaning of the new word that is made from combining the two parts. Some common suffixes are listed below to help you learn their meanings.

Suffix	Meaning	Examples
able, ible	able to, likely to	usable, sensible
er, or	one who, that which	teacher, actor
ful	full of	joyful
ize	to make	vocalize, finalize
less	without	homeless
ly	in the manner of	quietly
ment, ion, tion	the act of, result of, condition	contentment, action, invention
ness	state of, quality of	happiness
ous	full of, filled with	glorious
ward	moving, direction	forward, upward

Suffix Spelling Check

The following spelling rules will help you when you add suffixes to words. Since there are several exceptions to these rules, always check the dictionary if you are in doubt about the spelling of a word.

1. To add a suffix to a word that ends in a **silent** -e, *drop the final -e* if the suffix begins with a **vowel**.
   use / usable   sense / sensible   drive / driving   **Exception:** noticeable

2. To add a suffix to a word that ends in a **silent** -e, *keep the final -e* if the suffix begins with a **consonant**.
   care / careless   state / statement   advance / advancement   **Exception:** true / truly

3. To add a suffix to a word ending in a **consonant** plus -y, *change the -y to i* unless the suffix begins with i-.
   fly / flier / flying   dry / drier / drying   copy / copied / copying

4. To add a suffix to a word ending in a **vowel** plus -y, *do not change the -y to i*.
   key / keyed   joy / joyful

5. To add a suffix to a short word that ends with one vowel and one consonant, *double* the final consonant.
   hop / hopping   pop / popper   big / bigger   **Exception:** job / jobless

Resource Tool: LISTENING AND SPEAKING

Following Written Directions

It is important that you learn to follow written directions. Sometimes, you must read directions several times in order to understand what to do. Written directions are used for many reasons. Some of the ways you will follow written directions include following recipes, filling out forms, taking tests, and following "how to" instructions. You can see from the following examples why following directions is important.

Directions are especially important when you write a process, or "how to," essay. Notice the use of time-order words in the following "how to" essay.

Directions from City Hall to Ten Pins Bowling Alley

From the parking lot in front of city hall, take a left onto Main Street. Go straight on Main Street for about two miles. Before you intersect Hwy 32, turn right onto Maple Street. At the third stoplight, take a left onto Fifth Avenue. You will see Yummy's Ice Cream Parlor on the left as you are heading up the hill. Ten Pins Bowling Alley is the next large building just over the crest of the hill.

How to Change a Flat Tire

Before changing a flat tire, find a safe place to pull out of the flow of traffic. Stop on a level surface away from hills or curves. Next, turn on the car's hazard lights.

Then, retrieve the spare tire, the jack, and the lug-nut wrench. The owner's manual will have the location of these items if you are unsure where they are located. Next, remove the hubcap, if necessary, and loosen the lug nuts by turning them counter clockwise with the wrench. Do not completely remove the lug nuts yet. Position the jack and raise the car until the tire is about six inches off the ground. Then, remove the lug nuts and the flat tire. Place the lug nuts in the hubcap for safekeeping. Carefully put the spare tire on the car and replace the lug nuts by turning them clockwise.

Finally, lower the car until it rests on all four wheels and tighten the lug nuts, starting at the top and moving to opposite corners. Now, put all of the tools away and drive safely to a location where the flat tire can be repaired.

HANDS-ON ACTIVITIES

1. **Writing Connection:** Create a set of written directions for a student partner to follow. Observe as the partner follows your written directions. At the end of this activity, you and your partner will evaluate how easy the directions were to follow and how correctly the partner followed them. Analyze what went wrong if mistakes were made.

2. **Listening/Writing Connection:** Write down a set of directions given to you orally by a student partner. After you write the directions on paper, get with your student partner and evaluate the written set of directions. Did you write the directions down correctly? Did you leave out important information? Analyze whether the written directions match the oral directions.

3. **Literature Connection:** With your friends, read the speaking parts in a play. Follow the directions in parentheses that tell you how to speak (angrily, softly, loudly, etc.), where to stand/walk (walk to the center of the stage, stomp off the stage, etc.), or how to move your body (wave your arms, close your eyes, etc.).

4. **Science Connection:** In small groups, find an interesting science experiment in a science book. Describe the importance of following the directions for the experiment. Predict the outcome of the experiment. Discuss how the results would be different if the directions were not followed. Discuss the usefulness of the experiment. Write directions for an experiment of your own.

Following Oral Directions

Also important is training yourself to listen to oral directions well enough to follow them correctly. Oral directions are spoken directions. When you do not listen carefully, you waste time and make careless mistakes.

To find out how well you can listen and follow oral directions, select a partner and do the activity below. First, each of you will select a number 1 or a number 2. Then, for the activity, the person with number 1 will read the directions while his partner follows them. Use a large book to separate the partners so that the reader cannot see the finished picture. Then, the roles will be reversed. The person with number 2 will now read the directions for the activity while his partner follows them.

Compare the two pictures after both of you have completed the activity. Was it easier or harder for the first reader to follow the directions? Why? Do you prefer oral directions or written directions? Report the findings to your teacher.

STUDENT INSTRUCTIONS

Activity: Read these directions orally to your partner.

1. Today, you will follow oral directions to draw a tropical fish. I will read each step two times. You will have a short working time between each step.
2. Get out one sheet of notebook paper, a pencil, a black crayon, and an orange crayon.
3. Put your name and date in the upper right hand corner of your paper.
4. Draw a medium-sized square in the middle of your paper. This is the body of your fish.
5. Draw a triangle that touches the right side of the square with the point facing outward. This is the head.
6. Draw an eye in the middle of the head.
7. Draw a small heart-shaped mouth on the point of the triangle. Face the top of the heart outward.
8. Draw another triangle that touches the left side of the square. Have the point facing outward. This makes the tail.
9. Draw a smaller triangle with the point touching the left triangle. This makes the tail fin.
10. Draw fins on the top, bottom, and middle of the square.
11. Erase the right and left lines of the square to make the body parts join up.
12. Erase the pointed corners of the squares and triangles. Replace them with rounded edges.
13. Draw wavy vertical (up and down) lines on the body to put stripes on the fish.
14. Draw wavy horizontal (side to side) lines on the tail fin to put stripes on the tail.
15. Draw wavy vertical lines on the top and bottom fins to put stripes on the fins.
16. Go over all the pencil lines with the black crayon.
17. Color every other stripe orange.

HANDS-ON ACTIVITY

Social Studies Connection: Use the map below to write detailed directions from Point A to Point B. Select your Point A and Point B from places on the map, such as the library, the post office, the gas station, etc. Now, read your directions to a friend to see if he/she can follow them.

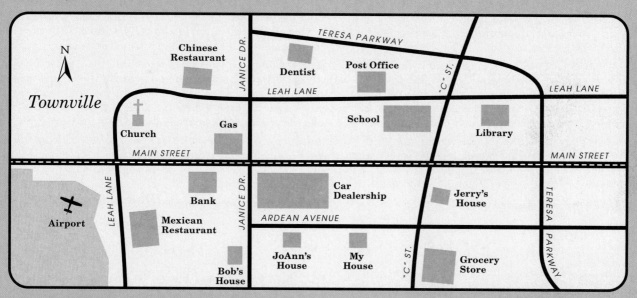

Resource Tool: LISTENING AND SPEAKING

Interviews

You conduct an interview when you ask a knowledgeable person a series of questions in order to get information about a particular subject. The information that is gathered from an interview is most often used for reports or articles. Family interviews can be used to document and preserve events rooted in family history. Community interviews serve the same purpose as they preserve the history of local events.

The type of interview you are conducting will determine the questions you ask. However, it is helpful to have a few general guidelines to help you conduct a successful interview. Use the suggestions below to help you plan an interview.

Guidelines for Conducting Interviews

1. Call the person you want to interview, explain the purpose of the interview, and make an appointment. Be courteous and be on time for the interview.

2. Write down the questions that you will ask during the interview. Make sure the questions are designed to get the information you need. Avoid asking yes-no questions because they do not give you enough information. The who, what, when, why, and where questions are always good to ask because they will provide plenty of details. (Examples: How do you feel about…, What do you think about…, Why did you…, What are the results of…, When do you expect…, What motivated you to…, etc.) Make sure your questions stay on the subject and are in good taste.

3. Take notes or use a tape recorder. If you take notes, leave plenty of space to write the answer to each question. If you use a tape recorder, ask permission first.

4. Make sure your notes accurately reflect what the person said. If you quote a person, be sure to place the exact words in quotation marks. If you are in doubt about any answers, repeat them to the person being interviewed to make sure your information is correct. This is especially important when recording dates or numbers.

5. Thank the person for the interview. Follow this up with a thank-you note expressing your appreciation for his time.

6. Write the article as soon as possible after the interview while the details are fresh in your mind.

7. If possible, give a copy of the article to the person you interviewed as a courtesy before it is published.

HANDS-ON ACTIVITIES

1. **Social Studies Connection:** Write a news article about something that is going on in your school. Are there any new students? Has any class gone on a field trip or had a special visitor? Is anyone working on an interesting project? Has anyone won an award? Interview a teacher and the principal. Make a list of the questions you will ask. Have your teacher approve your questions before the interview. Follow the interview guidelines when conducting the interview and writing your article. Publish the article you write in a school newspaper or in a class booklet.

2. **Science Connection:** Each student will research an assigned or a selected science topic. Half the class will be designated as the interviewers, and the other half as the "experts" who are being interviewed. All the experts' names are put in a basket. Each interviewer will draw an expert's name from the basket to interview. The expert and the interviewer will work together to develop a set of questions specifically designed for the expert's topic. Then, the interview begins, with the interviewer taking notes. Finally, reverse the two groups and repeat the process.

3. **Media Connection:** Interview a reporter from a local newspaper, magazine, or TV station. Include these questions in your interview: How do you find the person to interview? How do you know what questions to ask? Do you use a tape recorder or take notes? What determines how long you interview a person? How long does it take to write the article? What do you do to get the article ready for publication?

Resource Tool: LISTENING AND SPEAKING

Video Presentations

Making video presentations is a fun way to publish any writing, including tall tales, poetry, and book reviews. Some general guidelines that will help video presentations go smoothly are listed below.

Student Guidelines for Making Video Presentations

1. Check the posted schedule so you will know when it is your turn to present.
2. Stay seated until the current presenter has finished and the video camera is no longer recording.
3. When it is your turn, go to the designated area. Make all preparations necessary for your presentation before the camera begins recording.
4. When you are ready, look at the camera operator and wait for the signal to begin.
5. Introduce yourself and your presentation. Be sure to say your first and last name. Here are two examples.
   - Say, "Hello, my name is (*your first and last name*). The title of my story is (*the title of your story*)."
   - Say, "(*the title of your story*) by (*your first and last name*)."
6. Read clearly, slowly, and loudly enough for everyone to hear and for the equipment to record your voice. Read with expression. Do not be afraid to raise your voice and read with feeling. Even though you are reading from your paper, make an effort to look directly into the camera from time to time.
7. Do not make fast movements. If you move, give the camera operator time to follow you. If you make a mistake, correct it and keep going. Most people do not notice minor mistakes if the speaker recovers quickly and smoothly. It takes practice to become a calm and fluent speaker.
8. After you have finished, look at the camera operator and wait for the signal that the camera is no longer recording.
9. You are part of the audience when you are not presenting. The camera may also zoom over the audience from time to time. As a member of the audience, you must be as quiet as possible because the recording equipment will pick up classroom sounds and movements.

Teacher Guidelines for Pre-Filming

1. Set the equipment up and test it before the presentations begin.
2. Make sure a responsible adult is present to help with setting up the presentation area.
3. Rope or tape an area around the recording equipment and the person operating the camera. Only authorized persons should be in this area!
4. Tape down any cords or loose wires around the equipment so no one will trip over them.
5. Make sure you have a blank video. Keep an extra one on hand just in case something happens to the first one.
6. Place tape marks on the floor where you want the presenters to stand while they give their presentations.
7. If possible, do a test run. Film the area where the students will be presenting. Is the lighting good? Is there a glare from the sunlight or indoor lights? Is the background appropriate? Do you have plenty of space for the presenter? Do you have everything close by that the presenter might need without being in the camera's view?
8. Be relaxed so you can encourage and reassure your students. Presentations in front of a camera will provide students with invaluable experience and will develop poise and confidence.
9. Have a prior schedule posted so everyone will know when it is his turn to present.

Resource Tool: LISTENING AND SPEAKING

Guidelines for Evaluating Video Presentations

At the top of a sheet of paper, write the date and title of your presentation. Next, choose the evaluation prompt according to the way you made your presentation. For example, if you portrayed a character, use the evaluation section under Character Portrayal. For each number, write your answers and comments in complete sentences. Try to be as objective as possible. This self-evaluation will help you improve your next video presentation.

Character Portrayal	Illustration	Reading Dramatization
1. Explain why you made the choice to do a character portrayal.	1. Explain why you made the choice to use illustrations for your presentation.	1. Explain why you made the choice to do a dramatic reading of your story.
2. Which character did you choose to portray? Explain how you made your choice.	2. How did you illustrate your story? Did you use paint, markers, chalk, crayons, pencils, or other media? Were your illustrations easy for the audience to see? Did you use them effectively?	2. Were you aware of nonverbal cues in your presentation? Did you hold your paper so that your face could be seen? Did you look at the audience from time to time? Did you use facial expressions and body gestures effectively? Did you move around or did you stand still?
3. How did you look? (Describe your hair, face, and costume or outfit.)	3. Did you use any other props? If so, what were they? Did they add to your presentation? Did they distract from it?	3. Did you speak clearly and loudly enough to be heard? Did you use inflections in your voice to make the characters come alive?
4. Did you use any other props? If so, what were they? Did they add to your presentation? Did they distract from it?	4. Were you aware of nonverbal cues in your presentation? Did you hold your paper so that your face could be seen? Did you look at the audience from time to time? Did you use facial expressions and body gestures effectively? Did you move around or did you stand still?	4. How could you enhance your presentation? What would you change and what would you not change?
5. Were you aware of nonverbal cues in your presentation? Did you hold your paper so that your face could be seen? Did you look at the audience from time to time? Did you use facial expressions and body gestures effectively? Did you move around or did you stand still?	5. Did you speak clearly and loudly enough to be heard? Did you use inflections in your voice to make the characters come alive?	5. What is your honest opinion of your presentation? What were the strong points, and what areas needed improvement?
6. Did you speak clearly and loudly enough to be heard? Did you use inflections in your voice to make the characters come alive?	6. How could you enhance your presentation? What would you change and what would you not change?	
7. How could you enhance your presentation? What would you change and what would you not change?	7. What is your honest opinion of your presentation? What were the strong points and what areas needed improvement?	
8. What is your honest opinion of your presentation? What were the strong points, and what areas needed improvement?		

Resource Tool: Writing Invitations

Invitations

With all the commercial cards available today, the art of writing personal, unique, and individual invitations is almost obsolete. However, learning to write invitations is an important skill. An invitation should follow the same form as a friendly letter: heading, greeting, body, closing, and signature.

Before you begin writing an invitation, it helps to make an outline that includes specific information (what, who, where, when) in any logical order. Study the example of the outline and the invitation below.

An invitation will sometimes contain an RSVP. This is an acronym for a French expression that means "please respond," and a reply is needed. If a phone number is included, reply by phone. Otherwise, a written reply is expected.

Invitation Outline

1. What . . . . Tell what the event or special occasion is. A farewell party
2. Who . . . . Tell whom the event is for. . . . . For Terry Smith
3. Where . . . . Tell where the event will take place. At 635 Ohio Circle
4. When . . . . Tell the date and time of the event. . . . . On Friday, July 22, at 2:00
5. Whipped Cream . . . . A polite statement written to make the person feel welcome. . . . . . We hope to see you there!

Sample Invitation

> 635 Ohio Circle
> Randall, Montana 00033
> July 7, 20—
>
> Dear David,
>
> You are invited to a farewell party for Terry Smith. He is moving to Texas. The party will be at 2:00 on Friday, July 22, in our backyard at 635 Ohio Circle. Lots of games and food are planned. We hope to see you there!
>
> Your friends,
> Sam and Stan Turner

Check Your Understanding

Why do you send an invitation? _____

HANDS-ON ACTIVITIES

1. **Writing Connection:** Pretend you are giving a party or other event. First, make an invitation outline. Then, write, revise, edit, and illustrate an invitation for your event. (Ideas: costume or theme party, food-tasting party, sports party, book-club meeting, science/history/math/Spanish-club meeting, movie party, etc.)
2. **Social Studies Connection:** Study another culture to find out how the people use written invitations for special events. Create an invitation from another culture.
3. **Literature Connection:** Create an invitation to ask your friends or family to join a book club, attend a book fair or participate in a book-signing/swapping event.
4. **Science Connection:** Create an invitation to encourage your parents, relatives, and friends to visit a science exhibit you are sponsoring.

 **Resource Tool:** STUDY SKILLS

Test-Taking

Preparing for Tests

1. Keep up with daily work to develop an understanding of the material.
2. Pay attention during the class review. The teacher will usually highlight important information to study.
3. Ask questions about things you do not understand before the test.
4. Find out what testing format will be used (essay, true/false, multiple choice, fill-in-the-blank, etc.).
5. Begin studying several days before the test so you do not have to cram.
6. Use notes, worksheets, review sheets, etc., to help you. Reread your notes and look over references.
7. Create acronyms to memorize a series of items, using the first letters of each word.
8. If your teacher permits, tape-record lectures and/or notes. You can play them back as many times as necessary to help you learn the information.
9. Have a study-buddy. Find a classmate who takes his studies as seriously as you do. You can design a sample test for each other. Or, you can have oral reviews of the content to be covered on the next test.
10. You can design a lecture on the material to be covered on the next test. Then, you can "teach" a couple of your peers. Remember, you know it if you can teach it.

Taking the Test

1. Stay calm and do your best.
2. Read all directions carefully before you begin marking answers. Identify key words in the directions.
3. Go through your test and answer the ones you are sure about first.
4. Pace yourself. If you do not know an answer right away, come back to it later.
5. Utilize all your test time. Double-check your answers after you have finished.
6. Know how the test is scored. If you are penalized for wrong answers, answer only questions you are sure you know. If no points are deducted for wrong answers, make sure you've answered all the questions.

Test-taking Tips for True-False Tests

1. Read true-false questions carefully.
2. If a statement is <u>always</u> true, mark true. If it is only true sometimes, mark false.
3. Watch for tricky phrases such as: *it seems, I think, always, never,* and *maybe.*

Test-taking Tips for Fill-in-the-Blank Tests

1. Read and reread each question carefully.
2. If an answer bank is provided, check off answers as you use them.
3. Do not scratch answers out because you may need to read them again later.
4. Copy answers in the blanks correctly. Pay attention to correct spelling.
5. Write or print all answers as neatly as possible. Make sure each answer is legible.
6. If an answer bank is not provided, make sure you know whether to study for spelling as well as facts.

Test-taking Tips for Multiple-Choice Tests

1. Read and reread each question and any sample sentence or paragraph carefully.
2. Read all the answer choices carefully before choosing an answer.
3. Eliminate choices you know are wrong.
4. If more than one answer on a multiple choice test looks correct, mark the one that makes the strongest impression.
5. Write or print all letters as neatly as possible. Make sure each answer is legible.
6. If the test requires shading ovals, make sure each oval is filled in fully.

Test-taking Tips for Essay Tests

1. Read and reread each question or writing prompt carefully. Understand what kind of response is expected from the question or writing prompt.
2. Think about your purpose and audience.
3. Plan how you will organize your writing by jotting down ideas on a separate piece of paper. Use your favorite style of graphic organizer to organize your ideas.
4. Make sure the main idea is stated clearly in the topic sentence.
5. Use only details that support each of your main points.
6. If you have time, write a rough draft on another sheet of paper so you can revise and edit it.
7. Write the final essay as neatly as possible. Make sure every word is legible.
8. Reread the essay. Check one last time for correct punctuation, capitalization, and spelling.

Resource Tool: STUDY SKILLS

Handwriting Tips

There are two different kinds of handwriting: **manuscript** and **cursive**. When you first learn to write the letters of the alphabet, you print them in manuscript form. **Manuscript writing** means that each letter in a word is written separately. Sometimes, manuscript writing is called printing. After you have learned and practiced manuscript writing, you are taught cursive writing. **Cursive writing** means that you connect the letters within a word.

Whether you use manuscript or cursive writing, you should make your writing legible. **Legible** means writing that is neat and easy to read. Sloppy handwriting not only creates a negative impression, it often prevents clear communication.

Tips to Make Your Writing Legible

1. Make all similar letters uniform in height.
2. Use the correct slant and keep slant uniform.
3. Space letters and words correctly.
4. Connect the letters correctly.
5. Recognize unacceptable standards and redo the paper.

Other Handwriting Tips

1. **Use good writing posture.** Sit up straight with your feet flat on the floor. Your wrists should rest on the desk, but they should not support the weight of your body. Don't slouch.
2. **Hold your pencil correctly.** Place your pencil between the tip of your thumb and your index finger. The pencil will rest on your middle finger. Grip your pencil at the end of the painted wood, right above where the sharpened part begins.
3. **Position your paper correctly.** Place your paper in front of you, slightly slanted, and parallel with your writing arm.
4. **Anchor your paper so it doesn't slide.** If you are right-handed, put your left hand lightly on the top left corner of the paper to keep it from moving. If you are left-handed, use your right hand on the top right corner. Make sure your hand stays flat and relaxed.
5. **Continue to check your writing posture and your paper placement.** As you near the bottom of your paper, slide your paper up so your arms don't hang off your desk. Your elbows should always remain under your shoulders.

HANDS-ON ACTIVITY

In order to evaluate your writing posture, have someone videotape you as you are writing an essay. As you view the video, check how well you accomplished each of the areas under "Other Handwriting Tips."

1. Did you use good writing posture?
2. Did you hold your pencil correctly?
3. Did you position your paper correctly?
4. Did you anchor your paper?
5. Did you continue to check your writing posture and your paper placement?
6. Did you see any areas that needed improvement?
7. Did this evaluation help you make improvements?

Resource Tool: STUDY SKILLS

Guide for Cursive Handwriting Standards

In the samples below, the small **x** shows you where to start, and the arrows guide your starting direction.

Group 1 Letters: a, c, e, i, m, n, o, r, s, u, v, w, x
- All characters rest on the baseline and have an x-height that stops at the waist line.

a c e i m n o

r s u v w x

Group 2 Letters: b, h, k, l
- All characters rest on the baseline and have a tall thin loop that ascends to the cap line.

b h k l

Group 3 Letters: d, t
- Both characters rest on the baseline and have a single line that ascends to the cap line.

d t

Group 4 Letters: g, j, q, y, z
- All characters rest on the baseline, have an x-height that stops at the waist line, and have a looping tail.

g j q y z

Group 5 Letters: f, p
- **f** — The character has a tall thin loop that ascends to the cap line, descends below the baseline, and has a looping tail.
- **p** — The character rests on the baseline, has an x-height that stops at the waist line, and has a single-line tail that descends below the baseline.

f p

Capital Letters: A, B, C, D, E, F, G, H, I, J, K, L, M, N, O, P, Q, R, S, T, U, V, W, X, Y, Z
- All characters rest on the baseline and ascend to the cap line.
- The letters **J, Y, Z** have looping tails that descend below the baseline.
- Care should be taken to connect to lower case letters correctly.

A B C D E F G H I J K L M N

O P Q R S T U V W X Y Z

Resource Tool: STUDY SKILLS

The Dictionary / Thesaurus

Sometimes, studying involves looking words up in a dictionary. You may need to see if you have spelled a word correctly, or you may want to check a word's meaning. A **dictionary** gives you correct spellings, pronunciations, meanings, usage, and history of words.

A **thesaurus** is a type of dictionary that contains synonyms and antonyms for different words. Most writers use a thesaurus to find synonyms and antonyms that will make their writing clearer and more appealing.

Alphabetical order is important to know because words in a dictionary and a thesaurus are arranged in alphabetical order. There are two rules that help you put words in alphabetical order.

Rule 1: If the first letters of the words are different, use only the first letters to put the words in alphabetical order.

Rule 2: If the first letters of the words are the same, use the second letters to put the words in alphabetical order. If the second letters are the same, use the third to put the words in alphabetical order, etc.

Guide words are the two words listed at the top of each dictionary page. Guide words tell the first and last words on the page. If the word you are looking up can be put alphabetically between the two guide words, then the word is located on that page. As you look up a word in the dictionary, you will use the first letter of the word to find the section you need. After you have found that section in the dictionary, you can use *guide words* to keep you from looking at every word on every page.

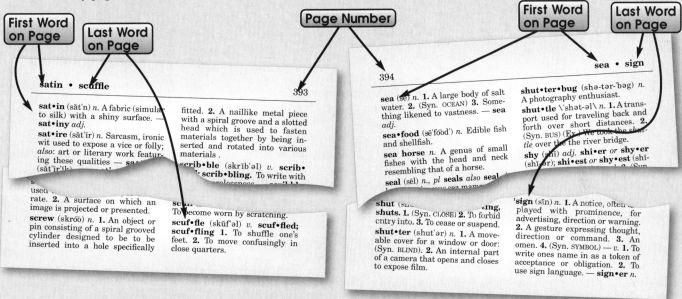

Entry words in a dictionary are the words in bold type that are listed in alphabetical order and defined. A dictionary provides many kinds of information about an entry word.

- pronunciation – tells how to pronounce a word. It is usually in parentheses at the beginning.
- part of speech – shows small *n.* for noun, small *v.* for verb, *adj.* for adjective, etc.
- meaning – gives numbered definitions of the word according to its parts of speech.
- example – gives sentences that use the entry word to explain a meaning. Shown as (Ex.)
- synonym – lists words that have similar meanings to the entry word. Shown as (Syn.)
- origin – tells when and where the word was originally used. Shown as [1350–1400 ME]. The date tells when the word was first used in its present form, and the initials tell the language origin. (ME stands for Middle English, Gr stands for Greek, Fr stands for French, L stands for Latin, Sp stands for Spanish, G stands for German, OE stands for Old English, etc.)

Some entries are slang words. The dictionary identifies slang words as nonstandard or informal. Slang words are not suitable for formal writing or speaking but may be used in casual speech.

Sample Entry Word

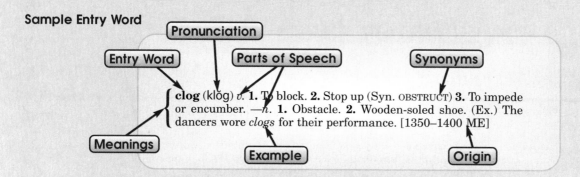

clog (klŏg) *v.* **1.** To block. **2.** Stop up (Syn. OBSTRUCT) **3.** To impede or encumber. —*n.* **1.** Obstacle. **2.** Wooden-soled shoe. (Ex.) The dancers wore *clogs* for their performance. [1350–1400 ME]

Check Your Understanding

1. How are words listed in a dictionary? _____

2. What are guide words in a dictionary? _____
   _____

3. What kind of information does the dictionary give for each entry word?
   _____

 **STUDY SKILLS**

The Library

When you visit a library, you need to know how the books are arranged. Most libraries have three main sections for books: fiction, nonfiction, and reference.

Fiction Section

Fiction books contain stories about people, places, or things that are not true even though the writer, or author, may use ideas based on real people or events. Fiction books are arranged on the shelves in alphabetical order according to the authors' last names.

Nonfiction Section

Nonfiction books contain information and stories that are true. You can find a nonfiction book on just about any subject. Nonfiction books are grouped together in numerical order, according to a call number. A call number is the number found on the spine of all nonfiction books.

Reference Section

The Reference Section is designed to help you find information on many topics. The Reference Section contains many different kinds of reference books and materials. Some of these references are listed below.

1. **Dictionary.** The dictionary gives the definition, spelling, and pronunciation of words and tells briefly about famous people and places. Words in a dictionary are listed in alphabetical order.

2. **Thesaurus.** The thesaurus is actually a dictionary of synonyms and antonyms. Words in a thesaurus are listed in alphabetical order. Most writers use a thesaurus to find synonyms and antonyms that will make their writing more exact and more appealing.

3. **Encyclopedia.** The encyclopedia gives concise, factual information about persons, places, and events of world-wide interest. Topics are arranged in alphabetical order in books called volumes. Each volume has a letter or letters on the spine that indicates the range of topics in that volume.

4. **Atlas.** The atlas is primarily a book of maps, but it often contains facts about oceans, lakes, mountains, areas, population, products, and climates in every part of the world.

5. **Almanac.** An almanac is a book that is published once a year and contains brief, up-to-date, factual information on important people, places, events, and a variety of other topics.

6. **Periodical.** Periodicals are magazines. The *Readers' Guide to Periodical Literature* is an index of magazine articles. It is a monthly booklet that lists the titles of articles, stories, and poems published in all leading magazines. These titles are listed under topics that are arranged alphabetically. The monthly issues of *the Readers' Guide to Periodical Literature* are bound together in a single volume once a year and are filed in the library. By using the *Readers' Guide*, a person researching a topic can know which back issues of magazines might be helpful.

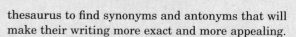

Card Catalog

The card catalog is an index to the books in a library. A book is listed in a card catalog in three ways—by author, by title, and by subject. An electronic index or traditional card catalog can help you find any book in the library. All three kinds of cards are arranged alphabetically by the word or words on the top line. The main difference in the cards is how the information is arranged.

Author Card	Title Card	Subject Card

586.3
Author: Pacton, James R.
  Title: Science for Kids and Parents
  Ill. by Charles Finley
  Children's Press, Chicago
  (c1990) 116p.
	586.3
	  Title: Science for Kids and Parents
	Author: Pacton, James R.
	  Ill. by Charles Finley
	  Children's Press, Chicago
	  (c1990) 116p.
		586.3
		Subject: Science Projects
		Author: Pacton, James R.
		  Title: Science for Kids and Parents
		  Ill. by Charles Finley
		  Children's Press, Chicago
		  (c1990) 116p.

Check your understanding

1. What is a card catalog? _____

2. What are the names of the three kinds of cards in a card catalog? _____

3. What are the three main book sections in the library? _____

4. How are fiction books arranged on the shelves? _____

5. How are nonfiction books arranged on the shelves? _____

6. What is a call number? _____

HANDS-ON ACTIVITIES

1. **Literature Connection:** Create a set of catalog cards for a favorite book. Share the catalog cards with your classmates.

2. **Writing Connection:** Choose a book in the library. Read a few pages from the middle of the book. Write a prediction of what you think happened at the beginning and end of the book. Then, read the book. Write how your predictions were similar and different from the original version.

3. **Drama Connection:** Choose a scene from your favorite book or play and act it out with several of your classmates.

4. **Art Connection:** Design your own library. Draw a diagram or floor plan to show where main areas would be located. You might even include a sketch to show what the outside of the library would look like. Share your drawings with family and friends. Write a newspaper article for the grand opening of your library. Tell about its main features, the services it will provide to the community, and the businesses and clubs that helped make this project possible.

5. **History Connection:** Research the history of the public library in the United States. Who started the first public library? What is the name of the largest public library and where is it located? What is the history of your community library? What interesting facts can you find about presidential libraries?

6. **Literature Connection:** Research the history of the Newberry and Caldecott books. Look up the Newberry and Caldecott winners. Make a list of the Newberry and Caldecott books you have read and the ones you would like to read.

Resource Tool: STUDY SKILLS

Parts of a Book

Do you know the parts of a nonfiction book? Actually, a book can be divided into three sections: the front, the body, and the back. Knowing the parts of a book will help you make full use of the special features that are frequently found in nonfiction books. The front includes these parts: title page, copyright page, preface, and table of contents. The body is the main section, or text, of the book. The back includes these parts: appendix, glossary, bibliography, and index. *(Note: For a more detailed description of the parts of a book, see Chapter 11, Lesson 6.)*

HANDS-ON ACTIVITY

Use the parts of a book to complete the puzzle below. Then, use your vocabulary words, science words, social studies words, or spelling words to make your own crossword puzzle or word-search puzzle.

Parts of a Book

Down:

1. Contains meanings of important words in a book.
2. Tells the reason the book was written.
3. Is the first section of a book.
5. Tells the publisher's name and city where the book was published. (2 words)
8. Is the second section of a book that contains the text of a book.
9. Is the third section of a book.

Across:

4. Contains titles of units and chapters. (3 words)
6. Gives exact page numbers for a particular topic.
7. Has the copyright date and ISBN. (2 words)
8. Contains extra maps in a book.
10. Is a list of sources used by the author as references.

Check Your Understanding

1. What parts of a book are located in the front? _____

_____

2. What parts of a book are located in the back? _____

_____

3. What is the text of a book called? _____

Resource Tool: STUDY SKILLS

The Table of Contents

Make your study time count by learning to use the shortcuts already available in a book. When you are looking for general information in a book, you can use a table of contents to help you find information quickly. A table of contents tells you four things.

1. What the book is about.
2. How many chapters are in a book.
3. The title of each chapter.
4. The first page of each chapter.

The main heading is *Contents*. The title of the first chapter is *"Selecting a Breed."* By reading over the rest of the chapter titles, you can tell that this book is about dogs.

The chapter numbers are the numbers on the left under the heading *Chapter*. There are eight chapters in the book. The beginning page numbers are the numbers on the right under the heading *Page*. The page number listed to the right of each title tells the **first** page of the chapter. Chapter 1 begins on page 2. To find the last page of Chapter 1, go to the page where Chapter 2 begins and back up one page number. Chapter 2 begins on page 18. Back up one number, and you will be on page 17. So, Chapter 1 ends on page 17.

Contents

Chapter	Title	Page
1	Selecting a Breed	2
2	Special Needs of Puppies	18
3	Feeding Your Dog	27
4	Exercising Your Dog	30
5	Grooming Your Dog	32
6	Veterinary Care	35
7	Teaching Your Dog Tricks	43
8	Special Needs of Older Dogs	53
	Index	54

Check Your Understanding

1. A table of contents tells you four things. What are they? _____

2. What is the title of the chapter that would tell you how often to feed your dog?

   _____

3. What is the number of the chapter? _____

4. On which page does Chapter 3 begin? _____

5. On which page does Chapter 3 end? _____

HANDS-ON ACTIVITIES

1. Make your own table of contents. Choose a topic that you know well enough to make up titles for your chapters. You could also look up information about a topic you are interested in. List the chapter titles in a logical order. Give each title a chapter number and beginning page number. Think of four questions to ask about your table of contents. Exchange papers with a partner. Answer the questions and evaluate what you have learned about the table of contents.

2. Choose a nonfiction book that has a table of contents. Before you study the book's table of contents, make up an original table of contents, using the information you think will be in the book. Compare your table of contents to the one in the book. Analyze the similarities and differences. Evaluate why a table of contents is important in finding information about a book.

Resource Tool: STUDY SKILLS

The Index

Do you know why an index of a book is important and how to use it? When you are looking for information about a specific topic in a book, you can use the index to help you find the information quickly. The index is located in the back of the book. It has an alphabetical listing of specific topics and tells on which page that information can be found. It is similar to the table of contents, but it is much more detailed. There are three main reasons to use an index:

1. When you want to find an answer quickly.
2. When you want to know the answer to a specific question.
3. When you want to know more about a subject.

There are **six features of an index** that you should know:

1. An index is located at the back of the book.
2. An index lists information alphabetically.
3. When an index lists key ideas in a book, they are called topics.
4. When an index lists specific information under a topic, it is called a subtopic.
5. The numbers following topics and subtopics tell on which pages the information is found.
6. Punctuation of page numbers appears in subtopics.
   - When you see a **dash** between numbers, say "**through**." (23–25 *means page 23 through page 25*)
   - When you see a **comma** between numbers, say "**and**." (23–25, 44 *means page 23 through page 25 and page 44*)
   - When you see a **semicolon**, it means stop. Go no further for pages on this subtopic.

Sample Index

Index

L	O	T
Leashes, 23–25, 44	**Obedience training,**	**Ticks,** 37
	collars in, 23–24, 43;	**Training,** *see* Obedience training.
	housebreaking, 25–26;	**Tricks,** 49–53
	leashes in, 23–25, 44;	
	for puppies, 23–24;	
	simple commands, 45–48;	
	special tricks, 49–53	

The index topic under the letter *O* is *Obedience training*. Notice that *Obedience* is the only word that is capitalized and the subtopics under it are indented. Each subtopic tells about the main topic *Obedience training*.

Page numbers are listed after each subtopic. The page numbers listed after the subtopic *collars in* are *23–24, 43*. The **dash** between the 23 and 24 is read as *23 through 24*. The **comma** between 24 and 43 is read as *and*. Together, it would mean that information about collars in obedience training is found on pages 23 through 24 and on page 43.

Check Your Understanding

How is information in an index listed? _____

HANDS-ON ACTIVITY

Choose two or three nonfiction books with indexes. Compare how the indexes are alike and how they are different. Exchange ideas with a partner. Write a paragraph to evaluate what you have learned about the value of the index.

Resource Tool: STUDY SKILLS

Reading Maps, Charts, and Graphs

Maps

Being able to read a map is an art unto itself. The more detailed the map, the greater the skill needed to interpret it. Virtually all maps have a legend for interpreting them. The legend includes such things as a distance scale, a set of symbols, and a collection of demographic information. The distance scale enables one to approximate the number of miles between two points. In addition to the distance scale, there is a set of symbols, which shows, among other things, types of roads, rest areas, medical facilities, historic markers, and airports. Finally, the demographic information contains the names of capital cities, populations, and land areas. A weather map has a legend that includes precipitation, highs and lows, fronts, and temperatures. Map information will vary, depending on the purpose of the map.

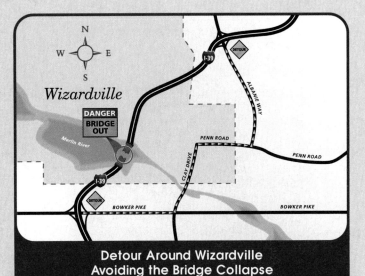

**Detour Around Wizardville
Avoiding the Bridge Collapse**

Because of a bridge collapse, I-39 is closed through Wizardville and traffic has been rerouted over some secondary roads. The detour connects with the interstate again three miles north of town.

Task:
1. The detour around Wizardville consists of how many secondary roads? _____

2. Motorists traveling north on the interstate will exit where? _____

3. Motorists traveling south on the interstate will exit where? _____

4. Is the damaged bridge in the northern, southern, eastern, or western part of town? _____

Hunting in State Forests

	October	November	December	January
Blackhorn Forest		Deer		Elk
Russian Olive Forest		Deer, Elk	Elk, Moose	
Persimmon Forest		Deer		Moose
Bayberry Forest	Antelope, Deer	Antelope, Deer, Elk		
Sassafras Forest	Moose			Elk

Game Legend:

Antelope: Deer: Elk: Moose:

Hunting in some of our state forests is limited to certain types of wild game and to certain months of the year. In some parks, hunting multiple types of game are permitted; in others, hunters are limited to just one type.

Charts

There are many different types of charts. Among others, there are meteorological charts (having to do with weather), navigational charts (having to do with air and/or ocean travel), and general information charts (having to do with facts and figures about some particular subject matter). Information in charts is usually easy to read and to understand because the facts and figures are arranged in columns and headings. Some charts contain directions for interpreting them. Other less technical charts are designed in such a way that interpreting them is self-explanatory.

Task:
1. What type of game may hunters kill in Russian Olive Forest? _____

2. In which forest is only one type of game hunting permitted? _____

3. In what months is hunting permitted in Sassafras Forest? _____

4. In which month can all of the game be hunted? _____

Graphs

Graphs reveal a wealth of information without making it necessary to read a series of paragraphs. A graph compares facts and figures in an easy-to-read format that can be read at a glance. Usually, a graph is accompanied by a legend that enables the reader to interpret it. Ordinarily, the purpose of a bar graph is to make a comparison between something past and present whereas the purpose of a pie graph is to show and compare the component parts that make up a whole. Sometimes, as in the case of a line graph, the intent is to show progression over a period of time.

Line Graph

Task: 1. Between 1996 and 2000, what was the percentage increase in high-speed Internet connections in the town of Quinceyville? _____

2. In what year did the number of households with Internet capability reach 50% for high-speed connections? _____

3. In the year 2000, what percentage of households had high-speed Internet connection? _____

4. What was the first year high-speed Internet connections were available to Quinceyville? _____

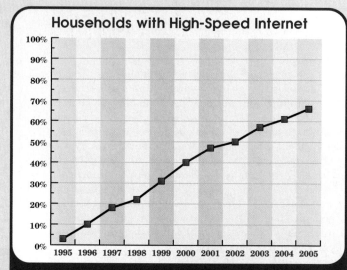

Households with High-Speed Internet

In Quinceyville, high-speed connections have become the rage in the past decade in households with Internet. High-speed connections have increased 3000%, from 2% of the households in 1995 to 66% in 2005, in this small coastal town.

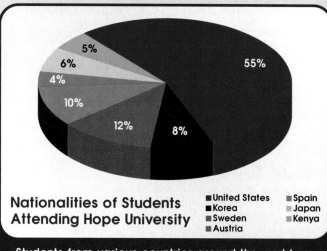

Nationalities of Students Attending Hope University

- United States
- Korea
- Sweden
- Austria
- Spain
- Japan
- Kenya

Students from various countries around the world are enrolled at Hope University.

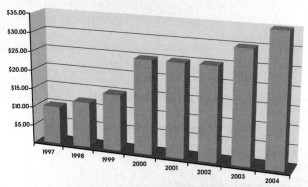

Yearly Subscription Newspaper Costs

Inflation has caused the price of newspaper subscriptions to increase.

Pie Graph

Task: 1. The fewest number of students attending Hope University come from what country? _____

2. What is the percentage of Japanese and Korean students attending Hope University? _____

3. What country is represented by 12% of its students? _____

4. How many countries are represented at Hope University? _____

Bar Graph

Task: 1. For how many years did the annual subscription price remain the same? _____

2. What was the cost of a subscription during those years? _____

3. The largest price increase took effect in what year? _____

4. How much did the newspaper subscriptions increase from 1997 to 2004? _____

HANDS-ON ACTIVITIES

1. **Math, Science, and Social Studies Connections:** Look at the local and national weather report in a newspaper or on the Internet. Find and cut out examples of a weather map, a bar graph, a line graph, and a chart. Mount these examples on poster board. Identify them by labeling each kind, and, then, write one or two sentences explaining each one. Compare the local information to national information. Discuss how the local and national maps, graphs, and charts are alike and how they are different. Exchange ideas with a partner. Evaluate what you have learned about the value of maps, graphs, and charts.

2. **Math, Science, and Social Studies Connections:** Make your own map, graph, or chart. Choose a topic that you can look up information about and display in a map, graph, or chart. You can put the map, graph, or chart that you make on construction paper or poster board. Make sure you organize and label the information so that it is easy to read. Think of four questions to ask about your map, graph, or chart. Exchange papers with a partner. Answer the questions and evaluate what you have learned about maps, graphs, and charts.

Resource Tool: STUDY SKILLS

Cause and Effect

A cause-effect relationship exists in everyday events and situations. If you think about these events and situations carefully, you can learn why or how one thing (**cause**) makes another thing (**effect**) happen. Practically every event in life is either the **cause of** or the **result of** some other event.

In other words, a cause is the reason something happens. An effect is the event that happens as a result of the cause. For example, a storm was the **cause** of the damage. The damage was the result, or **effect**, of a storm. When cause-effect or effect-cause sentences are combined, the words *because* or *since* are commonly used to connect them. Sometimes, sentences do not show a cause-effect relationship.

> **Example of the cause listed first:** Because of the fire, there was great damage. (CE)
>
> **Example of the effect listed first:** There was great damage because of the fire. (EC)
>
> **Example of no cause-effect relationship:** Mary has curly hair. She likes to read books.

Comprehension Activities

1. List two possible results (effects) that might result from the cause listed below.
   Cause—He wasn't at home.

2. Complete the missing part of the effect-cause and cause-effect relationships below.
   We stopped by your house because
   Because I forgot my homework,

3. Find an example of cause and effect in a book. Share your findings in cooperative learning groups.

4. Look for an article in the newspaper that shows cause and effect. Bring the news article to school.
   Explain the cause and effect relationship of the news article in a report to the class.

5. Make two effect-cause sentences and two cause-effect sentences.

_____

_____

_____

_____

Resource Tool: Technology

On-line Searches

Using the Internet for obtaining information is quick and effective. Many search engines exist on the Internet, and which one to use is a personal choice. For an example, assume you want more information about the doctor who was killed at the Alamo in the Texas Revolution. First, you need keywords for the search engine to use. In this case, "Texas" and "Alamo doctor" may be good first choices. Too many words limit the results; too few words result in too many "hits." Use quotation marks around any phrase that you want used as a group and not as independent words.

Go to your favorite search engine website on the Internet and enter your keywords in the appropriate line. Click "Search" or hit the "Enter" key. A list of websites, usually with the most appropriate ones first, will appear on your screen. Click on any website link that seems to meet your needs. A new page will appear from that website. If this is not the information you need, click the "Back" option on the tool bar to return to the search results and try a different site.

If you decide to use the information, you may choose to print it in order to retain a hard copy of the information. This printout will usually also have the web address, or URL (Universal Resource Locator), of the site in case you wish to return to the site at a later time for more information. One website will usually link, or connect, to other websites that have additional information. It is very easy to get distracted by irrelevant information, so remain focused on the topic.

Once you have found all the information you need from one website, return to the search result page and try additional websites. You may need to refine your search criteria. If you use the information in a report, make sure you document your source. If you use someone else's work without giving them appropriate credit, it is called plagiarism. Plagiarism is not only unethical, but it is illegal as well.

Be aware that all information on the Internet is not necessarily true. Most information is true and valuable, but a significant amount is completely or partially false. You should take the responsibility of verifying whether the information you obtain is valid before using it.

Privacy and the Internet

Since the Internet connects you to people all over the world, you must protect your privacy when using the Internet. Because you do not know if you can trust everyone who is connected to the Internet, some precautions are necessary.

1. All computers connected to the Internet should have a good software program for virus protection installed. It should be upgraded regularly.
2. Never enter ANY personal information about yourself or your family on ANY website. This includes names, addresses, phone numbers, and social security numbers.
3. Never agree to a personal meeting with anyone you meet on the computer. All safety rules designed to protect you from strangers apply when using the Internet.
4. Never go to websites that you know you should not see or that you are forbidden to use. If in doubt, don't go there.
5. Keep your parents informed. Tell your parents, guardian, or another responsible adult if something on the Internet makes you uncomfortable. Make sure a responsible adult has your password so that he/she can help keep you safe. Do not give out your password to anyone else.
6. Never use a web camera without permission.
7. Go to www.cybercrime.gov/rules for additional tips on how to use the Internet safely.

E-mail

E-mail, or electronic mail, is a great means for communicating with people across town or on the other side of the world. However, e-mail is different than regular mail. The guidelines below will help you use e-mail correctly.

1. Type an appropriate message title in the Subject line.
2. Keep your e-mail paragraphs short and to the point.
3. Try not to use special type fonts because some computers may not display them properly.
4. Put space between paragraphs by skipping a line.
5. Use appropriate spelling, capitalization, and punctuation.
6. Do not get in the habit of forwarding messages to everyone in your address book. Only forward appropriate messages to a minimum number of people.
7. Do not reply to the "to be removed from our mailing list" messages. This only verifies your e-mail address is valid and will result in even more SPAM, or unwanted e-mail.
8. Tell an adult immediately if you get an e-mail that scares you or upsets you.
9. If it is going to require some time to respond to an e-mail, you may wish to go offline, compose your message, and then "paste" it into your e-mail. This will minimize your connection time to the Internet.

Computer Terms

Whether you use a computer at home or at school, you will need to have a working knowledge of the most commonly used technology terms. Becoming familiar with computer terms and what they mean will be helpful as you learn more about computers. The definitions for the technology and computer terms below will guide you as you gain knowledge of how computers work.

Computer Files to Organize Writing

Think of your computer as a file cabinet that organizes and stores your writing in electronic folders. The number of folders you can create is almost unlimited. You can create separate folders for every type of writing that you do: stories, poems, reports, letters, and unfinished pieces. You can put these writing folders on your hard drive or copy your files onto other electronic storage devices. It is easy for you to add new documents or files throughout the year.

Bit	the smallest unit of measurement for information (This is sometimes referred to as binary code, which has two positions. It can be thought of as a computational quantity that takes on one of two values such as "0/1", "on/off" or "yes/no.")
Byte	a sequence of eight bits processed as a single unit of alphanumeric data that represents one character of information
Megabyte Gigabyte Terabyte	Megabyte (MB) is a unit of information equal to one million bytes. Gigabyte (GB) is a unit of information equal to one billion bytes or one million megabytes. Terabyte (TB) is a unit of information equal to a trillion bytes or one million gigabytes. Most computer memory and storage are referred to as megabyte, gigabyte, or terabyte.
CD-ROM	a portable storage medium for computers (It consists of a plastic-like, round disk upon which data or music has been burned by a laser. CD-ROM's typically hold approximately 700 megabytes of data.)
CPU	Central Processing Unit; the main brain of a computer system that contains the electrical parts that interpret and execute the commands necessary for data processing
cursor	a mechanism, usually a square or bar, blinking on a computer screen (The cursor indicates where the next character typed will appear or where the next command issued will be performed.)
data	pieces of information before they are formatted and organized into usable facts
disk drive	an internal computer component for accessing data stored on a floppy disk or a hard drive (The term "disk drive" is sometimes used to refer to a hard drive.)
document	an electronic file typically associated with a word-processing program
DVD	Digital Video Disc; a DVD is a computer-storage medium, similar in size to a CD-ROM, but holding approximately 4700 megabytes (4.7 GB) of data. (A single DVD is typically used to hold a full-length motion picture.)
floppy disk	a rectangular plastic portable storage medium used to store data for computers, holding approximately 1.44 megabytes of data (Early versions were flexible, hence the name "floppy disks," but current ones are rigid.)
font	a set of typeface glyphs, or letters and numbers (Fonts vary in size and artistic representation and can be used by word-processing applications on computers.)
hard copy	any electronic computer data file that has been printed on paper
hard drive	a storage medium for storing large amounts of data on a computer system (Typical hard disks now store thousands of megabytes, or gigabytes, of data.)
hardware	any part of a computer, or its accessories, that is physical, such as the keyboard, mouse, monitor, CPU, and printer
keyboard	an accessory for a computer. (It consists of typewriter-style keys, usually arranged in the standard keyboard arrangement, which is sometimes identified as QWERTY.)
menu	a list of options or commands shown on a monitor screen that is available to a user and allows the user to execute any command of choice

Continued on next page. >>>

Continued from previous page.

monitor	that part of a computer system that displays information on a screen and allows the user to interact with the system
mouse	a small input device used to position a cursor on a document and execute commands
printer	a computer accessory that prints hard copies of electronic documents
RAM	Random Access Memory; the most common computer memory used by programs to perform necessary tasks while the computer is on (This integrated circuit memory chip allows information to be stored or accessed in any order, and all storage locations are equally accessible.)
ROM	Read Only Memory; the contents of a memory chip that can be accessed and read but cannot be changed, also known as fixed storage (This chip allows the computer to start the system when it is turned on.)
software	programs that tell computers what tasks to accomplish, also referred to as Applications (Software programs are nonphysical components of a computer system and are written by human programmers.)

Word Processing Terms

Computer users must have a working knowledge of the terminology and commands used in word processing. These commands can be executed from a menu on the screen or by typing a series of keys on the keyboard.

close	a command that allows you to exit a document
copy	a command that puts a selected (highlighted) object or text into a computer's memory for pasting into another location
cut	a command that removes highlighted text and places it into a storage area for later use
delete	a key or a command that removes highlighted text (Deleted text is not saved for later use.)
find	a command that locates specified letters, words, or phrases in a document
font	a menu item that allows you to choose a typestyle (Times New Roman, Courier, etc.)
new	a command that creates a new document
open	a command that brings up and displays a document from existing files
page break	a command that ends a page wherever you want it to end and creates a new page
paste	a command that allows copied or cut text to be inserted at a different location in the current document or in another document
print	a command that produces a printout (hardcopy) of the current document
exit/quit	a command that exits/quits the current application
return	an "enter" key that sends the cursor to the next line
save	a command that keeps all changes in a document for later use
select	a command to highlight chosen text
shift	a key that allows capital letters to be typed (It is also used for various other commands.)
spelling	a command that checks the spelling of the words in a document
tab	a command or key that moves the cursor to the right at specified intervals

Internet Terms

Internet users must have a working knowledge of the terminology and commands used in searching the web or using e-mail. A list of common terms relating to the Internet is provided below.

address book	a list of e-mail addresses and other important information most frequently used by an individual
browser	an application to view web pages such as Netscape, Internet Explorer, etc.
chat room	a place for an interactive conversation through the Internet by using the keyboard
cookies	software technology that collects (gathers) information of all users that visit a particular website
download	a process used to copy a file from the Internet to a user's computer
DSL	Digital Subscriber Line; a fast method of connection to the Internet
dial-up	a slower method to connect to the Internet
e-mail (mail)	electronic mail messages sent through the Internet
e-mail address	an electronic mail address for an individual computer user
forward mail	a process to send a copy of an e-mail message to another computer user
home page	the web page that appears when a web browser is started
IP address	a number assigned to a user's computer by a web server for the purpose of tracking the user's use or habits of what sites are visited
Internet	a world-wide collection of computers networked together
junk mail	unwanted e-mail, usually soliciting money (also called SPAM)
instant messaging	real-time, person-to-person interaction through the Internet
modem	a computer accessory that enables a computer to connect to other computers, such as the Internet, through a connection, using a standard telephone line or cable wire
news groups	an Internet group of users sharing an interest in a common topic
password	a series of unique characters that must be entered to access some websites, personal or company accounts, some files or directories, etc.
SSL	Secure Sockets Layers; a way to protect private information between web servers
search engine	an application used to find appropriate websites by entering in "keywords" of a subject
send	button (or option) that sends an e-mail into the Internet
SPAM	unwanted junk e-mail messages sent in large quantities
surfing	exploring the Internet
URL	Universal or Uniform Resource Locator; unique address used to identify a document, file, web page, web site, etc.
upload	a process of sending a file to another user's computer
virus	a disguised program that inserts itself into programs of other computers to perform a malicious action such as destroying data or an entire hard drive
www	World Wide Web; refers to the network of computers that make up the Internet
web address	*see* **URL**; characters keyed in a web browser to get to a particular website
web cam	an electronic camera device used to send images over the Internet

Glossary

A

Action verb: a verb that shows a state of action and tells what the subject does. (*Sara **runs** home.*)

Adjective: a word that describes, or modifies, a noun or pronoun; one of the eight parts of speech. (***That black*** *dog jumped on the bed.*)

Adverb: a word that describes, or modifies, a verb, adjective, or another adverb; one of the eight parts of speech. (*The employees worked **feverishly**.*)

Adverb exception: an adverb that modifies the verb but is located immediately before the verb. (*That dog **suddenly** ran after the cat.*)

Alliteration: the repetition of consonant sounds at the beginning of words; used mostly in poetry. (***Five fine feathered fowls***)

Analogy: a kind of reasoning based on comparing one pair of words with another pair of words that are related in the same way. (*hand : glove :: sock : foot*) (*purpose or use relationship*)

Antecedent: the noun to which a pronoun refers. (*The **cat** devoured **its** food.*)

Antonyms: words that have opposite meanings. (*black, white*)

Apostrophe: a punctuation mark (') used in contractions and possessive nouns. (*Harvey **won't** work on Saturday. **Mary's** car was parked in the street.*)

Appositive: a word, phrase, title, or degree used directly after a noun to rename it. (*Sally, **my best friend**, helped me with the decorations.*)

Article adjectives: specific adjectives (**a, an, the**) that come before a noun. (***A*** *bee stung me. I ate **an** orange at lunch. **The** paper was not delivered on time.*)

Assonance: the repetition of vowel sounds within words; used mostly in poetry. (*low moan*)

Audience: person or people that read, listen, or watch something.

Autobiography: nonfiction writing in which the author tells about his own life.

Auxiliary verb: *See* helping verb.

B

Biography: a nonfiction writing in which the author tells about another person's life.

Brainstorm: to develop, broaden, or elaborate ideas.

C

Capitalization: the use of capital letters in certain grammatical situations, such as to denote a proper noun or the beginning of a sentence.

Case: the position of nouns and pronouns in a sentence that shows whether they are used as subjects (*nominative or subjective case*), objects (*objective case*), or possessive words (*possessive case*).

Classification: the grouping of items into categories based on their similarities.

Clause: a group of words that has a subject and a verb. A clause that expresses a complete thought is an independent clause. A clause that does not express a complete thought is a dependent clause.

Colon: a punctuation mark (:) used to separate a sentence from a list of words or hours from minutes or words in an analogy.

Comma: a punctuation mark (,) used to separate items in a series, appositives, cities from states, dates, compound sentences, complex sentences, and in a variety of other grammatical situations.

Comma splice: a punctuation error in which two independent clauses are joined by a comma only. (*The doorbell rang**,** Jane answered the door.*)

Common noun: a noun referring to any person, place, or thing rather than to a specific person, place, or thing. (*desk, boys, playground*)

Comparative form: the form of an adjective or adverb that compares two people, places, or things. To make comparative forms, add -er, -ly, -ful or more to the simple form. (*slower, more generous*)

Comparison/contrast: a type of writing in which the author's purpose is to tell how things are alike and how things are different.

Complete predicate: the main verb and all the words that modify the verb in a sentence. (*That red car raced down our street.*)

Glossary

Complete subject: the subject noun or pronoun and all the words that modify it. (*That red car raced down our street.*)

Complex sentence: a sentence made by joining two clauses together: an independent clause and a subordinate clause. (*The windows lock **when the store is closed.***)

Compound sentence: a sentence containing two independent clauses and no dependent clauses. (*The girls rode the motorcycles, **and** the boys rode the four-wheelers.*)

Compound subject: two or more subjects in a sentence that are joined by the words and, or, or but. (***Michael** and **Judy** worked on a project in science class.*)

Compound verb: two or more verbs that are joined by the words and, or, or but. (*Michelle **sang** and **danced** in the talent contest.*)

Conjunction: a word used to connect other words, phrases, clauses, or sentences. The three most common conjunctions are **and**, **or**, **but**; one of the eight parts of speech. (*Sally **and** David played the violin in the recital.*)

Contraction: a word formed by combining two words and adding an apostrophe to replace the letter or letters that have been left out. (*did not / didn't*)

Coordinate conjunction: a word that connects words, phrases, or sentences of equal importance. The three most common coordinate conjunctions are **and**, **or**, **but**. (*The weather was sunny, **but** the wind made it cool.*)

Creative writing: a type of writing in which the author's purpose is to entertain through stories, poems, plays, etc.

D

Declarative sentence: a sentence that makes a statement. (*I went to work with my dad.*)

Degree of comparison: adding er, est, more, most or making a word change to an adjective or adverb so that it shows a comparison to something else. (*big, bigger, biggest / beautiful, more beautiful, most beautiful / bad, worse, worst*)

Descriptive writing: a type of writing in which the author's purpose is to describe.

Direct object: a noun or pronoun that receives the action of the verb in a sentence. A direct object tells what or whom after the verb. (*Amy took her **books** to the library.*)

Double negative: a grammatical error involving the use of two negative words in the same sentence. (*The plumber **can't** find **nothing** wrong with our sink.*)

E

Editing: the fourth step in the writing process. Editing involves checking and correcting mistakes in spelling, grammar, usage, capitalization, and punctuation.

Exclamatory sentence: a sentence that expresses strong feeling. (*My car is on fire!*)

Expository: a type of writing in which the author's purpose is to explain or inform.

F

Fact: a specific statement that can be looked up, measured, counted, or otherwise proven. (*John is six feet tall.*)

Fiction: stories about people, places, or things that are not true even though the author may use ideas based on real people or events.

Figurative language: *See* Figure of Speech.

Figure of speech: a poetic device, sometimes called figurative language, that uses words to create images that compare one thing to another. Three figures of speech are simile, metaphor, and personification.

First person point of view: the writer writes as though he is personally involved in what is happening. The writer uses the personal pronouns I, we, me, us, my, our, mine, and ours. (***We** will leave for **our** vacation.*)

Fragment: an incomplete sentence. A fragment is missing one or more of the core parts: a subject, a verb, or a complete thought. (*After the game.*)

Future tense: the form of a verb that refers to a future action or future state of being. (*She **will ride** the bus home after school today. She **will be** a good teacher.*)

G

Genre: a category that identifies what type of writing a piece of literature is. (*essays, poems, short stories, plays, etc.*)

H

Helping verb: a verb or verbs that combine with a main verb. Helping verbs are also called auxiliary verbs. (*He **did** not help his brother with his homework.*)

Homographs: words that are spelled alike but have different meanings and/or different pronunciations. (*You have the **right** answer. Turn into the **right** lane.*) (*He will **lead** us to a safe place. The metal pipe contained **lead**.*)

Homonyms: words that sound alike but have different meanings and spellings. Homonyms can be a combination of homographs and homophones.

Homophones: words that sound alike but have different meanings and spellings. (*write, right*)

I

Imperative sentence: a sentence that gives a command and has an understood subject. (*Wash the dishes.*)

Indefinite pronoun: a pronoun that does not refer to a definite person, place, thing, or idea. (*anybody, everything*)

Indirect object: a noun or pronoun that receives what the direct object names. An indirect object tells to whom or for whom after the direct object. (*I gave **you** the invitation.*)

Interjection: a word or short phrase that expresses strong or mild feeling; one of the eight parts of speech. (*No! Oh my! Wow! No way! Great!*)

Internet: an international network of computers.

Intransitive verb: a verb in a sentence that does not have an object to receive the action. (*He **laughed**.*)

Inverted order: an adverb, prepositional phrase, or helping verb that is located at the beginning of the complete subject and modifies the predicate. (*<u>Today</u>, <u>we</u> / <u>went to school</u>. <u>During the play</u>, <u>Jan</u> / <u>sang a song</u>. <u>Did</u> <u>he</u> / <u>write that song</u>?*)

Irregular verb

Irregular verb: a verb that forms the past tense by having a vowel change or by not changing at all. (*I **know** his name. / I **knew** his name. Today, I **let** my dog eat a treat. Yesterday, I **let** my dog eat a treat.*)

J

Jargon: the language of a special group or profession.

Journal: a written record of personal thoughts and feelings.

L

Linking verb: a verb that connects the subject of a sentence with a word that renames or describes the subject. (*That man **is** a clown. That dress **was** beautiful.*)

M

Main idea: the most important idea in a paragraph or an essay.

Metaphor: a figure of speech that compares things by stating that one thing is something else. Metaphors use linking verbs such as am, is, are, was, and were. (*The **fog was a curtain** during the morning hours.*)

Modify: to describe another word. Adjectives and adverbs are words that describe, or modify, other words in a sentence.

N

Narrative: a type of writing in which the author's purpose is to tell a story.

Natural order: a sentence with all the subject parts located before the verb and the predicate parts located after the verb. (*<u>We</u> / <u>went to the school play yesterday</u>.*)

Nonfiction: information and stories that are true. Autobiographies, biographies, and reference books are nonfiction.

Noun: a word that names a person, place, thing, or idea; one of the eight parts of speech. (*Mother, desk, Alaska*)

O

Object of the preposition: the noun or pronoun after a preposition in a sentence. (*She rode down the **elevator** with her **friend**.*)

Glossary

Object pronoun: a pronoun that functions as an object of the preposition, a direct object, or an indirect object in a sentence. (Common object pronouns: **me, us, him, her, it, them, you**.) (*He gave **me** the ball. He went with **us** to town.*)

Opinion: a personal belief, judgment, or feeling held by one or more persons that cannot be checked or proven. (*John is a considerate young man.*)

P

Paragraph: a group of sentences that is written about one particular subject, or topic.

Parallel form: the wording of topics, subtopics, and details within sections of an outline so that they begin in the same way: as nouns, verbs, noun phrases, verb phrases, prepositional phrases, etc.

Part of speech: one of eight categories of words that have different functions within a sentence. The eight parts of speech are noun, verb, adverb, adjective, pronoun, preposition, conjunction, and interjection.

Past tense: a verb form that shows that something has happened in the past. (*The cars **raced**. The children **sang**.*)

Period: a punctuation mark (**.**) used at the end of a declarative or imperative sentence to signify the end of a complete thought. A period is also used at the end of abbreviations, initials, and after Roman numerals, Arabic numbers, and letters of the alphabet in an outline.

Personal pronoun: pronouns like *I, we, me, he, she, it, they*, and *you* that refer either to a person, people, or things.

Personification: a figure of speech used to compare things by giving human qualities to something nonhuman. (*The door eyed the visitor with contempt and refused to open.*)

Persuasive: a type of writing in which the author's purpose is to convince someone to agree with his/her opinion.

Plural noun: more than one person, place, thing, or idea. (*cats, glasses, children, women*)

Poetry: one of the oldest and most artistic forms of literature. Poetry is both visual and auditory and may include rhyme, rhythm, and various figures of speech.

Point of view: the writer's use of personal pronouns to show who is telling a story. First-person point of view uses the pronouns: *I, we, me, us, my, our, mine*, and *ours*. Second-person point of view uses the pronouns: *you, your*, and *yours*. Third-person point of view uses the pronouns: *he, his, him, she, her, hers, it, its, they, their, theirs*, and *them*.

Possessive noun: the name of a person, place, or thing that owns something. The possessive noun will have either an apostrophe before the s (**'s**) or an apostrophe after the s (**s'**). The apostrophe makes a noun show ownership. (Kim's car)

Possessive pronoun: a pronoun that shows ownership and takes the place of a possessive noun. (Common possessive pronouns: **my, our, his, her, its, their, your**.)

Predicate adjective: an adjective in the predicate of a sentence that modifies the simple subject. It tells what kind of subject. (*Her new dress is absolutely **gorgeous**!*)

Predicate nominative: another name for a predicate noun or a predicate pronoun.

Predicate noun: a noun located in the predicate of a sentence that means the same thing as the simple subject. (*Dad is an excellent **carpenter**.*)

Prefix: a word part added to the beginning of a base word to change its meaning. (***bi**monthly, **inter**state, **un**happy*)

Preposition: a word that shows the relationship of its object to other words in the sentence; one of the eight parts of speech. (*The little boy walked **beside** his mother.*) (*The Preposition Flow Jingle gives a list of common prepositions.*)

Prepositional phrase: a group of words that starts with a preposition, ends with a noun or pronoun object, and includes any modifiers of that object. (*The little boy walked **beside his mother**.*)

Present tense: a verb form that shows that something is happening in the present. (*The cars **race**. The children **run**.*)

Prewriting: the first step in the writing process. The planning and organization for writing is done during this stage.

Pronoun: a word that can take the place of a person, place, thing, or idea in a sentence; one of the eight parts of speech.

Glossary

Proofreading: part of the fourth step in the writing process. Proofreading involves checking sentences or paragraphs for mistakes in spelling, grammar, usage, capitalization, and punctuation.

Propaganda: an organized effort to spread ideas or information in an attempt to change the opinions and actions of a group of people. Propaganda usually contains some accurate facts along with exaggerations and untruths.

Proper adjective: an adjective that is formed from a proper noun. Proper adjectives are always capitalized no matter where they are located in the sentence. (*Mexican food, English language, French bread, Japanese maple*)

Proper noun: a noun that names a specific, or particular, person, place, or thing. Proper nouns are always capitalized no matter where they are located in the sentence. (*Charles is my dad. We are moving to Peru.*)

Publishing: the sixth step in the writing process. Publishing is sharing the final copy of a writing with others.

Purpose of writing: the author's reason for writing. The purpose of writing determines the organization of a piece of writing.

Q

Question and Answer Flow: an oral set of questions and answers used to find the function of each word in a sentence.

Quotations: the exact words spoken by someone in a piece of writing. Quotation marks (" ") are used to indicate a direct quotation. Quotations are also called dialogue in narrative writing.

R

Regular verb: a verb that is made past tense by adding an –ed, –d, or –t ending. (*want, wanted; race, raced; mean, meant*)

Repetition: saying or doing something again and again.

Revision: the third step in the writing process. Revising is the process of improving the content and meaning of a sentence or paragraph.

Rhyme: the sound-alike quality of words, regardless of their spellings (*do/few, made/paid*). Rhyme may be of two types: end rhymes and internal rhymes. Rhyme is often used in poetry.

Rough draft: the second step in the writing process. A rough draft is a first attempt at putting all prewriting ideas from a Prewriting Map into sentences and paragraphs.

Run-on sentence: a grammatical error that occurs when two or more sentences are written continuously without the required punctuation.

S

Second-person point of view: used in giving directions. The writer uses the pronouns you, your, or yours almost exclusively to name the person or thing being addressed. (*You may leave now.*)

Semicolon: a punctuation mark (;) used to join two independent clauses in a compound sentence.

Simile: a figure of speech that compares things by using the words like or as. (*Jeff is as tall as a giraffe. My brother jumps like a frog.*)

Simple form: the form of an adjective or adverb that is used when no comparison is made. (*pretty, fast, good*)

Simple predicate: another name for the verb in a sentence. (*Our soccer team played well yesterday.*)

Simple sentence: a sentence having three core parts: a subject, a verb, and a complete thought.

Simple subject: another name for the subject noun or subject pronoun in a sentence. (*Our soccer team played well.*)

Simple tense: the present, past, and future tense of verbs. (*walk, walked, will walk*)

Singular noun: only one person, place, thing, or idea. (*cat, glass, child, woman*)

Slang: informal language used in everyday conversation. It is not considered appropriate in formal writing. (*dude, cool*)

Stanza: divisions of a rhyming poem.

Strophe: divisions of a poem that does not rhyme.

Subject noun: a noun that tells who or what a sentence is about.

Glossary

Subject pronoun: a pronoun that tells who or what a sentence is about. (Common subject pronouns: **I**, **we**, **he**, **she**, **it**, **they**, **you**.)

Subordinate clause: a clause having a subject and a verb but not expressing a complete thought. (*When the bell rang for class.*)

Subordinate conjunction: a connecting word that introduces a subordinate clause. (*after, before, since, etc.*)

Suffix: a word part added to the end of a base word to change its meaning. (*care**less**, advance**ment**, joy**ful**, hugg**able**.*)

Superlative form: an adjective or adverb that compares three or more people, places, or things. To make the superlative form, add –est or most to the simple form. (*fast**est**, **most** nervous*)

Synonym: words that have similar, or almost the same, meanings. (*guess, surmise*)

T

Tall tale: a humorous story that makes use of exaggeration, but it also includes believable events and situations.

Tenses: the forms of a verb that show when an action takes place. (*present tense, past tense, future tense.*)

Third-person point of view: the writer writes as though he is watching the events take place. The writer uses the pronouns he, his, him, she, her, hers, it, its, they, their, theirs, and them. (***He** bought **his** new car today.*)

Topic: a word or group of words that tells what something is about.

Topic sentence: a sentence that states the main idea of a paragraph or essay.

Transition word: a word or phrase that shows a link between sentences and paragraphs. (*The Transition Words Jingle gives a list of common transition words.*)

Transitive verb: a verb that transfers action to a direct object in a sentence.

U

Underlining: a form of punctuation appropriate for the titles of books, magazines, works of art, ships, newspapers, motion pictures, etc.

V

Verb: a word in a sentence that expresses action (*see* action verb) or a state of being (*see* linking verb); one of the eight parts of speech.

Voice: the aspect of writing in which the writers' thoughts and personal viewpoints are clearly and genuinely revealed.

W

World Wide Web: a network of computers that makes up the Internet.

Writing process: the steps it takes to plan, write, rewrite and publish a final paper. Steps in the writing process include pre-writing, writing a rough draft, revising, editing, writing a final paper, and publishing.

sharing poetry, 469, 473, 478, 482

preparing for, 399

reading your writing aloud, 99, 128, 161, 193, 225, 257, 286, 317, 349, 371, 374, 398–399, 400, 401, 418, 463, 502, 503

share times, 128, 161, 193, 225, 257, 286, 317, 349, 374, 398, 418, 469, 473, 478, 482

speak clearly, 99, 402–403, 525, 526

research report, 502–503

telling a story, 402–403, 525

video presentations, 525, 526

Spelling

homonyms, 90, 546

prefixes, 521, 547

plurals of nouns, 299–300

suffixes, 521, 549

Statement, 40

Story.

See Writing, creative; narrative

Subject

complete, 41, 81, 545

noun, 25, 548

pronoun, 109, 110, 510, 549

simple, 81–82, 548

understood, 110

Subject-verb agreement, 86–87

Subtopic, 450–453

Suffix, 521, 549

Supporting sentences.

See Sentences, supporting

Synonyms, 19, 549

T

Table of contnets, 342, 534, 535

Tall tales. *See* Writing

Technology, using 540–543

Tenses of verbs. *See* Verbs, tenses

Tests, taking, 528

Thank you notes. *See* Letters

Thesaurus, 531

Titles, 13–14, 16, 56, 135–136, 167–168, 197–198, 200–201, 231, 275

Topics, 48

Topic sentence, 53–54, 134, 166, 196–199, 229, 258–259, 549

Transition words, 94, 103–104, 509, 549

Transitive verbs. *See* Verbs, transitive

U

Underlining

definition of, 549

in editing exercises, 116, 123, 212, 434

punctuation rule, 16

V

Verbs

action, 24, 25, 544

be, 140, 510

helping, 140, 141, 510, 546

irregular, 185, 210, 546

jingle, 24, 507

linking, 324, 349, 395, 546

main, 141

plain form, 86–87

principal parts, 185, 246

regular, 185, 210, 548

tenses, 209, 238, 242, 549

transitive, 206–207, 226, 287, 549

Vocabulary, 20–21, 516–518

Voice, 64, 549

W

Word analogies, 20–21, 516–518, 544

Writing

cause and effect, 539

comparison and contrast essay, 351–352

descriptive paragraph, 259

expository essay, 133–136, 165–168, 545

expository paragraph, 53–56, 60, 545

how-to essay, 522

journal, 12

narrative, 290–291, 318–319

persuasive essay, 198–201, 229–231

persuasive paragraph, 197–198

research report, 483, 499

tall tale, 375–376, 549

Writing across the curriculum.

See Across the curriculum

Writing conferences, 97, 127, 159, 191, 223, 255, 284, 315, 346, 372, 397

Writing process

editing, 66–67

final paper, 69

prewriting, 57

publishing, 98

revising, 64

rough draft, 61

Writing prompts, 191, 223, 284, 498

Level 6 Sources Cited

"Albert Einstein." nobelprize.org. Nobel Foundation. <http://nobelprize.org/nobel_prizes/physics/laureates/1921/einstein-bio.html>.

Anagnost, George T. "US Supreme Court: Sandra Day O'Connor." Answers.com. Answers Corporation. The Oxford Companion to the Supreme Court of the United States. Copyright © 1992, 2005. Oxford University Press. 15 Dec 2006. <http://www.answers.com/topic/sandra-day-o-connor?cat=biz-fin>

"Alexander Graham Bell-Biography." About.com: Inventors. About, Inc. New York Times Company. 9 Jan 2007. <http://inventors.about.com/library/inventors/bltelephone2.htm>.

Annett, Will. "Adventures in Cybersound." Australian Centre for the Moving Image. 9 Jan 2007. <http://www.acmi.net.au/AIC/Baird_Annett.html>.

"Baird, John Logie." Encyclopaedia Britannica. 2004 ed.

Bankard, Bob. "Profiles in Black History." phillyburbs.com. Calkins Media Incorporated. 11 Jan 2007. <http://www.phillyburbs.com/bhm/banneker1.shtml>.

"Bartholdi, Frederic-Auguste." Encyclopaedia Britannica. 2004 ed.

"Beethoven, Ludwig van." Encyclopaedia Britannica. 2004 ed.

"Bell, Alexander Graham." Encyclopaedia Britannica. 2004 ed.

"Bill Gates." Microsoft. 2007. Microsoft Corporation. 10 Jan 2007. <http://www.microsoft.com/presspass/exec/billg/default.mspx>.

"Booker T. Washington." Booker T. Washington Inspirational Network. 10 Jan 2007. <http://www.booker-t-washington.com>.

"Cherokee." Encyclopaedia Britannica. 2004 ed.

"Clarence Birdseye." Birds Eye Foods. Birds Eye Foods, Inc. 5 Dec 2006. <http://www.birdseyefoods.com/corp/about/ClarenceBirdseye.asp>.

"Coca-Cola Company, The." Encyclopaedia Britannica. 2004 ed.

"Conan Doyle, Sir Arthur." Encyclopaedia Britannica. 2004 ed.

"Country Music." Microsoft® Encarta® Online Encyclopedia 2007. © 1997–2007 Microsoft Corporation. 11 Jan 2007. <http://encarta.msn.com>.

"Ferdinand Magellan." Microsoft® Encarta® Online Encyclopedia 2007. © 1997–2007 Microsoft Corporation. 11 Jan 2007. <http://encarta.msn.com>.

"Garrett Morgan." About.com: Inventors. About, Inc. New York Times Company. 10 Jan 2007. <http://inventors.about.com/library/inventors/blgas_mask.htm>.

"George Washington Carver." Microsoft® Encarta® Online Encyclopedia 2007. © 1997–2007 Microsoft Corporation. 10 Jan 2007. <http://encarta.msn.com>.

"Guglielmo Marconi." SolarNavigator.net. 1999. Solar Navigator® 15 Jan 2007. <http:www.solarnavigator.net/inventors/guglielmo_marconi.htm>.

"Gutenberg, Johannes." Encyclopaedia Britannica. 2004 ed.

"Helen Keller Biography." Helen Keller Kids Museum Online. American Foundation for the Blind. 15 Jan 2007. <http://www.afb.org/braillebug/helen_keller_bio.asp>.

"Henry Ford." Microsoft® Encarta® Online Encyclopedia 2007. © 1997–2007 Microsoft Corporation. 15 Jan 2007. <http://encarta.msn.com>.

Hood, Tomas. "Louis L'Amour - a fans tribute." newWebMakers.com. June 01, 2006. Tomas Hood. 5 Dec 2006. <http://newwebmakers.com/ll>.

"Jack London." Encyclopaedia Britannica. 2004 ed.

"James Watt." The Great Idea Finder. 13 Dec 2006. <http://www.ideafinder.com/history/inventors/watt.htm>.

Jaukovic, Milan. "Most Expensive Paintings Ever." Auguste Renior Gallery. Alvilim. 17 Jan 2007. <http://www.renoir.org.yu/most-expensive-paintings.asp>.

"Jefferson, Thomas." Encyclopaedia Britannica. 2004 ed.

"Joan of Arc, Saint." Encyclopaedia Britannica. 2004 ed.

"Joseph Farwell Glidden." New Perspectives on the West. PBS.org. © 2001. The West Film Project and WETA. 13 Dec 2006. <http://www.pbs.org/weta/thewest/people/d_h/glidden.htm>.

Kepos, Paula. "Kroc, Ray." Nutrition and Well-Being A to Z. Advameg, Inc. 17 Jan 2007. <http://www.faqs.org/nutrition/Biographies/Kroc-Ray.html>.

"Kipling, Rudyard." Encyclopaedia Britannica. 2004 ed.

"Kroc, Ray." Encyclopaedia Britannica. 2004 ed.

"L'Amour, Louis." Encyclopaedia Britannica. 2004 ed.

"Laura Ingalls Wilder." Microsoft® Encarta® Online Encyclopedia 2007. © 1997–2007 Microsoft Corporation. 17 Jan 2007. <http://encarta.msn.com>.

"Leonardo da Vinci." Encyclopaedia Britannica. 2004 ed.

"Lewis, C. S." Encyclopaedia Britannica. 2004 ed.

Lewis, David. "Irving Berlin." The Guide to Musical Theatre. 1994–2006. 15 Jan 2007. <http://www.nodanw.com/biographies/irving_berlin.htm>.

"Liberty, Statue of." Encyclopaedia Britannica. 2004 ed.

"Louis Braille Biography." AFB-American Foundation for the Blind. 17 Jan 2007. <http://www.afb.org/Braillebug/Louis_braille_bio.asp>.

"Mark Twain." Microsoft® Encarta® Online Encyclopedia 2007. © 1997–2007 Microsoft Corporation. 23 Jan 2007. <http://encarta.msn.com>.

"Martin Luther King, Jr." Nobelprize.org. The Nobel Foundation. 23 Jan 2007. http://nobelprize.org/nobel_prizes/peace/laureates/1964/king-bio.html>.

"Marva N. Collins Biography." Marva Collins Seminars. Copyright © Marva Collins Seminars 2006. 13 Dec 2006. <http://www.marvacollins.com/biography.html>.

"Michelangelo." Microsoft® Encarta® Online Encyclopedia 2007. © 1997–2007 Microsoft Corporation. 23 Jan 2007. <http://encarta.msn.com>.

"Morse, Samuel F. B." Encyclopaedia Britannica. 2004 ed.

"Mozart, Wolfgang Amadeus." Encyclopaedia Britannica. 2004 ed.

"Navajo Code Talkers." Infoplease. Pearson Publishing. 23 Jan 2007. <http://www.infoplease.com/spot/aihmcode1.htm>.

Newbold, Ken. "Benjamin Banneker: A Brief Biography." 17 May 2004. The James Madison Center. James Madison University. 13 Dec 2006. <http://www.jmu.edu/madison/center/main_pages/madison_archives/era/african/free/banneker/bio.htm>.

"Newton, Sir Isaac." Encyclopaedia Britannica. 2004 ed.

"Nobel, Alfred Bernhard." Encyclopaedia Britannica. 2004 ed.

"Paul Revere." Microsoft® Encarta® Online Encyclopedia 2007. © 1997–2007 Microsoft Corporation. 23 Jan 2007. <http://encarta.msn.com>.

"Plan Approved and Fund Raising Undertaken." Statue of Liberty. 25 Sept 2000. National Park Service. 15 Dec 2006. <http://www.nps.gov/history/history/online_books/hh/11/hh11c.htm>.

Sahlman, Rachel. "Jacques Costeau." Spectrum Home & School Network. IncWell.com. 11 Jan 2007. <http://www.incwell.com/Biographies/Cousteau.html>.

Schneider, Elaine. "Ludwig van Beethoven: Biography." essortment.com. 2002. 15 Dec 2006. <http://www.essortment.com/all/beethovenbiogra_rxef.htm>.

"Schulz, Charles." Encyclopaedia Britannica. 2004 ed.

"Sequoyah." Encyclopaedia Britannica. 2004 ed.

Sherry, Suzanna. "US History Companion: O'Connor, Sandra Day." Answers.com. Answers Corporation. The Readers Companion to American History, Eric Foner and John A Garraty, Editors. 1991 © Houghton Mifflin Company. 15 Dec 2006. <http://www.answers.com/topic/sandra-day-o-connor?cat=biz-fin>

"Sitting Bull." New Perspectives on the West. PBS.org. © 2001. The West Film Project and WETA. 8 Feb 2007. <http://www.pbs.org/weta/thewest/people/s_z/sittingbull.htm>.

"Sousa, John Philip." Encyclopaedia Britannica. 2004 ed.

South, A. "First Woman to Win the Nobel Prize." Helium. Helium, Inc. 11 Jan 2007. <http://www.helium.com/items/869637-marie-curies-unprecedented-radioactivity>.

"Stanton, Elizabeth Cody." Encyclopaedia Britannica. 2004 ed.

"Stephen Foster." Microsoft® Encarta® Online Encyclopedia 2007. © 1997–2007 Microsoft Corporation. 8 Feb 2007. <http://encarta.msn.com>.

"Thomas Edison." Microsoft® Encarta® Online Encyclopedia 2007. © 1997–2007 Microsoft Corporation. 9 Feb 2007. <http://encarta.msn.com>.

"Tompkins, Sally Louisa." Encyclopaedia Britannica. 2004 ed.

"Wal-Mart Stores, Inc." Alliance to Save Energy. 2005. The Alliance to Save Energy. 9 Feb 2007. <http://www.ase.org/content/article/detail/3065>.

"Walton, Samuel Moore." Encyclopaedia Britannica. 2004 ed.

"Webster, Noah." Encyclopaedia Britannica. 2004 ed.

Webster's Encyclopedic Unabridged Dictionary of the English Language. New York: Random House, Inc., 1996.

Webster's II New College Dictionary, Boston: Houghton Mifflin Company, 2001.

"Whitney, Eli." Encyclopaedia Britannica. 2004 ed.

"Who2Biography: Sandra Day O'Connor, Jurist." Answers.com. © 1998–2006. Who2, LLC. 15 Dec 2006. <http://www.answers.com/topic/sandra-day-o-connor?cat=biz-fin>

"Who Was Sitting Bull?" Sitting Bull Monument Foundation. © 2007 Sitting Bull Monument Foundation. 8 Feb 2007. <http://www.sittingbullmonument.com/whowassittingbull>.

"William Shakespeare." Microsoft® Encarta® Online Encyclopedia 2007. © 1997–2007 Microsoft Corporation. 9 Feb 2007. <http://encarta.msn.com>.

"Women in History, Jane Addams." Lakewood Public Library. 9 Jan 2007. <http://www.lkwdpl.org/wihohio/adda-jan.htm>.

"Wright, Wilbur and Orville." Encyclopaedia Britannica. 2004 ed.